INFORMATION MANAGEMENT

INFORMATION MANAGEMENT

The Organizational Dimension

edited by
MICHAEL J. EARL

OXFORD
UNIVERSITY PRESS

OXFORD
UNIVERSITY PRESS

Great Clarendon Street, Oxford OX2 6DP

Oxford University Press is a department of the University of Oxford.
It furthers the University's objective of excellence in research, scholarship,
and education by publishing worldwide in

Oxford New York

Athens Auckland Bangkok Bogotá Buenos Aires Calcutta
Cape Town Chennai Dar es Salaam Delhi Florence Hong Kong Istanbul
Karachi Kuala Lumpur Madrid Melbourne Mexico City Mumbai
Nairobi Paris São Paulo Singapore Taipei Tokyo Toronto Warsaw

with associated companies in Berlin Ibadan

Oxford is a registered trade mark of Oxford University Press
in the UK and in certain other countries

Published in the United States
by Oxford University Press Inc., New York

First published 1996
First published in paperback 1998

British Library Cataloguing in Publication Data

Data available

Library of Congress Cataloging in Publication Data

Information management : the organizational dimension / edited by
Michael J. Earl.
Includes some papers presented at conference organized by the
Oxford Institute of Information Management and sponsored by PA
Consulting Group, held at Templeton College, Oxford.
Includes bibliographical references.
1. Management information systems—Congresses. 2. Information
technology—Management—Congress. I. Earl, Michael J.
II. Oxford Institute of Information Management. III. PA Consulting
Group. HD30.213.1537 1996 658.4'038—dc20 95-39381

ISBN 0-19-825760-0 (hbk)
ISBN 0-19-829452-2 (pbk)

5 7 9 10 8 6 4

Printed in Great Britain
on acid-free paper by
Biddles Ltd., Guildford and King's Lynn

PREFACE

In one sense this book is a sequel to an earlier volume—*Information Management: The Strategic Dimension*. That 1988 book brought together some early research, interspersed with company case histories, on how information technology (IT) could be strategically deployed in firms and on how to bring some concept of strategic management to the information systems (IS) function. At the time of writing this preface (1995), more substantive work in these domains has been done by scholars and the strategic impact of IT on firms, markets, and sectors is becoming clearer day by day.

'The Organizational Dimension' of IT may have a longer pedigree than 'the strategic dimension'. Almost since computers first entered the commercial world, writers have been fascinated about whether computing and other information technologies would change the shape and functioning of organizations. Many of the predictions of the first thirty years have not materialized or are taking longer to manifest themselves than was expected. Conversely, especially in the last decade, the pervasiveness of information technology has brought about changes in how we conceptualize the organization and in how many managers and specialists work. Often there is a correspondence between new organizational terminology and the language of IT. Networked organizations, inter-organizational alliances, distributed organizations, and the intelligent or knowledge-based corporation are examples.

All this speculation and analysis is predicated maybe at a conceptual level on organizations being seen as systems or structures of communication and information processing. In this light, new information technologies might allow us more choice in organization design and the ability to increase our information and communication channels.

So the organizational dimension of information management as seen through the domain of organization theory is continuously unfolding. In truth, this aspect is the minor (in chapter count) contribution of this volume. Most of the chapters are concerned with organizing the IS function— or to be more descriptively accurate—organizing IT activities, for by 1995 it is apparent that at least as much information systems effort and investment is in the hands of 'users' as under the control of the IS function.

Why, then, is so much of this volume devoted to the organization of a technological activity? One response is that repeatedly we find that when studies are done of the scope, the application, the use, or the impact of IT, the enabling or constraining factors are more often organizational rather than technological. Another related answer is that in the apparently simple matter of managing a specialist function like IS, organizational questions abound.

There are two other explanations. The contributors to this volume hail from business schools where managerial (often organizational) issues are often at the heartland of their agenda. Secondly, in part, the heritage of this volume—like its predecessor—is connected with an annual conference held at Templeton College, Oxford, organized by the Oxford Institute of Management and sponsored by PA Consulting Group. This event brings together academics and IS directors to discuss and examine contemporary questions of information management. Some of the chapters were originally presented as papers at these conferences.

Others were specially written or solicited. The editor's move from the University of Oxford to London Business School provided both a need and an opportunity to enlarge the volume! The Centre for Research in Information Management thus has contributed too. I owe a special thank-you to Linden Selby who not only has worked diligently at the word processor but has continuously reminded me to 'get the book done'. I hope that both ends of the M40[1]—and their extended networks—appreciate the alliance. I am grateful to all the contributors.

So to return to 'The Organizational Dimension'. Section I looks at some of the organizational horizons made possible by information technology. The next section tackles some of the challenges that face organizations who want to exploit IT in innovative and strategic ways. Section III examines some of the eternal questions of how to organize the IS function, including under perhaps the most threatening environment of all, a merger.

Many managers experience both the risks and rewards of IT at the project level. In Section IV the contributors look at various aspects of project management and systems implementation. The next section examines some contemporary management questions on the agendas of chief information officers (CIOs) and their IS departments. The postscript seeks to integrate the volume through a framework of analysis dubbed 'organizational fit'.

Finally, the question with which we might have started: what is the purpose of this volume? There are perhaps three:

1. To provide some personal, but authoritative overviews of information management questions to help and guide other researchers and academics.
2. To provide perhaps more detailed and carefully argued papers on key managerial questions than are often available to managers thinking through their information management dilemmas.
3. To put into the public domain a few papers which have been well received in conferences, but not published elsewhere.

---

[1] The M40 is the motorway which links London and Oxford. When first built and carrying the traffic volumes of a country by-road, it was often alleged that civil servants proposed and encouraged its construction so that they could travel quickly from Whitehall to arrive for dinner at 7p.m. at their old college! The same was said of the M11 between London and Cambridge.

I hope all these constituencies find the volume useful. In measuring the effectiveness of information systems, we often fall back on 'usage' as a proxy measure of value. I am told that the prior volume has been 'well-thumbed' by many of its buyers. May readers' thumbs be well exercised again!

Michael Earl

London Business School
January 1995

CONTENTS

LIST OF TABLES

LIST OF FIGURES

LIST OF CONTRIBUTORS

Paul Anand
Reader in Decision Theory, School of Social Sciences, De Montfort University.

Cynthia Mathis Beath
Associate Professor of Management Information Sciences, Edwin L. Cox School of Business, Southern Methodist University.

David Boddy
Reader in Management Studies, University of Glasgow.

J. Daniel Couger
Distinguished Professor, Management Science, University of Colorado.

Michael J. Earl
Director, Centre for Research in Information Management; Andersen Consulting Professor of Information Management, London Business School.

Brian Edwards
Research Associate, Oxford Institute of Information Management, Templeton College, Oxford.

David Feeny
Director, Oxford Institute of Information Management, Templeton College, Oxford.

Guy Fitzgerald
Cable and Wireless Professor of Business Information Systems, Birkbeck College, University of London.

Stephen L. Hodgkinson
Andersen Consulting, Melbourne, Australia.

Blake Ives
Constantin Distinguished Professor of MIS at the Edwin L. Cox School of Business, Southern Methodist University.

Mary Lacity
Professor in Management Information Systems, University of Missouri, St Louis; Visiting Fellow at Oxford Institute of Information Management, Templeton College, Oxford.

Jane C. Linder
Director, Business Development, Polaroid Graphics Imaging, USA.

Martin Lockett
Senior Principal, American Management Systems UK Ltd., London.

Peter Morris
Director, Special Projects, Bovis Ltd.; Associate Fellow, Templeton College, Oxford.

Enid Mumford
Emeritus Professor of Organizational Behaviour, Manchester Business School.

Jeffrey L. Sampler
Assistant Professor, Centre for Research in Information Management, London Business School.

James E. Short
Assistant Professor, Centre for Research in Information Management, London Business School.

David J. Skyrme
Research Associate, Oxford Institute of Information Management, Templeton College, Oxford.

Michael Vitale
Foundation Chair in Information Systems and Head of Information Systems Department, University of Melbourne.

Leslie P. Willcocks
Fellow in Information Management, Oxford Institute of Information Management, Templeton College, Oxford.

SECTION I

FOREWORD

Information Management enthusiasts tend to claim that IT has changed, or will change, organizations both in structure and behaviour. The more sceptical organizational theorists often argue that fundamentals of social organization will defeat any technological forces. Their more open, but critical, colleagues, may suggest that IT tends to enable organizational change, but very much in the spirit of an almost dialectic journey between organizational adaptations and experiment on the one hand, and technological diffusion and learning on the other. Other theorists see a convergence of information and organization, as exemplified by the work of Galbraith (1973). This school can be called the information processing view of organizational design.

Certainly, in the 1990s models of organizations carry labels which seemingly represent a convergence of information management and organizational theory. Examples include networked, virtual, and knowledge-based organizations. It is interesting to compare such developments with predictions made in the past. For example, Leavitt and Whisler (1958) over thirty years ago identified some trends which have come to pass but they did it in the language of their time, including concern with centralization and decentralization. So it is probably appropriate that the first chapter of this volume explores the relationship between information technology and organization structure. Here Sampler takes a dispassionate view, surveying and evaluating some of the most influential writing and the more rigorous research on this question. He reminds us that enquiry in this area needs to be done with great care. His important conclusion is that the romantics and the realists is this area may be reconciled if we begin to study where the theory and practice of information processing and organizational design do converge—and where they differ.

In the next chapter Anand writes a similar essay to examine the impact of information systems on decision-making. He focuses on the contemporary technology of groupware and efficiently surveys some of the IS research to-date, injecting critical perspectives from decision theory and microeconomics. This is an important area to develop if we are to advance the use of information systems in managerial decision-making. It needs work in both the rational paradigms of decision theory and the more behavioural studies of how information is actually used and decisions actually taken.

In the third chapter of this section Earl explores some information management characteristics of knowledge-based organizations. Drawing on two contrasting case studies, he presents propositions on knowledge as a strategic resource and discusses possible differences between data, information, and knowledge. He then goes on to consider what is involved in knowledge management. Appropriately for this volume, he argues that the organizational domains are as important as the technological ones.

The first half of the 1990s has seen the heavy promotion of a seemingly new management idea: business reengineering. The IT industry and IS functions in large corporations have been very active in developing both concepts and practice in this area. An important contribution has been the development of process thinking. Hence common labels for this activity have been business process reengineering or business process redesign (BPR). In the fourth chapter Earl provides a breakdown of the key elements of BPR and emphasizes two: the construct of process and the challenge of change management. He argues that these lie respectively in the domains of organization design and organizational behaviour. Implicit, therefore, in the paper is a warning against development and use of technocratic models of BPR and a plea for seeing and applying BPR with lenses from 'organizational science'.

The final chapter in this section looks at global organizations. Some information management writers have argued that global business only becomes feasible and viable if supported by global IT infrastructures. Some strategy theorists, for example, Porter (1986), suggest that information and communications technologies increase the options for how to organize efficiently and effectively on a global scale. Earl and Feeny report on case study research which aimed to find out how much different forms of globalization depended on information systems and what particular management challenges were presented. They conclude that whatever information systems are required, the biggest challenge is that they generally have to cross several organizational boundaries. National boundaries are less of a challenge. The consequence is that the organization of the IS function in global business is a central question of strategic management. Such information management questions have been ignored by writers on business strategy and international business. Perhaps this is one reason why the organizational dimension of information management is in need of continuous, empirical research.

References

Galbraith, J. R. (1973), *Designing Complex Organizations*, Reading, Mass.: Addison-Wesley.

Leavitt, M. J., and Whisler, T. L. (1958), 'Management in the 1980s', *Harvard Business Review*, vol. 36, no. 1, pp. 41–8.

Porter, M. E. (1986), 'Competition in Global Industries: A Conceptual Framework', in M. E. Porter (ed.), *Competition in Global Industries*, Boston: Harvard Business School Press.

1

Exploring the Relationship Between Information Technology and Organizational Structure

JEFFREY L. SAMPLER

Introduction

Over thirty-five years have passed since academics began speculating on the impact that information technology (IT) would have on organizational structure (Leavitt and Whisler 1958). The debate is still on-going, and both researchers and managers continue to explore the relationship between IT and organizational structure. This relationship is becoming increasingly complicated by both the rapidly changing nature of IT and the increasing environmental turbulence faced by many organizations. As organizations need to process more information under these uncertain conditions, IT is one possible way for organizations to increase their information processing capability. However, other, more organizational tools are also at their disposal for processing more information. These include task forces, lateral relationships, self-contained work groups, and slack resources (Galbraith 1973). Thus, the relationship between IT and organizational structures is not a simple one.

However, the relationship between IT and organizational structures is definitely a topic worthy of investigation for both academics and practitioners. Organizational structure is one of the key variables affecting how firms' strategies are implemented (Chandler 1962). Thus, an appropriate organizational structure is critical in achieving performance. In addition, an organization's structure and established routines are one form of organizational memory. Thus, structure is a critical factor not only in what organizations learn, but how this information and/or knowledge is retained. Increasingly, as the ability of a firm to compete is based on its ability to learn (Senge 1990), then the issue of appropriate organizational structure assumes even greater importance, and to the extent that IT impacts this, or enables new organizational arrangements, then this too must be understood.

The purpose of this chapter is to explore different perspectives on the relationship between IT and organizational structure. In describing these various perspectives, previous research will be summarized, and then evaluated according to a variety of criteria. Finally, suggestions for future research and managerial implications will be discussed.

Perspectives on the Relationship Between IT and Organizational Structure

Despite much academic and managerial attention, no clear-cut relationship has been established between IT and organizational structure. Instead, there is a variety of perspectives, which may be summarized around five principal positions: (1) IT leads to centralization of organizational control; (2) IT leads to decentralization of organizational control; (3) IT has no uniform impact on organizational control, but instead this relationship is determined by other factors; (4) organizations and IT interact in an unpredictable manner; and (5) IT enables new organizational arrangements, such as networked or virtual organizations. Each of these views will be discussed in order to compare assumptions and findings so that a more integrated perspective can be derived from which future recommendations can be developed.

IT Causes Centralization

The early work by Leavitt and Whisler (1958) made ground-breaking predictions of the impact that IT would have on organizations. Among their predictions were that by the 1980s advances in IT and scientific management practices would cause the number of middle managers to decrease, top management to assume more of the creative activities, and that large organizations would centralize organizational control and decision authority. Some have recently argued that many of Leavitt and Whisler's predictions were realized during the 1980s (Applegate *et al.* 1988), as evidenced by the radical downsizing of middle management in many organizations and the large amount of real-time information available to executives in many organizations.

Others have also suggested IT would lead to centralization of control and decision-making because of the ease with which IT allowed the accurate transferal of information to senior management (Hoos 1960; Mann and Williams 1958; Reif 1968; Whisler, 1967, 1970*a*, 1970*b*). In addition to the earlier work by Leavitt and Whisler (1958), Whisler expanded and supported these arguments through both additional theoretical work (1967) and case-based research within insurance firms which revealed that the introduction of IT led to a recentralization of previously decentralized decision authority. In other early empirical work by Reif (1968), based on his findings from three case studies, introduction of IT also led to centralization. However, Reif also noted that IT-related shifts towards centralization were affected by: (1) type of information being processed; (2) existing managerial reporting relationships within the organizational hierarchy at the time of IT implementation; and (3) organizational function in which IT was introduced (Reif noted greater centralization in production functions than in marketing functions).

Later research also indicated that the introduction of IT caused centralization, but the consistency of findings was often mixed. For example, in Robey's (1981) study of eight companies, only a few of the cases suggested that IT led to centralization. One case in particular was that of a British glass manufacturer. This offered evidence of centralization in control and power through the introduction of sales monitoring and budget-preparation computer information systems. In a study of five Italian firms the introduction of IT led to: (1) the centralization of control for production; (2) the consolidation of departments in some of the firms; and (3) delegation of decision authority to lower levels of the organization in several of the firms studied (Roveda and Ciborra 1981). Finally, in a study which focused specifically on the impacts of IT on the work-group, work-groups in manufacturing and insurance organizations that used IT extensively were found to be more centralized than work-groups that did not use IT extensively (Leifer and McDonough 1985).

IT Causes Decentralization

Not long after Leavitt and Whisler's article (1958), several articles were published that refuted the earlier claims that IT causes centralization (Anshen 1960; Burlingame 1961). Instead, they suggested that IT causes decentralization, because IT will take over routine decision-making at the lower and middle levels of the organizational hierarchy, and in so doing will free up individuals at these levels to focus their attention on less-routine problems (Klatsky 1970). Also, IT can cause decentralization, because the ability to consolidate large amounts of information through computer systems, and make it available to top management in a cost-effective manner, can also be used to distribute this same information across the lower levels of the organization. Such availability of information has the potential to empower these workers to make their own decisions.

Several empirical studies have supported the assertion that IT causes decentralization. For example, the results from Klatsky's study of US employment agencies revealed a strong relationship between IT and the decentralization of decisions associated with hiring. Two methodologically well-constructed studies used the manufacturing sector as a source of data. Blau *et al.* (1976) studied 110 manufacturing plants and found that the location of a computer *within* the manufacturing plant was associated with decentralization, while the location of the computer *outside* the manufacturing facility was associated with centralization. At this time, location of the computer was a good indication for access to data-processing and information systems. Thus, the more general conclusion was that computers in factories resulted in a decentralization of decision-making authority from corporate headquarters to plant managers. These finds were reinforced in another study of manufacturing industry. Pfeffer and Leblebici (1977) studied thirty-eight manufacturing firms and controlled for both size of the firm and environmental characteristics. Their results indicated that IT caused organizations to adopt a decentralized decision authority structure.

Organizational Characteristics Influence Use of IT

The two arguments discussed above have been variations on the theme that IT determines or strongly constrains organizational decision and control structures. Markus and Robey (1988) refer to this as the 'technological imperative' (see Fig. 1.1). The importance of this view is not whether IT results in the centralization or decentralization of organizations, but that IT is viewed as the independent variable, which in turn effects the dependent variable, organizational structure.

An alternative perspective is to view organizational structure as determined by the situation under which the organization operates. Here, organizational characteristics determine the information processing needs of the organization, and computer information systems are one method of fulfilling these information requirements. Other potential ways to fulfil information needs are through creating slack resources, designing self-contained work-groups, or initiating task forces to facilitate lateral communication (Galbraith 1973).

Thus, under these assumptions, organizational characteristics, such as information processing needs, determine how IT will be used. Suppose that two organizations are identical (e.g. same industry), except that one introduces three times as many new products as the other every year. The one introducing more new products will have higher information-processing needs, because management must determine the demand for these products as well as face more complex production, distribution, and marketing problems.

If one takes the view that there is latitude in how to apply IT to organizations (Buchanan and Boddy 1983), then one major thrust of research operating under the assumptions of the organizational imperative (Markus and Robey 1988) is concerned with locating key contextual variables that influence how IT is applied (see Fig. 1.1). Here it is assumed that IT is the dependent variable and that the independent or causal variable is managerial intent and organizational characteristics. Integrating the work of Woodward (1965), Perrow (1967, 1970), and Child (1973), Robey (1977,

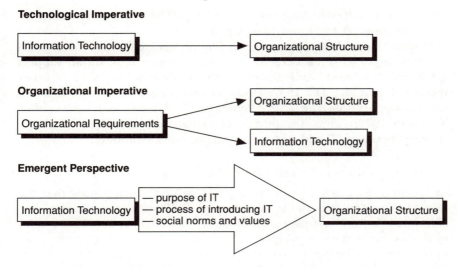

Technological Imperative

Organizational Imperative

Emergent Perspective

Fig. 1.1. *Perspectives of the relation between organizational structure and information technology (adapted from Markus and Robey 1988)*

1981) argued that organizational structure is determined by more fundamental influences than IT, such as environmental uncertainty, manufacturing technology, and organizational size.

In building on Galbraith's work, which developed an information-processing view of organizations, Daft and colleagues (Daft and Lengel 1986; Daft and MacIntosh 1978, 1981) argued that organizational information needs varied with task variety and knowledge about the task. These task characteristics influenced the type of media appropriate for transferring information associated with the task. They proposed that un-analyzable or non-routine tasks require the use of 'rich' media, such as face-to-face meetings, which are capable of conveying equivocal and complex information. Conversely, computer information systems are more appropriate for transferring information that has less equivocality associated with it.

Another possible contingent factor affecting organizational design is task interconnectedness (Thompson 1967). An example of highly interconnected or coupled tasks would be the materials procurement and production departments in a just-in-time manufacturing environment. Loosely coupled tasks would be the legal department and the production department in the same organization.

Robey (1981) and Malone and colleagues (Malone 1987; Malone and Rockart 1991; Malone *et al.* 1987) have examined the ability of IT to support lateral communication and improve co-ordination. Malone and colleagues argue that the ability of IT to support co-ordination will result in the development of new co-ordination intensive structures. However, conditions under which such co-ordination-intensive organizational arrangements are desirable have yet to be fully developed.

Despite the intrinsic appeal of this line of research, empirical support for these arguments has been limited. Some studies have shown support (Daft and MacIntosh 1981; Specht 1986), while empirical tests of other models (Galbraith 1973, 1977; Tushman and Nadler 1978) have received mixed support (Morrow 1981; Penley 1982; Triscari and Leifer 1985; Tushman 1979). Thus, the pursuit of explanatory models for the relationship between IT and organizational structure continues.

IT and Organizations: Unpredictable Interactions

In recent years a school of thinking has evolved which argues that the uses and consequences of the introduction of IT emerge in an unpredictable manner from complex social interactions. Markus and Robey refer to this as the 'emergent perspective' (see Fig. 1.1). Building on the work of Salancik and Pfeffer (1978) and Giddens (1979, 1982, 1984), scholars argue that the perception, (and hence the use), of IT is subjective and that the meanings associated with IT are socially constructed (Fulk *et al.* 1990). Orlikowski and Robey (1991) assert that IT plays a dual role in organizations. First, IT possesses an objective set of rules and resources that both enhances and constrains the roles of workers within organizations. At the same time, because IT alters the roles and social fabric of work, it possesses a unique cultural-specific component. Thus, the interaction between these dual roles for IT will determine how IT is used and viewed within organizations. This set of properties cannot be predicted a priori, but instead evolves as a unique social norm evolves within an organization.

Thus, in the emergent perspective, technology is viewed not just as providing a technical capability, but also as altering the social fabric of the organization. Because of this complex interaction, making predictions about the relationship between technology and social norms requires detailed understanding of both the proposed uses and features of IT and the evolving organizational processes around the use and implementation of technology.

IT Enables New Organizational Arrangements

Much of this research which has focused on the relationship between IT and organizational structure has assumed that the organization is a stand-alone entity that is separated and buffered from environmental change (Thompson 1967). However, as shifts in the environment and customer demand occur more frequently (Pine 1993; Stalk and Hout 1990), organizations have been forced to develop new models of operating in order to be able to respond to market demands. In order to be more responsive or 'fleet of foot' organizations have increasingly adopted new organizational arrangements, such as networked organizations (Miles and Snow 1987; Nohria and Eccles 1992; Snow *et al.* 1992), strategic alliances (Hamel *et al.* 1989), and virtual corporations (*Business Week* 1993).

At the same time that market forces are requiring organizations to adopt different arrangements and structures, the capabilities of IT to support many of these new arrangements is also becoming increasingly affordable for most organizations. At the heart of many of these geographically diverse and fleeting configurations is the ability of IT quickly and cheaply to transmit data, thus effectively eliminating barriers of time and distance that would previously have been impediments to organizational adaptation.

Increasingly, organizations are developing information systems that are not limited to the originating organization, but use IT to link with companies outside their organization, such as suppliers or customers in their product value chain. Such inter-organizational information systems (Johnston and Vitale 1988) allow firms to share a richer set of data in a real-time fashion, and effectively establish an ongoing linkage or relationship, which is one of the purposes of a traditional organization. Examples of these inter-organizational information systems are well established in both American and European retail settings, for example, Wal-Mart and Proctor and Gamble and Asda and Proctor and Gamble respectively. In these cases the retailer and supplier not only perform electronic ordering and invoicing, but also the retailer provides forecasting information to manufacturers better to enable them to meet demand, and avoid stock outages in the stores.

To date, the establishment of such inter-organizational systems and electronically created organizations has required the participating organizations to invest in the communication infrastructure necessary to create the communication linkages. However, with the explosion of electronic communication occurring over publicly provided communication infrastructures, such as Internet, these types of non-traditional organizational arrangements will undoubtedly become more frequent. Also, the possibility of richer types of communication, such as voice, image, and data, occurring over a publicly provided digital communication infrastructure, for example, 'the Information SuperHighway', provides the opportunity to expand the appropriateness of such electronically enabled networks. In such an environment it is vital for both researchers and managers to understand the capabilities and limitations of such arrangements. For example, how does organizational learning occur in a networked or virtual corporation? Such issues will be at the heart of investigation into the next century.

Summary

Figure 1.1 summarizes the perspectives described above about the interactions between IT and organizational structure. Clearly, past research has

suggested very different relationships, with a different set of managerial practices associated with each. The question arises whether both IT
researchers and practitioners should continue to view this area of inquiry
as one with no clear solutions. Alternatively we might ask whether there
are recommendations that can be made to guide both future research and
managerial practice in this area. The next section seeks to take an initial
step in this direction.

Analytical Lenses for Critiquing the IT-Organization Structure Literature

In this section six different analytical lenses will be used to interpret and
critique the literature summarized in the previous section. The lenses
used are: (1) unit of analysis; (2) task; (3) nature of IT; (4) conceptualization of organization; (5) period of data collection; and (6) alignment
between IT and organizational structure.

Unit of Analysis

Many of the research studies which have set out to determine the relationship between IT and organizational structure have suffered from one particularly worrying defect. They have sought to make statements about the
implications of IT on the organization as a whole, yet studied information
systems that impact only part of the organization. For example, common
types of information systems that have been studied are sales monitoring
or customer ordering systems (Robey 1981). Clearly, these types of systems
will affect different functions and different levels of personnel in varying
manners. It is difficult and probably inaccurate in many cases to make
observations at a local level and then generalize findings to an aggregate
or organizational level.

   Thus, we must seek to align the impact of the information system under
evaluation with the appropriate level of organizational impact. If one wants
to make statements about the organization as a whole, then one must
study computer information systems that impact the entire organization.
In addition, the manner in which workers interact and the tasks performed
in the information system must be similar. Clearly, this is a very rigorous
set of hurdles for inquiry. An alternative is to reduce the organizational
level of IT impact to the area in which the information system is used in
a homogeneous, or at least fairly consistent, manner. Therefore, rather
than examining the relationship between IT and organizational structure,
the more appropriate level of inquiry may be between IT and the organizational sub-unit.

   Tushman and Nadler (1978) have asserted that organizations can be viewed as being composed of departments or sets of groups, which they refer to as sub-units. They further argue that this perspective on organizational structure suggests that the appropriate unit of analysis is the organizational sub-unit. Thus, rather than attempting to characterize the organization as a whole, the more important issue may be what are the optimal organizational arrangements for the various organizational sub-units, such as R&D, production, and marketing, and what are the appropriate mechanisms used to co-ordinate these interdependent sub-units. Similarly, the appropriate question may be to ask what is the impact of IT on an organization's sub-units and how can IT be used to facilitate co-ordination among these various sub-units.

This view is consistent with others who have suggested that part of the natural evolution of organizational growth is for organizations to form specialized units that are created to deal with specialized tasks or specific aspects of the organization's environment (Lawrence and Lorsch 1967). Through creating these specialized sub-units, organizations also must be concerned with how to integrate these sub-units in order effectively to run the entire organization (Lawrence and Lorsch 1967; van de Ven *et al.* 1976), that is, decisions about how to link activities of different production sub-units or share product design staff across sub-units must be decided.

In summary, analysis of the relationship between IT and organizational sub-units should result in a more accurate matching of the scope of impact of IT with the affected area of the organization. In addition, analysis at the organizational sub-unit level may allow for more accurate comparisons across similar sub-units within organizations, which will facilitate a cumulative and hopefully more generalizable set of recommendations. Conducting research at the organizational sub-level also may be more relevant as more organizations continue to focus on alternative forms of organizational arrangements, such as networked or virtual organizations. In these cases the organization focuses only a few activities and seldom conducts all procedures necessary to develop products.

Task

A second lens though which to evaluate existing literature describing the relationship between IT and organizational structure is through the type of task that is studied. Clearly few organizations perform only a single task. Unfortunately, much of the literature in this area often only examines a single task and then generalizes the impact of IT on this task to the organization as whole. An alternative approach would be to more clearly define the nature of the task along several dimensions.

One possible dimension for defining tasks would be around the structuredness of the task (Gorry and Scott-Morton 1971; Simon 1960), that is, how well understood is the task, or is task knowledge in codified or tacit form (Kogut and Zander 1992). The greater the structuredness of the task, the more likely the task knowledge is to be in codified form. More structured or less equivocal tasks are more likely domains for computerization (Gorry and Scott-Morton 1971; Daft and Lengel 1986). Less structured or more equivocal tasks may be less well suited to the application of IT. For example, studying the tasks in a payroll system would probably produce different results from a similar analysis of new product development. Thus, the impact of IT on the organization may be due to the nature of the task under analysis rather than some intrinsic property of the organization or IT.

A second possible dimension for defining tasks is the organizational level at which the task is performed, that is, operational, control, or strategic (Anthony 1964; Gorry and Scott-Morton 1971). The organizational level of the IT-impacted task is an important consideration in examining the effect of IT upon an organization, because the same IT system may be used for different purposes throughout the organization. For example, a computer-integrated manufacturing system (CIM) could have different effects if the task examined was the nature of production work compared, say, with top-management decision-making. If the production work becomes highly automated as a result of CIM, then the system may be used to empower the workers better to plan their own work, because they are aware of the work-flow in the entire plant. Alternatively, if the impact of CIM is examined by exploring the nature of top-management decision-making, then one might see this task centralized, because of the availability of real-time information in easily accessible form, such as through an executive information system (EIS).

Thus, as both researchers and practitioners attempt to understand the relationship between IT and organizational structure, the nature of the task that IT is impacting must be consistent across the various studies if comparative findings are to have any meaning. Two dimensions of the task that are important in determining consistency are the structuredness of the task and the location within the organization at which the task is performed.

Nature of IT

Research exploring the relationship between IT and organizational structure has been a fundamental question for over thirty-five years. However, during this time the capabilities and varieties of IT have changed dramatically, and in interpreting research on IT and organizational structure one must be clear exactly what type of IT is under consideration.

Several characterizations of IT have been developed by previous researchers. For example, Robey (1983) categorized IT into these types of systems: administrative, production scheduling, and central co-ordination systems. He also noted that these different types of systems had different effects in organizations. In particular, he noted that systems designed merely to automate existing procedures did not tend to result in any organizational changes. Thus, not only is the type of IT important, but so is the organization's purpose in using this technology.

Markus and Robey (1988) noted that previous researchers have described IT using such dimensions as batch processing versus administrative systems, decision support versus decision-making, and administrative versus technical systems. Thus, IT may be described in terms of how the user interacts with the technology, the extent of support, and the type of function supported. However, technology use within an organization is characterized by all of these dimensions, and probably many more. It is vital to understand which are the key dimensions for the technology under investigation. These dimensions may vary with the organization's purpose for using the technology and how long the technology has been used within the organization. Thus, making comparisons about the use of IT across organizations is not a simple process, but is often contextually bound by these and other characteristics.

Because of the many characterizations of IT, some researchers have chosen not to examine the type of IT used, but rather measure the extent of IT usage. Often this is operationalized by broad metrics, such as amount of money spent on IT. Of course, just because organizations spend the same amount of money on technology, this does not imply that they are actually utilizing the investment to the same extent.

The dimensions of analysing IT are also influenced by the nature of the impact that IT has in the organization. One perspective on this is Kling and Scacchi's (1982) characterization of IT in terms of 'discrete-entity' or 'web' models. IT can be described as discrete-entity if it has fairly well-established boundaries of influence and change. An example of such a system would be a computerized payroll system. On the other hand, web models describe IT which have impacts that are much harder to define, such as a customer database. Here the set of users who access a database and their reasons for doing so are much more ill-defined than in the case of the users of a payroll system.

It seems clear that there are no established methods for defining IT. However, this is absolutely necessary if comparative studies of the influence of IT on organizational structures are to occur. In addition, as new generations of IT become available, such as multi-media, then new dimensions of IT will be required in order to fully describe these very powerful and malleable IT tools.

Conceptualization of Organization

In the previous section we explored the different ways in which IT has been defined in research exploring the relationship between IT and organizational structure. Here we explore the other principal component of these studies, the organization, and will review various theories that have been used to describe or characterize organizations.

As a starting-point for exploring perspectives on organizations I will discuss four characterizations of organizations proposed by Malone (1985): rationalist, motivational, political, and information processing.

The rationalist perspective assumes that organizations are composed of intendedly rational agents, all of whom are working towards a common goal. This goal is typically an economic one, and often is profit maximization. The major objectives of the firm under this set of assumptions is focusing on economic efficiency and rational behaviour and structuring of the firm. In the rationalist perspective of organizations the impact of IT on the organization would be explored through examining changes in work and job roles, because IT allows work to be performed more efficiently or in new and different ways.

The motivational perspective realizes that workers may have interests that are divergent from those of the owners or managers of the organization, but assumes that these varying goals can be aligned through the appropriate design of individual jobs. The underlying assumption is that if jobs are sufficiently interesting and motivating, then employees have greater job satisfaction, which will result in better performance. Under these conditions, the primary focus for the impact of IT in organizations is its impact on individual jobs and the enhancement or routinization of the tasks performed.

The political perspective on organizations assumptions that the organization is not one monolithic group of people, but is instead composed of different interest-groups which may have conflicting goals that cannot be resolved through negotiation. Conflict resolution occurs through the use of power, and power determines the direction the organization will take. Here, the utilization of IT revolves around the shifts in the balance of power within the organization. The assumption is that those presently in control will use IT to reinforce or enhance their existing position of power, rather than being used to change the organization if this would result in a decrease in power.

The information processing perspective focuses on communication patterns and information flows within organizations. This approach shares the same assumptions as the rational perspective—mainly that individuals are rational and working toward a common goal. Under these assumptions, the introduction of IT is mainly concerned with changes in the nature of information processing and communication within organizations, especially with regard to the amount and location of information processed.

The previous characterizations of organizations have viewed the organization as a static framework of normative or behavioral relationships. An alternative conception of organizations is that organizations are continuously evolving over time. As stated by Barley (1986: 80): 'Through this interplay, called the process of structuring, institutional practices shape human actions, which, in turn, reaffirm or modify the institutional structure. Thus, the study of structuring involves investigating how the institutional realm and the realm of action configure each other.' Giddens (1979) refers to this process of actions defining structures and structures constraining actions as structuration. The investigation of how IT and organizational structure mutually influence and constrain each other (Orlikowski and Robey 1991) is thus a very different perspective than much of the previous work investigating the relationship between IT and organizational structure, which assumed that the nature of influence between IT and organization was unidirectional, not bidirectional.

Period of Data Collection

Previous research exploring the relationship between IT and organizational structure has used a variety of methods in collecting data. Some research has used survey instruments to sample a variety of firms at a particular point in time, while other studies have used in-depth case-based data on a few firms to inform their conclusions. Is one method more appropriate than the other for collecting information about this relationship?

At the heart of this question is how are the IT-based changes in organizations best observed—through a snapshot or through videotape? Also at issue is whether one wants to detect changes over time, or rather to understand and follow how those changes occurred.

If the objective of the research is merely to denote differences or changes over a period of time, then survey research may be the most appropriate method for investigation. However, this type of research is not without its complications. Of critical importance is the lag period between when IT is introduced into a firm and when changes occur. Obviously this does not occur overnight, and different firms may change at different rates. An additional problem in developing a sample of firms to survey is the date at which the IT was introduced. Unless this occurred at a similar time across all organizations, then interpreting the results may be problematic and not truly reflect the impact that IT has had on the organization, because of time-related issues around when technology was introduced.

If the objective of the research is to denote the pattern of change over time rather than just the resultant effect, then longitudinal data-collection methods such as case studies or repeated surveys are more appropriate. Some of the problems with this research are generalizing the results from a few firms to have implications and meaning for a larger set of firms. Also, it is unclear how long an observation period is necessary to follow the pattern of IT-related organizational change. Longitudinal or event studies research is absolutely necessary if one takes a structuration view (Giddens 1979; Orlikowski and Robey 1991) of IT and organizations. Here it is assumed that technology and organizations simultaneously constrain and change each other, and that organizations evolve over time. Again, the generalizability of these results to firms in general is difficult, because many of the findings may be contextually dependent on social and behavioral norms within the studied organizations.

Alignment between IT and Organizational Structure

Research evaluating the relationship between IT and organizational structure has assumed that IT will either reinforce or aid in shifting the organization to a new structure, for example from centralized to decentralized. The underlying assumption is that the relationship between IT and organizational structure is static. In other words, an IT-based change leads to a single impact or shift in organizational structure—an intervention occurs and a new stable structure results.

However, if one instead assumes that IT and organizations have an ongoing interaction and simultaneously constrain and change each other (Orlikowski and Robey 1991), then the idea of alignment takes a different perspective. For example, the hand-held computers (HHCs) that were given to route salespersons to automate the order-collection function in Frito Lay first had a centralizing impact as information from the entire sales force was centrally consolidated for production decisions. However, over time this information was then made available to lower levels and different functions better to inform their decisions, and resulted in a decentralizing tendency. Thus, the same information systems may have different impact on the organization at different points in time. In other words, the relationship between IT and organizational structure is time-dependent. In addition, this relationship may also be dependent on the rate of evolution of IT users' skills, as a more robust skill-set will allow IT to be used in different ways. It is therefore increasingly necessary to assume not that the relationship between IT and organizational structure is static, but that it changes over time. Future research must begin to address what factors (e.g. social norms) influence how this relationship will evolve.

Discussion and Conclusions

It is now apparent that the relationship between information technology and organizational structure is not easily described. This is because the introduction of IT seldom occurs in isolation; rather it is often accompanied by many changes—work practices, skill-sets, and authority relationships to name a few. To further complicate matters, it seems clear that the use of IT is not a static phenomenon, but instead constantly evolves as new uses for the technology are developed.

Furthermore, technology also has been changing rapidly. The price–performance improvements in semiconductor technology are unparalleled. In addition, new types of technology, such as multi-media, are springing forth. At the same time, the usability and power of software also has greatly improved. Together, these changes have shifted the fundamental emphasis away from computation towards communication and co-ordination of activities. With this as a primary objective of IT, the impact of technology will become more amorphous in many organizations.

Indeed, the fundamental assumption of much of the previous research has been that IT alters organizational structure, the idea being that IT and organizational structures are separate entities. Increasingly, this argument is invalid—IT is becoming the organizational structure, because it is increasingly the principal source of information transmission. This is especially true in many of the new organizational forms that are evolving—networked organizations and virtual corporations. In these arrangements IT is often the enabler that allows them to exist. Without IT's capability to remove time-and-distance barriers in a cost-effective manner such arrangements would not be viable. Thus, the critical agenda for researchers and practitioners is to begin exploring where and how IT and organizational structure are the same and where they differ, rather than assuming that they are separate.

References

Anshen, M. (1960), 'The Manager and the Black Box', *Harvard Business Review*, vol. 38, no. 6, pp. 85–92.

Anthony, R. N. (1964), *Planning and Control Systems: A Framework for Analysis*, Harvard Business School, Division of Research.

Applegate, L. M., Cash, J. I., and Mills, D. Q. (1988), 'Information Technology and Tomorrow's Manager', *Harvard Business Review*, vol. 66, no. 6, pp. 128–36.

Attewell, P., and Rule, J. (1984), 'Computing and Organizations: What We Know and What We Don't Know', *Communications of the ACM*, vol. 27, pp. 1,184–92.

Barley, S. R. (1986), 'Technology as an Occasion for Structuring: Evidence from Observations of CT Scanners and the Social Order of Radiology Departments', *Administrative Science Quarterly*, vol. 31, pp. 78–108.

Blau, P. M., Falbe, C. M., McKinley, W., and Tracy, P. K. (1976), 'Technology and Organization in Manufacturing', *Administrative Science Quarterly*, vol. 21, no. 1, pp. 20–40.

Buchanan, D. A., and Boddy, D. (1983), *Organizations in the Computer Age: Technological Imperatives and Strategic Choice*, Aldershot: Gower.

Burlingame, J. F. (1961), 'Information Technology and Decentralization', *Harvard Business Review*, vol. 39, no. 6, pp. 121–6.

Business Week (1993), 'The Virtual Corporation', (8 Feb.), 36–40.

Chandler, A. D. (1962), *Strategy and Structure*, Cambridge, Mass.: MIT Press.

Child, J. (1973), 'Predicting and Understanding Organization Structure', *Administrative Science Quarterly*, vol. 18, pp. 168–85.

—— (1984), 'New Technology and Developments in Management Organization', *Omega*, vol. 12, no. 3, pp. 211–23.

Daft, R. L., and Lengel, R. H. (1986), 'Organizational Information Requirements, Media Richness and Structural Design', *Management Science*, vol. 32, pp. 554–71.

Daft, R. L., and MacIntosh, N. B. (1978), 'A New Approach to the Design and Use of Management Information', *California Management Review*, vol. 21, pp. 82–92.

—— (1981), 'A Tentative Exploration into the Amount and Equivocality of Information Processing in Organizational Work Units', *Administrative Science Quarterly*, vol. 26, pp. 207–24.

Fry, L. W. (1982), 'Technology-Structure Research: Three Critical Issues', *Academy of Management Journal*, vol. 25, pp. 532–52.

Fulk, J., Schmitz, J., and Steinfield, C. W. (1990) (eds.), *A Social Influence Model of Technology Use, in Organizations and Communication Technology*, London: Sage Publications.

Galbraith, J. R. (1973), *Designing Complex Organizations*, Reading, Mass.: Addison-Wesley.

—— (1977), *Organization Design*, Reading, Mass.: Addison-Wesley.

George, J. F., and King, J. L. (1991), 'Examining the Computing and Centralization Debate', *Communications of the ACM*, vol. 34, no. 7, pp. 63–72.

Giddens, A. (1979), *Central Problems in Social Theory: Action, Structure and Contradiction in Social Analysis*, Berkeley: University of California Press.

—— (1982), *Profiles and Critiques in Social Theory*, Berkeley: University of California Press.

—— (1984), *The Constitution of Society: Outline of the Theory of Structure*, Berkeley: University of California Press.

Gorry, G. A., and Scott-Morton, M. S. (1971), 'A Framework for Management Information Systems', *Sloan Management Review*, vol. 13, pp. 55–70.

Hamel, G., Doz, Y., and Prahalad, C. K. (1989), 'Collaborate with Your Competitors—and Win!', *Harvard Business Review*, 67/1 (Jan.–Feb.), 133–9.

Hoos, I. (1960), 'When the Computer Takes Over the Office', *Harvard Business Review*, vol. 38, no. 4, pp. 102–12.

Huber, G. P. (1990), 'A Theory of the Effects of Advanced Information Technologies on Organizational Design, Intelligence, and Decision Making', *Academy of Management Review*, vol. 15, no. 1, pp. 47–71.

Johnston, H. R., and Vitale, M. R. (1988), 'Creating Competitive Advantage with Interorganizational Information Systems', *MIS Quarterly*, vol. 12, no. 2, pp. 153–65.

Klatsky, S. R. (1970), 'Automation, Size, and the Locus of Decision Making: The Cascade Effect', *Journal of Business*, vol. 43, no. 2, pp. 141–51.

Kling, R., and Scacchi, W. (1982), 'The Web of Computing: Computer Technology and Social Organization', *Advancer in Computers*, 21, New York: Academic Press.

Kogut, B., and Zander, U. (1992), 'Knowledge of the Firm, Combinative Capabilities, and the Replication of Technology', *Organization Science*, vol. 3, no. 3, pp. 383–97.

Lawrence, P., and Lorsch, J. (1967), *Organizations and Environment*, Cambridge, Mass.: Harvard University Press.

Leavitt, H. J., and Whisler, T. L. (1958), 'Management in the 1980s', *Harvard Business Review*, vol. 36, pp. 41–8.

Leifer, R., and McDonough, E. F. (1985), 'Computerization as a Predominant

Technology Affecting the Work Unit Structure', *Proceedings of the Sixth International Conference on Information Systems*, 238–48.

Malone, T. W. (1985), 'Designing Organizational Interfaces', in Proceedings of the CHI '85 Conference on Human Factors in Computing Systems, San Francisco: Association for Computing Machinery, 66–71.

—— (1987), 'Modelling Coordination in Organizations and Markets', *Management Science*, vol. 33, pp. 1,317–32.

—— and Rockart, J. F. (1991), 'Computers, Networks and the Corporation', *Scientific American* (Sept.), 128–36.

Malone, T. W., Yates, J., and Benjamin, R. I. (1987), 'Electronic Markets and Electronic Hierarchies', *Communications of the ACM*, vol. 30, pp. 484–97.

Mann, F. C., and Williams, L. K. (1958), 'Organizational Impact of White Collar Automation', Annual Proceedings of Industrial Research Associates, 59–68.

Markus, M. L., and Robey, D. (1988), 'Information Technology and Organizational Change: Causal Structure in Theory and Research', *Management Science*, vol. 34, no. 5, pp. 583–98.

Miles, R. E., and Snow, C. C. (1987), 'Network Organizations: New Concepts for New Forms', *California Management Review* (Spring).

Morrow, P. C. (1981), 'Work Related Communication, Environmental Uncertainty, and Subunit Effectiveness: A Second Look at the Information Processing Approach to Subunit Communication', *Academy of Managment Journal*, vol. 24, pp. 851–8.

Nelson, R. R., and Winter, S. (1982), *An Evolutionary Theory of Economic Change*, Cambridge, Mass.: Harvard University Press.

Nohria, N., and Eccles, R. G. (1992), *Networks and Organizations*, Boston: Harvard Business School Press.

Orlikowski, W. J., and Baroudi, J. J. (1991), 'Studying Information Technology in Organizations: Research Approaches and Assumptions', *Information Systems Research*, vol. 2, no. 1, pp. 1–28.

Orlikowski, W. J., and Robey, D. (1991), 'Information Technology and the Structuring of Organizations', *Information Systems Research*, vol. 2, no. 2, pp. 143–69.

Penley, L. E. (1982), 'An Investigation of the Information Processing Framework of Organizational Communication', *Human Communication Research*, vol. 8, pp. 348–65.

Perrow, C. (1967), 'A Framework for the Comparative Analysis of Organizations', *American Sociological Review*, vol. 32, pp. 194–208.

—— (1970) *Organizational Analysis: A Sociological Review*, Belmont, California: Wadsworth.

Pfeffer, J., and Leblebici, H. (1977), 'Information Technology and Organizational Structure', *Pacific Sociological Review*, vol. 20, no. 2, pp. 241–61.

Pine, B. J. (1993), *Mass Customization*, Boston: Harvard Business School Press.

Reif, W. E. (1968), *Computer Technology and Management Organization*, Bureau of Business and Economic Research, College of Business Administration, University of Iowa, Iowa City.

Robey, D. (1977), 'Computers and Management Structure: Some Empirical Findings Re-Examined', *Human Relations*, vol. 30, pp. 963–76.

—— (1981), 'Computer Information Systems and Organizational Structure', *Communications of the ACM*, vol. 24, no. 10, pp. 679–87.

—— (1983), 'Information Systems and Organizational Change: A Comparative Case Study', *Systems, Objectives, Solutions*, vol. 3, pp. 143–54.

Rovenda, C., and Ciborra, C. (1981), 'Impact of Information Technology upon Organizational Structures', in *Microelectronics, Productivity, and Employment*, ICCP #5, Paris: OECD.

Salancik, G. R., and Pfeffer, J. (1978), 'A Social Information Processing Approach to Job Attitudes and Task Design', *Administrative Science Quarterly*, vol. 23, pp. 224–53.

Senge, P. M. (1990), *The Fifth Discipline*, New York: Doubleday.

Simon, H. A. (1960), *The New Science of Management Decision*, New York: Harper & Row.

—— (1973), 'Applying Information Technology to Organization Design', *Public Administration Review*, 268–78.

Snow, C. C., Miles, R. E., and Coleman, H. J. (1992), 'Managing 21st Century Network Organizations', *Organizational Dynamics* (Winter), 5–20.

Specht, P. H. (1986), 'Job Characteristics as Indicants of Information Systems Requirements', *MIS Quarterly*, vol. 10, pp. 271–87.

Stalk, G., and Hout, T. M. (1990), *Competing Against Time*, New York: Free Press.

Thompson, J. D. (1967), *Organizations in Action*, New York: McGraw-Hill.

Triscari, T., and Leifer, R. (1985), 'Information Processing in Organizations: An Empirical Test of the Tushman–Nadler Model', paper presented at the Academy of Management National Meeting, San Diego.

Tushman, M. L. (1979), 'Impacts of Perceived Environmental Variability on Patterns of Work-Related Communication', *Academy of Management Journal*, vol. 22, pp. 482–500.

—— and Nadler, D. A. (1978), 'Information Processing as an Integrating Concept in Organizational Design', *Academy of Management Review*, vol. 3, pp. 613–24.

van de Ven, A., Delbecq, A., and Koenig, R. (1976), 'Determinants of Coordination Modes Within Organizations', *American Sociological Review*, vol. 41, pp. 322–38.

Whisler, T. L. (1967), 'The Impact of Information Technology on Organizational Control', in C. A. Myers (ed.), *The Impact of Computers on Management*, Cambridge, Mass.: MIT Press.

—— (1970a), *The Impact of Computers on Organizations*, New York: Praeger.

—— (1970b), *Information Technology and Organizational Change*, Belmont, Calif.: Wadsworth.

Woodward, J. (1965), *Industrial Organization: Theory and Practice*, London: Oxford University Press.

2

Groupware in Decision Support

PAUL ANAND

Introduction

The scope, rules, and technologies of organizational decision-making are changing rapidly—issues such as business reengineering, globalization, teamworking, networking, subcontracting, and privatization are just a few examples of the way in which organizations are now forced fundamentally to revise the way they design the nexus of internal and external relations that govern corporate life. The old idea of individuals relating through hierarchical direction and coming together on set occasions continues to wane under the rise of persuasion and negotiation as norms of social interaction. Finally, the exploitation of information technologies can transform the opportunities for such interactions to occur.

It is perhaps decision-making in groups that best allows us to explore some of these changes. In this chapter I shall review some of the ideas behind the growth[1] of what has variously come to be known, *inter alia*, as collaborative working, group decision support, and groupware. Figure 2.1 shows the growth of interest in groupware and compared with other decision support technologies. The aim of the paper is to sketch an understanding of what group decision support is, and why we might need it and what we know about its effects. To understand the potential scope and impact of groupware, we do need to examine both theories of decision-making and the diffusion and adoption of new technologies.

The Decision-Making Task

Although good managers do much more than make good decisions, a broad view of the decision-making process provides a useful starting-point from which to understand what groups must do. The following list is a generalization of a taxonomy due to Herbert Simon (Sprague 1980):

[1] I am very grateful to Michael Earl for comments on earlier draft. Fig. 2.1 shows the growth of interest in Groupware compared with other decision support technologies. Human interface systems are those which rely on the use of human intermediaries—e.g. telephone banking.

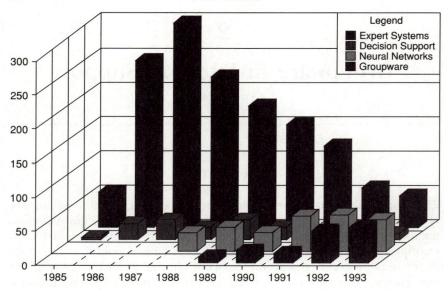

Fig. 2.1. *Interest in decision support technologies as measured by media coverage*

- information gathering;
- problem innovation;
- option selection;
- implementation;
- evaluation;
- feedback, learning, and refinement.

Information gathering or scanning becomes more important as the rate of change in the environment speeds up. The activity is one in which successful entrepreneurs are particularly adept (Gilad *et al.* 1988), and which provides inputs both for day-to-day activities as well as ideas about what I shall call 'problem innovation'. The higher up the managerial tree a person progresses, the more the job moves away from solving problems defined by others towards the crystallization of new problems which establish parameters within which others must act. With their emphasis on problem solving, academic tests of competence are usually a poor guide to the various skills and procedures required to fulfil this function of problem innovation (see de Bono 1977).

Option selection is what classical decision theory is all about (Anand 1993), and merits little further comment except perhaps to say that though quantitively phrased, many of decision theory's ideas have practical value as qualitative guidelines. More important is the question of implementation which came to the fore as an issue when people noticed that plans and consultants' reports had a habit of gathering dust rather than providing support for change. Many of the problems associated with implementation can be solved just by taking into account the decision-making of a wider class of decision-makers than might otherwise be the case (as an excellent introduction to information systems implementation by Farrell and Broude (1987) shows). In a sense, there is nothing mystical about implementation: it just requires a more comprehensive account of stakeholders (Mitroff and Linstone 1993) and their interests, though without a separate and explicit implementation stage decisions may collapse rather quickly. The final items, evaluation, feedback, learning, and refinement are really part of one process though the emphasis varies between organizations. Some public sector bodies are primarily keen on evaluation, though for reasons which have more to do with accountability than with learning.

We can also think of decision styles as being summarized, *inter alia*, by the amount of *time* given to each of the activities. In comparison with Japanese firms, Western organizations tend to spend less time scanning and more on implementation and error correction. Although the Japanese are noted for a 'right first time' attitude, they are also able to react to new information very quickly and indeed the strictures of social pressure seem to be designed to ensure this.

The Need For Group Support

Having defined what decision-making is, it will be useful to recall what we know about the possible problems that can reduce the effectiveness of group activities. The list of problems is long enough to encourage modesty even in the most resolute.

A Catalogue of Errors

Groups consist of individuals who are prone to error and they might serve either to compensate or compound the mistakes which limited information processing capacities lead us to make. Just saying that humans have limited cognitive capacities does not lead us very far, except perhaps to the suggestion that automated information processing might be an improvement, though we know that the simplistic 'automate' view does not curry favour in the managerial decision-making of organizations. More interesting is the fact that we make errors in a systematic way, a result we might exploit either by seeking to reduce the degree of bias in our own decisions or by using our knowledge of those biases in the decision-making of others.[2]

Logical Reasoning

Most of us would say that we were reasonably logical, though there is plenty of evidence that we are not. One experimental research programme related to the development of artificial intelligence arose from work which showed that individuals could not act on a problem which required only the simplest understanding of logical relations (Wason 1968). The resulting puzzle, how we solve everyday problems with more complex structures correctly, was partly answered by a theoretical development due to Shank and Abelson (1986), who argued that we perform mental logic tasks by learning how to solve problems in similar contexts—keeping the logical structure and defamiliarizing the context causes us to behave as if the problem were new. More recently still, experimental work by Perkins (1986), based on naturalistic reasoning and critical thinking, shows that arguments are judged inadequate by others for a few basic reasons:

sparse situation modelling involves a number of errors due to over-simplification of the decision problem, whilst *use of evidence* problems arise when people give arguments that are, in some way, inadequate to their evidential premises.

Probabilistic Inference

Another major research programme examining our ability to make decisions under conditions of risk or uncertainty finds that we often make systematic errors when estimating chances. Sometimes, as in the case of over- or under-weighting of small probabilities, it is difficult to be categorical about the desirability of the practice. Perhaps low probability disasters should be given more than their probability-weighed consequences suggest and perhaps they should be ignored as planners and statisticians sometimes suggest. However, there are occasions when behaviour gives a stronger indication of error. The representative heuristic, for one, leads to irrelevant information biasing judgements that would otherwise be correct. When subjects are given a rather bland description of a 30-year-old person selected at random from a group of engineers and lawyers in the proportions 70 : 30 and asked the probability that the person is an engineer, they tend to ignore the essential base probabilities and offer probabilities of 0.5.

A second source of bias is due to the availability or otherwise of relevant instances. US citizens asked whether they believe murder or suicide the more likely cause of death offer murder, although suicide is actually one-

---

[2] Using proneness to cognitive bias, in and of itself, raises no ethical issue through the end to which it is used might—and that is no different from anything else.

OBSERVABLE ANTECEDENTS   OBSERVABLE CONSEQUENCES

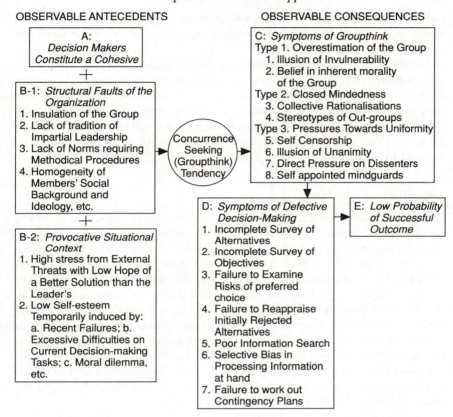

Fig. 2.2. *Theoretical analysis of grouplink. After Essex and Lindoerfer, 1989*

and-a-half times more likely. It seems it is easier to recall instances of the former however, either because of the way we store information or for social reasons (e.g. reporting frequency.)

Groupthink

In an intriguing analysis of US foreign policy-making, Janis (1972) and Janis and Mann (1982) proposed a model of defective decision-making in groups which identifies three key elements: a highly pressurized and often time-constrained decision-making problem; a strong group; and a weak organizational structure (see Fig. 2.2). The idea simply is that groups can tend to generate and promote behaviour in their members that serves to filter out undesirable information and unprejudiced evaluation. The main consequences of groupthink are: incomplete survey of alternatives, incomplete survey of objectives, failure to examine risks of preferred choice, failure to reappraise initially rejected alternatives, poor information search, selective bias in processing information available, and failure to work out contingency plans.

Decisions in which losses might be substantial are especially susceptible as groups are only weakly conditioned to follow good decision-making rules by the organization in which they operate. (Press statements by the US military during the war with Iraq seem to suggest they now consciously take steps to avoid the problem.) Groupthink is, to a large extent, the result of groups failing to perform different components of the decision-making process to a high enough standard.

Organizational Failure

There are many views about the ways in which organizations fail, and here we mention just two. The first, due to the 'garbarge can' theory of organizations, suggests that problems and solutions flow through organizations along two essentially different and independent lines. Both occur at random and the co-existence of a problem and the availability of its solution is, in part, a matter of luck so that there is, potentially, an opportunity to consciously manage these flows. A second view (Brown 1983), depends on the idea that productive interfaces between departments within organizations and between organizations themselves require a certain level of conflict. Too much conflict leads to a breakdown of relations, but there are dangers from relations that are too cosy also (see Fig. 2.3). Information requirements are, however, sometimes discussed in a way that pays little attention to the emotive and political uses to which data is often put.

Types of Group Decision Support

In deciding what is and what is not a support for groups, one has to ask what distinguishes a group from a set of individuals. Mere membership is barely adequate, though it helps raise the question of whether we think organizations should support informal as well as formal groups. One of the features of conventional meetings is that a number of individuals can interact very quickly and by this criterion three people communicating and responding immediately via e-mail would, in informational terms, be close to a conventional meeting, wherever they were located around the world at the time.

Decision Conferencing

As a response to the 'dust-gathering' syndrome from which consultant reports can suffer, decision analysts began in the late 1970s to involve cli-

A. PRODUCTIVE CONFLICT

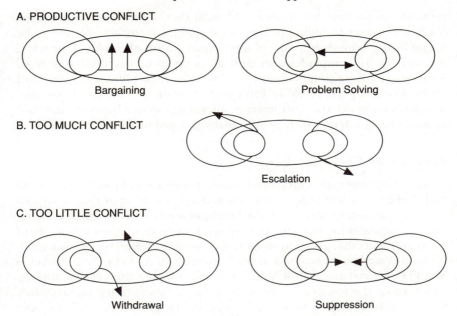

Bargaining   Problem Solving

B. TOO MUCH CONFLICT

Escalation

C. TOO LITTLE CONFLICT

Withdrawal   Suppression

Fig. 2.3. *Dynamics of interface development. After Brown (1983)*

ents in the application of the techniques they were using. Commonly a facilitator, who in some respects takes on the role of chair (Weiss and Zwahlen 1982), will identify a group of key stakeholders and take them through a process that often lasts two days and takes place away from the normal working environment. Using software versions of frameworks that can be applied to a very wide class of decision problems, the facilitator helps a group build a picture of the decision that confronts it. The model is both a visual representation of options, criteria, and trade-offs and a shared mental picture of issues, the robustness of which can be tested in real time using sensitivity analysis. Consensus building and establishing 'buy-in' are key objectives for facilitators.

Teleconferencing

A number of IT developers have explored the business potential for supporting groups with the aid of live audio-visual links. The emphasis is on communication,[3] and a variety of devices are available ranging from purely audio equipment to video systems that start from freeze-frame and go up to two-way full motion video. There is relatively little serious academic

---

[3] A number of vendors claim that qualitative benefits are only weakly perceived by potential users (Johansen 1988).

research on the benefits of these, although their rapid uptake during the 'Gulf war' serves to highlight the fact that their main benefits are to be found in the opportunity cost of alternatives. When the risks of air travel are high, or for companies with high travel needs between different fixed locations, there are simple if substantial benefits to be obtained, as the Ford Motor Company has found in Europe. Such systems have also been used in marketing to external customers by allowing potential buyers to view and in some cases interact with people making a product presentation.

Computerized Conference Rooms

In many ways, the main difference between computerized conference rooms and decision conferencing is one of emphasis, for most of their components are common to both. Here the emphasis tends to be on the fit between room design and information technology: human facilitation is just one of the ingredients that go up to support the meeting. Different software modules developed by researchers at the University of Arizona (Nunamaker *et al.* 1989), for instance, support different tasks ranging from brainstorming, which allows the creation of private idea lists to be submitted anonymously to an overhead display that can be seen by the group, through to topic analysis via group wordprocessor. These ideas can then be prioritized with the aid of tools that permit simple voting or multi-attribute evaluation and subsequent policy formation and development activity may draw on software that helps groups use standard conceptual frameworks, such as Porter's value chain analysis.

Use of Group Decision Support Systems

Are these tools being used? Evidence concerning the location and use of GDSS based on a survey of 135 US organizations appears in Beauclair and Straub (1990) and of those sampled,[4] 45 per cent were actively using the technology.

Those using interfaced conferencing mentioned on average four uses, the main ones being: the aggregation of data from different sources (65 per cent), the sharing of statistical analyses (44 per cent), strategic planning (42 per cent), and policy writing (38 per cent). A principal components analysis showed three clusters of usage: administration (policy writing, hiring, strategic planning, report sharing, team building, and voting), planning (forecasting and modelling), and data aggregation (an item separate from the rest).

The computerized conference room seems to be associated with activities

---

[4] The population comprised members of the Data Processing Management Association. See also the review in Sabherwal and Grover (1989).

that reflect the duties of senior managers. The three most commonly cited applications were strategic planning (86 per cent), brainstorming (57 per cent), and forecasting (43 per cent). Components analysis shows different clusters. The most important group includes aggregation of data, unstructured decision-making, forecasting, strategic planning, and modelling. Hiring decisions, policy writing, and structured decisions form a second group, whilst sharing statistical analyses and voting comprise a third category. Whilst plausible, these groupings would seem more difficult to interpret than for interfaced conferencing.

Only five organizations reported the use of teleconferencing: two utilities, two financial institutions, and a government body. With such a small sample generalization is impossible, though the pattern of use was broadly in line with that reported for the computerized conference rooms, except for a greater emphasis on team building.

Overall, the picture is one in which interfaced conferencing is employed primarily for structured decision problems whilst computerized conferencing is used to support less structured planning. Automated voting appears to be of little importance in either situation.

Evaluation of Group Decision Support

Although the evaluation of certain benefits (like time-savings) may be relatively simple, establishing changes to, say, the quality of decisions made requires a theory that enables us to make the with/without comparisons required. Several benefit areas deserve a few final comments: consensus and commitment, decision quality, time savings, cost savings, equity, satisfaction. The first three benefits are difficult to measure let alone quantify in bottom-line terms, though they may be of most value to both the organization and its senior executives.

Consensus and Commitment

The most elegant demonstration that consensus and commitment can result from groupware is available from the decision conferencing work pioneered for both public and private sectors by Larry Phillips at the London School of Economics and members of the Decision Techtronics group based in Albany, New York. Here the production of stable agreements to which signees will adhere seems to be the result of involving key stakeholders and letting everyone be seen to 'have had a say'. The decision focus of such conferences often results in groups comprising members from a wider set of constituencies than routine organizational practice might allow. This contributes to more informed decision-making and reduces the scope for the pursuit of individual or departmental interests at the expense of organizational issues. These are valuable benefits for senior management groups, but a critical success factor seems to be the quality of facilitation which currently depends on the possession of a rare mix of communication and analysis skills.

Decision Quality

To determine effects on decision quality it is helpful to decompose the decision into the basic elements noted at the start of this article. In an early attempt to estimate the value of group interventions, Hoffman (1982) breaks the decision process down into five categories: problem definition and objective setting, constraint identification, solution generation, evaluation, and implementation. Options become more or less attractive as discussions progress and on this depends their acceptance by the group. The degree of individual commitment however depends on an individual's own evaluation and the final decisions usually emerge early on with subsequent discussion providing a reinforcement role. Discussions themselves may be categorized along three dimensions. First, they may be directed towards the decision task in hand or they may be focused on actions designed to foster and maintain group cohesion and identity. Secondly, some issues are handled more implicitly than others—for example, activities relating to the group dynamics are difficult for group members to surface and deal with explicitly. Thirdly, the arguments used may depend on pre-existing rules and norms or they may be more *ad hoc* and specific to the problem in hand.

These dimensions add further insight into what it is that decision-making groups do which might be amenable to support, and provides a background against which we might evaluate experiments and field studies, of which there is an increasing number. We should not forget in all this that the key raw ingredients are the people. Jarvenpaa *et al.* (1988), for example, compare a computerized conference room with an unsupported group using expert evaluations of completeness, clarity, overall and specific handling of issues. A variety of GDSS-related hypotheses proved insignificant although team differences were substantial: in that case it was the people (not the supports) who made the difference to decision quality. The extensive work by the Arizona group at IBM (Vogel *et al.* 1989), on the other hand, showed specifically that non-task interactions were reduced over all stages of the decision-making process and that there were improvements in terms of idea generation, issue identification, goal achievement, and perceived fairness of the process.

Time and Cost Savings

Time (and related cost) savings are difficult to substantiate with experimental methods, though field studies by Nunamaker *et al.* (1989) and Post

(1993) find substantial financial savings due to more focused meetings. At IBM, Nunamaker found time savings of around 50 per cent when compared with chairperson estimates of conventional meeting times. In his work, Post actually costs these out and finds an *ex post* return on investment of 170 per cent.

Equity and Satisfaction

Early accounts of GDS emphasized the scope for democratic decision-making and in some situations, ranging from parliaments to game shows, computerized voting has served useful purposes. Within organizations, however, the emphasis on democracy is beginning to seem slightly off the point and with its impact being limited to certain cultures. Equal participation may be in a group's interests early on in the decision-making process but it serves no obvious purpose later on when key members of the group are moving to closure. A more subjective approach to process evaluation which has been used extensively relies on subjective responses to attitudinal questions. Comfort with support tools depends to some extent on familiarity with information technology, but it is worth remembering that this is only a sufficient condition for the continued use of support tools. Attitudinal measures are no substitute for proxies or surrogates or the performance benefits discussed above. Often an innovation is tried because of the enthusiasm of an individual. This is a precious and time-limited resource which must at some stage be supplanted by the more mundane but ultimately longer-lasting vehicles of routine and procedure. The issue is raised by El Sherif and El Sawey (1988) at the end of their work for the Egyptian government, but it is one on which the IS community needs much more research.

Future Developments

At this point in time a few issues stand out as being under-explored but possibly of considerable interest. First, it seems likely that the communications and presentation aspects will come to the fore, as they have with so many other successful information technologies. Secondly, a couple of papers recently combine group decision support with ideas about expert opinion pooling of the kind associated with iterative Delphi techniques (Kettlehut 1991 and Vickers 1992). At face value it would seem plausible to think that the existence of IT networks might now make the use of experts more feasible than hitherto. Thirdly, attempts to apply GDSS ideas to negotiation are just beginning to emerge (Jarke *et al.* 1987). Given the complexity of negotiation as a cognitive activity, the area seems particularly amenable to, and in need of, support.

No doubt Group Decision Support will continue to develop, transform itself, and combine elements and ideas from other technologies as do most decision support systems. Whilst there are few general rules to go by, one of the features of decision support systems seems to be that the expected benefits change substantially as the technologies move out of the laboratory and into corporations. This makes the case as much for empirical investigation as for technological research and development.

References

Anand P. (1993), *Foundations of Rational Choice Under Risk*, Oxford: Clarendon Press.

Beauclair, R. A., and Straub, D. W. (1990), 'Utilizing GDSS Technology: Final Report on a Recent Empirical Study', *Information and Management*, 18/5 (May), 213–20.

Brown, L. D. (1983), *Managing Conflict at Organizational Interfaces*, Reading, Mass.: Addison-Wesley.

de Bono, E. (1977), *Opportunities*, Harmondsworth: Penguin.

El Sherif, H., and El Sawy, O. A. (1988), 'Issue Based Decision Support Systems for the Egyptian Cabinet', *MIS Quarterly*, 12/4 (Dec.), 551–69.

Esser, J. K., and Lindoerfer, J. S. (1989), 'Groupthink and Space Shuttle Challenger Accident', *Journal of Behavioural Decision-Making*, vol. 2, pp. 139–47.

Farrell, K., and Broude, C. (1987), *Winning the Change Game*, Los Angeles: Breakthrough.

Gilad, B., Kaish, S., and Ronen, J. (1988), 'The Entrepreneurial Way with Information', in S. Maital (ed.), *Applied Behavioural Economics*, Brighton: Wheatsheaf.

Hoffman, L. R. (1982), 'Improving the Problem Solving Process in Managerial Groups', in R. A. Guzzo (ed.), *Improving Group Decision Making in Organizations*, New York: Academic Press, ch. 5.

Janis, I. L. (1972), *Victims of Groupthink*, Boston: Houghton Mifflin.

—— and Mann, L. (1987), *The Free Press*, New York: Macmillan.

Jarke, M., Jellassi, M. T., and Shakun, M. F. (1987), 'Mediator', *European Journal of Operational Research*, vol. 31, pp. 314–34.

Jarvenpaa, S. L., Rao, V. S., and Huber, G. P. (1988), 'Computer Support for Meetings of Groups Working on Unstructured Problems', *MIS Quarterly*, vol. 12, pp. 645–66.

Johansen, R. (1988), *Groupware*, New York: Free Press.

Kettlehut, M. C. (1991), 'Using a DSS to Incorporate Expert Opinion in Strategic Product Development Funding Decision', *Information and Management*, vol. 20, pp. 363–71.

Mitroff, I. I., and Linstone, H. (1993), *The Unbounded Mind*, New York: Oxford University Press.

Nunamaker, J. F., Vogel, D., Heminger, D. R., Martz, B., Gorhowski, R., and McGoff, C. (1989), 'Experience at IBM with Group Support Systems', *Decision Support Systems*, vol. 5, pp. 183–96.

Perkins, D. N. (1986), *Knowledge as Design*, Hillsdale: Erlbaum.

Phillips, L. D. (1984), 'A Theory of Requisite Decision Models', *Acta Psychologica*, vol. 56, pp. 29–48.

Post, B. Q. (1993), 'A Business Case Framework for Group Support Technology', *Journal of Management Information Systems*, vol. 9, pp. 7–26.

Sabherwal, R., and Grover, V. (1989), 'Computer Support for Strategic Decision Making Processes', *Decision Sciences*, vol. 20, pp. 54–74.

Schank, R. C., and Abelson, R. P. (1977), *Scripts, Plans, Goals and Understanding*, Hillsdale, NJ, L. Erlbaum.

Schuman, S. P., and Rohrtbaugh, J. (1991), 'Decision Conferencing for Systems Planning', *Information and Management*, vol. 21, pp. 147–59.

Silver, M. (1991), *Systems that Support Decision Makers*, Chichester: John Wiley.

Sprague, R. H. (1980), 'A Framework for Research on Decision Support Systems', in G. Fick and R. H. Sprague (eds.), *Decision Support Systems*, Oxford: Pergamon.

Vickers, B. (1992), 'Using GDSS To Examine the Future of European Automobile Industry', *Futures*, vol. 24, pp. 789–812.

Vogel, D. R., Nunamaker, J. F., Martz, B., Grohowski, R., and McGoff, C. (1989), 'Electronic Meeting Experience at IBM', *Journal of Management Information Systems*, vol. 6, pp. 25–43.

Wason, P. C. (1968), 'Reasoning About a Rule', *Quarterly Journal of Experimental Psychology*, vol. 20, pp. 273–81.

Weiss, J. J., and Zwahlen, G. W. (1982), 'The Structured Decision Conference', *Hospital and Health Services Administration*, vol. 27, pp. 90–105.

Wright, G. (1984), *Behavioural Decision Theory*, Harmondsworth: Penguin.

3

Knowledge Strategies: Propositions From Two Contrasting Industries

MICHAEL J. EARL

Introduction

It has been argued by Bell (1979) and others that knowledge is the key resource of the post-industrial era and that telecommunications is the key technology. Employment categories have been reclassified to accommodate knowledge-working (Porat 1977) and some analysts have argued that knowledge workers already form the dominant sector of western work forces (OECD 1981). Computer scientists are prone to suggesting that knowledge-based systems can yield abnormal returns. For example, Hayes-Roth *et al.* (1983) claim that knowledge is a scarce resource whose refinement and reproduction create wealth and, further, that knowledge-based information technology is the enabler that turns knowledge into a valuable industrial commodity. It could be argued whether knowledge is scarce, particularly as it can be created, reproduced, and shared with as much chance of multiplying value as depleting it. Indeed, economists who are concerned with allocation and distribution of scarce resources—and also who make assumptions about availability of perfect or costless information— do recognize these unusual qualities, classifying knowledge as a public good (Silberston 1967). What is of interest, therefore, as the information society unfolds, is whether we can learn anything about knowledge, its value, and knowledge-working from companies who are exploiting information technologies in new domains which have the character of knowledge processing.

Two case studies—Shorko Films and Skandia International,[1] are used here inductively to build a set of propositions about knowledge and its management. *Ex post*, they can be seen as examples of firms who built knowledge-based strategies which were enabled by IT. In Skandia's case there is evidence that this was an explicit strategic intent in an information-intensive industry, namely reinsurance. In Shorko Films the strategy could be better

[1] See two case studies, CRIM CS93/2 Skandia International and CRIM CS93/3 Shorko Films SA, Centre for Research in Information Management, London Business School, Sussex Place, London NW1 4SA.

described as an emergent one, following the language of Mintzberg and Waters (1985), in the manufacturing sector, namely chemicals.

Skandia International built a risks/claims/premiums database to be shared and maintained worldwide and accessed by a corporate data communications network. Essentially they built an encyclopaedia on all reinsurance business in chosen niche sectors. This was available to their underwriters anywhere and they could use decision support tools and analysis and enquiry routines to explore patterns over time, work within parameters learnt and codified through experience, and select profitable business taken at sensible prices. The explicit strategy, explained in the 1988 Annual Report, was the building of a platform of 'know-how' and taking the lead in information and communications initiatives across the sector. Although in a somewhat esoteric industry, the Skandia case can be seen as an investment in product/market data or information or knowledge (a definitional conundrum to be discussed later). The plant operators were re-trained in computing, statistical analysis, modelling, and polymer science in order to do these process and product analyses. Knowledge-building through IT at Skandia International allowed them to pursue a niche strategy, specializing in those reinsurance classes which generated high information processing and required high analysis.

Shorko Films built a distributed process control system to try and optimize—or at least improve—factory efficiency in the plastic film-making business. Data was collected by a series of electronic nodes (in concept a network) on many parameters of the production process and optimization was pursued on-line and in-line. However, this crucially provided the opportunity to construct a historical database of product/process experience that could be analysed to learn how to make further improvements in the process. Moreover, a better understanding of the interaction between process and product allowed Shorko to specify and develop new products, make product range profitability decisions, and work out how to satisfy customers' specialized requirements. Knowledge-building through IT at Shorko Films allowed them to pursue a competitive strategy of differentiation, exploiting their better understanding of process and its relationship to product, with the intent of yielding premium prices. Previously they had been caught in a seemingly hopeless task of low cost production demanded by the parent.

Both cases can be seen as demonstrators of Zuboff's (1988) concept of informating. Indeed, Shorko is a replication (or technology transfer) of the early directions Zuboff traced in the paper and pulp industry, and the IT investments began with an automating scope before the value of informating was recognized. The process management database became the model or image of the firm's operation, the line operators became knowledge-workers analysing and manipulating information, the distinction between managers and workers became blurred, and the nervous system was the distributed process control electronics. Skandia is not unlike Zuboff's description of her financial services research sites. The database was not here the source of product development, but it was the generator of product decisions. The underwriters have developed new information processing skills using IT tools and the worldwide network was a transmitter and receiver of knowledge. These characteristics will be examined later.

More than 'informating', however, Skandia and Shorko can be seen as evolving cases of *knowledge as strategy* or knowledge strategies. This concept is not novel. After all, science and technology are a critical basis of competition in many industries, for example, chemicals or electronics, and know-how is often the foundation in industries like engineering, contracting, or consultancy. Indeed, innovation, today perceived as a generic need in all industries, can be seen as knowledge-dependent, whilst the concept of core competences, popularized recently by Prahalad and Hamel (1990) as an alternative strategic paradigm to conventional product-market thinking, is close to the construct of know-how. What perhaps is interesting is that as information technology becomes pervasive and embedded in organizational functioning, new opportunities for building competitive strategies on knowledge are becoming apparent. This chapter, therefore, seeks to develop by induction some thoughts on knowledge strategies. The vexed question of what is knowledge is a good starting-point and an attempt is made to analyse and classify information systems from a knowledge perspective. Some observations on the strategic value of knowledge are made and thereby also on the relative value of different types of information system. The two cases also are suggestive of what is required if knowledge is to be managed as a strategic resource, and so a model of knowledge management is proposed and developed.

The concept of 'knowledge as strategy' or 'knowledge strategies' invites theorizing. Case studies such as these allow us to explore ideas, describe emerging phenomena, examine experience, and develop propositions. They are a useful means of developing grounded theory (Glaser and Strauss 1967) in new areas of interest.

Knowledge

The possible need to distinguish between data, information, and knowledge was suggested above. In the 1960s and 1970s many workers devoted considerable time and energy trying to define information and proposing distinctions from data. Delineation was not always easy or helpful, and different disciplines brought alternative characterizations. Where computer science and management science converged, data were perhaps seen as events or entities represented in some symbolic form and capable of being processed. Information was the output of data that was manipulated, re-presented, and interpreted to reduce uncertainty or ignorance, give surprises or insights, and allow or improve decision-making. However, it was perhaps for many, but not all, safer to leave conceptualization and definition of *knowledge* to philosophers and to recognize that knowledge was potentially an even more complex phenomenon than information.

This is not to say that workable definitions and taxonomies were beyond us. For example, mathematical theories of communication (Shannon and Weaver 1962) were found to be helpful in delineating levels of information processing. Micro-economics analyses of uncertainty (Knight 1921) were insightful in relating information to decision-making. Epistemology (Kuhn 1970) potentially provided some discipline in thinking about knowing. And as data processing and MIS advanced, we at least became both conscious of, and largely comfortable with, the differences, similarities, and ambiguities of data and information.

In the late 1970s and the 1980s developments in artificial intelligence, expert systems, intelligent knowledge-based systems, and their complementary challenges of knowledge engineering and symbolic representation and manipulation have perhaps likewise stimulated us to reassess knowledge. Indeed, the very hyperbole and confusion surrounding these technologies and techniques have demanded some conceptual classification. Now we are at least conscious of the difficulties as the challenges of these branches of computer science have become apparent, and so again we can be tolerant of the conceptual murkiness.

This chapter does not seek to resolve these mysteries! However, to propose knowledge as a strategic resource, some conceptualization is required. And these two case studies do, perhaps, demonstrate some interesting— or at least debatable—attributes of knowledge.

We should perhaps first separate knowledge from intelligence. At the everyday level we observe that knowledge can be acquired, whereas intelligence is more elusive. The two are connected: intelligence is required to produce knowledge and in turn knowledge provides a foundation upon which intelligence can be applied. Those who have worked in the area of artificial intelligence (AI) generally argue—in the spirit of this lay observation—that AI is concerned with formal reasoning and thus needs not only to represent evidence symbolically but to build inference mechanisms employing techniques from pattern recognition to heuristic search, presumably falling short at inspiration and serendipity. AI, like intelligence itself, is essentially generic, general purpose reasoning and easily hits constraints of physical and social complexity. In the context of this essay, however, as suggested later, the concept of designing and building more intelligence into organizations is not rejected.

Knowledge, by contrast—and to be equally 'lay' or trite—is what we know, or what we can accept we think we know and has not yet been proven invalid, or what we can know. Expert systems developers have preferred often to talk of 'expertise', which is commonly defined as knowledge about a particular (specialist) domain (Hayes-Roth *et al.* 1983). These workers point out that experts—and potentially expert systems—perform highly because they are knowledgeable. The appeal of expert systems is that they can codify both established public knowledge and dispersed, often private or hidden knowledge and make it available to a wider set of users. For example, a bank developed expert systems for lending in order to capture the hard-won credit and risk analysis capabilities admired of loan officers about to retire and thereby to be able to disseminate it to young successors and collapse a forty-year training curve. Indeed, at Skandia one intent was the spreading of underwriting skills and experience from senior to junior underwriters and from country to country. Expert systems essentially codify and arrange such knowledge into 'if . . . then' rules.

One source of knowledge for these rule-based systems is 'science', the published, tested definitions, facts, and theorems available in textbooks, reference books, and journals. However, experts develop and use expertise which go beyond this. They develop rules of thumb, assimilate and cultivate patterns, conceive their own frameworks of analyses, and make educated guesses or judgements. This is also the stuff of expertise and is another layer of knowledge, perhaps less certain than that we might call 'science'. It is more private, local, and idiosyncratic; it is perhaps better called judgement. We often pay considerably more for judgement than science. Interestingly, we use analysis and enquiry tools, decision support systems, and modelling techniques to develop this layer of knowledge. And these applications have some knowledge in them, based on science or previously discovered working assumptions. They are not performing reasoning in the strict sense because they are application-specific or use limited rationality. But they bring some measure of intelligence to bear on the generating of knowledge.

How does this discussion relate to the Shorko and the Skandia cases? We can imagine that at Shorko the distributed process control system contained—or could contain—rules based on physics and the chemistry of polymer/copolymer relationships in making plastic film. Furthermore statistical process control parameters were built in to recognize unacceptable deviations and variances together with signals to indicate where intervention or caution were required. There was science and there was judgement.

In Skandia, the core risks/claims/premiums database contained no science. But there were surrounding applications and decision support tools which contained rules based on actuarial science and judgement embodied in limits on acceptable risks and prices, together with underpinning trends and patterns to indicate probable outcomes. There were also procedural rules on data input and access. A second generation of expert systems was being generated to improve risk analysis. The core of the 'platform of know-how', however, was quite simple: it was the capturing and archiving of all transactions in order not to lose experience from which learning could be gained. Indeed, business was bought in order to build a comprehensive experience picture. If a risk seemed unattractive, the lowest proportion possible was taken on in order to collect all future experience on risks and claims. The value of these, in some sense undesirable, business transactions was the information content.

We can see the same phenomenon in Shorko. After installing the distributed process control system a decision was made to buy further computer power and a process management system was installed to enable the capturing and archiving not of just the last thirty-two hours of data but of a year's experience for analysis. In other words, experience was seen to have value and experience can be thought of as untapped knowledge. It can also be current, continually updated, and often situation-specific. The same was true for Skandia's reinsurance database. Other companies can do the same thing, but the experience-base will reflect each firm's particular business strategy.

So we can posit three levels of knowledge: science (which can include accepted law, theory, and procedure), judgement (which can include policy rules, probabilistic parameters, and heuristics), and experience (which is no more than transactional, historical, and observational data to be subjected to scientific analysis or judgemental preference and also to be a base for building new science and judgements). This allows us to postulate two models. The first is a hierarchy of knowledge in Table 3.1 where each ascending level represents an increasing amount of structure, certainty, and validation. Each level also represents a degree or category of learning. Experience requires action and memory, judgement requires analysis and sensing, whilst science requires formulation and consensus. It will be proposed below that this hierarchy has strategic implications.

This classification could be argued to be synonymous with the distinctions between data, information, and knowledge. The lowest level is the equivalent of transaction data (and transaction processing systems). The middle level is the equivalent of information in the classical sense of reducing uncertainty to make decisions (and thus equivalent also of decision support systems). The highest level is knowledge where use is constrained only by its availability or the intellect to exploit it (and thus approximate to the classical expert system or what some call intelligent knowledge-based systems). This mapping of one taxonomy on another allows us to derive another model, Figure 3.1, which attempts to describe the differences between data, information, and knowledge.

In the cases of Shorko and Skandia, the core transaction systems could be seen as no more than data. Shorko's distributed process control system collected real-time process measurements. Skandia's SARA system collected all reinsurance transactions worldwide. Skandia's decision support

Table 3.1. *Levels of knowledge*

Metaphor	Knowledge state	Typical components
Science	Accepted knowledge	Laws, theorems, and procedures
Judgement	Workable knowledge	Policy rules, probablistic parameters, and heuristics
Experience	Potential knowledge	Transactions, history, and observation

system inventory and Shorko's reskilling of operators into data analysts were converting data into information. However, both businesses were basing their competitive strategy on understanding their operations on chosen territories better than their rivals. Their goal was a knowledge capability for Skandia, 'the platform of knowhow', for Shorko, 'we didn't know enough about the process'.

Strategic Value of Knowledge

What do these two cases tell us about the strategic value of knowledge? Both investments yielded strategic advantage. In Skandia this strategy was intended: the chief executive officer pursued a vision of being a niche player in information-intensive risks. At Shorko the strategy was discovered—or it emerged, to use Mintzberg and Waters' (1985) term. The CEO pursued process automation as a means of surivival but then learnt that the information (to become knowledge) base offered a route to product and process differentiation.

At Skandia the value of their know-how has been put to the test in two ways. First, they will buy business transactions to capture the potential knowledge (or experience). Knowledge is not often free—it is bought or generated by transaction processing systems and decision support systems; it incurs production costs. Secondly, when approached to sell their reinsurance systems Skandia had a clear policy. It might sell the transaction processing architecture but not the decision support and input/output routines, for these contain the second (workable) and perhaps eventually third (accepted) levels of knowledge. The transaction processing architecture gives the capability to capture potential knowledge, but it does not contain knowledge and the potential will be considerably firm-specific. A firm which buys this architecture will begin to collect data which reflects its chosen strategy, not Skandia's. The only concern that Skandia might have is, will another firm be better at exploiting potential knowledge than they are? We can be sure, however, that Skandia would not sell the database, for this is their store of potential knowledge which could be valuable to a look-alike rival.

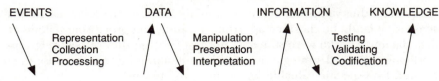

EVENTS DATA INFORMATION KNOWLEDGE

Representation
Collection
Processing

Manipulation
Presentation
Interpretation

Testing
Validating
Codification

Fig. 3.1. *Towards conceptualizing knowledge*

Shorko's IT investment has not been market-tested in this way, but we can observe that whilst their new knowledge is not free, it did not cost much. The accepted level, the science, will have been in the public domain and is, generally speaking, a public good; costs here are low or zero. One could conceive of an application package being developed at this level if there were a big enough market for automation of processes based on polymer science. The workable level usually depends on IT and IS which are not large-scale and resource intensive; decision support tools, for example, need not be too expensive. Shorko's analysis systems, including a packaged Process Management System, were not expensive; investment in operator re-skilling, however, was not trivial. The potential level—in Shorko's case, capturing experience—was not conceptually complex but it did require more infrastructure than the other levels. This was the distributed process control system comprising 1,000 nodes each line and a central processor. Without this infrastructure the Process Management System was useless (equally, setting up the worldwide transaction system SARA was the high-cost investment for Skandia). Fortunately the prior IS investments at Shorko yielded automation benefits and the transaction processing systems at Skandia had helped them be a low-cost producer. The strategist, then, needs to be aware of the knowledge potential of automating and transaction processing systems.

Where does this lead us? We note that the cost of each level of knowledge is likely to diminish from potential through workable to accepted. Even in knowledge-based research and development, this seems to hold true. For example, pharmaceutical researchers might buy accepted knowledge bases relatively cheaply, but the cost of molecular modelling and the like, scanning available knowledge and analysing experimental experience, is high. This means the investor in knowledge as strategy must be confident of the returns if the knowledge required is not a public good.

Indeed, the value question is interesting. Everybody in principle can tap and exploit the science or accepted level of knowledge, or at least they can if it is not under protection of patents, copyright, or some similar mechanism. Of course, protected accepted knowledge may be extraordinarily valuable; the patent or copyright is a value-locking constraint. The potential level or experience level is also an investment strategy open to all, subject to affordability (which does mean that there are barriers to entry), but the more differentiated or niche is your competitive strategy, the more unique and thus value-holding the potential of experience becomes. In this sense what could be classified as ordinary transaction processing systems at Skandia and Shorko were strategic, not just because they respectively supported and created strategic thrusts (the outcome), but also because they created firm-specific valuable knowledge (the means).

The value of judgement or workable knowledge is also potentially very high. It is this *use* of the databases at Skandia and Shorko which makes the difference. Of course, the necessary tools and skills can be developed by many firms. But without the databases, such tools have no foundation. In this sense the underpinning infrastructure becomes the all-important strategic capability. We further should note that expert systems—combining accepted and workable knowledge—which can be complex and costly to build—were in their infancy at Skandia and non-existent at Shorko. Much more modest decision support systems and analyses and enquiry tools were the key weapon at Skandia. Screen-based analyses and the education of operators in information-based analysis and inference skills (with a vision of modelling and exploration work to follow) were the armoury at Shorko. This is not expensive in IT terms; it is demanding of human resource development. Indeed, Skandia stressed the importance of complementary investment 'in the personnel side' and Shorko were sending their operators to college to learn polymer science, computer science, and mathematics.

A proposition therefore is that if strategy is based on knowledge, the value of each level in the classification of Table 3.1 increases downwards; so also does the cost. The cost of the experience level, when based on transaction processing systems, only becomes relatively low and acceptable because there are joint costs. At this level, knowledge often can be the by-product of automation. Otherwise the costs can become very high. The potential value of transaction processing systems is only realized by investment in decision support systems (or expert support systems following Luconi *et al.* 1986) and judgement skills. The accepted knowledge level is the basis of human and organizational functioning. It is also a foundation upon which new industries have grown and existing ones adapt. However, without further development it is not a source of sustainable competitive advantage; conversely, transaction processing systems which capture relatively more firm-specific experience or potential knowledge can be; but only if exploited by decision support systems at the workable knowledge level. This apparent value of transaction processing systems helps explain why many retailers have invested in EPOS, why they and financial service companies have launched credit and charge cards, and why reservation systems are not just about channel warfare and inventory management. It also explains how American Express can grow a substantial insurance business and banks develop ever-more products. Transaction processing systems and their databases become a source of product and process innovation.

Knowledge Management

This inductive analysis also suggests that knowledge-building is a multi-faceted endeavour. At its simplest, it requires a combination of technological and social actions. Figure 3.2 is an attempt at a model of knowledge management. For a business to build a strategic capability in knowledge, the proposition is that at least four components are required: knowledge systems, networks, knowledge workers, and learning organizations.

The Skandia and Shorko cases demonstrate the *systems* that are required: Skandia's core transaction processing system, SARA, and Shorko's distributed process control system captured experience; Skandia's corporate database and Shorko's Process Management System archival database stored, stewarded, and made accessible the experience; the decision support tools and screen-based analyses exploited it. In Skandia everyone had to use the system in underwriting to ensure all relevant data was captured; at Shorko data collection was in-line and automatic. In Skandia the database had to be corporately managed—even though regions could manipulate subsets of it for their own use—to ensure its comprehensiveness and validity. At Shorko the archive period had to be extended. Decision support tools were already important at Skandia and were to become so at Shorko.

Capture systems can be concerned with product/markets (Skandia) or operations and processes (Shorko). We could also conceive of environmental data capture and should perhaps note that executive information systems increasingly serve this purpose by tapping into external databases, or by assembling environmental news—as described by Applegate (1988) at Phillips 66.

Networks appear to be significant in knowledge capture, knowledge building, and knowledge dissemination. At Skandia a corporate world-wide network both captured underwriting transactions to update the corporate database and disseminated knowledge-based parameters, knowledge-based trends, and knowledge tools. In Shorko the distributed process control system of 1,000 nodes per production line can be seen as an intensive local intelligence network. There is no evidence in these cases of external networks. However, we can observe how in knowledge-intensive communities such infrastructure is valued. The academic community is an exemplar. Possibly the most common and pressing demand in my own institution is faculty access to the Internet and related communications net-works which transcend organizational boundaries. Knowledge-building is facilitated by networked interchange of papers, hypotheses, data, gossip, and messages. And to draw on another case study company, Digital Equipment Corporation is renowned for its heavy use of Easynet—with at one time 100,000 users and traffic doubling each year in the 1980s. This facilitates internal administrative efficiency but it also contributes to more creativeness through

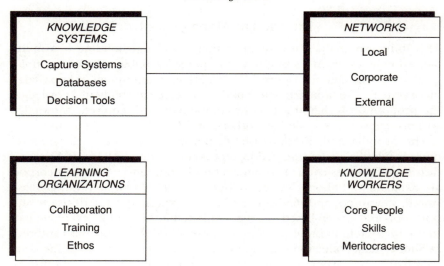

Fig. 3.2. *Knowledge management*

sharing of engineering problems and their solution, collaborative product development, and building of alliances with third parties.

The *knowledge workers* component is the people challenge. At Shorko the automating phase of their IT investment first of all displaced people. Those who remained, however, became core assets; their experience, their continuous knowledge acquisition, and their skills arguably made them more valuable to the organization than before. At Skandia, perhaps surprisingly, some of the IT professionals were found to be peripheral (or surplus to requirements). The bulge needed to build their IT infrastructure was by 1991 no longer necessary and they contributed only the fabric for knowledge as strategy. We would expect that those who remained would often be those with the skills to build the systems to support the judgement level of knowledge. Meanwhile the underwriters remain core not only as the selling and operations resource but as the analysers, interpreters, and exploiters of knowledge and contributors of experience.

The underwriters at Skandia and the operators at Shorko, however, have needed new skills. As proposed by Zuboff (1988) and discovered by Stymne (1989), those who *use* the new levels of information (or knowledge) provided by IT tend to be upskilled rather than deskilled. Computer-mediated work requires a higher level of skill. At Shorko the operators went back to college. In Skandia underwriters underwent 'intensive internal and external training'. We can note, from another case described by Nolan (1990), that as multimedia technology was used to train staff at Federal Express, the system also tested their competence. If the requisite level was met, the employees' remuneration was increased. This is illustrative of the trend to pay not for time or results or effort but for knowledge.

These tendencies, then, begin to suggest a move towards organizational meritocracy. The CEO at Shorko noted how workers became employees and foremen became managers. Blue-collar workers become white-collar workers, increasingly indistinguishable in their work and responsibility from managers. If workers whose self-respect and perhaps power was based on what they knew about a process now have to give up that knowledge to a system, and thus to all, they are perhaps entitled to be rewarded in status, pay and authority for their contribution. The same principle could be 'extrapolated' on Skandia. An underwriter who progressed by his private knowledge is now contributing to, and working on, systematic knowledge. We can see knowledge-based technology as not only a democratizing force, as in Shorko, but as an equalizing force where technical and knowledge-based skills entitle you to join the meritocracy and sharing knowledge entitles you to stay.

These trends at the individual level have their implications at the organizational level, for knowledge is only maximized if the organization can learn. There are several perspectives which could be drawn upon here from Argyris and Schon's (1978) research on organizational learning to Senge's (1990) more recent development work on enabling organizations to learn. The Shorko and Skandia cases give both weak and strong signals on what may be required *in learning organizations.*

First, we see indications of the need for collaborative organizational functioning. In Shorko the operators had to work as a team to build the process knowledge (and the system) and to operate the new production lines environment. Furthermore, they were working with both technical specialists and management in these endeavours. In Skandia there was a 'high degree of decentralization to offices and underwriters'. However, the strategy depended on connecting these units and co-ordinating reinsurance business. The system and network forced this level of collaboration and Skandia resisted attempts to fragment it. We can look elsewhere for stronger signals of collaborative working where knowledge is strategy. Digital use skill-based virtual teams in product development and business projects by bringing key people across their Easynet network. Indeed, one of the images of the networked organization is the ability to cross internal and external organizational boundaries to exchange information, break down established positions and demarcation lines, locate relevant skills or experience, and create synergies of shared talent. In another case I have examined, IKEA, the Swedish retailer, the decentralized, near to sources of supply, profit-centre evaluated buying managers use the data network to share knowledge about potential suppliers and product development.

Secondly, the skill requirements of knowledge working noted earlier create demands for training and personal development. The visionary CEO of Skandia explained that 'we are introducing powerful computer and communications systems in IT while making improvements on the personnel side'. The production manager in Shorko said 'you can't invest in technologies if you don't invest in people, especially in training'. It is evident that the need is not just for technology-use training, but also for knowledge processing skills, such as analysis, reasoning, and deduction. This may also mean 'remedial' education on the accepted, scientific, knowledge level which underpins the business: risk and actuarial techniques for Skandia's underwriters, polymer science for Shorko's operators. However, education is always remedial in a sense, for as potential knowledge becomes workable knowledge and perhaps becomes accepted knowledge, the implication is clear. Education in learning organizations is continuous.

Finally, a third requirement was hinted at earlier. There needs to be an ethos of knowledge as strategy. If organizational members are to share knowledge, collaborate, and be willing to learn continuously, the incentive and support must be present. Indeed, if we regard organizations as networks of contracts which govern exchange transactions between members having only partially overlapping goals—as described and analysed by the transaction costs economics framework of organization (Williamson 1975)—why should members in different locations, roles, levels, and career stages subscribe to a knowledge-based strategy? The very uncertainty and complexity of knowledge domains, the information assymetries built into organizations, and the opportunism available to the informed would suggest that, in the mixed interest settings of firms, actors can selfishly withhold, distort, or exploit knowledge.

One response is that information technology can help mediate this challenge by lowering the costs of information processing required for co-ordination and control (Ciborra 1987). This would include operational costs of knowledge acquisition, storage, and sharing but also of management control processes required to implement knowledge-based strategies. The two cases suggest at least three other notable facets of knowledge as strategy when a transaction costs perspective is adopted.

In Shorko the operators saw that the system was the summation of their very own collective and best knowledge and experience. However, they had a dramatic incentive to support the strategy-survival. Indeed, it also seems likely at Skandia that the bold vision which built the organizational and IT capabilities necessary for its platform of know-how was borne out of the survival crisis that the international division faced in 1984. In short, we can posit the notion of the superordinate goal which can perhaps win over knowledge opportunism and 'deviance'. Of course, survival can be analysed within the transaction cost framework—workers, all workers, are discounting their price in the short run, either in the hope of reinstating the longer term employment contract or, for most of them, conceding in the short run to authority, in the hope of gains to come.

The second facet is that knowledge constructs combined with strategic change provide a rhetoric for managerial action and power. De Pierrefeu recalls in Shorko how 'I explained that everything would change', and he and his team spent considerable time in building a new ethos—personified in a physical way by making the process control centre the new and bright hub of the factory. In Skandia the new ethos was partly created or reinforced by the rhetoric of knowledge, namely, the repeated references and tutorials in the annual reports and the use of the metaphor of 'know-how'.

Gowler and Legge (1983) have argued persuasively that rhetoric can be a powerful tool of management, both symbolically and more instrumentally. Earl (1983) too has demonstrated how the language, roles, and rituals of specialist, technical endeavours and activities are one armoury of management.

The third facet is more mundane. We can perhaps posit that the two cases show another potential of the experience and transaction processing level of knowledge in Table 3.1. Physical transaction data in Shorko and basic business transaction data in Skandia is less vulnerable to manipulation and withholding than the fabric of systems at the higher two levels. The data are structured, their collection is more automatable, there is less human intervention and quality control is easier. Of course the processing, interpretation, and use of these data—at the judgement and science levels—bring opportunities for 'games-playing', but there is an inherent visibility and robustness in experience level data upon which they may be built.

So a knowledge ethos seems necessary if knowledge-based strategies are to be pursued. The appeal of the superordinate goal and the management of rhetoric may be useful political devices to employ in this regard. IT may help by reducing the transaction costs of co-ordination and control required to buttress knowledge as strategy. Finally, transaction processing systems may have another source of knowledge value; they may have inbuilt properties of 'objectivity' which limit the potential to subvert the knowledge ethos.

Conclusions

The Skandia and Shorko cases can be seen, respectively, as examples of IT supporting a competitive strategy and of IT creating a new strategic option. Underpinning them both, however, is investment in knowledge and the realization that knowledge can be a strategic resource. Information technology has made knowledge-based strategies much more feasible and these two cases indicate that databases and networks supported by decision support tools are crucial enabling requirements.

It seems, however, that not all knowledge is the same. Three levels of knowledge, representing increasing degrees of certainty, structuredness, and validation can usefully be recognized: accepted knowledge or science, workable knowledge or judgement, and potential knowledge or experience. All of them rarely come free, but each level in that order seems to increase in cost—not in terms of discovery or cumulative investment over time, but more in terms of collation and exploitation by IT.

Expert systems and databases which codify or provide accepted knowledge are likely to be derivatives of a public good and of useful, but not often firm-specific, value. Decision support tools which craft and make available workable knowledge are likely to be more private and thus competitively valuable. Transaction processing systems which capture potential knowledge and arrange it in databases are likely to be firm-specific and continuously providing a source of strategic value.

This classification could be alternatively expressed as data, information, and knowledge. However, the earlier classification helps point out that 'knowledge' exists at each level and that in a strategic, competitive sense the direction of value is counter-intuitive. Data processing or transaction processing systems may contain potentially high knowledge value—in excess of either MIS and decision support systems or expert systems and knowledge-based systems. Also transaction processing level systems may be the most expensive. Fortunately the cost bind implied by this analysis is often mitigated by the fact that data processing yields joint benefits of an automation kind and information processing joint benefits of a decision-making kind. Whilst, therefore, Zuboff's (1988) concept of 'informating' can be seen as an alternative and more strategic option to 'automating', we can note that often the IT infrastructure is common. The trick therefore is to recognize and pursue the knowledge opportunities in the firm's (current and planned) information technology and information systems infrastructure.

This leads on to the capabilities required of the firm if knowledge is to be a basis of strategy. They are both technological and organizational. Knowledge systems comprising capture devices, databases, and decision tools are required. These are commonly built and used through communications networks local, corporate, and external. The users become knowledge workers. These become core personnel through their knowledge and IT-mediated work. Their skills have to be enhanced and more meritocratic structures rebuilt. Accordingly, at the organizational level collaboration in knowledge development and use is essential, continuous training in knowledge and knowledge skills has to be provided, and a knowledge-based ethos is required to lead, reward, and support exploitation of knowledge as strategy.

The vision for this is particularly apparent in Skandia. The enactment is particularly apparent in Shorko. If Bell (1979) and others are right, these firms are not oddities; they are interesting prototypes of the firm in the post-industrial or information or knowledge economy.

References

Applegate, L. M. (1988), *Phillips 66 Company. Executive Information System,* Harvard Business School Case Study 9–189–006. Publishing Division Harvard Business School Press.

Argyris, C., and Schon, D. A. (1978), *Organizational Learning: A Theory of Action Perspective,* Reading, Mass.: Addison-Wesley.

Bell, D. (1979), 'Thinking Ahead: Communication Technology—for Better or for Worse', *Harvard Business Review* (May–June).

Ciborra, C. U. (1987), 'Research Agenda for a Transaction Costs Approach to Information Systems', in R. J. Boland, Jnr., and R. A. Hirscheim (eds.), *Critical Issues in Information Systems Research,* New York: J. Wiley & Sons.

Earl, M. J. (1983), 'Accounting and Management', in id. (ed.), *Perspectives on Management,* Oxford: Oxford University Press.

Glaser, B. G., and Strauss, A. L. (1967), *The Discovery of Grounded Theory: Strategies For Qualitative Research,* Chicago: Aldine Publishing Co.

Gowler, D., and Legge, K. (1983), 'The Meaning of Management and the Management of Meaning: A View from Social Anthropology', in M. J. Earl (ed.), *Perspectives on Management,* Oxford: Oxford University Press.

Hayes-Roth, F., Waterman, D. A., and Lenat, D. B. (1983), 'An Overview of Expert Systems', in id. (eds.), *Building Expert Systems,* Reading, Mass.: Addison-Wesley.

Knight, F. H. (1921), *Risk, Uncertainty and Profit,* Chicago: University of Chicago Press.

Kuhn, T. (1970), *The Structure of Scientific Revolutions,* Chicago: University of Chicago Press.

Luconi, F. L., Malone, T. W., and Scott-Morton, M. S. (1986), 'Expert Systems and Expert Support Systems: The Next Challenge for Management', *Sloan Management Review* (Fall).

Mintzberg, H., and Waters, J. A. (1985), 'Of Strategies, Deliberate and Emergent', *Strategic Management Journal,* vol. 6.

Nolan, R. L. (1990), 'The Knowledge Work Mandate', *Stage by Stage,* vol. 10, no. 2, pp. 1–12, Nolan Norton & Co.

OECD (1981), *Information Activities, Electronics, and Telecommunications. Technologies: Impact on Employment, Growth and Trade,* Paris: Organization for Economic Development.

Porat, M. U. (1977), *The Information Economy: Definition and Measurement,* Washington DC: Office of Telecommunications, US Department of Commerce.

Prahalad, C. K., and Hamel, G. (1990), 'The Core Competences of the Corporation', *Harvard Business Review* (May–June).

Senge, P. M. (1990), *The Fifth Discipline,* New York: Doubleday.

Shannon, C. E., and Weaver, W. (1962), *The Mathematical Theory of Communication*, Chicago: University of Illinois.

Silberston, A. (1967), 'The Patent System', *Lloyds Bank Review*, no. 84.

Stymne, B. (1989), 'Information Technology and Competence Formation in the Swedish Service Sector', Institute for the Management of Innovation and Technology, Stockholm School of Economics.

Williamson, O. E. (1975), *Markets and Hierarchies: Analysis and Antitrust Implications*, New York: Free Press.

Zuboff, S. (1988), *In the Age of the Smart Machine*, New York: Basic Books.

4

Business Process Reengineering: A Phenomenon of Organization

MICHAEL J. EARL

Introduction

Business Process Reengineering (BPR) is the latest management recipe being offered for the survival of Western businesses. Also known as Business Process Redesign, Process Innovation, and various combinations of these keywords, it has become the subject of best-selling books, a new practice area (sometimes trademarked) for consultants, a phenomenon upon which most business academics feel they should have a view, and a growing endeavour in many companies. The protagonists seem convinced that it is a new approach to improving business performance even if it may be a synthesis of recent and not-so-recent ideas. The cynics feel that they have seen it before in different guises and stress the apparent naïvety of some of the component concepts. Meanwhile some companies claim that 'it has worked for them', even if some did not realize it was BPR they were practising!

In this chapter BPR is 'deconstructed' into six elements and, as argued in an earlier paper (Earl and Khan 1994), three are seen as 'new' thinking and three as 'old'. This provides a visual model (Fig. 4.1) of two domains and a structure for this paper. However, one element in each domain is seen as the key to understanding BPR and assessing its viability. In the 'new' domain it is argued that *process* is the distinctive conceptual contribution or breakthrough offered by BPR. In the 'old' domain *change management* is seen as the element which makes or breaks BPR projects in practice.

So why is Business Process Reengineering dubbed 'a phenomenon of organization' in the title of the chapter? First, it is argued that process is a concept of *organizational design*. There are several attributes of process, but they are essentially ways of conceiving organization or indeed of organizing. Secondly, it should be clear that change management rests on an understanding of *organizational behaviour* and on practising many of the principles and skills of that subject area. In at least two senses, therefore, 'reengineering' is an unfortunate title: it does not reflect the complex, social nature of either the distinctive underpinning concept of BPR or the essential practical challenges required to make it happen.

The Phenomenon

Business Process Reengineering has been promoted as a business techno- logy. The popular writers (Davenport 1993; Hammer and Champy 1993) will admit that so far methodologies are immature and implementation more challenging than the concept. Nevertheless, organizations have BPR groups, consultancies are developing reengineering tools and techniques, and business schools are developing courses in the area. The claim is that through the 1980s some well-known companies—Xerox, Ford, IBM, Cigna, Texas Instruments—were quietly revolutionizing the way they were doing business. Orders of magnitude improvement in operational and admin- istrative performance were being realized, and when field visits were made to these companies they were found to be engaging in at least three endeavours. First, they were radically redesigning or reengineering key business activities, often, it has been claimed, as though operating on a greenfield site. Secondly, they were applying the concept of process in this reengineering which is an input–output activity view of business, not a functional, responsibility centred, and structural view. Thirdly, they were usually exploiting information technology to redesign the process in a way which was not possible before the information era. This was new, it was argued, achieved outstanding results, and seemed to be something that western companies could do well.

In a sense, therefore, the concept belongs to the managerial journalism domain, although the two early seminal articles (Davenport and Short 1990; Hammer 1990) appeared in journals which provide an interface between business schools and practitioners. The former exposition used a metaphor of new industrial engineering and sought to define the activity of BPR and suggested a high-level methodology. The latter was more of a polemic, namely, that because many business processes had never been explicitly designed or engineered in the first place, firms' performance improvement schemes were often suboptimal. Furthermore, application of IT had often automated old, inefficient, and cumbersome business practices with little benefit, a claim and message which are valuable in their own right.

These articles also propelled and helped legitimize the concept of BPR, creating a market for consultants and a new recipe for one group of managers in particular, the IT directors. The early promotion of BPR was largely due to IS academics and consultants and explicitly suggested that it was very much an information systems endeavour. However, it soon became obvious that the concept and evolving practice had roots in a number of disciplines but nevertheless had contemporary appeal.

Antecedents of Business Process Reengineering

It is often recognized that our keyword, 'process', has a history, although it is variously and sometimes vaguely defined. We talk of process control, and certainly process as well as techniques have been emphasized in the quality movement (Garvin 1988; Juran 1964). We talk of management processes and often process is seen as a complement to structure in management and organizational theory. Process skills and process consultancy have been emphasized in the human relations and management of change schools (Schein 1969). And in the field of innovation it is mandatory to distinguish product innovation from process innovation. Indeed, inattention to the latter is seen by some to explain why western firms have been outperformed by some rivals in certain industries (Clark and Fujimoto 1991).

Perhaps five sets of ideas underpin the early development and current conceptualization of Business Process Reengineering:

1. *Competitiveness* is a current theme. New standards of operational performance were set through the late 1970s and 1980s, marked by quality programmes, customer service philosophies, time-based competition, and cost management. Often attributed to 'Japanese Management' or 'continuous improvement' or other somewhat magical metaphors, two related arguments were then heard. First, application of these ideas and techniques may allow firms to catch up with best of class rivals, but industry leadership and abnormal performance required more of a breakthrough management philosophy. The apparently radical and high impact concept of BPR was a candidate. Indeed, this thinking drove Xerox Corporation's[1] BPR initiatives as they sought to regain leadership in the photocopier industry.

Secondly, claims are made that radical, big-bang approaches to performance improvement may be the forte or preferred change management style of many western companies. It may be a strategy based on capability, one, it is suggested, that can 'beat the Japanese'. It is a belief expressed by some top managers and it is never far away in Davenport's (1993) exhortations, especially when he hints that western companies could add their focus on results to the more eastern focus on process to good effect.

2. *Information technology* is very much part of the 'architecture' of business

---

[1] See Centre for Research in Information Management Mincase Study CRIM MC93/3, London Business School, 1993.

process reengineering. Implicit very often is that reengineering or redesign requires or is enabled by IT. The potential of telecommunications to reduce the costs of co-ordination across organizational boundaries, or indeed to increase the scope or intensity of co-ordination is one contribution. Another is the development of shared databases (and systems) to provide information to those who need it in line (or in-process).

It is intriguing that the IT industry—particularly the IT management consultants—has in many ways developed the technology of BPR and certainly created the market. There is always a fine balance between hype and rhetoric serving as propaganda, illusion, and myth in a cynical, self-serving campaign or being essential to promote new ideas, educate managers about them, and build confidence and credibility in them. In 1989 one consultant acquaintance described BPR as 'the best product we ever developed'. More recently another managing partner on the launch-day of his practice's book on BPR commented: 'We always write a book to create a market.' Whatever stance we take on these market machinations, one observation we can make is that the IT industry needed an idea to replace the tired 1980s slogan that IT created competitive advantage.

3. *The rebirth of operations management* also may have contributed to the acceptance of BPR. The quality, customer service, time-based competition and cost management movements all rejuvenated operations management (in both manufacturing and service contexts) in business schools and consultancies and returned performance improvement to management agendas. One consequence is that the early BPR literature has drawn on seminal works in the Operations Management domain, such as Juran (1964), Takeuchi and Nonaka (1986), Womack *et al.* (1990). Another is that there is usually some discussion about whether these ideas can contribute to BPR, should complement it, or are a subset of it. A more important consequence perhaps is that managements were ready to countenance the concept and promise of BPR. It came at the right time.

4. *Strategic management*: one possible antecedent that was notably absent in the early development of BPR was any theory of strategy. In focus, it was largely internal to the firm, concentrating on improving performance of the business as historically conceived. It was not explicitly about product-market strategy or the 1980s new industrial economics conceptualization of competitive strategy (Porter 1980). More recently, however, the possibility of BPR changing business or industry scope was brought to our attention by Short and Venkatraman (1992) who extended the concept of BPR into Business Network Redesign, discussed below. This is concerned with redefining the boundaries of the firm, changing supplier and customer relationships, and repositioning the firm in the market place.

Strategists are, of course, concerned about superior performance and BPR does connect with the business turnaround literature, for example, the recent work of Stopford and Baden-Fuller (1994), if seen as a technology of strategic change. And in the 1990s strategic management theory has embraced resource-based views of the firm (Wernerfelt 1994). These see capabilities and competences (Prahalad and Hamel 1991) as assets the enterprise can nurture to outperform, and perhaps differentiate from, rivals. So if BPR is about building, improving, and rethinking core capabilities or activities, it can be seen as strategically legitimate.

Also if strategy is seen in the military parlance of 'how do we achieve goals' rather than 'what do we do', BPR can be seen to be in the domain of strategic management. Indeed, one pharmaceutical company now expects strategic business units to formulate two complementary strategies. The first is the product-market strategy concerned with positioning. The second is the process strategy concerned with what critical processes must be improved to achieve the desired position.

So strategic management may not have been strictly an antecedent. Indeed, strategists have probably been late entrants in the field. However, BPR does connect with today's strategic agendas and thinking.

5. *Organizational rethinking*, as already argued, is perhaps the final, dominant theme. Exponents of BPR refer to today's inheritance of efficiency-driven models of organization from the industrial and scientific management eras. The concern of mass production to create task-efficient work design and the need to develop specialist skills led to functional and also often centralized organization design in the images of Frederick Taylor and Henry Ford. However, as time-based competition, quality control, customer service, and cost management become imperatives, the 'functional stovepipe' legacy was seen to impede co-ordination, teamwork, interdependence, and removal of unnecessary buffers and slack resources. Horizontal or lateral views of organization emerged, not in the classic project management or matrix form but in activity, task-oriented, interdependent, and systemic form. Indeed, this process view of organization is resonant of the systems view of organizational design and the task views of work design.

Another model of organization is also challenged. The divisional and responsibility accounting movement pioneered in the likes of General Motors and DuPont is also found wanting. If radical performance improvement requires collaboration and interdependence, if candidate routes are teamwork or individual empowerment, and if the focus is on the customer and buyer values, then both the bottom line culture and the departmental or divisional loyalties generated by responsibility centre structures can be impediments. The process view of organization thus becomes more a model of partnership and collaboration.

Whether BPR survives or not as a management technique, we can expect that process concepts will have re-entered, and to a degree reshaped, our organizational thinking. The process axis or dimension of organizational design has been given a boost and concern has returned to building, maintenance, and enactment of management processes.

Six Fundamentals of Business Process Reengineering

The six fundamentals of BPR can be portrayed as the star in Figure 4.1. This representation is derived in a sense from a deconstruction of the phenomenon influenced by three sources:

1. the existing literature;
2. field studies of BPR in practice;
3. experiences reported by leading-edge companies.[2]

The result is a structural model of two triangles. One represents what is perhaps new about BPR in concept. The other comprises what is old, but by no means trivial, about it in practice. Some of the practical challenges in the old triangle are complicated by the three elements in the new triangle; others are eternal issues of business improvement and strategic change.

Transformation

The typical promise of BPR is that a quantum leap in business performance is available and that the organization will have to be reengineered or redesigned to achieve this goal. Taking years out of product to market time, months out of lead times, and 50 per cent or more out of resource buffers or headcount are typical goals. Radical thinking, unconstrained analysis, and greenfield concepts of design are encouraged. A comprehensive and one-step turnaround is suggested. These are the characteristics of transformation which, as Hammer and Champy (1993) opine, carry risks. In other words, there is a spirit of revolution more than evolution and it is not unusual to contrast BPR with continuous improvement. Table 4.1, due to Earl and Khan (1994), provides such a comparison building on an earlier analysis by Davenport (1993).

Such a perspective implies that BPR is more top-down, analytical, and comprehensive than the bottom-up, emergent, and local emphases of continuous improvement. This is perhaps plausible if BPR seeks to challenge or move away from 'business as usual', and it implies a design engineering approach to organizations. However, it does raise some questions about how BPR should relate to strategy-making—not only business strategy, but functional strategies, especially those for IT.

Case evidence suggests a variety of experiences to date. In some companies BPR projects are strategic initiatives in that they have evident top management support, have significant resources allocated to them, are accompanied by internal propaganda programmes, and attack performance

---

[2] Particularly at a workshop participated in by US and European Companies in the Centre for Research in Information Management, London Business School, Oct. 1993.

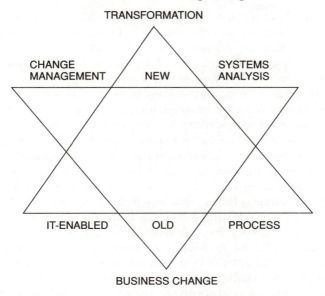

Fig. 4.1. *Six fundamentals of Business Process Reengineering*

Table 4.1. *The transformational scope of Business Process Reengineering*

	Continuous process improvement	Business process reengineering
Change	Incremental	Quantum leap
Focus	Current practice	Start again
Frequency	Continuous	One shot
Scope	Narrow, within function	Broad, cross-functional
Participation	Bottom up	Top-down
Risk and rewards	Low to moderate	High
Type of change	Work design	Structure, culture roles
Role of IT	Incidental	Key enabler
Aids	Ideas and suggestions	Methods and tools

issues widely acknowledged to be at the core of firm competitiveness. These are commonly CEO-led and can perhaps be seen as strategic projects—even if they are totally unconnected to formal strategy-making processes. In one company they were spawned after the CEO had taken his team on a study tour of Japan; in another they arose out of a top-management retreat to consider how to meet and then exceed world-class benchmarks of performance. In another, a new CEO was searching for ways of turning round his company and he personally analysed signific-ant dimensions of performance. It is noticeable in both hard and soft ways that benchmarking is often both a stimulus for BPR and a component of methodology. This increasingly includes benchmarking best-of-class companies, both inside and outside a particular industry.

In other companies strategic planning processes have incorporated BPR. One corporation was described earlier where strategy-making is separated into two sets: product market strategy and process strategy. Both constructs are reviewed and resourced for each business unit. In another company business process reengineering project proposals are assessed and prioritized against the current strategic goals of the firm. In another company business strategic planning reportedly was temporarily suspended in place of business process planning. These all have a top-down character where strategic management does expect and include BPR initiatives.

Another BPR-strategy linkage may also be achieved through the Information Systems Strategic Planning Process. One company now will only approve IS projects if they are conceived as, or are part of, BPR projects. Indeed, Business Process Redesign can be one way of formulating IS strategies, forcing IS initiatives to be grounded in the business and integrated with other business changes.

A further approach is aggressively to seek to change the management processes of the firm with the hope that managers will realize the need for, and be motivated towards, business process reengineering. Two such companies in the food-and-drink sector have been discovered where the CEO instituted new performance measures and responsibility accounting. In the food company this was explicitly to force executives to rethink standards and consider BPR as a means of achieving different benchmarks of operational performance. In the drinks company introduction of a new brand equity performance measurement system led weight to arguments to redesign core supply chain and sales processes.

Further research on the BPR-strategy linkage is important, especially if BPR is concerned with achieving sustainable competitive advantage and is not to be seen just as improvement projects with particularly ambitious goals.

Process

The fulcrum and distinctive element of BPR is process. Indeed, BPR was defined by Davenport and Short (1990: 11) as the 'analysis and design of work flows and processes within and between organizations'. Most writers stress this attention to processes and Davenport and Short (1990: 12) defined a process as 'a set of logically related tasks performed to achieve a defined business outcome'. It is generally argued that business processes have two important characteristics: they have internal or external customers and they cross organizational boundaries. Already the argument made earlier that process is an organizational construct should be apparent. To help develop that argument, it is perhaps fruitful to demonstrate and explain the character and scope of business processes that are reengineered using examples. In our research[3] we have identified four possible process types.

1. *Core processes* are those central to business functioning, which relate directly to external customers. They are commonly the primary activities of the value chain. For example, the order fulfillment process is becoming a classical area of attack as manufacturers reassess lead time standards. Through most of the 1980s Xerox Corporation had matched best-in-class standards of cycle times through programmes of continuous improvement in each activity of the supply chain. To achieve market leadership, however, optimization of each step in the chain was not enough. Optimization of the total inventory management and logistics process was required. A multi-functional design team analysed Xerox's supply chain to address the interrupts between each step. The order fulfillment process was redesigned on top of the underpinning functional organization, which was retained, by simplifying material flows, information flows, and time-consuming activities and by seeking co-ordination with a supply chain management adviser system which provides rapid access to cross-functional data in the existing transaction processsing systems. Service levels improved from 75 per cent to 97 per cent and cycle times were reduced by 70 per cent with inventory savings of $500m.

In the Xerox case, therefore, we see a process axis of organization being introduced on top of a functional one. Here the process axis emphasizes flows across departments, functions, and responsibility centres. It is a task interdependence model of organizations which required new forms of co-ordination. Organization design becomes concerned with performance optimization from the customer perspective.

Texas Instruments has recently done much the same thing in its mission to speed up lead times for customized semiconductors. The original manufacturing organization had been designed to make essentially generic wafers for multiple customers. The maturing of the market-place to requirements for customized wafers to single customers and unique applications presented new challenges. For example, wafer production lead time could exceed the end-product life-cycle! The functional and geographical fragmentation of the typical manufacturing process included transit through fifteen buildings, over 15,000 miles, on eight planes and fourteen trucks requiring forty customs signatures and tracked through eighteen databases. Redesign of this process—treating all world-wide establishments as 'a virtual factory' and processing orders through a reservation system—has allowed TI to achieve cycle time reductions of 70 per cent with an intent to achieve over 95 per cent reductions.[4]

[3] At Centre for Research in Information Management at London Business School, researchers involved have been James E. Short, Jeffrey L. Sampler, Bushra Khan, and the author.
[4] See Centre for Research in Information Management Case Note MC93/12 London Business School, 1993.

The TI case again is concerned with optimizing flows and with task interdependence but introduces a concept of virtual organization by using information systems to allocate work globally and provide the requisite co-ordination. A customer case manager is the link between the customer and the virtual factory, adding another dimension of organization to process—namely new roles of liaison, integration, and ultimate customer ownership.

In the services sector the well-documented examples of Mutual Benefit Life's insurance underwriting design adopted similar logic, using the case manager concept and reducing the administrative steps involved. Productivity improvements of 40 per cent are reported (Hammer 1990; Davenport and Short 1990). In the UK, National Vulcan Engineering Insurance collapsed policy issue time from sometimes up to three months to twenty-four hours, reduced administrative steps from forty to six, and staff from thirty to three. Important here was provision of integrated policy processing systems to rationalized branch offices.

In these cases we see the emphasis on work simplification and rationalization. It is perhaps a turbo-charged version of the 'organization methods' movement of the past, a return to work-design ideas of organization theory.

2. *Support processes* have internal customers and the back-up (or 'back office') of core processes. They will commonly be the more administrative, secondary activities of the value chain. The redesign of Ford's accounts payable processing reportedly achieved headcount savings of 80 per cent (Hammer 1990). Here a cumbersome paper-based activity involving purchasing, suppliers, accounts payable, goods receiving, and data processing was replaced by an automated process based on one shared database, networking linkages between all parties, and an information flow designed around accounts payable data conformance not exceptions.

Another route to administrative efficiency is provided by the shared services organizations. Baxter Healthcare, for example, has combined and centralized many of its accounting and related services (Short and Konsynski 1992). Creating a separate internal services line of business was one way to yield economies of scale in administration after the Baxter-American Hospital Supply merger.

These examples add two more organizational concepts to process. In Ford an administrative process is seen to be one essentially of information processing. It can be improved or automated by the application of IT. More important, it can be reconceptualized as a virtual process held together by a shared database. In Baxter a new organizational unit, or line of business, is actually created, not eliminated. It is a centralization and rationalization of low value-adding activities, but in a sense outsourced to a new organization. This is organization design writ large.

3. *Business network processes* are those which extend beyond the boundaries of the organization into suppliers, customers, and allies. Identified through

the IS historiography of Baxter Healthcare by Short and Venkatraman (1992), redesigning external processes in that company had the potential to redefine the business scope and reposition the firm in its industry value chain. The evolution of American Hospital Supply's (now a division of Baxter) on-line order processing system from ASAP through ASAP Express to Valuelink represented increasingly forwards integration with customers' inventory, distribution and logistics processes.

Here we see the relocation of activities across trading organizations. We can view the resultant organizational configuration as business alliances, value-added partnerships, or networked organizations. Or we can see the Baxter case as electronic integration of two organizations. Finally, we can recognize in Baxter's forward integration the elimination of other organizations' activities or businesses through disintermediation. In Business Network Processes the mission, roles, and boundaries of organization can be redesigned.

4. *Management processes* are those by which firms plan, organize, and control resources. A particularly comprehensive example is provided by National and Provincial Building Society,[5] who redesigned both their organization and the roles within it on process lines. This accompanied redesign of core business processes, but a process-based organization design was established partly continuously to help initiate process thinking and organically adapt core and support processes. Structures, jobs, committees, and performance measures were redefined; even organizational language was redesigned so that, for example, jobs became roles and committee meetings became events.

In the N&P case we see not only organization and management being redesigned before attention to business processes, but a theory being applied that management processes are the key to a viable organization which adapts. In this particular example, rhetoric and language were important instruments of BPR—a deeper, cultural view of reengineering.

These cases demonstrate that process is an organizational construct in at least seven ways:

1. a unit of organizational analysis;
2. a matter of organizational configuration;
3. a systems view of organization;
4. a cultural, symbolic view of organization and management;
5. an information processing view of organization;
6. a work-design view of organization;
7. a 'natural but taken for granted' function of organization.

As a *unit of analysis*, or frame of reference, it focuses on activity, for example, order fulfillment. Essentially a horizontal or lateral form, process

---

[5] See forthcoming Centre for Research in Information Management Case Study, London Business School, 1995.

encapsulates the need for interdependence, integration, and co-ordination of tasks, roles, people, departments, functions, and soon required to provide an internal or external customer with a product or service. It is this view which presents a stark contrast with functional or responsibility centre pictures of organization and highlights how the twentieth-century business may well have evolved into a series of 'functional stovepipes' or responsibility centre 'hand-offs' as traditional processes are enacted. To restore the process axis, some firms have redesigned their functional structures into process responsibilities with process directors heading them up. Others, like Xerox, have superimposed the process axis on the existing structure to form a two- or three-dimensional matrix.

Configuration is concerned with shape, topology, and boundaries. Business network processes demonstrate this conceptualization of organization where processes transcend the historic boundaries of the firm as the activities of the value-chain are redistributed according to who does what best. Once we draw or chart the process in question—logistics and inventory management in the Baxter case—it becomes both irrelevant and difficult to think in terms of boundaries, especially in terms of asset ownership, job or role belonging, and activity location. The firm's value chain has to be seen as a wider value system.

Thus the *systems* view of organization is demonstrated by process. Indeed, the interdependent, interactive, boundary-crossing, superordinate goal conceptualization of process is essentially a systems model. Furthermore, as we shall see later, BPR has rediscovered the concepts and tools of systems analysis—including socio-technical systems thinking. A process has inputs, processing, and outputs, just as do the simpler conceptualization of systems. We can also see the processing component as value-adding activity which suggests that the value chain is a process model and that collapsing of value chains (Rockart and Short 1988) is essentially an exercise in BPR.

More important, perhaps, is that this input-process-output thinking inevitably has led to concern with flows, material, information, time, decision, and work flows. Such flow-based systems analysis leads firms to discover that processes have subprocesses just as systems have subsystems. One pharmaceutical company recognizes four levels of process analysis: business processes with an external customer, such as new product development; processes which go to make up a business process, such as clinical trial supplies; subprocesses which are recognizable, delineated, but factored down lower level processes such as drug release; and activities or tasks which take place within any of these, such as producing a certificate of analysis.

Once the systems view of process is promoted other ideas seem to fit it. Thus teamwork, especially across boundaries, is incorporated. Roles, which stress contribution and interrelationships, displace jobs. Case management and liaison roles are created. And it is the need to, and challenge of, creating responsibilities around activity systems rather than functions or responsibility centres that leads to the call for process owners, process sponsors, and process measures. Above all, perhaps, the notion of process (or system) optimization is encouraged in that process is a way of promoting the higher goal which challenges local optimization at functional, departmental, divisional levels because this becomes sub-optimal at the process (or higher system) level. We hear of functional performance or task execution which are best of class, but when these optimized units have to work together, the overall result in customer service, product to market time, or whatever is uncompetitive.

The *cultural symbolic* view of organization and management demonstrated by process is partly apparent from the new 'process' language and roles just mentioned. The language and rhetoric of process can be used to achieve cultural change. 'Process' has a somewhat neutral but imperative ring to it and can be used to galvanize organizations into more co-operative and commercial working. Attention to management process appears to put managing back on the design agenda, recognizing that things do not necessarily just happen. There may be a sense of formalizing previously informal ways of operating. In the National and Provincial case a management 'theory' was being tested: construct the organization around management processes and a higher performing, self-adapting business will result. We see process becoming a grand management theory, a new style 'Theory Z' (Ouchi 1981) perhaps.

Process as an *information processing* view of organization is demonstrated in at least four ways. First we see that information flows are critical in processes as a means of integration and co-ordination. In both Texas Instruments and Xerox information systems were necessary to provide a process world view to actors in the process and to provide co-ordination. This connects with Malone and Crowston's (1994) view that IT can reduce costs of organizational co-ordination or enable more intensive (or better?) co-ordination structures. It also relates to Galbraith's (1977) theory of organization design, where increased information processing capacity is required to handle increased uncertainty, in BPR cases often the uncertainties of task interdependence. Information systems or organizational designs can be used to tackle uncertainty; in these cases the process-based organizations were made possible by complementary information systems.

The Ford payables case shows that information-intensive processes can be transformed, with redundant steps being obliterated by the application of IT. A shared database made radical reorganization possible.

The Texas Instruments, Ford, and Baxter cases also show that 'virtual' or 'network' organizational forms can evolve once process thinking is applied. Finally, our examples of reengineering both business and management processes have demonstrated that 'empowerment' to key actors in the process line, especially to customer-facing case managers, can be vital to making sure the process dimension works. Empowerment implies provision of all necessary information to fulfil this role. Process-based organizations become involved with redistribution of power and thus of information.

The *work-design* view of organization is exemplified by the early thinking on BPR. Hammer (1990) was concerned with abnormal efficiency improvements by obliterating work activities. Davenport and Short (1990) used the metaphor of industrial engineering, which in a sense was a call to revisit the world of work study, organization and methods, and industrial engineering with today's tools. Much of the emphasis was on work design, job design, and efficiency. For some there was a fear of a return to 'scientific management'. For others it was an opportunity to reintroduce socio-technical systems analysis to the design of the workplace. By 1995 we do hear of managers applying 'reengineering' thinking and practice locally to work design, in departments, sections, and offices. Particularly in customer-facing localities, it may make very good sense.

Finally the '*natural, taken for granted*' view of organization may be one of the most important legacies of the BPR movement, one that seems to have been overlooked perhaps because it appears mundane. Processes are real and how the business works. However, they have been forgotten or ignored in large organizations. More often their managements concern themselves with functions, business units, regions, and the like—the structures by which we describe and analyse organizations. Yet processes are visible and tangible, and are how things get done. Paradoxically, on organograms and in policy manuals they are invisible and unrecognized. Yet a small businessman would probably describe his business and analyse it in terms of processes. Ask a general manager of a large firm how orders are fulfilled or even invoices handled and he or she may well reply with difficulty; processes are how businesses function but they are commonly unknown. My recommendation to some managers of large firms on BPR study teams often has been this: 'If you want to see how your processes could be reengineered and do some design benchmarking, go and visit some small firms.'

So process invites or comprises several organizational perspectives. Before leaving the subject, are our four process types anything more than an exercise in descriptive labelling? Already, some firms are recognizing different process types because they require different design approaches, carry different risks, and have different scopes. Our four types are represented in Figure 4.2. Here it is posited that we can more easily analyse, model, and predict processes and their redesign if they are relatively structured. High structuredness means we understand them, they are easily described, we can prescribe rules for them, and be reasonably certain of achieving the goals that the reengineering is seeking. Low structuredness in contrast implies more complexity and uncertainty and therefore risk. On the

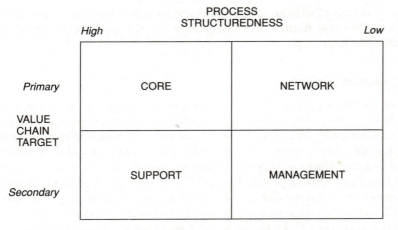

Fig. 4.2. *Typology of processes*

opposite axis, we can distinguish between primary and secondary activities of the value chain. Primary processes are how we do business and they have external customers; their impact is likely to be strategic in the sense of competitiveness and competitive positioning. They are the means by which we can turn around a business. Secondary processes are how we administer and manage and are internally focused. They may improve internal efficiency and have indirect effects on business performance. They are more concerned with planning and control than with daily competitiveness. The scope and character of change differ between primary and secondary activities. The four types of process delineated earlier neatly fit this model.

Core processes are usually well known and can be modelled. In other words, structuredness is high. They also, by our definition, are central to business functioning and commonly affect external customers; we recognize them as primary value chain activities. Business network processes are their extension into trading partners. Here the understanding of need, the impact of extending this process and the strategic outcome are somewhat uncertain—structuredness is lower. Support processes can be seen as relatively trivial to understand; structuredness is high, and by definition they are secondary value chain activities. Management processes are secondary (or tertiary), but because they greatly involve the complexities of social behaviour, are concerned with decision-making under uncertainty, and are more knowledge-based than task-based, their structuredness is low.

The framework may therefore inform us about relative risks, strategic impact, methodological choice and change management procedures. However, more valuable process taxonomies may emerge. In particular, this one is not grounded in models of organization. Because we argue that process is a construct of organization, this is unfortunate! Research and development of process frameworks based on views of organization ought to be a valuable next step.

Information Technology

Some business process reengineering has depended on very little investment in information technology. For example, Xerox Corporation's reengineered logistics management process apparently required only a relatively simple decision support system or model on top of existing information systems. Conversely, writers have suggested that the whole gamut of information technologies can be enablers of redesigned business processes. Hammer and Champy (1993) even suggest that reengineering teams should think inductively, that is, consider what IT allows us to do. Certainly there are two recurrent IT elements in BPR applications. Shared databases (or systems) are often essential in integrating functions and ensuring different actors in a process view their world and activities in the same way. Secondly, networking not only allows this integration or co-ordination but also enables both collection and dissemination of data through a process.

The claim, however, is that by understanding and harnessing IT we can redesign business processes in hitherto non-feasible ways. Davenport (1992) provides a list of opportunities, but this and others can perhaps be summarized (Table 4.2) under three economic contributions that IT generically offers (Earl, forthcoming). The critical opportunities are, first, obliterating (to use Hammer's language) activities which grew up before the IT era, and second, redesigning activities and processes because time and space can be collapsed, boundaries crossed, and information systems improved and made more accessible.

So applications of IT may be crucial to reengineered processes. Some also may be valuable in the actual design stages. Modelling is the primary example—to portray processes, analyse information, material, work, decision, activity, and timeflows, and to test alternative designs and their impact. Systems dynamics (Forrester 1961) is becoming an important tool for BPR teams and other tools (see below) are being developed.

It is commonly pointed out, however, that IT also can be a constraint on BPR, principally because of the legacy of architectures built to serve the past. Where data and systems architectures have been built to serve local, functional needs (or indeed the specific requirements of responsibility centres), there may be limits on process integration. Incompatible data, non-communicating systems, and inconsistent models are typical. The famous 'functional stovepipes' are embedded and perhaps preserved by our IT architectures. Thus process-oriented architectures, emphasizing lateral data models, interfacing systems, integrating communications, and process 'objects' and the like are called for—and these can take some time

Table 4.2. *IT opportunities in Business Process Reengineering*

Technology	Economic scope	Process opportunities
Computation	Reduce costs of production	Automating data dependent tasks Disintermediating information processes Eliminating activities
Communication	Reduce costs of co-ordination	Collapsing time and space Integrating tasks and processes Distributing and collecting data/information
'Infoware' (Databases and systems)	Reduce costs of information	Monitoring processes and tasks Analysing information and support decisions Archiving and making sense of experience and expertise Modelling and conceptualizing processes

to build. Yet the functional and responsibility centre information requirements do not disappear. As one company put it, 'there is danger of replacing functional stovepipes with process tunnels'. So it is likely that we need to learn much more about IT architectures. For these, alongside applications and tools, can enable BPR, but can also constrain it or displace one functionality with another.

We now turn to the 'old' elements of the BPR model in Figure 4.1, each at least as challenging as the new ones.

Business Change

It should be apparent by now that process thinking and the enabling potential of IT are necessary but not sufficient in BPR. To realign operations, administration, management, or inter-firm relationships with process is likely to require a fundamental shift in the way the whole business or organization thinks and works.

The real yet formally invisible process axes of organization either reassert themselves over, or become complementary to, the functional and responsibility axes. This may create new roles or it may, as in National and Provincial Building Society, substitute multi-dimensional, adaptive roles for task-specific, responsibility-delineated jobs. Job design and role domains become part of BPR.

Work and tasks are redesigned too. They may be widened, taking on lateral, interdependent, and collaborative aspects. They may be designed around information processing or knowledge-sharing. New skills and structures may be required, impacting jobs and roles.

In their wake, controls and performance measures may have to be redesigned to emphasize process goals, collaborative or teamwork behaviour, and new dimensions of performance. Indeed, they may be defined more in terms of buyer values and customer perceptions (since processes have customers). Such refinements may motivate the newly intended employee, manager, or group behaviour. But rewards and compensation may have to match too. For example, one insurance company made 25 per cent of employee compensation dependent upon policy and claims processing performance.

Indeed, responsibility and authority may be redistributed from vertical lines to horizontal lines and with them information, as argued earlier. Here the connection is made with 'empowerment' as enriched jobs, wider roles, case managers, and semi-autonomous work groups reappear.

Were all these changes to be necessary, it becomes apparent why some writers argue that nothing short of a culture change is required. For process thinking begins to look in practice like a radical departure from old norms and values. In case studies we have found it is often important to demolish the old props and determinants of organizational and employee behaviour, even if it is still unclear what new performance measures, controls, and rewards are required. Some companies have found that new roles and work organization are sufficient. Peer pressure is enough of an incentive and reward and more effective than very formal controls.

What stands out is how many variables may have to be redesigned. Business Process Reengineering is perhaps another case of socio-technical systems thinking: we have to combine a sense of good fit between both technological and social variables in our design. Figure 4.3, reproducing Leavitt's (1964) model, seems to describe the challenge well. Optimizing one can be sub-optimal in total. It is perhaps significant that this model became the core and driving conceptual framework for MIT's Management in the Nineties programme (Scott-Morton 1991). The model could drive a research agenda for testing the feasibility of BPR as a concept and providing help on design and implementation. It is interesting to note that other derivatives of the model have been developed by consultancies, stressing in particular the variables of strategy, processes, technology, and people. For them the message has been that IT or technological change projects require multiple skills and an integrative approach. If the concept of BPR achieves no more than this it will have been valuable.

Change Management

Indeed, once a BPR project is seen through Leavitt's lens, it becomes clear that the key challenge is change management. This is not new. As argued earlier, it takes us fully into the domain of organizational behaviour again. To ignore the change management challenge in understanding and thus

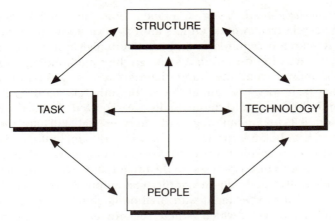

Fig. 4.3. *Leavitt's view of organizations*

seeking to apply BPR is hardly to know BPR at all. It is salutary to quote from the last pages of Hammer and Champy's best-selling book:

We have written only a little about how organizations actually make reengineering happen. A methodology for conducting a reengineering effort, the orchestration of the change campaign, the design and timing of releases of newly-redesigned processes, and tactics for dealing with the most common problems that arise in implementation are issues that go beyond the scope of the single book.

Implementation, it seems is the most complex part of all.

Perhaps four characteristics distinguish BPR from many change projects:

1. the underpinning concept of process adds new complexities;
2. there is no universal or proven methodology;
3. the transformational element is significant;
4. the apparent or assumed association with IT.

The *process* element seems to lead to a number of critical success factors. Because processes cross so many boundaries, a process sponsor is required to lend commitment, provide resources, oversee the project, be a resolver of conflicts, and pursue the superordinate goal. Case study evidence indicates that this is often the CEO. He or she may also need a process champion who is the full-time manager of the change, living it and fostering integration among those who are redesigning the process and will operate it. Indeed, there may also be a process owner who will be the executive responsible and accountable for the redesigned process which is dependent upon contributions from people in dispersed units and with other loyalties too. And to unite and drive all those involved, firms have been keen to create process visions which explain and remind what the change is seeking to achieve. Education has an important role here.

BPR *methodologies* are being developed. Some are high-level stage or project life-cycle frameworks. Others are based on tools, techniques, and models. Research is required to evaluate alternative approaches. Leading-edge firms have often found that some guiding methodology is required in order to move beyond the intent, that tools are needed for analysis (see later), that teamwork is essential due to the inherent nature of the processes, and also because different skills are required. In particular, communication skills, team-building, and interpersonal skills are mentioned by companies as being important as analytical, design, and creativity activities. In addition, consultants may be valued for either asking the politically incorrect questions or for process (in the organizational development sense) consultancy skills, especially in conflict resolution. A common approach currently, as firms experiment with methodologies, is to build BPR centres of excellence out of which skilled 'reengineers' will be migrated into different parts of the business. These are people who can replicate BPR experience.

The *transformational* element of BPR emphasizes the need for leadership, often from the CEO as sponsor. Many writers emphasize the importance of setting abnormal or outrageous goals. Here benchmarking is potentially important not only for establishing goals, but to render them believable and to give a sense of matching the best rival or beating the enemy. The politics of change is further pursued through rhetoric. Language becomes important as firms coin campaigns like 'breakthrough', 'turnarounds', 'world class', and the like. At SmithKline Beecham, whose logo is 'SB', the BPR programme is encapsulated in 'Simply Better'.

But if we are dealing with transformational change, what is the appropriate theory to adopt? For example, there is respectable evidence which indicates that strategic change is often incremental, emergent, unplanned in the formal sense, and based on learning through small gains (Mintzberg 1987; Quinn 1977). All these characteristics seem closer to continuous improvement than to BPR as currently propagated. Equally, many practitioners and academics would doubt, from experience, the probability of success in implementing large, massively orchestrated, and formally pioneered planned change projects. Also we may note that the apparent successes of 'Japanese Management' in achieving change are based more on continuous improvement philosophies, and yet BPR is held up as a technology with which to outperform such economies.

On the other hand, the systematic, rational, comprehensive approach to BPR may work where typically the focus is on internal, perhaps better understood, and more controllable activities (structured) than the external, dynamic, and uncertain areas (unstructured) of competitive product-market strategy-making. We need more research on these matters.

Also, if BPR is about transformational change it is likely to be political. Resources, status, roles, information are reallocated and there are potential winners and losers, proponents and opponents. Some of the popular treatises are surprisingly quiet about this or offer an almost apolitical view—or argue for macho leadership from the top. There are many BPR sponsors, champions, and consultants who have rediscovered the politics of change and there are many managers and employees who have refined their counter-implementation strategies.

The association of BPR with *information technology* is more problematic. Most firms who have attempted BPR soon realize that, because of the arguments above, the IT function should not drive these projects. IS managers may know more about how the firm's processes work than others, the redesigns may be heavily IT-dependent (and may not), the tools of systems analysis and development may be relevant, and the project management experience of the IT function may be invaluable. IS managers may even have an objective and relatively neutral view. However, mostly it is important that the project is seen and managed as a *business* project and the sponsor and owner at least will come from outside IS. Conversely all the above-mentioned qualities of IT and IS underscore that the IS function cannot be excluded from BPR teams and they also explain why some BPR centres of excellence are outgrowths of the IS function. We are also seeing IT managers being asked to lead BPR projects because of their project management experience and perhaps because they do bring some independence to the politics of change.

Finally, there is more than one famous case of apparent Business Reengineering which never happened or which was aborted. BPR may have begun life in the rationalist, technocratic world of some consultancies. I am reminded of one consultancy which was asked to talk about their experiences of BPR projects rather than sell the folklore. 'Ah—there is a problem', was the reply; 'we have worked with many management teams but none of the ideas have yet been implemented.' The change management dimension of BPR demands the contribution of organizational behaviour specialists. This is happening. But it also may also require better theories and principles of transformational change.

Systems Analysis

It has already been argued that 'process' is a systems concept and it is interesting to note that many of the tools of systems analysis are being resurrected or refined. A common technique in BPR is to do flow analyses of processes. We have encountered work flow analysis, activity flow analysis, material flow analysis, time flow analysis, and information flow analysis. In management process redesign, the construct of decision flow analysis is appealing too. There are at least three types of flow analysis involved:

1. techniques borrowed from industrial engineering such as time analysis or value analysis;

2. techniques borrowed from information systems development such as flowcharting;
3. new techniques using modelling software or software engineering tools (such as object-oriented representation) to portray and map processes.

To these analysis techniques we should add simulation and business modelling. Often based on systems dynamics methodology originally developed by Forrester (1961), teams build computer-based models to describe processes, evaluate alternative designs, and test the likely behaviour of the reengineered processes. Indeed, models may be one way of demonstrating to potential sponsors and owners how a reengineered process will work.

Another method borrowed from IS practice is prototyping. This involves building a trial system in order to test live the effect, analyse the interrelationships in the Leavitt lens of business change, learn from trial and error some of the benefits, and assess the viability of any technology. Prototyping was originally seen as a way of testing systems in use and as a means of organizational learning (Earl 1978). Indeed, we now hear the term 'organizational prototyping'.

The use of these tools and techniques has not only brought in skills of information systems to BPR teams. We are seeing the re-emergence of operations research, organization, and methods and industrial engineering, often within the IS function. Another contribution of the BPR movement is that firms are re-learning that it pays to analyse the business first, before designing computer systems. The 1970s and 1980s saw systems designers take the place of systems analysts in many IS departments. We might have asked 'where have all the systems analysts gone?' They are returning, but from different and relevant disciplines.

So the three 'old' challenges are very much ones of implementation and they explain why BPR is not easy. For this reason competitive advantage may accrue to those firms who are able to 'pull it off'.

Conclusions

BPR has been 'deconstructed' into six elements which are grouped into the new domain and the old domain. Experience is beginning to show that there is appeal in the new domain. IT-enabled transformation along process lines seems to fit the demands of today's competitive world. There could be strategic sense in BPR from the perspective of building resource-based, excellent capability advantages. And putting 'process' back into large organizations may be overdue.

However, experience is also showing that the substantial challenges of

BPR lie in the old domain. BPR is about multi-dimensional change in business, very much of a socio-technical nature. It requires the tools of systems analysis and IS departments are reskilling accordingly. Implementation rests on the ability to manage change.

In our six-element model (or star) of BPR, two elements have been emphasized. *Process* was examined at length and is argued to be a construct of organization design, from several viewpoints. The implication for practice is that to achieve all the full promise of BPR, managers and consultants must understand process as organization and exploit the lessons of organization theory. Researchers could help by studying processes through organizational lenses and enhancing our frameworks for analysis and design.

Change Management too was emphasized and the obvious point made that to understand how to reengineer business processes in practice needs deep knowledge of the principles and skills of *organizational behaviour*. The contribution of research, therefore, could be to improve our models of transformational change. In information management in general, and in the current wave of BPR, the available knowledge-base on managing change has often seemed wanting. The result commonly has been naïve prescriptions. As is always the case, both the design and implementation of change—in information systems and more widely—rest particularly on the organizational dimension.

References

Clark, K. B., and Fujimoto, T. (1991), *Product Development Performance: Strategy, Organisation and Management in the World Auto Industry*, Boston: Harvard Business School Press.

Davenport, T. H. (1992), *Process Innovation: Reengineering Work Through Information Technology*, Boston: Harvard Business School Press.

—— and Short, J. E. (1990), 'The New Industrial Engineering: Information Technology and Business Process Redesign', *Sloan Management Review*, 31/4 (Summer), 11–27.

Earl, M. J. (1978), 'Prototype Systems for Accounting, Information and Control', *Accounting, Organisations and Society*, vol. 3, no. 2, pp. 161–72.

—— (1994), 'The New and the Old of Business Process Redesign', *Journal of Strategic Information Systems*, vol. 3, no. 1, pp. 5–22.

—— (forthcoming), *Management Strategies for Information Technology*, 2nd edn., London: Prentice Hall.

—— and Khan, B. (1994), 'How New is Business Process Redesign?', *European Management Journal*, vol. 12, no. 1, pp. 20–30.

Forrester, J. W. (1961), *Industrial Dynamics*, New York: J. Wiley.

Galbraith, Jay R. (1977), *Organization Design*, Reading, Mass.: Addison-Wesley.

Garvin, D. A. (1988), *Managing Quality*, New York: Free Press.

Hammer, M. (1990), 'Reengineering Work: Don't Automate, Obliterate', *Harvard Business Review*, 90/4 (July–Aug.), 104–12.

—— and Champy, J. (1993), *Reengineering the Corporation: A Manifesto for Business Revolution*, New York: Harper Collins.

Juran, J. M. (1964), *Managerial Breakthrough*, New York: McGraw Hill.

Leavitt, H. (1964) *Applied Organisation Change in Industry: Structural Technical and Human Approaches*, New York: J. Wiley.

Linder, J. (1986), *Frito-Lay Inc: A Strategic Transition (A)*, Harvard Business School Case Study 9–187–065.

Malone, T. W., and Crowston, K. (1994), 'The Interdisciplinary Study of Coordination', *ACM Computing Surveys*, 26 (Mar.), 87–119.

Mintzberg, H. (1987), 'Crafting Strategy', *Harvard Business Review*, 66/4 (July–Aug.), 66–75.

Ouchi, W. G. (1981), *Theory Z: How American Business Can Meet the Japanese Challenge*, Reading, Mass.: Addison-Wesley.

Prahalad, C. K., and Hamel, G. (1991), 'The Core Competence of the Corporation', *Harvard Business Review*, vol. 63, no. 3, pp. 79–91.

Porter, M. E. (1980), *Competitive Strategy*, New York: Free Press.

Quinn, J. B. (1977), 'Strategic Change: Logical Incrementalism', *Sloan Management Review*, 20/1 (Fall), 7–21.

Rockart, J. F., and Short, J. E. (1988), *Information Technology and the New Organisation: Towards More Effective Management of Interdependence*, Centre for Information Systems Research Working Paper 180, Sloan School of Management, MIT.

Schein, E. (1969), *Process Consultation: Its Role in Organisation Development*, Reading, Mass.: Addison-Wesley.

Scott-Morton, M. S. (1991) (ed.), *The Corporation of the 1990s: Information Technology and Organizational Transformation*, Oxford: Oxford University Press.

Short, J. E., and Konsynski, B. (1992), *Baxter International: Shared Services in Albuquerque*, Harvard Business School Case no. 9–193–016.

Short, J. E., and Venkatraman, N. (1992), 'Beyond Business Process Redesign: Redefining Baxter's Network', *Sloan Management Review*, 34/1 (Fall), 7–21.

Sloan, A. O., Jnr. (1964), *My Years With General Motors*, New York: Doubleday.

Stopford, J. M., and Baden-Fuller, C. (1994), *Rejuvenating the Mature Business*, 2nd edn., Boston: Harvard Business School Press.

Takeuchi, H., and Nonaka, I. (1986), 'The New New Product Development', *Harvard Business Review*, 65/1 (Jan.–Feb.), 137–44.

Taylor, F. W. (1911), *Principles of Scientific Management*, New York: Harper and Row.

Wernerfelt, B. (1994), 'A Resource-Based View of the Firm', *Strategic Management Journal*, vol. 5, no. 12, pp. 171–80.

Womack, J. P., Jones, D. T., and Roos, D. (1990), *The Machine That Changed the World*, New York: Rawson Associates.

5

Information Systems in Global Business: Evidence from European Multinationals

MICHAEL J. EARL AND DAVID F. FEENY

Introduction

In the literature of international business a recurring theme is the need for co-ordination of operations and their management in global organizations. Such co-ordination is indeed central to the whole concept of globalization. Co-ordination of activity in order to achieve supra-national efficiencies is argued by many writers to distinguish the global business from the 'multinational' (Bartlett and Ghoshal 1989) or 'multidomestic' (Porter 1986). And co-ordination in the strategic planning domain is at the heart of the 'strategic intent' which defines global businesses for Hamel and Prahalad (1989).

These authors have expanded on the nature and complexity of global co-ordination required in the successful organizations of the future. Such organizations, it is claimed, exhibit the simultaneous achievement of global scale, responsiveness to markets and governments, world-wide transfer of learning, and innovation (Prahalad and Doz 1987; Bartlett and Ghoshal 1989). In place of organizational uniformity, each geographical unit will have a distinctive role within the overall business (Hamel and Prahalad 1985; Bartlett and Ghoshal 1989). In the 'transnational' corporation of Bartlett and Ghoshal the organization is neither centralized nor decentralized; it represents an integrated network in which there are intensive and complex interactions between physically remote but interdependent units.

As Porter (1986) recognizes, the ability to co-ordinate globally is seen to be dramatically increased through advances in information technology (IT). The wide-scale use of IT is also implicit in Bartlett and Ghoshal's (1987) vision of the transnational as an organization in which there is 'collaborative information sharing and problem solving, co-operative support and resource sharing, collective action and implementation'. So information systems would seem to be an important component of global competitive strategy. Egelhoff (1988) has touched on this in his work on the complexity of global organizations. He has applied information processing models of organization, such as the work of Galbraith (1973), Huber (1989), and Thompson (1967), to MNC's and concludes that high information processing requirements are likely and could easily be ignored in formulating international business strategies (Egelhoff 1991). Hagström (1991) shows through case study research in SKF that information and communication flow requirements tend to grow as a multinational organization evolves.

However, there has been little empirical research done, through the information systems perspective (i.e. looking at IT applications and studying the IS function.[1] Ives and Jarvenpaa (1991) executed a survey to test emergent alignment of IS management with global business strategies but otherwise there has been little examination of the practice of exploiting IT to enable co-ordination in a globally-managed business. In this chapter we examine some of the forms in which IT may contribute, the enabling conditions, and the obstacles to success, based on case study research in four European-based corporations.

The Potential Role of IT in Global Business Management

Before exploring these case studies, we sought to establish more specifically what might be the theoretical contribution of IT. The starting-point was consideration of the three imperatives of global operation identified above—global efficiency, local responsiveness, and transfer of learning. In other words, we take a model of business strategy and speculate on the need for different sorts of information systems in the spirit of a model of strategic fit.

The search for *global efficiency* implies that the organization must be able, within each relevant function, to co-ordinate and consolidate its activity to achieve available economies of scale. A key requirement would seem to be the collection of comparative performance information from locations around the world to support decisions on how effectively to allocate resources and source requirements. This need may be facilitated by building a global data network, collecting and providing access to information which conforms to some globally applied data standards. Organizations often wish to go further, to implement standard application systems worldwide, in order to ensure the integrity of information, facilitate the transfer of activities and people, and perhaps achieve scale economies in systems development and processing. Conceptually, however, the base requirement is for the definition and communication of standard data.

Achieving *local responsiveness*, on the other hand, implies limits to standardization. The expectation is that organizations will want to identify some

---

[1] We use 'IT' to describe information technology and 'IS' as a shorthand for information systems. IS is also used to describe the information systems function. We are conscious how varied and loose terminology is in this domain.

Table 5.1. *Global information systems*

Business imperative	IT contribution
Global efficiency	Data networks; data standards; common systems
Local responsiveness	Production systems to manage variety; networks to support collaborative development
Transfer of learning	Functional communications networks; knowledge bases/systems
Global alliance	Inter-organizational systems

level of standard/core product, but also provide a variety of optional features which may be present or absent in the delivered product depending on local, legal, or market conditions. Thus the 'world car' or 'global TV' becomes tailored to suit the requirement of each market segment— 'glocalization' in the vernacular. Global IT investment to support this environment may include production scheduling and control systems to support the management of high variety and IT and communications networks to facilitate the efforts of dispersed marketing/engineering/manufacturing groups who are tasked with developing the next generation of global core products or creating the required local derivatives. These capabilities would need to be planned and developed at global level, to interface with and supplement local systems which meet local needs, especially national sales activities.

The co-ordination required for *transfer of learning* would seem to be along functional dimensions, across multiple locations involved in research and development, marketing, service, and so on. Communication networks providing electronic mail, and computer and video conferencing facilities to support informal dialogue among professionals are the obvious IT contribution. Construction of globally accessible knowledge bases or knowledge systems may follow, as examples of best practice or scarce expertise are recognized and codified for distribution to others who can use or build upon them.

Finally, the potential IT contribution may be extended beyond the organization. For example, Ghoshal (1987) has described how an organization may extend its economies of scope through *external alliances* between companies with different skills and cultures. Inter-organizational information systems can provide new opportunities to operationalize this concept. In the vertical dimension, Benetton use IT to support what Johnston and Lawrence (1988) call Value Adding Partnerships with manufacturers and retailers. In the horizontal dimension, Konsynski and McFarlan (1990) have described the global 'information partnerships' between airlines, hotel chains, and car rental companies.

Table 5.1 summarizes these propositions on the potential contribution of IT to the pursuit of global business strategies. It served as a framework for analysing the history, current use, and development of global information systems in our case study companies. The ideas it contains seem straight-forward enough, but we were already aware from prior work with global businesses of a significant gap between the propositions and common practice. While this gap might be merely a function of deficiencies in the framework, an alternative explanation was that global information systems present difficult organizational and implementation problems. Consequently, IS organization and management issues were also a focus of our fieldwork.

The Research Design

Given the complexity and emerging nature of the global business field, it was our view that a large-scale empirical study was inappropriate at this stage. Instead we sought to build insights into the reality, potential, and problems of IT contribution through in-depth investigation of a small number of businesses which were known to have pursued global management capabilities over a number of years.

Four such businesses were selected, to represent a variety of global business contexts and potential co-ordination needs. For the first, in re-insurance, transfer of learning was the primary global driver, with global efficiency of information processing a secondary goal. For the second, in electronics, supra-national economies of scale in R&D and manufacturing were paramount; however, there were concerns about responsiveness to local market requirements and accordingly a possible need for sharing of learning both within and across functions—for example, from marketing to design. In the white goods industry our case study business was among those promoting global competition, seeking out economies of scale and scope while maintaining responsiveness to residual heterogeneity between national markets. By contrast, in the chemicals industry the product was already a global commodity—but our case study business had set out to improve responsiveness in an industry traditionally organized to achieve efficiency. Figure 5.1 illustrates the approximate positioning of the case study businesses on the familiar efficiency/responsiveness grid. It demonstrates that we set out to examine a mix of global strategy contexts, including two where industry positioning was changing. Furthermore, in all four cases there was some level of attempt to simultaneously achieve global efficiency and market responsiveness—and indeed the transfer of learning. In this sense each business aspired towards the transnational positioning of Barlett and Ghoshal (1989).

Our case study businesses also exhibited a mix of organizational structures, driven by a combination of business need and organizational heritage.

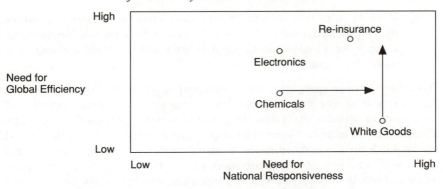

Fig. 5.1. *Strategic positioning of case study companies*

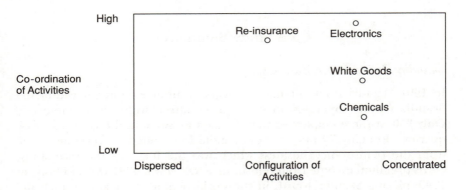

Fig. 5.2. *Organizational positioning of case study companies*

In Figure 5.2, Porter's (1986) co-ordination/configuration framework is used to suggest their overall positioning in this respect. While Bartlett and Ghoshal focus on organizational capabilities required and achieved, Porter is concerned with organizational arrangements. His framework is primarily designed to explore the operation of value chain activities but it serves here to demonstrate the contrasting co-ordination/configuration patterns of our case studies.

In combination, Figures 5.1 and 5.2 confirm that our case study businesses were concerned with global management capability, beyond multinational/multidomestic operation. The need for co-ordination was implicit in at least some dimensions of their functional activities, and hence a potential IT contribution existed. Our basic questions for these businesses became:

1. What information systems (applications of IT) are in place or under development to support the global strategy of the business?

2. What IT infrastructures (networks, data bases) are in place or under development to enable the desired levels of cross-border functioning?
3. How is the IS function being managed in the global context, and with what results?

To address these questions, we conducted in each business a series of interviews at senior management levels, examined archival evidence of information systems evolution and plans, and documented experience of operational activity. General management executives were interviewed to establish an understanding of industry context, business strategy, and perceived and potential contribution of IT. IS management was questioned about IS history, strategy, organization, and key issues. Operational management described usage of information systems in place, and experience of co-ordination needs, policies, and problems.

Case Study Summaries

Skandia Re-Insurance Business

In 1991 Skandia International[2]—a major insurance company within the Skandia Group—operated in eighteen countries with 3,800 employees. Only 350 of these employees were located in Sweden, the Group's headquarters. Roughly 70 per cent of Skandia International's revenues came from the re-insurance business which was the focus of the case study. Gross premium income from reinsurance was MSEK 9341 ($1.5 billion) in 1990, placing Skandia fourth in the world behind the giant Munich Re, Swiss Re, and General Re.

The re-insurance market was seen as naturally global, large (more than $40 billion) but mature and cyclical. The market was in slow decline as direct insurers reduced their purchases of re-insurance through backward integration. Entry barriers were low ('a tough mind and a pen'), so that during cyclical upturns new entrants increased rivalry and created over-capacity. In 1991 there were an estimated 1,250 competitors world-wide. In this difficult market Skandia's strategy was summarized as follows by (former) CEO Hans Dalborg:

We strive for profitability before volume and are realigning ourselves towards areas in which we can offer clients superior services. We are focusing our efforts on advanced actuarial techniques and products as well as on administrative and consulting services. At the same time we are introducing powerful computer and communication systems while making improvements on the personnel side. Together these measures will help us keep costs in check and will give us a base

---

[2] Further detail can be found in a case, 'Skandia International', by M. J. Earl, in C. Ciborra and T. Jelassi (eds.), *Strategic Information Systems: A European Perspective*, J. Wiley & Sons, 1994.

for new product development. The objective is to keep volume where it is, or expand in a controlled way in areas where profit potential is very good—concentrating on technically advanced niches.

Skandia operated a relatively flat organization structure, with most employees operating from a network of local offices as underwriters or support staff. Each local office was a profit centre, operating within the strategy and policies laid down by Stockholm headquarters. Monthly accounting figures were reported to Stockholm via a common general ledger package.

As can be detected from Dalborg's statement, these global policies extended beyond business goals and strategy to the field of information systems. In the words of corporate controller Sten Lundqvist, 'the essence of our offensive competitive strategy is to build information in a structured way over many years, and then take risk and return decisions'. A corporately developed and owned system called SARA (System for Advanced Reinsurance Assistance) tracked reinsurance treaties and conditions; accounted for and managed money flows; stored treaties, risks, and claims; and handled credit. SARA was available on-line at all local offices, supported by a standard set of analysis and enquiry tools. Underwriters accessed SARA for decision support, entered deals, and updated the central database on-line to Stockholm. In 1991 Skandia was encouraging and co-ordinating experimental investments in expert systems, triggered by an initiative in the USA, to help distribute underwriting expertise to new and dispersed staff. The database therefore was the repository of experience-based knowledge on risks, claims, and prices. It was updated and disseminated to offices over the global data network. The decision support tools, some with resident expertise in them, enabled underwriters to be both responsive and shrewd in taking on risks. SARA and its related systems were thus fundamental to the global business strategy and operations of Skandia.

While IT resources and investment had reached a peak during the development of SARA, the company continued to regard IT as a strategic resource. Skandia was one of the three initiators of RINET—the value-added network being developed for information exchange in international insurance and re-insurance. Skandia set out to be a leader in improving information flows in the industry because it had an incentive to do so.

These examples demonstrate how IS was itself a globally co-ordinated function within Skandia's re-insurance business. Corporate policy vested ownership of all local equipment and support staff with corporate IS; there were globally defined technical architectures for the IT networks and applications; two preferred IT vendors were recognized world-wide, with central co-ordination of purchasing; a central register was maintained for all data and programmes. This strong co-ordination of IT in the re-insurance business was very much a conscious choice, not a chance legacy of history. Indeed, IS and IT policy issues were formally taken at alternate board meetings of Skandia International. A recent proposal from the

US business unit to devolve IS responsibility had been firmly rejected by the board because it was felt that central control of IS strategy, development, and operations was essential if risk management was to be optimized, information processing costs minimized, and crucially, data managed as a corporate resource to transfer underwriting learning. By contrast, IS organization for Skandia's Life and General insurance business had long been decentralized, in line with the nature of those businesses which were responding to a variety of local, national markets.

Philips Display Components

In 1991 Display Components was a major business unit within the Components Division of the Philips Corporation, with annual revenues of around Fl 4 billions (US $2.3 billions). With global responsibility for development and manufacture of picture tubes for TV sets and computer monitors, Philips DC employed around 19,000 personnel in factories and offices around the world.

Like Skandia, Philips DC competed in a market that was large (100 million tubes/annum worth US $15 billions), global in nature, and relatively mature. Western Europe was the largest market area, followed by North America and Japan. Because of economies of scale in development and production, competition was concentrated, with four global companies accounting for more than 50 per cent of industry output. Philips DC was the leading producer, closely followed by Toshiba and Matsushita. These same corporations were of course prominent in TV set-making, but in practice set-making and tube-producing subsidiaries operated on a trading basis, with set-making plants sourcing their TV tubes from producer plants in the same region.

The market for computer monitors was smaller, around US $9.5 billions in 1991, but growing strongly at around 25 per cent per annum. The market was heavily concentrated in the Far East, reflecting that region's strength in microcomputer systems. Competition was less concentrated in this segment, with Philips DC perceived to be 'one of the pack'.

The strategic question for Philips DC in 1991 was summarized by executive management as 'choosing where we want to be and what we want to have'. The concern was that Philips DC was too influenced by Europe where its dominant market share could only decline over time. Future business success was dependent on capturing market share elsewhere— particularly in the Far East, which included the large Japanese TV market and the critical market for computer monitor tubes.

To this end, Philips DC had a number of strengths to deploy. Its current product offering was rated (at least in Europe) as better than the industry average on every customer criterion except price, and Philips were perceived as technology leaders over time. Philips already had a manufacturing presence in all of the four key continental markets of the world. But three aspects of market responsiveness were identified for special attention:

- Since success increasingly came from being the chosen partner of successful set-makers, the Philips culture needed to develop further from a technology orientation to a customer one.
- 'Closeness to the customer' must extend in a physical sense to the R&D function; poor performance in the Far East was linked to the lack of a development group based there to be able to develop local derivatives.
- Product time-to-market must be significantly reduced, with rapid handover from development to manufacturing despite the geographic separation involved.

Industry scale economies and globally oriented Japanese competition had resulted in Philips DC becoming the first business to move away from the corporation's historic emphasis on autonomous national subsidiaries. During the 1980s decision-making was increasingly centralized into the Philips DC Head Office. However, by the end of 1991 a new organizational pattern had emerged to balance global coherence with customer responsiveness. Under this new regime (which also reflected wider corporate changes towards profit centre autonomy, cost, and quality emphases), three levels of responsibility were emphasized:

- Business Unit HQ was responsible for R&D and Strategic Marketing, therefore controlling the global core product stream.
- Four geographic Regions were each responsible for the manufacture, sale, and distribution of the core products within their territories.
- Each Plant had a mission to manufacture and distribute one or more core products to customers in its Region, tailoring core products where necessary to meet customer needs.

At the beginning of 1992 it was not clear that IS was yet anchored securely in the new organization. A number of IT studies and developments were in progress but they were not explicitly focused on global issues or the emerging global business strategy. IT resources were thinly scattered across HQ, Regional, and Plant levels; IS managers were rarely embedded into the key management teams at each level; Philips DC was largely dependent for IT development and service on resources elsewhere, a legacy of the historic IS structure which was aligned to Corporate, National, and more recently Divisional levels within Philips.

A further legacy of this structure was a set of common transaction processing systems across the corporation, notably in order processing, production planning and control, and logistics management. While the imposition of these systems in the 1970s and 1980s had caused resentment in some businesses, it did create an unusually coherent infrastructure which, in principle, global business units could exploit to considerable benefit. For example, Philips DC had no difficulty in taking an order from a customer anywhere in Europe and allocating it to whichever plant was appropriate. However, by 1991 a number of operational systems were due for replacement and questions were being raised over future levels of standardization. Could a Regional requirement for the co-ordination of logistics, for example, be met through Regional data standards and local systems, or did it necessitate a common world-wide logistics system?

A higher-order information management agenda was put forward by one member of the Philips DC Executive Management team, who believed IT had a further and critical contribution to make in four areas:

- enabling the co-ordination of increasingly geographically dispersed product development, based on distributed access to a consolidated design data base;
- providing information to support the optimization of supply vs. demand, across the various production sites;
- supporting goods flow management within the vertical manufacturing and supply chain;
- providing to management better information on global activity of competitors.

The Electrolux White Goods Business

With forty-three factories in fifteen countries and a turnover of more than US $5 billions, white goods was the dominant business of the Electrolux Corporation in 1991. It was also a pioneer of globalization in an industry where received wisdom had held that national differences prevented products such as refrigerators and washing machines from selling across borders. Electrolux had built its global business through more than 200 acquisitions, including large units like Zanussi (1984), White (1986), and Thorn EMI Appliances (1987). These acquisitions had been energetically and rapidly integrated into a complex new organizational structure. Despite setbacks (Baden-Fuller and Stopford 1991), Electrolux had been sufficiently successful to convince others of the global potential of white goods, notably Whirlpool with its acquisition of the Domestic Appliance business of Philips. The industry now comprised a combination of global giants such as Electrolux, Whirlpool, and Matsushita; and aggressive National/ product specialists such as GEC's Hotpoint and Merloni's Ariston—who, in turn, were beginning to seek global alliances.

Electrolux has been a case study target for others interested in international business, including Ghoshal and Haspeslagh (1989), and Lorenz (1989) who wrote a series of articles which positioned Electrolux as the epitome of Bartlett and Ghoshal's transnational organization. Features of the organizational structure for white goods in 1991 included:

- product divisions, responsible for development and manufacturing; each had a specific international mission, delivered through a number of dispersed sites;
- international marketing units which each controlled a number of national and international brand names; working through nationally based sales companies which operated an arms-length/trading relationship with product divisions;
- country organizations, headed by strong country managers with 'primary responsibility' for all the development, manufacturing, and sales units in their territory;
- centralized service functions, including IT, which provided specialized expertises across the corporation.

In most respects the culture stressed decentralization, with production sites, sales units, and service functions all operating as profit centres. It is clear that a number of tensions are built into such a structure, which can be pictured as a multi-dimensional matrix. But, according to Bartlett and Ghoshal, Electrolux operated not as a formal matrix but through overlay of a series of microstructured mechanisms on top of a distributed asset structure! Certainly there was little evident co-ordinating bureaucracy: rather, an emphasis on a culture which expected agreement seeking, galvanized by a series of corporate strategic initiatives, and monitored by a small number of high-level executives such as the three responsible for international marketing.

The strategy this 'impossible organization' was designed to deliver had the classic transnational components (Ghoshal and Haspeslagh 1989):

- achieving global scale volume to ensure long-term survival;
- building/maintaining 'adequate' share in all markets through local presence and responsiveness;
- developing 'insurmountable' competitive advantage through faster development of better products by multidisciplinary design teams; and through transferring/leveraging product concepts, components, and manufacturing techniques across markets and borders.

This most transnational of our case studies also showed the most extensive exploitation of IT, at least in terms of the global information systems framework of Table 5.1. The Electrolux Forecasting and Supply system (EFS) supported business-wide co-ordination of demand, production, and distribution—across functions, profit-centres, and national borders. A common Financial Reporting System (FCS) provided comparative information for performance assessment. Standardization on the ODETTE protocol for Electronic Data Interchange (EDI) allowed co-ordination of internal and external suppliers across different plants. The IT contribution to faster development was based on a common/shared CAD system;

and IT was integral to the extensive investments in flexible manufacturing systems made at the Susequana and Porcia plants in Italy to achieve
flexibility of production. Only in respect of the transfer of learning was
an IT contribution less in evidence, with little apparent enthusiasm, for
example, for using the electronic mail system; but the presence of a group
subsidiary to supply and install all factory level automation ensured transfer of functional learning within that field.

This alignment of IT investment with business need had been achieved
even though the IS function was not formally integrated into the organization and management structure of the white goods business. As already
noted, the dominant unit in Electrolux's IS function took the form of a
corporate subsidiary and profit centre, with minimal IT resources being
located in production and sales units.

A number of other factors, however, seemed to have enabled the alignment of IS strategy with the white goods global business thrust:

- White goods were (by far) the dominant customer of the corporate
  IS unit, and therefore critical to its success.
- IS initiatives consistently paralleled and evolved with major business initiatives (for example, EFS was first created in support of a
  corporate-wide inventory reduction programme); this ensured the
  line management support required to implement tough changes such
  as the imposition of standard product coding.
- The centralized nature of the IS group simultaneously ensured that
  a standard and coherent technical architecture was put in place as
  applications developed.
- The central IS group remained lean (150 employees in a corporation of 153,000) and committed to pragmatic evolution rather than
  revolution; standards and new developments went no further than
  necessary. For example, EFS interfaced with existing local order
  processing systems.

Overall, the IT effort at Electrolux demonstrated the focus and drive
which may be considered the hallmarks of effective IS strategy-making.

Eurochem[3]

In 1991 Eurochem comprised four business units producing commodity
chemicals with a combined turnover of around £2.3 billion. Each business unit had global responsibility for its product range. But a combination
of scale and scope economies, history, health and safety, and environmental factors meant the business units shared production sites. Indeed, in

[3] The company in the chemical sector requested anonymity on the basis that our findings
were a fair representation but captured a business in transition.

a common industry pattern, production sites and technologies and facilities were often shared with rival chemical companies.

The 1991 organization resulted from a series of evolutionary steps which had rationalized the acquisitions made in the 1970s and 1980s. The progressive emphasis in these steps had been devolution from a centralized, functional structure to business units with the aim of increasing accountability and cost control in a commodity-based industry. Most service functions had now been migrated to business unit control to establish value for money; one of the most recent changes was the devolution of the IS function.

Alongside this process of decentralization, group business strategy continued to stress leadership in process technology as the route to cost advantage and market leadership. Since price was determined by market conditions, low cost production was essential to long term survival. However, a common ordering pattern was for customers to select a chemicals supplier to meet their forward needs during a contract period, with actual deliveries being made against call-offs, and at prevailing market prices. Therefore, in the shorter term and at business unit level customer service was an important parameter of competitive strategy.

It was a particular attempt to create a service edge that had attracted our interest in Eurochem. In 1984 the company decided to develop a new computer-based Order Processing System which would provide 'comprehensive facilities to manage order processing, distribution, stock control, and invoicing' across the business, replacing a plethora of systems inherited through acquisition. In the classic pattern of IT innovation (Runge and Earl 1988), the system was championed by a senior line manager in the commercial function who saw it as the solution to a business problem ('we like your products, but we can't get hold of them'). He won the support of an executive sponsor who steered the proposal through the Board. Another parallel with IT innovations elsewhere was set when the project development was put under the original champion, who contracted with external hardware and software suppliers to the exclusion of the in-house IS department. For a number of reasons the order processing system went through an often traumatic development history, with major overruns in timescale and budget; but by 1991 the system was installed and in use across the commodity businesses.

Opinions of the benefits and value of the system varied widely. In the opinion of the original champion it had not only succeeded in putting Eurochem on a par with, or ahead of, the best chemical company and distributor competition; it had also been a stimulus to the internationalizing of the company. Others were much less convinced, complaining that it was a high-cost system which would be of limited value until it became a more authoritative source of inventory and market data. More mundanely, a sales office manager opined that the system was too slow to provide the planned immediate response to customer telephone calls. Some of the specialty chemicals businesses doubted that they required this sort of system.

With the latest changes to the IS organization the ownership of the system had been devolved from Group level to the business unit processing bulk chemicals. With its thousands of customers and hundreds of products, this was the business where the system's capabilities were most relevant. The business unit agreed to provide the system service to its sister businesses, some of which were expressing dissatisfaction with it, expressing the belief that they could find a cheaper/better alternative to meet their own particular needs. Of course if any one business discontinued its use of the order processing system there would be adverse cost consequences for the others. The question would be asked more loudly of whether a common system had in fact been necessary for interfacing four distinct groups of businesses to the plants that served them. In short, the original rationale, the anticipated benefits, and the current need for a common order processing system were not agreed across the chemical businesses.

While order processing attracted most of the attention, it was not the only common system in Eurochem. It had in fact been preceded by the creation of a management accounting database. More recently a standard Maintenance and Materials system had come up for consideration; but a proposed common approach to Payroll had been rejected as poor value for money. With seemingly ever stronger profit centre focus, and the accompanying devolution of most IT resources and responsibilities to business units (a small IT policy unit remained at the centre, reporting to the controller),[4] it seemed unlikely that new initiatives which involved cross-business co-ordination and co-operation would either emerge or be supported.

Discussion

Global Alignment

Our four cases demonstrate more differences than similarities, as the research design intended. Collectively, however, we believe that they do suggest that information systems are necessary to support or enable certain global business strategies. In Table 5.2 we compare the descriptive evidence against our normative matrix presented in Table 5.1. Different levels of investment in IS for co-ordination are evident, but each company has recognized at least some need. (The question-marks represent systems not yet agreed and developed or systems which in principle could have

---

[4] Subsequently this unit was closed down and an investigation initiated into how to downsize the entire IS function across the businesses.

Table 5.2. *Investments in global information systems*

Business imperative	Investment in information systems at			
	Skandia	Philips	Electrolux	Eurochem
Global efficiency	General ledger SARA reinsurance assistance system	Order processing Logistics system production, Planning and control ?Supply/demand balance	EFS FCS CAD EDI	MAS ?Order processing
Local responsiveness		Order processing Logistics system ?Competitor information	EFS FMS EDI	?Order processing
Transfer of learning	SARA reinsurance assistance system Reinsurance decision support and expert systems	?Design database	?CAD	
Global alliances				

supported a global business imperative). Each type of global thrust, or business imperative, is represented except the development of global alliances. As we anticipated, companies differed in terms of their particular global strategies.

At Skandia, operating in a global market-place, the intent was to differentiate by building and exploiting a world-wide platform of knowledge within parameters of low cost operation. SARA and the Ledger systems, therefore, support global efficiency, but more particularly SARA and its surrounding decision support systems provide transfer of learning. Our model in Table 5.1 predicts these IS investments plus the emphasis on world-wide standards which the central IS group enforced.

Electrolux also fairly well demonstrates the model. By design and some good fortune, they have developed or acquired information systems and technologies to support the three dimensions of the 'transnational'. EFS, the Financial Control System, and EDI Standards all facilitate the pursuit of global efficiency. EFS and EDI also provide the co-ordination to serve local responsiveness from one or two production sites. The flexible manufacturing technologies also aid responsiveness. The CAD system provides functional co-ordination across sites to transfer design and development knowledge.

In Philips DC we find information systems present which are capable of supporting the same three transnational thrusts. However, their management team, with new and increased responsibility through the parent's decentralization programme, were only just beginning to agree the critical success factors required to operate globally and perhaps thereby agree on IS requirements. The systems inheritance in production and logistics looked promising.

Eurochem neither fits nor deviates from our model because their (global) business strategy was not clear. Organizational devolution in response to corporate business was prompting hard questions, not only about its strategy, but the appropriate structure and the requisite information systems. This is not a context in which alignment is likely to be found, nor be capable of evaluation.

Our study could have ended with the above descriptions and evaluation. We could have concluded that global business strategies are likely to benefit from or need investment in IT and IS and claimed support for our normative model of global information systems requirements. However, not all the companies were investing equally in IT and two clearly demonstrated better adjustment between IS and their global business strategy than others. Indeed, collectively the four cases do not provide overwhelming evidence that a global IT platform is necessary to do business globally as the industry hype often claims. We offer two explanations for this situation, one relatively commonplace, the other more novel.

First, there needs to be a *global business vision* shared among the top management team. Skandia and Electrolux largely fulfilled this requirement. Philips DC and Eurochem did not. Now it is the gospel of consultants and many academics that before a firm can formulate its IS strategy it needs a business strategy. So the need for a global vision may be only a special case of the wider problem. Indeed, it may not be just that information systems should not be forgotten in global strategy-making, as Egelhoff (1991) suggests, but more fundamentally that you cannot consider appropriate IS requirements until the vision of competitive strategy at a global level is developed and agreed.

However, it is well documented that information strategists often find business strategies absent, disputed, or unclear (Earl 1993). The IS function often has either to work with the organization to explicate both levels of strategy or to await for them to emerge (Earl 1993). Consequently it is clear that whether an IS strategy is derived from the business strategy, is formulated integrally with it, or emerges by an incremental and evolutionary process, it only happens through organization.

The second condition therefore is that *IS organization structure* promotes integration of business and IS strategy. This integration was particularly clear at Skandia where the IS function's centralized structure and wide-ranging powers both enabled and reflected its role in business strategy. At Electrolux the positioning of IS as a service business and profit centre was consistent with corporate culture. More important, the dominance of the white goods business ensured that IS gave the highest priority to understanding and meeting its needs. We are not clear that a smaller business unit would have been equally well served by these arrangements. In contrast, our two case study businesses were clearly handicapped by a lack of organizational integration. At Philips years of change had left the IS function fragmented and struggling to catch up with the business unit structures. Lack of IS representation on key management teams was a particular problem during a period of formative strategic thinking. Even the agreed IT initiatives were making slow progress, lacking resources and active support from business management. Finally, at Eurochem the IS function faced a major repositioning challenge. From being a group level function with executive support for development of the order processing system, it had to migrate to business unit level, where doubts about its contribution and performance had always existed. But unless it repositioned quickly and successfully it would be unlikely to make much contribution to the group's new thinking and development.

The importance of a shared business vision and especially of alignment and integration of the IS function may, then, seem simple or obvious propositions. However, it is not unusual for quite different issues to be emphasized by writers on global IS management. For example, McFarlan (1992) stresses the disparity of standards in equipment, provision, and service around the world. We suggest that this is no more than a technical, operational issue, the IT equivalent of the controller's need to handle multi-currency accounting. As in other functional areas perhaps, the challenging issues are managerial and organizational. In the case of IT and IS, however, there is undue complexity because information and information systems not only cross national borders, but those between functions, business units, profit centres, and sites. This is the inevitable corollary of the role of information systems in global businesses being that of co-ordination. Information management, as we discuss below, has to cross many levels and borders of the organization.

Information Management in the Global Business

The need for alignment between business and IS organizations has already been noted in the global context by Ives and Jarvenpaa (1991), but this was a top-level mapping, associating different configurations of IS and IT with the different globalization categories of Bartlett and Ghoshal, namely, international, multinational, global, and transnational. Beneath these labels, and in contrast to the neat and tidy configuration implied by the familiar SBU of the 1980s, the organizational arrangements for global business management appear to us to be both varied and complex. Whereas the global business unit (GBU perhaps) in principle has the characteristics of the SBU—product homogeneity, market delineation, identity of competitive forces, strategic control of resources—the four case studies demonstrate how organizational forms may vary as these ideas are played out across national borders. In Skandia Re-insurance there is a relatively simple and single line of business, centre-driven strategy, profit centre discipline, hub-and-spoke configured organization. By contrast, Electrolux dub themselves 'an impossible organization but the only one that works'. The organization is multi-dimensional, with different market, product, functional, and geographic axes, overlaid by a strong profit centre control architecture. It can be sensibly described at the level of the white goods business, but in reality it comprises many interacting entities and its operation relies on myriad boundary-crossing activities and mechanisms. Meanwhile, in Philips and Eurochem organizational history has left complicating legacies which hinder the working out of a neat and tidy configuration. The GBU, then, is apparently a complex phenomenon with which to achieve alignment.

The four case study businesses were all moving towards the transnational model of Bartlett and Ghoshal (1989), which involves simultaneous pursuit of several global capabilities. One consequence suggested by these authors and others writing on the history of international management is that the organizational design of functions becomes critical. Each function may have to be designed differently, dependent upon which global driver is most relevant to its domain. Since IT is a means to different ends—supporting these different functional activities or enabling them to be done differently—the IS function has first to align with a mix of functional strategies. But crucially IT can then be instrumental in welding these organizational axes together. We emphasize once more that the co-ordination role is essentially this, the enabling of cross-boundary as well as cross-border integration and interaction. For example, at Philips and Electrolux information systems were necessary in interfacing geographically based sales units into product based manufacturing plants; at Eurochem the interface was between product based businesses and geographically oriented plants! So how to organize the IS function to both align with and integrate across different functional strategies is both a critical and non-trivial question—and may be the single most important issue in understanding the implications of globalization for IT.

Curiously, achieving the required organization fit may become easier if the question is first made more complex, if the different aspects of IT management are identified for potentially separate organization design decisions. We suggest that each of our case studies, even the more successful, might have benefited from adoption of Earl's (1989) distinction between three strands of information strategy:

- Information Systems (IS) Strategy—the choice of applications, of *what* is to be delivered to the business;
- Information Technology (IT) Strategy—the choice of technical platform, of *how* applications are delivered;
- Information Management (IM) Strategy—the adoption of policies which determine *who* holds what mission, authority, and responsibility.

In particular, our case studies suggest that IM Strategy must be determined at or above the top organizational level of the global business. Skandia had identified that, because the re-insurance (as distinct from the insurance) business had global character with clear global IS opportunities and needs, a very strong mandate had to be given to the IT director, together with appropriate administration arrangements. In Electrolux the IS function was corporate and so had little difficulty in taking an aggregate view of the white goods business. In consequence, at Skandia and Electrolux global IS strategy was being delivered (for example, the SARA and EFS systems respectively); and global IT strategy was in place and robustly protected—not just by the IS function but by top management. By contrast, at Philips DC and Eurochem the IM issues were not yet resolved and this helps to explain why the business/IS strategy connections were not consistently made, and why questions of whether certain applications should be common across the business were so difficult to address.

The rationale for this proposition about IM strategy ownership should be clear. From the case study evidence, we propose that global information systems are needed to cross both borders and boundaries within the transnational organization. To develop the appropriate IS strategy, a business vision must be set and shared at the level of the global business. To deliver the IS strategy, an IT strategy/architecture is required—data standards, application interfaces, computer compatibilities, communications topologies—which is independent of any one function, country, profit centre, or operating unit. Top-level ownership of IM strategy provides the platform, the decision framework, from which all this can be achieved.

Having a global IM strategy does not, of course, mean that all applications must be global and common, or that every piece of equipment must be prescribed by a monolithic global architecture. On the contrary, a successful global IM strategy enables application and technology decisions to be made at various organizational levels without prejudicing global business strategy. The third framework developed during our research (depicted in Table 5.3) concentrates on these questions of IS and IT strategy ownership level. Conceptually it might be employed after the global IT application set has been developed, perhaps assisted by using the model in Table 5.1 to explicate the information requirements. In practice, the framework seems to stimulate further application thinking in its own right.

Table 5.3. *Information system ownership—system scope*

System Objective	Global	Regional	Local
Efficiency			
Responsiveness			
Learning Transfer			

Two examples can briefly illustrate the framework's use. At Electrolux EFS is essential to delivering the global aspirations of the white goods business: both IS and IT specifications must be set at global level. On the other hand, order entry is seen as a local application: its functionality (IS aspects) can be determined by local management, but interface into EFS requires that each local system must be designed within a global technical (IT) specification. Secondly, at Philips DC reorganization of the logistics function raises the question of what combination of IS and IT responsibilities for the relevant applications will best align with daily operational control which is local and with policy co-ordination which is a regional responsibility.

We therefore suggest that our four case studies demonstrate something of the need for, and nature of, alignment between global business and information strategy. The resolution is not as straightforward as speculative practitioner and academic articles suggest (for example, Reck 1989; Karimi and Konsynski 1991; Alavi and Young 1992). The frameworks we have introduced address the need to surface, analyse, and action a set of information management issues as a function of the business strategy and organization. When Egelhoff (1991) calls for greater attention to information requirements in global businesses, we have to agree. However, firms may need the sorts of frameworks of analysis we have proposed to identify and justify requisite information systems. They certainly need to address information management strategy—the IS organization and ownership questions—at the organizational design stage. The contrasting and changing contexts we have encountered emphasize the importance of this type of analysis. However, they also leave unanswered the question of whether the 'transnational' is yet a robust prescription for the challenging economic environment of the 1990s. Nevertheless, information systems appear to be one important means for achieving the potential advantages implied by the transnational model.

Implications and Conclusion

The aim of the study reported here was to explore how IT was being deployed in pursuit of global business strategies in four firms. Each case study business had some characteristics of the 'transnational' and each was at a different stage of evolution. We now venture some implications of our findings for research and practice.

Implications for Research

The global information systems challenge appears to be more complex than commonly suggested, and the solutions far from neat and tidy. The critical questions seem to be ones of information management strategy, in particular about organizing the IS function appropriately. These are not new questions, nor are they technological *per se*: in some ways they are general management questions. It is perhaps interesting to note that Bartlett and Ghoshal (1991) recently argued that management and organization studies have contributed significantly to understanding international business. They may be of similar value in studying international aspects of information systems.

One way of doing such managerial research is through case studies. They allow multi-disciplinary, integrative enquiry. We suggest they also can provide a necessary dynamic lens on global IS. It seems likely from our four case studies that the archetypal IT applications—as, say, predicted by our framework in Table 5.1—are not yet widely in place. Firms are still discovering their global IS requirements and thus IT applications are evolving. Longitudinal case studies—not least further monitoring of events in the four firms reported here—therefore could be valuable if theory development is in part making sense of firms' actions.

Another direction for research is to extend investigations into the transnational organization. The multidimensional thrusts of the transnational form seem to involve high co-ordination and thus require intensive information processing. IT would seem to offer considerable potential in meeting these challenges. Our studies show some, but not widespread, investments in IT as transnational strategies unfold. Thus three related questions arise. What is the contribution of IT in practice *and* what other means of information processing—social and organizational in particular—are commonly deployed? Then it becomes important to know which mechanisms are more effective and yield more sustainable advantages.

Two other research opportunities may be mentioned. The use of interorganizational systems to enable or support global alliances was not evident in this study. It still could be a rich area of enquiry. Finally, in examining how IT can enable new ways of doing and managing global business, individual IT applications may be a more fruitful level of analysis than the business unit.

Implications for Practice

We have argued from case study evidence that there are no easy and straightforward prescriptions for practitioners involved with global information systems. However, we have concluded that a useful starting-point is to formulate a global business strategy first, before any sensible IT decisions can be made. (We also have opined that few, rather than many IT applications will be required). 'Strategy before Systems' is a beloved adage of consultants and is hardly noteworthy advice. However, perhaps only one of our case firms, Skandia, had managed to adopt this rational approach where a CEO had formed and pursued a business vision that was significantly dependent on IT.

Such top down, business-led strategy-making in IT is rare and difficult to achieve. Commonly a much more organizational approach is required (Earl 1993), where management teams work continuously—or are specially brought together—to analyse business problems, agree business imperatives, and identify a strategic theme, including the IS requirements, which is implemented over several years. There were elements of this in Electrolux; it was perhaps beginning in Philips, and maybe it was needed in Eurochem.

This perspective on IS strategy-making leads to a third implication for practice. If a global business strategy is in place and the IS strategy has been aligned with it, the Information Management (IM) strategy must then also match to ensure implementation and prevent global IT policies being eroded by local behaviours. Skandia is an exemplar. However, if the global business strategy is not yet clear and therefore no IS strategy has been formulated—or if determination of the IS strategy is hindered by legacies from the past—our cases suggest that attention is then best directed to IM strategy. By defining the roles, relationships, and processes for managing IS, alignment of global IS and business strategies may then evolve. In particular, it seems crucial to ensure that these IT decisions are made at or above the level where the global business strategy is to be formulated and debated.

The final recommendation for practice is that in resolving these questions our frameworks for analysis may help. They were prompted and refined by the case study evidence and could help managements identify and address the key questions of global information strategy.

Conclusion

Co-ordination of operations and management is commonly seen to be the hallmark of global businesses. Information technology in principle extends the horizons of co-ordination and reduces its cost, and thus information systems are likely to be important investments for any global business. Some were present in each of our case study firms.

The co-ordination need is found to be across business entities, functional boundaries, and national borders. Thus information often becomes a shared and common asset and information systems have to cross many organizational domains. This creates considerable management challenges and organizational complexity for the IT function. It is this complexity—often in a context of slowly evolving global business strategy—that stands out. There may be some special difficulties in applying IT globally—regulatory constraints, national infrastructure development, multiple vendors, conflicting standards—but they seem likely to be trivial compared with the management and organizational issues which arise.

This complexity provides an opportunity for those firms whose competitive strategy is partly based on global IT applications. Sustainable advantage may be gained by those who effectively resolve these questions. The complexities of information management may also provide an arena for those researchers who wish to study the realities of how transnational organizations function.

References

Alavi, M., and Young, G. (1992), 'Information Technology in an International Enterprise: An Organising Framework', in S. Palvia, P. Palvia, and R. M. Zigli (eds.), *The Global Issues of Information Technology Management*, Harrisburg, Pa.: Idea Group Publishing.

Baden-Fuller, C. W. F., and Stopford, J. M. (1991), 'Globalisation Frustrated: The Case of White Goods', *Strategic Management Journal*, vol. 12, pp. 493–507.

Bartlett, C. A., and Ghoshal, S. (1987), 'Managing Across Borders: New Organizational Responses', *Sloan Management Review*, 29/1 (Fall), 43–53.

—— (1989), *Managing Across Borders: The Transnational Solution*, Cambridge, Mass.: Harvard Business School Press.

—— (1989), 'A New Kind of Organization', *PA Issues*, no. 10, PA Consulting, London.

—— (1991), 'Global Strategic Management: Impact on the New Frontiers of Strategy Research', *Strategic Management Journal*, special issue (Summer), 5–16.

Earl, M. J. (1989), *Management Strategies for Information Technology*, London: Prentice Hall Int.

—— (1993), 'Experiences in Strategic Information Systems Planning', *MIS Quarterly*, vol. 17, no. 1, pp. 1–24.

Egelhoff, W. G. (1988), *Organising the Multinational Enterprise: An Information Processing Perspective*, Cambridge, Mass.: Ballinger Publishing.

—— (1991), 'Information Processing Theory and the Multinational Enterprise', *Journal of International Business Studies* (third quarter), 341–68.

Galbraith, J. R. (1973), *Designing Complex Organizations*, Reading, Mass.: Addison-Wesley.

Ghoshal, S. (1987), 'Global Strategy: An Organising Framework', *Strategic Management Journal*, vol. 8, pp. 425–40.

—— and Haspeslagh, P. (1989), 'Note on the Major Appliance Industry in 1988', *INSEAD-CEDEP Case Library*, INSEAD, Fontainebleau, France.

Hagström, P. (1991), *The 'Wired' MNC: The Role of Information Systems for Structural Change in Complex Organizations*, Institute of International Business, Stockholm School of Economics, Stockholm.

Hamel, G., and Prahalad, C. K. (1985), 'Do You Really Have a Global Strategy?', *Harvard Business Review* (July–Aug.), 139–48.

—— (1989), 'Strategic Intent', *Harvard Business Review* (May–June), 63–76.

Huber, G. P. (1989), 'A Theory of the Effects of Advanced Information Technologies on Organizational Design Intelligence and Decision-Making', *Academy of Management Review*, vol, 15, pp. 47–71.

Ives, B., and Jarvenpaa, S. L. (1991), 'Applications of Global Information Technology: Key Issues for Management', *MIS Quarterly* (Mar.), 33–49.

Johnston, R., and Lawrence, P. R. (1988), 'Beyond Vertical Integration—The Rise of the Value-Adding Partnership', *Harvard Business Review* (July–Aug.), 94–101.

Karimi, J., and Konsynski, B. R. (1991), 'Globalization and Information Management Strategies', *Journal of Management Information Systems*, 7/4 (Spring), 7–26.

Konsynski, B. R., and McFarlan, F. W. (1990), 'Information Partnerships—Shared Data, Shared Scale', *Harvard Business Review* (Sept.–Oct.), 114–20.

Lorenz, C. (1989), 'Electrolux Management', *Financial Times* (19, 21, 23, 26, 28, 30 June).

McFarlan, F. W. (1992), 'Multinational CIO Challenges for the 1990s', in S. Palvia, P. Palvia, and R. M. Zigli (eds.), *The Global Issues of Information Technology Management*, Harrisburg, Pa.: Idea Group Publishing.

Porter, M. E. (1986), 'Competition in Global Industries: A Conceptual Framework', in M. E. Porter (ed.), *Competition in Global Industries*, Boston: Harvard Business School Press.

Prahalad, C. K., and Doz, Y. L. (1987), *The Multinational Mission: Balancing Local Demands and Global Vision*, New York: Free Press.

Reck, R. H. (1989), 'The Shock of Going Global', *Datamation* (1 Aug).

Runge, D. A., and Earl, M. J. (1988), 'Using Telecommunications-Based Information Systems for Competitive Advantage', in M. J. Earl (ed.), *Information Management: The Strategic Dimension*, Oxford: Oxford University Press.

Thompson, J. D. (1967), *Organizations in Action*, New York: McGraw Hill.

SECTION II

FOREWORD

When this volume's predecessor was published, terms like 'strategic information systems' and 'IT for competitive advantage' were very much central to the hype of IT in the 1980s. Many managers since have become cynical and sceptical about the strategic potential of information technology, partly because it always seemed to be the same case studies that were presented on how firms could and should discover strategic advantage in IT. *Information Management: The Strategic Dimension* started to correct some of this naïvety, but did not doubt that IT was a strategic matter.

In that volume, Earl and Runge argued from Runge's research that seeking competitive advantage from IT was partly dependent upon organizational processes of innovation. This work and the early results of two projects reported in the current volume were important in influencing Earl's paper in *The Strategic Dimension* on IS strategy formulation, where he proposed a multiple methodology which included some technique and some process. So in some ways, Section II here takes off from where those papers ended. Evidence from research on 'strategic information systems' and 'IS strategic planning' and 'business strategy-making' is collated to try and understand how to mobilize the organization to achieve the full horizons of IT capability.

Ives and Vitale studied strategic information systems in the late 1980s. First they disclose some less well-known examples of IT being used for competitive advantage. More particularly they cast doubt on the use of techniques and frameworks, and argue that organizational mechanisms and processes may have more promise. Interesting is how important it is for users and line managers to take the initiative, and for IS professionals to change their traditional attitudes and practices. To encourage these changes, Ives and Vitale contend that general managers need to create a context for discovery, experimentation, and innovation. This includes elements of organization design, control systems and incentives, and management and organization development programmes.

Lockett presents some similar findings and recommendations, using the paradigm of innovation as his framework. Drawing on a one-company study of successful and failed IS innovations, he identifies technical and organizational factors which matter. He also suggests how innovation processes in IS can be managed, drawing on his subsequent experiences of information management. I am pleased that we have been able properly to put this work into the public domain for the first time.

Earl's chapter on strategic information systems planning draws on more recent research. His five approaches to planning were published in 1993, when it was suggested that one approach—the organizational approach—outperformed the others. The chapter here seeks to elaborate on the organizational approach with practical advice for managers. It is characterized as being the pursuit of themes by teams. A number of ideas, derived from further work on IS planning, are proposed on how the organizational approach can be managed.

In the final chapter of this section, Earl, Sampler, and Short present evidence from four firms on alternative strategies for mobilizing business process reengineering initiatives. They propose a 'process alignment model' as a framework for analysis and then derive a taxonomy of BPR strategies, each differing substantially in process scope, strategic theory, information systems contribution, and change management and control. This case study evidence suggests a rich variety of BPR practice and a future agenda for research.

A common thread of this section is that IS strategy—broadly defined—is less to do with analysis and techniques and more to do with process and learning by doing. This is consistent with the 'capability' or 'resource-based' school of strategic management which sees strategy formulation as an organizational matter rather than just an exercise in analysis based on industrial economics. It provides convincing support for bringing an organizational dimension to information management and it helps demonstrate that research on the process of strategy is as important as research on strategy content and methods.

References

Earl, M. J. (1988), 'Formulation of Information Systems Strategies: Emerging lessons and Frameworks', in M. J Earl (ed.), *Information Management: The Strategic Dimension*, Oxford: Oxford University Press.

—— (1993), 'Experiences in Strategic Information Systems Planning', *MIS Quarterly*, vol. 17, no. 1, pp. 1–24.

—— and Runge, D. A. (1988), 'Gaining Competitive Advantage from Telecommunications', in M. J. Earl (ed.), *Information Management: The Strategic Dimension*, Oxford: Oxford University Press.

6

Strategic Information Systems: Some Organization Design Considerations

BLAKE IVES AND MICHAEL VITALE

Introduction

Strategic information systems (SIS) is one in a string of miracle cures offered up by the information systems community to an increasingly wary audience of senior managers and directors. SIS is one of the alphabetic elixirs of information technology alongside DBMS, DSS, EIS, and AI. Unlike the others, which focused primarily on internal efficiency, the SIS cure is usually targeted specifically at a firm's products, customers, distribution channels, or suppliers. Information technology (IT), we were told in 1984, can be used to erect barriers to entry, lock in customers and suppliers, produce new products and new distribution channels, and in some cases, restructure an industry (McFarlan 1984).

Some SIS success stories (American Airlines, Merrill Lynch, and American Hospital Supply) became well known and frequently told, occasionally in versions that include 'benefits' that have not always been carefully documented. After a period of initial euphoria, practitioners and academicians alike then began to question the validity of the SIS concept. Can information technology, so easily purchased in the open market, ever produce sustainable competitive advantage? And even if it can, can SIS initiatives be deliberately fostered, or do they result instead from gradual increments in quality built from a series of false starts, minor improvements, and subtle repositionings of the technology within a competitive milieu?

As later generations of SIS stories surfaced, and more rigorous analysis was employed to draw firmer conclusions (Runge 1985; Lockett 1987), we have looked at scores of cases in which information technology was purported to offer competitive advantage. At a cursory glance, the answer to the above questions appeared to be 'no'—no sustainable competitive advantage, and limited opportunities for information systems management to unearth new competitive opportunities. However, a closer look at the case suggests that IT *can* play a strategic role and that organizational redesign *can* foster innovative applications.

The first question, that of sustainability, has been addressed by others

(Feeny and Ives 1990; Clemons 1986) and still deserves attention. We focus the bulk of our discussion, however, on the organizational design opportunities.

IT and Sustainable Competitive Advantage

Porter noted that sustainable competitive advantage is 'the fundamental basis of the above-average performance in the long run' (Porter 1985). Any advantage gained from information technology appears almost by definition to be non-sustainable. Most technology is readily available on the open market and, due to rapidly decreasing costs, is often cheaper for the latecomer than for the first mover. The firm that pursues a strategy of being an IT follower may be able to improve considerably on the design of a predecessor's system and, with fourth-generation productivity tools, might do so in short order. In fact, we have found numerous examples of competitors responding quickly and effectively to the initiatives of an IT leader. The case of MBS Textbook Exchange is an illustrative example of this form of competitive follow-the-leader.

MBS sells used textbooks to college bookstores, who resell them, at relatively high profit margins, to students seeking an alternative to new texts. At term-end the bookstores buy books from students, selling those they have no use for to used book firms such as MBS. MBS began to make aggressive use of IT in the early 1980s. They were the first firm in the industry to provide customers with a toll-free number for placing orders, the first to introduce a computerized inventory, the first to provide an itemized receipt for books sent them by college bookstores, and the first to provide college bookstores textbook managers with an integrated information system for managing the textbook acquisition process. (Previously, textbook managers, typically last on the priority queue for new system applications, used limited manual systems.) TEXTAID, developed by MBS and provided free-of-charge to college bookstores, gives the manager a system for tracking faculty book adoptions, ordering books, shelving books, and even for repurchasing them from students. In exchange for a free copy of TEXTAID, the bookstores agree to provide MBS with its most sought-after resource used books. But the IT innovations developed by MBS soon were not unique. Today all of their major competitors offer systems similar to TEXTAID. Moreover, competitors typically developed their software for a personal computer, whereas MBS had to spend time and money converting TEXTAID from the minicomputer on which it was originally offered to a pc when enough capability became available.

Though at first glance the MBS case seems to illustrate the non-sustainability of competitive advantage from information technology, it actually serves to demonstrate several counter-arguments.

IT can win Market Share

During the 1980s MBS Textbook Exchange went from being a small player in used textbooks to become one of the two biggest firms in the industry. Information technology was the driving force behind that gain in market share. Although their technological innovations were copied, it was not before MBS had effectively differentiated themselves in the market-place. While competitors eventually achieved comparable levels of service, customers did not rush away from MBS. MBS has maintained and built upon their market lead.

IT Can Be Good for the Industry

The technological innovations first introduced by MBS, and later copied by most of their competitors, turned the used-book companies into the most potent distributors serving the college bookstore market-place. Publishers of new books focus their attention on the professors—who actually make book adoption decisions, and therefore have considerably less clout with bookstores than the used-book providers. Through IT, the used-book companies were able to offer a 'one-stop' distribution channel to college bookstores—taking a store's total order for a particular book, filling it with highly profitable used books when those are available, and then acting as an intermediary between the bookstore and the publisher to fill the remainder of the order with new books.

IT Can Provide First Mover Advantages

A textbook manager would gain little from having two TEXTAID-like products simultaneously. Unless an alternative system is considerably better or cheaper, the first one installed is probably not going to be replaced. Textbook managers who adopted a system later were as likely to choose a competitive offering as TEXTAID, but those who were early adopters are usually still using TEXTAID. With customers having considerable investment in training, or in historical data now readily available only through the system, first mover advantages can be quite important.

IT Innovations Can Continue

TEXTAID was not MBS's first innovative use of IT, nor will it be their last. The company subsequently announced a system designed to do for trade books what TEXTAID provided for texts. The International Trucks Division of Navistar relied on a similar series of carefully spaced innovations in their own competitive application of information technology (Navistar Corporation 1986).

Navistar's FOCUS information system provides valuable guidance to the fleet owners who are important Navistar customers. An initial version helped the fleet owner choose between gasoline- and diesel-powered trucks. Subsequent versions helped the owner estimate the garage space required for maintenance, build an inventory of spare parts, and determine the appropriate number of maintenance personnel. The original version of FOCUS was innovative, and the subsequent enhancements have made it difficult for competitors to respond effectively.

An innovative application of information technology may produce only a six-month advantage over an aggressive competitor, but that six months may provide an effective window for implementing additional functionality while picking up market share. Many of the innovative applications we looked at have come from firms with a history of innovation.

IT Can Leverage Strengths or Exploit Weaknesses

An investment in information technology that is based on an already established distinction between a firm and its competition will be much more difficult and expensive for competitors to duplicate. Navistar, for example, based the initial version of FOCUS on data they had been collecting from customers for years, initially to help Navistar's own engineers design better trucks. Eventually, however, management saw that the historical data could be leveraged in a new way. The competition, without such historical data, started from a decided disadvantage. Here, of course, the definition of 'information technology' is considerably broader than just that which can be bought in the market-place. Historical data on existing customers can be a powerful source of leverage.

Organizing for Strategic Advantage

We are confident that information technology has provided some firms with significant sustainable competitive advantage, though probably only under one or more of the conditions listed above. The second question—can the information systems (IS) executive foster innovative applications of IT—is similarly challenging, and was our research focus.

Ideation Workshops

Such efforts in the past have generally focused on 'process' rather than on 'organizational' issues. Early on it became clear that internally focused planning methodologies such as IBM's Business Systems Planning (IBM 1981), developed to help align a firm's IT investments with the organization's broader goals and objectives, would not be particularly effective in seeking out the two or three applications of IT that could differentiate a firm in the eyes of its customers. In place of such alignment planning methodologies came ideation workshops (Rackhoff *et al.* 1985). Such sessions, often multi-day gatherings of IT and/or user managers, were based on conceptual frameworks that drew attention to customers, products, distribution channels, and suppliers (Ives and Learmonth 1984; McFarlan 1984; Porter and Millar 1985; Wiseman 1985).

This literature has focused primarily on the frameworks, with little attention given to the underlying processes that the frameworks support. In addition to deciding which frameworks to employ, decisions need to be made concerning the list and role of attendees, the purpose and source of the facilitator, the length of the sessions, the illustrative cases to be used, and perhaps the availability and suitability of automated tools (Ives *et al.* 1986; Sullivan and Smart 1987) that might be used to support the process. There are also important questions about how one transforms a list of creative ideas into a justified project, and that project into a viable system.

Perhaps partially because of inattention to some of these issues, facilitated ideation workshops have apparently not proven particularly useful in unearthing innovative applications of information technology. Very few of the innovative applications of which we are aware have been produced by such sessions. In the future such sessions may prove more successful, but the innovation-seeking processes themselves seem in need of some innovation.

New Levers for Competitive Applications

From our examination of purported strategic applications of IT, we have formulated some initial thoughts concerning the organizational 'levers' that seem to accompany the design and development of successful systems. The list should be viewed as tentative and suggestive rather than proven or prescriptive.

A Vision for Information Systems

A remarkable number of our examples include a senior level manager who had articulated a specific vision of the business problem that IT was being asked to address. George David, chief operating officer at Otis Elevator, expressed a desire that any sales person in the organization should be able to order an elevator within a single day. At USAA, CEO Robert McDermott stated as an objective that all customers calling the insurance company be able to accomplish their task with a single call. At Fidelity Investments, CEO Ned Johnson desired to have Fidelity's mutual funds priced each hour rather than at the end of the day.

These and the other visions we have collected are remarkably similar in several ways. They relate to a business problem or opportunity, not to technology. They are fairly specific and easily measured. They effectively communicate what is desired but not how it is to be achieved. And, finally, the customer is included somewhere within each vision.

For the executive with responsibility for multiple lines of business, such specific visions are more difficult. Here one is more likely to find, and excuse, vision statements such as, 'we will lead our industry in the use of advanced computing technology'. Such statements are considerably less operational than the specific visions discussed above, but some senior executives have attempted to bring such generic visions to life. The CEO of a large electronics company, seeing some years ago that his firm was among the last in the industry to make effective use of embedded micro-processors, rented a large hall and filled it with competitors' products that contained embedded chips. A tiny section of the room highlighted the paltry number of the firm's own offerings. The executive then assembled in that room all the firm's product designers from around the world. As the designers paraded through the hall, they quickly grasped the CEO's vision.

IT executives with responsibility for multiple lines of business face a similar generic vision problem. They may believe that IT can play a significant role in the businesses for which they are responsible, but lack the time and the knowledge required to formulate a specific vision for each business. To address that problem, Malcolm MacKinnon, head of information systems at Prudential Life Insurance Company of America, tried a unique method of presenting IT. He pulled together a travelling road-show that wove several dozen advanced technologies into a vignette involving a potential insurance client. Much of the demonstration was live, with the remainder simulated or videotaped. MacKinnon's audience, senior insurance managers, were able to see new technology in a familiar business setting and have a better opportunity to formulate their own IT visions.

Separating SIS From IS

Several organizations we have studied have found it helpful to move responsibility for strategic systems out of the traditional information systems department. Some years ago the Buick Division of General Motors, for instance, developed EPIC, a multi-function videotext system for use by dealers when making sales presentations. EPIC was the product of a separate group set up within Buick, reporting directly to Lloyd Reuss, then the division's general manager.

At the John Hancock Mutual Life Insurance Company in Boston, their StarView system was developed over a two-year period by a small team reporting to self-styled 'IS renegade' Alex Malcolm, who operated largely outside the influence of the company's large IS organization. StarView was a

PC-based workstation that let corporate benefits managers instantly analyse health claims activity and send electronic mail to their Hancock account representatives. Malcolm claimed:

Speed and creativity are the keys to successful strategic-systems development—and that's why the MIS department is not the place for it . . . Attitudes that would interfere with the effective development of strategic systems are the norm in MIS departments, where conservative management styles are rewarded and the successful execution of a plan is valued more than the idea from which the plan was made. (Malcolm 1987)

A separate group for SIS development and implementation offers several advantages. Many strategic systems are developed iteratively, based on close contact with users and—frequently—with outside customers instead of on formal specifications. A separate group unfettered by procedures and standards intended for more traditional kinds of applications will probably do better at this kind of development than a group that must change its style from project to project. In addition, a smaller group will find both internal and external communication faster, and is likely to be more responsible about maintaining the security that can be vital to achieving that important initial advantage over the competition.

An SIS group outside the main IS area can be staffed, managed, and controlled in ways designed specifically to encourage innovation. Non-technical people from user areas find it easier to join such a group for a time, then rotate back to an area outside IS. Similarly, technically oriented individuals may view an SIS group as an excellent bridge to a position in a user area. Focus on customers, both internal and external, appears extremely important to SIS success, and is easier to maintain in a group oriented solely to strategic systems.

Finally, it may be easier to evaluate the relative importance of both mainline IS applications and 'strategic systems' if they are developed by different groups. This situation allows clearer separation of the costs, and creates built-in advocates for the benefits, of the two types of system.

New Justification Approaches

Perhaps no issue related to SIS has been more hotly debated than that of project justification. Traditional IT applications have commonly focused on internal efficiencies and have therefore been evaluated using traditional ROI criteria. SIS applications tend to focus more towards the revenue side of the business, where quantification is often more challenging. Runge (1985) found that only 20 per cent of the applications he studied had gone through traditional project review and screening processes. Our own findings mirror those of Runge. Strategic systems tend either to be approved at high levels, often with minimal justification (another reason for pulling the SIS group out of the traditional IS department), or to be buried in other parts of the budget. The Buick EPIC project, for example, was approved directly by Reuss, with no attempt at cost–benefit analysis. John Hancock's StarView project was staffed and developed under a budget granted for a completely different system.

The ability to build prototypes using fourth generation software or off-the-shelf packages can permit 'market tests' before substantial monies have been invested, thus allowing a multi-step justification process. For example, Hewlett-Packard pilot tested their 'Sales Productivity System' by giving portable computers to 5 per cent of their field sales personnel (Taylor 1987). The portables were loaded with various productivity tools, most of which were off-the-shelf software products adapted for HP application. By designing the test carefully, HP executives inexpensively demonstrated the productivity improvements possible through the use of portable computers. Based on the test data, HP equipped its entire sales force with portables. In addition to gains in sales force productivity, HP received an interesting and unexpected benefit. Customers aware of, and curious about, the HP pilot tests were anxious to learn of the results—and some subsequently purchased the Sales Productivity System for their own sales force.

Packaged software and prototyping tools require relatively low fixed initial costs, making it possible to 'market test' a system before incurring the large variable costs associated with multiple sites or users. It is often possible to see considerable functionality, and see it in operation, before spending significant monies.

Project Champions

An interesting, though not surprising, finding of recent work is that project champions play a significant role in the design and implementation of innovative uses of IT. Project champions have been found to be instrumental in many other forms of R&D innovation. In his study of thirty-five customer linkage applications, Runge found that in 29 per cent there was an identifiable project champion, usually drawn from the user area, and having minimal background in IT (Runge 1985). In 1987 Lockett, drawing from a study of twenty-nine applications selected from a single firm, found that most of the successful applications were nurtured by a champion. Projects that failed were usually without a champion, and projects whose champion had moved on to another job were at great risk. Lockett's study is reported in more detail in the next chapter. In some cases the champion was positioned high enough in the organization so as to be able to move the necessary organizational mountains. In other cases the champion was supported by a more senior project sponsor.

Project champions may view themselves as fighting for their innovation against all odds, or they may have been charged with bringing a project to fruition, perhaps against their best wishes or better judgement. In the former case, we have often found them placing the 'DP Bureaucracy' high on their list of barriers to progress. One champion complained: 'The IS guy went nuts when I told him I wanted to let our salespeople and distributors have online access to our product database.' Another complained that: 'The people down in IS can think only in terms of COBOL, IMS, and six figure cost estimates.' A third champion, trying to pull together a system with little financial support, complained that the rates charged for central computer time were preposterous, and he was seeking funding for his own computer.

Identifying and assisting project champions may prove to be one of the most useful strategies that information systems managers can employ to foster innovation. Specific techniques by which this might be done are discussed in Beath's chapter in this volume.

New Approaches Towards Requirements Determination

We found that determining the requirements for the SISs that we studied was often done in non-traditional ways. Both Fidelity Investments and GM's Buick Division formed interdisciplinary groups to consider the implications of regulatory, market-place, and other changes. In particular, the groups were charged with exploring new opportunities made available for the competitive use of IT. The initial concepts for the hourly pricing and EPIC systems originated with these high-level study groups. John Hancock used focus groups of internal and external customers to help refine the features of proposed strategic systems, in much the same way that a consumer goods company might use such groups to refine a new product concept.

Prototyping, the rapid building of part of a proposed system that users can test, can, as described above, lower development costs and decrease development time. At another level prototyping can also be seen as an effective tool for communication between users and developers. Such communication is always carried out with an abstraction tool of some sort, for example, a system chart or a set of written specifications. A prototype system is also an abstraction, but has the dual advantages of being more easily understood by the user and more easily changed by the developer. Thus prototyping, appropriately applied, is an effective technique for refining specifications by promoting mutual learning on the part of users and information systems staff.

At some point this mutual learning can bring the 'user' and the 'developer' so close that these terms distinguish prior roles rather than current activities. The devolution of information systems to line organizations has similarly blurred these distinctions. Some of the companies we have studied already have reached the point where the majority of new information systems—and *all* systems of strategic significance—are being developed by user groups.

New Development Methods

Organizations are using both technical and organizational approaches to promoting user development. On the technical front, the phenomenal spread of low-cost end-user computing has put powerful technology on the desks of many middle managers. Easy-to-use tools, such as Apple's HyperCard, various expert system shells, and the armoury of software that comes with today's personal computers, have made user development technically feasible as well as affordable. John Hancock and Hewlett-Packard were among the companies who were early in encouraging user development, based initially on off-the-shelf building blocks. Some of these components are simply commercially available software packages; others are applications based on packages, such as Lotus 1–2–3 worksheets; still others are programmes written from scratch by one user and then shared with others. Given the appropriate incentives and a reasonable tracking mechanism, end-user tools and reusable building blocks can significantly promote user development.

IS managers are generally aware that user-built software tends to lack many of the features promoted by professional training and experience with the technology. User-written code may be without structure and full of bugs; the software may make inefficient use of the hardware and will almost certainly be without documentation and adequate provisions for backup or other security mechanisms. Sometimes only the IS manager's sense of propriety is at risk; the system will then be used in a specific, perhaps one-time, situation and then discarded. In other circumstances a system is intended for ongoing use and should be improved with the features common to professionally-developed software. The key is recognizing which systems will be used often enough to justify further attention, then convincing users to participate in an improvement process that may bring few immediately obvious benefits. Since users typically feel pleased and proud about software they have designed, some sort of incentive-based control is appropriate.

One large investment bank which we have studied was relying almost exclusively on users for initial systems development, then used its large, experienced IS staff to bring these systems to production quality. The staff were organized into so-called 'SWAT Teams', modelled conceptually after the Special Weapons and Tactics teams used by urban police forces to deal with unusual situations. The SWAT Teams operated on the basis of never refusing a user request. They worked investment bankers' hours to meet urgent needs, thereby building close working relationships and confidence among users. In the rapidly changing investment banking environment, user development is virtually a necessity if IT is ever to play a strategic role; the SWAT Teams are one way of combining the benefits of user development with the necessity for 'bullet-proof' software that can be relied upon in the process of analysing and negotiating billion-dollar deals.

Cross-Fertilization (Job Rotation)

New methods for determining requirements and developing software, while undoubtedly important, are relevant only given an adequate supply of concepts for new systems. We observed several mechanisms that appeared to have been repeatedly successful in stimulating such concepts. Among these mechanisms, cross-fertilization through job rotation was perhaps the least practised and yet the most effective.

As is often the case, the terminology used to describe the purchaser and owner of an information system is a good clue to the system developer's thinking. Only after 'user' came to be popularly applied to drug addicts did IS groups begin to abandon the term in favour of 'customer'. In fact the customers of most IS groups for a long time were accountants and other internal processors of highly structured information. When the IS focus moved towards other 'customers', including those external to the firm, many IS groups found themselves poorly positioned to know what was going on outside their own area. For example, during a consulting assignment with a hospital supply company, the authors interviewed physicians, nurses, pharmacists, and other customers. The client's IS manager asked to accompany us on one of our visits to a local hospital. Although he had to return to his office to attend to some pressing details after a half-day of interviews, the manager expressed gratitude for the opportunity; during his seven years with the company he had never been inside a hospital. Upon hearing this story during an SIS workshop, the IS manager of a large distribution company remarked that his staff would never be in such circumstances; he insisted that all IS employees spend at least one day in the field during their careers with the company. When pressed, this IS manager admitted that to date only one-third of his staff had found the time to put in their required eight hours.

Such anecdotes are particularly unfortunate given the very real benefits we have seen accrue from circumstances—some planned, others opportunistic—in which IS staff become familiar with their customers' business.

One large communications company has a service centre that answers billing inquiries from customers. The company's service is offered nationwide and is subject to various tariffs in each location. Traditionally the clerks who staffed the centre relied on manual listings of the tariffs, stored in some ten feet of notebooks that were constantly out of date. During a clerical strike the service centre was staffed temporarily by IS employees. Appalled by the centre's inefficiency, the IS employees returned to their normal jobs with the determination to improve customer service by automating the service centre. On their own, the IS group developed an easy-to-use system, complete with colour graphics and pull-down menus, that accesses the tariff information on-line. The new system can also access databases of service information stored in several locations across the country.

A car rental firm similarly used labour unrest as an opportunity for familiarizing its IS staff with the situation faced daily by counter clerks at its airport offices. Whenever the clerks in a particular city went on strike, the company would require IS staff to assist in staffing the affected location until the labour dispute could be resolved. By working directly in the clerks' situation the developers learned first-hand about deficiencies and potential improvements in the existing systems.

A large defence contractor that also produces consumer goods followed a more deliberate path towards job rotation. Personnel from the corporate R&D labs are routinely moved into divisional IS groups to serve as product champions for new applications that have been prototyped in the lab. One such application is an expert system used by field technicians who are fixing large, complex air-conditioning systems. This system incorporates both expert systems technology and remote predictive diagnostics, another technology on which the R&D lab had worked. The application was moved at an early stage from the laboratory to the service division, and a chief developer went along with it. When the system was fully implemented, this individual could choose whether to return to the lab or stay with the line division. In either case, cross-fertilization occurs.

There are, of course, some concerns associated with the practice of job rotation. It is generally easier for staff, at least at lower levels, to move out of IS than it is to move in, since the latter often requires some specialized technical skills. At higher levels, the salaries typical of IS managers may render them overpaid for those user-area jobs that they are qualified to perform. The reputation of some IS organizations is such that a transfer to IS may be seen, as it was in one large insurance company with which we are familiar, as a demotion.

Companies with established job rotation programmes in areas outside IS will have a head start on addressing these issues. IS managers in organizations having no tradition of job rotation may have to be selectively opportunistic in promoting cross-fertilization until the accumulated weight of positive experience convinces management to establish a formal programme.

Reward Systems

A firm's reward system may be a tool for fostering innovation and creativity, or it may actually serve as a barrier. For example, a large manufacturer of consumer products had established a separate group to focus on strategic applications. The members of the group expressed concern to one of the authors that they were not being properly rewarded for their activities. In those cases where the group had successfully 'sold' the concept for a competitive application to a user area, the users had taken the system development and implementation away from the original group, apparently wishing to manage such important projects themselves. The only projects that stayed with the development group were those for which no project champion had emerged—in other words, the projects most likely to fail. These were the projects on which the group was evaluated.

Reward systems can be designed to foster innovation and responsiveness to users. At the large investment bank mentioned previously, SWAT Team members receive bonuses that may exceed their annual salary. The users they work for have considerable input into determining the size of the bonus cheques. An 'old line' insurance company recently promoted to director of marketing the project champion who had just forced a dramatically new, IT based, insurance product upon his often-resistant colleagues. The executive vice-president who made the promotion decision used it as an opportunity to signal the new role he expected IT-based product innovation to play in the organization.

Emerging Technology Groups

Over the last few years firms as diverse as Air Products and Chemical Inc. and the Massachusetts Mutual Life Insurance Company have established special groups with responsibility for introducing new information technology into the organization. Cash and McLeod (1985), among others, argued persuasively for the creation of such 'emerging technology' (ET) groups. In our research, however, we found no examples of strategically important systems that had been originated by such groups. Runge (1986) reported similarly negative findings, and there is some evidence that ET groups are not effective. For example, the senior IS executive at a large commercial bank disbanded an ET group after it had repeatedly failed to find user sponsors for the technologies that it was investigating. The executive then established a second such group focused on a narrower range of technologies; within months this group was facing similar problems.

In view of the theoretically consistent and intuitively plausible published support for the ET concept, why have such groups not achieved more notable success? In some organizations, groups concentrating on things like emerging technologies are regarded as niceties that can be done without in lean times. An ET group in this sort of company is unlikely to attract the staff or attention necessary for success, even if it survives long enough to develop some ideas. More far-sighted organizations may still have difficulty developing adequate understanding of the business among ET staff who have by definition spent most of their time concentrating on technology. Similarly, it may be difficult for a group perceived as primarily technical to get an audience with the appropriate managers.

Anderson (1987) suggests that ET groups can achieve technical success and attract management attention through a process that considers both general and technological developments and specific business issues. The process begins with scanning the environment for technological opportunities, then performing 'triage' to identify those technologies most appropriate to the particular firm. This process may of course be extremely complicated in a large organization; we recommend that the triage be based on the information-intensive portions of the business, particularly in areas where an information bottleneck is standing in the way of better customer service, improved quality, closer relations with suppliers, and so on. Once a short-list of technologies has been created, Anderson recommends convincing a key line group to examine each technology as it may tie into their particular business. After some initial experience with a technology, its use can be expanded to other areas.

There are clearly many issues related to the staffing, organization, management, and control of ET groups that are beyond the scope of this chapter. We will confine ourselves here to repeating Anderson's (1987) suggestion that such a group work under a 'sunset clause' that requires them to find a line sponsor for a new technology within a short period of time—the retailer Sears, Roebuck & Co uses six months—or abandon the technology. Such sunset clauses tend to enforce a useful market discipline on what could otherwise become an inappropriately technology-focused group.

Conclusion

The observations and recommendations in this paper are based on our interviews and visits with companies in a wide variety of industries, ranging in size from small entrepreneurial start-up ventures to the very largest US manufacturers. In part we have extrapolated from what we did *not* see, for example, strategic information systems that grew out of the formal ideation frameworks described in the published literature. One can always argue that we looked in the wrong ways or in the wrong places, and indeed it is virtually certain that important systems have in fact been conceptualized and developed following the use of such frameworks.

We believe that organizations sometimes reach a stage of such high potential that almost any spark will ignite a flame of innovation. In such circumstances virtually any methodology that encourages participation will serve to bring out ideas for new systems. In this regard, as well as in their ability sensibly to classify known examples, the frameworks are useful tools for the IS practitioner.

Other organizations sometimes seem to be at the opposite end of the spectrum: so wary and unimaginative that no method, no framework stimulates many good suggestions for strategic systems. The environmental and business circumstances of such organizations may nevertheless contain considerable opportunity for the increased use of IT.

A traditional way of realizing such opportunity is to bring new people in from the outside, either as consultants or as permanent employees, to develop and implement systems. This approach is occasionally effective but tends to be expensive and potentially disruptive. We recommend instead that companies pursue a long-term approach combining effective organizational structure with appropriate management systems and technology to build and maintain focus on the competitive use of IT.

Far from being an outdated fad or 'buzzword', SIS remain part of the nature of competition in the 1990s and requires the integration of information technology and business practice. In the course of our study we talked with and visited numerous organizations that have used information technology repeatedly to out-distance the competition, gain market share, and exploit their existing advantages. We believe that other organizations can achieve such results, at least in part by following one of the paradigm examples described here.

References

Anderson, H. (1987), Presentation at Conference of the International Centre for Information Technologies, Washington, DC (June).

Buday, R. S. (1989), 'IW Roundtable: Strategic Systems', *InformationWeek* (11 May), 31.

Cash, J. I., Jnr., and McLeod, P. L. (1985), 'Managing the Introduction of Strategic Information Systems Technology', *Journal of Management Systems*, 1/4 (Spring), 5–23.

Clemons, E. K. (1986), 'Information Systems for Sustainable Competitive Advantage', *Information and Management* (Nov.), 131–6.

Feeny, D. F., and Ives, B. (1990), 'In Search of Sustainability: Reaping Long Term Advantage from Investments in IT', *Journal of Management Information Systems*, 7/1 (Summer), 27–46.

IBM (1981), *Business Systems Planning: Information Systems Planning Guide*, IBM Corporation, GE20–0527–3 (July).

Ives, B., and Learmonth, G. P. (1984), 'The Information System as a Competitive Weapon', *Communications of the ACM*, 27/12, (Dec.), 1,193–201.

Ives, B., Sakamoto, G., and Gongla, P. (1986), *S*P*A*R*K: A Facilitative System for Identifying Competitive Applications of Information Technology*, IBM Los Angeles Scientific Centre, Scientific Report G320–2789, May.

Lockett, M. (1987), *The Factors Behind Successful Innovation*, Research and Discussion Paper RDP 87/9 Oxford Institute of Information Management, Templeton College, Oxford.

Malcolm, A. (1987), 'MIS May Not Be Suited to Develop Strategic Systems', *InformationWeek* (11 May), 80.

McFarlan, F. W. (1984), 'Information Technology Changes the Way You Compete', *Harvard Business Review* (May–June), 98–103.

Navistar Corporation (1986), 'Focus: Programs to Analyze Truck Efficiency Performance and Costs', International Trucks Brochure.

Porter, M. (1985), *Competitive Advantage*, New York: Free Press.

—— and Millar, V. E. (1985), 'How Information Gives You Competitive Advantage', *Harvard Business Review* (July–Aug.), 140–60.

Rackoff, N., Wiseman C., and Ulrich, W. A. (1985), 'Information Systems for Competitive Advantage: Implementation of a Planning Process', *MIS Quarterly*, 9/4 (Dec.), 285–94.

Runge, D. A. (1985), 'Using Telecommunications for Competitive Advantage', unpublished doctoral dissertation, Oxford Institute of Information Management and Magdalen College, Oxford University.

Sullivan, C. H., Jnr., and Smart, J. R. (1987), 'Planning for Information Networks', *Sloan Management Review* (Winter), 39–44.

Taylor, T. C. (1987), 'Hewlett Packard Gives Sales Reps a Competitive Edge', *Sales and Marketing Merchandising* (Feb.), 36.

Wiseman, C. (1985), *Strategy and Computers: Information Systems as Competitive Weapons*, Homewood, Ill.: Dow Jones Irwin.

7

Innovating with Information Technology

MARTIN LOCKETT

IT and Business Change

Information technology is becoming recognized as an important business weapon. As well as traditional data processing applications designed to increase business efficiency through cost-reduction, information technology is being used to improve effectiveness, for example, through improved information for decision-making and faster speed of response to the customer. More radically, IT can be a key component in doing business in new ways and even transforming a business or sector.

It is clear that while developing IT systems is a necessary condition for success in such cases, it is by no means sufficient. The question, therefore, is how new products, services, processes, and ways of working involving IT can be managed to obtain business benefits. Today the availability and cost of information technology are not the major constraints on its effective application in business. The potential applications of information technology which can be cost-justified and are technically feasible far exceed the capability of organizations to exploit these opportunities.

But while this potential is large, there are many cases of projects which fail to meet their objectives and produce limited business benefits, as well as exceeding budgets by large margins. Cases in which millions or tens of millions of pounds have been spent in IT systems with little or no result exist in many organizations. A recent analysis of top US companies was conducted by Nolan, Norton & Co covering recent major projects which failed to achieve their objectives on time and to budget. In only 9 per cent of projects was technology the major blockage, while in 78 per cent it was people issues. However, typically the focus of planning had been on technology rather than people and organizational issues.

So the capability of information technology is less of a limiting factor than the recognition and implementation of business opportunities for change involving information technology. Given this context, determining the factors behind success (and failure) in innovations making use of information technology is an important precondition of effective use of IT for business advantage and for organizational learning about how to achieve business benefits. This chapter is based on research to identify the factors behind successful innovation in projects involving information systems in a large multinational company. This work was done at the Oxford Institute of Information Management. Subsequent consulting work with Nolan, Norton & Co in other major companies and financial institutions developing and implementing business-driven IT strategies has provided insights on how to make these ideas practical.

The Innovation Framework

Industrial Innovation

The research started from the hypothesis that the factors behind success and failure in innovation involving information technology would be similar to those previously identified for product and process innovation in industry. These studies include Science Policy Research Unit (1972), Rothwell (1977), Roussel (1983), Shanklin and Ryans (1984), Kanter (1985), Cooper and Kleinschmidt (1986), and Fischer *et al.* (1986). Innovation is defined as the commercial application of a new technology—as opposed to invention of new ideas (Freeman 1974). These studies have shown a number of factors to be particularly important in successful industrial innovation:

- good understanding of customer and end-user needs by those involved in development;
- the use of external information, skills, and contacts by systems developers and customers;
- senior management sponsorship, commitment, and involvement (by both developers and customers);
- the existence, and relatively senior position, of an internal champion;
- effective, but not necessarily fast, technical development of the system.

Based on this background of industrial innovation studies, this research took IT projects as the unit of analysis. Projects were viewed as similar to other technical innovations, which to be successful must combine technological development with a market opportunity, whether internal (process) in the sense of changing business processes or external (product) by providing new marketable products or services. It was hypothesized that the organizational process of innovation would explain much of the variation in success between projects.

Research Design

In order to limit some of the variations in technology and to concentrate on applications designed to increase effectiveness and gain competitive advantage, three areas were chosen:

- Expert Systems;
- Production and Research Management Systems;
- Sales and Marketing Systems.

Within these areas a total of twenty-seven projects were selected to give: (i) varying degrees of success and failure; (ii) wherever possible matched pairs of projects which used similar technology but had different degrees of success; (iii) a range of operating divisions and locations within the company. Two further projects in decision support and manpower planning were used to pilot the research instruments, making a total of twenty-nine projects. For each project the aim was to interview: (i) *system developers*, usually from the information systems function; (ii) internal *customers*, a manager responsible for the commissioning and/or use of the system; (iii) *users* of the system, where applicable. This approach was used to obtain the often differing perspectives of information systems professionals and those in business functions using the systems. It also enabled cross-checking of the data.

Each interview lasted from thirty to ninety minutes. No one refused to be interviewed. However, it was impossible to conduct some interviews as staff had left the company, were unobtainable, or worked in locations which it was not possible to visit. Relevant documents were also obtained for many of the projects.

For each project the following areas were examined:

- PROBLEM RECOGNITION: the process of recognition and definition of a problem;
- PROBLEM CHARACTERISTICS: the characteristics of the problem tackled;
- PEOPLE CHARACTERISTICS: the developers, customer, and end-users of the project;
- INNOVATION PROCESS: the management of the innovation process;
- SUCCESS OR FAILURE: the success of a project was assessed in terms of:
    achievement of goals of those involved
    extent of use by ultimate end-users
    impact on business *efficiency*
    impact on business *effectiveness*
    strategic impact of system

In the case of projects which were not yet working commercial systems, an assessment of the prospects for the system was obtained from those interviewed. For projects which were not implemented or stopped after implementation, the reasons for stopping the project were explored.

Results

Is Technology the Constraint?

The results confirmed the starting-point of the study, that the availability and cost of information technology are not the major constraints on business. In 70 per cent of the projects cost was not a significant constraint. Only in a 15 per cent minority of the projects was the availability of technology a significant problem delaying its application in the past. As expected, technical problems during systems development were higher with projects for which technology availability was an obstacle.

But while the availability and cost of information technology were not major constraints, the projects certainly were innovative and used technology new to the users, the systems developers, or both groups. As rated by those involved in the projects, the technology used was either significantly or completely new to users, while on average having significant new elements for system developers. The majority of these new elements were in the software and user interface area, as well as in applying new information technology to the particular application area. Thus the projects were cases of innovation at least at the business unit level—and in some cases are seen more widely as innovative examples of the business application of information technology.

New technology from the viewpoint of users and systems developers was associated with technical problems in the project and greater time taken and higher cost over-runs. However, overall the newness of the technology in itself had a small positive association with project success. Thus there is little evidence that the newness of technology itself has a major impact on overall success and failure of information technology innovation. Rather, it appears that the benefits from projects which pay off are substantial relative to the technology costs and come from the business change which technology makes possible. Achieving these benefits requires *both* targeting the business areas where cost and revenue gains would be highest *and* successfully managing business change.

Champions and Sponsors

If technology does not explain the success and failure of IT innovations, what does? The clearest factor to emerge from the research was the existence in successful projects of a project *champion* in the relevant function within the business. In almost every failed project the lack of a champion was evident, or there was moving of a project champion in cases where the new incumbent did not take over the champion role. But why are champions so important?

A champion in the business rather than the information systems function is able to co-ordinate the project and guide it towards relevant business goals. This increases the chances of success for two reasons: (i) by influencing the design of the system to make it meet user and business needs more closely; and (ii) by providing impetus for the implementation of the project. Such a champion, therefore, manages the project in a way more likely to achieve business objectives than one which either is championed from within the information systems function or has no clear leadership.

In the event of problems during the development of the project, a champion is able to gather support for the project if he or she believes it to be viable. However, some champions are not at a sufficient level in the organization to be able to allocate adequate resources on their own initiative. A second role of *sponsor* is important here—a senior manager who takes an interest in the project, makes some commitment to it, and reviews its progress. Two patterns emerged which were associated with successful project development: first, a relatively senior champion, and secondly, a more junior or less enthusiastic champion backed by a more senior sponsor. So, while sponsors were important, they are not a substitute for a champion actively involved in a project.

Thus the existence of a champion, combined with a sponsor where appropriate, was the single most important factor for success. This confirms the findings in technical innovation research—as well as the experience of many companies in implementing both IT strategies and other programmes such as quality initiatives. However good the technology or strategy methodology, it is actually business commitment to change which has the greatest influence on business success or failure.

Problems of Formalization

In recent years there has been great stress placed on the need for formal controls over information systems projects—starting with formal approval followed by structured development methods and formal project structures. This degree of formalization has been intended to avoid the problems of cost and time over-run. However, this research showed such formalization to be positively associated with both costs and elapsed time exceeding budgets and expectations. This was particularly true of projects using formal project management structures. Further, there was little association between these formal structures and success or failure. Thus, at first sight formal management processes appeared to have done little if any good.

A detailed examination revealed a more complex pattern in which formalization in the later stages of a project was associated with success while early formalization had the opposite effect (cf. Kanter 1985, on technical innovation). Qualitatively, this was confirmed by cases of success which took place outside the 'proper' channels for approval and systems development. In these a champion often worked informally with the information systems function to produce a prototype or initial working system. In a number of cases corporate rather than divisional resources were used—again to some degree outside normal procedures. On the other hand, in two of the projects with earliest formal approval and highest visibility there were serious problems and the systems were implemented late and were rejected by users after development.

The best explanation lies in the costs of exit from projects which are not meeting business objectives. Early formalization tends to freeze a project in a particular form and to make it more difficult for those involved to stop as this involves 'public' admission of failure. Also real checkpoints tend to be months apart on large projects. In contrast, unapproved projects using discretionary resources have to gain continual approval from those involved. Thus commitment is built on both sides over time and deciding not to pursue the idea does not count as a 'failure' as it is less visible. In such projects it is also easier to change approach: for example, the focus of the project or the information technology tools used. Such changing of approach was associated with project success.

Underlying these problems of formalization is the nature of systems aimed at effectiveness through faster and better decision-making or aimed at gaining competitive advantage. In these it is difficult to define precisely in advance what will meet business needs, especially where the technology or the application—or both—are new to those in the business. Early formalization tends to make it more difficult to change approach, for example, as a result of better understanding of business needs or market opportunities. It also makes stopping a problematic project more difficult. However, at later stages formalization becomes important as in project implementation at large—lack of formal approval and integration into the planning and operations of the business function concerned tends substantially to reduce the impact of the project on business results.

Thus the problems and management requirements for successful IT projects differ during their development. Two broad phases can be distinguished: a *development* phase lasting from the initial idea generation to the development of an initial working system, and an *implementation* phase in which a system is implemented fully within the business. Between these there is often a period of refocusing to clarify the business goals which can be achieved and the technology and organizational change which will realize these benefits. These two phases of development and implementation will now be discussed in more detail and are graphically represented in Figure 7.1.

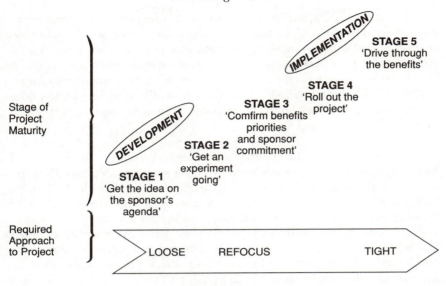

Fig. 7.1. *Stages in innovative projects*

The Development Phase

In the development phase of a project, four main areas are of interest and were found to be associated with project success: (i) the *origin of ideas* for projects; (ii) the *nature of the problem* tackled; (iii) the nature of the *development team*; and (iv) the use of *prototyping methods*.

Origins of Ideas   Taking the origins of the projects, there was a small positive relationship between success and between ideas coming from business rather than the information systems function. What was clearer was a positive association between championing of the project and ideas coming from the business. Also there was a predominance of projects in which there was some form of joint initiative in formulating ideas. In this, organizational structures facilitating discussion and initial investigation of such ideas from both business and information systems viewpoints seemed to be beneficial. One such structure was through an information systems professional responsible for liaison with a business function, in effect in an 'account manager' role.

Problem Characteristics   In the area of problem characteristics it was found, not surprisingly, that if the problem involved quantification, it was more likely to succeed. The opposite was true of problems involving substantial judgement. Generally, the better the understanding of the problem structure involved in the project, the higher the level of success. The same was true of expert systems—refuting the view that expert systems are able to tackle unstructured problems. Rather, expert systems were most applicable for structured problems involving relatively routine judgement, often combined with some quantification. More generally, understanding of the business processes involved in the area tackled was an important factor in success.

The Business–IS Gap The ability to understand business problems and hence develop information-technology based solutions depended on the nature of the development team. In particular, success depended on bridging the gap between (i) business managers who often knew little about information systems and had not been involved in previous projects, and (ii) information systems professionals often unaware of detailed business needs. In successful projects this gap was bridged within the development team—there had to be no significant gap in understanding and communication between those involved. The most critical area was converting business needs into functional specifications of information systems requirements, for example, a production manager specifying the information needs to analyse plant performance.

Here past experience of a project champion was useful in some of the projects—though they were regarded as tough customers to please by the information systems function. Where this was not the case someone had to fulfil this role—typically either someone from the business area being moved into information systems in mid-career, or an information systems professional with a long working relationship in the business area. So, in the early stages of a project the quality of the staff in the development team is truly cross-functional rather than being essentially from the information systems area.

Prototyping and its Problems The use of prototyping methods was associated with project success. Prototyping in this context is the development of small systems of restricted scope and/or functionality which users can test for themselves. The system design develops through an iterative process of evaluation followed by a further prototype system. Particular gains come from enabling business managers and staff unfamiliar with information systems to see what can be done and thus to refine the specification of the functions of a desired system. Prototyping also enabled user interfaces to be tested before they were finalized—thus meeting user needs better.

Using prototypes enabled changes of approach to be made at an earlier stage in a project. This meant the cost of change was lower as the technical design of the system was still undecided. It also enabled business users to see if information technology could produce benefits without the cost of trying to specify and produce a full system—thus making it easier to stop a project which turned out not to be as promising as expected. However, analysis of the research results indicated that while a certain amount of prototyping gave positive results, a high level of prototyping gave no more benefits—and probably gave less. Why was this?

There were two main problems which arose from prototyping, both connected with the transition between the development and implementation stages of a project. The first was the nature of prototyping tools which are intended to enable rapid development (within days) of prototype systems. While these tools (for example, Lotus 123 and '4th generation languages') were highly productive at the early stages of projects, they were often inappropriate for future use of computer hardware leading to higher costs and response time problems. Also they were usually not the tools for future maintenance of the system.

The second problem of prototyping was that associated with the 'freezing' of a specification at an appropriate stage. Having had the freedom to make changes quickly and easily in the early stages, there was a problem in moving towards a working system which would be more stable. This was necessary not only for the technical reasons outlined above but also for other reasons such as needing a final design to train users. In very few cases was it appropriate to continue prototyping methods into the implementation of the project. Thus, while prototyping was a useful tool in the early stages of a project, there was a need to move away to the implementation phase of a project.

The Implementation Phase

The analysis above suggests that for successful development of an information technology project from an initial idea to a working system, a prototyping approach with a small, high quality cross-functional team probably works best. In addition, there is a need to be prepared to stop or change the approach towards projects in which initial ideas do not work out. However, in the study there were a number of cases in which projects reached an initial working system but did not achieve the commercial use or business benefits foreseen by their initiators. Five factors appeared important in implementation.

Project Ownership A major reason for this was the lack of management support and commitment among those who would be using the system. Again, the roles of champions and sponsors are vital. For while a champion from the information systems area or one in a boundary spanning role could push an idea forward into an initial working system, wider implementation relied on commitment from the business function itself. Thus, either a reasonably senior champion or a lower level champion combined

with a high-level sponsor had a much better chance of success. In particular it was necessary for the implementation of the system to become part
of the planning and operations of the business function. In short, ownership
of the project had to be in the business rather than the information systems functions.

The model shown in Figure 7.1 shows what can happen to gain the
commitment of senior management when they do not give full commitment from the start. Having got the idea on the sponsor's agenda, the
champion pushes through an experiment or pilot whose benefits can be
used to persuade senior management to commit themselves to the implementation of the project as a whole.

Managing the Transition   The management and technical requirements in
the implementation phase differ from those in the development one. On
the management side the marketing of the project becomes critical in
ensuring it will actually be used both internally and sometimes externally,
especially for projects in the sales and marketing area. Technically, the
requirements of the system change to include reliability and its delivery to
users in a suitable form.

Delivering the System   The delivery issue was a major one in some projects
as prototypes had been developed on hardware to which most potential
users did not have access. For example, customer access to Viewdata[1] was
lower than predicted at the start of one project—meaning either a limited
customer base or the need for a new method of delivery, for example, on
a personal computer. More generally, part of the marketing of a project
could include persuading users that it is worth buying additional hardware. An established information technology infrastructure obviously helps
provide a base for delivery as well as making it clearer when new hardware
and system software will be needed. Software licensing conditions could
pose problems, especially if use of a personal computer meant buying full
licenses for software which would not be used regularly.

As a result, it was easier for projects to succeed when they built on
existing systems rather than requiring major new investment, especially
when use of the system was not continuous—as was the case in most
projects directed at improving management effectiveness and gaining
competitive advantage. Sometimes this was impeded by the difficulty of
linking new systems to existing ones, especially in the expert systems area.

User Interface   This also meant that the user interface was an important
aspect of business. With irregular use, often by managers with other competing priorities, it was necessary to ensure that the system fitted in with their
methods of working. In cases where other systems were used, a common

---

[1] Viewdata is Videotex technology.

user interface was popular. For example, one project used an interface similar to Lotus 123 with which many users were familiar although it was written in a standard computer language. In another, local sales offices had problems with a system for one product line which did not use the same interface as the system for others.

Maintenance Maintenance of systems was another issue. In some expert systems projects prototypes were abandoned after an assessment of the maintenance needs for a full system. This problem was particularly acute as maintenance of an expert system and other prototyping tools often provided poor maintenance capabilities. Responsibility for maintenance was a potential organizational difficulty while the need to re-key data from other manual or computer systems was another obstacle. Other organizational issues posed problems in some projects, for example, whether or not to give customers a copy of a marketing system or to keep it under the control of sales representatives and other internal staff. Perhaps the most serious was the loss of a champion through moving jobs before a project had been implemented and gained acceptance.

Many but by no means all of these problems can be foreseen in the development phase—for example, user interface, delivery, maintenance, and some organizational problems. In other cases it is the integration of the innovative information technology project into the business function which is critical. While linked to the development phase, the management needs in this implementation phase differ significantly. However, projects which were implemented fully often gave much higher benefits than originally envisaged, though taking longer to implement and sometimes costing more than expected.

Conclusions

We can identify four sets of conclusions from the above results.

1. IT is Technical Innovation

The results from the research broadly confirm that the factors identified for technical innovation also apply to information systems projects. In particular, the existence of a strong project champion in a business area (rather than in information systems) is critical to success. Good understanding of end-user needs by system developers is another important factor, as are mechanisms for communication with the business users of the system. Senior management sponsorship and commitment was another success factor, but dependent also on the existence of a champion. Use of external sources of information and contacts was not a major factor in success, though less successful projects were associated with low use. Effective development was essential, and in successful projects this often involved an initial phase with a relatively small project team working over a longer period of time to define what would actually produce business benefits.

2. An R&D approach?

The structures and processes for evaluating information systems in many organizations assume that both costs and benefits should be certain—and that the benefits are obtained more or less automatically from the implementation of an IT system. As a result, cost-saving projects are likely to be ranked higher than those where benefits are less certain and therefore are seen as riskier. This research showed that projects designed to increase effectiveness and gain competitive advantage involved significant risk but also have the potential for major business benefit. Highly formalized controls will deter innovation at its early stages, though they are necessary for successful implementation of large projects. Also budget pressure on the information systems function often means reducing the 'slack' resource available for discretionary use in investigating potential opportunities.

This is understood in other areas of technical innovation, and is recognized in the management of research and development (R&D). The same principle can be applied to information technology innovation. This would involve the generation of a relatively large number of ideas, of which some will be selected for further investigation. Then using prototyping or similar methods, these ideas can be tested and those with greatest potential selected for implementation. This process of continual selection and rejection of potential projects contrasts strongly with the tendency in many companies towards early formal approval of information technology projects whose costs and benefits are assumed to be certain.

In the management of information technology innovation, such an 'R&D approach' means that two processes are important: (i) the identification of opportunities for significant potential business gains; and (ii) the rejection as early as feasible of those which will not realize these gains. It is also important to recognize that if more risky projects are to be tackled, those considered must have higher potential gains than less risky ones—there is no point in aiming for high-risk, low-benefit projects.

3. A Climate of Innovation

Even if such changes were made to formal procedures, there are still substantial organizational obstacles to more successful information technology innovation. Probably most important is that of the climate of attitudes towards innovation and risk-taking. In many organizations risky projects are avoided as a result of the costs to those involved of failure— in terms of prestige and career advancement. Stopping a project is often seen as an admission of failure, rather than a good management decision after investigation. Thus, for effective innovation there must be a tolerance of failure for risky projects and a climate which favours risk-taking when the benefits can be high. So while involvement in successful projects should be rewarded, failure up to a certain level should be accepted.

4. Developing Organization Capability

Even if the changes in organizational processes recommended above are implemented, there is still a need to develop an organization's capability for information technology innovation. This involves two aspects: the first within the information systems function, and the second within the business as a whole.

Within the information systems function there is obviously a need to ensure that some discretionary resources are available for the early development of project ideas. This could be done by reserving a proportion of the information systems function budget for such development work. However, those involved in such areas will need a high level of business awareness, probably gained through coming from, or working closely with, a business function. This also implies that many existing information systems professionals will need education in areas such as marketing. In addition they will need high-productivity prototyping tools to use in the early phases of a project. Ideally, these tools should be able to be used as a basis for commercial working systems in the future—with perhaps a proportion of the system needing rewriting if performance is an issue. It may also pay to use hardware inefficiently in order to reduce the lead times in implementing projects and increase the utilization of scarce staff resources.

More generally within the business, there is a need to spread awareness of the potential uses of information technology for effectiveness and competitive advantage. Education is one method, but its payoff is likely to be greatest if it can be concentrated on senior management (potential sponsors) and also on potential champions. In the longer term substantial benefits are likely if management development involves some time in the information systems function. Also staff could be recruited into the information systems function from business areas and then trained in the use of prototyping and other tools. In all these mechanisms, the payoff will not be quick and will require commitment from both business and information systems functions.

Ten Steps to Successful IT Innovation

What are the practical steps which could be taken to increase both the level and chance of success of IT innovation with substantial business benefits?

To conclude, ten steps are proposed to promote successful innovation involving information technology:

1. See IT projects as innovations whose benefits come from the business change which IT makes possible, not primarily as the technical implementation of systems.

2. Allocate part of your IT budget to R&D. Focus this resource on high-quality IT staff working with managers on business needs.

3. Ensure different management processes and controls at different stages of projects—looser for development and tighter for implementation phases.

4. Insist on a cross-functional project team involving both IT and all relevant areas of the business. Ensure the right mix of skills to bridge the IT–business gap.

5. Only use new technology if it is absolutely necessary to achieve the business benefits: there is huge potential in what you already have and what is widely available in the market-place. Go for 'clever use of technology, not clever technology'.

6. Be prepared to experiment with alternative technology approaches and to change after an initial review; even try two alternatives competing against each other.

7. Explicitly include personal commitment and organizational factors in assessing projects—as well as ensuring clear accountability for achieving the benefits. Remember that a business champion is the number-one factor in success and the easiest way to stop a wayward project.

8. Be prepared to stop projects early—and refocus others rather than ploughing ahead. The bigger the project, the more necessary and the more difficult this is!

9. Split IT development into 'bite-sized chunks' with a deliverable scheduled after a maximum of a few months—and do not move forward unless the business recognizes that value has been delivered.

10. To build a long-term capability to innovate successfully, reduce the barriers between business and IT by: educating senior management on how to manage IT; developing business awareness of information systems staff; and increasing the interchange between information systems and other functions in the business, particularly for high-fliers.

References

Cooper, R. G., and Kleinschmidt, E. J. (1986), 'An Investigation into the New Product Process: Steps, Deficiencies and Impact', *Journal of Product Innovation Management*, vol. 3, pp. 71–85.

Fischer, W. A., Hamilton, W., McLaughlin, C. P., and Zmud, R. W. (1986), 'The Elusive Product Champion', *Research Management* (May–June), 13–16.

Freeman, C. (1974), *The Economics of Industrial Innovation*, Harmondsworth: Penguin.

Kanter, R. M. (1985), *The Change Masters: Corporate Entrepreneurs at Work*, London: Unwin.

Rothwell, R. (1977), 'The Characteristics of successful innovators and technically progressive firms', *R&D Management*, 1/3 (June), 191–206.

Roussel, P. A. (1983), 'Cutting Down the Guesswork in R&D', *Harvard Business Review* (Sept.–Oct.), 154–60.

Science Policy Research Unit (1972), *Success and Failure in Industrial Innovation*, London: Centre for Study of Industrial Innovation.

Shanklin, W. L., and Ryans, J. K. (1984), 'Organising for High-Tech Marketing', *Harvard Business Review* (Nov.–Dec.), 164–71.

8

An Organizational Approach to IS Strategy-Making

MICHAEL J. EARL

Introduction

For many IS executives strategic information systems planning (SISP) continues to be a critical issue (Niederman *et al.* 1991). It is also reportedly the top IS concern of chief executives (Moynihan 1990). At the same time it is almost axiomatic that information systems management be based on SISP (Synott and Gruber 1982). Furthermore, as investment in information technology has been promoted to both support business strategy or create strategic options (Earl 1988; Henderson and Venkatraman 1989), an 'industry' of SISP has grown as IT manufacturers and management consultants have developed methodologies and techniques. Thus SISP appears to be a rich and important activity for researchers.

The literature recommends that SISP target the following areas:

- aligning investment in IS with business goals;
- exploiting IT for competitive advantage;
- directing efficient and effective management of IS resources;
- developing technology policies and architectures.

It has been suggested (Earl 1989) that the first two areas are concerned with *information systems* strategy, the third with *information management* strategy, and the fourth with *information technology* strategy. According to survey-based research to date, it is usually the first two areas that dominate chief information officers's agendas. Indeed, SISP has been defined in this light (Lederer and Sethi 1988) as 'the process of deciding the objectives for organizational computing and identifying potential computer applications which the organization should implement'. This definition was used in the investigation reported here into SISP activity and experience in twenty-seven UK companies.

Five different approaches to strategic information systems planning were found, and one—the *organizational approach*—appears to outperform the others. Reported by Earl in 1993, the study is summarized in the first part of this chapter. Then in response to queries since the results were first published, the organizational approach is described and explained in more detail, based on both the earlier work and more-recent observations.

The original research was done in 1988–9. First, case studies captured the history of six companies previously studied by the author. These retrospective case histories were based on accounts of the IS director and/or IS strategic planner and on internal documentation of these companies. The cases suggested or confirmed questions to ask in the second stage. Undoubtedly, these cases influenced the perspective of the researcher.

In the second stage, twenty-one different UK companies were investigated through field studies. All were large companies that were among the leaders in the banking, insurance, transport, retailing, electronics, IT, automobile, aerospace, oil, chemical, services, and food-and-drink industries. Annual company revenues averaged £4.5 billion. They were all headquartered in the UK or had significant national or regional IS functions within multinational companies headquartered elsewhere. Their experience with formal SISP activities ranged from one to twenty years. The scope of SISP could be either at the business unit level, the corporate level, or both.

Within each firm the author carried out in-depth interviews, typically lasting two to four hours, with three 'stakeholders'. A total of sixty-three executives were interviewed. The IS director or IS strategic planner was interviewed first, followed by the chief executive officer or a general manager, and finally a senior line or user manager. Management prescriptions often state that SISP requires a combination or coalition of line managers contributing application ideas or making system requests, general managers setting out direction and priorities, and IS professionals suggesting what can be achieved technically. Additionally, interviewing these three stakeholders provides some triangulation, both as a check on the views of the IS function and as a useful, but not perfect, cross-section of corporate memory.[1]

The further description and analysis of the organizational approach is based on re-examination of the original data and on case study observations and *ad hoc* discussions with CIOs since 1990.

The Concept of Approach

Three findings led to the conceptualization of *approach*. First, data was collected on what SISP methods had been adopted in the twenty-one companies. It was hoped to be able to correlate methods with success, context, and problems. Unfortunately, nine of the companies had tried three or more methods. On average, 2.3 methods had been employed and

---

[1] For more detailed description of the methodology see Earl (1993).

it seemed that the longer the company had been involved with SISP, the more methods they had tried. In other words, it was very difficult to trace or disentangle cause and effect where more than one method had been used.

Secondly, however, it became clear that methods were only part of the armoury used in SISP. Interviewees described different emphases in how the IS function worked with the firm, changes in behaviour as a new CIO was appointed, reactions to different successes and traumas, intended and unintended effects, and so on. It seemed that *approach* captured this multi-dimensional investment in SISP more graphically and accurately than the term 'method'.

Finally, as well as collecting scores or ratings in SISP experience to date—the average self-reporting score (1 = low and 5 = high) being 3.73 and the modal score 4.0—ways in which SISP had been unsuccessful were also recorded. Sixty-five different concerns were discovered and an inductive and subjective cluster analysis classified them into three almost equal (in frequency) categories. The five most frequent concerns cited are:

Rank order	Unsuccessful features
1.	Resource constraints
2.	Not fully implemented
3.	Lack of top management acceptance
4.	Length of time involved
5.	Poor user–IS relationships

The frequency of concern by type and stakeholder interviewed are shown in Table 8.1. It is apparent that concerns extend beyond method or technique and that one view of effective strategic information systems planning is investment in method, process, and implementation. This conceptualization can be thought of as an approach (Figure 8.1).

Method concerns centred on the SISP technique, procedure, or methodology employed. Firms commonly had used proprietary methods, such as Method 1, BSP, or Information Engineering, or applied generally available techniques such as critical success factors or value chain analysis. Others had invented their own methods, often customizing well-known techniques. Among the stated concerns were lack of strategic thinking, excessive internal focus, too much or too little attention to architecture, excessive time and resource requirements, and ineffective resource allocation mechanisms. General managers especially emphasized these concerns, perhaps because they have high expectations but find IS strategy-making difficult.

Implementation was a common concern. Even where SISP was judged to have been successful, the resultant strategies or plans were not always actioned or fully implemented. Even though clear directions might be set and commitments made to developing new applications, projects often

Table 8.1. *SISP concerns by stakeholder (%)*

Total citations			IS directors ($n = 21$)		General managers ($n = 21$)		User managers ($n = 21$)	
			Citations		Citations		Citations	
45	36	Method	14	36	18	44	13	28
39	31	Process	9	23	11	27	19	41
42	33	Implementation	16	41	12	29	14	31
126	100	TOTAL	39	100	41	100	46	100

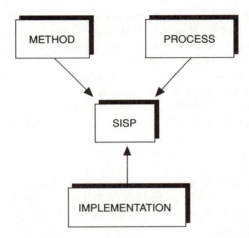

Fig. 8.1. *Necessary conditions for successful SISP*

were not initiated and systems development did not proceed. This discovery supports the findings of earlier work (Lederer and Sethi 1988). Evidence from the interviews suggests that typically resources were not made available, management was hesitant, technological constraints arose, or organizational resistance emerged. Where plans were implemented, other concerns arose, including technical quality, the time and cost involved, or the lack of benefits realized. Implementation concerns were raised most by IS directors, perhaps because they are charged with delivery or because they hoped SISP would provide hitherto elusive strategic direction of their function. Of course, it can be claimed that a strategy that is not implemented is no strategy at all—a tendency not unknown in business strategy-making (Mintzberg 1987). Indeed, implementation has been proposed as a measure of success in SISP (Lederer and Sethi 1988).

Process concerns included lack of line management participation, poor IS–user relationships, inadequate user awareness and education, and low management ownership of the philosophy and practice of SISP. Line managers were particularly vocal about the management and enactment of SISP methods and procedures and whether they fit the organizational context.

Analysis of the reported concerns, therefore, suggests that method, process, and implementation are all necessary conditions for successful SISP. Indeed, when respondents volunteered success factors for SISP based on their organizations' experience, they conveyed this multiple perspective (see Table 8.2). The highest-ranked factors of 'top management involvement' and 'top management support' can be seen as process factors, while 'business strategy available' and 'study the business before technology' have more to do with method. 'Good IS management' partly relates to implementation. Past research has identified similar concerns (Lederer and Mendelow 1987), and the more prescriptive literature has suggested some of these success factors (Synott and Gruber 1982). However, the experience of organizations in this study indicates that no single factor is likely to lead to universal success in SISP. Instead, successful SISP is more probable when organizations realize that method, process, and implementation are all necessary issue sets to be managed.

Prompted both by the list of concerns and narrative histories of planning-related events, the focus of the study therefore shifted. The object of analysis became the SISP *approach*. This we viewed as the interaction of method, process, and implementation, as well as the variety of activities and behaviour upon which the respondents had reflected. The accounts of interviewees, the 'untutored' responses to the semi-structured questions, the documents supplied, and the 'asides' followed up by the interviewer all produced descriptive data on each company's approach. Once the salient features of SISP were compared across the twenty-one companies, five distinct approaches were identified. These were then used retrospectively to classify the experiences of the six case study firms.

SISP Approaches

An approach, then, is not a technique *per se*. Nor is it necessarily an explicit planning study or formal, codified routine, so often implied in past accounts and studies of SISP. As in most forms of business planning, it cannot often be captured by one event, a single procedure, or a particular technique. An approach may comprise a mix of procedures, techniques, user–IS interactions, special analyses, and random discoveries. There are likely to be some formal activities and some informal behaviours. Sometimes IS planning is a special endeavour and sometimes it is part of business planning at large. However, when members of the organization describe how decisions on IS strategy are initiated and made, a coherent picture is gradually painted where the underpinning philosophy, emphasis, and

Table 8.2. *Success factors in SISP*

Rank order	Success factor	Respondents selecting	Primary frequency	Sum of ranks	Mean rank
1	Top management involvement	42	15	160	2.55
2	Top management support	34	17	140	2.22
3	Business strategy available	26	9	99	1.57
4	Study business before technology	23	9	87	1.38
5	Good IS management	17	1	41	0.65

influences stand out. These are the principal distinguishing features of an approach. The *elements* of an approach can be seen as the nature and place of method, the attention to, and style of, process, and the focus on, and probability of, implementation.

We label the five approaches as business-led, method-driven, administrative, technological, and organizational. They are delineated as ideal types in Table 8.3. Several distinctors are apparent in each approach. Each represents a particular philosophy (either explicit or implicit), displays its own dynamics, and has different strengths and weaknesses. Whereas some factors for success are suggested by each approach, not all approaches seem to be equally effective.

Business-Led Approach

The underpinning 'assumption' of this approach is that current business direction or plans are the only basis upon which IS plans can be built and that therefore business planning should drive SISP. The emphasis is on the business leading IS and not the other way round. Business plans or strategies are analysed to identify where information systems are most required. Often this linkage is an annual endeavour and is the responsibility of the IS director or IS strategic planner (or team). The IS strategic plan is later presented to the board for questioning, approval and priority-setting.

General managers see this approach as simple, 'businesslike' and a matter of common sense. IS executives often see this form of SISP as their most critical task and welcome the long-overdue mandate from senior management. However they soon discover that business strategies are neither clear nor detailed enough to specify IS needs. Thus interpretation and further analysis become necessary. Documents have to be studied, managers interviewed, meetings convened, working papers written, and tentative proposals on the IS implications of business plans put forward. 'Homespun' procedures are developed on a trial-and-error basis to discover and

Table 8.3. *SISP approaches*

	Business led	Method driven	Administrative	Technological	Organizational
Emphasis	the business	technique	resources	model	learning
Basis	business plans	best method	procedure	rigour	partnership
Ends	plan	strategy	portfolio	architecture	themes
Methods	ours	best	none	engineering	any way
Nature	business	top down	bottom up	blueprints	interactive
Influencer	IS Planner	consultants	committees	method	teams
Relation to business strategy	fix points	derive	criteria	objectives	look at business
Priority setting	the board	method recommends	central committee	compromise	
IS role	driver	initiator	bureaucrat	architect	emerge team member
Metaphor	it's common sense	it's good for you	survival of the fittest	we nearly aborted it	thinking IS all the time

propose the IT implications of business plans. It may be especially difficult to promote the notion that IT itself may offer some new strategic options. The IS planners often feel that they have to 'make the running' to make any progress or indeed to engage the business in the exercise. They also discover that some top executives may be more forceful in their views and expectations than others.

Users and line managers are likely to be involved very little. The emphasis on top-level input and business plans reduces the potential contribution of users and the visibility of local requirements. Users, perceiving SISP as remote, complain of inadequate involvement. Because the IS strategy becomes the product of the IS function, user support is not guaranteed. Top management, having substantially delegated SISP to the specialists, may be unsure of the recommendations and be hesitant to commit resources, thus impairing implementation.

Nevertheless, some advantages can accrue. Information systems are seen as a strategic resource and the IS function receives greater legitimacy. Important strategic thrusts which require IT support can be identified, and if the business strategy is clearly and fully presented, the IS strategy can be well aligned. Indeed, in one of the prior case study companies which adopted this approach a clear business plan for survival initiated IT applications which were admired by many industry-watchers. However, despite this achievement, the IS function is still perceived by all three sets of stakeholders as poorly integrated into the business as a whole.

Method-Driven Approach

Adherents of this approach appear to assume that SISP is enhanced by, or depends on, use of a formal technique or method. The IS director may believe that management will not think about IS needs and opportunities without the use of a formal method, or the intervention of consultants. Indeed, recognition or anticipation of some of the frustrations typical of the business-led approach may prompt the desire for method. However, any method will not do. There is typically a search for the 'best method' or at least one better than the last method they adopted.

Once again, business strategies may be found to be deficient for the purpose of SISP. The introduction of a formal method 'rarely' provides a remedy, however, because it is unlikely to be sufficiently robust or comprehensive for formulating business strategy. Also, the method's practitioners are unlikely to be skilled or credible in such work. Furthermore, as formal methods are usually sponsored by the IS department, they may fail to win the support or involvement of the business at large. Thus a second or third method may be attempted, as help or inspiration is sought to elicit or verify the business strategy and to encourage a wider set of stakeholders to participate. Often, a vendor or consultant plays a significant role. As the challenges unfold, the criteria of the 'best' method evolve and often are concerned with the qualities of the consultants as much as the technique. The consultants often become the drivers of the SISP exercise and thus have substantial influence on the recommendations.

Users may judge method-driven exercises as 'unreal' and 'high level' and as having excluded the managers who matter, namely themselves. General managers can see the studies as 'business strategy-making in disguise' and thus become somewhat resistant and not easily persuaded of the priorities or options suggested by the application of the method. IS strategic plans may then lose their credibility and never be fully initiated. The exercises and recommendations may be forgotten. Often they are labelled the 'xyz' strategy, where 'xyz' is the name of the consulting firm employed; in other words, these strategies are rarely owned by the business.

It is not clear that formal methods will always fail. A *succession* of methods achieved little in the companies studied. Managers often judged that each method had been good in some unanticipated way for the business or the IS department. For example, in one firm it showed the need for business strategies and in another it informed IS management about business imperatives. In the former firm, IS directors were heard to say the experience had been 'good for the company—showing up the gaps in strategic thinking'! Nevertheless, formal strategy studies could leave behind embryonic strategic thrusts, ideas waiting for their time, or new thinking which could be exploited or built upon later in unforseen ways.

Administrative Approach

The emphasis here is on resource planning. The wider management planning and control procedures are expected to achieve the aims of SISP through formal procedures for allocating IS resources. Typically, IS development proposals were submitted by business units or departments to committees who examined project viability, common system possibilities, and resource consequences. In some cases resource planners did the staff work as proposals ascended the annual, hierarchical approval procedure. The administrative approach was the parallel of, or could be attached to, the firm's normal financial planning or capital budgeting routine. The outcome of the approach is a one-year or multi-year development portfolio of approved projects. Typically no application is developed until it is on the plan. A planning investment or steering committee makes all decisions and agrees any changes.

Respondents identified significant downsides to the administrative approach. It was seen as not strategic, through being 'bottom-up' rather than 'top-down'. Ideas for radical change were not identified, strategic thinking was absent, inertia and 'business as usual' dominated, and enterprise level applications remained in the background. More emotional were the claims about conflicts, dramas, and games-playing—all perhaps inevitable in an essentially resource allocation procedure. The emphasis on resource planning could lead to a resource constrained outcome. For example, spending limits were often applied and boards and CEOs were accused of applying cuts to the IS budget as though only the IS function suffered.

Some benefits were identified. Everybody knew about the procedure; it was visible and all users and units had the opportunity to submit proposals. Indeed, a SISP procedure and timetable for SISP was commonly published as part of the company policy and procedures manual. The encouragement to users to make application development requests did produce some ideas for building competitive advantage. Also it seemed that truly radical, transformational IT applications could arise in these companies despite the apparently bottom-up and cautious procedure. They emerged when the CEO or finance director broke the administrative rules and proposed and sanctioned an IS investment informally.

By emphasizing viability, project approval, and resource planning, the administrative approach also produced application development portfolios that were implemented. Not only financial criteria guided these choices. New strategic guidelines such as customer service or quality improvement also could be influential. Finally the administrative approach often fitted the planning and control style of the company. IS was managed in congruence with other activities which permitted complementary resources to be allocated in parallel. Indeed, unless the IS function complied with procedures, no resources were forthcoming.

Technological Approach

This approach is based on the assumption that an information-systems oriented model of the business is a necessary outcome of SISP and therefore analytical, modelling methods are appropriate. The Technological approach is different from the method-driven approach in two principal characteristics. First, the end-product is a business model (or series of models). Secondly, a formal method is applied based on mapping the activities, processes, and data-flows of the business. The emphasis is on deriving architectures or blueprints for IT and IS and often information engineering terminology is used. Architectures for data, computing, communications, and applications might be produced and Computer Aided Software Engineering might be among the tools employed. A proprietary technology-oriented method might have been used or adapted in an in-house style. Both IS directors and general managers tend to emphasize the objectives of rigorous analysis and of building a robust infrastructure.

This approach is demanding in terms of both effort and resource requirements. These also tend to be high profile activities. Stakeholders commented on the length of time involved in the analysis and/or the implementation.

User managers reacted negatively to the complexity of the analysis and the outputs and reported a tendency for technical dependencies to displace business priorities. In one case, management was unsure of the validity and meaning of the blueprints generated and could not determine what proposals mattered most. A second study of the same type, but using a different technological method, was commissioned. This produced a different but equally unconvincing set of blueprints.

These characteristics could lead to declining top-management support or even user rebellion. In one firm the users called for an enterprise modelling exercise to be aborted. In one of the case study firms, development of the blueprint applications was axed by top management three-and-a-half years after initiation. In another, two generations of IS management departed after organizational conflict concerning the validity of the technological model proposed.

Some success was claimed for the technological approach. Benefits were salvaged by factoring down the approach into smaller exercises. In one case this produced a database definition and in another an IT architecture for the finance function. Some IS directors claimed that these outcomes were valuable in building better IT infrastructures.

Organizational Approach

The underpinning assumption here is quite different. It is that SISP is not a special or neat-and-tidy endeavour, but is based on IS decisions being made through continuous integration between the IS function and the organization. The way that IT applications were identified and selected was described in much more multi-dimensional and subtle language. The approach was not without method, but methods were employed as required and to fit a particular purpose. For example, value analysis had been used, workshops arranged, business investigation projects set up, and vendor visits organized. The emphasis, however, was on process, especially management understanding and involvement. Sometimes a major SISP method had been applied in the past, but in retrospect it was seen to have been as much a process-enabler as an analytical investigation. Executive teamwork and an understanding of how IT might contribute to the business were often left behind by the method rather than specific recommendations for IS investment.

Organizational learning was important and evident in at least three ways. First, IS development concentrated on only one or two themes, growing in scope over several years as the organization began to appreciate the potential benefits. Examples of such themes included a food company concentrating on providing high service levels to customers, an insurance company concentrating on low-cost administration, and a chemical company concentrating on product development performance.

Secondly, special studies were important. Often multi-disciplinary senior executive project teams or full-time task-forces were assigned to tackle a business problem from which a major IS initiative would later emerge. The presence of an IS executive in the multi-disciplinary team was felt to be important to the emergence of a strategic theme, for he could suggest why, where, and how IT could help. Teamwork was the principal influence in IS strategy-making. Indeed, the organizational approach could be characterised as 'themes with teams'.

Third, there was a focus on implementation. Themes were broken down into identifiable and frequent deliverables. Conversely, occasional project cost and time overruns were acceptable if they allowed evolving ideas to be incorporated. In some ways, IS strategies were discovered through implementation.

These three learning characteristics can be seen collectively as a preference for incremental strategy-making. Indeed, quite often strategic planning and any sort of long-term plans were 'taboo'. Line managers were expected to be developing or improving the business through practical projects. Sometimes the IS function was mandated and organized to work closely with the line. In other organizations the senior IS executives strove to get involved with the business.

Respondents reported some disadvantages of this approach. Some IS directors worried about how the next theme would be generated. Also, because the approach is somewhat fuzzy or soft, they were not always confident that it could be transplanted to another part of the business. Indeed, a new CEO, management team, or management style could erode the process without the effect being apparent for some time. One IS director believed the incrementalism of the organizational approach led to creation of inferior structures.

Evaluating the Approach

The five approaches appear to be different in scope, character, and outcome. Table 8.4 differentiates them using three delineating parameters and offering slogans as caricatures.

The parameters can be translated into the following questions to help an organization position itself and diagnose its SISP approach in use:

   i.   What is the underpinning assumption in the way IS strategic planning is done?
  ii.   What is emphasized in the way SISP is done?
 iii.   Who has the most influence on the outcomes of SISP?

Strengths and weaknesses of each approach are contained in Table 8.5. It is also possible to indicate the apparent differences of each approach in

Table 8.4. *Five approaches summarized*

	Business led	Method driven	Administrative	Technological	Organizational
Underpinning assumption	Business plans and needs should drive IS plans	IS Strategies will be enhanced by use of a formal SISP method	SISP should follow and conform with the firm's management planning and control procedures	SISP is an exercise in business and information modelling	SISP is a continuous decision-making activity shared by the business and IS
Emphasis of approach	The business leads IS and not vice-versa	Selection of the best method	Identification and allocation of IS resources to meet agreed needs	Production of models and blueprints	Organizational learning about business problems and opportunities and the IT contribution
Major influence of outcomes	The IS planners	The practitioners of the method	Resource Planning and steering committees	The modelling method employed	Permanent and ad hoc teams of key managers including IS
Slogan	Business Drives IS	Strategy Needs Method	Follow the Rules	IS Needs Blueprints	Themes with Teams

Table 8.5. *Strengths and weaknesses of the SISP approach*

	Business led	Method driven	Administrative	Technological	Organizational
Strengths	Simple	Methodology	System viability	Rigor	Becomes normal
	Business first	Plugs strategy gaps	System synergies	Infrastructure	Implementation
	Raises IS status	Raises strategy profile	User input	Integrated tools	IS–User partnership
Weaknesses	*Ad hoc* method	User involvement	Non-strategic	Management support	Regeneration
	Management commitment	f(Method)	Bureaucratic	Partial implementation	Soft methodology
	f(Business Strategy)	Implementation	Resource-constrained	Complexity	Architecture

Table 8.6. *SISP approaches v. three conditions for success*

	Business led	Method driven	Administrative	Technological	Organizational
Method	Low	High	Low	High	Medium
Process	Low	Low	Medium	Low	High
Implementation	Medium	Low	High	Medium	High

terms of the three factors suggested in Figure 8.1 as necessary for success: method, process, and implementation. Table 8.6 attempts such a summary. Here, in the business-led approach, method scores low because no formal technique is used; process is rated low because the exercise is commonly IS dominated; but implementation is medium because the boards tend to at least approve some projects. In the method-driven approach, method is high by definition, but process is largely ignored and implementation barely or rarely initiated. In the administrative approach, only a procedure exists as method. However, its dependence on user inputs suggests a medium rating on process. Because of its resource-allocation emphasis, approved projects are generally implemented. The technological approach is generally method-intensive and insensitive to process. It can, however, lead to some specific implementation of an infrastructure. The organizational approach uses any method or devices that fit the need; it explicitly invests in process and emphasizes implementation.

In Table 8.7 the SISP success scores reported by each respondent are tabulated by stakeholder and approach. Analysis of variance tests indicate that differences between approaches are significant, but differences between stakeholder sets are not. This is one indication that *approach* is a distinct and meaningful way of analysing SISP in action. We also see that no approach differed widely from the mean score of 3.73 across all companies.

The most intensive approach in terms of technique (technological) earned the highest score, perhaps because it represents what respondents thought an IS planning methodology should look like. Conversely, the business-led approach, which lacks formal methodologies, earned the lowest scores. There are, of course, legitimate doubts about the meaning or reliability of these success scores because respondents were so keen to discuss the unsuccessful features.

Accordingly, another available measure is to analyse the frequency of concerns reported by firm, assuming each carries equal weight. Table 8.8 breaks out these data by method, process, and implementation concerns. The organizational approach has the least concerns attributed to it in total. The business-led approach was characterized by high dissatisfaction with method and implementation. The method-driven approach was

Table 8.7. *Mean success scores by approach*

	Business led	Method driven	Administrative	Technological	Organizational
Total means	3.25	3.83	3.6	4.00	3.94
IS directors	3.50	4.50	3.6	4.25	4.00
General managers	3.00	4.00	3.4	4.00	4.17
Line managers	3.25	3.00	3.8	3.75	3.66
Number of Firms	4	2	5	4	6

Note: 5 = high; 1 = low.

Table 8.8. *SISP concerns per firm*

	Business led	Method driven	Administrative	Technological	Organizational
Method	2.75	2.5	2.8	1.75	1.33
Process	0.75	3.0	1.6	2.50	2.16
Implementation	2.75	1.0	1.6	3.00	1.83
TOTAL	6.25	6.5	6.0	7.25	5.32
Number of Firms	4	2	5	4	6

Table 8.9. *Competitive advantage propensity (applications per firm)*

Approach	Competitive Advantage Application Frequency
Business led	4.0
Method driven	1.5
Administrative	3.6
Technological	2.5
Organizational	4.8

perceived to be unsuccessful on process and, ironically, on method, while opinion was less harsh on implementation, perhaps because implementation experience itself is low. The administrative approach, as might be predicted, is not well-regarded on method. These data are not widely divergent from the qualitative analysis in Table 8.6.

Another measure is the potential of each approach for generating competitive advantage applications. Respondents were asked to identify and describe such applications and trace their histories. No attempt was made to check the competitive advantage claimed or to assess whether applications deserved the label. Although only 14 per cent of all such applications were reported to have been generated by a formal SISP study, it is interesting to compare achievement rates of the firms in each approach (Table 8.9).

Method-driven and technological approaches do not appear promising. Little is ever initiated in the method-driven approach, while competitiveness is rarely the focus of the technological approach. The administrative approach appears to be more conducive, perhaps because user ideas receive a hearing. Forty-two per cent of competitive advantage applications discovered in all the firms originated from user requests. In the business-led approach some obviously necessary applications are actioned. In the organizational approach most of the themes pursued were perceived to have produced a competitive advantage.

These three quantitative measures can now be combined to produce a multi-dimensional score. Other scholars have suggested that a number of performance measures are required to measure the effectiveness of SISP (Raghunathan and King 1988). Table 8.10 ranks each approach according to the three measures discussed above (where 1 = top and 5 = bottom). In summing the ranks, the organizational approach appears to be substantially superior. Furthermore, all the other approaches score relatively low on this basis.

Thus, both qualitative and quantitative evidence suggest that the organizational approach is likely to be the best SISP approach to use. The organizational approach is perhaps the least formal and structured. It also differs significantly from conventional prescriptions in the literature and practice. It is therefore examined further in the rest of this paper.

<table>
<thead>
<tr><th></th><th>Business led</th><th>Method driven</th><th>Administrative</th><th>Technological</th><th>Organizational</th></tr>
</thead>
<tbody>
<tr><td>Success score ranking</td><td>5</td><td>3</td><td>4</td><td>1</td><td>2</td></tr>
<tr><td>Least concerns ranking</td><td>2</td><td>3</td><td>4</td><td>5</td><td>1</td></tr>
<tr><td>Competitive advantage potential ranking</td><td>2</td><td>5</td><td>3</td><td>4</td><td>1</td></tr>
<tr><td>Sum of ranks</td><td>9</td><td>11</td><td>11</td><td>10</td><td>4</td></tr>
<tr><td>Overall ranking</td><td>2</td><td>4</td><td>4</td><td>3</td><td>1</td></tr>
</tbody>
</table>

Table 8.10. *Multi-dimensional ranking of SISP approaches*

The Organizational Approach in Practice

Since the research underpinning this article was first published, both practitioners and academics have asked for more enlightenment on how the organizational approach works and on how to recognize it. The following ideas are based on: the original fieldwork; subsequent observations in other organizations; and on using the five-approaches framework in workshops to help organizations diagnose their SISP and discuss ways to improve it. We first analyse the organizational approach in more detail and then propose a second framework which can be used to help organizations examine what may need to be done to adopt the organizational approach.

The organizational approach can comprise six sets of characteristics: process, technique, structure, implementation, philosophy, and context.

Process

The emphasis of this approach is on process more than method. In particular, *teamwork* is important, notably the use of multi-disciplinary teams, including IS professionals, in an *ad hoc* or continuous manner. Four types of team can be recognized.

1. Management teams Characteristically, the IS executive is in the management team at any level—corporate, region, business unit, or site. The potential outcome is that when business issues are discussed at weekly, monthly, or special meetings the IT consequences or possibilities are discussed. Conversely, IT issues can be raised and the business implications discussed. The hope is that IS thinking becomes integrated with business thinking as a *normal* component of management behaviour.

One company ensures that at every management team meeting IT is put on the agenda so that IT implications and issues are not forgotten. Another board which meets four times a year devotes considerable time in alternate meetings to IT; one meeting discusses technology policies and the implications for the business; the other meeting reviews business developments and discusses the IT consequences. The implication of this aspect of teamwork is that IS managers should be full members of management teams, a finding of a study of effective IS organization (reported by Earl *et al.* in Chapter 10 of this volume).

2. Task forces Firms in the study who were following the organizational approach often were ardent believers in task forces. These had four characteristics. By definition, they were temporary and *ad hoc*. They were formed to tackle a business problem not an IS issue. They were multi-disciplinary, but included a senior IS executive because increasingly not only was IT seen as one of the potential solutions to business problems but IS executives were seen as bringing good understanding of how the particular business (or business area) or process worked. Finally, they were commonly initiated by, and reported to, the CEO. Since the study, we have observed some task forces now being chaired by a CIO, again because of his or her knowledge of the problem area or because the CIO has been found to be a good team leader.

Task forces were an important element of IS strategy-making, because the study of a problem would lead to an attack, in which IT applications were a part. These often evolved into a theme. Task forces also can bring multi-functional sponsorship of a theme—more powerful than having one singular, heroic sponsor.

3. Improvement groups   Another potential contributor to IS strategy-making are improvement groups like quality circles, value analysis committees, and so on. These are standing or semi-permanent teams at all levels charged with suggesting and making continuous improvements in focused areas of the business. It is from such groups that a potentially valuable IT application can emerge. Once recognized (see below) it may evolve into an ever bigger thrust or strategic change or theme. Possibly the firm in the study with the most advanced form of the organizational approach had several of these groups and the CIO had won the mandate to make sure that a systems analyst or consultant was a member of each one. As the CIO said: 'When the next theme emerges, we'll be there because I have an IS guy in every team and group.'

4. Project teams   It might seem odd to include IS project teams in this analysis. However, when diagnosing a firm's SISP, I have often also asked the managers present to describe the IS management processes in place when they developed an IT application which everybody thinks of as a success story—or alternatively to describe the characteristics of the golden era of IS. A recurring factor is the importance of IS project teams. Often the real business requirement behind the success story, the unfolding specification, and the requisite efforts of implementation were attributed to formation of an IS project team that comprised committed, knowledgable users, was driven by, or reported into, a top-level sponsor, and was very much a partnership experience between the IS function and the users. In retrospect that project was seen to have been the engine-room of a strategic theme and the dominant element of the IS strategy.

So teams and teamwork are important and it seems that one aspect of integrating the IS function with the organization is ensuring that IS professionals are members of all teams that matter. In turn, this implies that an important skill of IS executives, project leaders, and systems analysts or consultants is team-building and teamwork. Teams may not be led by IS managers, but IS professionals cannot only help teams be more effective, but can use them to advantage in IS strategy-making.

A second aspect of process is *education*. Although the learning emphasis of the organizational approach is also characterized by, and dependent on, teamwork, evolution of themes, IS–user partnership, studies, retreats, visits, and the like, education itself is important. It is commonly evident in four ways.

1. *Management teams participate in educational events.* These include retreats to analyse the business and examine IT opportunities, often facilitated by an outsider. Formal one-off seminars are also typical, where the management team collectively undergoes information management education on topics relevant to its business. These can be important vehicles for orchestrating change and building a platform of common understanding and language in the future exploitation of IT. They may even discover and agree the beginnings or direction of a theme.

2. *Study teams visit demonstrations of technologies and applications often in IT vendor premises* or other exemplar organizations. Such visits give the opportunity not only to see IT in action, but probe others' experience and, of course, build confidence from seeing what are in a sense reference sites. This activity can be important in recognizing and agreeing how an IT solution can help solve a business problem.

3. *The CIO puts education on his own agenda*, namely seeking opportunities to increase the IT awareness and understanding of individual executives. This also can involve visits to other sites, taking a partner to conferences and arranging 'tutorials' with well-known outsiders. This process can be a valuable means of the CIO influencing others to own and develop an idea for IT investment.

4. *Strategy studies are sometimes seen as learning activities rather than just exercises in business analysis and strategy formulation.* Often studies which yielded disappointing results, for example, application of a consultant's SISP methodology under the method-driven approach, are recognized, after the event, as having been valuable in moving an organization's awareness of IT and strategic thinking a step further. The idea may not be resurrected for some time, but a candidate IT application may have been created in latent form waiting for the appropriate opportunity to arise.

In short, education at the right time in the right way appears to be an important component of the organizational approach. Another is *partnership*, or the positive building of relationships between the IS function and users at all levels. It is particularly important for those who are charged with plotting strategic direction in IS to foster close relationships with key line and functional executives. This may not only ensure that IS professionals are brought into teams, but that IS managers or user managers can initiate ideas and discuss them with counterparts. It is also a means to education since IS specialists begin to learn more about the business and user managers begin to learn something about technology matters. Above all, partnership is important in establishing both information technology and IS managers as normal. Normalization is important in ensuring IS strategy and business strategy are integrated and in avoiding IT being seen as different or a residual. We can predict that to build partnerships, IS managers need good social and organizational skills.

Another related process investment is devising schemes for IS specialists to 'get about' the business. This can improve their business and organizational knowledge, initiate alliances with line personnel, and perhaps prompt new application ideas. One firm does this by sending an IS specialist to fill an operational job when a key employee is absent. Another has a programme whereby all IS personnel spend two days in an operational job each year.

Technique

Methods or techniques are not unimportant in the organizational approach, but they do not drive it. There is no formal method required for, or inherent in, the approach, but there is an eclectic view of techniques. For example, when study teams are at work, they may use any of the following:

1. *IS Strategy techniques* such as value chain analysis or critical success factors or more focused methods such as the customer resource life-cycle to analyse a problem, the business, or an improvement area and identify IT solutions or opportunities. They may even scan the literature, consultants, and academe for the appropriate method.

2. *Other management techniques* such as value analysis, statistical analysis, or simulations to probe a problem and examine options.

3. *Creativity techniques* such as brainstorming, lateral thinking, and the like to break out of conventional solutions and business as usual momentum.

4. *Conventional systems analysis techniques* to describe and map the business and detect obvious problems or areas for improvement. These include analysis of information flows, decision flows, time flows, material or work flows, and process mapping.

The important point is that none of these is mandatory or preferred. When an investigation is under way the appropriate method is sought and used. Indeed, more than one may be used and outside help from vendors, consultants, or academe sought at different stages of the evolution of the IS strategy or theme.

Structure

A key element of the organizational approach is devolution of IS management and development. Devolution means more than decentralization in at least three ways.

First, it does mean a tendency towards *decentralization* of IS management and development so that both the formulation and development of IS strategy can be close to business unit thinking and the playing out of competitive strategies.

Secondly, however, it can involve *dispersal* of IS personnel down to the level of departments so that there is daily interaction between operational managers and IS. Then IT opportunities can be spotted or responded to. Examples include putting a permanent systems analyst in the marketing department (not least to raise the profile of IT in marketing) or putting systems personnel on trading floors and dealer desks in investment banks to help continuously in developing new instruments or information services.

Thirdly, some organizations are now aligning development with another axis of organization, namely *business processes*. If organizations are being designed around processes or temporary structures being created to attend to process reengineering, this could make sense, for the rationale of devolution is that IS personnel help develop IT opportunities wherever they arise in the organization.

Implementation

An indicator of the organizational approach is the emphasis on implementation. This is seen in three ways:

1. IS strategies are actually *implemented* in contrast to the experience of other approaches. This is partly because, in the organizational approach, firms tend to identify the themes that have evolved and have been implemented as their IS strategy—in other words *ex post* rationalization. However, the themes would not have grown if they were not seen as being of significant business value. Nevertheless, a recurring characteristic of firms adapting the organizational approach is that delivery or implementation is important, that a strategy is more than concept, and often that focusing on implementable strategies was a last-chance policy after a period of user frustration and aborted IT investments or strategic analyses. Also where teams and task forces sponsor a theme, they generally expect early results.

2. Implementation is *continual* (or frequent). There seems to be a preference for implementing in small steps, perhaps in six-monthly modules. One firm drew a theme or strategy as a plum tree. The tree had plums (modules) which would be delivered in stages. There are obvious benefits in this policy. It reduces risk of time-and-cost overruns, technology mistakes, and mis-specifications. It gives users confidence in the delivery capability of IS. It may yield some early benefits or essential functionality. And it allows the organization to revise its requirements as the theme evolves or as managers learn what is possible next.

3. Implementation through this incremental learning becomes the means of strategy-making. Implementation is not separate from, and consequent

upon, analysis and design. And small wins accumulate to become strategic thrusts and build organizational capability and confidence. So IS strategy-making becomes *evolutionary*. In analysing both the organizational approach and data collected contemporaneously on how competitive advantage IT applications originate, it seems evident that evolution, not big bang, is most likely to work. Many stunning competitive applications evolved out of user requests, simple IT-based tools and weapons used in the market-place or straightforward transaction processing systems which underpinned a key activity of the business.

Figure 8.2 captures this evolutionary, organizational learning cycle. A business problem (sometimes a simple application opportunity) is attacked with IT. Users begin to suggest how the system can be improved. As it evolves, a new level of understanding and a strategic theme (or thrust) is identified. Larger scale investment in IT behind the theme is made (and other business changes initiated too) and the scope and scale of invest-ment grows bigger in a sort of virtuous circle[2]. It can be thought of as experiential learning or even strategic prototyping.

Philosophy

The organizational approach discovered in the firms studied was not con-scious. It may have been adopted by design, as a set of perhaps common-sense steps, but it was not conceived of—either *ex ante* or *ex post*—as a coherent or holistic approach. But in characterizing and classifying it there are some distinctive emphases which perhaps make up a 'philosophy'. Three are noteworthy.

1. These firms do not necessarily have IS strategies, plans, or applica-tion development portfolios. They pursue one or two *themes* for several years, evolving as described above. A theme often emerges from an attack on a problem, a simple application idea, or a half-formed vision. It often can be described by a pithy statement or slogan which has a business intent, not an IT orientation. Themes are usually stated in business language. Examples include 'to be the firm that is easy to do business with', 'to halve product to market time', 'to never have our items off the retailer's shelf', 'to be number one in service'. A theme, therefore, encapsulates business change involving other functions besides IT. A theme brings focus and is likely to consume a substantial proportion of IS development resources. However, it is never set in concrete—the direction may be clear, but the route is flexible and the goals refined over time. A good indicator of a theme is that nearly everybody in the organization knows about it.

2. The organizational approach often exists in a culture of *anti-strategy* and anti-planning. There may be no formal business planning processes and

[2] A case study by the author, Shorko Films SA (Centre for Research in Information Man-agement at London Business School Reference CS93/3) describes such a history.

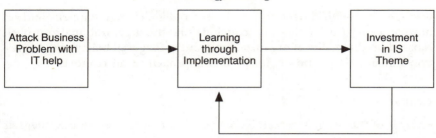

Fig. 8.2. *Experiential learning*

strategy may be a taboo word. To quote one firm, 'strategic planning is counter-cultural, but we do need some direction for IS and to take a multi-year view'. The idea of a theme was their way of coping. This informal and processual view of strategy-making may seem light on management, but there is evidence (see later) that it is effective and the most probable dynamic of strategic change.

3. There may be a period of *no IS strategy* because there is no theme. 'We seem to have exhausted the last thrust and IS has gone off the boil', was one typical line manager comment. In another company the CIO remarked: 'IS has gone off the front page. We need another theme. However I am not anxious. We could do with a period of consolidation and when the next theme emerges we'll be there . . .'

4. In the organizational approach, IS strategy (*what to do*) matters more than IT strategy (how to do it). The incremental and evolutionary nature can lead to imperfect and perhaps fragile infrastructure. There can be insufficient advanced notice on the architectural qualities required. This conflict can be managed in three possible ways:

i. The periods of no theme and consolidation described above can be used for remedial work on infrastructure.

ii. As one firm had done, a shadow architecture team can be monitoring how a theme evolves, constantly reassessing the architecture, thus shaping technical designs of the theme continuously.

iii. A theme may have to be reverse engineered. Once the theme is fully implemented it is replaced by a project to re-architect the whole application set. In this sense the journey of theme discovery by implementation is a strategic prototype and the re-architecting becomes the traditional systems development life-cycle phase. In other words, firms may have to be prepared to pay for the cost of experiential learning.

This 'philosophy' is somewhat at odds with traditional prescriptions of the IT industry. It also may fit uneasily on how IT management believe organizations should behave. However, when senior executives and line managers pause to reflect on how most strategic change happens and on how we seem to learn, they may conclude that the organizational approach is based on the reality of organizational and managerial behaviour. A question remains. Does the organizational approach fit all contexts?

Context

Analysis of the original research data and subsequent case studies suggests some of the contexts where the organizational approach may be best suited. There are also perhaps two hostile environments.

1. Some firms have reached the organizational approach, almost by trial and error, when others have failed. In particular, two forces seem influential. The need for IS to focus on streams of deliverables after a period of dissatisfaction was mentioned earlier—this was the trigger for adopting the organizational approach in a food company. The second is the realization that unless the IS function works with and within the organization, it will always be ripe for criticism and either isolation or takeover.

The trial-and-error arrival at the organizational approach is partly supported by data from the original research. Firms adopting this approach had many years experience of SISP. However, no association between SISP experience and approach was found because some firms with similar length of SISP experience were adopting other approaches.

2. One multinational's culture was that neither business units nor managers could be dictated to. Thus adoption of a universal SISP method would be resisted. Instead, guidelines were issued on managers' responsibilities in IT and the characteristics of a sound IS strategy. A mix of processes and initiatives followed but was typified by IS planning and IS plans becoming subsumed within normal business planning and business plans. In other words, this company did not set out to reify SISP as a separate activity, and the managers integrated IS planning into business planning. This could result in the ultimate state of IS-business alignment. One characteristic, and perhaps aim, of the organizational approach to SISP is that there are no IS strategic plans (or planning), just business plans (and planning) which consider IT.

3. The insurance company where strategy and planning were countercultural has been mentioned. This is not uncommon. Teams, themes, incrementalism, and implementation are softer, lower profile, and credible alternatives to the heavier models of planning that some executives fear.

4. A chemical firm traditionally made progress and pursued change through alliances between top executives. The CIO set out to build a strong relationship with the CEO of the division regarded as the source of future earnings growth and the head of the function regarded as the core capability of the firm. These initiatives led to two themes which consumed much of the IS budget for several years. In other words, the organizational

approach may well suit and need the more political aspects of organizational behaviour. Recognizing this, the CIO of an automobile company made sure he had a continual dialogue with his CEO and that each year he identified a major project (or theme) which the CEO could sponsor.

5. A Swedish firm tended to pursue strategic change through company-wide programmes initiated every three years or so. Quality management and inventory reduction are examples of these quite operational programmes. The corporate IS function saw its role as 'latching on' to these programmes as themes. In this way IS was not only being aligned with business need, but was explicitly being no different from the rest of the firm.

6. Another political perspective on SISP approaches inevitably is to analyse power bases. One hypothesis goes as follows. The business-led approach represents top management power at work. The method-driven approach could be symptomatic of the IS function seeking to wrest some power (or influence) from top management. The finance and control function may possess most power when the administrative approach is in use. The technological approach may indicate that the IS function has considerable power (or thinks it has) based on specialist knowledge and control of IS resources. The organizational approach could indicate a shift of power to line management and the users (or in a more Machiavellian way, the IS function seeking to lead from behind).

This political perspective becomes significant when contexts which are hostile to the organizational approach are identified. Two may be recognized.

1. Where there is a strong financial planning and control regime, characterized by most planning being through budgetary planning and capital budgeting mechanisms and the finance and control function driving most business planning decisions, the administrative approach to SISP seems to fit. In contrast, the emergent and more informal aspects of the organizational approach may not be tolerated or sanctioned.

2. A change of CEO and management regime, especially in distress situations, can undermine the organizational approach if the mood changes to one of bottom-line orientation, hard-nosed analysis, and organizational restructuring or downsizing. This happened in a food company. A new CEO was nervous that the systems in place, which had resulted from an organizational approach to SISP, were poorly integrated and not robust enough for an era of fast consumer response. An SISP study by a software company, akin to the technological approach, recommended 'wall to wall' integrated applications built around one database. The CIO advised against this strategy, but was overruled. The project eventually failed for technical reasons and because some of the systems did not match the way the business had to work. 'It was the biggest mistake of my career', conceded the CEO, who also recognized that the former heritage of the organizational approach had been effective enough.

These contextual propositions are not intended to suggest a contingency theory of SISP (i.e. which approaches work where), but they may indicate where the organizational approach is most likely to work or fail. The fact that on a multi-dimensional evaluation it seems to outperform other approaches suggests that it would be helpful to understand what mechanisms can be used to shift from any of the other four approaches to the organizational approach.

Shaping the Approach

In Figure 8.3 we suggest five levers that can be pulled to move towards the organizational approach: positioning of the IS function, the processes used to integrate IS with the organization, the procedures used in the firm's formal planning and control armoury, the people involved, and finally the SISP philosophy being encouraged. It should not escape readers that there are five 'P's to pull (the 5P model)! Figure 8.4 suggests some of the factors that can be managed to adopt the organizational approach—or perhaps to adapt any of the other approaches in use. It builds on the idea of power gained in turn through responsibility, influence, authority, knowledge, and credibility.

The *positioning* levers can be seen as options on the distribution of IS responsibility in the organization and the responsibility retained by IS management. The *process* levers are those which can influence users, management, and the organization, especially their perception of what IT can do for the business and how the IS function can help. The *procedures* levers refer to the instruments of both business planning and control and of information management. These distribute or restrict authority. The *people* levers refer to the types of people who may be needed for different approaches and the skills required. These decisions help govern the level and distribution of knowledge, always an important element of power. Finally, the *philosophy* of SISP being encouraged affects the pragmatics of how organizations exploit and manage IT. The philosophy mediates the tensions between concepts and action, between espoused theories and theories in use, and between the interests and values of IS and those of users. In short it builds the credibility required of SISP and the IS function. When used as a diagnostic and prescriptive framework to help firms move to the organizational approach, this model often emphasizes the real challenges in behaviour change that are required.

The Organizational Approach in Theory

There is some supporting evidence in the literature for the likely effectiveness of the organizational approach. The arguments are diverse but worth assembling.

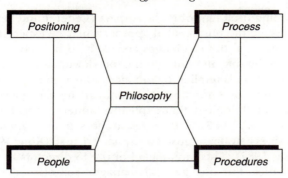

Fig. 8.3. *Five levers*

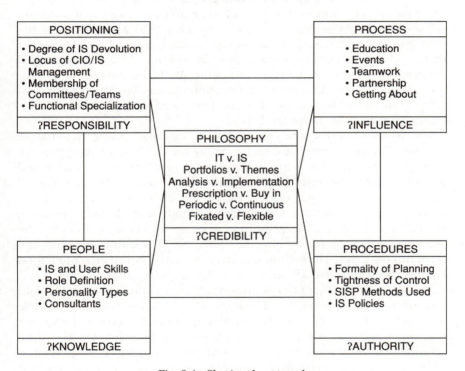

Fig. 8.4. *Shaping the approach*

Difficulties encountered in the business-led approach to SISP have been noted by others. The availability of formal strategies for SISP cannot be assumed (Bowman *et al.* 1983; Lederer and Mendelow 1986). Nor can we assume that business strategies are communicated to the organization at large, are clear and stable, or are valuable in identifying IS needs (Earl 1989; Lederer and Mendelow 1989). Indeed, the quality of the process of business planning itself may often be suspect (Lederer and Sethi 1988). In other words, while the business-led approach may be especially appealing to general managers, the challenges are likely to be significant.

There is considerable literature on the top-down, more business-strategy oriented SISP methods implied by the method-driven approach, but most of it is conjectural or normative. Vendors can be very persuasive about the need for a methodology that explicitly connects IS to business thinking (Bowman *et al.* 1983). Other researchers have argued that sometimes the business strategy must be explicated first (King 1978; Lederer and Mendelow 1987). This was a belief of the IS directors in the method-driven companies, but one general manager complained that this was 'business strategy making in disguise'.

The administrative approach reflects the prescriptions of bureaucratic models of planning and control and general management literature offers some insight on these in practice. Quinn (1977) has pointed out the strategy-making limitations of bottom-up planning procedures. He argues that big change rarely originates in this way and that, furthermore, annual planning processes rarely foster innovation. Both the political behaviour stimulated by hierarchical resource allocation mechanisms and the business-as-usual inertia of budgetary planning have been well documented elsewhere (Bower 1970; Danziger 1978).

The technological approach may be the extreme case of how the IT industry and its professionals tend to apply the thinking of computer science to planning. The deficiencies of these methods have been noted in accounts of more extensive IS planning methods and, in particular, of information engineering techniques. For instance, managers are often unhappy with the time and cost involved (Goodhue *et al.* 1988; Moynihan 1990). Others note that IS priorities are by definition dependent on the sequences required for architecture building (Hackathorn and Karimi 1988; Inmon 1986). The voluminous data generated by this class of method has also been reported (Bowman *et al.* 1983; Inmon 1986).

The organizational approach does not fit easily with the technical and prescriptive IS literature, but similar patterns have been observed by the more behavioural studies of business strategy-making. It is now known that organizations rarely use the rational-analytical approaches touted in the planning literature when they make significant changes in strategy (Quinn 1978). Rather, strategies often evolve from fragmented, incremental, and largely intuitive processes. Quinn believed this was quite the natural, proper way to cope with the unknowable—proceeding flexibly and experimentally from broad concepts to specific commitments.

Mintzberg's (1983) view of strategy-making is similar. It emphasizes small project-based multi-skilled teams, cross-functional liaison devices, and selective decentralization. Indeed, Mintzberg's view succinctly summarizes the organizational approach. He argues that often strategy is formed, rather than formulated, as actions converge into patterns and as analysis and implementation merge into a fluid process of learning. Furthermore, Mintzberg sees strategy-making in reality as a mixture of the formal and informal and the analytical and emergent. Top managers, he argues, should create a context in which strategic thinking and discovery mingle, and then they should intervene where necessary to shape and support new ways forward.

In IS research Henderson (1989) may have implicitly argued for the organizational approach when he called for iterative, ongoing IS planning processes to build and sustain partnership. He suggested partnership mechanisms such as task forces, cross-functional teams, multi-tiered and cross-functional networks, and collaborative planning without planners. Henderson and Sifonis (1988) identify the importance of learning in SISP and de Geus (1988) sees all planning as learning and teamwork as central to organizational learning. Goodhue *et al.* (1988) and Moynihan (1990) argue that SISP needs to deliver good enough applications rather than optimal models. These propositions could be seen as recognition of the need to learn by doing and to deliver benefits. There is, therefore, a literature to support the organizational approach.

Conclusions

The original study which led to identification of the five SISP approaches provided two general lessons. The first was that SISP required more than method alone. The more holistic view of method, process, and implementation—an 'approach'—has implications both for practice and future research. For practitioners, the concept of approach can be helpful in recognizing and managing all the factors required for effective IS strategy-making. For researchers, it seems that broader-based and more processual and experiential studies of SISP could be valuable.

The second general lesson is that stakeholders matter. The study underpinning this paper was the first one on SISP known to have formally addressed users and general managers as well as IS professionals. So both the concept of approach and the taxonomy of approaches may be a multi-dimensional view in another sense. It is interesting to note that when workshops have been conducted with the firms studied in order to diagnose and develop their SISP practice, another insight has materialized. If only the IS professionals are asked to position their firm in the taxonomy, their view rarely agrees with my own positioning of the firm. However, when users and general managers are also bought in, a long debate ensues and always they conclude that the firm has been adopting the approach which I originally attributed to them. There is a lesson here for practitioners who only see things happen through IS eyes and for researchers who only talk to IS personnel.

The two specific contributions of the study are the taxonomy of approaches and the tentative finding that the organizational approach is most effective. Since the study was done, further work has not unearthed a sixth approach, although clearly the approaches as presented are ideal types. Some firms have tried to construct hybrid approaches but have not yet reported success. So, in practice, the taxonomy can be used to diagnose a firm's SISP practice and experience. Then it can be used to identify strengths and weaknesses and improve the approach in use. Or a mix-and-match experiment can be tried, seeking the best of different approaches. Alternatively, firms can invest in the organizational approach.

Researchers can use this framework further to test effectiveness of SISP approaches, seek contingency or situational theories of SISP, and of course validate it further. They can also follow the proposition that the organizational approach is more effective and shift their attention to more behavioural studies of SISP. They could also do work on how to operationalize the organizational approach more definitively.

This chapter, however, has begun to operationalize the implications of the original study in two ways. It documents many of the on-the-ground actions that firms who have adopted the organizational approach tend to initiate. Secondly, it provides a further framework for considering how to shape a particular SISP approach and, especially, how to move towards the organizational approach. By focusing on the power and politics of IS management, it may also underline the challenges.

References

Bower, J. L. (1970), *Managing The Resource Allocation Process: A Study of Corporate Planning and Investment*, Division of Research, Graduate School of Business Administration, Boston: Harvard University.

Bowman, B., Davis, G., and Wetherbe, J. (1983), 'Three Stage Model of MIS Planning', *Information and Management*, 6/1 (Aug.), 11–25.

Danziger, J. N. (1978), *Making Budgets: Public Resource Allocation*, Beverley Hills: Sage Publications.

de Geus, A. P. (1988), 'Planning as Learning', *Harvard Business Review*, 66/2 (Mar.–Apr.), 70–4.

Earl, M. J. (1988) (ed.), *Information Management: The Strategic Dimension*, Oxford: Oxford University Press.

—— (1989), *Management Strategies for Information Technology*, London: Prentice Hall.

—— (1990), *Strategic Information Systems Planning in UK Companies: Early Results of a Field Study*, Oxford Institute of Information Management Research and Discussion Paper 90/1, Templeton College Oxford.

—— (1993), 'Experiences in Strategic Information Systems Planning', *MIS Quarterly*, 17/1 (Mar.).

Goodhue, D. L., Quillard, J. A., and Rockart, J. F. (1988), 'Managing the Data Resource: A Contingency Perspective', *MIS Quarterly*, 12/3 (Sept.), 373–91.

Goodhue, D. L., Kirsch, L. J., Quillard, J. A., and Wybo, M. D. (1992), 'Strategic Data Planning: Lessons from the Field', *MIS Quarterly*, 16/1 (Mar.), 11–34.

Hackathorn, R. D., and Karimi, J. (1988), 'A Framework for Comparing Information Engineering Methods', *MIS Quarterly*, 12/2 (June), 203–20.

Henderson, J. C. (1989), *Building and Sustaining Partnership Between Line and I/S Managers*, CISR Working Paper, no. 195, Center for Information Systems Research, Massachusetts Institute of Technology (Sept.).

—— and Sifonis, J. G. (1988), 'The Value of Strategic IS Planning: Understanding Consistency, Validity and IS Markets', *MIS Quarterly*, 12/2 (June), 187–200.

Henderson, J. C., and Venkatraman, N. (1989), *Strategic Alignment: A Framework for Strategic Information Technology Management*, CISR Working Paper, no. 190, Center for Information Systems Research, Massachusetts Institute of Technology (Aug.).

Inmon, W. H. (1986), *Information Systems Architecture*, Englewood Cliffs, NJ: Prentice-Hall.

Karimi, J. (1988), 'Strategic Planning for Information Systems: Requirements and Information Engineering Methods', *Journal of Management Information Systems*, 4/4 (Spring), 5–24.

King, W. R. (1978), 'How Effective is Your Information Systems Planning?', *Long Range Planning*, vol. 1, no. 1, pp. 7–12.

Lederer, A. L., and Mendelow, A. L. (1986), 'Issues in Information Systems Planning', *Information and Management*, 10/5 (May), 245–54.

—— (1987), 'Information Resource Planning: Overcoming Difficulties in Identifying Top Management's Objectives', *MIS Quarterly*, 11/3 (Sept.), 389–99.

—— (1989), 'Co-ordination of Information Systems Plans With Business Plans', *Journal of Management Information Systems*, 6/2 (Fall), 5–19.

Lederer, A. L., and Sethi, V. (1988), 'The Implementation of Strategic Information Systems Planning Methodologies', *MIS Quarterly*, 12/3 (Sept.), 445–61.

—— (1991), 'Critical Dimensions of Strategic Information Systems Planning', *Decision Sciences*, 22/1 (Winter), 104–19.

McFarlan, F. W. (1981), 'Problems in Planning the Information System', *Harvard Business Review*, 59/5 (Sept.–Oct.), 142–50.

—— and McKenney, J. L. (1983), *Corporate Information Systems Management: The Issues Facing Senior Executives*, Homewood, Ill.: Dow Jones Irwin.

McLean, E. R., and Soden, J. V. (1977), *Strategic Planning for MIS*, New York: J. Wiley & Sons.

Mintzberg, H. (1983), *Structure in Fives: Designing Effective Organizations*, Englewood Cliffs, NJ: Prentice-Hall.

—— (1987), 'Crafting Strategy', *Harvard Business Review*, 66/4 (July–Aug.), 66–75.

Moynihan, T. (1990), 'What Chief Executives and Senior Managers want from their IT Departments', *MIS Quarterly*, 14/1 (Mar.), 15–26.

Niederman, F., Brancheau, J. C., and Wetherbe, J. C. (1991), 'Information Systems Management Issues for the 1990s', *MIS Quarterly*, 15/4 (Dec.), 475–500.

Quinn, J. B. (1977), 'Strategic Goals: Plans and Politics', *Sloan Management Review*, 19/1 (Fall), 21–37.

—— (1978), 'Strategic Change: Logical Incrementalism', *Sloan Management Review*, 20/1 (Fall), 7–21.

Raghunathan, T. S., and King, W. R. (1988), 'The Impact of Information Systems Planning on the Organization', *OMEGA*, vol. 16, no. 2, pp. 85–93.

Synott, W. R., and Gruber, W. H. (1982), *Information Resource Management: Opportunities and Strategies for the 1980s*, New York: J. Wiley and Sons.

9

Relationships Between Strategy and Business Process Reengineering: Evidence From Case Studies

MICHAEL J. EARL, JEFFREY L. SAMPLER, AND JAMES E. SHORT

Introduction

It is not unusual for management research to lag behind management practice; in some ways it is inevitable. Business Process Reengineering (BPR), it is claimed, was pioneered in a few large corporations in the 1980s (Hammer and Champy 1993). It was first described and explained at the turn of the decade (Davenport and Short 1990; Hammer 1990) and since then an evolving stream of research has been reported (Caron *et al.* 1994; Davenport and Stoddard 1994; Grover *et al.* 1994). This paper reports results from case-study research on relationships between BPR, business strategy planning, and information systems (IS) planning. These questions are particularly relevant due to the rapid escalation in the size and scope of reengineering projects.

Our work has been guided by the following questions:

- How have business process reengineering initiatives evolved in organizations?
- How has planning for BPR been integrated with strategic business planning? And with IS planning?
- Is there evidence that the character, scope, and size of BPR projects depends on the degree of integration between BPR, strategic business planning, and IS planning?
- To what extent has the degree of planning integration between BPR, strategic business planning, and IS affected change management policies and practices in firms undergoing BPR?

In approaching these questions we have surfaced a number of definitions of business process reengineering. Reengineering has been defined by consultants practising it as an approach to planning and controlling 'radical' organizational change. BPR has meant redesigning existing business processes and implementing new ones. 'Business processes' have been defined as 'logically related tasks performed to achieve a defined business outcome' (Davenport and Short 1990), where processes are 'any activity or group of activities that take an input, add value to it, and provide an output to an internal or external customer' (Harrington 1991). We will refer to business process reengineering in its current practice usage as approaches for initiating and managing 'radical' changes in existing business processes. However, we note also the importance of organizational change theories and their implications for intervention techniques, such as reengineering, which disrupt established work routines, resource dependencies, and human resource policies (Gersick 1991; Pfeffer and Salancik 1978; Tushman and Romanelli 1985).

Framework for Analysis

Although a relatively new field of inquiry, there are theory-based perspectives through which we can study emerging practice in BPR. Below we review four perspectives—organizational processes, strategy, IS, and change management and control, which provide grounding for our investigation into planning integration.

Process

Processes are intrinsic to organization design. Academics and practitioners alike have long used process concepts to distil and elaborate characteristics of organization structure, work-role behaviour, and resource interdependence (Mohr 1982; van de Ven and Poole 1990; Victor and Blackburn 1987). In organizational process research, for example, Weick (1979) has argued that organizations construct processes from a set of 'cycles' using 'assembly rules'—in short, organizations build routines based on goal-directed rules and procedures, where rules are seen as constraints on action (Drazin and Sandelands 1992). Other researchers have defined processes as co-ordination systems for managing resource dependencies in firms, using ideas from computer science and co-ordination theory to map process hierarchies and resource co-ordination (Malone and Crowston 1994).

Definitions of business processes have looked chiefly at the structure and specific ordering of work, using ideas from industrial engineering and, in some circumstances, from systems dynamics where the process focus crosses firm boundaries (Forrester 1961). Thus Davenport (1992) defines business processes as 'the specific ordering of work activities across time and place, with a beginning, an end, and clearly identified inputs and outputs'. The process objective is customer value added: processes are the structure by which organizations do what is necessary to produce value for customers. Such definitions generally have implied process hierarchies. Davenport separates 'operational' from 'management' processes; others define 'core' and supporting processes using ideas borrowed from value chain analysis (Kaplan and Murdoch 1991).

Reengineering practitioners have expanded the key ideas in business process redesign to include concepts of incremental and radical change in organization structure, work role behaviour, task interdependence, human resource policies, and rewards (Hammer and Champy 1993). This evolution of practice-based ideas, grounded in the 'organizational experiments' under way, has led organization theorists to call for increased academic research into business processes and their relationships to organization form (Daft and Lewin 1992). Whether one regards this as a case of theory leading practice or practice leading theory (Barley *et al.* 1988), the interest in process-based work seems clearly to call for greater understanding of this domain.

Strategy

Strategy researchers have continued to debate both the sources of competitive advantage and firm performances (the 'content' of strategy) and models of the strategic planning process (the 'process' view). In firm performance two contrasting perspectives are dominant: one looks to the importance of external market factors in predicting firm performance; the other looks to factors internal to the organization.

The external 'industry forces' view derived much force from the work of Porter (1980), who applied principles of industrial economics to strategy. The dominant principle is that (industry) structure determines the conduct (strategy) of firms, and the collective conduct of firms then determines the overall performance of firms in the industry (Bain 1968). Under these assumptions, strategy was concerned mainly with the placement of products in desirable market niches and defending those niches (Porter 1980). A second perspective has been the resource-based view of the firm, which emphasizes unique combinations of resources that firms employ to obtain above average rates of returns (Barney 1986; Rumelt 1974; Wernerfelt 1984). Extensions of the resource view have shifted the focus from unique tangible resources as competitively advantageous, to a focus on intangible assets, such as knowledge (Winter 1987), core competencies (Prahalad and Hamel 1990), or learning (Senge 1990) as the primary source of advantage.

Whether internally or externally derived, these models of firm performance give little emphasis to shifts in information technology that devalue existing resources or market positions (Sampler and Short 1994), or radical change approaches, such as reengineering, which disrupt established resource dependencies and/or processes of resource allocation.

At the heart of the second debate is whether strategy formulation and strategy implementation are distinct, separable activities. Many models of strategic planning assume this distinction and posit that strategy formulation initiates strategy development (Mintzberg 1990). Strategy is then implemented through a 'series of subactivities which are primarily administrative' (Andrews 1982).

Alternatively, other researchers hold that strategy formulation and implementation are not separable, that is, 'thinking cannot be separated from doing' (Mintzberg 1990). Here the argument is that strategies emerge incrementally over time (Mintzberg and Waters 1985). The IS planning literature has also been influenced by the incremental view (Earl 1994).

The two views have obvious implications for BPR. For example, is process reengineering a means of achieving resource-based competitive advantage? When implemented, can it help create or sustain advantageous product-market positions? Moreover if these are the goals of BPR projects, how might BPR planning methodologies relate to contrasting models of the strategy-making process?

Information Systems

As the scope and importance of IS has increased within firms, IS planning agendas have evolved to broader strategy and organizational concerns (Venkatraman 1991). Interrelationships between IS and other organizational functions have led to various approaches and methodologies for planning integration (Cash *et al.* 1983; Earl 1987; Henderson and Sifonis 1988; King 1978; King and Zmud 1983; Lederer and Mendelow 1989; Pyburn 1983; Ward 1989).

Henderson and Venkatraman (1993) recast much of the earlier planning work in developing their proposed business-IS strategic alignment model (SAM). The SAM model is more comprehensive in that it extends the concept of alignment from the firm's business and IS strategy domain to the decisions undertaken by managers to design organizational units and the internal work processes and information flows necessary to execute strategy. However, the SAM framework was developed before attention to reengineering and process redesign rekindled interest in the enabling role of IT in process innovation and change (Davenport 1992). The question thus presents itself: what are the implications of BPR for the strategic alignment model?

Change Management and Control

BPR projects imply organizational change. Indeed, their goal may be strategic change. At present, however, there is no coherent theory of change within BPR research (Earl and Khan 1994). The debate centres around whether radical or incremental change is most effective and how such shifts occur within organizations.

Much research has argued that the introduction of innovations or radical shifts must be paced with a gradual, persistent introduction into the organization. The logic is to allow for a period of adjustment to, and understanding of, the capabilities and implications of the innovation and/or radical change (Hage and Aiken 1970; Hughes 1971; Rogers 1974). In contrast, others have argued that following the introduction of an innovation, the period of adaptive behaviour and change is relatively short (Tyre and Orlikowski 1994). This suggests that radical shifts may have to be executed quickly rather than gradually.

The decision of how to introduce an innovation is further complicated by the behavioural implications for those affected by the change. The typical radical change approach associated with BPR is to determine the new optimal procedures through various techniques and then to implement optimized procedures quickly (Hammer 1990; Hammer and Champy 1993). Such sweeping structural changes are intended to change behaviour rapidly, but they also create uncertainty and insecurity (Tushman *et al.* 1986). The contrary view is that people or team building interventions, which are slower than structural interventions, will result in greater building of commitment (Beer 1980).

The reengineering practitioners (Davenport 1992; Hammer and Champy 1993) also argue that performance measurement and management controls can help motivate and reinforce desired process-oriented behaviours. Research is tentative on this front, but the balanced score-card systems of Kaplan and Norton (1992) which stress internal metrics of excellence and learning as well as external measures, may provide a way forward. An alternative perspective is to recognize that controls and performance measures can be used to drive strategic renewal (Simons 1994) including, presumably, BPR.

As described in Figure 9.1, these four perspectives ground our framework for analysis. In our preceding discussion we acknowledge that we may have implicitly suggested that effective integration of BPR, strategic business, and IS planning requires an alignment between the four domains. In this sense, business process reengineering does prompt an added dimension for strategic alignment models such as that of Henderson and Venkatraman (1993). Thus Figure 9.1 suggests a tentative 'process alignment model'. Its conceptual value may be either a revised alignment framework or an argument for adding a process dimension to existing alignment models. We address this question again at the end of the paper.

We turn now to assess qualitatively the interrelationships of the four domains in our case studies. We first outline our case methodology and case selection criteria. We then discuss the cases themselves, after which

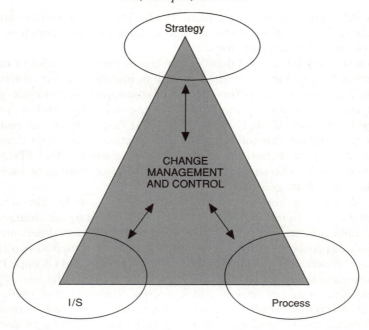

Fig. 9.1. *A framework for analysis*[1]

we derive and present a taxonomy of BPR strategies suggested by our analysis.

Methodology

We conducted four in-depth case studies over two years (1993–4) to help us understand how firms define and manage the relationship between business strategic planning, process reengineering projects, and IS strategic planning. Three of the four firms are large, diversified companies with significant market shares in their respective industries. The fourth is a mid-sized firm, ranked in the second half of the twenty largest building societies in the UK.

The unit of analysis in our company case studies was reengineering projects, defined as projects of at least six months' duration, incorporating dedicated personnel with the objective of using process-based concepts and tools to analyse, make recommendations upon, and change an existing business process. We conducted lengthy, semi-structured interviews in each company with three to ten interviewees, the number depending

[1] We are tentatively calling this the *Process Alignment Model.*

on the size and complexity of the reengineering project or projects under study. All interviewees were senior executives and/or line business managers with responsibility for strategic business planning, IS planning, and/or process reengineering. Where applicable, the entire reengineering team, composed generally of five to nine individuals, was interviewed at least once. In one case the entire senior management team, including the chief executive officer, was interviewed.

Interviews were supplemented by archival studies of reports, memoranda, and presentation materials in each firm. We gathered case-level data consistent with the logic and steps outlined in case-study methodologies as described by Campbell (1975), Eisenhardt (1989), and Lee (1989), although work reported at this stage must be considered preliminary. In two companies large-scale reengineering initiatives had been broken down into defined projects, and here we were able to look specifically at project work through its full cycle of planning and implementation. However, in the two other case studies reported the reengineering initiatives were in different stages of execution. In the pharmaceutical company, for example, the firm (described later) had just completed the planning phase and was moving into project implementation.

We selected the four case studies from a larger research effort under way studying sixteen reengineering projects in twelve firms. In each project a minimum of four stakeholders were interviewed: project (reengineering) sponsor, project manager (operational), major customer, and business planner. On projects involving a clearly defined IS support role, the IS project manager or systems development manager was interviewed. Our survey instrument[2] includes items in five areas: actors (roles) involved; project tasks (activities, tasks sequences); time (synchronization of activities; event criticality); resources (process-based methods and tools, IT support); and planning integration (relationship of project planning to business strategic and IS planning).

Our four 'archetypal' cases were selected on both analytic and practical grounds. Following Eisenhardt's (1989) discussion of theoretical sampling, we chose cases to help illustrate four 'polar types' of planning integration observed in the larger sample. As Pettigrew (1992) and others have argued, given the limited number of cases that can be studied in many areas, and particularly here in the BPR-planning integration area, it makes sense to choose extreme cases where the focus of inquiry is 'transparently observable'. Moreover, practically speaking the sixteen projects under study in the larger research effort were not all completed (many are multi-year efforts). We have elected in this paper to report on work in progress and on our observation of polar types with the view that this analysis will contribute to our emerging understanding of BPR planning integration.

---

[2] Available from the authors.

Case Study Results

We turn now to describing our four cases, presented in two parts. The next section presents each case and details observations on planning integration. The section thereafter presents an aggregate analysis of all cases, organized by key factors emerging from the interviews and our analysis.

Organization 1—Semiconductor Manufacturing

Organization 1 is a large semiconductor manufacturing firm. Radical shifts in semiconductor product and process technologies have fundamentally changed the industry in recent years. Increasing demand for specialized (custom) chips has dramatically shortened product life-cycles for mainstay commodity products, accelerating time-based competition across the industry.

By the late 1980s, senior business unit executives at Organization 1 recognized that the company would have to derive the majority of its future revenues from custom-manufactured products. The problem was 'how to get there from here'. A long string of process improvement and quality programmes throughout the 1980s had been initiated with mixed results. Few interviewees disputed the importance of these efforts, but, likewise, fewer still felt that the efforts had been entirely successful.

A broad business unit reengineering programme was begun in early 1990, supported by a new, internal process engineering competency group. Composed of functional managers, business analysts, and software developers experienced in manufacturing operations, systems analysis, and the then-growing interest in specialized reengineering practices, the group was responsible for developing internal competencies in process concepts, methodologies, and tools necessary for reengineering practice. By late 1990 the group had grown to twenty-three full-time professionals.

Working with group-level and key functional managers, the internal process engineering team defined six core semiconductor business processes. These processes included strategy development, product development, customer design support, manufacturing development, and customer communications. A sixth process, order fulfilment (OF), was selected as the first core process for reengineering. Three characteristics of OF contributed to its selection: first, the large number of customer-facing interfaces and handoffs in the process; secondly, the implications for time compression, cost efficiencies, and improved customer interaction in simplifying the interfaces; thirdly, the view that the benefit/risk of tackling OF was more easily calculated than for the other core processes. OF was defined broadly as starting with a customer need for a specific product, and ending with the receipt of the product at the customer's site. To document the OF process, and the effect of interventions on the order flows of semiconductor products, the team used process decomposition and analysis techniques suggested by industry research and developed internally by the process engineering team. Following three months of intensive work, the team recommended to senior management that process improvement activities already under way were insufficient: OF required redesign.

Group management's decision to completely reengineer OF was formalized in late 1992. The reengineering team continued work on disaggregating and defining key workflows and documenting 'best in class' performance in each process category. For example, for the order entry process the team used airline reservations agents as the benchmark process. Team members visited several travel reservations systems (TRS) to evaluate reservations procedures and agent workflows. An early comparison showed that while a typical reservations agent could book a complex travel agenda in under twenty minutes, the semiconductor firm's 'reservations activities' involved many individuals and could take as long as two weeks to schedule an order.

The team completed its analysis by mid-1993, recommending a two-phased implementation plan including process education for employees and 'showcase' pilot projects to provide 'proof of concepts' to build support for reengineering change initiatives. Interviewees reported that several problem areas have arisen as the business unit moves further into reengineering implementation: first, the high-level process mapping exercises are moving quickly to more granular sub-processes, where negotiations on resource utilization, workflows, and management responsibilities are more operationally complex. Resistance among functional managers is increasing as trade-off decisions on component lot sizes, line speeds, and inventory holding becomes more complex to negotiate. Secondly, dependence on better information technology in areas including information access, software development, and communications is escalating rapidly, partly driven by the increased need for functional managers to negotiate trade-off decisions.

Thirdly, new metrics for process improvement have invariably been added to existing functional metrics, thereby increasing complexity in measurement and control. As one senior manufacturing manager told us, 'increasingly our jobs will be to simplify the measures of performance as we move to the next level of redesign. We've tended to do the reverse—to add metrics while keeping the old ones around for comfort. In many cases, the two tell you to do different things. It's not always clear how to sort them out.'

The decisions taken at Organization 1 emphasize the importance of manufacturing operations and supply chain logistics in reengineering. Strategy formation was seen classically as product–market–customer segmentation, and the implications of changing product technologies in customer use. Reengineering was defined chiefly as functional integration and metrics to measure end-to-end cycle time improvement. IS's role largely was to contribute skills in systems analysis as part of the broader reengineering methodology developed by the process engineering group.

We select the label 'engineering strategy' to describe the activities undertaken by Organization 1. This strategy is related to industrial engineering and process engineering projects where the goal is optimization of workflows and the precise scheduling and co-ordination of interdependent work tasks and related activities. The BPR projects evolved independently of formal business or strategic IS planning, yet the project strategy could achieve strategic change. The engineering strategy appears to be the generally implied approach to BPR in the majority of cases and literature to date.

Organization 2—Property and Casualty Insurance

Organization 2 is a large, multi-line property and casualty insurance company. This industry has been hit by a variety of competitive threats in the last decade, ranging from severe earthquakes, storms, and other environmental hazards, to declining profitability in traditional product and service lines in many customer segments. Some insurers have aggressively targeted niche market segments in mature product areas with favourable results. But many of the older, traditional carriers have faced steadily eroding market share, and losses.

Organization 2 has lost money in the Property and Casualty (P&C) market since the late 1980s, with subsequent downgrading of the firm's Standard and Poor's bond rating. Interviewees reported that numerous reorganizations, most focused on realigning headquarters and field staff ratios and responsibilities, had failed to take the required effect.

In the early 1990s the decision was made to reorganize the P&C division into multiple business areas and to restructure field operations to change customer and agent (distributor) relationships. In this decision, the initial planning sequence began classically with business strategy and structure. Product service market areas, and their respective field operations implementation, were refocused and reorganized. This was led by senior management—the sponsor was the P&C division president.

The second initiative focused on reengineering division level, 'macro' business processes (planning phase). This effort, led jointly by IS systems personnel and line business managers, defined upwards of fifteen different processes using structured process decomposition techniques developed by the team and taken from various industry sources. The project team itself, which ranged from six to ten individuals over the course of the initiative, followed a participative design strategy to maximize employee ownership of the results. The team gathered data from a large percentage of the total number of employees in the business unit (almost 20 per cent), through surveys, interviews, customer workshops, 'brown paper' process modelling sessions, and other meeting and data input formats. The methodology and process analysis approach emphasized workflows and their associated information flows within the business unit.

Following the process design and reengineering phase, the team turned to implementation activities, focusing on several cross-functional 'streams' keyed to expected impact on revenue performance. For example, streams focused on underwriting, claims, and producer (new business) processes, supported by IS. The implementation plans for the various projects were timed between twelve and twenty-four months.

The emphasis and procedures taken at Organization 2 emphasize a classic top-down strategy–bottom-up implementation approach. Reengineering was initiated after decisions regarding business strategy and structure were taken. The participative approach to generating process designs and reengineering alternatives across the division emphasized both senior management and team concerns with implementation effectiveness. IS's roles in this effort were judged by interviewees as contributing process analysis (systems analysis) skills, as providing adequate communications and information access to support redesigned business processes, as 'broker' between multiple business functions coming together in the new process design. With the exception of greater emphasis on process as opposed to purely systems design, these IS roles are well-understood responsibilities in any large, cross-functional systems project.

We denote Organization 2's activities as 'Systems Strategy'. IS planning has largely driven BPR initiatives and systems analysis is a central activity. Providing information access and communications is a goal of business and systems (architectural) design. The success of such a strategy is heavily dependent on the state of partnership between business and IS professionals in the firm. Surveys, interviews, 'brown paper' modelling sessions, and the like organized by Organization 2 can be seen as necessary prerequisites to build and sustain the required partnership.

Organization 3—Pharmaceuticals

Organization 3 is a large, diversified pharmaceuticals firm. In response to the many changes in health-care policy and administration taking place in the USA and Europe over the last decade, this firm, like its primary competitors, has acquired several related health-care businesses and focused on improving internal operations. Company profitability has remained strong, even given the state of industry flux, but there is widespread concern that the industry at large is entering a period of reduced profitability amid increased regulatory unrest.

In early 1992 the company's CEO announced a broad corporate initiative focused on the company's core values, its leadership practices, and the linkages of these values and practices to daily work. The initiative followed top executive visits to manufacturing and service firms in Japan, Europe, and the USA. While not formally a benchmarking exercise, the trips served to heighten senior management attention to innovative practices implemented in selected 'best in class' firms.

A decision was made soon thereafter to rethink the firm's strategy and operating plans, with emphasis on strategic planning, process integration, and 'breakthrough projects' targeted at new product development (discussed below). Interviewees noted that the clear emphasis of management was on 're-energizing' the link between planning and action. 'The problem', one interviewee noted, 'was that too often plans were thrown over the wall for implementation without clear guidelines for action and followup. This was recognized as an old problem that had to be solved.'

A dedicated cross-functional team, composed of line business and IS managers, was put together in mid-1992. The team made an early commitment to new group-oriented software products then coming onto market. The software served two key purposes: as the team's own internal workflow analysis system; and as the team's project archive. The team's immediate activity over the next ten months was to develop a high-level planning methodology with the stated emphasis on explicitly linking planning activities to 'measurable outcomes'.

The team devised an 'integral 10 : 3 : 1 planning cycle', composed of a ten-year planning forecast, three-year requirements for capabilities development, and one-year 'breakthrough' reengineering projects. The ten-year planning forecast developed both business (customer, product, market) and process strategies, where processes were defined as major operational activities supported by sustaining processes. For example, operational processes included drug discovery, drug development, and drug launch, supported by sustaining processes including human resources, finance, and information technology.

The ten-year plan included requirements for three-year 'core capabilities' development, these capabilities serving as platforms for breakthrough process improvement projects. 'Breakthrough' projects were in turn implemented through multiple, one-year reengineering projects. For example, as part of the ten-year forecast, the team defined three core business processes for new product development: product creation, demand creation, and order fulfilment. Within these three core business processes, three-year requirements for five breakthrough projects were defined. For product creation, they were drug discovery, and drug development; for demand creation, they were new product launch, and life-cycle management; and for order fulfilment the project was supply chain management. For each breakthrough project, processes were identified for one-year reengineering projects. For example, within drug development reengineering projects were defined for clinical trial supplies, clinical study processes, and regulatory dossier preparation. In all cases the process analysis approach emphasized workflows and their associated information flows across functional units.

The strategy planning–process integration approach was piloted in 1993. Two pilots were run sequentially to allow refinements to be transferred from pilot one to pilot two. Interviewees report that the 10 : 3 : 1 planning framework: (1) legitimizes investment in process capabilities as an important element of competitive strategy at the business unit level; (2) provides a defined sequence of activities integrating strategy and process planning objectives; (3) tends to locate the selection criteria for breakthrough projects away from political or other considerations; and (4) 'more rationally' drives reengineering project selection. Adopting the framework, interviewees noted, was widely understood by most line business managers to have elevated the process concept into the strategy domain.

Regarding IS's role, again as we saw in Organizations 1 and 2, a major activity was to contribute systems analysis and project management skills to the team planning effort. An added role was to influence and facilitate the team's investment in group support software for internal workflow co-ordination and project data archiving.

We denote Organization 3's planning approach 'Bureaucratic Strategy' because it relies on formal planning procedures and co-ordination of interdependent sub-tasks reminiscent of rule-based approaches falling under a mechanistic model of organization (Emery 1969; Galbraith 1973). Such models have been shown to be robust in hierarchically co-ordinating large numbers of interdependent sub-tasks, but have limited capacity to re-examine and/or remake decisions. Organization 3's efforts to 'informate' the planning process with group-oriented software can be seen to address part of the problem of effective lateral decision processes (Galbraith 1973). However, the team's charter did not include re-examining managerial decision-making, even if adoption of the group-oriented software could be viewed as a precursor to exactly this issue.

Organization 4—Building Society

Organization 4 is a mid-sized building society in the UK, providing mortgage loans to home buyers and financing these mortgages through savings accounts with different terms, rates, and tax benefits. Industry deregulation in the late 1980s found larger, nation-wide building societies entering banking and insurance markets. While several of the mid-sized building societies intended to follow suit, a downturn in the economy and uncertain profitability in several larger firms forestalled many of these efforts, Organization 4 among them.

In mid-1990 Organization 4 began a series of internal changes to prepare for the expected, though postponed, entry into new financial markets.

The traditional centralized head office, working through a region and branch structure, was reorganized into product divisions better able to specialize in different product markets and absorb newly acquired businesses (much of the growth in this industry in the late 1980s had come through acquisitions and mergers). This added cost in the short run and increased fragmentation in a company unused to the idea of differentiated, and at times competing, product market strategies. There was also concern over profitability. The company had survived in the economic downturn, but turnover was below projections.

Market shifts and structural change in the organization set the stage for what senior management described as 'an organizational experiment' built around the radical reshaping of management processes. The top dozen senior managers in the company were called together for a week-long retreat and asked to bring their problems and solutions with them. The mission and goals were still to drive the organization, but management processes—the way in which managers around the company came together to set business strategy, develop implementation plans, allocate people and resources, and measure progress, were to change. The company's leadership wanted to do more than designate teams and other cross-functional, co-ordination mechanisms—the intent was to reshape the processes by which managers worked on a day-to-day basis in the firm.

The first step was to design a new set of management processes which emphasized decision-making and communications flows across managers in the company. This necessitated two major changes across the organization (the 'organizational experiment'): a new way of describing how work was done, and a complete replacement of old definitions of what was done. In brief, all job titles were thrown out, and a new language for organizational roles, meetings, and teamwork was introduced. For example, all 'jobs' were redefined as 'roles'; 'meetings' were recast as 'events'; 'team members' became 'team players'. The intent was to reinforce a new way of working by introducing a new 'corporate language' for describing work.

At the senior management level, the executive team defined three 'macro' management processes: the Direction Management Process (DMP), which included business development and customer relationships; the Implementation Management Process (IMP), which defined the required capabilities to implement decisions taken by the DMP; and the Understanding Process (UP), discussed in more detail below. Examples of the IMP process included process architecture (somewhat analogous to the process engineering function in a manufacturing organization), customer engagement processes, process quality measurements, customer satisfaction processes, and risk management.

The direction management and implementation processes were themselves defined within a company-wide Understanding Process (UP). The

Understanding Process involved a substantial commitment by managers, supervisors, and employees continuously to appraise and solicit interaction and comments from all personnel in the firm. The goal was continuously to surface issues and problem areas across the entire company every two weeks. The output to the cycle was 'understanding events', typically large meetings (often company-wide) involving all levels of management held when an internal 'issueometer' reached a pre-specified level (the 'issueometer' was a 'problem metric' devised to assess the frequency and severity of issues raised in the bi-weekly cycle). Of course, company-wide or otherwise very large 'understanding events' were not required at every two-week cycle, but the intent of the system was to allow different groupings of 'team players' to call for events as circumstances dictated. The frequency of events varied widely according to need, but in one IMP project seven understanding events were held in the first two weeks to clarify direction and allocation of team resources.

The image created by these process definitions and cycles of management participation in direction, implementation, and understanding processes is one of continuously appraising what (the DMP) and how (IMP) work was done. This echoes Deming's (Walton 1990) Plan-Do-Check-Act (PDCA) sequence—indeed, many of the pictures produced by Organization 4 describing the cycling of managerial work in the DMP, IMP, and UP processes are reminiscent of Deming's point that PDCA cycles represent work on processes, not on specific tasks or problems (the assertion is that processes can never be 'solved', only worked on, and in this cycle problems get solved).

The new process design was rolled out in 1993. As noted, implementation required new role definitions for all employees, new forms of personnel assessment and development, new payment systems—in short, a different culture of managerial operations. Resistance to these changes had been tempered by scepticism that the new design would actually take hold, but as implementation rolled out, a number of managers and employees left, uncomfortable with the changes. A relatively small percentage of employees was asked to leave (under 5 per cent). A year after the 'experiment', work-force retention has been surprisingly high (over 80 per cent), although much of this can perhaps be explained by regional employment patterns in the UK and the depressed state of financial services employment generally.

Interviewees reported that one or two problems were the most difficult: the changes required in personal attitudes about how work was completed and evaluated (for example, how individuals worked with each other became an explicit determinant of pay); and the uncertainty created in focusing first on how things were done, not on what was done. Managers and employees long accustomed to working on specific problems, tasks, and/or processes found the emphasis on events, communications, and

Table 9.1. *BPR strategies*

BPR strategies	Process perspective		Strategy perspective		IS perspective		Change management perspective	
	Process paradigm	Process attributes	Strategic motive	Strategic scope	Dominant IS contribution	IS expertise	Change initiation	Change sponsor
Ecological	Process as management design	Decision responsibilities and decision flows	Dynamic adaptation	Enterprise	Process consciousness	Systems modelling	Vision	CEO
Bureaucratic	Process as core capability	Value chains and work flows	Resource capability	S B U	Process construction	Systems awareness	Strategic planning	S B U management team
Systems	Process as systems opportunity	Information systems opportunities and information work flows	Information leverage	Cross-functional information-intensive activities	Process co-ordination	Systems analysis	IS planning	Process owner
Engineering	Process as work flow optimization	Work roles activities and work flows	Benchmarking and efficiency	Cross-functional operations-intensive activities	Process integration	Systems design	Operational problem	Line management

direction-setting difficult and time-consuming. The perception among many who left was that 'little work was getting done'. The belief among those making the changes was that attention to 'how' (e.g. processes) meant that the 'right work was getting done'.

The role of IS in the changes to organization design was minimal in terms of technology. Few projects concentrated on systems per se—those that did focused on customer information (the Customer Requirements Implementation Process was one example). However, interviewees believed that IS personnel brought important systems thinking to the process design, although this expertise was often poorly communicated.

More important than the role of IS in supporting the process change was the role of the process change on IS. The IT function was reorganized around processes, including systems development, information design, and customer systems. The Systems Development process team developed and used a rule-based system development methodology incorporating object-oriented design. When the company producing the object-oriented software went into liquidation, Organization 4 acquired the intellectual rights to the product.

In the first year of the new organization costs fell and profits rose by over 60 per cent in a flat mortgage market. The result quelled many a sceptic, although top management at Organization 4 believe that the 'experiment' is still very much in its early stages.

We denote the strategy undertaken at Organization 4 'Ecological', as the scale and pattern of attempted change is reminiscent of Hannan and Freeman's (1989) work on organizational ecology (in particular, their contention that organizations are structured systems of routines). Much of Organization 4's efforts to redefine roles, processes, and communications presupposes the view that structural inertia (conditions that impede change) must be overcome by changes of state in structured routines. This is much the sense of Organization's 4's 'experiment' in evolutionary change.

Four Strategies for BPR

The four cases selected can be seen, we argue, as archetypes of different BPR strategies. Using the four domains outlined in our conceptual framework illustrated in Figure 9.1, these strategies are presented as 'polar types' in Table 9.1.

The 'Engineering Strategy' typified by Organization 1 has the characteristics of an improvement project driven by identification of an operational problem where process reengineering is one part of the required business change. We have seen similar characteristics in a BPR programme in a major photocopier company. In both cases it was clear that the firms were no longer competitive in order fulfilment. Benchmarking of best-in-class lead times and inventory management influenced reengineering goals and helped make the case for radical performance improvement. Cross-functional teams of line managers were assembled to design new and integrated cross-functional and cross-entity production, logistics, and inventory processes. Workflow analysis identified redundant steps and time buffers, plus activities which were performed well from a local perspective, but not from a global process level. In each case, one particular IT application was required in the reengineered process. In the semiconductor company it was a world-wide 'reservation system' for order taking and scheduling. In the photocopier company it was a supply-chain decision support system to inform all managers in the nodes between functional organizations and supply-chain processes of time and resource interdependencies across the chain.

The 'Systems Strategy' typified by Organization 2 identifies reengineering opportunities through IS planning, where often investment priorities are positively weighted in favour of BPR projects. For a period in Organization 2 when information systems proposals were made, those with apparent BPR potential were subjected to short 'fly-by' feasibility studies involving benchmarking, rough benefits assessment, and evaluation of management willingness to change. If the outcome was promising, a fuller review of strategic needs, operational performance, and systems requirements was commissioned. In a food-and-drink company the corporate IS group had authority to review all business unit IS plans. If an opportunity was found to initiate a BPR study, a corporately funded consulting team was sent in to do much the same sort of business systems analysis as in Organization 2.

As described earlier, the project work in Organization 2 then took on the character of what one observer has called 'doing information systems work properly'. We see in the systems strategy the application of systems analysis skills at the process level and an emphasis on both workflows and information flows, using traditional and more modern flowcharting techniques. Providing information access and communications for co-ordination becomes the goal of systems design. Projects, however, are most probably led by managers who have performance responsibility for the process, but work in close partnership with the IS function.

The 'Bureaucratic Strategy' uses formal strategic planning to promote and legitimize the idea of formulating and investing in process capabilities as one element of competitive strategy at the SBU level. As epitomized by Organization 3, business strategy-making comprises both product-market-customer decisions and process decisions, the latter concerned with the building of core capabilities to support the former. Typically, the focus of a BPR project becomes a breakthrough activity in the primary value chain, thereby having potentially high customer impact.

In our archetypal case, IS expertise raised BPR awareness by arranging management team seminars and workshops, typically employing both external consultants and in-house BPR expertise. Where breakthrough reengineering projects were identified, the IS function was involved in building new or replacement process infrastructures including IT applications, operational procedures, and performance metrics. Momentum, however, depends on continued commitment of the management team, and, critically, sponsorship and championship by one of its members. Otherwise token or ephemeral BPR initiatives can result in compliance with the formal strategic planning regime.

The 'Ecological Strategy' of Organization 4 is much more of a holistic, cultural approach intended to raise process consciousness and establish a new routine of managerial decision-making. The espoused logic is that if management decision-making processes are redesigned to engage all levels of the organization, BPR initiatives—and related continuous process improvements implemented through specific implementation projects—will result. In Organization 4 the CEO and top-management team began this by creating three 'macro' processes: the Direction Management Process, the Implementation Management Process, and the Understanding Process.

New language and roles were defined to achieve culture change and to raise process consciousness. In two large FMCG (fast-moving consumer goods) companies we have found CEOs who changed the performance measurement systems to emphasize customer service, product development time, quality, and brand share. In both cases, line managers then turned to BPR as a means of initiating performance improvement on these metrics.

In our archetypal case, the CEO believed that he and the management team were engaged in an 'organizational experiment' to achieve a vision of continuous, dynamic adaptation. The IS function had a limited and relatively late role in this endeavour. Systems were to be adapted to report on, and render more visible, process performance. As BPR initiatives were identified, CASE-based modelling software was used to reconceptualize core processes. We select the label 'Ecological' because of the emphasis on creating deep-seated process thinking throughout the organization in the pursuit of organizational adaptation.

These four strategies suggest that there is a richer and wider set of BPR practices being deployed in organizations than has been documented hitherto. Implications arise for both research and practice.

Implications and Conclusions

The research underpinning this paper was done in the spirit of grounded theory (Glaser and Strauss 1967), exploring reengineering initiatives in the field to examine interactions or integration of planning processes and BPR. Following the advice of Eisenhardt (1989), we have selected four distinctive case studies from our sample which demonstrated substantial and interesting variation across the four domains of the framework for analysis in Figure 9.1. The cases suggest four strategies for BPR which we have structured as a taxonomy of polar types or clusterings (Table 1) which can be identified in cases other than those presented here.

Inevitably, a taxonomy based on such inductive and interpretative enquiry is tentative. Nevertheless we suggest that there are several implications for reengineering practice and some potentially promising directions for further research.

Implications for Practice

First, the taxonomy reinforces the view that there is more than one way of initiating and implementing BPR. We do not, at this stage, offer any contingency theories to propose in what contexts each of the BPR strategies may work. Indeed, there may be an element of choice here, particularly as demonstrated by our examples of the ecological strategy, where the CEOs pursued very personal campaigns to change their organizations. Nor can we claim that any strategy is more effective than others. However, our data suggest that the Engineering and Systems strategies may result in more definitive and enduring BPR projects. In contrast, the Bureaucratic and Ecological strategies may have created more widespread process and BPR awareness in the organizations in question.

Indeed, each strategy does appear to favour, produce, or imply a different concept of process. The levels of analysis and the motivations, that we labelled in Table 1 process attributes and process paradigm in use, are substantially different. We do not make any value judgements about each, but we do suggest that the taxonomy is useful in extending whatever process thinking managers and reengineers initially adopt. For example, the more conventional view of BPR, represented by the Engineering strategy as cross-functional workflow optimization, has instant, practical appeal. Considering information systems developments as vehicles for BPR—or BPR as a means of implementing more viable systems—is potentially a further valuable political insight implied by the Systems strategy. Seeing BPR as a means of building requisite, core capabilities, as depicted in the Bureaucratic strategy, is both a way of identifying and selecting reengineering projects and a vehicle for reminding management that business strategy comprises more than just product-market analysis and positioning. Seeing BPR as an opportunity to rethink management processes and improve decision-making, as embodied by the Ecological strategy again widens the reengineering opportunity set as well as suggesting the creation of an organizational context in which BPR projects may be propagated.

The different strategic perspectives also serve to remind practitioners that there may be alternative sources of competitive advantage to that of best-in-class operational performance implied by the Engineering strategy. Indeed, the Systems, Administrative, and Ecological strategies may create in turn more sustainable sources of competitive advantage. The Systems strategy may do so by leveraging firm-specific information assets, the Bureaucratic strategy by aligning process investment with product-market positioning, and the Ecological strategy by achieving deeper-seated changes in managers' mindsets, ultimately manifesting itself in higher quality decisions.

The enabling role of information technology is seen to vary within each strategy, implying that not all BPR projects require substantial investment in IT. An important but not necessarily dominant investment in IT applications is likely under the Engineering and Systems strategies respectively. The idea of process architectures seems to fit the Bureaucratic strategy, especially where core operational capabilities are being laid down. Under the Ecological strategy, information systems are required for quite different purposes, either for modelling new ways of thinking or to direct attention to process metrics in performance measurement.

For IS managers in particular, we also can suggest that the requisite skill set will vary. Creative systems designers may propose sophisticated solutions for process integration within Engineering strategies. The skills of systems analysis, including the rediscovered techniques of operations research, industrial engineering, and organization and methods, can help convert IS projects into more radical BPR exercises under the Systems strategy. Besides building architectures, we have seen IS personnel very much acting as reengineering educators and consultants under Bureaucratic strategies. The expertise—technical and behavioural—of modellers may be required in the Ecological strategy.

Finally, practitioners probably will recognize the importance of sponsorship in Business Process Reengineering, but our taxonomy proposes that the level and character of sponsorship vary widely. In our cases, where CEO sponsorship really mattered was in the Ecological strategy. Other line and staff managers become candidates for sponsorship under the other three remaining strategies.

Directions for Research

Several of the implications for practice also prompt questions for further research. However, the overriding need is to test the taxonomy further for completeness, robustness, and content. Completeness may be addressed by replicating our investigation on a larger sample of BPR initiatives. Testing for robustness of the four (or more) polar type strategies requires more classical research methods, starting with operationalization of our four domains into measurable constructs. Then tighter cluster analysis can be done and tests of association carried out between the BPR strategies and the suggested components.

There also may be a prior or complementary need to test our conceptual framework for analysis—that is, to refine further our 'process alignment model'. This implied the need for integration between the domains of process, strategy, information systems, and change management and control. Certainly, by using this framework for analysis a degree of alignment is suggested in each of our four strategies. The operationalized constructs discussed above could be employed in tests of alignment.

Both academics and practitioners are likely to be interested in more evaluative research. It would be interesting to examine whether any particular BPR strategy outperforms others. Tests of success are notoriously difficult in the planning arena; a variety of quantitative and qualitative assessments would be required of both the process and outcomes of the strategies.

Finally, some obvious contingency tests are possible. For example, are certain BPR strategies associated with differences in planning and control style, organization size, external environment, industry sector, or information processing contexts? Indeed, are they mutually exclusive?

Conclusion

These directions for further research could be important in advancing Business Process Reengineering from the status of a contemporary phenomenon to a more robust management practice with stronger theoretical foundations. We submit that understanding of linkages between Business Process Reengineering and strategic planning is likely to rest in the four domains which made up our initial framework for analysis: process, strategy, information systems, and change management and control. Our taxonomy could provide a useful platform for researchers interested in carrying out more field studies of BPR and strategy. In the meantime it also offers some managerial implications for those actually engaged in business process reengineering. Finally, in a volume devoted to the organizational dimension of information management we might conclude by suggesting that our taxonomy represents different levels of organizational analysis of business process engineering in action.

References

Andrews, K. R. (1982), *The Concept of Corporate Strategy*, Homewood, Ill.: Irwin.
Bain, J. S. (1968), *Industrial Organization*, 2nd edn., New York: Wiley.

Barley, S. R., Meyer, G. W., and Gash, D. C. (1988), 'Cultures of Culture: Academics, Practitioners, and the Pragmatics of Normative Control', *Administrative Science Quarterly*, vol. 33, pp. 24–60.

Barney, J. B. (1986), 'Strategic Factor Markets: Expectations, Luck and Business Strategy', *Management Science*, vol. 32, pp. 1,231–41.

Beer, M. (1980), *Organization Change and Development*, Santa Monica, Calif.: Goodyear Publishing Co.

Campbell, D. T. (1975), ' "Degrees of Freedom" and the Case Study', *Comparative Political Studies*, vol. 8, no. 2, pp. 178–93.

Caron, J. R., Jarvenpaa, S. L., and Stoddard, D. B. (1994), 'Business Reengineering at CIGNA Corporation: Experiences and Lessons From the First Five Years', *MIS Quarterly*, vol. 18, no. 3, pp. 233–50.

Cash, J. I., McFarlan, F. W., and McKinney, J. L. (1983), *Corporate Information Systems Management: Text and Cases*, Homewood, Ill.: Irwin.

Daft, R. L., and Lewin, A. Y. (1992), 'Where are the Theories for the "New" Organizational Forms? An Editorial Essay', *Organization Science*, vol. 4, no. 4, pp. i–vi.

Davenport, T. H. (1992), *Process Innovation*, Boston: Harvard Business School Press.

—— and Short, J. E. (1990), 'The New Industrial Engineering: Information Technology and Business Process Redesign', *Sloan Management Review*, vol. 31, no. 4, pp. 11–21.

Davenport, T. H., and Stoddard, D. B. (1994), 'Reengineering: Business Change of Mythic Proportions?', *MIS Quarterly*, vol. 18, no. 2, pp. 121–7.

Drazin, R., and Sandelands, L. (1992), 'Autogensis: A Perspective on the Process of Organizing', *Organization Science*, vol. 3, no. 2, pp. 230–49.

Earl, M. J. (1987), 'Information Systems Strategy Formulation', in R. J. Boland, Jnr., and R. A. Hirscheim (eds.), *Critical Issues in Information Systems Research*, Chichester: J. Wiley.

—— (1994), 'The New and the Old of Business Process Redesign', *Journal of Strategic Information Systems*, vol. 3, no. 1, pp. 5–22.

—— and Khan, B. (1994), 'How New is Business Process Redesign?', *European Management Journal*, vol. 12, no. 1, pp. 20–30.

Eisenhardt, K. M. (1989), 'Building Theories from Case Study Research', *Academy of Management Journal*, vol. 35, no. 4, pp. 699–738.

Emery, J. C. (1969), *Organizational Planning and Control Systems*, New York: Macmillan.

Forrester, J. W. (1961), *Industrial Dynamics*, Cambridge, Mass.: MIT Press.

Galbraith, J. R. (1973), *Designing Complex Organizations*, Reading, Mass.: Addison-Wesley.

Gersick, C. J. G. (1991), 'Revolutionary Change Theories: A Multilevel Exploration of the Punctuated Equilibrum Paradigm', *Academy of Management Review*, vol. 16, no. 1, pp. 10–36.

Glaser, B. G., and Strauss, A. L. (1967), *The Discovery of Grounded Theory: Strategies for Qualitative Research*, New York: Aldine Publishing Co.

Grover, V., Fiedler, K. D., and Teng, J. T. C. (1994), 'Exploring the Success of Information Technology Enabled Business Process Reengineering', *IEEE Transactions on Information Management*, vol. 41, no. 3, pp. 276–83.

Hage, J., and Aiken, M. (1970), *Social Change in Complex Organizations*, New York: Random House.

Hammer, M. (1990), 'Reengineering Work: Don't Automate, Obliterate', *Harvard Business Review*, vol. 90, no. 4, pp. 104–12.

—— and Champy, J. (1993), *Reengineering the Corporation: A Manifesto for Business Revolution*, New York: Harper Business.

Hannan, M. T., and Freeman, J. (1989), *Organizational Ecology*, Cambridge, Mass.: Harvard University Press.

Harrington, H. J. (1991), *Business Process Improvement*, New York: McGraw Hill.

Henderson, J. C., and Sifonis, J. G. (1988), 'The Value of Strategic Planning: Understanding Consistency, Validity and IS Markets', *MIS Quarterly*, vol. 12, no. 2, pp. 187–200.

Henderson, J. C., and Venkatraman, N. (1993), 'Strategic Alignment: Leveraging Information Technology for Transforming Organizations', *IBM Systems Journal*, vol. 32, no. 1, pp. 4–16.

Hughes, W. R. (1971), 'Scale Frontiers in Electric Power', in W. M. Capron (ed.), *Technological Change in Regulated Industries*, Washington, DC: Brookings Institute.

Kaplan, R. B., and Murdoch, L. (1991), 'Core Process Renewal', *The McKinsey Quarterly*, vol. 2, pp. 15–26.

Kaplan, R., and Norton, D. (1992), 'The Balanced Scorecard: Measures that Drive Performance', *Harvard Business Review* (Jan.–Feb.).

King, W. R. (1978), 'Strategic Planning for Management Information Systems', *MIS Quarterly*, vol. 2, pp. 27–37.

—— and Zmud, R. W. (1983), 'Managing Information Systems Policy Planning, Strategic Planning and Operational Planning', *Proceedings of the Second ICIS* (Dec.).

Lederer, A. L., and Mendelow, A. L. (1989), 'Coordination of Information Systems Plans with Business Plans', *Journal of Management Information Systems*, vol. 6, no. 2, pp. 5–19.

Lee, A. S. (1989), 'A Scientific Methodology for MIS Case Studies', *MIS Quarterly*, vol. 13, no. 1, pp. 33–50.

Malone, T. W., and Crowston, K. (1994), 'The Interdisciplinary Study of Coordination', *A C M Computing Surveys*, vol. 26, no. 1, pp. 87–119.

Mintzberg, H. (1990), 'The Design School: Reconsidering the Basic Premises of Strategic Management', *Strategic Management Journal*, vol. 11, pp. 171–95.

—— and Waters, J. A. (1985), 'Of Strategies, Deliberate and Emergent', *Strategic Management Journal*, vol. 6, pp. 257–72.

Mohr, L. B. (1982), *Explaining Organizational Behaviour*, San Francisco: Jossey-Bass.

Pettigrew, A. M. (1992), 'The Character and Significance of Strategy Process Research', *Strategic Management Journal* (special issue), 5–16.

Pfeffer, J., and Salancik, G. (1978), *The External Control of Organizations*, New York: Harper and Row.

Porter, M. E. (1980), *Competitive Strategy: Techniques for Analysing Industries and Competitors*, New York: Free Press.

Prahalad, C. K., and Hamel, G. (1990), 'The Core Competence of the Corporation', *Harvard Business Review* (May–June), 79–91.

Pyburn, P. (1983), 'Linking the MIS Plan and Corporate Strategy: An Exploratory Study', *MIS Quarterly*, vol. 7, no. 2, pp. 1–14.

Rogers, E. M. (1974), *Diffusion of Innovations*, New York: Free Press.

Rumelt, R. P. (1974), *Strategy, Structure and Economic Performance*, Cambridge, Mass.: Harvard University Press.

Sampler, J. L., and Short, J. E. (1994), 'An Examination of Information Technology's Impact on the Value of Information and Expertise: Implications for Organizational Change', *Journal of Management Information Systems*, vol. 11, no. 2, pp. 59–73.

Senge, P. M. (1990), *The Fifth Discipline*, New York: Doubleday.

Short, J. E., and Venkatraman, N. (1992), 'Beyond Business Process Redesign: Redefining Baxter's Network', *Sloan Management Review*, vol. 34, no. 1, pp. 7–21.

Simons, R. (1994), *Levers of Control: How Managers Use Innovative Control Systems to Drive Strategic Renewal*, Boston: Harvard Business School Press.

Tushman, M., and Romanelli, E. (1985), 'Organizational Evolution: A Metamorphosis Model of Convergence and Reorientation', in L. L. Cummings and B. M. Staw (eds.), *Research in Organizational Behaviour*, Greenwich, Conn.: JAI Press, 171–222.

Tushman, M., Newman, W., and Romanelli, E. (1986), 'Managing the Unsteady Pace of Organizational Revolution', *California Management Review* (Fall), 29–44.

Tyre, M. J., and Orlikowski, W. J. (1994), 'Windows of Opportunity: Temporal Patterns of Technological Adaptation in Organizations', *Organization Science*, vol. 5, no. 1, pp. 98–118.

van de Ven, A. H., and Poole, M. S. (1990), 'Methods for Study Innovation Development in the Minnesota Innovation Research Programme', *Organization Science*, vol. 1, pp. 313–35.

Venkatraman, N. (1991), 'Information Technology-Induced Business Reconfiguration: The New Strategic Management Challenge', in M. S. Scott-Morton (ed.), *The Corporation of the 1990s*, Oxford: Oxford University Press.

Victor, B., and Blackburn, R. S. (1987), 'Interdependence: An Alternative Conceptualization', *Academy of Management Review*, vol. 12, no. 3, pp. 486–98.

Walton, M. (1990), *Deming Management at Work*, New York: G. P. Putnam & Sons.

Ward, J. M. (1989), 'Integrating Information Systems into Business Strategies', *Long Range Planning*, 20/3 (June), 19–29.

Weick, K. E. (1979), *The Social Psychology of Organizing*, 2nd edn., New York: Random House.

Wernerfelt, B. (1984), 'A Resource Based View of the Firm', *Strategic Management Journal*, vol. 5, no. 12, pp. 171–80.

Winter, S. G. (1987), 'Knowledge and Competence as Strategic Assets', in D. Teece (ed.), *The Competitive Challenge*, Cambridge, Mass.: Ballinger, 159–84.

SECTION III

FOREWORD

In the 1980s the IS function grew rapidly in many organizations, sometimes becoming the largest function in information-intensive firms. In the 1990s economic, technological, and organizational factors are combining to change the shape of the function and to often lead to 'downsizing'. IS *activities*, however, still continue and sometimes grow; specialists may no longer be the dominant group but users may have many more information-oriented responsibilities. So how to organize IS remains an important issue for IS executives, general managers, and line managers alike. Some valuable research of practical benefit on these matters is reported in this section.

The organization of IS can be seen in two dimensions: the centralization versus decentralization question and the issue of users versus specialists. The first is addressed by Earl *et al.*, where the evidence suggests that *effectiveness* in IS is dependent upon the IS function being designed to fit the characteristics, especially structure, of the host organization. This may seem like common sense, but at least four significant further points are made. First, *efficiency* in IS is not so dependent on organizational fit. The operational, service, or utility activities of IS can be run efficiently anywhere, within or without the organization. Then combining the efficiency and effectiveness criteria, Earl *et al.* suggest five ideal types of IS configuration and how they should be selected. The drivers of change in organizing IS, however, are not only seen to be the characteristics of the host organization but the track record or heritage of IS performance. Finally, in most multidivisional organizations the federal form is seen to be the most viable. Not only does it provide a means of balancing centralization and decentralization, but it allows less costly structural changes to be made over time. And as Earl *et al.* show, change seems to be continual.

Feeny *et al.*, using data from the same project which underpins the first chapter in this section, address the user–specialist dimensions. They find that integration of users and specialists is important whatever the structural configuration of IS. This is because there are differences between the two groups, each of which may have different roles, bringing different capabilities to the different activities of IS. Feeny *et al.* propose a contingency model of user–specialist integration, where the determining factor is relative maturity of the information technology in question. By 'relative' they mean the degree of experience of using and managing a particular technology in a particular organization. This hypothesis is closely related to the underpinning of both 'stages theories' and assimilation frameworks of managing IS. However, the Feeny *et al.* model seems to provide insights on a number of issues related to all information technologies throughout their life-cycle.

Hodgkinson picks up the federal IS organization, by examining the role of the corporate IS group. He documents what they seek to do and suggests twenty-six possible activities. The extent and emphasis of these activities is found to relate to another characteristic of the host organization, namely, strategic management style. Two contrasting IS management styles are then suggested. Identifying which style is appropriate could be the way to resolving two eternal IS management questions: do we need any centralized or corporate IS activities and if so, of what kind? Hodgkinson, within his analysis of the role of corporate IS groups, also makes an important distinction between activities to do with the strategic management of IT and those to do with provision of central services.

This distinction has some relevance in the next chapter. Willcocks and Fitzgerald examine the impact of outsourcing on the shape of the IS function. Whether outsourcing of IT activities makes sense is a topic reserved until a later section. The fact is that many large organizations have turned to outsourcing of IT in whole or in part and this raises the question of the shape and roles of the 'residual IS organization'. Evidence from UK case studies is analysed to propose seven key tasks such units may need to undertake.

A major discontinuity in IS organization can be the implementation of a merger or acquisition. Not only is the evidence on the financial returns of mergers worrying, but we do hear anecdotes of these marriages not being consummated due to IT difficulties. Linder studied in depth the merger experience of two banks. She found the reality differed substantially from the rhetoric. When it comes to merging IS, the potential for drama and conflict is high. Linder found that the merging IS functions became competitive and that thus, not surprisingly, political behaviours ensue. Technical integration was not usually the problem: organizational matters dominated, and as managers focused on internal integration of IS departments the information requirements of the market-place—new products and services—were ignored.

Linder identifies several risk factors in mergers and acquisitions and identifies some important lessons for managing through each episode of the IS marriage. Merging IS, from this perspective, becomes a project and some of her ideas provide a good linkage to the next section.

10

Configuring the IS Function in Complex Organizations

MICHAEL J. EARL, BRIAN EDWARDS, AND DAVID F. FEENY

Introduction

How to configure the Information Systems (IS) function in large, complex organizations appears to be an eternal management issue (Dickson *et al.* 1984; Niederman *et al.* 1991). This is because it is inherently difficult and because circumstances change. Commonly phrased as a centralization versus decentralization question, it is also often perceived by managers as the issue which most impedes their organization's ability to get value for money from IT.

The two basic arguments are often expressed thus. Centralization of the IS function is necessary to reap economies of scale, ensure the ability to integrate applications or share data, and optimize the use of scarce resources. Conversely, decentralization of the IS function is necessary to ensure that IS responds to real business needs, to encourage managers to get involved with IS, and often to add control of IS resources to the autonomy that local units possess. These arguments may appear to be no different from the normal tensions of the centralization versus decentralization debate at large. However, often there are at least two special characteristics at work. First, information *technology* does raise important questions of scale, infrastructure planning, risk, and change. Secondly, information *systems* can often be an emotional issue. Since information is often at the heart of power, arguments about the control of information processing can seem critical in the politics of organizational design. Indeed, nowadays information systems are something everybody has a concern about and thus can be guaranteed to stimulate a debate—at least in complex organizations.

By complex organizations we mean large, multi-business unit corporations. The authors studied fourteen such companies in Europe in 1987. We were attracted to studying the configuration of the IS function for three reasons:

1. We had observed that it was a recurring issue in many organizations we knew.

2. Very little empirical research had been reported in the literature—
   nor has been since.
3. We noted an apparent conundrum. In at least one sector, there
   were several different configurations in place.

This sector was the automobile sector. In the UK, the then-British Leyland
group had first made its IS function a separate profit centre and subsidiary, BL Systems, subsequently known as ISTEL.[1] It was then sold off in a
management buy-out, but supplying information services to Leyland companies and to the market-place in general. In contrast, General Motors
had acquired an IS company—EDS—to provide information services both
inside and outside the corporation. Ford, however, relied on its own IS
function, which was centralized at regional level. Meanwhile, Volvo had
recently decentralized much of the IS function from a central bureau to
its product divisions.

So one sector displayed at least four IS configurations. So did one major
British company. British Petroleum then had a central IS bureau (ISS)
which ran corporate utilities and could bid for divisional IS work. ISS
could develop up to 10 per cent of its activity level to external clients.
There was also a corporate IS policy-setting group (ISA). BP then owned
a software business, Scicon. In addition, each line of business had its own
IS function. So if the configuration of the IS function should be aligned
with the host organization, the BP example suggested this might be quite
a complex matter.

However, other forces seemed to influence the configuration of IS. One
was technological change, evidenced by the ever-increasing distribution of
hardware, reducing costs of telecommunications, and increased availability of software. These trends appeared to increase the feasibility of devolving IS to business units, or sharing and networking information services,
or giving more information processing autonomy to end-users.

Another, sometimes emotional, force was IS performance. If end-users
or business units became disenchanted with a central or corporate IS function, the pressure built up for both decentralization and distribution of
information processing. Alternatively, whatever the current configuration,
if IS was perceived not to be performing some change in structure was
prescribed.

So the research questions were:

1. Is there a preferred way of configuring the IS function?
2. Are there any factors which shape the configuration of IS and give
   guidance on a preferred solution?

The 1987 study suggested answers to both these questions. It also yielded
another insight. However decentralized a company's IS function became,

---

[1] Subsequently ISTEL was acquired by AT&T.

we noticed that often end-users perceived IS to be centralized in that often they felt remote from, and disenchanted with, the IS specialists. We realized that often past work had confused or conflated two organizational axes of importance in IS (Fig. 10.1). There is the centralization versus decentralization question but also the users versus specialists question. This paper addresses the first. A companion paper tackles the second.[2]

Since 1987 our research has continued, especially in case-study mode, because the configuration issue arises in ever new forms. Consider the following examples from the 1990s:

* A decentralized conglomerate with strong interests in publishing and leisure industries began to wonder if for the first time a group IS presence was required. It was evident that media technologies—important across the group—were converging with other information technologies. Concerns arose about transfer of learning across IS departments and also the ability to pursue new business opportunities based on technological convergence, but which required collaboration or integration between business units.

* A petrochemical company decentralized most of its IS activities, including downsizing its corporate IS department on a grand scale. As the group IT steering committee ran out of steam and the residual corporate IS group found it difficult either to discover a vision for corporate-wide IS or to pursue IT initiatives, the question arose whether now to complete the decentralization started two years earlier. However, the CEO worried that possible group synergies might be lost in the long run if no central IS presence was retained.

* A health-care products company found that it had to integrate the selling and distribution of products across five divisions in order to compete effectively with a more centralized, integrated rival and to satisfy the one-stop purchasing habits of its customers. A new IS organization across these five divisions had to be created to meet this challenge.

* A branded consumer products company created a reporting level of four sectors between head office and its former product divisions. The IS function was asked how it would respond when hitherto there had been both a corporate IS group and divisional IS units.[3]

* An oil company comprised three regional groupings each with its own IS organization. The CEO was looking for cost savings through rationalization and downsizing. Despite external advice that achieving group-wide economies of scale in information processing rarely worked, the company set up one global IS configuration.

We see in these cases, first, that continuing technological change can induce new questions about the configuration of IS. Next we see the belief

---

[2] See Chap. 11 by Feeny, Earl, and Edwards in this volume.
[3] This is documented in a case study, 'Grand Metropolitan PLC', Centre for Research in Information Management Case Study CS93/1, London Business School, 1993.

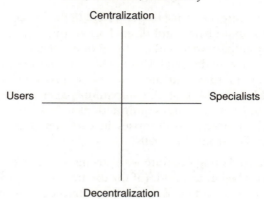

Fig. 10.1. *The two dimensions of IS configuration*

that IS can contribute to synergy even in quite decentralized organizations. We also see that quite often competitive strategies force a rethink of IS organization and that it is not uncommon to see consolidation of information processing, not necessarily at the centre, but at some intermediate level. The consumer brands company reminds us that as new organizational forms evolve, the IS function may have to realign itself. Finally, we see that the increasing demand for more efficient information processing can lead to a rethink of IS configurations.

In other words, the policy question of how to configure the IS function is not likely to go away. In this chapter drawn from our original research we suggest some organizational design principles which may stand the test of time. We also discuss some trends and experiences evident in more recent cases we have studied.

Theoretical Foundations

The IS Literature

The early information systems literature often related the issues of chargeout and responsibility accounting to the question of decentralizing or centralizing the IS function. In those days (Dearden and Nolan 1973; McFarlan *et al.* 1973), the evolution of mainframe computing tended to dictate relative centralization of hardware, but there was some choice on the location of IS development activities and management planning and control of IS. Chargeout was seen as one way of introducing more accountability into centralized mainframe environments and perhaps practices varied with an organization's position on the Gibson and Nolan stage model of EDP growth (1977).

When distributed computing became possible, new organization possibilities emerged. Buchanan and Linowes (1980) developed an analytical framework for resolving these configuration choices. They proposed a generic set of IS activities and classified them into operations, development, and control, implying choices at each level. They indicated what might be centralized or decentralized but, as has been the tendency since the distributed era, perhaps failed to distinguish between the user–specialist axis and the centralization–decentralization axis in analysing IS configurations.

The recognition that IT could be a strategic resource and was beginning to shape competition in certain sectors led McFarlan *et al.* (1983) to propose their strategic grid. This implied that organizations or their segments could be approaching and managing IS differently according to the strategic dependence on, and future importance of, IS. This notion that IS management, and thus configuration, could vary by firm was developed by McFarlan and McKenney (1983), when they suggested that choices were influenced also by host-organization structure, geographical spread, and the management control system. Zmud *et al.* (1986) posited the idea of an 'information economy' in organizations as the IS function's monopoly of IT resources weakened. They observed that responsibility for different technologies and different aspects of IS was migrating to local organizational units and to different specialist groups. This was leading to governance issues and possibly the need for federal approaches to IS configuration.

La Belle and Nyce (1987), reporting on a configuration exercise in Manufacturers Hanover Corporation, described how the tensions between centralization and decentralization of IS had led to such a federal resolution. This exercise had been prompted by Manufacturers Hanover's creation of a new decentralized business sector structure on the one hand and the realization that earlier decentralization of IS had created impediments to information-sharing and applications integration on the other.

Contemporaneously Dearden (1987) had predicted the withering away of the IS function as end-users took over much of their own information processing and many larger scale utility and development activities were outsourced to third parties. Dearden certainly spotted two key trends, but the iconoclastic scenario he painted had not come to pass by 1992, which was the time-scale he predicted. Von Simson (1990), in contrast, three years later claimed that a degree of recentralization of the IS function was happening as firms strove for increasing systems and technological integration, economies of scale, and maximizing the use of scarce specialists. He argued for a federal configuration in complex organizations or what he called the 'centrally decentralised' IS organization.

Organization Theory

Most of the above contributions have been inductive, interpreting trends and events in the evolution of the IS function. However, the centralization versus decentralization question is not new and more universal insights may be available from the literatures of organization theory and general management.

Lawrence and Lorsch (1967) introduced their language of differentiation and integration to describe how organizations respond to technology and market factors. They pointed out that organizations deal with their external environment by creating units—often 'divisions'—which each seek to master a particular part of the firm's environment (or a particular technology). Lawrence and Lorsch described these units as differentiated because of inevitable differences in 'cognitive and emotional orientations' between them, as well as their contrasting specialist skills. Differentiation, however, leads to a need for integration, in particular, collaboration between units in the interests of the organization as a whole. Consequently, as Lawrence and Lorsch found, organizations facing turbulence in their technologies and markets need to achieve high differentiation and high levels of integration simultaneously. This was not likely to be achieved simply by formal organizational hierarchy to resolve conflicts, but more by creation of specific roles, liaison devices, and management processes working towards integration.

The implications of Lawrence and Lorsch for configuring IS may be these. IT is a core technology for many enterprises today and is also a source of environmental turbulence. The creation of (differentiated) specialist IS units is therefore to be expected. However, these are unlikely to be effective unless special management processes and organizational devices are created to integrate these units with the host organization. Secondly, if there are differentiated business units with their own IS units, business unit integration may depend partly on the provision of information systems. Furthermore, there will be a need for some collaboration or integration across the local IS units.

Williamson's (1975) transaction-costs approach to questions of organizational design suggests that any given set of transactions can be conducted internally or externally. Choice depends on which option is more efficient, incurring the lower transaction cost. Organizations exist and grow because not all transactions can be efficiently subcontracted to the market. Williamson's organizational-failure framework shows that external contracting can be inefficient when various combinations of environmental and human factors prevail. These include environmental uncertainty combined with Simon's (1955) 'bounded rationality' of organizational decision-making; 'small numbers' of bidders combined with supplier or market 'opportunism'; and 'information impactedness' or asymmetry between parties combined with opportunism, small numbers, or bounded rationality. Williamson then classifies a number of available organizational forms: Unitary or Functional Enterprise (U-Form), Holding Company (H-Form), Multidivisional (M-Form) and its derivatives, and Mixed (X-Form). He concludes that for organizations in complex environments the pure M-Form leads to superior performance: divisions have autonomous responsibility for operations, whilst corporate management confines itself to giving strategic direction, designing internal controls to achieve congruence between autonomous business unit behaviour and corporate goals, and seeking optimally to manage and allocate cash resources.

Interpreting Williamson for IS management, we can posit that organizations will continue to retain at least a partial in-house IS function since the factors which warn against contracting out are often present in abundance for IT. Secondly, for complex (or multi-business unit) organizations, the M-Form structure for the in-house IS function would seem optimal. Such a structure would comprise location of some IS activities within business units plus maintenance of a central IS group concerned with policies in the interests of the organization as a whole.

A related economics perspective on organizational design comes from agency theory (Jensen and Meckling 1976). This distinguishes principals— often conceived of as shareholders or employers or superiors—from agents, who may be the corresponding managers, employees, or subordinates in an agency relationship. The development of agency theory has recognized that the values and interests of the principal and agent can differ, that often agents have informational advantages over principals and that incentives need to be constructed to engineer appropriate behaviour. Also the theory distinguishes between 'decision control' (the ratification and monitoring of decisions by principals) and 'decision management' (implementation of ratified decisions and generation of proposals for resource utilization). Clearly, in the centralization versus decentralization debate the corporate office is the principal and the business unit the agent. This leads into addressing the balance between direction and control and autonomy and responsiveness. In the IS context, agency theory can inform us about the need for reserved powers, for monitoring of risks and for corporate information reporting. It is perhaps interesting that LaBelle and Nyce (1987) talked of the search for an equilibrium point between central control of policy and resources and decentralized ownership of information processing.

Such a concept of balance is inherent in federal models of organization as advocated, for instance, by Drucker (1964) and more recently spelled out in terms of subsidiarity, interdependence, uniform ways of doing things, separation of powers, and twin citizenship by Handy (1992). Indeed, we might note that Vancil and Buddrus (1978) even recognize that the decentralized form of organization is a balancing act of 'managerial ambiguity by design'. In other words, federal structures are likely to be commonplace amongst complex organizations but will need considerable managing and subtlety in design. IS configurations may follow suit and may never be quite neat and tidy, certainly not permanent, and always in need of processes to accompany structure.

To return to Lawrence and Lorsch, their contribution built on the work of Burns and Stalker (1961) and Woodward (1965), in that they were advancing a contingency theory of organizations, namely that different environments, technologies—and other variables—were likely to require different organizational designs. This thinking influenced management control theory, and in 1980 Otley proposed a model whereby the firm's environment and perhaps strategy influenced the design of organizational and control arrangements which with other intervening variables (such as managers' abilities) would influence organizational performance. We adapted this framework for our 1987 study (Fig. 10.2) as a way of both exploring alternative IS configurations and of seeking whether any particular factors shape a preferred set of arrangements. This underpinned our methodology and is developed in the next section.

Methodology

In 1987 fourteen large European organizations were examined from the following sectors: insurance, oil and chemicals, automobiles, food and drink, chemicals and pharmaceuticals, electronics, paper, retailing, aerospace, and local government. The investigation comprised field studies, normally interviewing a senior 'IS executive', a senior user manager (and if he managed a local unit, his IS manager), and a senior corporate executive to whom IS reported. Interviews were semi-structured, following a questionnaire, but also encouraging discussion and reflection. Through these interviews and with back-up work, more structured data were collected either of a descriptive nature or in the opinion/satisfaction-rating mode.

Each organization was complex in the sense of comprising multiple business units and large (sales revenue from £1 billion to £27 billion). The fourteen organizations represented a continuum of IS configurations from centralized to decentralized; indeed, they represented all the forms in Table 10.1 which we discuss below. IS budgets ranged from £13 million to £200 million. Our entry-point was through the IS director and he selected the other interviewees—a possible sample bias. However, we did find that non-IS executives were far from reluctant to take a critical (in the strict sense) view of IS activities and performance.

The model in Figure 10.2 drove our data collection. It proposed five independent or contingent variables which might influence what we soon called IS organizational 'arrangements', although configuration, or structure, was our focus and is the emphasis reported here. We did find that, for example, organizational and control choices were interrelated. We were also conscious of the Lawrence and Lorsch observation that processes, policies, and personal action as well as structure are involved in resolving the centralization–decentralization debate (or more correctly differentiation and integration). 'Arrangements' became our collective noun for these organizational features.

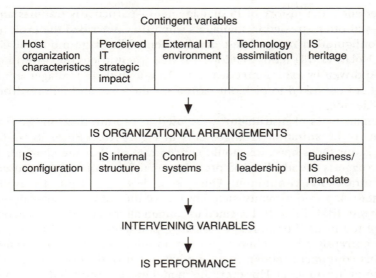

Fig. 10.2. *A contingency model of IS organization*

The contingent variables were suggested by the theoretical foundations above.[4] Host organization characteristics were defined as structure and management style. Respondents were asked to select which of Williamson's (1975) six organizational forms best described their organization's structure. We used an instrument from past IS research to capture interviewees' perceptions of the organization's preferred management style. This was Pyburn's (1983) four categories of planning and control decision behaviour, namely personal informal, personal formal, written formal, and written informal.

Respondents were asked to position their firm on the McFarlan *et al.* (1983) strategic grid as a way of capturing the perceived IT strategic impact. The Gibson and Nolan stage model was used to try and capture technology assimilation. Benchmarks were developed for six categories of IT to help respondents position the firm in one of the four stages of initiation, expression, formalization, and maturity.

The external IT environment was assessed by asking respondents to classify the significance of a number of established and emerging technologies. Since some writers argue that technology development has influenced IS configuration, this seemed important. Technologies assessed included personal computers, local area networks, expert systems, and mainframe computing.

IS heritage was the fifth independent variable and was more a prejudice of the researchers than a contingency suggested by the literature. In our

---

[4] The instruments used to represent these variables can be found in Feeny *et al.* (1989).

experience, the history of IS management—particularly traumas and crises—was often stressed by managers when they described the evolution of IS configuration or the latest development. The stage model of Gibson and Nolan (1974) tends to adopt this view when it sees the 'growth curve' being driven by experiential learning. In our study IS management interviewees were asked to pick out significant successes and failures from the past decade.

Similar types of instrument[5] were used to capture data on the five elements of organization arrangements in Figure 10.2. Since IS configuration is our focus here, we should concentrate on this one element. Table 10.1 suggests five idealized IS organizational forms on the centralization–decentralization continuum. These were developed from a consultancy framework previously constructed by one of the authors—Edwards—in his work with IBM. Table 10.1 seemed to contain all the configurational options suggested in the literature. We asked respondents to identify which form they currently adopted and to give an opinion on any future trend.

This contingent model, then, guided our investigation and generated research instruments. However, the model was not intended to be a straitjacket in our enquiry, just as we do not suggest that it provides a deterministic explanation of IS configuration. The aim was to discover guidelines for the organizational design of the IS function and to capture what were the important lessons and trends in the centralization versus decentralization debate. The expectation was that at least some of the independent variables would appear significant and that exploration of both the dependent and independent variables would demonstrate why they were important and how they could be satisfied. Use of such a multi-variate framework and the semi-structured mode of enquiry might lead to largely interpretative results of a propositional nature, but the investigation and analysis were being disciplined by a prior line of argument suggested by the literature and past research.

It did seem important to make some assessment of IS performance in assessing different IS configurations, and we chose two traditional constructs from management thinking: efficiency and effectiveness. As the specification of these measures became clear during the fieldwork, they are more appropriately explained in the next section.

Results

Trends in Configuration

The sample of organizations investigated deliberately represented a spectrum of IS configurations. Table 10.2 records how many of each ideal

---

[5] See Feeny *et al.* (1989).

Table 10.1. *Five ways to structure IS*

- *Corporate Service*: IS is a unified function reporting to corporate management. There may be distributed equipment, but it is under the operational control of central IS. If business units have people whose focus is systems they are best described as formal IS contact points, or negotiators.
- *Internal Bureau*: IS is again unified as described above, but it is run as a business within the organization and reports similarly to other business units. Its business is wholly or largely with other business units in the group, which it charges for its services. Business units may or may not be constrained to use the Internal Bureau to the exclusion of all other suppliers.
- *Business Venture*: Similar to the IS business unit, but there is a clear mission to obtain significant revenue for itself (and ultimately therefore for the group) by selling products or services outside the group as well as inside. Indications of this mode would be published tariffs, marketing literature, dedicated external salesmen, some products which are not employed internally at all, or external revenue targets.
- *Decentralised*: IS is a distributed function. Each business unit contains its own IS capability under its own control, or elects to employ commercial data services. There is no central IS unit or responsibility except for the support of corporate headquarters functions. Corporate management review the unit's capital and budget submissions for IS only to the extent required by general financial planning and control procedures.
- *Federal*: IS is a distributed function, with each business unit containing and largely controlling its own IS capability. However, there is in addition a central IS unit reporting to corporate management which has responsibility for defined aspects of policy and architecture across the organization, and which may deliver some common or shared services. It may or may not be coincident with the IS unit for corporate HQ.

form (from Table 10.1) existed in the sample in 1983 and in 1987 when we studied them. It also presents a forecast four years on, based on an interpretation of the respondents' comments on current concerns and significant trends. We have also added a 1993 column which records the situation (according to our own monitoring) six years after the study. The *federal* form is seen to dominate in recent years. However (to be discussed later), the 1993 version of federal in some cases is more decentralized than in 1987.

In the ideal federal form the IS function is co-ordinated from the centre, but IS activities are divided between central and distributed units. Many shades of the federal configuration are possible with different patterns of resource and responsibility distribution. In six of the eight federal structures encountered in 1987 much or all of the operational services were provided from the centre. Each of the federal structures had evolved from a previously centralized form where the initial evolutionary step generally was to install an IS manager and/or user support resources in business units. In this scenario, devolution of development resources may follow, but devolution of operations usually does not because the existing

Table 10.2. *Trends in IS configuration*

IS configuration	Number in sample			
	1983	1987	1981 (outlook)	1993 (actual)
Corporate service	5	2	1	1
Internal bureau/ business venture	4	3	0	0
Federal	3	8	9	9
Decentralized	2	1	4	4

service is generally well regarded. In most cases a strong development capability had been retained centrally in order sometimes to develop common application systems for use across the organization and often to provide a contracting bespoke service. Central development teams, however, seemed to meet with far less success than centralized delivery services.

In the period since 1987 (both forecast and 'actual'), the federal structure looks to be the most stable form as well as the most common in the sample. It can be adapted to align well with most forms of complex, multidivisional organization. It perhaps represents a design space in which compromises can be accommodated, balances evolve over time, different types of IS resource get distributed differently, and multiple dimensions of most organization structure be serviced. In the two cases where the federal structure was perhaps under threat in 1987, it was because the host organization was moving towards being a clear holding company structure and the need for any IS unit at the corporate level was being questioned. In both cases a reduced corporate IS unit survives, focusing on policy matters and pursuing any remaining economies of scale in information processing (for example, data communications networks).

In contrast, the pure corporate service form of IS structure has been waning. Only one instance in the sample has survived, because it sits comfortably within the centralized UK structure of its host organization. Indeed, the future of the corporate service IS structure is probably only assured within centralized host organizations, as may be found in the retailing sector, for example.

Although only a marginal decline in the number of internal bureau or business venture forms was recorded in 1987, they were predicted to decline further in the outlook period, did so, and are judged to be unstable. Internal customers of the sample bureau and business venture structures generally were nervous about relying heavily on market-oriented IS units for important services and were seeking to reduce their dependence on them. They also expressed concern that such units can soon lose touch with, and become less well informed about, their host organization, its units, and their needs. In the case of the business venture forms, customers also feared they might allocate their key resources to more lucrative sectors outside, or alternatively use internal customers as 'guinea pigs' for product and staff development. It should be noted, however, that the outlook prediction of decline in business unit or business venture structures does not imply that they will cease to exist. Rather they will cease to be the dominant structure in an organization's overall mix of IS arrangements. Indeed, they could become one of the sources of supply in a federal IS structure.

The decentralized form in the sample had reduced from two to one. In the company which had rescinded its decentralization of IS, a powerful corporate headquarters wanted to bring in controls over IS in line with its grip in all other areas of activity. However, the decentralized structure would seem to have a good fit in holding companies and it could become the dominant IS form in those organizations. Three host organizations originally were trending in that direction, in addition to the one clear case already within the study sample. The trend was fulfilled by 1993, notably in corporations with a holding company mentality and where the future of component businesses was perpetually uncertain.

This analysis suggests that only the centralized, decentralized, or federal configurations are likely to survive or be the options that corporations select. A centralized IS function seems to make sense in a purely centralized host organization. Equally, a decentralized IS function seems to fit the structure and spirit of purely decentralized hosts. In more complex organizations, the federal IS configuration seems to offer best fit and be very adaptable. These arguments collectively suggest that host organization characteristics may be a key contingent variable when configuring the IS function. Of course, the bureau or business venture would fit any decentralized or federal host organization in that it becomes a line of business. However, experience seems to show that making a business out of IS is not what organizations should be doing—the rest of the business suffers because integration of the differentiated unit seems to break down or be inhibited.

The Contingent Factors

Host organization characteristics, then, seem to influence IS configuration. The 1987 study deliberately examined a spectrum of IS configuration. What was not anticipated was the degree of change in *host organizational design and characteristics* most had recently experienced. Ten out of thirteen organizations had undergone major change in structure and control in the first half of the 1980s. Mostly, there had been a new emphasis on business and business unit definition, usually in terms of product groupings, together with a clearer delineation of responsibility and authority between the centre and the business units, resulting in greater operational autonomy for the business units and often a flatter overall organizational structure. The tendency for management style to be personal rather than written (Table 10.3) may suggest similar organizational contexts. At the same time formal styles exceed informal, suggesting also clear and felt accountabilities. The stimulus for change was increased external demands for performance in the midst of a fiercely competitive environment.

This trend can be seen to accord with Williamson's (1975) recommendations for the effective structuring of multi-divisional organizations. This business unit structuring also seemed to be facilitating the linking of IS to business strategy, much as suggested by Earl (1989) in his distinction between IS or applications strategies, which are the responsibility of business units, and IT or delivery strategies, which are largely the responsibility of the IS function, often at a higher level in the organization. In short, then, redesign of organizations' structure and control seemed to have been commonplace, emphasising devolution to business units, with possible benefits in IS strategy formulation.

Exploration of IS success and failures to trace *IS heritage* also suggested a clear pattern. The most consistently claimed success was the creation of high-quality and professionally managed data centres and networks. Of failures mentioned, more than 50 per cent of organizations mentioned user management hostility or indifference to IT and IS. References to specific major application development projects were made by eleven out of the thirteen organizations, but there was near equality between claims of success and verdicts of failure.

Interviewees had no difficulty in recalling successes and failures; such assessment seems normal. Indeed, in ten out of thirteen organizations a significant review and redefinition of the IS function had occurred sometime in the previous eight years. In seven cases the resulting configuration included a change of ownership for some or all of the IS resources. In eight cases a crisis of confidence in IS was reported as having reached main board level. Typically the configurational change involved devolution of IS development and/or support resources to the business units. However, the established operations capability—efficiently run data centres and networks—was usually retained intact to provide some or all of the required activity on a service basis. One case was resolved during the period of the fieldwork when three out of four business unit managers told the group executive that they did not want the responsibility of running their own operations facilities. More than once, business executives were heard to say 'we don't want the hassle of running data centres and networks'. This seems to be justified also by their intuitive reasoning of 'if it ain't broke, don't fix it'. In short, then, IS successes and failures appear to be readily observed and recalled in organizations. More important, serious failures of a crisis-of-confidence kind in the IS function seem to lead to

Table 10.3. *'Management style responses' (%)*

	Formal	Informal
Personal	69	28
Written	3	0

significant shifts in configuration of IS (perhaps as common sense would predict).

The proposed independent variable *IT strategic impact* was perceived to be high by most organizations. Two-thirds assessed the strategic impact of current IS to be high, whilst 80 per cent felt that planned IT applications were of strategic importance. Where business managers had a different perception from IS managers, it was the former group who rated IT strategic impact more highly, which is perhaps surprising. Thus most organizations perceived the strategic impact of IT as high, and this may not be a useful distinctor in explaining alternative IS configurations. Indeed, subsequent studies by the authors have found that the strategic grid may not be a useful instrument in research. For example, if examining corporations, each business unit may position itself differently. More recently it seems that most organizations have found themselves to be in the strategic quadrant. Thus perhaps the McFarlan *et al.* strategic grid was useful when there were leaders and laggards in recognizing or feeling the strategic impact of IT. In 1993 the diffusion of strategic impact may be widespread. Equally, the 1980s trend towards business unit devolution in host organizations (and the competitive pressures which commonly caused it) may have sharpened management's attention to, and understanding of, the strategic threats and opportunities of IT. In short, the strategic impact of IT, at least as measured by the McFarlan *et al.* strategic grid, does not seem to influence the configuration of IS activities.

All interviewees were able to position themselves on *technology assimilation* curves with ease. A universal picture emerged in 1987 of organizations facing different stages in the stage model for different technologies, with transaction processing, data communication, and scientific computing being at more advanced adoption stages than office or physical automation and end-user computing (Table 10.4). There were no observable differences in alternative IS configurations. It seemed that all organizations were having concurrently to manage multiple technologies through quite different IS management practices and regimes. This variable may impact the detail and disaggregation of IS management but it does not appear to have a comprehensive or universal impact on overall IS configuration.

The variable *external IT environment* was less revealing. Interviewees selected an average of 5.5 contemporary technologies or issues from a list of 13 as presenting important threats or opportunities. However, no

Table 10.4. *The assimilation of six strands of IT**

Technology	Assimilation reported: Stage 1–4		
	Mean	Median	Inter-quartile range
Business transaction processing	3.1	3	3– to 3+
Data communications	3.0	3	3 to 3+
End-user computing	2.5	2	2 to 3
Office automation	2.1	2	2 to 2+
Scientific computing	3.0	4	2 to 4
Automation of physical/build processes	2.4	3	2 to 3

Note: * When recording responses to this question we found it necessary to qualify a straight numeric response on some occasions. For example, an organization which had manifestly reached and recognized the Control stage, but had so far only partially succeeded in establishing controls, would be classified 3–.

distinguishing trends by technology or organization could be detected. Expert systems were most mentioned and have no obvious implications for structuring the IS function at large. The next three most quoted technologies were telecommunications-based. Rather than point to a preferred structure of the IS function, many observers (for example, Keen 1986) suggest that telecommunications increase the options and allow, for example, decentralization and centralization of both business operations and IS to coexist. External IT environment was proposed as a contingent variable because certain technologies in the past seem to have influenced the thinking and structuring of IS organizations. To a degree telecommunications may have been one such technology in the 1980s, in that where organizations had their own wide area network it was inevitable under central management. However, some organizations did not have corporate networks or chose to operate through third parties, either group-wide or at business-unit level.

We concluded in 1987 that the capability and diversity of available and new technologies perhaps were felt through two of the other contingent variables—IT strategic impact and technology assimilation—which in turn had no influence on IS configuration at the enterprise-wide level. Another interpretation in retrospect is that the external IT environment would be of secondary importance behind the driving variables of host organization structure and IS heritage. (For example, centralized network management is probably not needed in a decentralized organization and not credible if centralized IS groups have a bad reputation, but does appeal in terms of economies of scale and removing the anxiety from business units). A third interpretation is that, as key technologies evolve, the deterministic influence on IS configuration decreases, but that if different technologies are at different stages of evolution, a mixed impact on IS configuration (bringing more pressure for a federal IS function) is likely.

In short, our 1987 conclusions do not alter. Field studies pointed towards host organization characteristics followed by IS heritage as being the independent factors which most influence the configuration of the IS function. Our measure of strategic impact of IT suggested no relationship. Both technology assimilation and the external IT environment (which may be related) could influence the detail or disaggregation of IS configurations, but not the overall organization design choice. They may have much more to do with the user–specialist axis.[6]

Efficiency and Effectiveness

These measures not only allowed us to assess the validity of the contingency relationships, but also to examine what is the key to making them work. Efficiency in the IS context can be seen as the consistent provision of high quality and low-cost IS service. Effectiveness we defined as the successful exploitation of IT in support of business needs. These were partly assessed by asking respondents, especially users, to judge their organization's achievement levels on the criteria in Table 10.5.

Efficient IS organizations had to score highly on the first two criteria in Table 10.5. Also, they had to possess a high level of specialist skill in the IS function, be at an advanced stage of assimilation of established technologies, have clear arrangements for tracking and introducing new technologies, and apply sophisticated chargeout procedures.

Surprisingly perhaps, there seemed to be little difference in the levels of efficiency achieved by the sample organizations. It was difficult to distinguish between user-satisfaction ratings, other than by role of respondent. All IS sponsors and general managers gave a rating of 'largely satisfactory' (grade 2) whilst all finance directors and controllers opined that service levels had 'some key weaknesses' (grade 3) except one, who conceded a score of 2.5. One technical director gave a 'highly effective' rating of 1.

The researchers' more descriptive evaluation of technology assimilation and the other indicators were no more revealing as discriminants. Furthermore, a subjective overall assessment of each organization suggested little distinction amongst the organizations. The tentative, bold implication was that the provision of quality IS service at an acceptable cost was no longer a major issue in large corporations. Efficiency in IS apparently can be achieved by any large organization if it is prepared to commit adequate resources to the activity. Perhaps hardware and software products had

---

[6] See Chap. 11 by Feeny, Earl, and Edwards in this volume.

Table 10.5. *IS performance ratings*

Criterion	Highly effective— a key asset	Largely satisfactory	Some key weaknesses	Poor or badly exposed
Efficiency				
Cost of service provision				
Quality of service provision				
Effectiveness				
Achievement of system benefits				
Application implementation				
Relating use of IT to business needs				
Business management awareness of IT				

become so much more reliable, and installation management practice so improved, that efficiency could be expected and was becoming an industry norm.

Some users did claim dissatisfaction with IS technical achievement in the area of large application project development. Other respondents claimed success. However, successes and failures were reported in each pattern of IS arrangements. Thus major IS project development may still have been inefficient in several firms, but is was not clear that any particular pattern of IS arrangement would help remedy this deficiency.

The important conclusion drawn was that the operational activities of IS, and many of the development activities, could be located anywhere in an organization—centrally, at sector or regional level, or in business units—if efficiency was the criterion. Since the study the evidence has not changed, except that we can now say that these activities can be located anywhere inside or potentially outside the organization. There may be relative efficiency differences between internal or external IS rivals, but there is no rule which suggests absolute efficiency in IS, in terms of operations and large-scale applications developments, associated with either centralization or decentralization.

If there are historical, economies of scale, or critical-mass reasons for having a centralized IS operations-and-development group, it can work in either a centralized or decentralized host organization. In the latter context, however, the effectiveness analysis adds some other considerations.

Effectiveness was assessed by using the remaining criteria in Figure 10.5 and by recording successes and failures in the following areas: linking IS strategy to business needs, IS contribution to business in comparison with key competitors, achievement of system benefits, and awareness by business managers of IT capability. The views of IS and business interviewees within each organization were checked for consistency. Substantial contrasts in IS effectiveness were identified within the sample organizations and were confirmed by the researchers' subjective impressions formed by the interviews.

As the amalgam of effectiveness indicators used focuses on how well the IS function and the business relate to each other, they can also be seen as measuring *integration*, to refer back to Lawrence and Lorsch (1967). Thus these performance data were used to classify the twenty business units assessed across the fourteen sample organizations into categories of high, medium, and low integration. We examined more than one business unit in some of the more complex organizations. Five situations were classified as showing high integration, ten as medium, and five as low. The 'high' and 'low' were then compared in terms of their IS arrangements and clear distinctions were apparent. The following characteristics of IS arrangements were present in all the high situations and absent in all the low situations:

i. Business unit management perceived that future exploitation of IT was of strategic importance, as indicated by respondents' positioning on the strategic impact grid.

ii. An IS executive was established as a full member of the management team or board for the business unit concerned.

iii. There was ongoing education for business unit management in the capability and potential of IT. This might be achieved by formal programmes and/or continuous updating from the business unit's own IS executive.

iv. There was a top-down planning process in the business unit for linking IS application strategy to business needs. Also the business unit leader was both leading and promoting the exploitation of IT.

v. Some IS development resource was positioned within the business unit, but not necessarily all that was required. The business unit had some capability for systems development and the skill and knowledge base to subcontract development to other internal or external suppliers. Importantly, if a business unit identified an urgent and critical IS requirement, it could propel and develop it with some local resources.

vi. The introduction or piloting of new technologies took place at business unit level under business unit control. (Conversely, doubts were often expressed about the effectiveness of central experimental or R&D units for IT). It seems that business evaluation of new technologies is best done by relevant business units who understand their own product-market opportunities.

vii. There was a cost centre rather than profit or investment centre control regime for IS within the business. Chargeout procedures were relatively unsophisticated, at levels 6 or below on Allen's continuum. (A possible explanation of this tendency is that whilst profit centre management of IS can help focus on efficiency of service, it can also create a transactional relationship between IS and their users, thereby impeding effectiveness). IS resources were not free in cost centre regimes, but pricing did not become an emotional issue.

The discovery of these distinguishing factors suggested that corporate IS management should be concerned primarily with effectiveness. Whereas any set of IS arrangements could, it seems, foster efficiency, there were clear indications that only certain patterns of IS arrangements were conducive to effectiveness. These help clarify which are the significant factors and relationships in our proposed contingency framework.

The important recurring feature in the analysis of high integration or effectiveness contexts is that the pattern of IS arrangements is aligned with business units. In particular, IS management and development responsibilities are devolved to business units. We conclude, therefore, that *it is essential that IS arrangements should align with the key characteristics of the host organization.* Whether the host organization in traditional structural parlance is centralized or decentralized, the management of IS and at least some development resources should align with the overall distribution of managerial responsibility and authority. This pattern should then be backed up by IS education, IS planning processes, executive leadership, and a cost centre control regime for IS.

The business unit and business venture configurations for IS thus are likely to be ineffective because in both structure and process they cannot easily achieve these success factors. It becomes clear that there is no harm in allocating IS management and resources down to business units in decentralized organizations. In centralized organizations, all IS resources can also be centralized with no loss in effectiveness. We could conceive of minimal IS management and development resources being allocated to functions in centralized contexts—functions being the analogues of business units. For federal IS configurations, it is clear that business units should have at least an IS manager and minimal IS development resources and concentrate on the success factors. We still have to suggest what should be done, perhaps minimally at the centre of a federal configuration.

The Federal Centre

We analysed IS policies in use in the study companies. There was a high incidence of IS policy throughout. Executives running federal IS configurations emphasised policies seeing them as both a need and a rationale of federalization. Ten 'enabling' policies and eight 'restraining' policies were present in more than half the organizations and are listed in descending frequency below:

Enabling Policies	*Restraining Policies*
1. Negotiation of group discounts	1. Technical compatibility standards
2. Shaping IT vendor relationships relationships	2. Defining business units' freedom to procure and run IS
3. Chargeout rules	3. Use of common systems
4. Identifying and orchestrating a group IS 'guru'	4. Security, disaster recovery, etc.
5. Whether and how to develop common systems	5. Conformance to industry standards
6. Reviewing IS potential in business units	6. IS standards of competence
7. Taking initiatives on asset sharing	7. IS job specifications
8. Legal and tendering procedures	8. Selling IS services externally
9. Managing IS human resources groupwide	
10. Developing centres of excellence in business units	

It appeared from this data and subsequent case study work that group IS goals in federal configurations divide into two:

1. ensuring good practice and efficiency throughout the corporation; and
2. supporting corporate organizational and business goals.

Using Earl's (1989) taxonomy of strategy questions, the first is to do with Information Management Strategy and often can be expressed as: 'how can we make sure that corporate executives can sleep at night, and that we are running a competent IS function?' The second is to do with Information Systems Strategy, and in its wake Information Technology Strategy, and is concerned with supporting or enabling group synergies. We can now distil the practices and policies of the organization studied into two sets as shown below. They become the probable concerns of the federal centre of IS.

GOAL 1: *Ensuring good practice and efficiency throughout the group*
- IS education initiatives
- Review of business unit IS strategies
- Standard setting for development and operations
- Audit of quality and security
- Career management of senior staff

- Consultancy report for small businesses
- Clearing house for technology and applications information
- Management of IT vendor support and conditions

GOAL 2:   *Supporting corporate organizational and business goals*
- Definition of information infrastructure to support group efficiency, business integration, organizational flexibility, and knowledge sharing
- Identifying and commissioning systems which encourage desired co-operation or necessary integration across internal boundaries
- Identifying and commissioning systems which capture distinctive competences and transfer them across business units

The pragmatics learnt from case studies of federal IS configurations are equally important. To achieve the first goal, corporate IS staff must be first-class and their expertise maintained. To put it colloquially, head office visitors must be better than the visited. Secondly, processes are required to create, review, monitor, and enforce IS policies. To achieve the second goal, the central IS group needs a clear mission backed by corporate officers. They will not receive this support if the corporate business and organizational goals are unclear. These can usually be stated in terms of what value-added does the corporation or group bring to the business units.

The Federal Balance

If we combine the necessary conditions for effectiveness in IS at business-unit level with the responsibilities required at the federal centre and recognize that there are choices on how to configure IS resources for efficiency, we are able to produce a matrix of guidelines as in Table 10.6. We see the federal IS configuration as insisting on each business unit being charged with working out and implementing its own IT application needs. The centre oversees the best practice in IS and formulates policies on infrastructure that are required to add value to or provide synergy for the corporation as a whole. Often history, economies of scale, critical mass, and removal of worry from business units will lead to some centralization of IT operations. This is not unlike the federal form of IS governance suggested by Zmud *et al.* (1986).

1987 Conclusions

Our conclusions in 1987 have been restated as they emerge in this paper. They could be summarized thus:

1. The federal IS configuration seems most stable and flexible for complex organizations. We have shown what it might look like.
2. Business unit and business venture IS configurations are not recom-

Table 10.6. *Federal arrangements*

	Local	Central
Essential	IS executive in management team IS strategic planning	IT vendor and acquisition policy Architectural and technical standards
	IS education of managers Executive leadership for IT	Technical and quality assurance Delineation of local responsibilities
	Some IS development capability Piloting new technologies	IS human resource development Chargeout and control policies
Possible	Some IT operations capability	IS development consultancy IT operations capability Common systems development Co-ordinating IS development throughout the function Co-ordinating IS across business units

mended. This is for reasons of effectiveness (and integration) rather than efficiency (or differentiation).

3. Centralized IS configurations suit centralized host organizations. Decentralized IS configurations suit purely decentralized host organizations.
4. A primary contingent factor in configuring the IS function, therefore, is host organization characteristics. We emphasized structure; style and culture may be important too.
5. IS heritage is also influential. Crises and failures do beget, and need, changes in configuration. Indeed, they may often be signalling that the IS function is not aligned with the host organization.

We also concluded in 1987 that organizations should avoid drastic 'U-turns' in configuring IS. The cost and disruption are enormous. We see in the next and final section, however, that change, as they say, tends to be constant. However, for complex organizations, which were the primary focus of our study, we suggest that federal IS configurations provide enough design space to adapt to circumstances. They may be difficult to manage, but they are preferred to wide swings of the centralization–decentralization pendulum.

Recent Developments

Since the 1987 study the authors have continued to study the configuration of the IS function. We can detect at least seven trends:

1. the increasing adoption and finessing of the federal configuration;
2. the creation of intermediate levels of the federal configuration, here called consolidation;
3. the construction of IT-based services divisions;
4. the rise in outsourcing;
5. the recognition of new axes of organization;
6. the continued distribution of information processing to end-users; and
7. the continuing change in configuration.

Each is addressed briefly below.

Federal Sophistication

The variety of options within the federal model was identified earlier. This has turned out to be the practice. We see some firms who have recentralized some of their IS activities, commonly for four reasons:

1. To regain economies of scale or simply to rationalize. A common concern is to introduce control of software standards and centralize buying simply to save costs on software licensing. Another has been rationalizing data centres, given that efficient operations can be run anywhere and the decreasing cost of communications makes some hub-and-spoke architectures viable.
2. To get control of architecture and thus infrastructure so that cross-functional and cross-business unit application and data integration or connectivity are possible.
3. To facilitate or ensure that processes are in place to share experience and learning about both IT application and IS delivery across the group.
4. To monitor and improve standards of IS performance in all business units and review or coach component businesses on how strategically to exploit IT.

Apart from the first, these drivers do not normally involve reconstruction of 'heavy' central IS groups. Sometimes the team is from one to four people. Indeed, some federal configurations have become more decentralized. Four influences are apparent here:

1. The desire to devolve decision-making to business units on what IT applications to develop and how to implement them.
2. The desire to remove corporate head-count and cost either by outsourcing central IS operations centres or distributing them to business units.
3. The unclear added value not only from corporate IS groups, but large chunks of corporate offices in general.
4. The continued decentralization of the host organization.

Finally, some federal configurations are hybrids of the other configurations. Three examples are illustrative:

1. Some operational centres of federal organization now have a business venture mission to larger or lesser degrees. They sell services outside as well as inside and usually have no monopoly within their host.
2. One company with two divisions has a centralized IS group in one division and a deeply decentralized one in the other. The IS director of the former looks over the latter and has two consultants to help the smallest segments.
3. One group decentralized all its IS activities including a corporate bureau. Because the group executive wanted peace of mind through monitoring the decentralized activities and believed in providing coaching for local managers, it did, however, appoint a group CIO—on a part-time basis.

In short, the federal configuration has no standard topology or organization chart.

Consolidation

The federal configuration is not just as in Figure 10.3(a), but can be as Figure 10.3(b). At least four related drivers explain the trend towards consolidation of information processing at intermediate levels of the organization:

1. Where business units are having to collaborate to produce or distribute product families or present a common face to a customer. This happened in one decentralized business who had to compete with a centralized rival who was providing 'one stop shopping' to its customers. It was too painful, slow, and unnecessary to bring decentralized product centres together, but a shared information system centre and distribution function was superimposed over the five business units to achieve the same results.
2. As organizations look to take cost out of internal administration, we see information-based activities being consolidated across business units. These shared service organizations provide economies of scale and may accompany redesign of administrative processes. Common accounting centres are examples.
3. As corporations find themselves competing globally, we observe the need to co-ordinate IS strategy-making, IS development, and sometimes IT operations across business units and countries in order to support strategies for global efficiency or to transfer knowledge and learning. This requires some intermediate consolidation of IS.

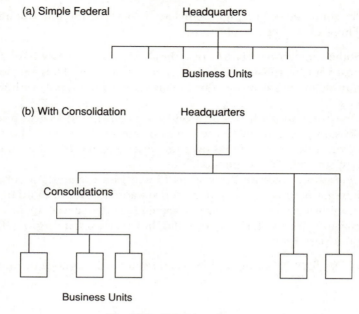

Fig. 10.3. *Federal configurations*

4. There may be simple manageability drivers. Two are becoming
    popular. One is coping with size or reach by creating, for example,
    regional data centres to serve whatever business units or functions
    exist in that region. Another is creating an IS configuration inde-
    pendent of the host organization with the hope of IS becoming less
    of a road-block to organizational change. The theory is that opera-
    tions and development centres are created (almost as bureaux) to
    serve a set of business units wherever located and however imper-
    manent. If a unit changes its position in the organization chart or
    merges or splinters, there is not an IS impediment because IS activ-
    ities and assets are not located within and owned by the business
    unit; they are corporate but central utilities.

All these consolidated forms can fit within the federal model.

Service Organizations

Apart from shared service centres, some corporations are now adding
information-based functions or businesses to IS to create a bureau or business venture. This can be seen at Barclays Bank, where credit-card processing, money-transmission services, global custody, and the like now were
joined with information services as a line of business to provide sources
inside or outside the host organization. However, they are not necessarily

the only IS unit in the group. Responsibility for IS development and management at Barclays, for example, was devolved to business units. The latter can also buy IS services from the market-place. Again, this is one form of the federal configuration. In the case of Barclays Bank, this organization was broken apart again within two years.

Outsourcing

The growth of the third-party market-place and organizations' desire to reduce information processing costs has encouraged outsourcing. This may or may not be a good idea (Earl 1991), but reminds us that IS configurations now extend beyond the traditional boundaries of the host organization. Outsourcing of operations and development is an option available to all four ideal IS configurations. However, what seems to be emerging is that outsourcing is just one partial answer to information services supply and rarely totally displaces the whole IS function. It certainly does not remove the need for managing either efficiency or effectiveness of IS and so, although outsourcing may lead to downsizing of the IS function, it does not necessarily alter the centralization versus decentralization axis of IS configuration.

New Axes

However, new axes are appearing. The most contemporary one is 'business process'. Where firms are engaged in business process redesign, not only may business operations and management be reallocated to key processes, but process-oriented (often cross-functional) systems are required too. We are then seeing IS management positions and development teams being allocated to these business processes and reporting to the business process sponsor or executive. These could prove to be temporary units, but currently they introduce a new axis at any level of the host organization. They may increase the 'federal' proportion of information resources in essentially decentralized or functional organizations.

End-Users

Particularly the distribution of computing, combined with networking, client-server architectures, and the like are not only putting more power and application capability into the hands of users, they are increasing the technological experience and knowledge of users. So at any level of the centralization–decentralization axis we see a shift in responsibility towards end-users. Indeed, over 50 per cent or more of IT resources may now be located outside the IS function. This has at least three implications. We do have to re-analyse the specialist–user axis. Secondly, the authority given to distributed users has to be considered carefully. This explains why infra-structural responsibility and reserved powers are being relocated to the centre in some organizations and reinforcing the good sense of federal configurations. Such a move also is reflecting the need to control costs.

Continual Change

We have tracked substantial organizational change in five of the original field study companies. It thus seems unlikely that IS configurations can or should remain static for long. Curiously, however, none of these can be reclassified on our continuum in Table 10.1. We could, therefore, suggest that the outline configuration of IS in complex organizations is settling down. However, it seems that the detail is always changing. One federal configuration is now more decentralized because the host has become deeply decentralized. Another federal configuration has intermediate or consolidated levels now because business units are combining into product groups. One federal configuration has coped with a merger which has introduced regional units for global manageability reasons. In contrast, another federal configuration has split into two federal patterns because of a de-merger. Finally, a group which was becoming decentralized after a business venture phase is now more decentralized because it was acquired by a conglomerate. It is notable that host organization characteristics seem to be very influential.

Conclusion

Six years on, our principal propositions have not been revised. There seem to be five ideal forms of IS configuration, of which three seem more viable than the others. The federal configuration seems the best fit with most complex organizations. It is varied in form and, as we suggested, seems to be very flexible and adaptive. As we have tracked organizations over the last six years, the federal configuration has been able to accommodate some recentralization or deeper decentralization or consolidation.

Host organization characteristics certainly appear to drive IS configuration. The most significant influence pre- and post-1987 seems to have been wider organizational change. Of course this may be driven by business strategy as much as preferred management theory. However adjustments within one of our archetype configurations—particularly the federal structure—may be due also to technological change and assimilation, the economics of information processing, and the requirements of IS strategy. IS heritage may remain a mediating influence, but as firms' IS management experience grows perhaps we can expect fewer major crises resulting in configurational revolutions.

Outsourcing, alongside other aspects of downsizing, now appears to be affecting the size of the IS function, but not dramatically affecting configuration. However, the total scale of IS activities seems likely to grow further, partly as more capability is put into the hands of end-users and partly as other, newer technologies—particularly media and image technologies—converge with what was conceived of as IT in the 1980s. We therefore should not expect the issue of configuring the IS function and IS activities at large to go away.

References

Allen, B. (1987), 'Making Information Services Pay its Way', *Harvard Business Review* (Jan.–Feb.).

Buchanan, J. R., and Linowes, R. G. (1980), 'Making Distributed Data Processing Work', *Harvard Business Review* (Sept.–Oct.).

Burns, T., and Stalker, G. V. (1961), *The Management of Innovation,* London: Tavistock Publications.

Dearden, J. (1987), 'The Withering Away of the IS Organization', *Sloan Management Review* (Summer).

—— and R. L. Nolan (1973), 'How to Control the Computer Resource', *Harvard Business Review* (Nov.–Dec.).

Dickson, G., Leitheiser, R., and Wetherbe, J. (1984), 'Key Information Systems Issues for the 1980s', *MIS Quarterly* (Sept.).

Drucker, P. F. (1964), *The Concept of Corporation,* New York: John Day & Co.

Earl, M. J. (1989), *Management Strategies for Information Technology,* New York: Prentice-Hall.

—— (1991), 'Outsourcing Information Services', *Public Money and Management,* 11/3 (Autumn).

—— Feeny, D. F., Hirschheim, R. A., and Lockett, M. (1986), *Information Technology Executives and Development Needs: A Field Study,* Research and Discussion Paper RDP 86/10, Oxford Institute of Information Management, Templeton College, Oxford.

Feeny, D. F., Earl, M. J., and Edwards, B. (1989), *IS Arrangements to Suit Complex Organizations: An Effective IS Structure,* Research and Discussion Paper RDP 89/4, Oxford Institute of Information Management, Templeton College, Oxford.

Gibson, C. F., and Nolan, R. L. (1974), 'Managing the Four Stages of EDP Growth', *Harvard Business Review* (Jan.–Feb.).

Handy, C. (1992), 'Balancing Corporate Power: A New Federalist Paper', *Harvard Business Review* (Nov.–Dec.).

Jensen, M. C., and Meckling, W. H. (1976), 'Theory of the Firm, Managerial Costs and Ownership Structure', *Journal of Financial Economics* (Oct.).

Keen, P. G. W. (1986), *Competing in Time; Using Telecommunications for Competitive Advantage,* Cambridge, Mass.: Ballinger.

La Belle, A., and Nyce, H. E. (1987), 'Whither the IT Organization?', *Sloan Management Review* (Summer).

Lawrence, P. R., and Lorsch, J. W. (1967), *Organization and Environment: Managing Differentiation and Integration*, Division of Research, Graduate School of Business Administration, Harvard University.

McFarlan, F. W., and McKenny, J. L. (1983), 'The Information Archipelago—Governing the New World', *Harvard Business Review* (July–Aug.).

—— and Pyburn, P. (1983), 'The Information Archipelago—Plotting a Course', *Harvard Business Review* (Jan.–Feb.).

McFarlan, F. W., Nolan, R. L., and Norton, D. P. (1973), *Information Systems Administration*, New York: Holt, Rinehart and Winston.

Niederman, F., Brancheau, J. C., and Wetherbe, J. C. (1991), 'Information Systems Management Issues for the 1990s', *MIS Quarterly*, 15/4 (Dec.).

Nolan, R. L. (1977), *Management Accounting and Control of Data Processing*, National Association of Accountants, New York.

Otley, D. J. (1980), 'The Contingency Theory of Management Accounting: Achievement and Prognosis', *Accounting Organizations and Society*, 5/4.

Pyburn, P. J. (1983), 'Linking the MIS Plan with Corporate Strategy: An Exploratory Study', *MIS Quarterly* (June).

Simon, H. A. (1955), 'The Behavioural Model of Rational Choice', *Quarterly Journal of Economics* (Feb.).

Williamson, O. E. (1975), *Markets and Hierarchies*, New York: Free Press.

Woodward, J. (1965), *Industrial Organization: Theory and Practice*, Oxford: Oxford University Press.

Vancil, R. F., and Buddrus, L. E. (1978), *Decentralization: Managerial Ambiguity by Design*, Homewood, Ill.: Dow-Jones-Irwin.

von Simson, E. M. (1990), 'The "Centrally Decentralized" IS Organization', *Harvard Business Review* (July–Aug.).

Zmud, R. Z., Boynton, A. C., and Jacobs, G. C. (1986), 'The Information Economy: A New Perspective for Effective Information Systems Management', *Data Base* (Fall).

11

Organizational Arrangements for IS: Roles of Users and Specialists

DAVID F. FEENY, MICHAEL J. EARL, AND BRIAN EDWARDS

Introduction

The commonest conceptualization of any organizational design is usually the 'structure' or vertical dimension—the definition of organizational units, the reporting relationships for each of them, and the distribution of responsibilities and authority. A second dimension, which may be less well defined in the design or its operation, is the 'process' or horizontal component—the way in which different organizational units work with each other when necessary to achieve organizational objectives. When organizational arrangements for IS are being considered, this second component takes on a particular importance because of the well-documented difficulties experienced between IS professionals and representatives of other parts of the organization. Problematic relationships are seen to arise regardless of choice of IS structure: corporations which demolish a central 'ivory tower' IS function by decentralizing resources into local IT units regularly find they have created a series of smaller ivory towers. Users still perceive the IS department as centralized because user–specialist relationships are inadequate. In this chapter we consider how organizational arrangements can foster effective working relationships between IS specialists and the 'users' they serve, irrespective of their positioning within a structural framework.

Users, IS Specialists, and Integration

A starting-point is to recognize that IS professionals typically possess—or at least are perceived to possess—particular personal characteristics which inhibit their working relationships with other members of the organization. Couger and Zawacki (1980) reported that IS specialists consistently demonstrated a higher need for constant challenge ('Growth Need Strength') but a lower need for interpersonal relationships ('Social Need Strength') than other professional groupings. Their findings have since been the subject of some academic debate (for example, Ferratt and Short 1986, 1988, 1990; Inmon and Hartman 1990), but among practitioners the perception of differences remains. In a survey of IS directors by Grindley (1991), 46 per cent reported that a 'culture gap' between IS professionals and business counterparts represented their most important challenge. The culture gap was demonstrated by contrasting approaches to tasks and problem-solving, which inhibited effective working relationships. The description remains consistent with the earlier findings of authors such as Edstrom (1977), Gingras and McLean (1979), and Zmud and Cox (1979) when they reported on the distinctive cognitive styles of IS professionals.

The importance attached to the culture gap by the IS directors may be readily understood when one considers how the literature of information management is permeated with appeals for the 'involvement', 'commitment', and even 'ownership' of those who are the intended beneficiaries of IT investments. The challenge is further underlined when Barki and Hartwick (1989) define the necessary 'involvement' as a 'subjective psychological state, reflecting importance and personal relevance'; it must be distinguished from mere 'participation' by users in IS-related activity. In the language of contingency theorists such as Lawrence and Lorsch (1967), we are seeking a high degree of 'integration' between groups (of users and IS specialists) who exhibit significant 'differentiation' in terms of personal attributes. Interpreting Lawrence and Lorsch, we may expect that distinctive personal characteristics may be expected to be consistently associated with the ability to master a set of fast-changing technologies. A group of IS professionals who are selected to be less 'differentiated' and easier to 'integrate' may lack the necessary technical proficiency.

To address the challenge of integration, Lawrence and Lorsch—and later Galbraith (1977)—suggested a range of integrating mechanisms. Many of these can be recognized in the various prescriptions proposed for the IS field over the years. These include integrative process designs, such as Mumford's (1983) ETHICS model for participative systems development; and the use of particular individuals as integrators, such as the 'hybrid managers' investigated by Earl and Skyrme (1992). In the context of systems development, the research of Taylor-Cummings (1993) has highlighted the importance to integration of contextual arrangements—users and specialists reporting to the same project manager, shared physical space, shared goals and incentives, and so on. Taylor-Cummings found a strong consensus on a set of 'goal' arrangements for IS development, but the practice of the organizations researched generally fell well short of their aspirations. There would seem to be two major reasons why organizations struggle to implement the integration arrangements they see to be most appropriate:

- First these arrangements are seen to be expensive and demanding of scarce resources. There is a strong temptation to compromise and settle for the 'practical' rather than the 'ideal'.

- Secondly, the 'ideal' arrangements may challenge the existing culture of the organization and/or the IS function. The arrangements may therefore be resisted or subverted (see, for example, Davidson's (1993) study of organizational attempts to introduce Joint Application Development workshops).

These difficulties may be diminished by a more targeted and selective implementation of such integrating mechanisms than is generally espoused. We propose a contingency approach, arguing that appropriate integration mechanisms are a function of the IS activity being addressed, and the maturity of the technology on which it is based. We argue that 'expensive' integration mechanisms based on teamworking are only required when uncertainty is high. As a technology and its application become familiar, then simpler, more contractual arrangements are not only adequate— they are actually superior.

In the remainder of this chapter we introduce a contingency model for managing relationships between users and IS specialists, and explore its implications. Our proposals are based on analysis of the organizational experiences we encountered during the Earl *et al.* study described in Chapter 10 above, and are further illuminated by the findings of other authors.

The Concept of Technology Maturity

The first proposition of our model is that integration mechanisms should vary with the maturity of the technology in question. The idea that information management processes should be a function of the relative maturity of the technology is not, of course, a new one. The Stage Theory of Gibson and Nolan (1974) suggested a pattern of practices for the management of computing, dependent on positioning relative to an S-shaped expenditure curve which serves as a proxy for organizational learning. Although Gibson and Nolan were at the time describing the evolution of the 'EDP Department', the department in 1974 was synonymous with the exploitation of a single broad strand of technology for business data processing. Gibson and Nolan themselves predicted that there would be 'more S-shaped curves as new EDP technologies emerge'. Subsequently McFarlan and McKenney (1982) detected the same pattern of assimilation for office automation, and other new technology capabilities; and Raho *et al.* (1987) pointed to a conceptual fit with the broader work on technology diffusion by Rogers (1962) and others. Henderson and Treacy (1986) used the McFarlan and McKenney model to suggest IS management perspectives appropriate to each phase of the assimilation of end-user computing. Our own model, therefore, follows well established precedents in proposing that *user–specialist relationships must be planned and managed separately for each distinctive technology, in the light of the relative maturity of that technology.*

The phrases 'distinctive technology' and 'relative maturity' elude precise definition, but our experience is that they do represent meaningful and helpful concepts in practice. In our field study of 1987 we distinguished between six areas of technology which we called Business Transaction Processing, Data Communications, End User Computing, Office Automation, Scientific Computing, and Automation of Physical/Build Processes. For each area we proposed benchmarks to denote an organization's position in relation to a four-phase model of assimilation. None of our interviewees had any difficulty with our methodology, either conceptually or pragmatically in terms of being able to locate their organization relative to our benchmarks. They readily accepted the implication that they could be, and often were, at different states of assimilation across these six technologies. They also anticipated that further distinctive technologies would emerge and require their own separate but similar patterns of learning, assimilation, and diffusion.

The 'relative maturity' of a technology can be considered with reference to the technology *per se*; to the application which the technology is being used to support; and to the organization which is using the technology. For example, a technology is classified as having 'low' maturity if it exhibits a high rate of change in terms of function provided, technical specification, and performance. As function and specification stabilize, it moves towards a classification of 'high' maturity even though price/performance may continue to improve. On the other hand, there is a real sense in which maturity is 'low' when a well-established technology is used to implement a radically new application, or when the implementing organization has little prior experience of the application or technology (even though both have been successfully exploited elsewhere). As we shall describe, the model can be used to suggest appropriate integration arrangements in each of these different contexts.

From User to Specialist Focus

The second proposition of our model is that integration mechanisms should vary: to engender teamworking between users and IS specialists when technology maturity is low; to co-ordinate the separate contributions of users and IS specialists when technology maturity is high. We describe this as a migration from a 'user focus' to a 'specialist focus'.

In the 'user focus' domain (see Table 11.1) the overriding objective is to identify and deliver the potential benefits of new technology, to search out 'instrumental effectiveness' (Thompson 1967). With high technological uncertainty it is inappropriate closely to specify tasks for individuals. Effective integration mechanisms will be of the type identified by Taylor-Cummings (1993), fostering collective effort towards a single shared goal expressed in terms of business benefits. While the goal may be a fixture,

Table 11.1. *Contrasting modes of integration*

	User focus	Specialist focus
Principal concern	Business benefits	Professional excellence
Operating style	Teamworking	Individual roles
Performance apprisal	Shared goal	Contractual responsibility
Leadership	User	Specialist

tactics and plans will change frequently as learning is achieved and uncertainty resolved; the team culture provides the flexibility to respond to such changes. The management style is consultative, to benefit from the perspective of each individual. But the leadership is effectively (and probably formally) invested on the user side, because the key question is 'can this type of technology bring business benefits?'—not 'which product/supplier is the leader in this technology?'

By contrast, in the 'specialist focus' domain the concern is to achieve IS professional excellence, the 'economic efficiency' which Thompson (1967) defines as performance of the specified task at minimum cost. The assimilation of the technology is sufficiently advanced for the 'demand' side of the equation to be clear. Hence users can be expected and obliged to state clearly their requirements; IS specialists can be charged with selecting and delivering the most appropriate technical responses. Rather than teamworking and a sense of communal responsibility, the emphasis is on defining individual responsibilities and the boundaries and interfaces between them. These are enshrined in a contract of service between users and IS specialists, which is the principal integration mechanism and may be the basis for formal chargeout of IS activity. Leadership passes to the IS specialist in the sense that the key question has become 'what is the best choice of technology (to meet a well defined need)?'

Integration by IS Activity

The third and final proposition of our model is that the transition from 'user' to 'specialist' focus should occur at different times for each main area of IS activity. Four such areas of IS activity are identified:

Delivery refers to the physical provision of IS service, the Operations function. It encompasses both direct service activities—such as data processing and communications networks—and also those activities which are required to sustain such a service—equipment planning and provision, fallback/recovery procedures, systems programming, and so on.

Support covers the assistance provided by the IS function to consumers of IS services. Activities include education, general advice and guidance, and help-desks for troubleshooting or resolving user problems.

Development reflects standard IS terminology for the activity required to produce the hardware and more especially the software for planned applications. This comprises the classical systems analysis, design, and implementation activities.

Strategy refers to the activities involved in determining the portfolio of applications which should be undertaken. The tasks in this area include identification of new application opportunities, evaluation of opportunities compared to business needs, financial assessment of proposals, and resource management in the light of priorities.

In each of these areas the IS function needs to interact with the user community, and may do so with the equivalent of either user focus or specialist focus. For example, in the 'Delivery' activity IS can provide qualified operators to work in a user-based team working on a departmental computer; or alternatively IS can respond to a user-prepared Service Level Agreement request, basing its response on whatever technical platform it believes to represent the best price/performance option. At the 'Strategy' level, Earl (1993) has identified five different approaches from his field research. The 'Organizational' approach, in which IS is part of the team pursuing a nominated business theme, is clearly equivalent to user focus; the 'Business Led' approach, in which IS attempts to identify IS investments based on top managements' statement of business strategy, qualifies as a form of specialist focus.

As depicted in Figure 11.1, we suggest that for each distinctive technology the transition from user to specialist focus follows the same sequence: starting with Delivery, followed by Support, and then Development. The assumption that this is the sequence in which learning takes place and uncertainty is resolved is supported by Curley and Pyburn (1982). In contrast to earlier hard-wired technologies, these authors suggest, information technologies require a relatively short period of 'Type A' learning (how to operate the technology) followed by a much more substantial period of 'Type B' learning (how to exploit the technology). Curley and Pyburn's emphasis on the prolonged nature of Type B learning can be related to the S-shaped boundary between the User Focus and Specialist Focus domains: the transition from User to Specialist focus can be expected to be fairly rapid in the case of Delivery; a much more gradual transition is likely to be appropriate in the Development phase as relatively familiar technologies can still be the platform for fundamentally new applications, involving high levels of uncertainty.

Interpreting the Model

To illustrate more clearly the potential contribution of the model, consider a particular technology at three points in time within its life-cycle.

In the *early* phase of the life-cycle, when maturity is low, users are con-

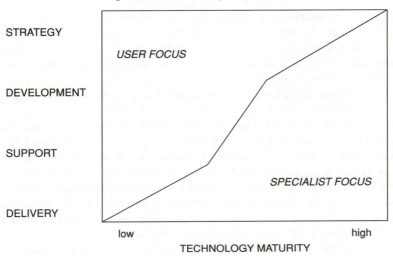

Fig. 11.1. *Contingency model of user–specialist integration*

fronted with a new and uncertain capability and the technology is characterized by rapid change. The model suggests that all areas of IS activity
should be guided by a user focus. The expectation is that a mixed team of
business and IS people is seeking to determine the potential value of the
new technology. Problems are addressed and resolved by face-to-face meetings within each team, requiring excellent communication between team
members. Indeed, Lockett (1987) suggests from his research that each
team must comprise a continuous spectrum of understanding between the
business and the technology to ensure that misunderstandings do not occur.
Each team will be led by a project champion from the user side (Runge
1985; Lockett 1987) who is directing and driving the project towards the
valued business goal. The reputation at stake is that of the project champion and therefore, with or without due debate within the team, the
ultimate authority is his—whether the decision involves the application
area to be tackled, the project design, or the equipment to be used. In
achieving successful innovation, such champions are not constrained by
established business or IS procedures in arriving at decisions. Most decisions
are dominated by considerations of effectiveness—speed, quality, risk-
minimization—rather than cost efficiency.

In the *middle* phase of the life-cycle some of the emphasis has changed
as the Delivery and Support activities migrate to the Specialist Focus domain.
The potential of the technology has been demonstrated, and early benefits are being achieved. It is time to ensure that those benefits are not
jeopardized by system failure, loss of data bases, or inferior service. Since
the direction of development of the technology is by now clearer, as is its

role within the business, it is also time to devise formal standards which will relate to its use. While the user still drives the application or 'IS' strategy, the specialist's insight is used to develop an 'IT' strategy or technical architecture which will allow the consistent and efficient exploitation of the technology across the business. The specialist also accepts clear management responsibility for the Delivery and Support activities, contracting to provide whatever level of service is required (and can be afforded) by a user who is now well informed of his needs in relation to established IS activity. However, the Development activity remains within the User Focus domain. The potential for further learning about how to use the technology requires a continuing emphasis on teamwork between users and specialist, supported by the use of interactive development processes such as prototyping. The Development 'contract' remains a soft one, with a sense of shared purpose to achieve a successful system, and no refusals to make specification changes, no litigious disputes.

Finally, in the *mature* phase of the life-cycle all IS activity except Strategy has migrated to the Specialist Focus domain. Strategy remains in the User Focus domain because it is still essential that IS is informed of, and responsive to, the changing needs of the business. The users are both uniquely able in, and ultimately responsible for, determining IS needs. However, once the Strategy is clear, the users are now sufficiently sophisticated in relation to this mature technology to be able (and to be required) to make a precise statement of their needs for new systems. These specifications are used to negotiate a formal Development contract with either an internal or an external supply source, enforced with financial penalty clauses applying when either side deviates from contract. We have reached a point where Development, Support, and Delivery are all contracted to the specialist. Formal charging procedures apply to all three areas—but the user is well able to exercise judgements about value for money, and an efficient market mechanism for further exploitation of that technology is in place.

Organization vs. Technology Maturity

There may be occasions when the technology maturity is relatively high in the general market-place, but a particular organization is seeking to exploit that technology for the first time. In these cases, the model can be used to provide a number of alternative prescriptions:

1. The organization concerned may properly ignore the fact that maturity is high in the market-place, and proceed on the basis that maturity is low in its own particular case. It will therefore adopt a 'User Focus' in all spheres of IS activity.

2. Alternatively, the organization may seek to bypass the inefficiencies of a 'User Focus' regime by buying in from the market-place experienced

IT management and staff. This may enable them to move immediately to 'Specialist Focus' in the Delivery activity. However, 'User Focus' will be required in the Support, Delivery, and Strategy areas because of the inexperience of the user personnel. One of the companies in our field study of 1987 had adopted this combination for a major new project with conspicuous success. In some cases the organization concerned may perceive that the application required is well established in the general marketplace, in addition to the technology on which it is based; there may be a 'package' solution available. Nevertheless, our model should be interpreted as counselling *against* moving directly to a 'Specialist Focus' in the Development area. Our experience is that high uncertainty surrounds the implementation even of a package when the user is inexperienced. Only if experienced/'mature' *users* are brought into the relevant area of the organization can a rapid transition to 'Specialist Focus' in the Delivery activity be planned with confidence.

Prescription vs. Practice

Our model provides guidance on what we believe to be effective arrangements for integrating the efforts of users and IS specialists. It is a prescriptive, not a descriptive, model. Hence it may be instructive to contrast the prescriptions of the model with generally reported experience of the assimilation of technologies.

Data Processing tended to spend its early days inside the controller's department—from the standpoint of both reporting line and applications emphasis. Integration between users and specialists was relatively straightforward within the department's boundaries. However, during the 1960s and 1970s the application portfolio broadened—with systems being developed for the use of many other departments—and reports of dissatisfaction accumulated. In 1970 Zani claimed that 'no tool has proved so disappointing in use'. As Bostrom and Heinen (1977) reported, attempts to explain the shortcomings consistently stressed behavioural rather than technical problems. Failure was associated with ineffective communications between users and developers (Edstrom 1977), and the dominant power of specialists who 'consciously or unconsciously directed the development and use of computing' (Bostrom and Heinen 1977). By contrast, success was associated with user rather than specialist origination of projects (Powers and Dickson 1973); a-priori involvement of users (Zmud's (1979) summary of previous research); and a fluid, iterative design process, characterized by collaboration between users and developers (Bostrom and Heinen 1977). In the language of our model, these are descriptions of failure stemming from Development under Specialist Focus while maturity is far too low; and prescriptions for success consistent with Development under User Focus. The welcome for prototyping techniques (Earl 1978;

Naumann and Jenkins 1982) confirms the contemporary need for User Focus. But prototyping is not a permanent panacea for all Development activity—it is unlikely, for example, to be the right tool for development of a replacement payroll system. When a relatively mature technology is applied to a well-understood application area, Development under Specialist Focus is entirely appropriate.

The literature reporting on *End User Computing* represents a sharp contrast to that on Data Processing. The introduction of personal computers is seen to be characterized by an extreme form of User Focus—with the specialist frequently absent from the partnership. Benson (1983) found that in only eight of twenty organizations surveyed did the IS department have a stated policy towards personal computers; and in only two was there any planned support for their users. But the issues to which Benson and others drew attention are not resulting in failures of application Development. On the contrary, Benson refers to user 'euphoria' and the development of further applications as familiarity with the technology increases. Gerrity and Rockart (1986) write of the critical importance of End User Computing, and refer to widely publicized benefits. The concerns that are highlighted relate to the other three areas of activity—Delivery, Support, and Strategy—and can be seen to arise from the absence of well-directed IS involvement. For the Delivery activity, the recommendations made (Benson 1983; Rockart and Flannery 1983; Gerrity and Rockart 1986) amount to a call for a Specialist Focus regime: there are critical issues of data provision and security, and a lack of documentation; standards are needed to enable efficiencies to be achieved in purchasing, operations, and support. On the other hand, Support apparently should remain a while longer under User Focus: distributed out to the users (Rockart and Flannery); with an emphasis on end-use rather than technology knowledge, plus strong interpersonal skills (Gerrity and Rockart). Finally, the Strategy activity has been overlooked. There is a critical need (Benson) for IS to persuade senior business management of the need for 'Top Level Planning' to ensure that the 'bottom up' movement does not lead to disruption and chaos. Gerrity and Rockart similarly highlight the need for a stated end-user strategy, and the pro-active targeting of critical applications. In short, End User Computing was typically introduced under a User Focus regime and suffered few birth-pangs; the model highlights where and how action needed to be taken as the technology matured.

The successful introduction of *Office Automation* can also be associated with the prescriptions of the model. For example, Meyer (1983) reporting on a study of thirty-five organizations, listed success factors which correlate closely with the definition of a User Focus regime: an Office Automation pilot should be clearly targeted at solution of an important business problem; implemented by a team which includes business, administrative, and IS staff, with an emphasis on collaboration and interpersonal skills; IS specialists should be seen as 'facilitators' rather than 'experts'. Interestingly, Meyer also concluded that IS rather than user control over equipment selection was not worth fighting for 'at this stage'. Such control was not associated with successful introduction, and could be counter-productive by alienating users. Curley (1984) also emphasized the importance of linking the introduction of Office Automation to an achievable and desirable corporate goal; and of allowing for/planning for user experimentation and learning rather than attempting early formalization of applications. By contrast, Hirschheim and Feeny (1986) suggested that the twenty Office Automation Pilots funded by the UK government were largely unsuccessful because of a focus on specific technologies and applications rather than business problems—tantamount to operating from the start under a Specialist Focus.

There are two other established strands of information technology on which it is difficult to comment because of the lack of research literature. A general view of *Scientific Computing*, consistently supported by anecdotal evidence, would be that it was introduced under a User Focus regime and has only slowly migrated any activity areas to Specialist Focus. As a result, Scientific Computing tends to be rated highly in terms of effectiveness—at least as measured by user satisfaction. In our own study of 1987, it was noticeable that the assimilation of Scientific Computing through the four-stage model was on average further advanced than any of the other five referenced areas of Information Technology. And yet Scientific Computing never featured among the 'war stories' revealed when we asked about the company's history and heritage of IT. It had been largely introduced and advanced by users (often 'scientific' ones), and the extent, scope and use had often gone unnoticed by the IS department. However, the efficiency of the Scientific Computing activity could be strongly questioned, with evidence of some organizations operating hundreds of lightly loaded minicomputers, representing so many different architectures that acquisition and maintenance costs were extremely high.

The case of *Data Communications* is intriguing, since for many businesses in the late 1980s it represented an unfamiliar technology despite quite a lengthy history in the overall market-place. The prescriptions of the model would therefore be to buy in specialist skills and operate Delivery under Specialist Focus; while maintaining a User Focus regime for Support, Development, and Direction. In practice this could be seen to have been an appropriate prescription in the UK life insurance industry (Feeny and Knott 1988). Three network provider companies targeted this sector and promoted the concept of links between insurance companies and intermediaries (distribution channels). Two of the three—IBM and British Telecom—were large companies offering technically sophisticated networks; but with preconceived ideas of how they should be used. Neither won significant business. The successful company—ISTEL—was very small by comparison and offered a relatively unsophisticated network based on viewdata; but they went beyond the network to provide an application service which they had jointly developed with the largest intermediary organization to address the key business requirement.

The Model and Sourcing Strategy

A further application of the model can be to provide input to decisions on the sourcing of IS activity. Lacity and Hirschheim (1993) have warned of the dangers of contracting out the entire IS function. Our model, adapted as in Figure 11.2, can help to guide a more selective use of the external market for IS services, taking advantage of its abilities without incurring unacceptable risks.

Wherever the model suggests that specialist focus is appropriate for a particular activity/technology combination, there is potential for what is normally called outsourcing. Since the business is sufficiently clear of its requirements to operate in Specialist Focus mode, it may reasonably choose to contract with an external rather than internal provider. The contract will specify performance of a well-defined task to required standards. Facilities management of data centres (delivery activities) are well-established examples; contracts to provide the Support activity for the organization's population of personal computers are also becoming common.

On the other hand, when the model prescribes a User Focus regime, the implication is that outsourcing will not be appropriate. There will be insufficient organizational learning in place for a robustly specified performance contract to be developed, and the buyer will face the problems identified in the classic works of Williamson (1975)—information impactedness, opportunist suppliers, future uncertainty, high switching costs. This does not mean that the external market should not be used at all. But the contract should now focus on needed resource rather than required task, and the resource acquired will be under internal rather than external management. 'In-sourcing' is one way of describing such a use of the market. One familiar example would be to bring in from a software house a technical specialist to join the in-house development project team. Such a resource should be acquired on a daily-rate basis, ideally with an incentive payment geared to achievement of the in-house team's own business goal. The objective is to maintain the teamwork culture of the User Focus regime.

Conclusions

We have presented a model whose purpose is to guide the management of new information technologies. It differs from one of the best-known

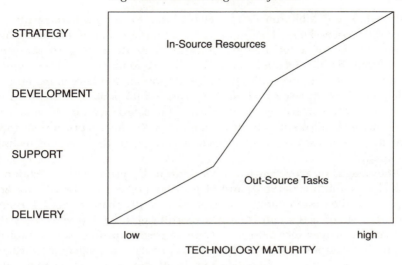

Fig. 11.2. *Sourcing strategy*

models–Nolan's (1979) six stages of assimilation—in a number of ways, but largely in taking each distinctive technology as a unit of analysis, whereas Nolan is concerned with the management of IS resources overall. The prescriptions of Allen (1987) for charging out IS services, and those of Dearden (1987) for contracting out, are also argued from the perspective of the IS function as a whole—mistakenly in our view. Allen's goal of 'Functional Pricing' and Dearden's belief in market contracting we see to be very appropriate to a mature technology—but only to a mature technology. Yet there is little to indicate that information technology in general can be treated as mature for decades to come.

Our model is more comparable with the original Gibson and Nolan (1974) Stage model (for Data Processing); or with McFarlan and McKenney's generalized four-stage model. However, neither is a very close match. The Gibson and Nolan model has little to say about users rather than specialists until Stage 3, when they recommend that analysts be devolved to user areas to act as conduits between users and programmers. Nolan (1979) did add a set of user awareness benchmarks to his expanded six-stage model, but the 'theory' continues to place far less emphasis than we do on user–specialist integration; users are relatively insignificant figures until Stage 4. Our own stronger emphasis on integration receives some support from the empirical testing of Nolan's stages by Drury (1983). Drury found that development of user awareness—alone of Nolan's five benchmark variables—was consistently and significantly associated with progress towards effective and efficient exploitation of data processing.

McFarlan and McKenney's model is closer to our own, but with two major differences. First, McFarlan and McKenney are describing four phases *in the early life* of a technology; our model is attempting to prescribe throughout the life. Secondly, McFarlan and McKenney do not distinguish as we do between Delivery, Support, Development, and Direction. Thus in their phase 3 an apparently complete transition takes place from an entre-preneurial to a control oriented group. Our categorization of IS activity into four areas allows for the prescription of the most appropriate form of management for each activity area, according to the status of techno-logy maturity.

Other stages of growth models continue to be proposed: for example, Mills (1983), Summer (1985), and Magal *et al.* (1988) all subscribe to such a model for the development of information centre management. It seems that the basic idea is a consistently powerful one for those who study the assimilation of new technology, despite consistent problems in establish-ing empirical support. Our own model is probably a particularly difficult one in terms of any formal validation. It sets out to be prescriptive, and its application clearly requires judgements to be made. What is a distinct-ive technology? What level of maturity has been reached? Where exactly is the boundary line between user focus and specialist domains? These may be further research questions. Yet the prescriptions of our model seem to be consistent with research-based findings.

Finally, we have found since our study in 1987 that managers in organ-izations—from both IS and the business side—consistently confirm that the ideals of the model relate to their experience and provide insights. These managers are confronted with more and more strands of technology to manage, and an increasing variety of options in terms of where to obtain resources and how to deploy them. The purpose of the model is to prompt both IS managers and user managers into asking critical questions about the management of each IS activity, and to provide them with first-level guidance on which management options are likely to be appropriate given the nature of that activity. At worst it should help organizations avoid mak-ing assumptions either that IS specialists should always be in control of all aspects of IT or that a user focus is always right.

References

Allen, B. (1987), 'Making Information Services Pay its Way', *Harvard Business Review* (Jan.–Feb.), 57–63.

Barki, H., and Hartwick, J. (1989), 'Rethinking the Concept of User Involvement', *MIS Quarterly* (Mar.), 53–63.

Benson, D. H. (1983), 'A Field Study of End User Computing: Findings and Issues', *MIS Quarterly* (Dec.), 35–45.

Bostrom, R. P., and Heinen, J. A. (1977), 'MIS Problems and Failures: A Socio-Technical Perspective', *MIS Quarterly* (Sept.), 17–32.

Couger, J. D., and Zawacki, R. A. (1980), *Motivating and Managing Computer Personnel*, New York: Wiley.

Curley, K. F. (1984), 'Are There Any Real Benefits from Office Automation?', *Business Horizons* (July–Aug.), 37–42.

—— and Pyburn, P. J. (1982), 'Intellectual Technologies: The Key to Improving White Collar Productivity', *Sloan Management Review* (Fall), 31–9.

Davidson, E. J. (1993), 'An Exploratory Study of Joint Application Design (JAD) in Information Systems Delivery', *Proceedings of the 14th International Conference on Information Systems* (Dec.), 271–83.

Dearden, J. (1987), 'The Withering Away of the IS Organization', *Sloan Management Review* (Summer), 87–91.

Drury, D. H. (1983), 'An Empirical Assessment of the Stages of DP Growth', *MIS Quarterly* (June), 59–70.

Earl, M. J. (1978), 'Prototype Systems for Accounting, Information and Control', *Accounting, Organizations and Society* (Mar.), 161–70.

—— (1993), 'Experiences in Strategic Information Systems Planning', *MIS Quarterly* (Mar.), 1–20.

—— and Skyrme, D. (1992), ' "Hybrid Managers": What Do We Know About Them?', *Journal of Information Systems*, vol. 2, pp. 169–87.

Edstrom, A. (1977), 'User Influence and the Success of MIS Projects: A Contingency Approach', *Human Relations*, vol. 30, no. 7, pp. 589–607.

Feeny, D. F., and Knott, P. (1988), *Information Technology and Marketing in the UK Life Insurance Industry*, Oxford Institute of Information Management, Research and Discussion Paper 88/5.

Ferratt, T. W., and Short, L. E. (1986), 'Are Information Systems People Different: An Investigation of Motivational Differences', *MIS Quarterly* (Dec.), 377–87.

—— (1988), 'Are Information Systems People Different: An Investigation of How They Are and Should Be Managed', *MIS Quarterly* (Sept.), 427–43.

—— (1990), 'Patterns of Motivation: Beyond Differences Between IS and Non-IS People', Issues and Opinions, *MIS Quarterly* (Mar.), 3–6.

Galbraith, J. R. (1977), *Designing Complex Organizations*, Reading, Mass.: Addison-Wesley.

Gerrity, T. P., and Rockart, J. F. (1986), 'End User Computing: Are You a Leader or a Laggard?', *Sloan Management Review* (Summer), 25–34.

Gibson, C. F., and Nolan, R. L. (1974), 'Managing the Four Stages of EDP Growth', *Harvard Business Review* (Jan.–Feb.), 76–88.

Gingras, L., and McLean, E. R. (1979), *A Study of Users and Designers of Information Systems*, IS Working Paper 2–79, Graduate School of Management, UCLA.

Grindley, K. (1991), *Managing IT at Board Level: The Hidden Agenda Exposed*, London: Price Waterhouse, Pitman.

Henderson, J. C., and Treacy, M. E. (1986), 'Managing End User Computing for Competitive Advantage', *Sloan Management Review* (Winter), 3–14.

Hirschheim, R. A., and Feeny, D. F. (1986), 'Experiences with Office Automation: Some Lessons and Recommendations', *Journal of General Management* (Winter), 25–40.

Inmon, J. H., and Hartman, S. (1990), 'Rethinking the Issue of Whether IS People are Different from Non-IS People', Issues and Opinions, *MIS Quarterly* (Mar.), 1–2.

Lacity, M. C., and Hirschheim, R. (1993), 'The Information Systems Outsourcing Bandwagon', *Sloan Management Review* (Fall), 73–86.

Lawrence, P. R., and Lorsch, J. W. (1967), *Organization and Environment: Managing Differentiation and Integration,* Division of Research, Graduate School of Business Administration, Harvard University.

Lockett, M. (1987), *The Factors Behind Successful IT Innovation,* Oxford Institute of Information Management, Research and Discussion Paper 87/9.

Magal, S. R., Carr, H. H., and Watson, H. J. (1988), 'Critical Success Factors for Information Center Managers', *MIS Quarterly* (Sept.), 413–25.

McFarlan, F. W., and McKenney, J. L. (1982), 'The Information Archipelago: Maps and Bridges', *Harvard Business Review* (Sept.–Oct.), 109–19.

Meyer, N. D. (1983), 'The Office Automation Cookbook: Management Strategies for Getting Office Automation Moving', *Sloan Management Review* (Winter), 51–60.

Mills, C. (1983), 'The Information Center', *DRS Journal* (Spring), 42–6.

Mumford, E. (1983), *Designing Human Systems for New Technology: The ETHICS Method,* Manchester Business School.

Naumann, J. D., and Jenkins, A. M. (1982), 'Prototyping: The New Paradigm for Systems Development', *MIS Quarterly* (Sept.), 29–44.

Nolan, R. L. (1979), 'Managing the Crisis in Data Processing', *Harvard Business Review* (Mar.–Apr.), 115–26.

Powers, R. F., and Dickson, G. W. (1973), 'MIS Project Management: Myths, Opinions and Reality', *California Management Review* (Spring), 147–56.

Raho, L. E., Belohlav, J. A., and Fiedler, K. D. (1987), 'Assimilating New Technology into the Organization: An Assessment of McFarlan and McKenney's Model', *MIS Quarterly* (Mar.), 47–57.

Rockart, J. F., and Flannery, L. S. (1983), 'The Management of End User Computing', *Communications of the ACM* (Oct.), 776–84.

Rogers, E. M. (1962), *The Diffusion of Innovations,* New York: Free Press.

Runge, D. A. (1985), 'Using Telecommunications for Competitive Advantage', unpublished doctoral dissertation, University of Oxford.

Summer, M. (1985), 'Organization and Management of the Information Center', *Journal of Systems Management* (Nov.), 10–15.

Taylor-Cummings, A. (1993), 'Bridging the User-IS Gap: Successful Integration Arrangements for Systems Involving Significant Organizational Change', unpublished doctoral dissertation, Oxford University.

Thompson, J. D. (1967), *Organizations in Action,* New York: McGraw-Hill.

Williamson, O. E. (1975), *Markets and Hierarchies,* New York: Free Press.

Zani, W. M. (1970), 'Blueprint for MIS', *Harvard Business Review* (Nov.–Dec.), 95–100.

Zmud, R. W. (1979), 'Individual Differences and MIS Success: A Review of the Empirical Literature', *Management Science* (Oct.), 966–79.

—— and Cox, J. F. (1979), 'The Implementation Process: A Change Approach', *MIS Quarterly*, vol. 3, no. 2, pp. 35–43.

12

The Role of the Corporate IT Function in the Federal IT Organization

STEPHEN L. HODGKINSON

Introduction

The organization, or reorganization, of IT activities is a perennial item on the agendas of the CIOs of large companies as they seek to ensure that their IT functions are aligned with an ever-changing business and technology environment. Consider these examples:

—The furniture group Silentnight created a new IT organization in 1990. Previously, each of the group's subsidiaries had an autonomous IT function, with no standardization or co-ordination of effort across the group. Management recognized that this approach failed to realize economies of scale and synergies between subsidiaries that were fundamentally quite similar—and led to much re-invention of the wheel and wasted effort. A central IT management group was created, tasked with formulating group-wide IT policy, standardization of IT purchasing, and the development of common core business systems.

—W. H. Smith, the UK based international retail group, 'tore up its centralized IT strategy and opted for a federal structure' in 1989. Responsibility for systems development was devolved from a central management services unit to the strategic business units. The central IT services unit was substantially downsized and refocused on strategic co-ordination rather than service delivery.

—The retail giant Storehouse created a centralized IT organization in 1988, only to reorganize in 1990 by devolving all IT resources to its divisional managements and closing down the corporate IT unit. The group chief executive stated that: 'Unambiguous profit accountability requires that the operating companies take greater responsibility for the support resources which underpin their businesses . . . We have therefore decentralized information systems and technology. This reduces head office overheads and allows the centre to concentrate on strategic issues, financial control, and performance monitoring.'

How can these events be explained? What forces drove the reorganization of IT activities in these companies? What organizational options are available? Is there a valid role for the corporate IT function in the modern, decentralized, multi-business-unit firm? Can a corporate IT function be justified in the face of pressure on corporate overhead costs and the desire of business unit managers for local control of IT? This chapter seeks to address these issues by describing the results of a study of the IT organizations of fifty of the largest companies in the UK.[1]

The Federal IT Organization

The diversified, multi-business-unit company is now the most common form of large business enterprise. Indeed, the vast majority of the companies in the *Times* listing of the largest 200 companies in the UK comprise more than three different lines of business. Most of these companies are managed in the decentralized manner originally identified in the early 1960s by authors such as Chandler and Sloan. The managerial philosophy of decentralization espoused by these authors, and many since, has become one of the fundamental principles of modern management—emphasizing location of responsibility for operational decisions as low in the organizational hierarchy as possible, whilst senior management retains responsibility for longer-term strategic decisions.

Coupled with this trend towards decentralization of management decision-making has been a trend towards increasing decentralization of IT activities (King 1983). Profit-accountable business unit managing directors now demand control of an important management resource—information technology (Boynton *et al.* 1992). Heightened strategic relevance of IT to business unit management, and technological developments that have enabled distributed computing, have led to the establishment of IT functions in divisional and business unit offices. The days when IT needs were met solely by a large centralized IT department are over for most companies. The 'IT function' now typically comprises a federation of numerous IT functions located at the head office, divisional and/or business unit levels simultaneously (Zmud *et al.* 1986).

The federal IT organization attempts to capture the benefits of both centralized and decentralized IT. In the federal IT organization, business units receive a responsive service from decentralized IT functions, whilst at the same time a corporate IT function provides group-wide IT services and exerts some degree of central leadership and control of IT activities. As Figure 12.1 implies, federal IT is not simply simultaneous centralized

---

[1] The study was doctoral research done at Templeton College in the University of Oxford, supervised by the editor.

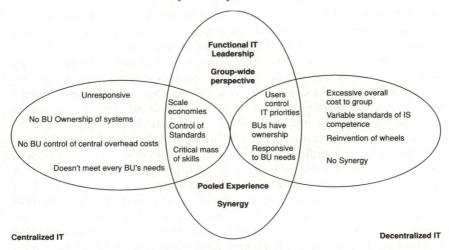

Fig. 12.1. *The federal IT organization attempts to capture the benefits of both centralized and decentralized IT*

and decentralized IT. In the federal IT organization the corporate IT department has some degree of explicit mandate to co-ordinate the IT activities of semi-autonomous business unit IT functions.

The Multi-Business-Unit Firm

By way of scene-setting, it is perhaps useful to reflect on some of the characteristics of the decentralized, multi-business-unit firm. This is the dominant organizational form of today's large companies (Channon 1973; Hill and Pickering 1986). The benefits of decentralization revolve around increasing the autonomy, accountability, motivation, and responsiveness of business unit managements—to which are delegated responsibility and authority for significant independent action. Decentralization brings decision-makers closer to the customer—closer to the information needed for effective decisions (Peters and Waterman 1982). Decentralization aims to improve operational flexibility and responsiveness to local market forces, and to encourage innovation by removal of bureaucracy.

Set against the benefits of decentralization, however, are the costs of lost integration of business activities, lost opportunities for synergy and cost-sharing between business units, and loss of central control. Some degree of central co-ordination and control is deemed necessary in most companies, and so business units have constrained autonomy—limited by the business needs of the overall company and top management's approach to corporate management. The ongoing challenge for top management is to strike a workable balance between, on the one hand, the benefits of decentralized decision-making and the responsiveness of business units to local market forces, and on the other hand, the benefits of central co-ordination, control, and integration of business activities (Lorsch and Allen 1973; Prahalad and Doz 1987). The way this balance is struck varies between companies, giving rise to a continuum of approaches to corporate management. At one extreme, top management may co-ordinate the activities of all business units and involve itself in the detail of their strategies—perhaps supported by hundreds of corporate staff. At the other, they may concern themselves with high-level direction only and the centre may comprise a mere handful of staff. Goold and Campbell (1986) provide a useful framework for describing a range of approaches to the management of multi-business-unit companies. They viewed the two main responsibilities of the centre as *planning* resource allocation and *controlling* business unit performance. Goold and Campbell used these two dimensions to analyse and describe the corporate strategic management styles of sixteen large international companies, identifying three dominant styles of corporate strategic management (see Table 12.1).

Goold and Campbell's framework provides a powerful description of the 'value adding' approach of the centre. As Porter emphasized, income is earned by the business units, while the centre inevitably adds costs and constraints. The challenge for the head office is to add sufficient value through planning and control activities to offset direct central costs and the costs inherent in constraining business unit autonomy. Strategic Planning style companies clearly have a different approach to central added value than Financial Control style companies, and we would expect this to have implications for the organization and management of the company's IT activities.

IT Organizational Fit

Many authors have asserted the need for the IT organization to 'fit' the company within which it resides—a common-sense notion and one that is consistent with wider organizational contingency theory. As a senior IT executive commented to me: 'IT is enough of a sore thumb to most executives as it is without an organizational miss-match as well . . .'

Empirical support for the necessity, or even existence, of such fit in the context of the federal IT organization is, however, rather scarce. Extant research in this area tends to deal mainly with strategies for distributed computing and the technology centralization vs. decentralization debate rather than with higher-level organization and technology management issues. In particular, existing studies have tended to ignore the existence of a grey area between the two extremes of centralization and decentralization, and the need to manage the portfolio of centralized and

Table 12.1. *Goold and Campbell's corporate strategic management styles*

Strategic planning	Strategic control	Financial control
Where the centre works with the business unit managers to develop strategy. It establishes extensive planning processes, makes substantive contributions to strategic thinking, and may establish a corporate strategy or mission that guides and co-ordinates developments across business units. Less attention is devoted to control. Performance targets are set in broad, strategic, terms (such as 'become a leading supplier'). Annual finance targets are seen as being less important than strategic objectives. The focus is on co-operative, collaborative, shared purposes and development of long-term strategic capabilities.	Where the centre prefers to leave the initiative in the development of plans to business unit managers. Plans are reviewed by the centre to monitor the quality of strategic thinking rather than for the centre to direct strategy. The control process is an important influencing mechanism for the centre. Targets are established for both strategic and financial objectives, and managers are expected to meet targets. The focus is on clear definition of individual strategic responsibility and motivation to achieve long-term competitive advantage. Strategic control companies combine moderate planning influence with tight controls.	Where the centre's influence is exerted mainly through the budget process. Little emphasis is placed on corporate review of strategies. Instead, the centre focuses on close review of the annual budget. Profit targets are set when the budget is reviewed. Performance is then closely monitored and careers are at stake if targets are not met. The focus is on clear definition of individual responsibility and on motivation to achieve challenging short-term results. Financial control companies combine a low level of planning influence with tight financial controls.

decentralized IT capabilities and competencies that exist in a large multi-business firm.

The Research Study

The research was aimed at improving our understanding of federal IT organizations in practice—focusing on the role of the corporate IT function. The research approach was exploratory, rather than aimed at testing an a priori hypothesis, and was carried out using an eclectic combination of two research approaches:

1. A postal survey of the largest 200 companies in the UK. A two-step mailing was used. The first step was a questionnaire sent to the

group IT director, aimed at collecting data on the characteristics of the IT organization. Fifty companies responded. Respondents were then sent a second questionnaire for completion by a senior corporate general manager, to collect data on the corporate strategic management style of the company. Twenty-eight matched pairs of questionnaires were collected. This provided a broad, but shallow, view of the IT organizations of large UK companies, and enabled identification of two variations on the federal theme.

2. In-depth interviews in eight companies selected from the original sample of twenty-eight. Four companies were selected from each of the two federal styles identified. Interviews were conducted with 105 group IT and finance directors, corporate IT managers, and divisional and business unit IT managers. This provided an opportunity to confirm the findings of the postal survey and explore the federal IT organizations of the sample in much greater detail.

This research approach sought to benefit from both the depth of insight afforded by interview-based research and from the broad coverage and generalizability of results afforded by larger-sample, questionnaire-based, research, as advocated by Harrigan (1983). The use of different survey techniques also provides some triangulation of results—confirming conclusions from several different perspectives.

Most respondents (88 per cent) had a federal IT organization of some sort—some simultaneous balance of both centralized and distributed responsibility for IT. Two distinct styles of federal IT organization were identified—based on two techniques for categorizing IT management style. First, the respondents were presented with a range of IT management, systems operations, and systems development activities and asked to rate each in terms of the amount of *responsibility* held at the head-office, divisional, and business-unit levels (All, Most, Some, or None). Secondly, they were presented with a list of strategic IT management roles and asked to rate the relative importance of each (on a Likert scale). These techniques provided a mechanism for classifying companies in terms of their IT management style—the way IT responsibility was allocated and the perceived importance of central IT management. Four distinct categories resulted: Centralized and Decentralized; and two federal styles—a 'strong centre/federal' style that was termed Strategic Leadership, and a 'weak centre/federal' style that was termed Strategic Guidance. Figure 12.2 shows the IT management styles of the companies studied.

These terms are used to convey first, the idea that in the federal IT organization the centre has a *strategic* IT management role—one focused on the longer term, on the development of a group-wide IT capability, and on the strategic management of a portfolio of IT resources—in addition to the more traditional tactical IT service provision role. Secondly, the

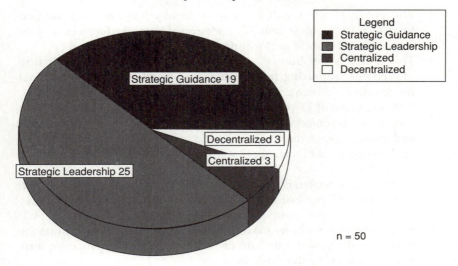

Fig. 12.2. *IT management styles of UK companies*

Leadership label conveys the idea of pro-active functional leadership, while the Guidance label conveys the idea of a less proactive advisory corporate role.

The two styles were explored in more detail during the case-study based research. Four companies were selected from those with a Strategic Leadership IT management style and four with a Strategic Guidance style. The case studies confirmed the existence of two distinct styles, and provided a richer understanding of the differences in the roles and responsibilities of the centre. The major characteristics of the two federal IT management styles are described in the next two sections.

The Strategic Leadership Style

In this style a substantial corporate IT function exists, ranging from thirty to 200 or more staff. Characteristics of Strategic Leadership style IT organizations may include:

- Corporate IT staff have an explicit mandate to add value from the centre. They are proactive in defining corporate IT strategy, formally reviewing business unit IT strategy, and in IT functional leadership activities.
- The group IT director/CIO is a senior executive who reports to the main board or to a senior board member—typically the finance director.
- A formally defined Corporate IT Strategy defines group-wide policy and standards for procurement and IT methods.

- The group IT director/CIO may be involved in assessing the performance of business unit IT managers. Under-performers may be replaced and poorly performing IT functions restructured.
- The centre is the hub of a group-wide IT organization, with firm 'dotted-line' reporting relationships and regular reporting between the group IT director/CIO and the business unit IT managers.
- A strong sense of IT community exists across the business units. Corporate and business unit IT managers meet regularly, both formally and informally, to discuss group-wide issues and share experiences. All business unit IT managers will likely know each other on a 'first name' basis.
- An explicit objective is to foster the development of uniformly high standards of IT professionalism across the business units—disseminating expertise from more- to less-competent business units.
- Synergistic behaviour and skills transfer across the business units are encouraged by corporate initiatives. The centre is a proactive initiator of change in the business units.
- Business unit IT managers are encouraged to have group-wide career paths, and to transfer between the centre and the business units.
- The centre may also provide a wide range of corporate IT services—many aimed at the creation of group-wide technology infrastructures, such as telecommunications networks and data centres.

The corporate IT function in Strategic Leadership IT organizations aims to proactively increase IT performance throughout the group. The aim is to develop a group-wide vision of how IT should be managed to maximize efficiency and effectiveness and then to roll this out across all the business units—creating a coherent group-wide IT organization.

Most Strategic Leadership style companies appeared to have evolved from previously Centralized structures—since when pressures from the business units over the cost and unresponsiveness of central services have led to the establishment of semi-autonomous business unit IT functions. The Strategic Leadership style aims to achieve an IT organization that enables *constrained* business unit IT autonomy—achieving business focus within a firmly defined environment of central direction and control.

The Strategic Guidance Style

In this style the corporate IT function is smaller and less proactive. The centre may only have one IS executive or a small number of staff. Its role is more focused on ensuring a minimum level of IT professionalism across the group and on correcting poorly performing business unit IT functions. Characteristics of Strategic Guidance style IT organizations may include:

Table 12.2. *The case study companies*

Companies with a strategic leadership style IT organization		Companies with a strategic guidance style IT organization	
Company A A £1,850M turnover international retail, beer and leisure group of 54,000 staff. The corporate IT function of 380 staff provides a full range of IT services to the group's companies. The IT organization is currently in transition from a Centralized to a Strategic Leadership style in response to the growing autonomy of recently established business unit IT functions.	*Company C* A £9,200M turnover global food, drinks and retail group of 152,000 staff. The corporate IT function of 150 provides mainly data centre operations services. All applications development is performed in the business units. The group IT director has a well-established global IT planning process and is active in most of the strategic IT leadership roles.	*Company E* A £2,600M international telecoms and information systems technology group of 36,000 staff. The corporate IT function of 450 staff provides extensive IT services to one of the large divisions, and has attempted to establish itself as the centre of the IT organization of the whole group, but this has met with active resistance from the other business units, who still operate largely autonomously.	*Company G* A £1,500M turnover transport, travel, and distribution group of 34,000 staff. The group has only one IT manager at the corporate level, who facilitates meetings of the business unit IT managers. These are aimed at establishing a co-ordinated approach to IT management practices across the group, but most business units remain highly autonomous.
Company B A £2,900M turnover international property, construction, engineering, and shipping group of 29,000 staff. The corporate IT function of 140 staff provides many traditional centralized services, but plans are well advanced to scale down the corporate resource in favour of business unit IT functions. A group IT director co-ordinates IT planning across the group.	*Company D* A £1,900M turnover retailing, distribution and television group of 35,000 staff. The corporate IT function was substantially downsized several years ago, and the 35 staff are focused exclusively on supporting the head office, strategic planning and co-ordination of semi-autonomous business unit IT functions.	*Company F* A £1,900M turnover industrial fibres, chemicals, and coatings group of 24,000 staff. The corporate IT function has been substantially downsized in recent years following management dissatisfaction with its costs and performance. It now comprises 13 staff who support the head office and provide consultancy support to the head office and some of the business units.	*Company H* A £4,700M turnover international food, food ingredients and agriculture group of 22,503 staff. The group also has only one IT manager at the corporate level, whose role is primarily to act as a consultant and 'trouble shooter' to the business units on behalf of the group finance director.

- Reviews of business unit IT strategies are less formal—perhaps only focused on problem business units and those with small IT functions that need specific support.
- The Corporate IT manager is less influential than the group IT director/CIO of a Strategic Leadership style company. The role is typically more advisory than directive and is reactive rather than proactive.
- Reporting relationships are variable and loose between the centre and the business unit IT functions. Competent IT functions may receive little attention from the centre.
- There is little sense of a group IT community. Business unit IT managers seldom meet the IT managers of other business units— many may not even know the names of all the other IT managers in the group.
- Standards of IT professionalism are variable across the business units—some high, some low.
- Minimal group-wide IT policy and standards may exist.
- Synergistic behaviour and skill transfer may be encouraged among some business units, but systematic efforts to propagate 'good ideas' group-wide are not common.
- Few corporate IT services are provided to business units.

The corporate IT function in Strategic Guidance style IT organization aims to ensure an acceptable minimum level of IT performance across the group's companies. The aim is to encourage propagation of good ideas where possible and to 'fix' the less competent business units on an *ad hoc* basis—rather than necessarily to roll out a common approach to IT management across the group.

Many Strategic Guidance style companies appeared to have evolved from previously Decentralized structures. The companies recognised that 'something is lost' when business units have totally autonomous and uncoordinated IT functions. Typical reasons cited were that technology and software diversity precluded systems integration, proliferation of technologies created excessive maintenance and support costs, standards of professionalism varied unacceptably across the business units, and opportunities for cost savings through co-ordinated procurement were lost.

A Corporate IT Roles Framework

A framework of the twenty-six most important corporate IT roles, the *Corporate IT Roles* framework, describes the two federal styles and distinguishes between them. The framework was derived from the case study data by a systematic post hoc analysis of the roles and responsibilities of each of the companies. This led to a reasonably exhaustive and mutually exclusive list of the corporate IT roles observed. Table 12.3 depicts the average extent to which each role is applicable in the Strategic Leadership and Strategic Guidance companies studied. The twenty-six roles in the Corporate IT Roles framework act in two fundamentally different dimensions:

- Strategic IT Management—roles A to T are those which enable the centre to oversee and promote the development of the entire group's information technology resources.
- Central IT Service—roles U to Z are those traditionally associated with a centralized IT function; provision of systems operations and systems development support to the business units.

In seeking to understand these strategic IT management and central IT service roles, it is useful to reflect on the reasons for the existence of a corporate IT function in a multi-business unit company. As Porter (1988) asserts, income is earned by the business units while the corporate head office inevitably adds costs and constraints: 'Corporate strategy cannot succeed unless it truly adds value to business units by providing tangible benefits that offset the inherent costs of lost independence.'

How does the corporate IT function aim to 'add value' over and above the costs and constraints it imposes on the business units? The Corporate IT Roles framework provides a useful perspective on this question— revealing that the strategic IT management and central IT service roles comprise fundamentally different approaches to adding value.

Strategic IT Management

In a manner similar to corporate strategic management (i.e. the high-level management of a portfolio of businesses), strategic IT management is concerned with the group-wide management of a portfolio of IT resources and capabilities. This involves many activities in common with strategic management, such as; organizational mission and goal formulation, formulation of strategies to achieve goals, strategy implementation, and strategic control.

The twenty strategic IT management roles are focused on four general areas of activity.

1. Formulating Group IM, IT, and IS strategy One of the main roles of the corporate IT function is to facilitate the definition of group-wide information technology strategy. A formally defined information-technology strategy provides the basis for a coherent approach to IT throughout the group—providing an agreed core set of policies about which to build the group IT organization. An essential purpose of the group IT strategy is to minimize the diversity of technologies and methods between the business units. When business unit IT functions have nothing, or very little, in

Table 12.3. *The corporate IT roles framework*

Strategic IT management roles	Strategic leadership	Strategic guidance
1. Formulation of groupwide information technology strategy and policy		
A. facilitate definition of group *IT management* strategy and policy	+ + +	+ + −
B. chair a meeting of BU IT managers to agree group IT strategy/policy	+ + +	+ + −
C. chair a meeting of BU MDs to promote and address IT issues	+ + +	+ + −
D. facilitate definition of group *IT architecture* policies and standards	+ + +	+ − −
E. prepare and promote a formal groupwide IT policy/standards manual	+ + +	− − −
F. facilitate definition of *IS application* strategy and policy	+ + −	− − −
2. Strategic Control		
G. ensure that BUs have effective IT functions—intervene if necessary	+ + +	+ + +
H. formally sign off significant IT expenditure by BUs	+ + +	+ + −
I. review BU IT plans to ensure integration with BU business strategy	+ + +	+ − −
J. review BU IT plans to promote and police group IT strategy	+ + +	+ − −
K. actively participate in the management of IT at the BU level	+ − −	+ + −
3. Functional Leadership		
L. review BU systems plans to challenge the quality of IT thinking	+ + +	+ + +
M. provide sponsored IT consultancy services to the BUs	+ + +	+ + −
N. proactively promote IT awareness to senior general managers	+ + +	+ + −
O. proactively identify and promote IT initiatives to the BUs	+ + +	+ − −
P. monitor competitor and IT trends, do R&D, & disseminate info to BUs	+ + +	− − −
Q. proactively organize IT skills training for business unit IT staff	+ + +	− − −
4. Promotion of Synergy		
R. foster synergy and experience sharing between BU IT functions	+ + +	+ + +
S. negotiate group-wide terms with vendors and service companies	+ + +	+ + −
T. facilitate the career development of IT professionals groupwide	+ + +	− − −
Central IT Service Roles		
U. provide voice and/or data telecoms to the BUs	+ + +	− − −
V. provide IT consultancy services to BUs on a commercial basis	+ + +	− − −

W. provide data centre ownership and/or facilities management services	+ + +	− − −
X. provide value added network services, such as email and office systems	+ + −	− − −
Y. provide applications development services to HQ and BUs	+ + −	− − −
Z. provide generic applications to BUs, e.g. payroll, general ledger	+ − −	− − −

Note: + + + *A key role*: A role which is well defined in the IT function's terms of reference and adequately resourced.
+ + − *To some extent applicable*: A role which is performed by the IT function but which is not necessarily formally defined with dedicated resources
+ − − *A minor role only*: It is not fair to say that the role is not performed at all, but it is not given much emphasis.

common there is little scope for attempting to achieve central added value. The establishment of a consistent approach to IT and some shared preferences for technologies across the business units is an essential precursor to many of the value-adding roles—providing the basic platform of commonality and shared experiences necessary to create an environment that enables synergy. One way of addressing these issues is to distinguish between Earl's (1989) three levels of information strategy.

IM strategy, which defines the IT organization structure and its management processes, is more formally defined in Strategic Leadership companies, but even Strategic Guidance companies have some degree of formal IM policy.

IT strategy, which defines technology architecture and standards, is common only in Strategic Leadership companies. Strategic Guidance companies tend to agree very high-level standards only—such as to attempt a focus on one or two preferred hardware vendors in order to reduce diversity and gain purchasing economies.

Corporate IS strategy, which defines corporate applications and group-wide systems, is given a relatively low emphasis in both styles. Some of the Strategic Leadership companies studied did have a limited number of group-wide systems, such as for financial reporting, general ledger, payroll, and personnel. None, however, were enthusiastic about group-wide *common* systems. In many cases corporate-level systems appeared to be legacies of a previous centralized strategy, and the systems were being devolved as the business units become more IT independent. IS strategy, therefore, is largely the concern of divisional and business unit IT functions.

The corporate IT function in the federal IT organization does not, however, necessarily decide and then dictate IT strategy. In both the Strategic Leadership, and (to a lesser extent) the Strategic Guidance companies, a key role of the centre is to facilitate a forum of the group's IT managers. Decisions on group-wide information technology strategy are typically made by the IT managers—with the corporate IT staff facilitating the process, researching issues, presenting options, and so on. This approach seemed to be important in order to ensure that the business unit IT managers are prepared to accept and voluntarily adhere to group-wide policies and standards. As one IT manager commented: 'Why wouldn't you adhere to a strategy or policy that you yourself were involved in creating?'

In Strategic Leadership companies, the corporate IT function also involved senior *general managers* in IT strategy decision making by chairing a high-level policy forum. This provided a vehicle for: (a) promoting integration between the IT function and the business; and (b) involving senior management in IT matters to promote IT awareness and commitment. This forum may take the form of a management board for the corporate IT function. This approach appeared to have much to recommend it, as it encouraged the board (which typically comprised senior head office and business unit general managers) to view the corporate IT function as their resource—rather than as a remote function 'owned' by the head office. Decisions made are therefore more likely to reflect group-wide needs rather than those of the centre only.

2. Strategic Control   The centre also exerts strategic control over the divisional and business unit IT functions by reviewing IT plans, formally approving significant IT investment, and reviewing the performance of business unit IT managers. Strategic control is aimed at ensuring, on behalf of the head office, that the business units have effectively and efficiently managed IT functions. The centre adds value by acting as a mentor, teacher, and if necessary, policeman—'encouraging' business units to think of the longer-term implications of their plans, offering specific advice, and preventing them from, as one group IT director put it, 'doing silly things'.

In Strategic Leadership companies, the centre takes a comprehensive approach to strategic control; proactively reviewing IT plans for quality of thinking, integration with business plans and conformance to group policies. The aim is both to ensure that the business units are making a professional job of IT and that they are doing it in the manner defined by the group's IM and IT strategy. In some companies the group IT director/ CIO also has a degree of influence over the business unit IT managers through the annual performance appraisal and group-wide career development programmes.

In Strategic Guidance companies the strategic control process is much less comprehensive—being limited primarily to challenging the quality of thinking behind business unit IT plans in a more *ad hoc* manner. Business unit IT plans are typically only reviewed, to ensure quality of thinking and 'reasonableness' of planned investment, as part of the IT capital investment approval process. The centre attempts to ensure that IT investment plans are well thought out and that the business units are making a professional job of IT, but is not too concerned about the details of how they go about implementation of the plans.

In both styles the centre may actively intervene to enforce strategic control. Strategic Leadership style companies in particular will restructure business unit IT functions, appoint new IT managers, and implement new IT management processes in the business units when necessary. This will often be the case following acquisition of a new company. The centre in Strategic Guidance style companies will also act to restructure business unit IT functions when necessary to correct major anomalies in performance.

It is important to recognize, however, that the corporate IT function will likely have only partial authority over the group's full IT resources. The perceived legitimacy of corporate control and intervention may not be high in the business units—depending on the corporate strategic management style. In most organizations the corporate IT function will need to exert influence and control over business unit IT managers without recourse to formal authority. A key success factor of federal IT is the ability of the group IT director/CIO, and the corporate IT staff, to establish an organization culture characterized by clear central leadership, participative decision-making, and frequent social contact between IT managers. Such a culture enables the corporate IT function to create a group-wide IT organization that will operate as a voluntary federation—minimizing the need for formal bureaucratic control from the head office.

It is important to recognize that the primary allegiance of most of the business unit IT managers will be to their individual business unit managing directors—with only a 'dotted line' relationship to the corporate IT function. The success of the relationship is largely determined by the ability of the group IT director/CIO to establish a clear vision for the IT organization and create a strong sense of shared preferences among the business unit IT managers by persuasion, negotiation, and open communication—by good old-fashioned *leadership*.

3. Functional Leadership The corporate IT function is also charged with the role of proactively promoting IT throughout the group—both to the general business community and the IT community. This is achieved by such activities as: promoting IT awareness among the senior managers with seminars and *ad hoc* consultancy; promoting specific IT initiatives to the business unit IT managers; disseminating information on industry trends and new developments; facilitating training for IT managers and actively facilitating the career development of senior IT staff; keeping the IT managers informed about industry developments; and providing sponsored consultancy to assist IT managers in specific areas. These roles are, in the main, performed only by Strategic Leadership companies. The functional leadership objective is to ensure that IT is being applied as effectively as possible across the group—to identify proactively and develop the key IT capabilities required to support, or enable, the group's core business competencies.

4. Promotion of Synergy A further objective of the corporate IT function is the promotion of synergy among the business unit IT functions—by both addressing ways of minimizing overall costs and maximizing 'mutual support' between the business units. Group-wide purchasing discounts are negotiated by the centre in most of the companies. A key role of the centre in both styles is the facilitation of communication and experience-sharing between business units. Communication reduces 're-invention of the wheel' costs and also speeds diffusion of innovation and the transfer of skills across the group. Interaction between the IT managers is significantly higher in Strategic Leadership companies, which place a high degree of emphasis on functional leadership and promotion of synergy. All the Strategic Leadership style companies studied held at least quarterly meetings of the business unit IT managers—usually chaired by the group IT director/ CIO.

Provision of Central IT Services

Provision of central IT services (roles U to Z) is largely confined to the Strategic Leadership style companies only. All the Strategic Leadership companies studied provided group voice and data telecommunications network services as the basis for a group-wide information technology infrastructure (though in some the network was operationally managed by a third party Value Added Network supplier); some provided central data centre ownership or facilities management services; some provided value added network services; some provided generic applications; some provided systems development services; and some provided IT consultancy services to business units on request.

In the Strategic Guidance companies, central IT services are not seen as a valid corporate activity. Those companies that do provide some degree of services tend to do so for historical reasons and plan fully to devolve the remaining services in the near future. The three main motivations for the provision of central IT services are:

1. To enable group strategic benefit through supporting the implementation of group IM, IT, and/or IS strategy; that is, to achieve group-wide benefits through systems integration, overall economies of scale, or maintenance of a critical mass of core competencies at the centre.
2. To deliver functional benefits to the business units by providing services that they would otherwise not have access to—perhaps

because of the high cost or poor service levels of public networks, or the difficulty of attracting specialist staff at the business unit level. The corporate service function is sometimes regarded as a 'skills centre' or 'centre of excellence'.

3. To deliver financial benefits to the business units. An efficiently managed corporate IT function may be able to achieve economies of scale that enable it to provide services to business units more cost-effectively than either the market or their own in-house IT functions. One company studied, for example, estimated that the planned merging of the data centres of a number of subsidiaries would save US $10 million per year in IT operations costs.

Because the service roles are concerned with the professional delivery of IT services, their perceived success depends on the effectiveness and efficiency of their management—just as for an external company providing the same services in the open market. In most companies these service roles are managed on a commercial basis, with the corporate IT service 'bureau' being established as a profit centre—though perhaps with a break-even target. Business units are charged for services they consume at negotiated prices. This encourages the corporate IT function to provide service levels and costs comparable to those available from other sources.

The provision of central IT services for strategic benefit, however, somewhat muddies this situation. A grey area may be created between the strategic IT management roles and the central IT service roles. Services provided in the interests of supporting corporate strategy may not be able to be fully charged to the business units. The strategy of one of the companies studied, for example, was to establish an integrated global business. The corporate IT function elected to fund the set-up costs of a telecommunications network as a corporate development expense and to offer discounted rates to the business units in order to encourage use the network.

Many IT managers in the study, however, commented on the need to keep a clear separation between the strategic IT management and central IT service roles. They emphasized two important points:

1. Poorly regarded central IT services can undermine the strategic IT management roles—meetings, for example, of the group's IT managers to decide on group-wide strategy often founder in disputes over the current chargeout rates or performance of the central resource.
2. Inclusion of the costs of the strategic IT management roles in the overall chargeout cost of the central resource can make it appear uncompetitively expensive to the business unit IT managers. The costs of centrally initiated strategies should not be 'hidden' in the charges made to business units for central IT services.

The message is loud and clear that the central IT service roles should be provided on a strictly commercial basis, and that strategic IT management related costs should be charged to business users separately or absorbed as a corporate overhead cost—typically funded from a corporate development budget.

Fit Between Corporate and IT Management Styles

The corporate strategic management style of the companies studied was defined using Goold and Campbell's (1986) instrument—allowing companies to be placed on a continuum ranging from the Strategic Planning style (relatively centralized) to the Financial Control Style (relatively decentralized). Corporate strategic management style was then compared with IT management style to evaluate the degree of fit between the overall strategic management style of the companies and that of their IT organizations. Figure 12.3 charts the relationships observed. A clear relationship was identified between the two dimensions. The Spearman Rank-Order Correlation Coefficient was calculated at 0.66 for the sample of twenty-eight companies in the postal survey, and 0.69 for the eight case study companies. This indicates a reasonably significant association, given the multitude of variables that impact the relationship.

Companies with a Strategic Planning corporate strategic management style preferred a Strategic Leadership IT management style. Companies with a Financial Control style preferred a Strategic Guidance IT management style. Companies who adopt a Strategic Leadership style seem to do so based on a firm belief in the strategic value of information technology and in the need to exert strategic control over this function. The finance director of a Strategic Leadership company, for example, commented: 'Information systems will be crucial to our future success. Systems and communications will provide the glue that holds a global company together.'

Companies which adopt a Strategic Guidance style, however, appear to perceive less value in IT management at the corporate level. The corporate executive in charge of IT in a Strategic Guidance company, for example, commented: 'IT is not central to our business.'

Why would a company adopt a Strategic Leadership style and not a Strategic Guidance one ... or vice versa? There are two main ways that corporate strategic management style influences IT management style: by top-down effects or by bottom-up effects.

IT management style is, of course, often directly influenced by the espoused mission, goals, objectives, and strategies of the board and senior executives. The following example illustrates a company whose IT organization was dramatically reshaped following such a top-down IT strategy study.

In a large retail group with a substantial corporate IT function, the IT director conducted a review of the IT organization in response to growth

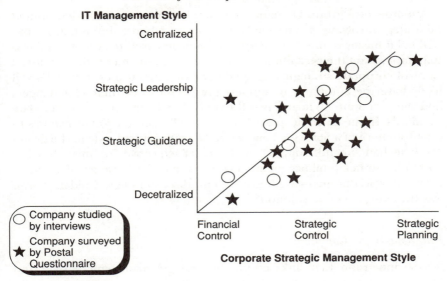

Fig. 12.3. *Fit between corporate and IT management style*

in the number of subsidiaries and increasing demands by the subsidiary managers for greater IT autonomy. The review was carried out, with the full support of the managing director, largely in secret. Once a conclusion was reached, a wide-ranging reorganization of the IT function was implemented within a period of months. The corporate IT function was considerably downsized, with staff relocated in the divisions, and a federal IT organization was established with firm central control of devolved IT functions.

Corporate strategic management style also acts indirectly by constraining the corporate IT management role to bounds of compromise which divisional and business unit managers are prepared to accept. This is a less obvious and more subtle effect. Those bottom-up effects represent the historical legacy of previous strategies and organizational structures—rather than the current intentions of the centre.

In a transport-and-travel group with mostly decentralized IT resources, growth by acquisition and a lack of central planning and co-ordination had led to proliferation of incompatible methods and technologies. Senior executives felt that the company was 'spending too much on IT and getting too little back'. The chief executive appointed a group IT manager, charged with the task of setting in place some degree of central policy control and realizing cost savings and synergies across the group's many autonomous IT functions. After two years little had changed—despite considerable top-down effort, the IT organization remained almost entirely decentralized.

Attempts by a group IT manager to implement a centrally determined IT strategy involving group-wide IT policies, standards, and initiatives may well fail if business unit IT managers are not prepared to accept standards that impinge on their traditional autonomy. In companies with a Financial Control corporate strategic management style, the business unit MDs will likely have the autonomy to support the decisions of their IT managers and the corporate IT manager will have little effective power to mandate standards. In the example above, the group IT manager's objective was to establish more of a Strategic Leadership IT management style in the group (and he had the full support of the chief executive for this), but the corporate strategic management style constrained the range of IT management style options—an almost decentralized Strategic Guidance style was the only workable solution.

Enthusiasm for Compromise

A key dimension that links corporate strategic management style and IT management style is the enthusiasm of the participants for *compromise*. Resolving the tensions inherent in the multi-business-unit firm inevitably requires compromise solutions—trading off detailed planning and entrepreneurial decision-making; strong central leadership and business unit autonomy; long-term strategic objectives and short-term financial objectives, and so on (see Fig. 12.4).

Tensions Inherent in the Federal IT Organization

In companies with a Strategic Planning corporate strategic management style, the centre has created an organization that supports the need to compromise in order to achieve the group's overall strategic objectives. In Financial Control style companies, the enthusiasm of managers for compromise is less—they are more focused on uncompromising achievement of clear financial targets.

Comparable statements appear to be true of IT management style. In companies with a Strategic Leadership IT management style, IT managers are encouraged to accept compromise; to trade off group-wide integration and standardization of hardware, systems, and methods against focused local independence; to trade off long-term group-wide strategies against short-term 'quick solutions' central group-wide IT initiatives against business unit autonomy, and so on. A business unit IT manager, for example, commented: 'I am accustomed to the need for co-operation between HQ and the business units . . . and the need to sub-optimize some local decisions for the sake of optimising an overall group position.' Another commented: 'Short term thinking is a real problem in my experience at the business

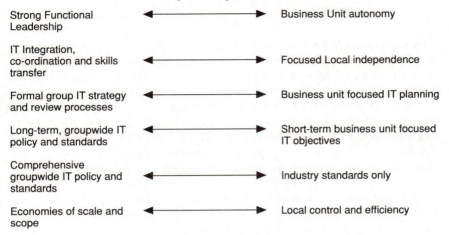

Strong Functional Leadership	Business Unit autonomy
IT Integration, co-ordination and skills transfer	Focused Local independence
Formal group IT strategy and review processes	Business unit focused IT planning
Long-term, groupwide IT policy and standards	Short-term business unit focused IT objectives
Comprehensive groupwide IT policy and standards	Industry standards only
Economies of scale and scope	Local control and efficiency

Fig. 12.4. *Tensions inherent in the federal IT organization*

unit level . . . corporate IT staff can encourage business units to take a longer term view of IT investments.'

In the Strategic Guidance IT management style, however, the business unit IT managers are not as enthusiastic about compromise—preferring instead to be clearly focused on the needs of their business unit only. The following comments are typical of business unit IT managers in the Strategic Guidance companies:

This company is self contained . . . I never saw the need for the corporate IT unit when it was created and have distanced myself from it from the outset. They may be adding value in other parts of the group so I'm not knocking them . . . its just that we have no need of them. We don't want to be slowed down by . . . and have to pay for . . . silly corporate initiatives.

Our business is different to the others . . . and quite stands alone . . . why should we comply with group standards that just make life harder for us?

It would seem to be difficult, if not impossible, for the corporate IT function sustainably to 'swim against the corporate current'. A Strategic Leadership IT management style would likely be unsustainable in a company with a Financial Control corporate strategic management style because divisional and business unit MDs and IT managers: (a) would not support the intangible costs of lost autonomy and compromised ability to meet the challenging financial targets set by the centre; and (b) would not tolerate the growth in central overheads required to fund the strategic IT management activities associated with the Strategic Leadership style. Conversely a Strategic Guidance IT management style in a Strategic Planning company would be unlikely to provide the functional leadership required to support corporate strategic planning and other 'value adding' objectives.

Conclusion

The study provided a clear description of the roles played by the corporate IT function in the federal IT organization—and draws a distinction between strategic IT management roles and central IT service roles. The strategic IT management roles are the key to the success of federal IT—creating the glue that binds together the semi-autonomous business unit IT functions. The transition from a fully centralized or decentralized IT organization to a federal one requires the establishment of these new management roles in the corporate IT function—strategic IT management roles aimed explicitly at the management of a portfolio of IT resources and capabilities across the group.

The evidence confirming the existence of fit between a company's corporate strategic management style and its IT management style confirms what is a largely common-sense conclusion. Common sense, however, is often not that common, and the study revealed a number of companies that went through periods of poor fit. Consider the following case.

A £1,900 million turnover UK-based company went through two major changes in its IT organization in a decade. The company had a decentralized Financial Control corporate strategic management style, and a history of largely decentralized approaches to IT. On the initiative of the group finance director, a substantial corporate IT function of eighty staff was established in the mid-1980s in the belief that there were certain benefits in central IT initiatives. The unit was charged with many of the roles characterized by the Strategic Leadership style. By the late 1980s, however, support for the corporate IT function's 'black hole club' initiatives waned and concerns about its costs and effectiveness precipitated a strategic review. The corporate IT function was closed down in 1990. The company now has a small team of ten at the centre operating in the Strategic Guidance style, which is more in tune with the objectives and management style of its senior executives.

Why did the company embark on the creation of a large corporate IT function that was plainly (at least in retrospect) at odds with its corporate strategic management style? Many factors were, of course, involved, but the conclusions of this study would probably have been useful input to decisions made by the board in the mid-1980s. It is not enough to have a general belief in the value of some degree of centralization of IT: economies of scale, enabling of integrated systems, and so on, as, for example, enthusiastically described by von Simpson (1990). What is needed is a sound understanding of the requirements of the company and the limitations and opportunities inherent in its corporate strategic management style.

The IT organization must strive constantly to ensure that it is demonstrably in-tune with the strategic management and organizational styles of its host. With growing recognition of the applicability of federal organizational models, it is crucial that the IT function understand the strategic IT management roles necessary to make federal IT organizations work.

References

Boynton, A. C., Jacobs, G. C., and Zmud, R. W. (1992), 'Whose Responsibility is IT Management?', *Sloan Management Review* (Summer), 32–8.

Chandler, A. D., Jnr. (1962), *Strategy and Structure*, Cambridge, Mass.: MIT Press.

Channon, D. F. (1973), *The Strategy and Structure of British Enterprise*, London: Macmillan.

Earl, M. J. (1989), *Management Strategies for Information Technology*, Hemel Hempstead: Prentice-Hall International (UK) Ltd.

Goold, M., and Campbell, A. (1986), *Strategies and Style: The Role of the Centre in Managing Diversified Corporations*, Oxford: Blackwell.

Hill, C. W. L., and Pickering, J. F. (1986), 'Divisionalisation, Decentralisation and Performance of Large United Kingdom Companies', *Journal of Management Studies*, 23/1 (Jan.)

Handy, C. (1992), 'Balancing Corporate Power: A New Federalist Paper', *Harvard Business Review* (Nov.–Dec.), 59–72.

Harrigan, K. R. (1983), *Research Methodologies for Contingency Approaches for Information Technology*, Hemel Hempstead: Prentice-Hall International (UK) Ltd.

King, J. L. (1983), 'Centralised versus Decentralised Computing: Organisational Considerations and Management Options', *Computing Surveys of the ACM*, 15/4 (Dec.), 319–49.

Lorsch, J. W., and Allen, S. A. (1973), *Managing Diversity and Interdependence: An Organisational Study of Multi-divisional Firms*, Cambridge, Mass.: Harvard University Press.

Peters, T. J., and Waterman, R. H. (1982), *In Search of Excellence*, New York: Harper Row.

Porter, M. E. (1988), 'From Competitive Advantage to Corporate Strategy', *The McKinsey Quarterly* (Spring), 35–66.

Prahalad, C. K., and Doz, Y. L. (1987), *The Multi-National Mission: Balancing Local Demands and Global Vision*, New York: Free Press.

Sloan, A. P. (1964), *My Years With General Motors*, New York: Doubleday.

von Simpson, A. M. (1990), 'The Centrally Decentralised IS Organisation', *Harvard Business Review* (July–Aug.), 158–62.

Zmud, R. W., Boynton, A. C., and Jacobs, G. C. (1986), 'The Information Economy: A New Perspective for Effective Information Systems Management', *Database* (Fall), 17–23.

13

IT Outsourcing and the Changing Shape of the Information Systems Function

LESLIE P. WILLCOCKS AND GUY FITZGERALD

Introduction

There has been considerable academic interest in recent years in three debates that come together in this paper.[1] The first concerns the causes, attributes, and consequences of emergent forms of organization, for example, Clark and Staunton (1990), Clegg (1990), Drucker (1991), and Whitaker (1992). The second focuses on structuring the information systems function, for example, Feeny *et al.* (1989), George and King (1991), and Hodgkinson (1991). The third relates to the reasons for, and the nature and impact of Information Technology (IT) outsourcing, for example, Buck-Lew (1992), Lacity and Hirschheim (1993), and Loh and Venkatraman (1992*a*, *b*, *c*). Our research programme from which this research paper is derived, in the form of thirty detailed case studies in the UK, has been conducted primarily through the lens of questions raised in the third of these areas. This has produced evidence that links the three debates in certain ways. In particular, we take two examples of the more radical (or 'total') forms of IT outsourcing occurring in the context of significant changes in broader organizational structure and strategy as a basis for examining the implications for Information Systems (IS) structures, management processes, and distribution of expertise in newer, emergent forms of organization.

In what follows, IT is used to refer to the supply of information-based technologies. IS is understood as organizational applications, more or less IT-based, designed to deliver the information needs of the organization and defined stakeholders. To introduce much-needed conceptual clarity we use the term 'IT outsourcing' narrowly—it is the commissioning of third-party management of IT/IS assets, people and/or activities to required

[1] Our thanks go to the sponsors of this research, Business Intelligence, to the survey respondents, and to the many managers we have been interviewing. Without their co-operation and generosity with their time this research would not have been possible.

result. So defined, outsourcing does not exhaust the ways in which markets can be used. Thus, a key distinction can be made between contracts that specify a service and result which the market is to provide ('outsourcing'); and contracts which call for the market to provide resources to be deployed under the buyer's management and control. Elsewhere we have described the latter as 'insourcing' contracts (Feeny *et al.* 1993).

For present purposes, 'total outsourcing' may be defined as where 80 per cent or more of an organization's formal IT budgets are spent on IT outsourcing. Other research suggests that, as at 1993, under 7 per cent of UK organizations that outsourced IT/IS did so on a total outsourcing basis. At the same time some 51 per cent of UK organizations outsourced some aspect of their IT/IS, and the market may be growing at up to 20 per cent per annum (Willcocks and Fitzgerald 1994). The findings presented here emerge from a larger, in-depth thirty-case study project that found six major factors helping to explain the degree of, and patterns in, IT outsourcing, and the degree of its perceived success or failure in UK organizations. These were: the degree of business uncertainty; whether the IT/IS system or activity was strategic or useful, a business differentiator or a commodity; the degree of in-house expertise compared to that available on the market; the degree of in-house 'technological maturity'; and the degree to which the system or set of activities were integrated with other systems and parts of the business, or relatively discrete and stand-alone (see Feeny *et al.* 1993; Willcocks and Fitzgerald 1993).

The purpose of the present research was to take the analysis further and harness the case studies to examine how organizations that have outsourced IT perceive and deal with the implications for organizing, managing, and staffing their IT/IS functions. The chapter first provides further detail of how our research was conducted, in the context of prior work by other researchers in this area. We then take two total outsourcing cases—British Home Stores and BP Exploration—and analyse in detail why IT outsourcing was pursued, how it was conducted, and the implications for the IT/IS function. Each case sees the development of a residual IS function. This construct is the subject of this chapter and the two case studies provide an opportunity for studying the parameters of this phenomenon. We then utilize evidence from further total and selective outsourcing examples to compare across the case studies the degree to which there are similarities and differences in how IT/IS functions are organized and managed after IT outsourcing.

While a variety of IT/IS outsourcing practice was revealed, the research does demonstrate that as organizations outsource an increasing amount of IT/IS, they move further toward the patterns of IT/IS organization and management found in our total outsourcing examples. In fact, the evidence suggests that across both total and selective outsourcing cases there is qualified support for a model put forward for BP Exploration, suggesting three ultimate roles in the residual IS function—those of 'informed buyer', 'business consultant', and 'integrator/architect/specialist' (Symons 1993). We then put forward a more detailed model delineating seven common tasks or roles that seem to be emergent as characteristic and integral to the running of the residual IS functions we have researched. We conclude by suggesting that if IT outsourcing continues to exhibit the growth trends emerging from our earlier survey work, then the residual IS functions and roles we have described may become common rather than untypical in the next few years.

Research on IT Outsourcing

Outsourcing IT has been the subject of considerable debate, not only at the level of how best it can be done (see, for example, Earl 1991; Willcocks 1994), but also in terms of its implications for organizational forms and management (for example, Grant 1992; Huber 1993; Quinn 1992). However, even by 1994 the UK phenomenon had not been the subject of detailed academic research, unlike in the USA (Apte 1990; Apte and Mason 1993; Clark and Zmud 1993; Klepper 1993; Lacity and Hirschheim 1993; Loh and Venkatraman 1992*a, b, c*). A number of detailed case studies have been produced on US corporations (see, for example, Buck-Lew 1992; Huber 1993; Moad 1993). More recently still there have been case studies produced from various European countries (for example, Auwers and Deschoolmeester 1993; Griese 1993; Heinzl 1993; Saaksjarvi 1993). However, even when researching total outsourcing as we have defined it, these academic studies tend not to focus in detail on the nature of what we have called the residual IS organization.

The research reported here forms part of a larger study of the outsourcing of IT/IS activities in the UK. The overall research approach harnessed survey and case study techniques. Mintzberg (1979) suggests that successful research requires both systematic and anecdotal data, that is, both hard and soft information, the hard to uncover relationships and the soft to help explain such relationships. Sympathetic to this view, our research design began with telephone interviews based on a relatively open-ended set of questions to validate the parameters for the study. A set of frameworks and hypotheses was then developed for testing. A detailed postal questionnaire was then administered. This was followed up by a series of semi-structured interviews with a range of participants involved in IT outsourcing, identified from both personal contacts, published sources, and from the database listings of a sponsoring research organization. The interviews relating to thirty organizations were then used, together with relevant published and internal documentation, to develop thirty case studies of IT outsourcing. We chose medium-to-large organizations from across industrial and private/public sectors, with experiences ranging from selective to total, self-declared successful or less successful IT outsourcing. The methodology sought to gain triangulation at two levels: first, at the level of the range of techniques employed; secondly, in interview sets and cases studies, by targeting respondents from senior management, IT, vendor, and user backgrounds.

In practice, the five total outsourcing cases we researched represent most of the (very few) large UK-based organizations operating total outsourcing contracts as at August 1993. For reasons of space we report in detail only two of the cases here, and these are written to show the contexts in which the demand for residual IS organizations can develop. We subsequently draw upon these and evidence from our twenty-eight other case histories to illustrate and substantiate our arguments concerning the reasons for, development, and characteristics of residual IS organizations in contexts of IT outsourcing.

Total Outsourcing: 1. British Home Stores—A Major High-Street Retailer

Background

In 1989 the company was heading for a financial loss and was deemed to have lost strategic direction. The business formula of the 1970s and 80s was no longer proving effective. A new chief executive was appointed to turn the company around. He put into effect a threefold strategy, first removing levels in the hierarchy, secondly decentralizing the organization, and thirdly, and in this context most importantly, focusing on the core competencies or skills of the business. These core skills were identified as essentially buying and selling, and from this analysis the philosophy of outsourcing was developed.

'We see the success of the company as doing the core things well. It is not an accident that the rest is outsourced. There are a series of outsourced non-core activities with people who we believe are world class at what they do. We intend to drive for good service and give them a hard time to get it. Ultimately we think we get a better service this way' (IT manager). This approach is based on an increasingly influential body of thinking in the area of strategy associated with core competencies, (see, for example, Prahalad and Hamel 1991; Quinn *et al.* 1990). One expression of this is that an organization can only be effective at a few core activities and that it should concentrate on developing these to a world-class standard and not dissipate its energy by trying to be world class in everything. The implication is that anything else should be eliminated, minimized, or outsourced. This is in marked contrast to other, earlier, strategic philosophies that were based on increasing market share and obtaining the resultant economies of scale, or seeking to build vertical integration to achieve control over all the elements in the vertical market.

This 'core competence' approach was duly applied in BHS, any activity that was not buying and selling becoming a potential candidate for outsourcing. For example, distribution was outsourced and reduced in size from 250 staff to three. Quality control, packaging, and design activities followed a similar pattern. Security and cleaning were, as at 1993, in the process of being outsourced; the only non-core activity still in-house was finance. The following comment sumarizes the company's outsourcing philosophy:

We have not completely finished the process but we are fairly close . . . We have left ourselves now with a lot of people buying and a lot of people selling and I should think, and I am guessing, less than 200 other people in a company that has got 14,000 full-time equivalent people. We as a company now manage contracts and demand service. Essentially I believe that you get a better service as a customer than you do as a boss, and I think all this stuff about losing control when you outsource is a myth. The evidence here is quite different, when I ask for something they jump. (senior company manager)

Detail

In the context of this corporate philosophy, the feeling of senior management was that IT was performing reasonably well in an operational sense but not really delivering on its potential for the business. IT outsourcing was seen as providing the opportunity for improvement by introducing rigour, and stimulating more detail and thought into what was really required for the business. It was also decided to decentralize IT/IS and make user management in the business much more responsible for the identification of what was required, the costs of achieving it, and ensuring that business benefits accrued.

The company addressed the issue of whether outsourcing IT would lead to losing competitive edge. Although IT was not identified as a core activity, this did not mean that it was not important to the company. However, senior management concluded that it was not the provision of IT itself but the way that it was used that might provide advantage, and that this could be harnessed irrespective of whether the IT itself was in-house or out. Some time was spent discussing whether all or just certain parts of the IT should be outsourced, but it was felt that if the company really believed in the philosophy it had to be total. So the decision was made to outsource the whole of IT, including the data centre, PCs, development, and support. A single contract was negotiated, worth £11 million over a contract period of almost eleven years. The deal started in January 1993 and involved the transfer of 116 people to the vendor.

The process involved the selection of a shortlist of vendors, not by issuing an open invitation to tender but by selecting four vendors that the company, based on its existing knowledge, felt to be capable of handling such a contract. The selected vendor was the one that was felt best to understand the philosophy and objectives of the company, especially in the area of development. Vendors treating it as basically a large data-centre deal with a few extras were felt to have misunderstood the company's real requirements. The selection was made on the basis of a compatible partner as well as competence. The company was very keen to enter a partnership with their vendor in terms of sharing risk and rewards. As will be seen, the type of relationship established with the vendor does have a number of implications for the type of residual IS organization and skills needed in-house. This notion of partnership was subsequently put to the test in a new area, with the vendor suggesting that they sell some IT equipment and software they have developed for the company to a third party on a partnership basis.

Almost all the details of the company's performance requirements in IT had already been defined in detail over the previous three years, especially the key requirements for their retail stores and for buying and merchandizing. This was felt to be an essential prerequisite. A series of hard negotiations was completed and the contract agreed and drawn up with help from outside legal specialists, the in-house legal activities having already been outsourced. The contract is a long one, and obviously, over this period, needed to be flexible. There are some penalty clauses for failure to meet service levels, but there are also benefit clauses which trigger extra payments if the vendor beats service levels significantly. There are guarantees of certain levels of spend in the area of systems development, the level of which declines over the period of the contract. If more people are required, this can be increased provided it is planned, that is, six months notice, otherwise extra people are charged at market rates. The planned rate is very much cheaper but this provides for flexibility and is an incentive for good planning. These details suggest that contract monitoring and conducting business relations with the vendor would be key in-house capabilities in any residual IS organization at BHS.

The benefits after the first year of operation were estimated to be 35 per cent savings on the computing hardware, although the company did not regard this as very significant in the long term as the prices of machines are declining rapidly anyway. For the rest it is about 5 or 6 per cent cost savings, but more importantly the company has shifted the bulk of £11 million from fixed to variable business overhead and given themselves financial, service, and technical flexibility. There are now only five IT jobs left in the company. One is the manager of the contract relationship. The other four are concerned with business development using IT, and getting close to the business. The transfer of people to the vendor was described by the company as having been remarkably smooth. The deals were relatively good, the contracts in terms and conditions were essentially the same as previously held, and people knew that the IT labour market had shifted over the previous few years from one favouring the employee to one where they were at some disadvantage. Some viewed the change as positive because IT was the core business of the vendor and they felt that there might be greater career opportunities with the vendor.

The company felt that previous outsourcing experiences within the organization were very important and had helped to smooth the way for IT outsourcing. It enabled them to understand the importance of putting the effort into building the contract and getting it right. It gave them the confidence to go for a long contract and seek a partnership rather than base everything on price considerations. The length of the contract is relatively unusual. It is long compared to most, but the company argued that if you are convinced by the philosophy and the deal you should ensure the benefits over the longer period. According to the company, short contracts are for companies that are experimenting with outsourcing and are not really convinced: 'If you do it for 3 years you are always thinking about what am I going to do after that, if you do it for 5 then you have to make absolutely sure you have a route back, and that precludes selling other things on the mainframe, so it has to be ten minimum . . . It is not about saving a few bob on the IT in the short term, it is about long term commitment' (company manager).

Summary

This is one of the relatively few examples of total outsourcing of IT that we encountered in our main research study, and perhaps the most notable, together with the BP Exploration case, where it was driven by the overall strategy of the company and not just for the cost-cutting reasons commonly encountered. IT was not seen as a core activity in the organization and therefore it was outsourced as a way of acquiring the world-class standards on IT that it believed could not be obtained in-house. The other significant, although related, factor was that the company sought a partnership with the vendor and entered a long-term contract to enable that partnership to develop and flourish. The previous experience of the company in outsourcing in other areas gave them great confidence in the way that they were able to deal with IT. IT was different but not that different; the general outsourcing lessons and principles from other areas were seen to be applicable. This level of experience may help to explain why so few people were retained to staff the residual IS organization. The company is still in the very early stages of the relationship and it remains to be seen what happens.

Clearly, total outsourcing here has produced a residual IS function. What are its parameters and the management roles required to operate this in-house function? The vendor became responsible for most aspects of BHS computing, including development. One hundred and sixteen people were transferred but five jobs were retained within BHS. These cover managing service level assessment and delivery (semi-clerical with some IT knowledge), and business development. The latter involves getting closer to the business and arriving at business requirement definitions. The jobs are filled by people who were all working in IT but have also worked elsewhere in organizations in recent years. According to Simon Hughes, IT manager at BHS: 'They are IT professional enough but they are not actually thoroughbred.' The vendor is responsible for managing systems specifications. Clearly these arrangements depend on a well-detailed contract and service level agreements being in place, and on the partnership element in the relationship, with the vendor having a close relationship with the BHS business end as well as the technical part of computing.

Total Outsourcing: 2. BP Exploration—A Major Energy Exploration Company

Background

This large energy exploration and production company has developed its current strategy in relation to the outsourcing of IT based on the company's overall philosophy and experience.[2] There were four important drivers in this context. First, there were steady reductions in BP profits leading to the company's first-ever loss in the early 1990s. BP came under heavy cash-flow pressures. Secondly, the overall business strategy has been one where outsourcing is a common way of operating; indeed, this is true for the industry as a whole. The applicable concepts, by 1990, once again were those of core competencies and the notion of the 'intelligent enterprise' (Prahalad and Hamel 1991; Quinn 1992). Senior management at BPX perceived its key competence as exploration; IT and other functions, such as accounting, were identified as support. Pursuing the logic of the argument, BPX outsourced not just its IT, but also the accounting function back in 1991. The overall outsourcing strategy was summarised thus: 'For us to remain, and in fact become an even stronger player in the exploration/production market in the next 10 years, we are going to need the skills of not just an in-house traditional organisation, but we need to move towards, what we would probably call, a constellation of partners' (senior manager).

---

[2] A teaching case study on BP Exploration documents this 'reengineering' of their IS function. See M. J. Earl and J. L. Sampler, CRIM MC93/11., London Business School, Centre for Research in Information Management.

Senior management also determined to shift core business from a relatively narrow focus that existed from the mid-1970s through to the 1990s, to much more diversified production. This required new skills and competencies as an organization. These could be developed internally, but it was felt that a better solution lay in developing partnerships with organizations that already possessed the relevant experience and skills. This can be identified as akin to the 'cloverleaf' approach described by Handy (1984). The third driver for their current approach to the outsourcing of IT was their view of IT and the problems they had experienced in relation to in-house IT. Historically the majority of people and resources in IT were focused upon infrastructure and applications, with only a very few people devoted to thinking about the role of IT, where it should be going, and how it could help the business. Having identified this as a problem area, the response was to move towards a complete inversion of the structure with the substantial resource being devoted to the role of 'IT thinking' and internal consultancy, supplemented by external information services. The applications and infrastructure were mainly outsourced to a number of partners and only a few key staff were retained in this area. Figure 13.1 illustrates the two different situations, although obviously it is simplified somewhat to make the point.

As one IT manager told us: 'it's a method of rebuilding the focus of your organization so that you start to focus on what is important to the company and not what's important to the traditional IT world.'

The attempt to change from the one structure to another was justified, it was argued, by the performance of IT in the organization. Under the first structure, performance of the IT/IS declined slowly over time and the focus was on the technology and the day-to-day activities. It could be improved from time to time by an injection of strategy or consultancy; this set it on a performance upturn for a short period, but inevitably it then would resume its previous decline. The second structure has, it was argued, the opposite performance slope, everything helping to push the business performance and focus in an upward direction.

The purpose of the internal consultancy structure supplemented by external partners with a core internal consultancy, i.e. putting your effort into 'IT thinking', is that you are constantly improving performance, you've got nothing established or set in concrete in your organisation, and so you find a steady but continuous improvement over time. That's what we've seen so far anyway on our performance indicators. Over about five years the difference in performance is actually a radical transformation. (IT manager)

The fourth driver for the organization was their existing experience with what they term 'traditional FM'. This had not been particularly successful. This was due to the problems of what was described as the 'cracks' between vendors, with the company ending up having to manage not only

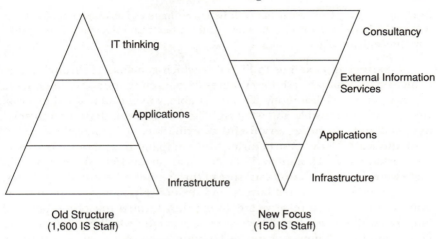

Fig. 13.1. *Reconstructing in-house capability: BP exploration*

each individual subcontractor but the relationships and interfaces between multiple vendors.

The combination of these factors led the company to seek a consortium of outsourcing partners to handle their IT. At the end of 1992 they identified three major partners and signed five-year contracts worth a total of roughly $35 million per year. All the partners were identified as capable of covering the company's requirements globally, which was identified as an important criterion. One partner was to handle the data centre operations, the second to develop and innovate in client server type systems, and the third managed telecommunications and wide area networks. BPX managers concluded that they needed different partners for different activities requiring differing skills, but all with the ability to work together, so eliminating the 'cracks' that had caused such problems earlier. They wanted them to work together as a kind of consortium to present a united interface to the company, and deal with any issues amongst themselves, minimizing BPX involvement. Part of the selection procedure was that the vendors get together and agree to this and establish how they would achieve it. The key to this was partnership not only between the client and the vendor but also between the vendors themselves.

The general manager of IT, John Cross, suggested that the IT restructuring and outsourcing partnership arrangements would save the company the cost of finding a new oil-field, or the equivalent of a £10 billion cash influx.

We've already halved our IT costs and next year's IT budget . . . will save another 30 per cent . . . and we will have only 10 per cent of our previous staff, 20 per cent of our mainframes, and 10 times as many Mips on the desktop . . . By the end of next year all the IT infrastructure will be in the hands of its outsourcing alliance partners. They deal with the suppliers, I don't buy technology any more, and I have no capital budget.

The partnership extends to IT policy which is managed through a particular board which has representatives from each vendor and, in general, policy is set in collaboration. 'This is valuable, you get some good external views on what's sensible and what isn't . . . They now understand our business well and can make very useful contributions' (IT manager).

At the start of the restructuring the company had about 1,600 people world-wide in IT and by 1993 they had about 150. About ninety of these were 'business consultants' spread throughout different physical sites. Twenty-five were 'informed buyers' and relationship managers for applications and infrastructure service delivery; they formed the prime point of interface with the vendors. There are ten managers who help to formulate IT strategy, though generally in collaboration with vendor partners. Twenty-five staff form a technology consultancy: 'We have retained some significant technical consulting expertise. We regard it as important. It's not so much a "doing" organisation now, but it is one which is capable of debating technical development routes with our outsourcing partners' (George Fish, BPX).

The company had high hopes for the new IT/IS arrangements. At the time of our research it was a little early to confirm whether these would be successful. However, the collaboration between the vendors was already seen to have worked well on a number of fronts and projects. The quality of the work and service had been rated highly on the performance measures in place and there had been no serious disputes. There was one situation where something that the company required had not been properly defined and it caused additional work for one of the vendors:

. . . it wasn't defined in the work we had actually set out. 'Sorry chaps we forgot to tell you about that'. They took us on trust and said okay we will have to absorb it, and actually I think this is what the partnership thing is about. Whether we will have a big issue in the future is a good question, but so far there have been lots of small pointers to indicate things are working well . . . I think because generally people sit down and are fairly open with each other. (IT manager)

Summary

This case is an example of the total outsourcing of IT, based on a number of factors. First, there were financial and cash-flow pressures. Secondly, the overall philosophy and strategy of the company placed the focus on core activities, which did not include IT. The implication was that IT should be outsourced. Thirdly, there was the company's desire to restructure and re-focus IT on the business and away from IT for its own sake. A further factor was their previous experience of outsourcing which suggested that a 'spot-contracting' relationship did not work; this led them to demand partnership relationships based on the sharing of risk and reward and including participation in policy-making. The sheer size of the company and the requirement to have more than one partner led to the desire for a consortium of partners that could work together which may be the direction that many large organizations will explore in the future.

All this has considerable implications for what IT/IS structure and management and technical capability should be left, or be developed in-house. BPX has developed their own form of residual IS organization, that relates to the particular multi-vendor form of IT outsourcing they have adopted for a complex organizational structure and set of business requirements. The BHS residual IS organization is on a smaller scale. The next section investigates whether there are elements of the residual IS organization which are common across these and other examples of radical and more selective forms of IT outsourcing.

Discussion: Redesigning In-House Capability

We have suggested elsewhere that: 'while the external market will over the years account for an ever higher percentage of IT activity, it is imperative that organizations retain the ability to manage their IT destiny' (Feeny *et al.* 1993). Our case studies confirm that even in situations of total outsourcing a minimum set of capabilities needs to be retained in-house. Symons (1993) has suggested from the BPX case that the ultimate roles for managing IT may well become those depicted in Figure 13.2. Certainly our own evidence goes some way to supporting this prediction, with organizations admitting to problems when these minimum capabilities are not in place.

The 'informed buyer' and 'business consultant' roles emerge as universally necessary in all outsourcing arrangements we have studied. However, in large organizations there emerges a difference in practice over where the skills are located—in a central IT/IS function or within the business division. It was also widely recognized amongst our case study respondents that control over strategy on IT and its business use should also stay in-house. Many organizations also preserved a technical capability in-house though there was some disagreement about how far technicians should have a watching rather than a 'doing' brief, and how far it is sufficient to have the technical capability spread through the people carrying out the other roles shown in Figure 13.2. Below we use the evidence from total and selective outsourcing examples to qualify and build upon the model shown in Figure 13.2.

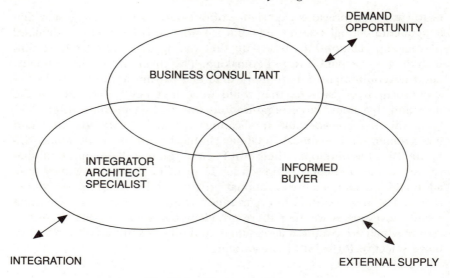

Fig. 13.2. *The ultimate IT roles?*

'Total' Outsourcing Examples

The experiences in two other total outsourcing examples we researched are pertinent. At NV Philips, the electronics company, the problem of who to outsource to and who to retain was handled in a different way from our two previous examples. By 1988 in the UK the information systems division had been rationalized and consolidated into three parts—a small business systems group, a software and development support group, and communications and data processing. Subsequently the 100 business systems staff were transferred into the business divisions thus guaranteeing that the demand side of IS was retained in-house. Subsequently the remaining supply side groups of some 320 IT staff were outsourced to wholly or partly owned companies. As at 1993, the UK had an IT director responsible for overseeing IT direction and policy, and relations with the two vendor companies. The role of the IT staff in the businesses is considered critical and they must have IT as well as management expertise. They also needed to develop contract management skills to deal with vendors: 'Philips have got control of their IT through business based IT managers which is absolutely critical and there is to be no abdication of that. They are now responsible for buying IT products and services from our two preferred suppliers' (John Bell, Philips).

Though the organization retains very little technical expertise, one of the reasons why these arrangements are more likely to be successful is that most of the vendor staff in fact are ex-Philips and have relevant IT and business knowledge of the company.

At Pilkington, the UK-based glass manufacturing multinational, after outsourcing head office systems operation and development in 1991, three key staff were retained at the centre. All had a group role to play, reporting to the board on IT strategy, standards, policy, infrastructure, and future technical developments and how they could be harnessed. They also offered consultancy to the business divisions within the group, helping to match any business development with an IT strategy and planning how it would be resourced. They also run the group's IT purchasing. There is also an important contract management role. The advice of the IS head at Pilkingtons is:

Distinguish clearly between the strategy, direction, control, information and communication needs on the one hand, and the service provision of information systems and technology. A very important part of what we were doing was not to outsource management and control and above all the direction and strategy. The experience we have had in some of our other operations worldwide where things have not gone as well as they should have is that the management tended to push everything out. (Bill Limond, Pilkington)

Both these examples, along with the BHS and BPX cases, largely support the Figure 13.2 model. However, the model is not clear on a major issue faced by organizations that totally outsource IT: how much technical expertise needs to be retained in-house and whether this should be on a small consultancy basis as at BPX, spread thinly through the organization as at BHS and Philips, or whether more in-depth coverage of certain skills bases should be provided. Some organizations in fact guard against risks and irreversibility of contract by going beyond both the 'thin spread' and technical consultancy routes. As one example, in 1990 First Fidelity Bank outsourced all data centre operations and systems conversions to EDS on a $450 million ten-year contract. Though EDS had a hire/fire power over the systems developers throughout systems conversions, 250 systems developers remained on the bank's payroll during and after the conversion projects. This was to protect the bank's ability to maintain new systems in the future (Moad 1993).

Selective Outsourcing Examples: What to Keep In-House

Varying degrees of the original IT/IS structure and skills are usually retained in situations of selective IT outsourcing. Nevertheless, amongst our researched histories of selective outsourcing we found new organizational forms and skill distributions run in parallel, consolidated into the existing IS function, or emerging into similar types of residual organization found in our total outsourcing cases. Below we give some illustrative examples of the changing nature and distribution of managerial and technical work and roles for the IS function in conditions of more selective IT outsourcing. We will then put forward what seem to emerge as the most typical structures and tasks of residual IS organizations after IT outsourcing.

Experience at the UK's Civil Aviation Authority suggested that the vital IS functions to retain in-house were strategic planning, evaluation, and decision-making, contract monitoring, and contract management:

Business analysis is also part of the function I wouldn't outsource. The most important part of any company is getting its requirement together. I think it is extremely dangerous to put that front-end to an outsourcing company. I came in as a contractor to set up an internal business, a consulting group, a fully paid employee who goes out into the business and helps to put down in a structured way what they really need both in terms of their strategy and their IT programme. Once we know in-house what we really need then from that point on, in principle, I would have no problem outsourcing. (Tony Summerfield, IT manager)

This largely supports the model shown in Figure 13.2. ICI Paints' experience pointed to the importance of having people who understand IT involved in the contract negotiations. Managing the external organization was also found to need a different set of skills—handling contracts, measurement, running review meetings effectively, taking action where necessary. Also people were needed who were capable of maintaining strategic control over IT, that is, over the way to apply IT to the business over three-to-five years. If strategic control is lacking the vendor may, for example, start to move the client's technical base to that which gives them greatest strength. That may not be best for the client and may also mean 'lock- in'. There is also an important 'informed buyer' role:

If you go into a shop and buy decorative paints you may go to a machine that mixes the colours for you. Those machines have a high IT content and all work on developing them is outsourced. We provide one person who in the contract negotiations worked 60 per cent on this. Now she spends 10 per cent of her time satisfying us as the informed buyer that they are doing a good IT job. She also understands what the business is trying to get out of that project and makes sure they are doing it in a way that we can integrate with the rest of our world. (Ed Jasnikowski, ICI Paints)

It is not always easy to identify what in-house capabilities are needed to manage outsourcing contracts. The case of a major US bank helps to develop a deeper understanding of the contract management role. In 1992 the firm outsourced its UK data centre on a five-year contract. The purpose was mainly to reduce costs and headcount. All staff transferred, including data centre managers. An in-house contract manager was appointed. The role was originally seen as managing the financial aspects of the contract, monitoring vendor performance, and responding to service requests. However, new roles were needed to co-ordinate the technology response across network, messaging, and applications development groups as well as the outsourced data centre: 'Very quickly the role I adopted changed from being a contract management role into a general technology services management role. As such, instead of one person worrying about how to fill the day on contract issues, it's become a small department with 2–3 people constantly looking at coordinating the total service response across the technology base' (contract manager, US bank).

The first year can also reveal omissions in the contract that help to generate a lot of unexpected work for in-house staff. Here the contract manager's work included sorting out data centre problems, licence reassignment, and contract interpretation:

I am not physically managing anyone in the data centre environment, but I am managing what's going on and the effects of what's going on. A lot of my time is being taken up as being not contract management but service relationship management . . . dealing with senior managers in the bank who are coming to me to explain service issues on a day to day basis. We are having to do lots of work we thought we had outsourced.

This was a common finding in our research, and indicates that once a contract has been signed there must follow a very active process of managing it. 'I was involved with central systems, EDI and telecommunications. Only the latter was outsourced, but it took up 70 per cent of my time over a 14 month period' (Malcolm Mckay, W. H. Smith).

On the other hand, some organizations manage to find ways of reducing the amount of active contract management required. Thus, from 1987 one of the leading UK high-street retailing companies started to plan to move from ICL to IBM mainframes. As a transitional move they outsourced the management of the ICL systems to ICL itself.

Obviously you do your courtship through the first year of the contract where you make sure they are doing what you want them to do, but in the end, because we are relatively stable in that environment, it's very easy to give it to them as a whole function. But they are a part of my team, they sit with my team, so to all intents and purposes they could be working for me. We have brought them into the organization almost, because they were running a very important production system for us, and it was important that they kept up to speed with what was going on around them as well. They also deal direct with the business users of the system . . . it's worked very well because they actually get a sense of responsibility for the service like the internal people. (IT manager, UK retailing company)

The outsourcing worked because there was a good management team provided by the vendor, ICL, and strong buy-in and trust. Also the retailing company operates a multi-vendor policy that keeps outsourcing vendors competitive. Furthermore, the vendor is treated as almost an in-house team, and the technology being managed by them was not problematical to either the vendor or the client. This is also not a total outsourcing arrangement; in-house staff existed who understood the outsourced systems, and indeed could take over the running of them if necessary. However, the company does practice more active contract management in less stable environments where service issues continually arise. As one example, there is regular monitoring of a contract with the vendor responsible for the maintenance of 3,000 head office PCs.

Making the Transition: Manager and Managed

In our cases of 'total' outsourcing where virtually all IT staff were transferred, there still remained issues concerning the competence and motivation of the remaining in-house team. This is an issue largely not dealt with in the Figure 13.2 model. Each member may be required to learn a whole new set of skills. For an IS executive, managing an IT department and its staff may be a very different type of task from the sorts of work detailed in the previous section. A critical element will be learning to become a manager of contracts instead of being a manager of people. The IS manager will also need to learn how to deal with the profit-and-loss margins of the business much more than before, and also how to deal with the vendor and leverage the alliance. As one commentator puts it: 'What outsourcing does is trade the hassles of managing IT and network operations for the hassles of managing alliances' (Ganz 1990). However, following the Figure 13.2 model, we found that the IS manager is usually released from most hardware and software procurement responsibilities. It was also usually the case that the IS manager can then also focus more on IT in the business.

However, lower-level staff often found themselves thrown in the deep end of service measurement and unfamiliar tasks in contract management on a day-to-day basis. Not only could this become quite onerous administratively, but also in terms of conflict if caught between user demands and vendor service on a poorly drafted contract, or where the vendor had been badly selected. It was suggested by many of our respondents in both total and selective outsourcing examples that an important element in managing staff was to be aware of such possibilities, make sure the staff know what they are going to be dealing with, and provide the necessary training, or recruit additional staff, where the work is new and likely to be administratively taxing. This seemed especially likely to be the case in the first year of any outsourcing contract. This again is an element not covered in the Figure 13.2 model.

Where outsourcing was done to bring in new skills or to remotivate or re-equip staff, a large number of staff still remained in-house. In such cases outsourcing and introducing vendor staff usually resulted in improved performance from in-house staff. However, where vendor staff worked closely with retained staff a number of problems could also arise. In one case we researched the vendor staff were ex-employees hired back to the client company. Their improved terms, conditions, and circumstances created resentments amongst in-house staff. A further emerging problem is the sense that in-house staff may have of having been left out of the outsourcing process. Two of our respondents explicitly mentioned this happening:

The funny thing was the 40–45 people remaining were the ones who were concerned. They wanted to know, why wasn't I good enough to sell off to FI Group, what's wrong with me. But we are getting there now. The attention given to the 100 people transferring tends to demotivate the others. Not exactly what you would expect. (Fraser Winterbottom, Whitbread)

There's always a perception that the outsourced people are better than the bank people. But that happens in any operation. I was talking to someone last year (1992) at the Stock Exchange where they outsourced a lot of their work to Andersens, and the Stock Exchange people felt very aggrieved about it. But in fact the Andersens people were worse off than they were. But perception is reality and you have to try to change that perception to change reality. (Brian Bath, Barclays Bank)

It emerged from our interviews that such perceptions rarely occurred where staff could be offered the option to stay or be transferred to the vendor. Conversely, where staff cannot be offered such a choice, managements of the new arrangements needed to be prepared to deal with their likely subsequent reactions, as described above, once performance of the contract began. Clearly there still needed to be active management of the in-house IT-related staff even in the most residual of IS organizations, a point not explicitly made in the Figure 13.2 model.

Structures and Tasks in Residual IS Organizations

From this discussion it is clear that organizations entering outsourcing, to whatever degree, at some stage identify the need to retain, change, and/ or develop different parts of their IT/IS structures, capabilities and skills to enable them to maintain the link between IT/IS and business prerequisites. In terms of structure we have seen the tendency, especially in the total outsourcing cases, to divide off IS demand from IT supply. In Philips, Pilkington, BHS, and BPX, for example, people with business analysis skills, able to elicit business requirements and also perform technical support functions, were pushed back into the business divisions. IT supply and services were totally outsourced. A small group of people were retained at the centre to fulfil a number of critical roles. These related to strategy, control, and responsibility, both for the running of the outsourcing contracts but also for ensuring that IT could deliver on current and future business requirements. This type of model could be fairly easily identified as latent and in some cases emerging, in even the selective outsourcing examples we have studied.

The research has also suggested that a number of critical tasks need to be fulfilled in residual IS organizations, though organizations seem to make different decisions on how many staff are needed to fulfil these tasks and where they are to be located in the organizational structure. Figure 13.3 summarizes these major tasks.

First, we identify the need for strategic IT thinking in relation to the business as a whole. All respondents stressed that IT strategy is too important to the business to be delegated externally. Even in situations where IT has been identified as a non-core and non-strategic activity, and this may have been the reason it was outsourced, it does not mean that this will always be the case. IT and IS strategy skills require a combination of an understanding of IT potential and business needs both currently and for the future. These are not traditional, purely technical skills. This is akin to the business consultant role shown in Figure 13.2. Even prior to any outsourcing, these skills have been difficult to identify and acquire. One of the reasons is that these people need to be a credible part of the business's senior management inside team, and this has presented a great problem for traditional IT people (Feeny *et al.* 1991). Wherever these skills come from and whatever the career paths, it is critical that companies recognize the need for such a capability. BP Exploration, for example, were very clear that although they now had no day-to-day operational IT expertise left in-house they certainly did retain expertise in the 'strategic direction' of their IT and felt that to do otherwise would be 'very risky'.

The second in-house capability identified from our case studies is for business development in relation to any areas outsourced. This may be regarded as strategic IT and business thinking at the application, or business function level. So, for example, a company that has outsourced its manufacturing systems must still be able to evaluate the manufacturing impact of new IT products on business in the future. Simply because the area has been outsourced does not mean that it can be ignored.

The ability to integrate systems, in both a business and a technical sense, is important when everything is in-house, but it was identified by our respondents as even more important when some systems and services have been outsourced. Without a systems integration capability the organization tends to end up with independent systems (islands of automation), that involve duplication, or exhibit gaps between systems, or both. The result is that the organization is unable to present a consistent business interface to its users and customers, and one part of the organization is often unaware of what the other parts are doing.

Contract management emerged as the most obvious ongoing requirement. There were two distinct views about this. The first argued for the ability to evaluate in detail how well the vendor was performing. Alternatively, it was argued that the strength of the relationship/partnership would maintain service delivery. In the first case, a significant number of people

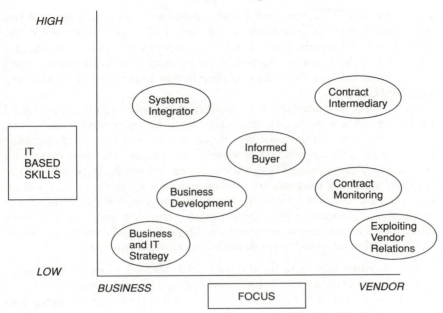

Fig. 13.3. *Tasks in the residual IS organization*

are needed in-house to monitor service performance. In the research we saw organizations at both ends of the spectrum and at many points in between. Tight monitoring is associated with high costs, because there are a lot of specialists checking all aspects of the service provision at regular stages in the process. In terms of risk it is relatively low, because the tight monitoring will pick up any problems and hopefully make sure they are rectified at an early stage, before too much damage is done to the business. The loose, end-result monitoring is lower cost, with fewer people involved, but is potentially higher risk because if things go wrong they will not be picked up until the end-results are seen by the users, or the business in general, or even more damaging, by end customers. A recommendation here would seem to be for an organization to retain a detailed monitoring function until it has been proved not to be necessary, that is, until a client–vendor relationship is strong enough to support delegation of quality control to the vendor.

The informed buyer role involves the capability to place contracts and negotiate deals effectively, including revisions and additions to the original contract. This is a crucial role where new requirements are not automatically undertaken in-house. The skills required are a combination of knowledge of the internal business, knowledge of the external market-place, and the ability to negotiate effective contracts. One person described their role in this way: '. . . if you are a senior manager in the company and you want something done, you come to me and I will . . . go outside, select the vendor and draw up the contract with the outsourcer, and if anything goes wrong it's my butt that gets kicked by you.' Sometimes the informed buyer role is provided by a central procurement function rather than as a specifically IT role.

One aspect of managing the contract that some organizations found problematical was managing the relationship between vendor and users. Should the user (end-users, user departments, and user management) deal directly with the vendors or should they operate through some kind of internal intermediary? It depended to some extent on the nature of the outsourcing being undertaken, and in many cases the users simply dealt directly with the vendors as if they were the employees of the client company. We found other organizations requiring users to deal with everything via an in-house intermediary. Organizations provided a number of reasons for adopting this contract intermediary approach:

- it provides one focus for the user, often termed 'one-stop shopping';
- users may demand too much and incur excessive charges;
- multiple vendors need co-ordinating in terms of responsibilities and users could not be expected to deal with this;
- the vendor demanded it;
- the users demanded it;
- it enables the easy monitoring of usage and service.

Whatever the reason, it was often a service provided by the remaining IT/IS department. In a number of cases it was a service set up after the contract had been running for a while and the users expressed dissatisfaction with dealing directly with vendors. Respondents also identified the need to exploit vendor relations at a level above the mechanism of any existing contract. This may involve aspects relating to business development opportunities, the sharing of risks and rewards, or simply discussions about each-other's business. One organization had a number of ways of achieving this, including an annual formal meeting: '. . . it's in both of our interests I believe to keep these things going and we formally, with our biggest suppliers, have a meeting once a year and these are done at very senior levels in both organisations and that works very well' (IT manager, major retail company).

Many of the above seven tasks are closely related and certain aspects overlap. In practice it is possible for some of them to be undertaken by a single person, perhaps the contract manager, but we identify them separately as tasks that need to be performed, rather than suggesting who should perform them.

Finally, the above discussion raises the question of what technical expertise needs to be retained in order to perform these tasks. Each element involves some IT expertise. On the strategy, business development, and vendor-relations side, it is basically an awareness of the potential of IT that is required.

For systems integration, it is a range of more technical IT skills, including an understanding of differing hardware platforms, databases, and architectures. For contract intermediary, it is an understanding of the current applications, including hardware and software. For contract monitoring, it is the ability to evaluate the conduct, advice, and recommendations of vendors, including pricing, that is important, and finally, for the informed buyer, it is a knowledge of the IT market and product offerings that is required. The need for in-house technical expertise was widely recognized, for example: 'We have retained in-house some significant technical consulting expertise; we regard it as important. It's not so much a doing organization now, but it's one which is capable of debating technical development routes with our out-sourcing partners' (George Fish, BPX).

Some of these skills are similar to those that an organization is likely to have had prior to any outsourcing; others may well be new and require developing. As one respondent remarked: 'You've got to be prepared to upskill your organization and to have an human resources policy which provides such training to people in the organization' (senior manager, BPX).

Quite a number of firms found themselves recruiting, though the right mix of skills and attitudes was not always easy to hire and recruitment of staff was not something that organizations entering outsourcing were always keen to contemplate. More than one organization recruited their contract manager from vendors on the basis of the benefits that accrue when the person knows the inside track.

Conclusions

The total IT outsourcing cases we researched were of large, multi-divisional organizations. Outsourcing was initiated by senior (not IT) management for three interrelated reasons. There were invariably considerable financial pressures on the business. Together with competitive pressures, these pushed the organizations into large-scale organizational changes, usually guided by the requirement to focus on core business and competencies. IT was identified as important but non-core. These wider organizational pressures led to a high degree of outsourcing of activities identified as non-core, including IT. Each organization developed a residual IS function, driving business analysis/consultant roles and some technical expertise into business divisions and tending to retain at the centre a mix of seven critical tasks spread amongst very few staff either retained, developed, or bought in. The cases we researched reported degrees of success with these arrangements, though all contracts were at quite early stages, and it is possible that these roles may need to be developed further. Getting the right balance of numbers of staff needed to carry out the tasks, where staff should be located, and the right amount of technical expertise distributed throughout the roles emerged as issues that were difficult to resolve, except as a result of experience in the specific circumstances of an ongoing contract.

These IS arrangements and roles were also latent and emergent to varying degrees in the selective IT outsourcing cases we investigated. In the public sector, the reasons for IT outsourcing were related to government market-testing pressures or to the development of emergent forms of organization in terms of privatization. In other selective outsourcing cases, the reasons were more related to financial pressures, the opportunities for cost savings, refocusing the efforts of in-house IT staff, and/or to technical reasons, for example, outsourcing in order to move off ageing mainframes and develop client/server architectures. IT managers were more prominent in decision-making processes in such cases.

By 1993 over 40 per cent of UK organizations had selectively outsourced IT and spent on average about 13 per cent of their IT budgets doing so. These organizations projected their IT outsourcing expenditure to increase to an average of 25 per cent of their IT budgets within the next five years. Organizations that had not previously outsourced IT were projected to undertake IT outsourcing at the rate of 6 per cent per annum (Fitzgerald and Willcocks 1993). These figures looked like being considerably higher amongst UK public-sector organizations. Studies of outsourcing suggest that total outsourcing may have mixed results but is not a declining phenomenon (see Lacity *et al.* 1995). In 1994 a number of large-scale total outsourcing deals were completed in both public and private sectors, notably at British Aerospace and the Inland Revenue. Much of this suggests that the residual IS functions we have described, or developments thereof—with their characteristic structures, roles, and distribution of technical expertise—will become commonplace, rather than novel, in the UK over the next five years.

References

Apte, U. (1990), 'Global Outsourcing of Information Systems and Processing Services', *The Information Society*, vol. 7, pp. 287–303.
—— and Mason, R. (1993), 'Global Disaggregation of Information Intensive Services', paper presented at the Outsourcing of Information Systems Services Conference, University of Twente, the Netherlands, 20–2 May.

Aucoin, P., Almay, F., Heise, R., Landry, R., Lichtenfels, P., Meneely, P., Ruggirello, A., Stout, E., Spurgeon, J., and Temple, R. (1991), *Internalizing the Vendors Resources: Outsourcing in the 1990s*, Boston: Chantico Publishing.

Auwers, T., and Deschoolmeester, D. (1993), 'The Dynamics of an Outsourcing Relationship: A Case in the Belgian Food Industry', paper presented at the Outsourcing of Information Systems Services Conference, University of Twente, the Netherlands, 20–2 May.

Buck-Lew, M. (1992), 'To Outsource Or Not?', *International Journal of Information Management*, vol. 12, pp. 3–20.

Clark, P., and Staunton, N. (1990), *Innovation in Technology and Organization*, London: Routledge.

Clark, T., and Zmud, R. (1993), 'The Outsourcing Decision Structure: A Dynamic Modelling Approach', paper presented at the Outsourcing of Information Systems Services Conference, University of Twente, the Netherlands, 20–2 May.

Clegg, S. (1990), *Modern Organisations*, London: Sage.

Drucker, P. (1991), 'The Coming of the New Organization', in W. McGowan (ed.), *Revolution in Real Time*, Boston: Harvard Business School Press, 3–15.

Earl, M. (1991), 'Outsourcing Information Services', *Public Money and Management*, 4 (Autumn), 17–21.

Feeny, D., Earl, M., and Edwards, B. (1989), *IS Arrangements to Suit Complex Organisations 1. An Effective IS Structure*, OXIIM Research and Discussion Paper 89/4, Oxford: Templeton College.

Feeny, D., Edwards, B., and Simpson, K. (1991), *Understanding the CEO/IT Director Relationship*, OXIIM Research and Discussion Paper 91/6, Oxford: Templeton College.

Feeny, D., Willcocks, L., Rands, T., and Fitzgerald, G. (1993), 'Strategies for IT Management—When Outsourcing Equals Rightsourcing', in S. Rock (ed.), *Directors Guide to Outsourcing*, London: Institute of Directors/IBM.

Fitzgerald, G., and Willcocks, L. (1993), *Information Technology Outsourcing Practice: A UK Survey*, London: Business Intelligence.

Ganz, J. (1990), 'Outsourcing: Threat or Salvation?', *Network Management*, vol. 10, pp. 24–32.

George, J., and King, J. (1991), 'Examining the Computing and Centralization Debate', *Communications of the ACM*, vol. 34, no. 7, pp. 63–72.

Grant, R. (1992), 'The Resource-based Theory of Competitive Advantage: Implications for Strategy Formulation', *Sloan Management Review*, vol. 33, no. 3, pp. 114–35.

Griese, J. (1993), 'Outsourcing of Information Systems Services in Switzerland—A Status Report', paper presented at the Outsourcing of Information Systems Services Conference, University of Twente, the Netherlands, 20–2 May.

Handy, C. (1984), *The Future of Work*, Oxford: Blackwell.

Heinzl, A. (1993), 'Outsourcing the Information Systems Function Within the Company—An Empirical Survey', paper presented at the Outsourcing of Information Systems Services Conference, University of Twente, the Netherlands, 20–2 May.

Hodgkinson, S. (1991), *The Role of the Corporate Information Technology Function in the Large Multi-business Company*, OXIIM Research and Discussion Paper 91/2, Oxford: Templeton College.

Huber, R. (1993), 'How Continental Bank Outsourced its Crown Jewels', *Harvard Business Review*, 65/1 (Jan.–Feb.), 121–9.

International Data Corporation (1991), *The Impact of Facilities Management on the IT Market*, London: IDC.

Klepper, R. (1993), 'Efficient Outsourcing Relationships', paper presented at the Outsourcing of Information Systems Services Conference, University of Twente, the Netherlands, 20–2 May.

Lacity, M., and Hirschheim, R. (1993), *Information Systems Outsourcing*, Chichester: Wiley.

—— and Willcocks, L. (1995), *Are Information Systems Outsourcing Expectations Realistic? A Review of US and UK Evidence*, Oxford Institute of Information Management Research and Discussion Paper 95/1, Oxford: Templeton College.

Loh, L., and Venkatraman, N. (1992*a*), *Diffusion of Information Technology Outsourcing: Influence Sources and the Kodak Effect*, Massachusetts Institute of Technology CISR Working Paper no. 245, Cambridge, Mass.: MIT (Oct.).

—— (1992*b*), 'Determinants of Information Technology Outsourcing: A Cross Sectional Analysis', *Journal of Management Information Systems*, vol. 9, no. 1, pp. 7–24.

—— (1992*c*), *Stock Market Reactions to Information Technology Outsourcing: An Event Study*, Massachussetts Institute of Technology Working Paper no. 3499–92BPS, Cambridge, Mass.: MIT.

Mintzberg, H. (1979), 'An Emerging Strategy of "Direct" Research', *Administrative Science Quarterly*, vol. 24, no. 4, pp. 582–9.

Moad, J. (1993), 'Inside an Outsourcing Deal', *Datamation* (15 Feb.), 20–7.

Prahalad, C., and Hamel, G. (1991), 'The Core Competence of the Corporation', *Harvard Business Review*, vol. 63, no. 3, pp. 79–91.

Quinn, J. (1992), 'The Intelligent Enterprise: A New Paradigm', *Academy of Management Executive*, vol. 6, no. 4, pp. 44–63.

—— Doorley, T., and Paquette, P. (1990), 'Technology in Services: Rethinking Strategic Focus', *Sloan Management Review*, vol. 31, no. 2, pp. 79–87.

Saaksjarvi, M. (1993), 'Outsourcing of Information Systems: Matching Organizational Forms and Organizational Roles', paper presented at the Outsourcing of Information Systems Services Conference, University of Twente, the Netherlands, 20–2 May.

Symons, C. (1993), Presentation at Creating Business Value for IT Conference, Oxford: Templeton College (June).

Whitaker, A. (1992), 'The Transformation in Work: Post-Fordism Revisited', in M. Reed and M. Hughes (eds.), *Rethinking Organization: New Directions in Organization Theory and Analysis*, London: Sage, 184–206.

Willcocks, L. (1994), 'Managing Information Systems in UK Public Administration: Issues and Prospects', *Public Administration*, 72 (Spring), 13–32.

—— and Fitzgerald, G. (1993), *IT Outsourcing: Preliminary Findings From Recent UK Research*, OXIIM Research and Discussion Papers, 93/10, Oxford: Templeton College.

—— (1994), *A Business Guide to Outsourcing IT: A Study of European Best Practice in the Selection, Management and Use of External IT Services*, London: Business Intelligence.

14

Mergers: The Role of Information Technology

JANE C. LINDER

Introduction

Mergers and acquisitions have had questionable success in recent years. Anecdotal sources report that 70 per cent of acquisitions do not meet the acquiring company's expectations and 50 per cent are outright failures (Carlyle 1986). More systematic research indicates that 50 to 60 per cent of acquisitions are later divested (Porter 1987) and that market share, profits, and return on equity in acquired units often decline (Bhide 1987).

These transactions are unsuccessful for a variety of reasons. Among these is difficulty in integration—a failure to bring two firms together in a way that creates value (Jensen and Ruback 1983; Lubatkin 1987; Salter and Weinhold 1979). Not all mergers and acquisitions intend to create value through operating synergies; some seek portfolio gains such as reduced financial risk, and others intend to restructure an acquired firm and resell it at a profit (Chatterjee 1983). However, if Bhide's statistics from 1981 and 1985 can be generalized, between 25 and 40 per cent of friendly acquisitions are intended to create operating (or business unit level) synergies (1987). The goal is to share or transfer skills or resources among business units. In these cases, effective integration is the gateway to value.

Much of the merger and acquisition literature has treated the process of integrating organizations as a 'black box' (for example, Rumelt 1974; Christensen and Montgomery 1981; Kusewitt 1985; Montgomery and Wilson 1986; Porter 1987). Using Mohr's words, the preferred approach has been 'variance analysis' rather than 'process analysis' (1982). This research focuses on what happens in between—how two companies and their information technology (IT) infrastructures are brought together. It attempts to draw links between the characteristics of the firms and business units involved in the transaction, the processes they use to integrate, and the outcomes they experience.

The purpose of the study is to understand the process and impact of IT integration in an acquisition or merger setting. There has been no systematic research in this area; the study is exploratory. The questions that guided this research are:

1. How do general managers integrate IT infrastructures effectively?
2. What role does IT play in the overall integration process?

The Study

The research was set in two 'super-regional' bank holding companies in one geographic area of the USA. The two companies had both been formed in the past three years by 'mergers of equals'. In addition, sixty-five identifiable banking institutions had become affiliated with, or absorbed by these two corporations during the 1980s.

A variety of IT projects were initiated to integrate systems within these corporations. Each of these systems projects crossed organizational boundaries, and most entailed major organizational change. In each case, the project involved the conversion and consolidation of two or more systems. Interview data were collected about thirty separate IT-related integration episodes, and two were observed from the initial planning stages through consolidation weekend and post-integration results. One hundred and thirteen different managers were interviewed and thirty project meetings were attended in the two corporations. (The study is described in more detail in Linder 1989.)

Management Objectives and the Role of IT

An effective integration process meets managers' objectives. What were these? Regional commercial banks merged and acquired in order to remain independent in an industry increasingly dominated by large players. The erosion of regulatory restrictions on pricing, products, and geographic expansion in this region in the 1980s created a competitive environment in which only the fittest would remain independent. To survive in this 'bank eat bank' world, institutions found they had to grow and remain relatively efficient to position themselves to be the buyers rather than the bought. Therefore, regional banks integrated the information systems of merged and acquired institutions to gain economies, leverage standard product lines across an expanding distribution network, and bring their disparate parts under control.

These performance objectives were not unrealistic *per se*. The nation's largest banks are, on average, slightly less profitable than mid-sized institutions, but some large banks earn considerably better returns than the average (Humphrey 1987, 1990; Rhoades 1986; Kolari and Zarkoohi 1987; Lawrence and Shay 1986). Clearly, information technology integration was critical to achieving growth with efficiency. It was intended to provide savings in its own right and was an essential precursor to operational cost improvements. Some managers also recognized its dominant influence in creating administrative coherence—in digesting a merged or acquired firm. By any measure, IT integration was a central task in the endeavour.

The Process of Integration—Rhetoric and Reality

Bankers described two ideal processes they used for accomplishing integration—one for acquisitions and another for mergers. *Acquisitions* often involved a large, experienced firm integrating a smaller bank. Managers outlined a co-operative process in which one partner clearly dominated the other and asserted that its information systems and operating procedures be adopted by its junior partner. The acquired firm accepted this directive because the other firm's managers were 'in charge'. The integration effort was implementation- rather than design-intensive as the smaller bank adjusted its practices to conform with its new parent, eliminated jobs, and consolidated options. Ideally, the acquiring bank's systems were technically and functionally superior to those of the acquired institution. If the latter had systems that were unique or innovative, these were adopted for the entire firm. New systems development, however, was avoided during the integration period in order to minimize technology-related risk.

Managers articulated an ideal *merger* process that was quite different. It was a collaborative approach in which equal partners joined together to design an operation that represented the best of both. The process of integration for a merger was more highly planning-intensive than for an acquisition. Ideally, partners devised a shared direction to which both could commit, then joint task forces selected the best systems, policies, and operating procedures around which to standardize. Once plans were complete, they proceeded to convert systems and remodel operations. The ideal processes for these implementation steps closely paralleled those for acquisitions.

In bankers' descriptions of both ideal mergers and acquisitions, capable, committed teams were fielded to implement systems changes in a way that was transparent to the customers, so that banking relationships were not endangered, and market share was largely preserved. Thirty-five to 45 per cent of the overhead expense of the consolidated partner was eliminated, resulting in significant improvements in overall return on assets.

The Reality

Reality differed dramatically from this ideal view, in most of the episodes reviewed for this research. The financial results of both corporations' mergers and acquisitions were mediocre. The savings produced by IT integration did not flow quickly or smoothly to the bottom line. On average, 17 per cent of the deposit share held in 1981 or later acquired by the study participants was lost by 1987, and the loss of income share was even more substantial.

These banks were not unique. A statistical analysis of all of the bank acquisitions in the region from 1981 to 1988 showed unspectacular performance (Linder and Crane 1991). On average, integrating banks lost competitive momentum. They lost assets, but did not improve their return on assets relative to their competitors. While they did reduce overhead expense significantly, their assets declined faster than expected. As a result, non-merging banks out-performed merging ones in reducing non-interest expenses relative to assets.

Just as financial results failed to match expectations, the actual process of integration bore little resemblance to the ideal described by managers. Most *acquisition* integrations failed to achieve the positive, co-operative process that executives sought. The acquiring firm's systems were neither technically nor functionally superior to those of the acquired firm, yet they were usually adopted. On-line systems were removed and paper-based processes installed. Integrated systems were dismantled, and fragmented, stand-alone applications were implemented to replace them. Training was insufficient to prepare branch and lending staffs to face customers competently. The integration was not transparent to the customers. Errors were made in accounts. In one telling example, a respected dentist's account statement was mailed to his office with the label, 'Doing Business as Marie's Massage Parlour'.

Executives of an acquired bank were not persuaded to accept the leadership of their new partner and commit their energies to the integration project. Some left. Some stood back and waited for the dominant bank to fail. Others actively sabotaged the project. The respected, co-operative local leader who was a central feature in an ideal acquisition process was not respected, not co-operative, or not even retained in many actual episodes.

Ideal *merger* episodes were as infrequent as ideal acquisitions. Among the banks studied, there was one. An executive explained: 'A merger of equals doesn't exist. It's a story book fiction. Both parties *act* as if they're equal while each one tries to gain control.'

The dominant feature of most so-called merger processes was contentiousness. The individuals in positions of authority were viewed with distrust by management from the other firm. As one manager said: 'Mergers are difficult because there is no single point of superior power.' Both sides predictably and aggressively argued to keep their own version of the *status quo*. The IT integration process was not perceived as an objective decision-making activity; each firm saw the other's initiatives as parochial—not driven by rational analysis, mutual benefit, or corporate good.

Actual merger and acquisition integration processes were almost indistinguishable in one respect: both were highly political. Twenty-six out of thirty episodes exhibited a characteristic pattern which only varied in the length and intensity of the infighting:

- Participants started off competing. They puffed, preened, and exaggerated their accomplishments. They avoided revealing weakness.
- Players used whatever means possible to gain advantage. They stalled, intrigued, fought openly, tested and rigged the playing-field. Differences were exacerbated and deadlines manipulated to win the contest.
- When they were convinced they could not win, players pressed for political compromises that simply maintained the balance of control.

Internecine warring was time-consuming and debilitating. In one particularly unfortunate case, adversarial wrangling between IT factions continued even as Federal regulators seized the bank's assets. In others, a 'corporate solution' was reached, but no individual was officially named responsible for the technology integration. In still others, the IT task force's 'decision' did not represent consensus, and did not generate commitment or even compliance from the participants. The common refrain in these episodes was that neither firm was willing to cede control to the other. The cost was in delay, in compromise solutions that did not serve the corporation, and in institutionalization of a rabid, back-biting style of management that inhibited commitment.

Technical Risk and Diversion

The problem was certainly not technical. Even though banks experienced a variety of systems hardware and software problems during integration, no single episode described in this study was counted a 'technical' failure. The technical difficulty of the project was, in fact, unrelated to integration effectiveness. A knowledgeable systems professional in each organization was asked to give a 'low–medium–high' assessment of the technical difficulty of each integration project that was then compared statistically to the overall integration effectiveness ratings. The result was a significant correlation *in the reverse direction*. In short, the higher the technical risk, the more likely the integration project was to be completed effectively. (See Table 14.1).

Integration projects did divert management attention from banking. Changing systems forced banks' operational routines and service delivery processes to change, and changing routines made the bank temporarily incompetent. For the period of the transition, management lost sight of

Table 14.1. *Statistical correlations among variables*
(Kruskal-Wallis Analysis by Rank)

Variables	Effectiveness	Differences	Absence of credible deadline
Technical risk	−9.4560**		
Balanced power	−14.3850***	15,798***	19.333***
Differences	−9.8970**		9.229**
Absence of credible deadline	−19.8860***		
Process	5.0777		
Process fit	16.7840***		

Note: *p ≤ .1; **p ≤ .01; ***p ≤ .001.

the market-place as the bank's attention was absorbed fully by its internal problems. Management simply did not have the capacity to attend both to the market and to a floor-to-ceiling renovation of their systems and operating habits.

The magnitude of the training effort was consistently underestimated. Managers mouthed the right words—'There's no such thing as enough training'—but only the most experienced integration teams had developed branch and operations training programmes that actually worked. Further, each bank paid considerable attention to training tellers and branch office staff, but most ignored management training. When new systems were implemented, managers were not taught what reports were available to them, what they meant, or how to use them. During the conversion period—often a stretch of several months—the information contained in the reports that did exist was suspect. Commercial lenders complained that they could not call the customers who were reported to be in arrears because of embarrassing data inaccuracies. The loss of control surprised and shocked bank management. They were unprepared for the effort and attention they were forced to devote to bringing the organization back under control.

A second kind of diversion also impacted bank performance. IT resources that were devoted to consolidating banks were unavailable for new product development, and so product innovation came to a halt. Again, the integrating bank was disadvantaged among its competitors.

The diversion of management and IT resources to systems integration was only part of the story, however. It was a temporary problem: for an experienced firm, an acquired bank with $300 million to $1 billion in assets could be integrated in about six months. The most active integrator in the study stated they actually spent only about 20 per cent of their systems resources on consolidations. This was significant, but not overwhelming.

Why Was IT Integration So Difficult?

Integration was not a process of collaborative or co-operative decision-making motivated by shareholder benefit culminating in excellent technical execution. Financial results were unspectacular, and the process of integration did not match managers' ideals in the majority of cases. Technology risk and management distraction did not account for the discrepancy between managers' expectations and their achievements. Why was IT integration so difficult?

Let me propose an analytical framework that helps to answer this question. It highlights the political risk of IT integration and links this analysis to process recommendations. We will consider three political risk factors: the balance of power between merging organizations, differences in strategy and style, and the presence or absence of a credible deadline. These risk factors are synthesized from the merger and acquisition literature.

Balance of Power Between Organizations

While the key players in the integration are often dependent on one another to some extent, this balance can vary. One can dominate the other because of superior size, skills, formal authority, or control of critical resources (Rumelt 1974; Jemison 1986*b*; Barney 1986). Alternatively, the distribution of power can be more evenly balanced. Balanced power among decision-makers presents a fertile environment for conflict (Pfeffer 1981).

Differences

The participants in a project can have divergent, strongly held beliefs about what should be done. These are opinions about objectives, business policies, or implementation strategies. Differences arise because of dissimilar histories, practices, values, and styles of the participating constituencies—so-called 'clash of cultures' (Sales and Mirvis 1984; Quinn and Kimberly 1984; Buono *et al.* 1985). They are intensified by distrustful, competitive, or negative attitudes between business units (Jemison 1986*a*). Disagreements are more likely to occur when one group must fail if another is successful (Pfeffer and Salancik 1978; Lax and Sebenius 1986).

Deadlines

Political risk increases when deadlines are too aggressive, too distant, and are vague or poorly defined. Deadlines that are too short allow little time for deliberation, for consulting all the interested parties, or for careful planning (Vroom and Yetton 1973; Kotter and Schlesinger 1979). The result can be poor decisions or inadequate commitment from the individuals who must implement them. Risk also increases when deadlines are distant or not compelling to the project participants (Gersick and Constance 1988). In this situation, projects are more likely to be effective when feasible, credible deadlines are set.

An analysis of the three risk factors leads to recommendations about the kind of integration process that is likely to be effective. The integration process is the method by which the risk factors described above are managed. It includes some people and excludes others; it has style—it can be autocratic or participative (Vroom and Yetton 1973). The process turns out results at a certain speed (Kotter and Schlesinger 1979). For it to be effective, the process must fit the situation (Quinn 1980; Haspeslagh and Jemison 1987). How do the political risk factors translate into recommendations for managing the IT integration process?

The schematic in Figure 14.1 shows the risk factors and the processes[1] that are used to manage them. On the left path of the schematic one group clearly dominates. To the extent time permits, the dominant group can market their decisions about what should be done and how implementation should proceed. Marketing is 'friendly persuasion'. The other participants feel they have some choice in adopting the decisions. In this way, marketing attempts to commit attitudes as well as behaviours. It is appropriate in situations in which the decision-maker can offer solutions with relative advantage (Rogers 1983) and can take some time to persuade others to 'buy in'.

Where action is urgent and/or persuasion is ineffective, mandates are called for. Mandates are unilateral decisions; the managers in charge give direct, enforceable orders. This approach is appropriate when meeting time constraints is more important to the success of the project than securing board participation in the decisions (Vroom and Yetton 1973). Mandates focus on achieving certain behaviours in the short run.

At the second step on the schematic no individual or group is dominant, but the participants basically agree about what should be done. Goals are clear and shared; decisions are obvious; the plan of action is acceptable to all. In this case, co-operation is appropriate. Despite the fact that authority and expertise are distributed, the participants can set realistic deadlines, assign responsibilities, and move forward.

At the third step power is balanced and the parties have major disagreements about what should be done. When they share a sense of timing, a negotiation process is effective (Gersick and Constance 1988). Negotiation is a collaborative, joint decision-making process organized around a specific deadline. Differences are resolved through active give-and-take.

---

[1] Processes are certainly more complex than the simple names and descriptions used here. The intent of this classification is to make categorical distinctions for analytical purposes.

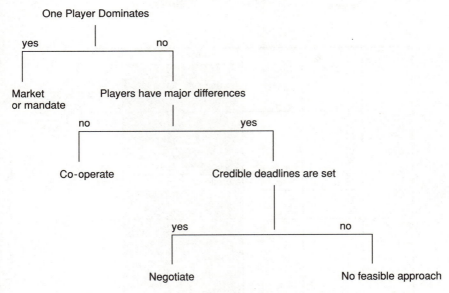

Fig. 14.1. *Political risk factors and process recommendations*

Negotiation is suited to situations in which there is disagreement over the best course of action and the commitment of the participants is critical to the success of the effort (Vroom and Yetton 1973; Eccles 1984).

On the farthest right path of the schematic power is balanced among the decision-makers. They disagree about an appropriate plan of action, and compelling deadlines are absent. No process appears feasible, given these constraints. Political risk is intense.

The framework points out several threats to the effectiveness of an integration project. First, the process can be mismatched with the political risks. For example, a manager could mandate a new information system despite major differences of opinion with colleagues who control important resources. Secondly, the political risk factors can be so constraining that there is no effective decision process. Finally, managers from different parts of the organization have every incentive to perceive the situation differently. When they disagree about the balance of power, the best plan of action, and feasible timing, the resulting conflict can push the process into the high-risk domain.

A Review of Thirty Episodes

The thirty IT integration episodes identified in this study can be evaluated in the light of the risk framework. They are arrayed in Figure 14.2 by

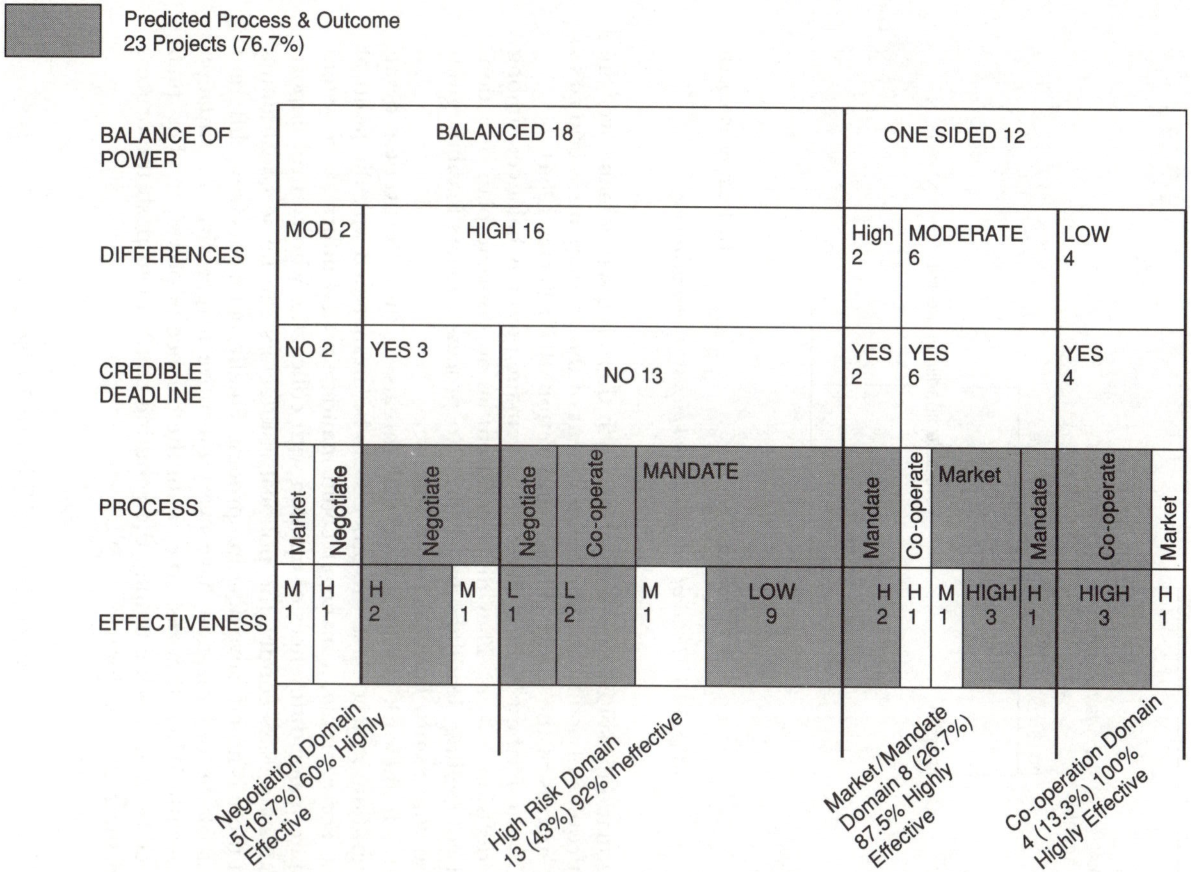

Predicted Process & Outcome
23 Projects (76.7%)

BALANCE OF POWER	BALANCED 18							ONE SIDED 12			
DIFFERENCES	MOD 2	HIGH 16					High 2	MODERATE 6		LOW 4	
CREDIBLE DEADLINE	NO 2	YES 3		NO 13			YES 2	YES 6		YES 4	
PROCESS	Market	Negotiate	Negotiate	Negotiate	Co-operate	MANDATE	Mandate	Co-operate	Market	Co-operate	Market
EFFECTIVENESS	M 1	H 1	H 2	M 1	L 1	L 2	M 1	LOW 9	H 2	H H 2 1	H M 1 1	HIGH 3	H 1	HIGH 3	H 1

Negotiation Domain
5/16 (16.7%) 60% Highly
Effective

High Risk Domain
13 (43%) 92% Ineffective

Market/Mandate
Domain 8 (26.7%)
87.5% Highly
Effective

Co-operation Domain
4 (13.3%) 100%
Highly Effective

Fig. 14.2. *Political risk factors, process and effectiveness of thirty IT integration projects (divisional scale represents the number of projects)*

political risk factors, with process and outcomes noted. (Several 'empty' columns are not shown in the figure.) The first three rows on the schematic are the political risk factors: balance of power, differences, and deadlines. The fourth and fifth rows further categorize the projects by process and effectiveness. Shaded areas in the bottom two rows indicate processes and outcomes that were hypothesized by the risk framework.

Effective integration projects did tend to use the process recommended by the risk framework (See Table 14.1). Seventy-six per cent of the projects (twenty-three of thirty) exhibited predicted processes and outcomes. However, two projects with balanced power and no credible deadline were unexpectedly effective with moderate differences. Of these two projects, the one in which a negotiation process was used was effective. One explanation of this result might be that moderate agreement on a course of action acts as an alternative to a credible deadline in enabling effective negotiation. Two additional projects used an unpredicted process but were nevertheless effective. Finally, two projects were less effective and one more effective than predicted, despite using the process predicted by the framework. We must conclude that factors other than those captured here are influential in some cases.

No single process was universally successful. A mandated process was effective in 23 per cent of the cases in which IS was used, while the other processes achieved good results 60 to 67 per cent of the time, generally supporting Nutt's findings (1986).

The highest risk category—projects with balanced power, high differences, and an absence of accepted deadlines—was the only group in which projects were likely to fail. Figure 14.2 shows that 92 per cent of the projects in this category were ineffective. None of the three processes used for these projects appears to have managed the risks effectively. For all other combinations of characteristics found in the study, a majority of the projects were effective.

'Acquisition' episodes—those with concentrated power—significantly outperformed 'merger' episodes. The former were highly effective in 92 per cent of the cases; the corresponding figure for the latter is only 17 per cent. This finding corroborates one repeated acquiror's claim that success lay in establishing the 'points of superior power' early in the game, then using them to make things change.

Finally, the three political risk factors were not independent; they were likely to be found together, producing a high risk context in which integration projects were likely to fail. (The statistics are shown in Table 14.1) Further, fully 43 per cent of the thirty projects studies fell in the high-risk category, more than any other type. Additionally, the most common process in this category was mandate—a process which managers described as their 'last resort'. Why did this occur?

Integration managers did not begin their task by taking an objective assessment of the relative power of the participants based on skills and expertise. A manager's assessment of his or her position was, in fact, highly coloured by perception and self-interest, open to manipulation, and established over time as the integration project played out. One executive said: 'It will take six months to sort out who is going to be a winner in this. Everyone is jockeying for position.' Because managers preferred control and independence in the high-stakes game of post-merger integration (Mohr 1982; Donaldson 1984; Jemison 1986a), they actively defended their turf, staged contests they were sure to win, hid their failures, and advertised others' problems. In other words, they did everything they could to tip the balance of power their way.

The level and intensity of reported differences was a tool in this agenda. When one organization found it could accept the other's leadership—and its definition of what needed to be done—IT issues were quickly resolved. When neither organization was willing to cede control to the other, so-called substantive differences were ardently proclaimed. There were no cases of balanced power and low differences among the projects.

Timing was used as a political instrument as well. Deadlines were 'externally' determined in only four of the thirty projects: in two, visible performance problems created urgency, and in two others, regulatory and legal problems constrained management from acting. For all others, deadlines were set by management, and reflected the preferences of the parties in control. One IT executive stated: 'Everything depends on timing. The systems decisions are being made [by our partner]. We're not in a position to make them because of all the [intrastate] consolidations we have to do. We're told that the architecture will be theirs because they're six months ahead of us.'

In some cases management constructed a false image of the balance of power to gain temporary control over people with critical skills. Projects in which one partner intended to dominate were billed, instead, as 'partnerships'. One manager described an information systems and back office integration this way: 'The façade is that we are tender and sensitive. The reality is that they will conform. No one wants to say it unequivocally. We set up false expectations for them. If you tell people how it is going to be, you will see them leave—we want to exploit them temporarily. When the jig is up, it creates a morale problem and a service problem.'

When key players could not or did not construct a shared view of the balance of power, the project was likely to end up in the high-risk category—neither firm willing to admit the other's dominance, differences ardently proclaimed, and deadlines posed to each player's advantage. In this situation the integration initiative collapsed into a self-fulfilling spiral of internal competition and political manipulation. One banker summarized the point by saying: 'Assuming you are in the political sphere forecloses opportunities in the rational one.'

This perceptual, manipulated view of means and ends also helps explain why mandate was the most common process in the high-risk domain. If one player actually dominated, mandate was an appropriate implementation process. As Figure 14.2 shows, it was effective in several projects of this sort. Players who *believed* themselves to have sufficient power to command others' behaviour used this tactic to close discussion in spite of resistance. When they misjudged their ability to gain control, the result was open confrontation, stalemates and sabotage, and ineffective projects.

Habits Increased Risk

Political behaviour and attributions fostered conflict, but a more subtle influence was also at work. Banks had elaborate repertoires of habits built around their particular strategic choices, organizational structures, and operating styles. Further, habits were more than emotionless, practised routines; they were value-laden (Schein 1961). In other words, banks that decentralized authority considered their organizational structure was right. Innovation-oriented banks scoffed at their conservative partners' reluctance to take risks. Risk-averse bankers, in turn, viewed their more entrepreneurial partners as impulsive and wasteful. Institutions that pursued the retail market found corporate bankers as impulsive and wasteful. Institutions that pursued the retail market found corporate bankers stuffy and élitist. Corporate bankers looked down their noses at their retail counterparts as unprofessional glad-handers. In short, the more potential synergy the combination promised—that is, the more complementary the organizations were—the more habits conflicted (Buono *et al.* 1985; Jemison 1986*a*, *b*).

Habits extended to management process as well. Banks with a consensual management style were comfortable with the negotiated process of mergers. Banks with a more aggressive, directive style were equally at ease taking charge of an acquisition. But directive managers ran participative task forces poorly; facilitating coaches resisted making tough, unilateral decisions, even when they 'knew' what process was called for in the situation they faced.

Habits were not only tacit and value-laden, but were imprinted on the information technology infrastructures of the organizations being integrated. Business policies were reflected in the kinds of systems that were built, the locus of IT decision-making, and the methodologies that were used. Joining systems created a clash between stable frameworks of accepted practices.

The following example illustrates how conflicting IT habits interfered with a project team's ability to work together on what was intended to be a 'quick win'. The task was to move an innovative system 'as is' from one bank to another. A joint project team was initiated between the fast-paced, centralized, entrepreneurial 'sending' bank and the slower, more deliberate, decentralized 'receiving' organization. The entrepreneurial bank's team members were accustomed to a prototyping approach with strong user direction, aggressive deadlines, and no formal specifications. The conservative institution's IT contingent used a standard life-cycle methodology with careful requirements review, sign-offs, and target dates that allowed time to involve affected departments.

The project was a disaster. One half of the team tried to prototype while the other tried to build a tight specification. The former sought a single, strong user champion; the latter scheduled 'endless' meetings to build consensus. A project that was initially estimated to require three months lingered on for a year-and-a-half with contentious meetings and missed deadlines. Furthermore, the team was blind to the reasons for its difficulties. Neither side could understand why the other was 'doing all the wrong things'. Their inability to see their own habits left both sides believing that the other was either inept or pursuing a political agenda. The result was confusion, mistrust, and mutual arrogance rather than the mutual respect that complementary skills theoretically provide.

Making IT Integration Work

Despite the debilitating influences of politics and habits, some projects succeeded. Organizations did change their assumptions and break their habits. Politically motivated, turf-battling task-forces did evolve into effective work groups which made hard decisions that served the corporation. Organizations that were stopped 'dead in the water' did catch the wind and begin to move forward again. How did management make IT integration work in these cases?

Three Anchors

An articulate executive explained the key to success simply: 'If you can keep the discussion rational, any problem can be worked out.' Each integration episode that reached a positive conclusion was anchored in one of three ways. Credible, respected leadership emerged; a credible, common direction was articulated; or a credible, compelling deadline was accepted. When all three were missing, the integration process was likely to be ineffective. At least one anchor was needed to 'keep the discussion rational'.

In two acquisitions that closely resembled managers' ideal view, the anchor was clear: one firm was in charge; its leaders dominated. This relationship was established from the outset of the process and accepted by the acquired institution. In one ideal merger, the anchor was equally clear. The common direction brought benefits to both firms; the joint mission was the keystone of the process.

Fourteen integration episodes were less than ideal, but did not end up in the unfeasible domain. In each of these, management found an anchor through the process. These episodes began as all others—with suspicion and mistrust. As managers anchored them, the processes gained clarity and order, and things got done.

In two episodes that were ultimately effective, credible leaders emerged from the integration task-force process. Because of their expertise and skill, these individuals became respected by participants from both original organizations. They were able to assume responsibility for a combined organization without engendering resentment. The second kind of anchor that executives used was a common direction. They delayed naming a single individual in charge of the IT project until a solid consensus had been reached about specifically what should be done. Between banks of equal size, newer, more sophisticated systems were the obvious choice of IT task-forces, and this superior technology sometimes provided the directional anchor that the team needed. The third kind of process anchor was time. Compelling deadlines drove competing groups to decisions they might not otherwise have been able to reach. As Allison said: ' "Solutions" to strategic problems are not found by research analysts focusing coolly on the problem. Instead, deadlines and events raise issues and force busy players to take stands' (1971: 168). Competitive urgency was used as a non-partisan wedge to break deadlocked discussions. When executives believed that the entire entity was threatened, they could sometimes put parochial issues aside.

Once the integration process was anchored by commitment to a common 'who', 'what', or 'when', the other elements were put in place. This step was critical to position the group to execute their plans. An IS executive analysed a particularly effective integration episode this way: 'We had the three things we needed to make changes: clear direction, a deadline, and the authority to make the decisions.' The result was something he called 'momentum'. The integration process was able to turn the organization, gather speed, and move again in a new direction.[2]

[2] Lewin (1947) and Schein (1961) described a change process as unfreezing, moving, and refreezing. The respondents in this study used very different language for the same three stages of change. To them, it was stopping, turning, and starting again. They described the first step in change as paralysis. The organization lost all forward momentum. People could not act—one executive called them 'rabbits, frozen in front of the headlights'. The second stage was not a change in the organization's position, but a shift in its attitudes, goals, and focus of attention. It was turning, not moving. Finally, the second stage was a slow process of getting moving again. The organization inched forward with uncomfortable new procedures as it tried to rebuild momentum. The distinction between this language and Lewin's and Schein's is subtle. It helps us remember, however, that an organization is a body in motion.

The Positive Role of IT

Information technology integration was difficult. The process costs were considerable; management attention was diverted from the market-place; conflicting habits and political wrangling drew many episodes off a rational course and resulted in unsatisfactory outcomes. Yet IT integration also had benefits. It provided a shared direction for the overall integration effort. Two executives independently made these remarks: 'To get the synergy of the merger [our CEO] had to fix the dilution and get rid of the redundancies. He decided to start with systems—it was an implementation tool.' 'The bank operations organization will be forced to consolidate because of the systems consolidation programme. If they are running the same programmes, they will have to work consistently. IS is the fulcrum of change.'

Because bankers were absolutely unanimous in their view that systems should be consolidated, IT provided a place to start in the overall process of bringing organizations together. Bankers used information technology as the frame for the integration project. It provided a common ground which, at the very least, enabled them to define and begin their work together.

Once in place, an integrated information systems environment became the foundation for a set of shared products and business practices. As systems formed the banks' manufacturing, service delivery, and management infrastructure, a shared applications platform was the basis for a single, new corporate style. The IT infrastructure was not singularly responsible for creating cohesion, but it ratified and implemented shared practices in visible ways throughout the combined firm.

Implications for Managing Bank Mergers and Acquisitions

The primary task in the process of integrating organizations was to define and implement a clear corporate direction, structure, and set of policies that would provide coherence and efficiency in the combined firm. IT change alone did not define a new order, but the IT integration project was a setting in which this issue could not be avoided. What are the implications for management?

Attend to Information Technology

Bank executives involved in mergers and acquisitions should be prepared to attend to IT integration. It will be a major endeavour that requires the attention of the most senior, and most competent management of the firm. IT integration presents an opportunity to alienate employees and abuse customers, but when managed deliberately, IT choices implement a new corporate order that promotes positive change. Attending to information technology can be particularly difficult, however, for executives who have considered it unimportant in the past.

Understand the Pitfalls

Some banks were habitually better suited to mergers than others; others' customary processes were more consistent with acquisitions. IT integration tended to be more effective when firms stayed within their competence. Managers should understand this bias. When they venture outside it, they should be prepared to mount an integration process which is alien to their structures and assumptions about how things should work. Nothing is more difficult. It requires a separate change management team with hand-picked members working under the authority of the CEO of the firm.

Executives can gauge the extent of habit-driven conflict between firms before they begin the IT integration process. A few simple questions about style can tip-off management to sources of difficulty in the integration. How is authority distributed in the firm? What is the status hierarchy? What is the firm's attitude toward risk? What strategy has been successful for them in the past? Knowing that one firm's answers to these questions differ substantially from the other's will not eliminate mutual disrespect, but it will at least alert management to likely sources and intensity.

Manage the Process

The key process management task in IT integration is to find a rational anchor. Build a perception of credibility for a leader, a direction, or a compelling deadline. The best of these three is a leader. Leaders at all levels in the organization can help avert the political morass by fostering co-operation, by focusing on the good of the corporation, and by stating, repeating, and then publicly counting the mutual benefits of the combination. Without this symbolic leadership the process devolves into a mosaic of self-interested political compromises. The single biggest error that management made in integration processes was failing to step up to this positive leadership role.

Executives must also deal with 'what about me' questions early in the process. Settle personal issues such as job security, pay, and benefits as quickly as possible so that people involved in the integration can concentrate on the task. When these questions linger unresolved they interfere with all other activities.

Execute with Care and Discipline

Systems development should be isolated from conversions. Post-merger conversions and major systems implementations are extraordinarily complex projects and should be spared the added burden of technical risk. Their scope should be aggressively managed to include only what is necessary. The good features of eliminated systems can be added to corporate applications as enhancements—after implementation. Activities which are not critical should be delayed—not forgotten, delayed.

Training is never sufficient. For front-line employees, provide practice. This is easier said than done. It implies the teller lines and platforms are fully staffed with trained people at all offices and that the firm has a full complement of experienced trainers. These staffing levels enable on-the-job rotation for at least some of the staff of a converting bank through offices where the systems they will be receiving are established. Attend to management training as well. Develop programmes for lenders, administrators, and trust executives who will have new systems thrust upon them.

An explicit 'aftermath' project should be created. Take the time to reassess where you are after the integration. Will the systems modifications that have been implemented stand the test of time? Are they technically secure? If not, reinforce them. Will management information flows support the ongoing conduct of business? If not, put solid ones in place. Mop the floors, complete the documentation, and finish the job right. Then take a few moments to stand on the platform that has been created and judge the view.

In Sum

This study paints a fairly dismal picture of bank mergers and acquisitions. This is not new or surprising; it reiterates prior studies. What is unique here is that we began to explore the sources of the problems. Bank mergers and acquisitions had mediocre results because achieving integration was extraordinarily difficult. Implementing common information technology infrastructures was a pivotal part of the process. Bankers' consensus on the wisdom of standardizing systems made it a unique common ground. But the indelible link between the IT infrastructure and organizational practices and the detailed, unambiguous change required to integrate systems made the IT project a forum in which the struggle for control was particularly intense. Effective integration projects were anchored to rationality by a credible leader, a common direction, and a compelling deadline. In these cases, new systems put new policies and practices in place. A common IT infrastructure formed the basis for a coherent, working organization.

References

Allison, G. (1971), *Essence of Decision*, Boston: Little, Brown and Co.
Barney, S. (1986), *Strategic Planning and Firm Performance*, unpublished paper, University of California.

Bhide, A. (1987), *The Causes and Conferences of Hostile Takeovers*, unpublished paper, Harvard Business School, Boston (Sept.).

Buono, A., Bowditch, J., and Lewis, J. (1985), 'When Cultures Collide: The Anatomy of a Merger', *Human Relations*, vol. 38, no. 5, pp. 477–500.

Carlyle, R. (1986), 'Mergers: A Raw Deal for MIS?', *Datamation* (15 Sept.), 60–2.

Chatterjee, S. (1983), 'Types of Synergy and Economic Value: The Impact of Acquisitions on Merging and Rival Firms', *Strategic Management Journal*, vol. 7, pp. 119–39.

Christensen, H. K., and Montgomery, C. A. (1981), 'Corporate Economic Performance: Diversification Strategy Versus Market Strategy', *Strategic Management Journal* (Nov.–Dec.), 327–43.

Crane, D., and Eccles, R. (1987), 'Commercial Banks: Taking Shape for Turbulent Times', *Harvard Business Review* (Nov.–Dec.), 94–100.

Cyert, R., and March, J. (1963), *A Behavioural Theory of the Firm*, Englewood Cliffs, NJ: Prentice-Hall.

Donaldson, G. (1984), *Managing Corporate Wealth*, New York: Praeger Publishers.

Eccles, R. (1984), *Creating the Collaborative Organization*, Harvard Business School working paper, no. 9–784–047, Boston.

Gersick, T., and Constance, J. G. (1988), 'Time and Transition in Work Teams', in L. W. Lorsch (ed.), *Handbook of Organizational Behaviour*, Englewood Cliffs, NJ: Prentice-Hall.

Graves, D., Haspeslagh, P., and Jemison, D. (1987), 'Acquisitions—Myths and Reality', *Sloan Management Review* (Winter), 53–8.

Heaton, G. (1984, 1983), 'Banking Structure in [the region studied]', *Federal Reserve Bank* [of the region studied], *Research Report 68* (Nov.).

Humphrey, D. B. (1987), 'Cost Dispersion and the Measurement of Economies in Banking', *Economic Review*, Federal Reserve Bank of Richmond (May–June), 24–38.

—— (1990), 'Why do Estimates of Bank Scale Economies Differ?' *Economic Review*, Federal Reserve Bank of Richmond (Sept.–Oct.), 38–50.

Jemison, D. (1986*a*), 'Process Constraints on Strategic Capability Transfer During Acquisition Integration', unpublished paper, Stanford University Graduate School of Business, 94305 (Nov.).

—— (1986*b*), 'Strategic Capability Transfer in Acquisition Integration', unpublished paper, Stanford University Graduate School of Business (Nov.).

Jenson, M. C., and Rubak, R. S. (1983), 'The Market for Corporate Control: The Scientific Evidence', *Journal of Financial Economics*, no. 11, pp. 5–50.

Kolari, J., and Zarkoohi, A. (1987), *Bank Costs, Structure and Performance*, Lexington, Mass.: Lexington Books.

Kotter, J., and Schlesinger, L. (1979), 'Choosing Strategies for Change', *Harvard Business Review* (Mar.–Apr.), 106–14.

Kusewitt, J. B. (1985), 'An Exploratory Study of Strategic Acquisition Factors Relating to Performance', *Strategic Management Journal*, vol. 6, pp. 151–69.

Lawrence, C., and Shay, R. (1986), 'Technical and Financial Intermediation in Multiproduct Banking Firms: An Econometric study of US Banks, 1979–1982', ch. 2 of *Technological Innovation, Regulation and the Monetary Economy*, Cambridge, Mass.: Ballinger Publishing Company, 53–92.

Lax, D., and Sebenius, J. (1986), *The Manager as Negotiator*, New York: Free Press.

Lewin, K. (1947), 'Frontiers in Group Dynamics: Concept, Method and Reality in Social Science', *Human Relations*, no. 1, pp. 5–42.

Linder, J., and Crane, D. (1991), *Bank Mergers and Acquisitions: Integration and Profitability*, Harvard Business School Working paper, no. 91–038 (Aug.).

Lubatkin, M. (1987), 'Merger Strategies and Stockholder Value', *Strategic Management Journal*, vol. 8, pp. 39–53.

Mohr, L. (1982), *Explaining Organizational Behaviour*, San Francisco: Jossey-Bass Publishers.

Montgomery, C. A., and Wilson, V. (1986), 'Mergers that Last: a Predictable Pattern?', *Strategic Management Journal*, vol. 7, pp. 91–6.

Pfeffer, J. (1981), *Power in Organizations*, Mansfield, Mass.: Pitman Publishing, Inc.

—— and Salancik, G. (1978), *The External Control of Organizations*, New York: Harper and Row.

Porter, M. E. (1987), 'From Competitive Advantage to Corporate Strategy', *Harvard Business Review* (May–June), 43–59.

Quinn, J. B. (1980), *Strategies for Change*, Homewood, Ill.: Irwin.

Quinn, R., and Kimberley, J. (1984), *Paradox, Planning and Perseverence: Guidelines for Managerial Practice in Managing Organizational Transitions*, Homewood, Ill.: Irwin, 295–313.

Rhoades, S. (1986), 'The Operating Performance of Acquired Firms in Banking Before and After Acquisition', *Federal Reserve Bulletin*, Board of Governors of the Federal Reserve System, Washington, DC, 20551 (Apr.), 1–32.

Rogers, E. (1983), *Diffusion of Innovations*, 3rd edn., New York: Free Press.

Rumelt, R. (1974), *Strategy, Structure and Economic Performance*, Boston: Harvard Business School Press.

Sales, A., and Mirvis, P. (1984), 'When Cultures Collide: Issues in Acquisition', in J. Kimberly and R. Quinn (eds.), *Managing Organizational Transitions*, Homewood, Ill.: Irwin, 107–33.

Salter, M., and Weinhold, W. (1979), *Diversification Through Acquisition*, New York: Free Press.

Schein, E. (1961), 'Management Development as a Process of Influence', *Industrial Management Review* (May), 59–77.

Sheshunoff (1987), 'Banks [of the region studied]', One Texas Centre, 505 Barton Springs Road, Austin, Texas 78704, (512) 472–2244: annual books 1982–9.

Tam, W., Arnold, C., and Lewis, B. (1987), 'Banking Structure [in the region studied]', *Research Report 70*, Federal Reserve Bank of [the region studied] (Dec.).

Vroom, V., and Yetton, P. (1973), *Leadership and Decision-Making*, Pittsburgh: University of Pittsburgh Press.

SECTION IV

FOREWORD

Often when one discusses with senior managers their experiences in, and attitudes to, IT, they are coloured by recent experience of an IS project that has been in difficulty. Successes may abound in the case studies we teach; they are rarer in the real-world cases that managers themselves recall. It is therefore perhaps appropriate that this volume contains a substantial section on IT project management and systems implementation. Indeed, many CIOs will observe that project management remains one of the key but elusive capabilities required in exploiting IT today. And in the media, it is failed projects that often give IT 'a bad press.'

Morris opens this section by presenting a historical perspective on project management—not just IT projects, but projects at large. He compares IT and non-IT projects and argues that often the former are more complex than the latter. It is the uncertain environment of IT projects which Morris particularly highlights and it is fairly well established in the IS literature that we should examine context when we choose project management techniques and information systems development methods.

In the IS project management prescriptive literature (McFarlan 1981; Davis and Olson 1984), we often describe and analyse context in terms of complexity, uncertainty, structuredness, and the like. Indeed, perhaps we already adopt Morris's mindset of the 'management of projects' rather then 'project management' when we recognize the roles of project sponsor and champion analysed later in this section. These too are seen by Morris as important factors in managing projects.

The other distinguishing factor in IT projects that Morris highlights is the degree of user-involvement required, not least because the 'product' of the system is often conceptual, vague, or ill-defined at the outset. This is, of course, one of the fundamental issues in IS, namely, establishing information requirements or user needs. Indeed, I sometimes think that it is *the* fundamental issue, even the only one that matters. It is the heart of systems development, it is perhaps the trickiest aspect of project management, and it is the question we are really addressing at a broad organizational level in strategic information systems planning. In the classical area of building user–specialist relationships, it is also a critical issue. 'Tell me what I can have', says the user. 'You can have anything', replies the specialist. This is the eternal problem of IS.

Such an analysis can be depressing. However, Morris provides some surprising comfort to IS professionals and CIOs. He suggests that project management in the IT industry, relatively speaking, is quite competent. He even suggests that other project-based industries could learn from the IT industry or the IS profession.

Boddy may bring the reader back down to earth. From his organizational behaviour perspective he examines technological change projects. At first sight readers might say to themselves that the analysis is obvious— a frequent criticism of social scientists who seek to make sense of social activity and who comprehensively and insightfully describe and analyse organizational and managerial practice. My response would be: 'read Boddy's checklist of how to manage technological change at least twice.' It captures so much of what must be done well and you will find that many of the infamous failed IT projects in recent years fell down on some of Boddy's 'principles'.

In the management of change and innovation literatures, the concept of the project champion is well known. Beath's research on IT project champions suggests that they are especially vital in the development and implementation of strategic information systems, and the pursuit of IS-based innovation. The role is not necessarily either official or formal, in that champions typically have less authority and responsibility than they need for their task. Interestingly, their role is as much about system initiation as implementation. They can be important in identifying a system need and then harnessing support for it. Champions, it seems, can be both visionaries and expediters.

Earlier research (Runge 1985; Lockett 1987) hints that project champions are sometimes somewhat piratical, pursuing an IT innovation against the odds and despite the dead hand of the IS function. Beath finds that equally they can work with IS, especially with the support of the CIO. In other words, a champion can be the CIO's best ally, playing a key role in the politics of IS strategies and innovation., Later in this volume Earl reports on how important it is for CIOs to develop good working relationships with peers and superiors. To this list of allies we can add actual or potential project champions. Interpreting Beath, those who may be champions can be identified as managers who have a reputation for innovation.

The role of project sponsor, on the other hand, would seem to be more formal. Indeed, Edwards is quite prescriptive on this topic in his paper, not only articulating the role but suggesting a number of activities which project sponsorship involves. He sees both the sponsor and the act of sponsorship very much as part of the formal apparatus of project management and, possibly, for all IT projects. His work is based on consulting experience and more systematic investigation, namely, retrospectively examining the management of both successful and failed projects. Anybody involved in managing IT projects should benefit from reading Edwards' persuasive analysis and advice.

Last in the section is a chapter by Enid Mumford, perhaps the first and most influential researcher and writer on user involvement in IS development. Here she describes and reflects on the implementation of a well-known export system, namely XSEL at Digital Equipment Corporation. We may well expect Mumford to argue for user participation, but it is interesting to see the scope of participation in an expert system project.

Two other ideas are striking in this chapter. First is the use of Beer's (1981) viable systems model to suggest characteristics of an effective systems development method. The second is the reminder that IS project teams involve group dynamics and thus the recommendation that tuition and skills in group behaviour are likely to be beneficial in implementing information systems. This connects with Earl's emphasis on teamwork in the organizational approach to strategic information systems planning.

This section spells out quite graphically both the nature and challenges of IS projects. It is clear that by definition they are business change projects and involve the management of change as much as the technical aspects of systems development. It is also clear that IS projects are significant exercises for several members of the organization, not just the developers and the eventual end-users. Project management or, more instructively, the management of projects is a significant activity for managers. Perhaps projects, IT and non-IT, often have been treated as separate from, alongside, or at arm's length from the daily, permanent endeavours of organizations—partly because they are special (indeed, perceived as specialist) events which are temporary. However, managers cannot easily abrogate project management responsibilities without increasing project risk. I find that most senior executives have not taken on, or been given, management of projects experience in their own management development.

Table [foreword]. *IS Project management key roles*

	Project manager	Project sponsor	Project champion
Role	Project planning and control	Project owner and fixer of last resort	Project implementator who makes things happen
Locus	With the project	Management team of application area	In the line of application area
Status	Formal role	Semi formal roles	Unofficial, informal role
Involvement	Full-time	*Ad hoc*	Part time
Qualities	Experience/ managerial	Faith/leadership	Fanaticism/ change agent

What is perhaps clear from this section is the existence of at least three roles in project management that managers can fulfil (see Table). It is possibly still an empirical question whether all three are necessary in all projects, but to use Edwards' argument, it seems unlikely that they are superfluous or damaging in most projects, and in many one can see their need. There remains a substantial research agenda on the roles, characteristics,

15

Project Management: Lessons From IT and Non-IT Projects

PETER W. G. MORRIS

Introduction

Information technology projects have a notorious reputation, in many respects justly deserved. Information technology touches us all, increasingly. We are seduced with the benefits that IT will bring but are often disappointed with delays in implementation, with costs which exceed budgets, and with poor operating performance. The record of some large information technology projects has been very bad and the consequences to the businesses which have come to rely on information processing for their operations can be enormously damaging.

Why do information technology projects have this poor reputation? Is it that IT projects are inevitably more difficult to manage? Or is it that those working on IT projects are in some primitive state of ignorance of the benefits that project management can bring them? The answer ought not to be the latter. It is often not recognized in fact that information technology was one of the pioneering industries in the development of project management and has remained at the forefront of the discipline throughout the years since its development.

We can date the emergence of modern project management from the Manhattan Project in World War II and, particularly, the USA's intercontinental ballistic and missile programmes in the early 1950s (Morris 1992). The essential 'project management' features of these programmes were:

1. an emphasis on identifying management as a separate special requirement;
2. the provision of that management by specialists, particularly firms of systems engineers and managers such as TRW who concentrated on (a) defining and accomplishing the overall needs of the system as a whole, and (b) doing so within specified time, to specified technical performance, and (frankly to a much lesser extent) within budgetary requirements;
3. the development of a series of planning and control techniques to assist in this systems and programme management effort, the earliest,

and to an extent still most well-known of these techniques, being
network scheduling—PERT and CPM most particularly.

In 1958, while the US Air Force and Navy were articulating a range of
project and systems management practices, P. V. Norden (1960) of IBM published a paper which has proved to be a landmark of its kind. Norden was
concerned explicitly with the predictability of R&D projects in his industry; it is one of the earliest pieces of work to concern itself with problems
of predicting accurately the times taken and the resources required to
undertake this kind of developmental work.

Further, the concerns of A. D. Hall, van Court Hare, and others at
organizations such as Bell Labs with systems engineering methodologies
in the late 1950s and early 1960s were of course to gain universal recognition as the best in this field. As such, they were to have an enormous
influence on the general development of systems engineering and management which was expanding rapidly through the 1960s. Both authors,
for example, are given due acknowledgement in the report of the US
Commission on Government Procurement of 1972. The Commission had
been formed at industry's request to review what had then developed into
a miasma of conflicting US government systems procurement practices.

The 1960s in fact saw a profusion of bureaucratic procedures for project management developed by government in the US defence-aerospace
industry—particularly by the US Air Force and NASA. The adoption of project management in the construction industries meanwhile was moving
much slower and was concerned almost exclusively with network scheduling—a technique the benefits of which were viewed with some scepticism.

By the late 1960s and early 1970s the information technology era was
again producing important writings on the field of systems and project
development, perhaps the most famous being Brooks's *The Mythical Man-
Month* in 1975—a classic on the problems of major product development.
Yet by the mid- to late 1970s it would not be a gross exaggeration to say
that many companies—possibly most—implementing information systems
were experiencing substantial project management difficulties. Projects
were often ill-defined and poorly executed. The result was all too often
substantial disappointment.

Why was this? Was the information technology community in some way
blind and deaf to what everybody else knew? Or were the institutional
circumstances in which IT projects are generally accomplished such that
project management simply could not be applied effectively? Is there really
something so intrinsically special, so difficult, about information technology projects that they are inherently more difficult to manage? Or could
it perhaps be that project management itself was not doing a good job in
articulating its practices?

It is my belief, and the purpose of this chapter to show, that in the last two of these questions there lie two extremely important points. First, project management has indeed not done a good job in articulating and communicating its essential insights. In fact I will argue in a moment that the very concept of project management as it is still generally thought of is flawed—that this concept is too narrow and that we would be much better advised to redefine its purposes in a top-down (or, perhaps better, outwards-in) way and to talk about the *management of projects* rather than *project management*. In the management of projects the focus of attention would be the project itself—its position in operation—rather than the traditional project management concerns of the on-time, in-budget, to technical specification accomplishment of a stated objective.

The second important point is that IT projects do indeed pose a particular class of management difficulty. The essence of this difficulty is the way that information technology is so intimately bound into its organizational context. As a result, issues of organizational effectiveness and user involvement are both more complex and more prominent in IT projects than they are in most other project industries. This puts much greater emphasis on the tasks of project definition and user involvement in IT than in other project situations.

Not 'Project Management' But 'Management of Projects'

Some time ago I was asked to assist the owners of the Trans Alaskan Pipeline System. The US regulatory authorities were claiming that the costs of building the pipeline were excessive—that at least $1.5 billion of its costs were due to negligence and mismanagement. The pipeline in fact had been initially estimated in 1969 as likely to cost around $960 million. At the time that the regulatory proceedings were initiated it was estimated that it would probably cost about $4.5 billion. When completed in 1977, it had actually cost about $8.7 billion. Much play was made by the regulatory authorities of this cost growth. This set me thinking about whether project cost growth necessarily implies mismanagement. I therefore collected all the data then available in the public domain, comparing the final costs with initial costs. I obtained data on 1,444 projects. To my surprise, there were only thirty or so projects whose final costs actually were the same as or less than the initial budget. (I subsequently expanded the database, and now have data on over 3,500 projects: the pattern still holds almost unchanged, although I suspect that the trend is in fact declining on more recent projects: Morris and Hough 1986.)

Analysis of this data immediately suggested two important findings. First, since the definition of what project management was supposed to be about was the on-time, in-budget, to technical specification accomplishment of a project, the data thus far showed that project management was not being exactly successful. (I readily admit that this conclusion may be challenged;

for example, to what extent was project management being properly implemented on these projects? Indeed, how valid is the data—to what extent
are escalation and contingencies included in the initial budget, when was
the initial budget made, to what extent were there scope or quantity
changes, and so on?)

Secondly, and perhaps more importantly, the data showed that the factors which were generally causing the final costs to exceed the original—
factors such as government action, inflation, strikes, technical uncertainty,
quantity order changes and scope changes, weather—were typically of a
strategic kind or were external to the project, or at least to the act of project
management as traditionally defined. And further, crucially, these factors
were typically not even mentioned in the writings on project management!

In short, project management had set itself a task—to bring a project in
on time, in budget, to technical specification—yet all the evidence showed
that projects appeared consistently to fail in this objective; and the causes
for that failure were typically factors which were not even being addressed
by project management.

Project management, I concluded, had to get away from its then preoc-
cupations with planning and control systems, organizational structures,
and issues to do with team working, and so on, and begin to learn how
to manage the external and strategic factors which were so clearly compromising its ability to perform. This was very much my concern and focus
of research in the 1980s.

This work has enabled a broad range of issues concerned with the
strategic management of projects to be articulated (Morris 1985b, 1986).
Amongst the most important pieces of work that we have accomplished,
I believe, is the study by Morris and Hough (1986) which identified the
preconditions of success and failure for projects. In this study we examined the question of how one should define success and failure and hence
how one should measure it; we reviewed all the writings by academics and
practitioners on what may lead to a project being successful or not; we
then supplemented these observations with eight longitudinal case studies
of different major projects—ranging from the Thames barrier, the UK
nuclear power programme, and a North Sea oil field, to Concorde, the
Giotto spacecraft, and the Advanced Passenger Train, and including also
the then-largest UK government public sector IT project, the computerization of the Pay-as-you-Earn taxation scheme (COP); and we finally concluded with a list of some ninety factors which influenced the chance of
a project being successful. These ninety factors we boiled down into twenty-
two preconditions of success.

Preconditions of Success in Major Projects

- Good positive client, parent company, and senior management attitudes, interrelationships, and commitment

- Comprehensive and clearly communicated project definition
  - prefeasibility, feasibility, and design study phases carried out in an orderly fashion with meticulous thoroughness
  - objectives related to participants
  - clarity not forced prematurely
  - premature over-commitment to project avoided
  - magnitude of task properly recognized
  - the project organized appropriately
- Good planning, clear schedules, and adequate back-up strategies
  - the broad 'systems' aspects of the project recognized
  - the project definition phased and developed as appropriate
  - sub-objectives identified, assessed, and developed clearly
  - full account taken of phasing, logistics, geophysical uncertainties, environmental problems, and the relationship between design and production
  - back-up strategies prepared for high-risk areas
- Good design/technology management, especially where there is technical uncertainty or complexity
  - the extent to which R&D is completed recognized as affecting the accuracy of the estimate
  - design tested adequately before final project commitment is made
  - interface management recognized as important where there are significant interdependencies
  - replication wherever possible
  - design 'frozen' once agreed.
  - switching design authority during different phases of project avoided
  - attention paid to detail
- Concurrency avoided where possible
- Effects of external factors on definitions of project success properly recognized (e.g. prices, regulation, technical developments, government/corporate changes)
- Full cognizance given to the potentially harmful effects of urgency
- Political support obtained
  - requisite sponsorship
  - political support for necessary management actions
  - nationalist aspirations constrained
- Community factors properly considered and controlled
- Full financial analysis of all project risks undertaken
  - Sponsors interested in success of project *per se*
  - availability of funding appraised in relation to perceived success of project at key review points
- The project appropriate to the size, complexity, and urgency of the project
- Innovations in contract strategy considered where appropriate (i.e.

design/production organization, form of contract, entry point of
contractor, form of competitive bidding)
  — contractors sufficiently experienced for the task
  — bid preparation time adequate
  — contractors made financially responsible for their performance
    as far as possible, though not unfairly penalized for factors outside
    their control
• Benefits of interference by owners in execution of contracts carefully
  assessed
• Firm, effective leadership and management from the outset
  — one person (or group) in overall charge, with strong overall
    authority
• Effective team working
  — competent personnel
  — teams' aims integrated with those of the project
• Communications excellent
• Resources adequate
• Labour practices consistent amongst and between contractors
  — site labour agreements considered
• Project controls highly visible, simple, and 'friendly'
• Full recognition given to quality assurance and auditing
• Recognition at all times that projects are built by people, none of
  whom are perfect

These twenty-two factors we have arranged as a model in a diagram-
matic form (Fig. 15.1).

The relationships in Figure 15.1 demonstrate how our conception of
project management differs considerably from what has previously been
available. Further, I intend to use this model as a basis for describing the
second of my theses, namely, that IT projects do represent a particularly
difficult and interesting class of projects to manage because of the way
they are so intimately embedded in their organizational context.

The model begins by stressing the importance above all else of positive
Attitudes, both between companies working on a project and from senior
management. It then emphasizes the primacy of the project's Definition.
By *Definition* we mean both the technical basis of the project—it's configuration and the technical uncertainties posed by the technology—and the
general planning which is needed for the project, such as strategies, and
so on. In addition, under Definition we should also emphasize the importance of design and configuration management.

The model then says that there are several factors, represented in the
boxes on the left-hand side of the figure, which may affect the viability
of the project Definition. These clearly should be monitored and managed since it will be impossible to realize a successful project if the project

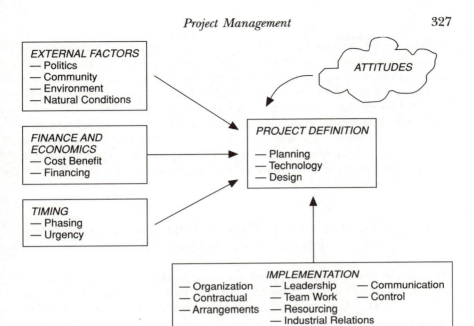

Fig. 15.1. *Factors affecting project success*

definition is no longer viable. The first of these factors is a group of *External* ones: government, community, general economic conditions, ecology, and so on. There have been a number of projects where these factors have proved so important that they have completely derailed the project, the US supersonic transport programme, for example (Horwitch 1982), and indeed virtually the entire US nuclear power programme. The second set of factors affecting the viability of project definition is that the project offer a sense of cost–benefit relationship and that the terms of the *Financing* of the project make sense. The last factor affecting the project definition is the project's *Timing*. Curiously, this aspect is often totally ignored in the project management literature which tends instead to dwell on scheduling methodologies. By Timing we mean the pace at which the project is developed: its urgency, its phasing, the placing of the strategic review points.

These three sets of factors, therefore, affect the viability of the project definition. The project itself must then be implemented using a range of concepts, tools, and techniques which have traditionally been thought of as the province of project management. These include matters of organizational structure responsibility and contract strategy, terms and conditions; issues of personal leadership and management style, resourcing, systems, and procedural conflict management and industrial relations, team-working, and matters of control and communication.

If the project as a whole is to be successful, then, all these factors must be the concern of the project's management; they must all be managed effectively. Project management is not just the Implementation issue, it is managing these together with matters of Definition, External Factors, Financing, Phasing, and ensuring, above all, positive Attitudes.

What is interesting about IT projects is that they demonstrate perhaps more clearly than almost any other project-based industry why this is so. For as I shall now show, IT projects require both careful relating to their environment as well as an extraordinary attention to detailed implementation.

Information Technology Projects: The Special Challenge of Heavy User Involvement

We can identify a range of project type industries. Such a range would include, but would not be limited to, building and civil engineering; power; petrochemical, pharmaceuticals, and oil and gas; the extractive industries; shipbuilding; information systems and telecommunications; and defence/ aerospace. These industries are primarily project orientated. A second list might include emergency and social services; entertainment; education; consulting; and so on: industries which are frequent users of projects although not necessarily organized primarily on a project basis.

The aerospace/defence and power industries put an enormous premium on technical excellence. The results of an air crash or of a leak at a nuclear power station are potentially catastrophic. Crucially, both the aerospace/defence and power industries are to an extent protected from rapid and substantial shifts in their environment. Both operate on long operational lifetimes for their products—quite typically ten to twenty years or more. When one then considers that the design and development period for major projects in these industries may well be of the order of seven years, one is looking at projects which have a lifetime of between twenty and thirty years in which the design of a particular product—a power station or an aircraft—will not have changed substantially. This is absolutely not the case in the information technology industry.

In the oil-based petrochemical industries, mining, and shipbuilding there is not the same shielding from environmental perturbation that there is in defence/aerospace and power, and yet the reality has been that since World War II these industries have, at least until about 1981–4, worked in an environment of a rising product price. Since the early 1980s the price of oil and most other primary commodities has fallen. This has caused projects in these industries to be reconfigured quite dramatically or even cancelled, and yet generally the projects themselves cannot be claimed to interact with their user environment dynamically in any degree. The design and development of a petrochemical project, for example, may well take three or four years and the operational characteristics of the plant will probably be unlikely to be altered for at least ten years, if at all.

The civil and building industries are the oldest project industries. By this, I am referring not to the pyramids or ancient henges but to the current institutional arrangements used in these industries which go back about 120 years to the time when the independent architect and consulting engineer roles were being formed. As a result, the building and civil engineering industries suffer from a number of project management anachronisms. They often do not have a single point of project authority, for example (Archibald 1976); they do not bring in all the relevant parties to a project at the appropriate time—I am referring particularly to the practice of not bringing a contractor input into the process early (Higgin and Jessop 1965; Morris 1973); design is not managed formally. In addition, and importantly for the argument I am making, the user satisfaction that building and civil engineering give us is often notoriously inadequate. The architect's inability to design a kitchen to the housewife's satisfaction is an old joke. The quality of our urban architecture and life in many buildings is frequently and roundly condemned.

Now consider information technology. IT is characterized to a degree not found in these other project-based industries by an intimate user involvement. And on top of this, information systems projects have a particular project management difficulty: their product is for large periods in people's heads. To be managed effectively, IT products must pay both extraordinary attention to their user requirements (external-strategic factors) and must pay rigorous attention to the mechanics of implementation.

All the other industries discussed so far have developed products which are used for several years under varying conditions with different degrees of satisfaction. Information Technology is fundamentally different in that its product—communication—generally involves an immediate or very short-term response. Unlike these other industries, then, IT has an intimate relationship with its users. Further, information systems are not configured as single, fixed products. Unlike, say, an aircraft, a power station, a petrochemical plant, or an office building, they can be implemented in many phases and can be modified considerably as they are so in order to respond to changing requirements. To a much greater degree than other projects, then, IT projects need to respond to External Factors.

The Management of IT Projects

Let me now amplify the characteristics of information technology projects using as a model the diagram shown in Figure 15.1.

External Factors

Although IT projects are liable to have to interact with their environment much more than in other industries, applications projects are likely to interact more than infrastructure projects. Applications projects are likely to be primarily business (environment) driven, whereas infrastructure projects will have a much heavier technological requirement constraining their flexibility. Hence, the trick on infrastructure projects is to choose technology having technical integrity while at the same time permitting applications consistent with the users' requirements. It has been suggested that doing this may be harder in those industries for which computer processing is essential since they may have been pushed into laying down their IT infrastructure before their business strategy was settled (Earl 1989).

Research has also shown that the leader of an applications project is likely to be a user/businessman whereas the leader of an infrastructure project is more likely to be a technologist (McFarlan 1981). In this regard, studies by McKinsey over the last twenty-five years have consistently shown that the IT and business cultures have always been 'out of sync'. There is now increasing evidence to suggest that the business and technological cultures are at last becoming synchronized.

No other industry, I would contend, places such demands on its project definition and project management behaviour being so intimately matched to the current and future strategic needs of its users' business strategy. It is not simply a question of relating user expectations and technology selection: it is a question of articulating these through the definition of organizational goals and business strategies. To the extent that these are incomplete or changing, then the project definition, and possibly the style of leadership, project timing, and cost–benefit relationship will all change. As they do, it is more than likely that the project implementation practices will have to change too.

Cost–Benefit Analysis

IT is often presented as an enabling technology, terms such as empowering, and self-governance being used to describe its advantages (Giuliano 1984). In the early days of IT projects there were many examples of information systems which were embarked upon with only the most loosely defined of rationales. All too often the result was much less than satisfactory.

There would seem now to be a growing trend towards concentrating on the hard benefits that IT projects will bring. A prominent retailer, for example, showed recently how, in order to demonstrate the value of an EPOS system, it was found desirable to demonstrate the benefits in terms of reducing the tendency to undercharge at the check-out tills. Benefits such as increased customer satisfaction were not included in the cost–benefit equation.

There is considerable evidence that this emphasis on 'hard' benefits is being widely adopted, yet there has to be concern that the pendulum may have swung too far and that we may be in danger of missing some of the softer, more difficult-to-quantify benefits. If these are not included in the project appraisal, important aspects such as competitive positioning, opportunity costs, marketing gains, and so on will be inadequately assessed; as a result, many marginal projects may not be initiated despite their important benefits.

Project Definition

Technical definition represents one of the most difficult and important challenges of managing IT projects. All the foregoing remarks on external forces, technical compatibility, and cost–benefit, for example, relate directly to issues of technical definition.

The practice of detailed risk assessment, whether considered as part of cost–benefit analysis or of project definition, is an important aspect of the management of projects. It is one which is probably done quite badly in several project industries. It certainly does not seem to be particularly well done in IT. Of the dozen or more major IT projects that I have examined, only one—the Government Data Network—appeared to have been put through a particularly rigorous risk assessment. (Risk was assessed separately before the project began on the different dimensions of feasibility, politics, finance, management and control, and commercial.)

One of the particularly difficult questions that IT projects face—as too do the building and civil engineering industries—is identifying who the user really is. On a large government project is it, for example, the minister, politicians in general, the permanent secretary, a regional manager, an office manager, the front-desk clerk, or the recipient? And which of these is involved in the project definition?

Also, what aspects of the total project are non-IT? There have been several well-known IT projects where the only part that went seriously wrong was the buildings section, and this because next to no thought had been given to this aspect. (The importance of defining the project in total and making sure all the bits properly interrelate and are managed correctly is a very old and important one in project management: the Space Station was essentially managed completely separately from the Shuttle programme until the Challenger disaster (Morris 1985a). Polaris system only went ahead once Edward Teller recognized that the designers of the missiles and the submarines had been erroneously using the wrong integration time frames for their respective technologies (Sapolsky 1972).

Most successful information systems are developed from existing systems. The problem with this, of course, is that developments off existing systems should only happen once the business strategy has been agreed, as we have seen; but further, there are many examples which show that it is important that, before implementing an existing system, great care be given to ensuring that the technical base of the system is sound. 'Don't automate a mess' is an important maxim on information systems projects.

Design Reviews, Configuration Management, Independent Verification, and Validation (I, V, & V) are all important IT project management practices. Most of these come directly to us from the US Department of Defence/ NASA and when carried out well are an essential part of IT design methodologies. It might, in passing, be observed that several construction-based industries—building, civil engineering, and several process ones too—are largely unaware of most of these terms and many of the practices they represent.

For projects having high technical uncertainty, prototyping makes sound sense. Sometimes, however, launching a project into full development without adequate prototype testing is seen as a necessary and justifiable strategy. Examples are frequently found in defence; pharmaceuticals is another industry where this practice is not uncommon. (The term 'concurrency' is used to describe the resultant state of simultaneous design, development, and implementation (Cochran *et al.* 1978). Certainly, IT projects have had their fair share of high technical-risk projects which have been developed without prototypes. The problem is, however, on both advanced technology telecommunications projects and on large information systems projects, that there is an irreducible minimum size of project. While the information system can be implemented in parts, in different parts of the organization for example, the system itself has to be developed in its overall form before it can be tested as a prototype.[1]

A particular problem facing IT projects is that of capacity. It is a problem which is not found to the extent or in the important form that it is in IT in other industries. The problem is that as an organization's needs change, management is quick to change its IT requirements. Capacity requirements may be suddenly increased as a result of new business, or a new marketing strategy, an acquisition, and so on, and the IT function is expected to respond accordingly. This may pose substantial technical problems, not just in the electronics of the process but in terms of staffing, training, facilities, and so on. Fortunately the modular nature of IT projects generally allows the system to change rapidly, but the basic systems design must have been prepared with this contingency in mind.

---

[1] This problem of an irreducible minimum size, incidentally, is one which plagues most of the project industries. It would, for example, have been more sensible to have developed the advanced gas-cooled reactor on a plant smaller than a 330 MW unit for direct production as the UK electricity generating boards did in the late 1960s. The problem is that power station sizes are not properly economic below 330 MW and the cost, as well as the time, involved in building a smaller prototype would have been truly questionable, as indeed would the resultant engineering and management experience.

Timing

In the same way that capacity may be something of an elastic quantity, so too overall IT implementation schedules may be treated with a certain amount of flexibility. While 'as soon as possible' is general practice, IT projects are typically implemented in phases, much more than projects are in other industries. (Indeed, in general, it would seem to be sound project management practice to implement in phases wherever possible. Smaller projects are easier to manage and in general pose less risk.) What is required, however, is for the overall implementation to make sense at a systemic level. This again drives us back to the point that IT projects need to be related to the strategy and business needs of the enterprise as a whole.

As already noted under Definition, in planning the overall implementation schedule beware of activities which initially do not seem critical or complex but which, like buildings, can suddenly become a critical path item.

The Computerization-of-PAYE (COP) project in the Inland Revenue illustrated dramatically one of the key issues in project management: when to begin implementation. On COP, no applications software was written until the programming staff were fully trained, the vendors' contracts had been proven to be fully in compliance, and all necessary middleware had been written. This refusal to begin coding until everything was ready became a point of some contention with the project manager, Steve Matheson, coming under intense pressure to begin coding before he felt the project was ready. To his credit he resisted the pressure, unlike the experience in many other projects.

The issue of whether to begin implementation before the project definition is secure is, of course, the heart of the concurrency issue. The question of whether concurrency is acceptable on projects is a very old one, going right back to the Manhattan Project itself. The debate essentially turns on whether the requirement to implement the project quickly is worth the certain disbenefits of rework, waste, frustration, possible error, and so on. Such a judgement must, of course, be contextual. Let no one imagine, however, that implementing a project before the design is stable (frozen) can escape these problems.

Project Implementation: 1. Organizational Matters

There is now considerable research evidence to show that top management support and project leadership are two of the most important factors in ensuring implementation success. Many projects these days have a senior management steering committee. In principle, this provides both organizational and contractual clout as well as ensuring the crucial tie-in to business strategy and the organization's real business needs.

Almost all the successful major projects that have been documented in recent times have benefited from strong leadership. Again, there is much research evidence on the attributes of leadership; albeit it is a skill which is not particularly easy to pass on. A role which seems to be particularly important on projects having an important external dimension, as this paper has argued IT projects generally have, is that of the project champion—someone who gains support for the project. In research that I have conducted I have found it necessary to distinguish between the internal project champion—that is, internal to the team—and the external project champion—somebody external to the project who is championing it within its wider environment.

Many major projects must pay considerable attention to issues of organization structure—questions of organization design, matrix versus project structure, and so on. Most IT projects would seem to work with a relatively small number of resources and be organized on a more purely project basis. This does not mean that interface management is not a problem; what it does suggest is that the organizational issues are rather those of interfacing between the project team and the many other organizational units interacting with the project. Further, this project–external environment integrating requirement is a more difficult one to manage than the more purely internal one commonly found in projects. Further, it again points to the need for some external champion/steering-committee structure to provide the necessary framework of managerial authority.

IT project personnel seem to work incredibly long hours. (So, in fact, do most project people!) But you can only try to get blood out of a stone for so long, and it is important therefore that IT project managers recognize the personal challenge that many of their staff may be encountering. There is plenty of evidence of course to show that people respond well to challenging environments; they should also be rewarded frequently—and not necessarily in monetary terms.

Project Implementation: 2. Control and Communication

Because of the intangible nature of so much software engineering, information systems projects have put considerable emphasis on creating organizational groupings whose task it is to monitor and control what is being developed. I, V, & V is an example. Indeed, Quality Assurance in general has received specific attention in IT for some time. The independent planning and control group is another core planning concept, frequently based on IT projects.

Many of the life-cycle controls that we think of as quintessentially project management are on software projects integrated into software methodologies. These methodologies include guidance on both the technical approach and on the project management practices and reviews to be adopted at each stage of the system development. This integration is unusual, and perhaps unique, to software. In general, such methodologies are very valuable although of course in their effort to be complete they can become overly complex, and if followed naïvely can be dangerous, like any methodology. One of the particular features of most methodologies, which again represents different practice from other project industries, is the extent to which the user is kept involved during the project.

Because of the complexity of most IT projects, and because of their need to gain user approval at frequent milestones, it is important to have from the outset an extremely detailed and careful definition of the project. Most IT projects use work-breakdown structures, task-responsibility matrices, and the like extremely rigorously. In this they are at one with the aerospace/defence; interestingly, however, these techniques are relatively unknown or under-utilized in the construction-based industries, which still have something to learn from this area I feel.

With projects defined carefully, it is possible to identify progress accurately. This helps in dealing with one of the great problems of IT project implementation—the '95 per cent complete' syndrome. It is much harder to be continually reporting 95 per cent complete, or 'it'll be complete in another two weeks', if the measurement period is itself only five to ten days long.

Special effort may be needed on IT projects to ensure formal integration. The idea of a project support office, or a systems integration function, is now frequently recognized as a means of integrating the development of the individual subsections of the project into an effective whole.

Conclusion

Having catalogued what appear to me to be the specific features of IT projects, I find that I am no longer surprised that they have caused such difficulty. And no doubt I have missed some factors, in which case my admiration for IT project managers must increase even further. For what the IT industry has done, to an extent not easily found in the other project industries, is to learn how to 'project manage' a particularly difficult class of technical challenge while at the same time facing up to the even harder question of ensuring that the project gives user satisfaction in an often fast-changing environment. That it has succeeded so often is a story worth telling!

References

Archibald, R. D. (1976), *Managing High Technology Programs and Projects*, New York: John Wiley.

Brooks, F. P. (1975), *The Mythical Man Month: Essays on Software Engineering*, Reading, Mass.: Addison-Wesley.

Cochran, E. G., Patz, A. L., and Rowe, A. (1978), 'Concurrency and Disruption in New Product Innovation', *California Management Review* (Fall).

Earl, M. J. (1989), *Management Strategies for Information Technology*, London: Prentice-Hall.

Giuliano, V. E. (1984), 'The Mechanisation of Office Work', *Scientific American* (Feb.), 149–58.

Hall, A. (1962), *Methodology for Systems Engineering*, Princeton, NJ.: Van Norstrand.

Higgin, G., and Jessop, N. (1965), *Communications in the Building Industry*, London: Tavistock Publications.

Horwitch, M. (1982), *Clipped Wings: The American SST Conflict*, Cambridge, Mass.: MIT Press.

McFarlan, F. W. (1981), 'Portfolio Approach to Management Information Systems', *Harvard Business Review* (Sept.–Oct.).

Morris, P. W. G. (1973), 'Organization Analysis of Project Management in the Building Industry', *Build International*, vol. 6, no. 6, pp. 595–616.

—— (1985a), *The Western Space Station: A Study in the Initiation of Major Projects*, Templeton College Management Research Paper MRP 88/5, (Mar.), Templeton College, Oxford.

—— (1985b), *Issues Raised in Seminars of the Major Projects Association December 1981– June 1984*, MPA Technical Paper, no. 1 (July).

—— (1986), 'Project Management: A View from Oxford', *International Journal of Construction Management and Technology*, 1 (June).

—— (1992), '*The Management of Projects: The History of Project Management 1950– 1990*', London: Thomas Telford.

—— and Hough, G. H. (1986), *Preconditions of Success and Failure in Major Projects*, Technical Paper, no. 3, Major Projects Association, Templeton College, Oxford (Sept.).

Norden, P. V. (1960), 'On the Anatomy of Development Projects', *IRE Transactions on Engineering Management* (Mar.), 34–424.

Sapolsky, H. (1972), *The Polaris System Development: Bureaucratic and Programmatic Success in Government*, Cambridge, Mass.: Harvard University Press.

US Government Printing Office (1972), *Report of the Commission on Government Procurement*, Washington DC.

van Court, Hare (1967), *Systems Analysis: A Diagnostic Approach*, New Jersey: Harcourt, Brace & World.

16

IT and Organizational Change

DAVID BODDY

Introduction

This chapter is based on the proposition that worthwhile results cannot be obtained from the current generation of IT products simply by installing expensive, state-of-the-art technology. Our studies of many applications of computing and information technology have included both successful and unsuccessful examples (Boddy and Buchanan 1986, 1987). The clear, practical lesson from this work is that the successful cases have usually been those where technological change has been accompanied by appropriate organizational change. The less successful ones have generally been those where projects have been dominated by technical considerations, with little or no thought given to organizational ones.

The information technology products now available have characteristics which make it possible to transform business performance by their imaginative use—yet which at the same time make the achievement of that potential more difficult to achieve. Managers are confronted by technological opportunities. To make successful use of those opportunities, many decisions (other than those of a technical nature) need to be taken during the course of the project. Studies of organizational change regularly show the importance of the 'promoter' or 'champion' who is willing and able to 'own' a new idea or product, to develop it into an operational form, and to get it accepted and embedded in the organization. Our research into the kind of decisions that need to be taken if IT projects are to be successfully implemented suggests that many of these issues have no obvious or powerful 'owner'—which in turn leads to the thought that they can provide valuable new roles for lively and outward-looking members of IS departments.

I begin by outlining very briefly those characteristics of information technology which open up new possibilities for business, and yet make their achievement more difficult. I then discuss in turn three major hurdles which need to be crossed if projects are to be successful. These are:

- managing the project;
- setting the right objectives;
- changing the organization.

Each of these hurdles will be outlined in turn, and reference made to the potential roles of the system staff in surmounting them. The paper concludes with some guidelines, based on our research, for the successful management of the organizational changes prompted by information technology.

Information Technology and Business Performance

Recent IT applications have characteristics which make them of much greater general significance to the management of an enterprise than earlier forms of computing:

Transaction based: this refers to the increased use of terminals to capture data at the place and time of the initial transaction. These replace dependency on the paper record, which may or may not have been keyed into a computer as a separate, later, and expensive operation. The significance of this is that it enables management to have much more computer-based information, more quickly, as a basis for many kinds of decisions.

Foreground tasks: the quality of the product or service provided to the customer is becoming ever more dependent on the use staff are able to make of their computer systems. This is in contrast to earlier, background applications, which were of little direct interest to the market-related operations of the business. Now the customer's image of the enterprise (in banking, public services, and increasingly manufacturing) is influenced by the computer systems in use.

Systemic nature: computer technologies increasingly display a systemic character, in that to get the full benefits from an installation, changes in many other parts of the organization are often necessary. Computer-aided manufacturing, for example, depends on quite major changes not only on the shop-floor, but also in maintenance, production control, process planning, tool engineering, and supervision.

Open-ended benefits: there is often an ambiguity about the potential benefits of new systems—which are frequently as novel to the company selling them as they are to the company installing them. This means that it is not unusual to hear managers drawing attention to benefits which they have achieved through computerization which were not envisaged when the initial capital expenditure was agreed. Equally, there are cases where the benefits achieved fall well short of those expected. Either way, the reasons more often lie with management decisions than with technical characteristics.

Open-ended costs: on direct and visible costs alone, information technology projects usually end up costing more than was originally expected. The inevitable upgrades and extra facilities, together with less tangible items such as training, disruption, and management time mean that an IT project can quickly become a major drain on resources. As such it is clearly of more than passing interest to senior managers.

Taken together, these characteristics add up to major opportunities. The ability of the new technologies to be used in foreground tasks and to generate rapid, detailed information, means that they can be used in ways that are strategically significant to the business. They can be used to do new tasks, offer new services, and enhance managers' decisions in ways that can materially change the perceived position of the organizations in its markets. At the same time, however, the costs can be high, and the greater the strategic benefits that are sought, the greater is the organizational upheaval that will probably be needed to bring them about. That in turn can be difficult to achieve, can generate opposition or apathy, and can undermine the potential benefits.

It has become progressively more necessary, therefore, for management not only to perceive the strategic potential of change, but also to appreciate the organizational changes that are needed to make it work. They *also* need implementation, which will usually be done by staff not fully aware of the strategic objectives. The major areas in which decisions need to be made are outlined in the following sections.

Managing the Project

Who's in Charge?

A safe assumption is that the direction a project takes will reflect the interests and preferences of the function or group to whom top management allocate project leadership. A good example of this occurred when a manufacturing company set out to reorganize its mainframe computing system, involving a move from a heavily centralized system to one in which computing services were provided at each of their several facilities.

The old system had, as is usually the case, been run by the finance function and, without a great deal of thought, the board decreed that the project to establish the new decentralized facility would also be run by the accountants. The new system worked adequately; but production and other line managers argued that they had been able to make very little contribution to its design. The effect was that in designing the system opportunities were missed to include facilities which would have been of great value to production staff at no extra cost.

A similar debate can occur over whether the project is led by a computer expert or a user. In general, successful applications have been those where the users have been in a dominant position in the project teams, with, of course, competent computer expertise available. A sure way to get a system that doesn't meet the practical requirements of a function is to give too much authority in shaping the project to the technical experts.

Finally, great care needs to be taken to ensure that project teams as a whole are not only balanced in terms of their representation from key areas, but also that they possess adequate team-working skills. We know of one project which failed dismally because it was entrusted to a project team which was not only functionally imbalanced, but which lacked the skills necessary to resolve problems, take decisions, and get action.

Who Do They Consult?

It is worth assuming (until it is proved otherwise) that the staff most closely involved with existing procedures have the best understanding of them, and thus, how a more advanced computer system could help. More-senior staff, at a distance, are not aware of, or have forgotten, the practical operating realities of daily work. If they take too dominant a role in designing and selecting new systems, there is a severe risk that they will computerize a myth rather than a real operation.

A successful example of involving staff in specifying a new information system occurred in a food company. They had previously installed a traditional management information system, producing huge quantities of print-out which no one used. A new senior management decided to abandon this system and to start again. They set up a series of temporary teams in all major areas of the factory, consisting of both operators and staff. Everyone was given the opportunity to think through their job, and to indicate what information would help them perform more effectively. This basic data was worked into a coherent specification, which system staff then used as their target. The final system, radically different from the one it replaced, was successfully implemented, and continues to be a daily help to staff at all levels. This was a difficult, and often chastening activity for the IS staff to take part in, but has been of great benefit to the company.

How to Develop Competence?

Contrary to popular belief, sophisticated equipment generally needs skilled, trained, and committed staff if it is to be used effectively. While most staff will be able to cope with the routine aspects of a new system with little or no training, potential benefits are lost if deliberate steps are not taken to develop, and to keep developing, competence.

We have often found companies which, having spent very large sums on hardware and software, regard training as a cost to be minimized or avoided altogether if possible. This is a false economy, which many have acknowledged in their discussions with us. Asked what lessons they have learned from a project, the one most frequently cited is that they would spend more time and money on training. Appropriate funds need to be built into the overall capital budget to ensure that acquiring competence is seen as being just as important as acquiring technology.

It is also important to ensure that people are given time to develop skills. If they, or their managers, are put under constant pressure for output above all else, training time will inevitably be diminished. Relying on other operators to do the training rarely works. Such people can certainly help the training and familiarization process; but they will experience unreasonable stress if they are expected to train other staff properly *and* meet their own output targets. Finally, it is important to consider what new competencies are needed by those less directly involved with the new system, as well as those who are operating it.

Setting the Right Objectives

An Operating or Strategic Emphasis

Whatever the technical characteristics of a new application may be, it is management which establishes what kind of contribution it will make to the business. In some cases the emphasis has clearly been on using the technology to improve operating performance in the production and delivery of current goods and services. The benefits sought have been those which could be measured, and where quantifiable improvements over current practice could be confidently expected. Thus, new technology is used if it promises to reduce labour costs, save energy, overcome bottlenecks in production, reduce scrap, and so on. In the same vein, computer technology has often been seen as a way of increasing the amount of control which can be exercised over operations, by allowing procedures to be specified more precisely, to reduce dependence on scarce skilled labour, or to ensure a more even and regular pace of work.

Elsewhere, the objectives have been different. Technology has been introduced to secure less-tangible benefits, such as improving the quality and timeliness of information available to managers, with the intention of enabling more confident decisions to be made. In other cases technical changes have been used to offer new or significantly enhanced products or services, and thus radically shift the position of the organization in the eyes of its customers or clients.

These two approaches can be labelled as having either an 'operating' or a 'strategic' emphasis (Benjamin *et al.* 1984; King 1986; Porter and Miller 1985). Which approach is taken is of vital signficance to the way the capabilities of IT are used in the organization, but is, by and large, independent of the technology. The key factor is senior managers' awareness of the scope for the strategic uses of emerging technology, *and* their willingness to embark on this much more difficult approach.

Adopting a strategic approach is a much greater challenge than using technology primarily to improve current operations. It presents those responsible for a project with new conceptual and organizational challenges. For example, managers need to have a global and consistent picture of the enterprise, and of how technical developments can be implemented which will radically change the kind of tasks it is able to do, and the services it is able to provide.

Exploiting this potential also requires managers who are able to conceive the operation of the organization as a whole, unconstrained by established departmental or other structures. Most managers are familiar with well-established lines of authority, and vertical information flows. Technology makes it possible to move information independently of established structures—and an ability to see and value this possibility is essential if the strategic capabilities are to be achieved.

Does the System Fit the Objectives?

Even if senior staff are aware of the strategic possibilities, there is a danger that those in charge of procurement and installation might unintentionally subvert those objectives. One company with which we worked planned, at senior level, to introduce an elaborate, highly automated manufacturing system, with a very clear set of strategic objectives in mind (quality, rapid response to design changes, ability to meet small orders quickly, and so on). These objectives were not fully appreciated down the line, where a series of decisions was taken about the details of the hardware, software, and operating layout which clearly reflected an emphasis on cutting costs rather than adding value. They ended up with an expensive system which, in practice, provided few benefits over that which it replaced, and certainly was not consistent with the strategic vision which had prevailed at the start of the project.

Does the Organization Encourage Strategic Action?

Senior management has a major role to play in creating a climate within the organization that encourages innovation in support of strategic objectives. Staff at middle levels need to be willing to make the effort and take the risks associated with technical change. Acting as the promoter or champion of a major technical change, especially if it needs to be accompanied by organizational change, puts the person concerned in a highly vulnerable position. He or she needs to master not only the technical aspect, but also be willing to argue the case through the organization, often in the face of indifference or outright opposition.

The position of the systems department in relation to the board will influence the contribution it can make. For example, at one company with very successful links between its computer strategy and the business development, the IT manager had been given responsibility not only for the mainframe, but also for office services, telecommunications, and a planned office automation system. He reported directly to a director in charge of several operating issues, who also had an interest in computing developments. This partnership ensured that the computer strategy was broadly consistent with the business strategy.

Changing the Organization

The more scope there is for computer technology to make possible big changes in the services offered, the more likely it is that there will need to be changes in the shape and style of the organization. Decisions need to be taken on these matters, as well as on those of a technical nature. What are the options, and what experience is there elsewhere?

Structures and Relationships

Technical change makes it possible to eliminate some functions, alter the importance of others, and create new ones—it becomes possible, and perhaps essential, to shake up existing boundaries of responsibility and existing relationships. For example, advanced manufacturing systems are greatly enhancing the role of support facilities like planning, tooling, and maintenance. Because of the much greater dependence of line managers on these facilities, two companies we have worked with are changing structures and reporting relationships to make these traditionally separate support systems closer to, and more answerable to, line management.

Technical change also makes it possible to link together successive stages of a process more closely, with data being transmitted automatically around the organization. There is a strategically important choice here: because a thing is technically possible does not mean it has to be implemented. For example, a hospital laboratory could have linked its automated analytical equipment directly to a newly installed computer system which stored information on patients, processed the results, and produced the reports on individual samples. Such a link would have made the later stages of the process somewhat more convenient; but it was rejected, as the analytical process would then have been completely dependent on the computer being up and running before work could start. This was judged an unacceptable risk, and a decision was taken in discussion between scientific staff and those designing the system to include a deliberate 'gap' in the system which would be filled by an operator, rather than introduce a fully automated procedure.

Management Style

Choices also arise over how the management style of an organization is changed as technology is introduced. For example, computer technology can be used either to centralize decision-making, or to decentralize it. The temptation is often to take the former option, those in positions of power generally taking the view that the more influence and control they have, the better the organization will work.

The fallacy of this presumption is well illustrated by the example of a decision taken by the board of a multinational company *not* to increase the centre's knowledge of the periphery. They were planning a new head-quarters building in which they would incorporate a significant amount of office automation. All the suppliers whom they invited to submit proposals tried to persuade the company to install systems which, as well as automating routine head office functions, would enable them to have direct computer links to all of their overseas subsidiaries. This would have enabled head office to receive much more frequent reports on matters like sales or oper-ating costs in their remote plants, thus, it was argued, improving manage-ment control.

The board decisively rejected such notions. The success of the business, they felt, had been based on giving substantial autonomy to local man-agers. They were accountable to the company in broad terms, and there was, of course, close monitoring of their quarterly and annual figures. But within those constraints they were left to run the business. Putting in direct computer links to head office would undermine that autonomy, and was therefore not implemented when the rest of the office automa-tion system was installed. This aspect of the business was well understood by the systems staff, who reflected it in their dealings with suppliers, and in the systems they eventually installed.

Work Organization

Having skilled committed people depends on ensuring that their jobs are organized in a way that complements rather than replaces human skill and experience. Many of the less successful applications of computer tech-nology have been those where work has been organized in a way that has led to boredom, inattention, and loss of interest among the staff con-cerned. Such attitudes cannot produce high performance.

Conversely, where decisions on work organization have ensured that the skills and experience of staff have been complemented by the technology, the effects have been highly beneficial. In such cases, staff have shown them-selves able and willing to accept responsibility, to work to overcome tem-porary difficulties in the system, to suggest valuable additional uses, and so on. By organizing work in a way that satisfies well-established motivational requirements of individual jobs, and grouping them together into natural work teams, companies have been able to achieve far more benefits from technical innovation than where such factors have been ignored.

Conclusion

In the preceding sections I have outlined the key areas where the right decisions need to be made if the potential of IT is to be realized. Many of these decisions do not obviously 'belong' to any particular part of the organization—and there is thus a danger that they might not be properly considered in the course of implementation.

IS staff with a suitable set of skills and inclinations could readily extend their roles here—and in doing so could make use of the following guidelines.

Nine Guidelines for Exploiting the Innovative Potential of New Computing Technologies and Information Systems

Purpose 1. Ensure that the use of new technology has a clear strategic focus which targets long-term market objectives and not just current internal operating problems.

2. Review and implement positive policies in areas like employment practice and investment appraisal, so that they encourage innovation and the strategic use of new technology.

3. When evaluating hardware and software options, make sure that you choose kit to fit the current and anticipated needs of the business.

People 4. Review work organization in relation to new technology, to encourage flexibility, creativity, and skills development.

5. Review management styles and working arrangements, to ensure that these are consistent with the strategic goals of the business, and with achieving the potential benefits of new technology.

6. Design support systems which are consistent with strategic aims, and which enable support staff to contribute in flexible and creative ways to the changing needs of the organization.

Process 7. Establish a clear project management responsibility to guide the often-protracted implementation process.

8. Plan the nature and timing of user involvement, to ensure that key staff establish 'ownership' of new equipment and procedures.

9. Develop a systematic training plan to equip users at all levels with the competence, in the form of new skills and knowledge, they need to exploit the innovative potential of technology.

References

Boddy, D., and Buchanan, D. A. (1986), *Managing New Technology*, Oxford: Basil Blackwell.

—— (1987), *The Technical Change Audit*, London: Manpower Services Commission.

Benjamin, R. I., Rockart, J. F., Scott-Morton, M. S., and Wyman, J. H. (1984), 'Information Technology: A Strategic Opportunity', *Sloan Management Review* (Spring), 3–10.

King, W. R. (1986), 'Developing Strategic Business Advantage from Informational Technology', in N. Piercy (ed.), *Management Information Systems: The Technology Challenge*, London: Croom Helm.

Porter, M. E., and Miller, V. E. (1985), 'How Information Gives You Competitive Advantage', *Harvard Business Review*, 63 (July–Aug.), 149–60.

17

The Project Champion

CYNTHIA MATHIS BEATH

Introduction[1]

The literature on strategic uses of information technology (IT) suggests that a very important, if not *the most* important, antecedent to a successful implementation of a strategic information system is a 'champion' for the new system (Runge 1985; Lockett 1987; Vitale and Ives 1988). We consider IT champions to be managers at fairly high levels of the organization who take on the responsibility for shepherding an IT innovation project through the development process. Champions are more than leaders and they are different from sponsors. Sponsors have the funds and authority to accomplish their goals (Vitale and Ives 1988). Champions, on the other hand, bring about change in their organizations in spite of having less than the requisite authority or resources. They push, they overcome resistance to change, they remove impediments to progress. In the end, they are usually seen as having been necessary to the success of the project, but the methods by which they achieve success sometimes run roughshod over organizational norms.

There seem to be two ways in which IT champions are important to successful implementations of strategic systems. First, strategic information technology ideas frequently require significant organizational upheavals. Successful implementation may require adjustments to reward schemes, changes in authority or responsibility patterns, and shifting of power centres (Markus 1984). An enthusiastic, visionary champion works around and through the organization, resolving turf disputes, overriding established norms, ignoring anguished cries of 'It won't work!' from those who stand to lose with the new system. Looking on, the IS manager may wonder who is right.

Secondly, IT champions may use the same techniques for cutting through bureaucracy on the processes of public review and rational investment which underlie most systems-development life-cycles. With competitive

[1] This chapter, given as a paper at the Oxford PA Conference in September 1990, is an early version of a paper published in MIS Quarterly (Beath 1991). The author wishes to thank Blake Ives, Brian Dobing, Macedonio Alanis, Rosann Collins, and Marianne D'Onofrio for their kind assistance on this paper.

advantage at stake, speedy implementation can be critically important. Successful champions break down bureaucratic barriers and drive change through the organization while the firm's competitors deliberate over the feasibility of an idea. To the IS manager, however, who has struggled to implement effective procedures for identifying, prioritizing, and approving projects, headstrong, hard-driving champions may be a nightmare come to life.

A strong IT champion can thus present the IS manager with a difficult challenge. How can the IT champion's organizational savvy, commitment, and energy be dovetailed with the normal IS planning process? What assistance should be offered to a champion, and what hindrances can be avoided?

An Information Technology Champion Support Agenda

The literature on organizational innovations and product champions offers a clear picture of what the champions are like, how they operate, and what kinds of organizational structures and environments foster championship. Innovation is an information-intensive process. Champions can be thought of as accumulators and bearers of the information needed to bring about a possible innovation in which the problem or the solution is not well understood. Champions are also distinguished by having the organizational clout and savvy needed to overcome resistance to organizational change (Schon 1963; Maidique 1980; Rogers 1983; Kanter 1983). They need information to evaluate, choose, and sell an innovation; resources to obtain the necessary information and to test and make transitions; and management support to guarantee both material resources and rewards for successful innovations.

Many of the organizational structures which are considered to be supportive of innovation are familiar to IS managers. IS, after all, is an agent of change in the organization. Principal among the innovation-fostering organizational structures are policies that facilitate change and reduce the risk of negative consequences, such as change-approval processes or experimentation policies. The systems-development life-cycle is such a policy. Other characteristics which foster innovations are: interconnectedness among units, because interconnectedness provides access to needed resources and support; openness to knowledge about functioning of the organization; slack resources for scanning, learning, and experimentation; network-forming devices such as job mobility, employment security and team-work, because of the increased channels of communication that result; and professionalism, because professionals place a premium on learning and their professional contacts give them additional communication channels (Zaltman *et al.* 1973; Kimberly and Evanisko 1981; Kanter 1983).

Table 17.1. *Seven ways to support IT champions*

Information for evaluation and persuasion
1. Help the IT champions to nail down what the information technology will do for the company, what the costs and risks of the operation and installation will be, how the technology might be experimented with, and how the transition to using information can be accomplished.
2. Help the IT champions to comprehend relevant parts of the application portfolio and help them to mine enterprise data.
3. Help the IT champions to fathom the organization's approach to change with respect to information technology.

Material resources
4. Make uncharged staff time available to the IT champions.
5. Loan or acquire computing technology for the IT champions.

Managerial support
6. Legitimate the IT champions' claims about the technology.
7. Help the IT champions to identify and make contact with potential coalition members.

It is possible to infer from this literature guidelines on how one manager, such as an IS manager, can help another manager champion an organizational innovation. In an earlier paper, we did just that. Table 17.1 summarizes seven ways we suggested IS managers can support IT champions (Beath and Ives 1988). The interesting thing about the list in Table 17.1 is that it does not include, and in some cases contradicts, many of the traditional concepts of how IS can best support its users. In the information category, for example, we might have expected to see 'Assist the IT champion in identifying strategic uses of technology' (Wiseman 1988); or 'Teach the IT champion a fourth generation language'. It is possible that brainstorming about innovative uses of technology and training in the use of personal computers are very useful for many users, but maybe not for IT champions. Champions, in most cases, have their own ideas.

In the Material Resource category, traditional suggestions might include 'Follow an orderly and rigorous approval process' and 'Select and enforce appropriate standards'. We propose, however, that IT champions value flexibility more than they value order and standards. With respect to Managerial Support, many IS managers seem to think their role is to 'Play devil's advocate—point out the weaknesses in the IT Champion's proposals'. They take the position that the only good proposal is a feasible, cost-justified proposal with a do-able schedule, which will run on existing hardware. Keeping an idea in the proposal stage until it reaches that condition makes the IS manager's job manageable.

Overall, we believe that IT champions seek a different support agenda than the one most IS managers are accustomed to delivering. To explore the support provided by IS for IT champions and their reactions to that support, a multi-phased research project was conducted in US companies.

The next section describes the research project. Following that, some early and potentially significant findings are summarized.

The Research Project

In the first phase of our research we conducted semi-structured interviews with seventeen IT champions and eleven of their IS counterparts (or other knowledgeable observers) at eleven firms. The interviews focused on critical 'championing' incidents related to strategic information systems. The thrust of the interview was to determine the nature of the support provided to the IT champion by his or her IS organization. After confirming that the system under discussion was of major importance to the organization, we asked the champion to describe an incident or period during which his or her 'championing' was critical to the system. Typically these were periods during which funding was approved, or organizational commitment to implementation was confirmed, or other go/no decisions were made. In no case was the champion only soliciting approval from his or her boss or his or her employees. To be a clear championing incident, we felt that the constituency being solicited should extend beyond the hierarchy in which the champion is embedded. Finally, the champion was asked open-ended questions about the support received from IS, followed by probes on the three types of support identified above—information, material resources, and managerial support. The champions also completed a follow-up survey.

In addition to interviewing champions, we also interviewed several IS managers who supported (or did not support) the IT champion, and other knowledgeable observers such as the senior project participants. In those interviews we confirmed that the system was important to the organization and that the incident described by the champion was properly understood. We also asked the IS managers to describe the support given to the IT champion. Each interview lasted about one-and-a-half hours.

We sought a sample which included both champions who had worked closely with IS and champions who had worked around or outside the IS group, perhaps with an outside consultant or vendor, or with his or her own development staff. We made contact with our champions either through IS managers that we knew well or through public affairs officers. In this way we hoped to reach some champions with unsatisfactory relationships with IS.

This paper is based on data from twenty-seven interviews. Of the seventeen champions we talked to, two were eliminated from our sample on the basis of our strategic system or championing criteria. Of the remaining fifteen champions, eight worked with IS and seven worked around or without IS. We also interviewed six IS managers about our champions—five of these supported champions who worked with IS, one described a champion who did not work with IS, and five other individuals were knowledgeable about champions or championing.

All but two of the champions work in Fortune 1,000 or equivalent size publicly traded corporations. The other two work in a medium-sized manufacturing company and a metropolitan utility. All the organizations have centralized IS organizations. The companies span the USA and are located in major metropolitan areas. The projects themselves ranged in size from tens of millions to tens of thousands of dollars, but all were, according to our informants, very important to their organizations.

Findings

What is Championing?

We started with the following definition of championing: champions establish organizational innovation in spite of having less than the requisite authority or resources. Our champions seemed to agree with this definition. They said things like: 'It's getting people to have a common view without feeling like their turf is being threatened', or 'I had to convince three [peer level managers] to take a chance'.

They called themselves cheerleaders, head coaches, czars, zealots, change agents, renegades. Championing is hard work. Said one: 'The frustrations of trying to champion something are incredible.' Describing the lengths to which he was driven, a normally mild-mannered executive said: 'I started agitating. I had to start insulting and badgering. You have to start making all sorts of noise, generally making a pest of yourself.'

Since innovation is an information-intensive activity, it follows that much of what champions do is teach, explain, and share with others the information they have gathered. As one champion reported: 'It wasn't so much that there was resistance to my idea, but rather that the need was unrecognized—it was a matter of education. Marketing had a problem and engineering had a problem but no one saw that these two problems were related and no one saw that it was possible to solve the two problems in one system.'

The role of champion as expediter came up in many of our interviews. 'If we'd tried to do this in the normal way, in committee meetings, with reports and decisions, it would have taken 3 years instead of 6 months. I made some wrong choices, but I had a vision and followed it and I made the choices.' Another said: 'We were into something that the company didn't know anything about. There was a lot to learn and not very much time. A champion was needed to expedite that.'

The role of champion as organization redesigner came up. As one IS manager reported: '[The champion] had taken two or three runs at this project; it was a toughie, but all the problems were on the user side—they had to change the way they do business, cross organizational lines, get people to work together, deal with turf battles. Once they got the political problems solved, it was a piece of cake, technically.' Another IS manager reported: '[X] was really a champion on this system—he got 200 systems installed in the field, in spite of the field. They fought him. He got them to use it without adjusting their compensation.' He might have added that the field likes the system now, too.

Champions Already Have a Vision: They Need Help Fleshing it Out

Champions may need a lot of information about the innovation they are championing, but not every champion needs an initial idea. As one IS manager put it: 'They're visionary. They work in concepts, because that's all you've got at that point.' Champions focus on information technology in terms of its benefits. IS, they say, may understand what the system will do, but not what its benefits can be. IS frequently is not alone in failing to understand the business benefits of the champion's vision, though. Just because the champion has a vision about using information technology does not mean he or she can articulate that vision to the right audience.

So, IT champions need plenty of help in fleshing out their visions. Sometimes they want help in the details of how the target technology operates. Said one champion: 'Our IS person told us what would work and what wouldn't.' The IS person said: 'I answered basic questions on what can or cannot be done.' Even more valuable, at times, is persuasive information. As one champion said: '[The CIO] was a translator between a business man's jargon or mind set and the technicians. He helped me frame questions, helped me understand the answers, and helped me translate the answers back into language that the senior managers were going to accept. This was the most important thing he did for me.'

When a new system uses existing data, IS involvement in the planning process is very important. IS can help the champion comprehend the application portfolio and mine enterprise data. As one champion noted: 'The system used a massive amount of data already in the portfolio and manipulated it in a complex way. The key to making it happen was on the IS side.'

Champions Need Help With the Life-cycle Process

Where IT champions worked with IS, rather than around IS, the champions frequently noted that IS had helped them fathom the organization's approach to information technology change, in particular in understanding the ins and outs of the project approval process. This is a different kind of information that IT champions need, but a very important one. Said one: 'The IS team member on our task force helped us understand their process, who determined priorities, how things got labelled "important". They showed us the need for a "Blueprint".' In this case the organization put great emphasis on projects that were part of an overall scheme or strategy known as a blueprint. After the task force produced a document boldly titled 'BLUEPRINT', project approval was obtained.

Champions are generally good at asking the right questions. As one champion described: 'Our liaison person described how the planning system—the way resources were allocated—actually worked. I asked him, what are the other users doing? How are they getting so much of the budget? He worked up a process for us, which we followed. We got a ninefold increase in the money allocated to new systems.' Several champions also mentioned that IS's help was valuable in estimating costs.

Champions Want the Best People

Staff resources, according to Kanter (1983), are the change agent's most important resource. On IT projects the special expertise that IS personnel have make them a critical resource. As one champion put it: 'Where [the CIO] offered me unprecedented support was in doing things that they said couldn't be done. Sometimes I would go to him and say we need more people on this and the technicians would say there are only 20 people who have the ability to work on this and I'd say we need 25 and then somehow [the CIO] would find 5 more qualified people.' In other cases it is the quality of staff that makes a difference. Several of our champions indicated that they were sensitive to the quality of staff assigned to their projects. 'We got better than average people for a project of this size', said one. Another said: 'We kept getting weak people assigned. All the power hitters went to another project.'

When they could get it, champions were grateful for uncharged staff time—'IS developed the budget that was presented to the steering committee, but didn't charge for this time.' One CIO told us that he sometimes charged staff time for developing proposals to education. Other times, he split the costs with champions. He also encourages his contractors, vendors, and consultants to spend free time with IT champions. As he points out: 'They can't find it in their own budgets, they have less flexibility, and we know how to work the approval process.'

Champions Want a Flexible Process, Not an Orderly One

IS managers usually manage their scarce and valuable human resources with project planning and approval processes and by insisting on technology standards. As one CIO told us: 'My philosophy is to keep the staff level stable and just do what can be done with that amount of resource; it cuts down on the less valuable projects, or creates pressure to redesign them so they are more valuable.' But IT champions, who want to change the organization in a hurry, put a premium on flexibility, with respect to both process and products. When IS demonstrates flexibility the IT champions really notice it. 'Having the mental flexibility to change the way to do business is very important', one said. 'We disagreed on some points at the beginning, but they were willing to test things and change.' In contrast another said: 'The IS people didn't want this added to their slate. Their slate was already full for the next 2 years. They were reluctant to offer assistance in selling an idea like this because they didn't have the resources to support it.' An interesting consequence of this battle is the tendency of champions to go it alone, by hiring consultants, by pushing for decentralization of IS resources, or by general bootlegging.

Some IT champions felt that IS was inflexible out of laziness or general truculence. As one put it: 'IS wasn't creative about designing the outputs. They were only creative about solving the job of building the system in the most efficient way. They complained when the specs changed, but the specs had to change if we were going to evolve an improved product. When you're doing something new, you need flexibility. When you want an idea IS tends to pull out what they know and what they're comfortable with.' One CIO noted: 'IS is more of a hindrance to champions than a help. IS is tradition-bound and turf-oriented with an attitude that no-one knows how to do things besides us. IS tends to find reasons why things won't work and put roadblocks in front of champions.' Some CIO's however, realize the value of being open to change. As one put it: 'The main thing IS did for the champion is—we listened.'

Other kinds of problems are generated by standard processes. One IT champion pointed out that, due to their ponderous development life-cycle, the IS people were reluctant to reconsider decisions. Several IT champions ran up against technology standards, such as bans on laser printing, restrictions on fourth-generation languages, or reluctance in dealing with additional vendors. 'The IS person kept arguing against our choice of package. I think he stooped to fogging sometimes, when in fact he did not understand the new technology we wanted, and the IS department still doesn't understand it.' Said one: 'IS didn't want Texas Instruments equipment, they didn't want to deal with another vendor. Then they weren't anxious to get involved with an outside software supplier. I think it was a matter of personal pride and professional jealousy. So then IS bid to develop the same system. They were more adversarial than useful, throwing up roadblocks.' The IT champion told us that IS's roadblocks had cost the organization several million dollars. The CIO agreed that IS had been balky, saying: 'There was a significant resistance in the early stages to the champion's proposal to use an outside software supplier.

Perhaps there was some element of discomfort with the idea that someone else can do it cheaper and faster.'

Two old hands at IT championing bemoaned the formality and rigor they find in their IS organizations today. 'I wouldn't be able to do today what I did then. MIS was pretty easy to manoeuvre and didn't offer resistance; I went directly to the programmers. Today I couldn't get to first base', said one. The other said: 'I don't think I could get this project approved today. The system is much more formal now. There's not as much listening.'

Champions Deeply Value Legitimation by IS Managers

We were struck by the frequency with which IT champions mentioned that they received, or didn't receive, managerial support from IS. In particular, IT champions are very sensitive about how their claims about technology are treated in public by IS experts. When legitimation was forthcoming, it was highly valued by the champions. They told us things like 'IS's support gave a validity that made it possible to get business support', and: 'The CIO said "He's right!" It validated the project from a technical standpoint', and '[The CIO] supported my analysis of what was wrong. He wasn't defensive. This was very important in convincing senior management that there was a light at the end of the tunnel. He had the prestige with senior management that was needed.'

Some CIOs understand the need for legitimation. One IT champion told us: 'In front of the steering committee the CIO's attitude was extremely supportive.' The CIO told us the rest of the story:

They had tried something similar a few years before and I expected this to be another disaster, but I thought that the downside risk was manageable, and the champion was my loyal friend. I made a pact to support him 100 per cent. I expressed my support formally to his boss and the executive VP's up the chain. I attended a presentation that the champion made from which IS support was inferred.

The project was approved, and was ultimately successful, to the CIO's happy surprise.

IS managers can also help IT champions by liaising with other managers in the organization. One champion appreciated that his IS liaison manager, who had credibility with a department whose co-operation was needed, had helped the champion deal with that department. Sometimes the other managers just need to be sold on the champion's idea, especially when resources that they might otherwise have a claim on will be used to implement the champion's vision. As one CIO told us, 'behind the scenes another IS manager was very effective in talking to other players, to people who had some voice in the funding decision. The IS manager went around and said, "here's what we're doing," communicating the vision,

keeping folks informed, building the case.' By contrast, in another case
where a coalition of users was needed to provide data for a champion, we
heard: 'The responsibility for this project got delegated four levels down
in the IS hierarchy. It wasn't a hot subject for IS. As a result, the four
people working on it could do very little to help us gain and maintain
commitment from our coalition of users.'

Champions Appreciate a Positive Atmosphere

Managerial support for IT champions sometimes comes in the form of a
co-operative atmosphere. Many champions praised their IS teams for being
co-operative: 'They were an ally.' 'We worked together. There was a sense
of esprit de corps, we're all in this together. An outsider wouldn't have
been able to tell the systems people from the business people.' 'IS was
enthusiastic, bringing excitement to the project.' 'The [CIO] agreed with
me, he agreed with what I said, he wasn't defensive.' Not unexpectedly,
lack of co-operation was an issue with IT champions: 'We were frustrated
by the lack of systems support.' 'IS wouldn't listen to what I needed; they
just couldn't hear it.' 'We saw the need, we worked up a proposal. IS grudg-
ingly assigned an analyst to listen to us.'

Most CIOs recognize the value of support and know how to be supportive. As one CIO put it, 'IS should put their weight behind a champion,
show that IS is a champion too. IS gains clout by doing this. Pitch the
champion's ideas up, down and around. IS should play a support role,
develop a partnership.' On the other hand, he pointed out: 'You do not
want to overdo it. You don't take an idea away from the champion. It can
be easy to overpower the champion, and you don't want to do that.' The
CIO needs the IT champion, he reminds us, to manage the organizational
politics that come with IT innovations.

Discussion

It is apparent from our interviews that IT champions strongly value assistance in fathoming the systems-development life-cycle, in fostering a flexible
implementation process, and in the legitimizing of their ideas about using
information technology. It is apparent that many CIOs currently deliver
on this innovation agenda, in spite of the fact that this requires them to
juggle resources and bend policies. Champions need and obtain special
treatment, in many cases, as we have seen here.

The CIOs successfully supporting IT champions spoke of the difficulty
of managing this process. Several paradoxes are evident in what they and
the IT champions told us. For example, in spite of the IT champion's
need for, and interest in, developing cost estimates for a project, the CIO

suggested that costs be downplayed early on. 'Focus on the value of the concept', one said. 'Forget cost at the beginning. Try to avoid "how much", "how long" questions. If the costs are reasonable, you want to do it. Say "yes" to ideas, and say "I'll get back to you if it turns out we can't".' It is particularly important to distinguish between the public and the private fleshing out of the project, he notes. It is possible to talk about cost and schedule privately with the IT champions, while focusing all public presentations on the impact of the idea, preferably the *strategic* impact.

The same CIO summarizes the managerial support concept eloquently:

Sell the idea. Say 'there's an idea worth pursuing' to everybody, every chance you get. Give it relevance, give it momentum. The first thing is to get people interested. The SECOND thing is to ask whether or not it's feasible. Some IS managers get those two reversed. Discount the negatives, or suggest that their resolution be postponed until later. Negatives are meaningless until you know what the idea is. IS should be there when the idea is presented—you don't have to say anything, just look positive.

The trick, of course, is to find the right champion. Not every person with an idea about using information technology is a potential champion who should receive this kind of treatment from IS. Champions are spokespersons with a reputation for innovating. Most of the ones we talked with had some hands-on experience with information technology, usually on PCs, but sometimes as programmers, project managers, or user liaisons. They were easily identified by their peers, however, and we suspect that their reputations for innovation are more important than any particular knowledge about information technology.

In summary, this chapter, drawing on innovation research, hypothesizes that IT champions want information, resources, and endorsement from their information systems departments, not new ideas, bureaucratic process, and arm's-length dealings. Our preliminary research findings suggest that IT champions strongly value assistance in fathoming the systems-development life-cycle, in fostering a flexible implementation process, and in legitimizing their ideas about using information technology. It seems that CIOs need IT champions and IT champions need CIOs.

References

Beath, C. M. (1991), 'Supporting the Information Technology Champions', *MIS Quarterly*, vol. 15, no. 3, pp. 355–72.

—— and Ives, B. (1988), 'The Information Technology Champion: Aiding and Abetting, Care and Feeding', in R. Sprague (ed.), *Proceedings of the 21st Annual Hawaii Conference on Systems Sciences*, 4, Kailua-Kona, Hawaii (5–8 Jan.), 115–23.

Brown, L. A. (1981), *Innovation Diffusion: A New Perspective*, New York: Methuen.

Kanter, Rosabeth Moss (1983), *The Change Masters*, New York: Simon & Schuster.

Kimberly, J. R., and Evanisko, M. J. (1981), 'Organizational Innovation: The Influence of Individual, Organizational and Contextual Factors on Hospital Innovation of Technological and Administrative Innovations', *Academy of Management Journal*, vol. 24, no. 24, pp. 689–713.

Lockett, M. (1987), *The Factors Behind Successful IT Innovation*, Working Paper RDP 87/9, Oxford Institute for Information Management, Templeton College, Oxford.

Maidique, M. A. (1980), 'Entrepreneurs, Champions and Technological Innovation', *Sloan Management Review* (Winter), 59–76.

Markus, M. Lynne (1984), *Systems in Organizations: Bugs and Features*, New York: Pitman.

Rogers, E. M. (1983), *The Diffusion of Innovation*, 3rd edn., New York: Free Press.

Runge, D. A. (1985), 'Using Telecommunications for Competitive Advantage', unpublished doctoral dissertation, Oxford University.

Schon, D. A. (1963), 'Champions for Radical New Inventions', *Harvard Business Review* (Mar.–Apr.), 77–86.

Vitale, M., and Ives, B. (1988), *Finding and Fostering Innovative Applications of Information Technology: The US Perspective. Part II: The Lessons*, Working Paper, Internation Center for Information Technologies, Washington, DC.

Wiseman, C. (1988), *Strategic Information Systems*, New York: Irwin.

Zaltman, G., Duncan, R., and Holbeck, J. (1973), *Innovations and Organizations*, New York: John Wiley.

18

The Project Sponsor

BRIAN EDWARDS

Introduction

Popular and academic commentary for many years has lamented the apparent fact that computer projects seem doomed to end up late, over-budget, and ineffective. Many have not even reached implementation, and their cancellation or suspension has been taken as further occasion for breast-beating by those involved in the complex business of bringing in new computer systems, and criticism from those demanding them. Of course there is an inevitable bias in the published stories, because good news is almost no news in any area of human activity. However, there is no doubt that many IT projects have indeed been unsatisfactory in their conduct, product, or result.

Therefore, in response to the at-least uncertain prospects for IT projects, much effort has gone into improving the general discipline and technology of delivering systems. This has not always produced a satisfactory outcome as seen by those who commissioned the work, however. One reason for the frequent disappointment can be found in the general misunderstanding of just what an IT project is. Properly, it is the *total* set of process, system, and relationship changes which are required to give effect to a new vision of how a piece of business should work.

Another mistake of some efforts to improve IT project management has been excessive concentration on the systems product which is the enabler for business change, at the expense of the total technical and business environment within which it has to be effective. A further mistake has been to rely too uncritically on the experience of managing projects in other spheres such as defence or construction.

For the purposes of this chapter let us take it that an IT project is defined as the total set of activities which have to take place to implement and take benefits from a new or changed set of business systems. It is by no means certain that the IT component is either the largest or the most difficult of the key activities concerned.

In the early 1980s a group of senior professionals in IBM United Kingdom gathered at their own initiative to share their experience of project problems. As the late Mike Pote, the then project management guru in IBM, said at the time: 'Everyone's concept of a project is shaped by the last one they were involved with.'

Fortunately the IBM group included people whose recent wounds had a wide diversity of characteristics, and it became clear that common themes lay less in the technical domain than in the commissioning and high-level management areas. As the base for this work on project management was commercial rather than academic, little citeable published material arose from it. An example of the management emphasis can, however, be seen in the IBM Project Assessment Checklist from that time (IBM 1986) which is still current. The insights developed influenced both the hands-on project management work performed by IBM people, and the Information Management work practised by the group of which I was then a member, IBM's Systems Management Consultancy Group. This experience, combined with the opportunity to participate over some years in a single major project which is described later, led me to a belief in the pre-eminent significance of the governance of projects as seen from the very top of the business. This can be personified in the role of a project sponsor or it can be described more processually as project sponsorship.

Accordingly, this chapter aims to examine the role of the project sponsor and the practice of project sponsorship. Sponsorship, as we shall see, is a wider concept than that of sponsor. But it is difficult, if the purpose of this chapter is to help practice, to separate the two. The Editor has suggested to me that especially in cross-functional projects, collective sponsorship helps, that is, the ownership of the business change by more than one person. However, he agrees with me that an acid test of whether meaningful sponsorship exists for a project is to ask who is *the* project sponsor, and certainly he has argued (Earl 1994) for having a top management sponsor in a Business Process Redesign Project, because fundamental issues may have to be resolved. Indeed, the Editor has described a project sponsor as a 'fixer of last resort' and I would support (and have quoted) this view. At the same time we must acknowledge that a sponsor is required to enable sponsorship, but that the practice of sponsorship may involve a number of tasks, and other people as well as the sponsor.

A working definition of the project sponsor might be: 'The member of senior management who is accountable for the effective implementation of all the changes involved in a major IT project, and for demonstrable delivery of their benefits, and who has the authority required to deliver them.'

It will be shown later that a number of projects have suffered or failed for lack of such sponsorship. Thus, an active search of literature and experience has been made to seek connections between sponsorship and success or failure.

It seems, however, there is only a little help available from the literature. No material has focused primarily on the role and contribution of a sponsor. Lockett, reporting in Chapter 7 of this volume on several projects in one organization, says that success requires either a champion who is adequately empowered, or otherwise a champion who is supported by an empowering sponsor, and suggests that both roles are necessary. Runge and Earl (1988) and Beath (1991) have discussed the role of a project champion in providing the drive needed to create the impetus for change, but in each case they concentrate largely on a person who has to compensate for the lack of all the needed authority. Those papers also concentrate on particular kinds of project, namely 'Telecommunication Based Information Systems' (TBIS) from Runge and Earl and 'strategic' projects from Beath.

Morris and Hough (1986) comment on the need for sponsorship and championship in major projects in general, and in one IT project studied in detail (Inland Revenue Computerisation of PAYE, COP), the role of the chairman of Inland Revenue and his steering committee was emphasized. In a later analysis, Morris (1995) lists twenty-one 'preconditions of success in major projects', in four of which sponsorship characteristics are implicitly or explicitly featured (see Chapter 16 in this volume).

A common feature of what has appeared seems to be that sponsorship is one of a number of aspects of project governance which has to be effectively established. It ranks alongside other disciplines and provisions for planning and controlling events. What follows is devoted to the idea that project sponsorship has a unique and pre-eminent role in the case of business change projects, of which the commonest these days have a significant or dominant IT component.

Proposition and Assumptions

Senior management involvement and commitment is frequently asserted as necessary for effective, well-directed, and rightly targeted IT strategies and IT projects. Less is said about how that is to be attracted, exploited, and efficiently employed.

The proposition is that *right use of the project sponsor is the way the achieve such senior management contribution to projects.* It is not contended that no project can succeed in the absence of sponsorship as it will be defined and developed, but it is suggested that the chances of success are so reduced that it is foolhardy to proceed without it.

A fundamental assumption is that life and management in a project environment *must* be different from that which is customary in the organisation's normal management style and behaviour. This is because the volume and rate of change which the organization has to contend with in a systems project will be far outside those which the 'normal' management approaches have developed to cope with. If an unaccustomed volume and

rate of change have to be accommodated, different norms of communication, decision-making, team behaviour, and mood are required. In particular, the mixture of objective and subjective aspects is important. It is
proposed that these are most difficult to deliver without the contribution
of the project sponsor.

A second characteristic of projects is that they are temporary organizations (Alloway 1976). Therefore, in some sense they have to be accommodated within the permanent and ongoing organization, which raises
tensions and conflicts in plenty. The role of champion can become important here to maintain project momentum. However, so does the role of
sponsor, often in resolving some of the tensions and conflicts. In the
minority of organizations in which a definition of the role has been attempted we can expect different versions. The set shown below is the
minimum:

The Role of the Project Sponsor (Edwards 1989)

1. Sponsor possesses **AUTHORITY** for anything done or changed within the project except in some cases the authority either to start or stop it. The authority
   normally exists by virtue of the sponsor's position in the business, but it might
   be specially and expressly delegated, for example, by the board.
2. Sponsor endorses the **BUSINESS CASE** for the project initially and repeatedly.
   Sponsor may be accountable to the ultimate owners of the organization for
   the satisfactory delivery of the business benefits. There is a section on Benefits
   Management later in this paper.
3. Sponsor is the highest level of formal **REVIEWER** of the project.
4. Sponsor is the source of **MOTIVATION AND INSPIRATION** for those involved
   as project workers and those invoked as receivers of the project's deliverables.

A corresponding minimal set of the activities through which the role is
fulfilled is:

Activities for the Project Sponsor (Edwards 1989)

1. Chair the Project Board (or whatever the top level review is called).
2. Be an available hotline for the project manager.
3. Perform walkabouts among workers and affected people.
4. Front the publicity for the system or service, through kick-off and branch
   meetings, publications and videos, and 'cutting the ribbon'.
5. Report the project at times of his/her judgement to the owners.

Some sponsors will want or need to become involved in further, more
specific activities. An example of a more active view of the sponsor is the
list of duties given by Parker (1990):

The Sponsor's duties are to:

- represent all potential users of his system;
- ensure that user requirements are clearly defined;
- develop and obtain approval of the business case;
- appoint the Project Administrator;
- establish which parts of the organization will bear the cost of the project and how the cost will be apportioned across users;
- approve and ensure availability of user support resource;
- identify Security, Auditability Requirements and Business Controls, e.g. access control, record counts, etc.;
- initiate a post-installation review after cutover to production status.

Normally the sponsor is a senior manager (in many instances the director) of a business area, for example, personnel, finance, or distribution. This essential role will be carried out in addition to his line capabilities.

Edwards's lists of roles and activities were distilled from experience or observation of satisfactory project implementations. By satisfactory, we mean that the project deliverables were available adequately close to plan and budget, the populations were adequately prepared, and benefits were achieved.

That evidence cannot be taken as other than experiential—just like evidence presented later about various patterns of failure. Accordingly, it seemed desirable to extend beyond experience into some more structured analysis of successes and failures from the history of IT projects, attempting to relate this analysis to how, if at all, sponsorship was exercised.

The Investigation

To examine the effectiveness of any aspect of project management or conduct it is necessary, of course, to have a view of what constitutes success or failure. In what follows it is required for 'success' that an IT project:

- implemented a system product which works;
- was achieved within known and acceptable cost levels and;
- delivered benefit.

None of this is to say that every component of a system has to be implemented precisely as originally conceived (nor that *only* such components are implemented). Nor does it say that original predictions of time and resource requirements have to be fulfilled precisely, provided that variances were noticed, accounted for, and accommodated. However, the fact that an installed system works, is used, and is liked by users is insufficient without evidence that substantive benefits have been achieved. (Smith 1990)

Sponsorship and sponsors, then were investigated by assembling evidence of management factors in significant IT projects. It should be stressed
that these were not all 'strategic' projects in the Beath sense. The common factor was their significant size in terms of one or more of: the
populations affected; the investment; the size of the system; or the degree
of change. The sources were:

- personal experience from consulting work, organized on a case-by-
  case basis.
- Written-up case studies, one from Morris and Hough (1986) about the
  computerisation of PAYE (COP) and one from Berry (1988) about
  EPOS in Boots the Chemist.
- Interviews carried out by the author to seek out the specifics of
  selected cases. In the interviews it was intended to achieve a balance
  of successful and unsuccessful projects, generally one of each from
  the same company. Twenty-one projects were examined from a range
  of industries: banking and insurance, retail, public sector, central
  and local government, manufacturing, and communications.

All the projects were active in the decade 1980–9. All had their development done in the UK except for one in the Republic of Ireland. Two of
the projects were for multi-country implementation.

The projects themselves covered a range of business objectives, including:

- productivity of clerical people;
- productivity of professionals;
- 'better' and more-accessible and timely financial information;
- enhanced customer service;
- better communications in the organization;
- more-effective and efficient manufacturing;
- ability to launch a new financial product (personal pensions);
- enhanced international and cross-border management;
- better retail stock and price management, and enhanced merchand-
  ized information.

Where possible, data were gathered from both business and IT representatives, and in some cases the sponsors themselves.

Project Sponsorship in Practice

In this major section the results of the research are first summarized.
Then some cases on 'how not to' are outlined. A 'model' project in Allied
Irish Banks is described, and finally we discuss why people in a position to
follow these prescriptions may not do so.

Findings from Twenty-one Cases

1. Not all huge projects fail. This observation is counter to folklore at least, if not received wisdom.

2. Not all failures are huge projects, in fact more were not.

3. When respondents are invited to describe a failed project, they tend to select a cancelled one. This is not surprising, because the failure is incontrovertible, unlike, for example, an alleged failure to deliver benefit. However, it is unfortunate that cancellation is so commonly identified as not simply a project which in due course was terminated, but a failure of management, people, and ideas. Sometimes cancellation is the appropriate course of action.

4. There is no monopoly of success or failure in public or private sectors, or any one industry type.

5. There was in three cases a connection between *extreme* technical complexity, lack of sponsorship, and failure. This requires more analysis than the present paper allows. But it is suggested that the extreme complexity results from attempting to meet utopian specifications of requirements in the absence of given priorities and any means of negotiating compromise. In none of the cases did the failure stem from inability to meet the technical challenge. Indeed, the concentration of management and resources on that challenge was so great that other exposures were either unnoticed or dismissed.

6. At the time of the analysis, *nine* projects could be rated successful, as defined earlier. Subsequently a further one was completed and was also successful.

7. In the successful projects there was a sponsor in place who conformed at least to the definition, role, and activities outlined earlier (from Edwards 1989), including the operation of a project review board.

8. Conversely, in no cases of failure had there been a sponsor with a board.

9. In all the successes the overall project manager came from the business rather than the IT community. (This is not to say that the project manager was necessarily devoid of IT experience; simply that he/she was seen as, and had been chosen as, a business person.)

10. In all the successes there was continuity—in the sense of the same sponsor and the same project manager for the duration of the project.

Caveats

Following this analysis and the widespread presentation of these results, contrary experience has been invited. There has been very little; however, the following have been offered.

1. Some writers have observed that it is easy to believe that if a system

works, is liked, and is used, it is successful, whatever the benefits. This is a fallacy: beware of it, particularly in office systems. The warning is useful, although the reservation cannot in fact be laid against any of the cases in the research sample. Benefits were attributed to the systems by their users.

2. When a project is successful, people are anxious to be publicly associated with it. In other words, you should expect managers to turn up and claim sponsorship credit for successful projects but to distance themselves when there is a failure. Again, this is not believed to be a defect of the analysis in this work because of the extent of peer commentary and approval that was recorded.

3. In one of the cases, both the attribution of success, and the identification of a sponsor as defined, can be challenged. In other words, there are plausible competing views.

The last caveat is almost a relief, because the apparently total correlation of a set of black-and-white situations can look suspicious. If we applied a statistical test of significance to this small sample, one grey project would probably not be influential. At worst, the level of significance or probability would alter. An IT director of development interviewed then put this in perspective: 'I don't say that you cannot succeed without proper sponsorship—but sponsorship does make success ten times more likely.' It should be noted that there were no obviously observable associations between success/failure and any other project data that were collected.

Case Studies in How Not To

From consultancy experience a number of instances of temporary or terminal project failure can be directly related to missing or deficient sponsorship.

Not having sponsorship in place at all In an important British food retailer an Electronic Point of Sale (EPOS) was mounted. This had full board authority, which had been secured as the direct result of persuasive championing by the IT director. Following authorization, the development and implementation processed without any mediation from a business sponsor or business-led review board. There had been no forum for reviewing the business case or what had to be done in business practices to deliver benefit. Nor were the trading people converted to the idea of a revolution in store practice or merchandise management.

The project was not aborted until millions of pounds had been invested in developing and testing the core systems, and some dozen sizeable stores had been converted to the new system. More than having no sponsorship, it was also a case which met the 'extreme technical complexity' model mentioned above.

Sponsor failing to identify sufficiently with the project In one of the biggest IT implementations of the 1980s there emerged a feeling among the senior management of the field staff who would have to receive and implement a new country-wide system that 'top management is not committed'. Indeed, this was asserted as one of the key exposures of the project when these were formally explored in workshops with senior field management. In fact there was an acknowledged sponsor in place, whose reaction to the news of this perception was: 'How can they say that; I'm £100 million committed!'

£100 million was by no means the total implementation investment required. The problem was the sponsor's lack of public identification with the project, and the lack of a business-based review board which would have triggered, and been one vehicle for, messages to the regions. The project was implemented, though very late and over budget. There was never clarity or confidence about the business case for it.

Trying to combine project sponsor and project manager roles A person who is senior enough in the business to provide the authority required as sponsor is not going to have enough time to provide the continuous project management as well. One or other role (or both) will suffer. To some degree Lockett in this volume has identified this risk.

One example is the tendency in some financial services institutions to appoint a 'project director' who is supposed to combine both roles. However, by virtue of his characteristic status, usually as assistant general manager (AGM), he has not the authority required.

In another industry, a project manager was promoted to the position hitherto occupied by the erstwhile sponsor of the project on the latter's early retirement. It was not possible simultaneously to assume the new, wider job responsibilities and pay proper attention to managing the project. Neither did the new incumbent carry conviction as sponsor. That project virtually stalled until a new project manager was appointed.

Trying to preserve conventional business habits or 'due process' even while recognizing the different nature of projects A project which involved reorganizing hundreds of sites and thousands of jobs had a demanding timetable that was imposed by government legislation. Its definition nevertheless included the requirement to operate 'according to due process of the authority'. That due process was excellent for the exhaustive reporting and minuting associated with democratic processes in local government, but could not have met the demanding timetable of a complex executive process. Part of the solution was to institute far more face-to-face and interactive processes for progress presentations and reviews.

Being soft on the business case If the organization fails, for whatever reason, to articulate a business case at the outset of a project, there will be no basis for assessing priorities or judging problems as it proceeds. There will be no yardstick by which to judge the acceptability of a jump in anticipated expenditure, or a time overrun. The longer that the project proceeds in this state, the more embarrassing—and therefore the more suppressed—becomes the lack of a business case. The project also becomes prone to the false argument that since we have already committed £X million to it, we would be foolish to stop now.

A further problem which follows from the lack of a business case is that there is no means of ranking system features. If, for reasons of progress or of cost saving, we wish to de-scope system function, where should we start? This was a problem in the EPOS system described earlier, with its unconstrained and unprioritized functional ambitions.

Establishing the role but no vehicle   In one case a very keen managing director was quite properly the sponsor of a business transformation project, and was seen to be so. But he had no review board, and no established route for communicating with the project manager. In his excitement he was therefore prone to interfere where he should not have, to make instant decisions on imperfect data, and to fail to communicate what he had done. This is perhaps an exemplar case of having a sponsor but not sponsorship.

Over-bureaucratizing sponsorship and the project review board   The organization sketched in the above case made precisely this error of over-compensation. One project became *fifty-three*, with a two-layer level of sponsorship and control, and a programme office bureaucracy. That worked no better than the previous state, either as a communications vehicle or as a decision-making structure.

Back-office director sponsoring front-office project   This is an emerging characteristic of some financial services institutions. Historically it has often been effective to set up a director of operations as sponsor of a project to enhance productivity and timeliness in the back office. Many of today's projects in this industry are, however, focused on the customer (rather than the policy or the account), on marketing, and on flexible product packaging.

Where an operations director is appointed as sponsor, he or she can lack both the authority needed to be effective with the marketing people, and the personal instincts which a sales-oriented sponsor would bring to the task of arbitrating priorities.

Failing to recognize multi-level sponsorship needs   Many an IT project has a corporate level of justification, system specification, and creation, but a distributed implementation. This can be a system like British Telecom's Customer

Service System (CSS), where the distributed elements were themselves major data centres in their own right. Or it can be one like the AIB system described later in this paper, which was implemented in many small provincial branches with a dozen hands or fewer.

Whatever the scale, there are sponsorship requirements at both corporate and distributed levels, *which are different.* Overlooking either can be disastrous.

Allied Irish Banks—A Case Study in How-to

Allied Irish Banks (AIB) is one of the two main clearing banks in the Republic of Ireland, headquartered and incorporated in Dublin. One of its four divisions as it was organized in the early 1980s was Domestic Banking, operating retail banking services throughout the Republic, in Northern Ireland, and in mainland Britain. At that time the management came to the conclusion that the growth in transaction volumes was such that it would soon put intolerable strains on staff and premises, since the resource requirement was certain to grow in proportion.

The bank was not naïve in IS terms. It operated automated cheque clearing, and branch account management was on an overnight basis on mainframes working in Dublin. An ATM network was in place. Branch automation had begun with back-office proof encoding machines. At the time in question, however, the bank's identification of on-line branch automation as the solution to the productivity challenge was very advanced for Europe.

On-line branch automation for AIB meant not only the on-line submission of enquiries, customer file updates, and so on, but also automating all 'value transactions' possible. These included cash withdrawals, lodgement of credits, and credit transfers, authorized through the use of a magnetically encoded bank card used at the branch counter and accredited through the use of a Personal Identification Number (PIN).

A business case was established for an on-line branch system, and a prime vendor was selected. From an early stage the bank had identified the need for what it called a 'Senior Review Body' to have oversight of the progress and general integrity of the development and implementation project. This was planned from the outset to be chaired by the chief general manager, Domestic Banking, Mr J. J. McAulcliffe.

The bank felt the need for an external mediator to assist the relationship between the Senior Review Body (SRB) and the vendor. I was privileged to hold this position for the life of the SRB, but I claim no credit for the invention of the SRB concept or its working.

The project had what could be termed a 'virtual' organization. The project workers and managers did not for the most part leave their formal reporting lines, but owed a temporary and overriding duty to the project for its duration. (A major exception to this was the full-time executive appointment of a banker as user project manager, supported by a small number of user staff representatives.)

There were two main groups of activity: those concerned with implementation, and those required to develop and prove the system products. Each of these groups was carefully defined as a number of sub-projects, each with an accountable manager. Examples of sub-projects from each group are shown below.

Sub-projects in Allied Irish Banks

Implementation Group of Sub-Projects (examples)
   Prototyping
   Branch physical installation
   Branch procedures Manual
   User testing
   Benefits management

Systems and Technical Group of Sub-Projects (examples)
   Develop phase 0
   Modelling/performance
   Develop phase 1
   Physical network
   Data centre
   Network management system
   Test on-line system

Alignment between these two groups of sub-projects was, of course, important. It was achieved both informally and formally through the device of having each group represented at the *other* group's routine progress meetings. In that way there were fewer surprises, and inter-group dependencies were quickly identified and managed.

As the project proceeded a number of different issues emerged as potentially critical aspects. Examples, in no particular order, were:

- reliance on the throughput performance of a key piece of equipment—the branches proof-encoder—for which this bank's implementation was to be the first in the world;
- quantification and confirmation of the business case for the project;
- coincident, enlargement of the group data centre;
- coincident intention to introduce 'cheque-retention', that is, discontinuing the practice of returning all cleared cheques to the drawer;
- training branch staff with minimal interruption to normal operations;
- identifying provincial subcontractors with the ability to carry out cabling for the bank equipment;

- the ability of the PTT to implement what was probably the largest leased line private network in the country at that time;
- coping with a change in the physical configuration of the vendor's branch terminal equipment which made it no longer fit the specially commissioned enclosures;
- maintaining conformance to a Technology Agreement made between all the major Irish banks and the relevant Bank Officials Association;
- determining when performance and reliability levels in the pilot installation sites were adequate to proceed with general roll-out;
- the acceptable rate and geographical distribution of that roll-out;
- how best to take advantage of a change in the vendor's options for machine configuration, balancing possible cost savings against contingent additional storage;
- questions raised about the basic productivity justification, when two city-centre branches were installed and failed initially to perform to expectations;
- the contribution required from the local branch manager which turned out to be crucial—in ensuring staff confidence and co-operation.

All of these were at various times raised as issues at the SRB, sometimes simply to flag the issues as possible exposures, but often to secure prompt and authoritative management decisions. It was the confident dispatching of those decisions which was impressive, and a clear example of how reliance on more conventional approaches to capital and people decisions could not have coped.

The SRB met every three to four months. The following people reported to it:

- the AGM in overall management control of the project (always);
- the manager of the systems group of sub-projects (always);
- the manager of the implementation group (always);
- managers of sub-projects which had come to a particular milestone, or a critical decision point.

Membership of the SRB included:

- chairman (chief general manager, Domestic Banking);
- general managers within Domestic Banking, representing regional branches, and central staff;
- group general manager for Technology, who had executed a championship role in the initiation and feasibility stages of the project;
- external consultant (this author).

The Senior Review body operated very much in Cabinet mode, and decisions were consensual. Once made, these decisions had behind them the authority of the chief general manager and, effectively, the board. At no time was the chief general manager referred to as the sponsor of the project, but in the terms of this paper that was precisely the role he exercised.

Project management is a special set of disciplines and management processes which is required when an organization is about to undertake a degree and rate of change that its normal management processes cannot cope with. It was interesting that there came a day when the SRB decided that the roll-out had been sufficiently proven and that the remainder of the implementation would be business as usual. That point arrived when over 90 per cent of the Irish Republic branches had been installed, but before the Northern Ireland installation had been started. One of the consequences was that the SRB was stood down at this point; interestingly, with a degree of ceremony.

The AIB on-line system has been satisfactory in performance, and in delivery of benefit. The implementation timetable which was achieved was not identical with that scheduled at the outset, but deviations in delivery of both function and branch installation were managed in an orderly way, and kept under review by the SRB.

Observation of the proceedings of the SRB convinced me that, however diligent and skilful the project workers and managers were, the satisfactory outcome could not have been accomplished without the SRB's contribution. That contribution was above all in providing decisive arbitration when it was needed, notably in matters of capital expenditure changes, and compromise between the ideal and the practical.

Had the SRB not been in place, it is likely that much time and effort would have been expended in attempting to meet some increasingly remote functional objective, and trying to operate within very constrained and arbitrary budget limits.

How to Set Up Sponsorship

Setting up a project sponsor should ideally be coincident, and intimately connected with, the commissioning of the project review board. This is because reflections on the role and requirements of the sponsor are illuminated by considerations of who needs to be on the board—and vice versa.

Setting up usually follows the key decision to proceed with the project. Until there is a clear commitment to implement a set of major changes for certain business objectives, the debates around the project proposals will probably be too speculative and imprecise for the team of people needed to oversee implementation.

It should not be imagined that either the board or the sponsor come instantly into full effectiveness on appointment. They learn it in action, but they can be assisted by brief induction training on the lines suggested in this chapter. They can also be assisted by inclusion of a 'non-executive' member of the board, the role to which I was apprenticed in AIB.

The key inclusions in the project review board (PRB) are:

- the sponsor;
- the reporting project manager;
- other reports of the project manager, usually representing the systems side and the business implementation side of activities;
- *informed* representatives of the main user communities at the most senior level possible;
- representatives of main provider functions, often including a financial director, and a senior representative of any truly vital vendor— for instance, the supplier of a critical software package.

It is not possible to preordain the remit of the PRB; the examples of concerns of the AIB board were described particularly to demonstrate the diversity of issues which may be legitimately addressed.

Why Don't Organizations Do It?

When an apparently obvious and uncontroversial prescription turns out to be far from universally followed we should ask why. Here are some reasons which have been heard of in real cases (R) with suggested responses from the author (A).

(R) Although the chief executive is the obvious sponsor for this particular project, because only at that level do all the needer and providers have a common head, he/she doesn't have the time to do it.

(A) Rightly implemented, the role does not always need much time. When it does, what in the CEO's work profile is so much more important than this project to justify the absence, especially if it is a high business change project?

(R) This is an IT infrastructure project and it does not affect the way the business is done so it doesn't need business sponsorship.

(A) If it is worth investing in, there must be a business case for it—and there may be a need for compromises in which a business view is needed, such as trading off flexibility against investment cost.

(R) This is only a branch equipment replacement programme which does not need strategic top management guidance.

(A) The above comment about business authority being required to arbitrate on priorities applies equally here. Also the need to justify and promote change to the user community applies at least as much to users who are being changed from one technology to another as it does to users being given technology for the first time.

(R) We have established the role of project director, and we have board authority for the project, so there is no case for a sponsor as well.

(A) The test is whether the director and his project board have authority *without reference* to change the resourcing, timing, or function of the project, to commit in trade union negotiations, and so on.

(R) This is such a little project; surely it does not need the paraphernalia of a sponsor and a board?

(A) Apparently little ones can have wide ramifications; but if it turns out truly to make only modest demands, there will be few meetings and they will be very short.

Discussion

The evidence appears very strong in favour of the contribution of a properly qualified and supported sponsor to the successful implementation of a major IT project. The extension of personal and anecdotal data by interview strengthened the case beyond expectations. There may be one significant reason for this: it is possible that, among the many features contributing to success, sponsorship stands in a special and superior position. This is because it lies within the sponsor's authority to amend or compensate for other project deficiencies.

The work has not examined at all the contribution of particular project management methods or habits within the systems and technology sub-project area. It makes no comment on them, beyond asserting that the reporting style and process must be communicable to the sponsor and project board level. This might sound like a statement of the obvious, but it is not unknown for people deliberately to obfuscate systems news for senior management.

Sponsors and Champions

A possible conflict that occurs to some people is that between the concept of sponsors and champions are people who drive through a major change project, taking a far more active and 'performance' type role than the sponsors we have been discussing. Inevitably there is overlap in definitions. Beath (1991) and Runge and Earl (1988) define champions as expressly *not* possessing a full spectrum of management authority, and achieving positive results in spite of this.

It should be noted that their work, and others' work that they report is particularly focused on innovation generally, and strategic systems of one sort or another. Not all major IT projects have the element of pioneering that requires the missionary champion's contribution, yet they can still transform the lives and activities of thousands.

Lockett's (1995) champion is rather different; Lockett asserts the need of voltage from a champion, who may or may not be empowered. If not empowered, Beath has agreed that sponsorship is not antithetical to championship. Lockett also recognized the importance of sponsors.

So it would seem that we do not have two contending principles; rather, two complementary ones. Focus will rightly be on the *championship* principle where the emphasis is on breakthroughs in business products, channels, customer relationships, and so on. Focus will be on *sponsorship* where there is a large number of employees or affiliates to be changed, a huge relative level of investment, and complex issues of prioritization *vis à vis* other business developments and imperatives.

Once the two characteristics—championship and sponsorship—are seen as complementary, it is possible to see that there need be no conflict. The exception would be if a reading of Runge (1985) led to the idea that we should deliberately engineer things to make sure that key players should be *denied* authority in order to keep them virile! But of course Runge's champions were both informal and unofficial, often promoting a project against the 'establishment'.

The assertion from this work is that the sponsor role cannot with safety be abandoned in general, and that there are unnecessary risks in doing so. It may well be that some sponsors may look a lot more like champions, and that some champions who are also overseen by sponsors may be the more visible member of the partnership.

Tasks of Sponsors

There will be many definitions of sponsorship tasks, some more inclusive than others, and all dependent on both the management culture and practices of the organization, and the specific models of project organization and management adopted.

The discussion so far should have suggested that the basic set of tasks to qualify as a sponsor is:

- assessing, ideally in a collegiate fashion, the project's state, and where appropriate reporting it upwards and outwards;
- reviewing alternative approaches to ameliorating problems or augmenting opportunities;
- taking decisions, again ideally in a collegiate fashion, and promoting and proclaiming them to the business and all others affected;
- performing all such leadership and marketing activities as fall to him or her in relation to the project;

- understanding the sources of benefit and working on the business to ensure that all necessary change is actioned to the point of demonstrable achievement;
- knowing when project status should stop, stopping it, and providing for life after project status.

It will be seen that this is a more comprehensive list than that given on page 362, but it is not intended to be an extension of those ideas so much as an elaboration, a better exposition of the same ideas.

Processes for sponsors

This is not the place to lay out a formal set of business processes for a sponsor, but it is important to describe three key modes of operation.

1. Interacting with the project management and community, either by planned intent or in response to hotline kinds of demand. It is vital that the project manager understand what can be expected of the sponsor so that the necessary enabling staff-work can be done.
2. Acting at the interface between the project and the business, which is primarily achieved through the PRB and associated staff work.
3. Interacting with the rest of the business on behalf of the project, but in areas which are by normal understanding outside the boundaries of the project. This could arise, for example, when other parts of the business are required to change their own business plans or priorities in order to enable the project to be fulfilled.

A feature of life in a project environment which has been insufficiently noted so far is that there are expenses, risks, and exposures involved in this way of working. (An extreme case of living under a wholesale project environment is being at war, where sacrifices may include loss of freedoms, acceptance of abnormal risk levels, and a modified approach to property rights, to put it mildly.)

This sheds a further light on the sponsor role, because he or she is at the interface between the project world and the 'normal' world and has to be the point of balance between them. How far can the business go in modifying prudence, economy, concern for the person, or whatever principle or practice that has to be suspended for the apparent good of the project?

Something else that may have to be suspended for the good of the project is certain individuals' normal accountability for business-as-usual issues. A board of a major company was taken aback recently when it was suggested that in order to put the required time and thought into a key project, the sales director might not be required to answer questions on the daily state of sales against plan, nor even to be aware of it.

Questions and Unknowns

At headline level, here are some questions which the work reported here does not answer.

- How do the prescriptions work for small projects?
- What is the largest number of major change projects that an organization can cope with concurrently?
- Is it possible to retrofit a project sponsor/PRB approach onto a project which hitherto has not had one? All of the successful projects in this research had their sponsorship in place from the beginning.
- How should sponsorship work where the project is major in terms of investment and of technical change, but user change is to be minimal or non-existent?
- Can a system be too big for subsequent management, even though through various devices or project governance and management it can be successfully implemented?

This last item is discussed more fully in the following section, as it appears to present a more profound problem.

Conclusions

The proposition put earlier was that it would be foolhardy, given what we now know, to proceed on a major business change project with an enabling IT component *without* properly commissioned sponsorship and a project board. A lot of evidence of effective good practice and of the effects of deficient practice has been presented. Is there some underlying connector which explains and justifies the findings and assertions from a basis in the very nature of IT projects?

A characteristic of IT implementation projects which perhaps differentiates them from some other kinds of 'project'—defence and construction, for example—is the continuing opportunity for compromise. This arises because of the trade-offs permanently present between elements such as function, capital cost, running cost, risk, flexibility in the solution, elapsed time, and so on. These trade-off often arise because it seems that there is more uncertainty about both the ends and means of IT projects than many other types (Beath 1988; Morris 1995).

To take one example of trade-offs, if things are running late there might be opportunities to stick to planned cutover by:

- implementing only some phases of the system function;
- accepting the risk of implementing as imperfectly tested rather than waiting for the ideal fit solution;
- diverting people from another part of the business to assist in training and implementation;

- accepting a more expensive but available component;
- dividing the project into sequential sub-projects.

The important feature all these have in common is that none of them is, or ought to be, the subject of a decision, exclusively within the project. This is because every one of them involves business impacts about which the most senior business people ought to be concerned. And the sponsor is the point of interaction between the project and the 'senior business people'.

The examples also illustrate the importance of the sponsor's accessibility to the project manager. The dilemmas illustrated above should not wait to be revealed until the next scheduled meeting of the project review board. It *may* be that the PRB meeting is the first point at which the issue is finally resolved, if there is a need for a consensual, 'cabinet' decision. But the resolution depends on a mutual staffwork between the sponsor and the project manager (at least), so that the issues are properly explored and the alternatives properly presented.

What has the work reported here added to our understanding of project governance? It has largely ignored the very extensive and professional set of project management methods and tools now available, and might appear simply to reassert the already obvious need for top management involvement. In response, I would emphasis that this chapter has sought to develop:

1. transformation of a generalized aspiration about top-management involvement into a much more specifically defined role;
2. extensive demonstration of the breadth of issues which a properly commissioned sponsor may be called on to address during the course of a project;
3. justification of the unique capability of the properly empowered sponsor to manage compromise;
4. many illustrations of how to do it, and how not do it, that should help practitioners to get it right.

An Outstanding Question

The previous section briefly alluded to one problem which the present work does not address, and which had the capability to negate or at least enfeeble all that a key change project has achieved. This is: how to manage an extensively integrated system after the period during which it was subjected to all the prescriptions we have so far outlined. This is a real problem, and it was presented by the project manager of one of the researched projects. The project was successfully implemented, albeit very late and with uncertain and uncertificated benefits.

The system was highly integrated from a database, an IT, and a system-function point of view. However, experience with running, maintaining, and enhancing the system has shown that the level of integration was proving to be a handicap, because there was no single point of ownership or arbitration for the system. During implementation there had been sponsorship at the very high level, but there was never any question of this being maintained after the system moved into regular production status.

Examples of the sort of problem reported were:

- how to establish priority among contending requirements for functional enhancements where different business areas are the bidders;
- how to determine the best way of amending technical details of a system where performance implications may favour one functional service at the expense of another;
- contention between the attraction of system stability, particularly as seen by the operators, and aspirations for new or changed functionality.

One of the other companies whose projects were under review in this work does possess an extensive and detailed bureaucracy of system ownership, which deals with issues of the after-life of a project. But that does not help in the question here, because that company tends to develop very function-bounded systems rather than the cross-functional integrated system type which presented the problem. In the case of Business Process Redesign, Earl (1994) has argued for the identification of process owners. Perhaps the analogy here is the nomination of a system owner.

The Final Claim—Why Does it Matter?

The justification for presenting and emphasizing these messages is quite simply that people are still running into trouble with IT projects, and that demonstrable deficiency in sponsorship is a major or sometimes key reason. The chapter has been written from a practitioner/consultant perspective, but the arguments do appear to relate to, and extend, the more obviously research-based literature of IS project management.

The hope is that these ideas of sponsors and sponsorship will contribute to increasing the success rate of IT projects. There are also some embedded questions for further research.

References

Alloway, R. M. (1976), 'Temporary Management Systems: Application of a Contingency Model to the Creation of Computer-based Information Systems', Exclusive Summary, Stockholm School of Economics (Nov.).

Beath, C. M. (1988), 'User Roles and Responsibilities', *Journal of Information Systems Management* (Fall).

—— (1991), 'Supporting the Information Technology Champion', *MIS Quarterly*, vol. 15, no. 3, pp. 355–72.

Berry, J. (1988), 'Implementing a Strategic IT Project: EPOS in Boots', presentation at the Oxford PA Conference 1988, Templeton College, Oxford.

Earl, M. J. (1994), 'The New and the Old of Business Process Redesign', *Journal of Strategic Information Systems*, vol. 3, no. 1, pp. 5–22.

Edwards, B. R. (1989), 'Project Sponsors: Their Contribution to Effective IT Implementation' (unpublished) the Oxford PA Conference 1988, Templeton College, Oxford.

IBM (1986), *IBM Project Assessment Checklist*, form no. GU59-5020, IBM United Kingdom Ltd.

Lockett, M. (1995), 'Innovating with Information Technology', in M. J. Earl (ed.), *Information Management: The Organizational Dimension*, Oxford: Oxford University Press.

Morris, P. G. W. (1995), 'Project Management: Lessons from IT and Non-IT Projects', in M. J. Earl (ed.), *Information Management: The Organizational Dimension*, Oxford: Oxford University Press.

—— and Hough, G. H. (1986), 'The Computerisation of PAYE', in *Preconditions of Success and Failure in Major Projects*, Major Projects Association, Templeton College, Oxford, ch. 10.

Parker, M. F. (1990), 'Managing Successful Applications', in T. J. Lincoln (ed.), *Managing Information Systems for Profit*, New York: John Wiley and Sons.

Runge, D. A., and Earl, M. J. (1988), 'Gaining Competitive Advantage from Telecommunications', in M. J. Earl (ed.), *Information Management: The Strategic Dimension*, Oxford: Oxford University Press.

Smith, J. E. (1990), 'Gearing IT in the Office to Business Needs', in T. J. Lincoln (ed.), *Managing Information Systems for Profit*, New York: John Wiley and Sons.

19

The Successful Design of Expert Systems: Are Ends More Important than Means?

ENID MUMFORD

Introduction

This chapter provides a case study example of the design of an expert system. The system was developed as a participative venture by a technical team and the future users who were sales staff. The author presents it as an example of how participation can assist the creation of shared values, commitments, and objectives in employment situations where relationships are traditionally contractual. The chapter shows how the success of the system was greatly influenced by the processes that were used in its design.

The Relationship of Means to Ends

In almost all situations the nature and success of the objectives achieved are related to the means used to attain those objectives. A recognition of the relevance of this statement to business has led to the writing of many books and articles on 'how to manage change' and 'how to influence people'. Weinberg (1985) defines the role of the consultant as 'the art of influencing people at their request'. Macoby (1976) describes the different strategies which managers use to achieve results. In his book *The Gamesman* he sets out the qualities of the modern chief executive as: 'one who is responsive to the requirements of various corporate departments, a person who can be trusted to protect the company's growth and profit, who can inspire employees and stockholders with a sense of purpose, who takes calculated risks, who is controlled and can control gifted technical people without dampening their enthusiasm for innovation.'

With some light modification this could also be a description of the qualities of someone who is concerned with the design and implementation of new technology. This might read as follows. He or she should be: 'responsive to the requirements of user areas, a person who can be trusted to protect the users' intersts, who can inspire managers, designers and users with a sense of purpose, who takes—and encourages others to take—well thought-out initiatives, who has self-control and can help others to achieve and accept control without losing their enthusiasm for innovation.'

Weinberg has formulated a number of 'laws of consulting', some of which are very relevant to the successful introduction of new technology. For example:

- Every prescription has two parts—the medicine and the method of ensuring correct use.
- No matter how it looks at first, it's always a people problem.
- If you use the same recipe, you get the same bread.
- Moving in one direction incurs a cost in the other.
- Effective problem-solvers may have problems, but they rarely have a single dominant problem.
- Nothing new ever works.
- It tastes better when you add your own egg.

But despite the books and good advice, it still seems to be the case that many systems designers believe that nothing more is required when designing a system than clear technical objectives and good technical design. Governments too seem to subscribe to the belief that because an exciting technical development has appeared someone will want to buy it. Yet there seems little evidence to support this assumption. On the contrary, it is more likely that new technology will not be introduced and accepted until a clear business need and benefit has been established. There must also be user conviction that its advantages outweigh any disadvantages.

What Are Change Processes and Why Are They Important?

Change processes are to do with interests, intentions, attitudes, emotions. They are also about participation, communication, motivation, and timing. As Weinberg says, they are more about 'know-when than know-how'. They are the means for making things happen. For changing lack of interest into excitement and enthusiasm. For translating old, rigid, organization structures into new, technology-centred, adaptive systems.

Without effective processes, change will not happen. Expensive systems may lie on the shelf unwanted and unused. Systems which benefit both managers and workers may be rejected because they are not understood.

Processes, then are about 'changing' the levers that are required to bring about change. When new technology is being introduced there is a need for changes in attitudes and behaviour. There is also a need for changes in organizational structures, procedures, and controls. Changing requires the ability to handle a great deal of complexity, to manage a wide variety of problems, and to bring new inputs and the altered bits and pieces of the old system together in a smoothly functioning, acceptable whole.

Successful change requires that change outputs are seen as necessary, important, desirable, and acceptable by those who will use or come into contact with them. This means that design must take place with a detailed knowledge of how each of these words is defined and interpreted by the future users of the system. System design methods and guidelines should pay as much attention to these 'process' factors as to methods for designing the technical part of the system.

In fact this nearly happens. There is a knowledge and an understanding gap. The design group which wishes to ensure that its expensive new system is easily and successfully implemented will not find this information in most of the books written on system design methodology. These assume that designing a system structure that works in a technical sense is sufficient and will ensure the system's future use and success. This is one of the reasons why so many carefully designed and costly systems never become operational.

Schein (1988) has described how a concentration on structure as opposed to process has dominated the management literature. This is also true of the computer literature, where great attention is paid to technical methods for building systems. Many of these are called 'structured design'. Schein argues that this approach is not wrong, but it is incomplete. Personalities, perceptions, and experiences will always influence what people do and how they relate to others. Ensuring that these relationships are positive, harmonious, and directed at a clearly formulated objective is an important part of the design process.

Processes, like computers, are the means to achieve desired ends. Whereas the computer system is an important means to enable a company to increase its business effectiveness, the social processes associated with its design are the means to arrive at a system that is good in business terms and also acceptable in human terms: a system that can be designed and implemented without excessive stress and tension and is non-threatening and easy to use. Ideally it should not displace or de-skill staff, and it must be simple to learn and logical to operate, while at the same time assisting the user to work more effectively.

As well as the primary objective of developing a good system, the social processes associated with design and implementation will have a number of sub-goals. Some of these will be related to enhancing the skill and knowledge of the members of the design group, so that they become increasingly competent in designing and in controlling the design process.

If users are important members of the design team, as they should be, then another sub-goal may be demonstrating to senior management the contribution that a participative approach can make to successful design.

A number of different processes are required when a new system is being created and a design team needs to be helped to acquire skill in all of them. Four that are particularly important are:

1. *Problem Solving.* The members of the design team must learn how to tackle and solve problems as a group; how to arrive at agreed solutions and how to take and implement decisions.

2. *Group Relationships.* The group must learn how to work together; how to become committed to both the 'group' and to the task; how to be supportive of each other and able to tolerate and handle conflict.

3. *Support Generation.* The group must learn how to gain support from other groups, in particular, powerful groups such as top management and the trade unions. They must understand how to exert influence and win friends.

4. *Knowledge Building.* The group must acquire new knowledge. This will include knowledge about their own company; about computer systems, organizational and job design, and design processes.

People can pick up this knowledge for themselves but a group that is new to design, or contains a mix of technical experts and users with different interests and perceptions, can benefit from having a teacher and helper work with them. The person in this role is often called a 'facilitator', and his or her role is to help the group members to acquire the knowledge listed above and apply it successfully to the design of a new system.

The Processes of Participative Design

In 1981 the author was invited to give a number of seminars on participative design at the Digital Equipment Corporation in Boston, USA. DEC was moving into expert systems at this time, and XCON, a tool to assist the accurate configuring of VAX computers in DEC's manufacturing plants, was in the process of being built.

Configuring is the process of ensuring that when a computer is being assembled all the necessary components are present and in the correct relationship to each other. This is a demanding and complex process, and before XCON existed many errors were made. One reason for these errors was mistakes made in the DEC sales offices. Before sending a customer's order to a manufacturing plant the salesperson has to configure the application. All the required items of equipment must be stated so that Manufacturing is informed of what is required and the customer is given the correct price for the system.

XCON was proving so successful that DEC decided to build a similar expert system, XSEL (Expert Selling), to assist the sales staff to configure accurately.

Bruce MacDonald, the project manager for the development of XSEL, decided that he wanted XSEL to be designed participatively and that he was looking for a method that would help him to do this. He decided that the author's ETHICS method (Mumford 1981, 1986) was the one to use.

His first step was to set up a formal participation structure and create a user design group from the XSEL technical project team, who were located in DEC's Intelligent Systems Technology Group (ISTG), and the future users of the system who were sales staff located in many sales offices throughout the USA. Clearly all of these could not attend design meetings and so a representative group would have to be created.

He sent a letter to all the sales offices describing the participative philosophy that was to be associated with the building of XSEL. He explained that the role of the User Design Group would be to integrate organizational, human, technical, and task-related factors into the design process in a *formal and organized manner*. He also explained his own role as project manager and facilitator. He would assist the group to define agenda items, keep focused on its task, ask critical questions, mediate conflict, and ensure that the system objectives and time targets were met.

Bruce had hoped to keep the User Design Group small, but he found that at the first meeting he had twenty-four people present—sixteen from sales offices and eight from ISTG.

Early Uncertainties

All new user design groups experience uncertainty at the start of a project. Participants arrive at the first meeting with no clear idea of their role or the task ahead, and with little confidence in their ability to complete this task. The facilitator too will have feelings of doubt and confusion, and Bruce was no exception. He was new to DEC, to expert systems, and to the role of the XSEL project manager. He had no experience of participative design or of acting as facilitator to a user design group.

He knew that he had to help the group master the four essential tasks ahead—acquiring knowledge to build the system, building the system and handling the problems associated with this, managing its own group relationships, and persuading external groups to support the project. He was unsure how best to do any of these things.

ETHICS enable him to solve the problems of the first three meetings by providing a structure for collecting information. The User Design Group members were asked to think about their work missions—what they were trying to achieve in their jobs. They were also asked to consider the extent to which the successful management of the configuring task contributed to the mission. They were then requested to describe the problems which hindered efficient configuring and caused them frustration and a reduction in job satisfaction.

Carnegie-Mellon University was building a prototype of XSEL for DEC. Soon after the first User Design Group meeting the members were given access to this in their sales offices. They were asked to try it out and send their comments to ISTG via a comments facility in the system.

Uncertainty was therefore reduced and knowledge-building started in two important areas—an intellectual consideration of the salesperson's mission and role and the importance and nature of the configuring task in these; and a practical test of XSEL in its embryonic state. This iterative mix of thinking and practice was to continue throughout the design and building of the system. It proved to be successful—the User Design Group saw themselves as both visionaries and entrepreneurs.

Once the prototype was seen to work, responsibility for building XSEL as an operational system was transferred to DEC. The ISTG group did the actual building of the system, responding all the time to the guidance of the User Design Group. The members specified what was required and tried out each version of XSEL as it was developed.

As the building and testing of XSEL proceeded it became increasingly clear to all those involved that systems design was a very complex process. For it to be successful there had to be a good integration between the technology, the users and their tasks and responsibilities, and the company. The choice and design of the technology must help the successful perform-ance of the selling tasks. The nature of this task must provide the users with job satisfaction, and the interaction of the technology and people variables must be a positive one that helped the sales offices to achieve their 'mission' of more effective selling and improved customer satisfaction.

Bruce MacDonald found that one of the most difficult aspects of using a participative approach was helping the User Design Group to be clear about its role. The members were very busy, pressurized salespeople who were not normally involved in the design stage of software development. Prior to XSEL they had merely rejected software which they did not find use-ful. Now they were required to improve it, and Bruce had to keep remind-ing them that they were in a development role. This required thought and judgement and the careful weighing of alternatives.

Once the User Design Group meetings were established, Bruce found that the interest of the sales-force in XSEL increased and more people wished to attend. This meant that the meetings became larger and more difficult to manage. There was also the problem of communicating what was taking place to members of the sales-force who were unable to be present. This was solved through DEC's electronic mail system. At the end of each meeting options that had been discussed were relayed to non-attending members of the salesforce and their views sought. Account was taken of these when the final decision on how to proceed with a particular aspect of system design was taken.

Competence Increases

Because XSEL was a very large and complex expert system containing many thousands of rules, its progress was slow. But by 1983 the User Design Group were reasonably happy with the performance of the system and attention was being paid to organizing necessary back-up activities. Sales offices had to be provided with hardware on which to run XSEL; there had to be a training programme to enable all sales staff to learn how to use it, and the system needed to be tested by a much larger pilot group. The User Design Group had to develop strategies and plans to accomplish all these things.

The Group had now become very knowledgeable about expert systems and how to build them. They were good at considering options and taking decisions, and a number of senior salesmen who had attended all the meetings had an influential role in the discussions. The members continued to approve of participation and were proud of what they had achieved.

External Problems

The achievements of the User Design Group did not mean that no problems had been experienced along the design route. There had been many of these, but most had been technical and capable of solution. In 1983 the Group began experiencing a number of problems which were a product of external events and attitudes. First, DEC underwent a major reorganization that caused some trauma throughout the company. Secondly, for XSEL to proceed further there was need for support from other groups in the Company. Senior management had to be convinced of XSEL's value and be prepared to finance its introduction throughout the USA. This would be a major investment. Thirdly, a number of sales offices had to agree to make the use of XSEL an integral part of their day-to-day activities.

Neither senior sales management nor the regional managers of the sales office had played any part in the participative processes. Neither did they know much about the system and what it had to offer. How could they be persuaded that XSEL was worth backing? The task of the User Design Group was now moving beyond systems development to problems of implementation and communication. The members decided that DEC's US Sales Management Committee must be approached and asked for its commitment to full-scale implementation of XSEL.

Bruce now had a personal dilemma. Should he talk to the Sales Management Committee as project manager of XSEL, or should one of the sales-force members of the Design Group make the case? If the Sales Management Committee was not convinced about the usefulness of XSEL then the system's future progress would be greatly slowed down. Bruce decided that the case for XSEL was best made by a salesperson, and the User Design Group chose one of its members to do this. He presented the arguments for XSEL excellently and the SMC gave its blessing to the company-wide implementation of XSEL in the USA.

In 1984 XSEL began moving slowly into some of the US sales offices, but the task of the Design Group was by no means over. As the number of users increased so more criticisms and ideas for improvement flowed in via the system's comments facility. All of these had to be evaluated and suggestions for changes made to the technical team. XSEL continued to grow in size and to become more versatile. Plans had to be made to link it to other automated systems which were being introduced into the sales offices.

XSEL was not generally introduced throughout the USA until 1985. Development continued thereafter and the User Design Group continued to meet at regular intervals to discuss and guide its progress. There was general agreement that it was a good system and provided financial bene-fits for the company, security from errors for the sales-force, and systems that meet their delivery dates and have no parts missing for customers. There is also agreement that participation played a major role in ensuring that these advantages were achieved.

Why Did the DEC Approach Work So Well?

To answer this question we need to consider both company effectiveness and individual needs. The cybernetic theories of Stafford Beer (1981) can throw some light on the factors that assist an organization to flourish. He has developed a five-tier hierarchical model (Fig. 19.1) which he calls the 'viable system'.

A design group is also a viable system. It requires a system-5 strategic control function to ensure that it is setting the right objectives for its activ-ities and formulating the best policies. It needs to ensure that these are in line with company objectives and policies. It also requires a system-4 intelligence-gathering function which enables it to collect relevant informa-tion. This information will include task-related inputs such as available methods and options, and also political news about external reaction to the design and building of the system. At system-3 level it requires an optimizing and monitoring activity to ensure that plans are successfully carried out. At the system-2 level there must be a means for keeping the design process on course by identifying the essential problems and avoid-ing or solving these. Level 1 has the essential task of designing, building, and implementing the system.

Each of these five system levels needs to communicate with the others,

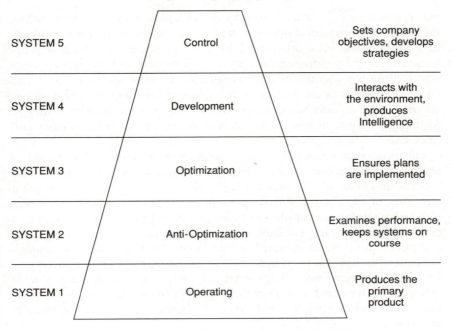

SYSTEM 5	Control	Sets company objectives, develops strategies
SYSTEM 4	Development	Interacts with the environment, produces Intelligence
SYSTEM 3	Optimization	Ensures plans are implemented
SYSTEM 2	Anti-Optimization	Examines performance, keeps systems on course
SYSTEM 1	Operating	Produces the primary product

Fig. 19.1. *Beer's five-tier hierarchic model: the viable system*

and the activities at all levels must be co-ordinated. This requires people to work closely together. It can be argued that if one group builds an expert system and another group implements it and uses it, then the feedback loops between the different levels of the viable system will not work smoothly. There are likely to be both co-ordinating and communication problems.

One way of getting the design task's viable system to work effectively is through bringing the different interests together in a single group. Burnand (1982) argues that agreement and shared objectives are assisted by: 'finding out other people's views and expectations and conforming or compromising with them, co-operating and co-ordinating one's activities with others, supporting others' views, and by bringing deviants into line with others by discussion and persuasion.' He also makes the point that sensitivity to problems arises from an awareness and understanding of other people's difficulties.

The DEC approach of involving other technical staff and future users in the design of XSEL made the development of a smoothly functioning viable system more possible. The strong feedback loops between intelligence gathering, design, and the testing of XSEL by sales staff reinforced the viability of the system.

From the company's perspective, participation assisted communication and the passing of information from technologists to users and vice versa. It brought groups with different interests together in a situation in which they could talk to each other, and this greatly helped the solving of problems in a new development activity. It highlighted and reinforced areas where there was identity of interest between technologists and users and enabled conflicts of interest to be brought out into the open and rationally discussed. It also assisted group learning and an understanding of feelings, interests, needs, anxieties, and hopes of the technologists and sales staff.

The process was assisted by the appointment of Bruce MacDonald as leader. He strongly believed in participation and was able to combine the control functions of a project manager with the teaching and motivating attributes of a facilitator. Burnand has defined leadership as having a central, linking role: helping develop and maintain group activity; helping a group to deal with its problems so that it continues and grows in stability and power and generates rewards for members and unit, and performance.

Leadership has also been described as containing two kinds of activities. First, initiating structure—helping set tasks, letting the group know what is expected of them and what they can expect of the leader. Secondly, showing consideration—helping with freedom, fairness, relationships, morale, and rewards.

The alternatives to this participative approach might have been either a 'let's guess' or a 'let's try it and see what happens' strategy. The first occurs when a group of technical designers build a system believing that they know what the future users want and that there is no need to involve or consult them. The second is when the technologists, without much prior consultation, produce a prototype of the final system for the users to play with. The first approach can lead to expensive disaster, the second to acceptance of a system that works adequately but does not really meet complex needs because these have not been identified and carefully thought through.

Participation appears to bring some clear advantages from a company point of view, but what are the advantages to the individual member of the design group?

Two advantages are that participation in group decision-taking brings with it feelings of personal freedom and control. Bion (1961) was one of the pioneers in group processes and he has described how groups can be helped to move from a state of uncertainty to one of maturity in which they are able to analyse situations, reach agreement, and take decisions. The mature group can work on a problem by seeking relevant data, building on experience, developing and applying principles, and generating support for their solution. This process gives the group a sense of progress and success. The mature group is also able to handle stress successfully.

But of course this does not always happen. Some groups may find themselves continually in conflict and unable to take decisions. Individual members then take refuge in behaviour such as 'passivity'—accepting what other people say, or 'fight or flight'—becoming embroiled in conflict or removing themselves from the group situation. These kinds of group react emotionally to stress. One of the functions of the facilitator is to help the groups he or she is working with to achieve maturity and avoid these kinds of problems.

From the individual's point of view, being in control means that he or she can exert influence. Psychologists tell us that this reduces stress. If we are in control of the roller-coaster, we don't want to get off.

Psychologists also argue that the pleasure of being in control does not come from the knowledge that allows us to hold that position, but from the excitement that comes from making things happen. There is a feedback loop between these two activities—the process of acquiring new knowledge makes it more possible to make things happen. Also, the more we have opportunities for working as a member of a group, the more our involvement with the group activity deepens.

Participation in group activity enables the individual to experience a number of benefits. There is a stronger sense of being able to exert control over events and a better knowledge of the environment to be controlled. As the group gets close to its desired objective, so enthusiasm, motivation, and excitement increases. The individual feels both competent and confident—he or she has succeeded in making things happen. There is a great sense of achievement.

Participation, then, assists self-development and increases knowledge. It makes the individual sensitive to potential problems and to the reasons for their occurrence.

The opposite to feelings of control are feelings of helplessness. The individual sees himself or herself as a passive victim, unable to influence events which are going to have a dramatic impact on work and life.

The cynical manager may now ask: 'What difference does it make how things get done as long as they get done?' The experience of designing XSEL suggests that there will be a number of differences. A participative approach means that the finished product is likely to be different, and the emotional response to the finished product is also likely to be different. In both instances the result may be better from the company perspective than would otherwise have been achieved.

Conclusions

Designing an expert system is a difficult and complex process. It requires the acquisition of new knowledge, the completion of a pioneering task, people working productively as members of a design group, and the generation of external support for the new system. All of these activities will be taking place simultaneously, although the emphasis may be different at each stage of the design process.

While handling these activities the design-group members will be engaged in an individual and group development process in which there is a progression from uncertainty—'what do we do and how do we do it?'—through increasing knowledge and competence, to maturity and confidence in their ability to tackle and solve problems.

Given the benefits of a participative approach, the interesting question is: 'Why is it not used more often?' Many companies say that they do involve the future users of new systems in their design, but closer investigation can show that this goes no deeper than an occasional communication or meeting to tell the users what is going to happen. Few companies use the more fundamental approach to participative design that DEC has found to be successful.

Alan Fox (1974) argues that this kind of participation requires 'high' trust relationships between management and employees, and this may be a factor. There may also be a reluctance on the part of technical experts to share the design task with the user. They may believe that their legitimacy depends on their not doing so. They are there to do, not to teach or involve.

Nevertheless, it is becoming increasingly difficult to keep the user at a distance and build good, acceptable systems. The XSEL User Design Group in DEC became convinced that the participative process which contributed to its design also contributed to its operational success. The message of this paper is that for design to be successful, means may be more important than ends.

References

Beer, S. (1981), *The Brain of the Firm*, Chichester: Wiley.

Bion, W. R. (1961), *Experiences in Groups*, London: Tavistock.

Burnand, G. (1982), *Via Focal Problems*, London: Leadership Ltd.

Fox, A. (1974), *Man Mismanagement*, London: Hutchinson.

Macoby, M. (1976), *The Gamesman*, New York: Simon & Schuster.

Miller, S. (1980), 'Why Having Control Reduces Stress', in J. Garber and P. Seligman (eds.), *Human Helplessness*, London: Academic Press.

Mumford, E. (1981), *Designing Human Systems*, Manchester: Manchester Business School.

—— (1986), *Using Computers for Business Success*, Manchester: Manchester Business School.

Schein, E. (1988), *Process Consultation*, Reading, Mass.: Addison-Wesley.

Weinberg, G. (1985), *The Secrets of Consulting*, New York: Dorset House.

SECTION V

FOREWORD

Perhaps the most striking and emotional issue in information management in the early 1990s has been the question of outsourcing IT activities. Large outsourcing deals in both the USA and UK have legitimized the practice in minds of several CEOs and put it on the agendas of CIOs. Equally, there have been smaller-scale horror stories of what can go wrong with 'unthinking' outsourcing. Lacity, Willcocks, and Feeny draw on their collective research on both sides of the Atlantic to write a managerial chapter on outsourcing strategy. They propose a framework for decision-making which breaks through some of the simplistic policy and practice rhetoric heard in organizations today. This framework may not have all the answers but it does provide a potentially valuable set of questions to avoid mishaps, to assess IS in the organization and to be more astute in sourcing decisions. It also offers more precise language and terminology in this very contemporary area of organizational challenge.

One idea which has caught on in some organizations is the development of 'hybrid managers' to help bridge the specialist activities of the IS function, whatever its future, with the business at large. Skyrme's chapter is an enthusiastic analysis of, and call for, hybrid managers. He inventories requisite skills and, learning from the experience of a sample of organizations who have pioneered the concept, suggests how hybrids can be developed.

If all Skyrme's ingredients are summated, it would seem that organization development and management development programmes on a grand scale are required. Perhaps all that this represents is putting professional human resource management into IS. There are some hints in the chapter that this can benefit the business beyond the intended goal of building bridges between IT and the business. Whatever a hybrid manager is, and whether or not it is a good label, the competences suggested may well be necessary for all managers in the information era.

Certainly some of the attributes of 'hybrids' are called for in the next chapter, by Couger. Here the driving force is the shift of information systems capabilities and responsibilities towards users. Couger sees this as the concern with wider domains of information processing as well as the growth of end-user computing. It was apparent in the late 1980s, at least in the UK, that often over 50 per cent of IT expenditure was in the hands of users. By 1994 we observe the phenomenon of 'power users', non-IT personnel who can design, develop, and operate their own information systems with scant help from the IT specialists.

Couger, who orginally wrote this chapter at the turn of the decade, posits three scenarios for the IS department as technology and applications become more dispersed. He then suggests the required changes in roles, skills, interests, and experience of IS personnel. This allows him to summarize for us the characteristics of the 'typical' IT professional as discovered in his many psychometric studies of programmers and analysts around the world. It becomes clear, in the new scenarios he paints, that many IS personnel and their managers will have to 'change their spots'. It is interesting to read this chapter alongside that by Willcocks and Fitzgerald on the 'residual organization', a construct triggered by outsourcing. Interpret the two and the agenda for change, in the IS Department, appears substantial.

Any organizational development of this sort in the information management domain is likely to be led by the IT director. Commonly known as the CIO, or *chief information officer*, this role began to be investigated in the 1990s. Prior work was largely speculative. The chapter in this volume by Earl is based on a comparative study of ten CIOs who had survived in the role and ten who had not. This 'discriminant analysis' produced ten possible 'critical survival factors' for CIOs. Subsequent work (Earl and Feeny 1994) argued that the abilities or actions of the CIO are crucial in ensuring that IT adds value to organizations. The survival factors suggest some of the requisite attributes.

Earl then goes on to speculate how the demands on the CIO will change into the next millenium. He argues that the job is unlikely to become easier. Even in a 'residual IS function', the challenges would appear to be many and diverse.

The final chapter in this volume is offered as an integrating denouement. The editor develops a framework first proposed in a more primitive mode in the predecessor to this volume (Earl 1988). Its purpose is to help analyse and guide the integration of IS with the organization. Dubbed the 'organizational fit framework', it is perhaps an alternative or complement to the Strategic Alignment Model of Henderson and Venkatraman (1993). Somewhat more pragmatic, it builds on Earl's (1989) delineation of IS, IT, and IM strategies and examines not only the linkages between these three constructs but also with the organization's business strategy set. It is labelled the 'organizational fit framework' because understanding the characteristics of the organization is seen as the starting-point. Information strategies can only be made and implemented by and through the organization. For this reason, it is hoped that the chapter provides a fitting epilogue to *Information Management: The Organizational Dimension*.

References

Earl, M. J. (1988), *Information Management: The Strategic Dimension*, Oxford: Oxford University Press.

—— (1989) *Management Strategies for Information Technology*, Hemel Hempstead: Prentice-Hall.

—— and Feeny, D. F. (1994), 'Is Your CIO Adding Value?', *Sloan Management Review* (Spring).

Henderson, J. C., and Venkatraman, N. (1993), 'Strategic Alignment: Leveraging Information Technology for Transforming Organizations', *IBM Systems Journal*, vol. 32, no. 1, pp. 4–16.

20

Sourcing Information Technology Capability: A Framework for Decision-Making

MARY C. LACITY, LESLIE P. WILLCOCKS, AND DAVID F. FEENY

Introduction

In the years since Eastman Kodak in 1989 announced that it was outsourcing its entire IT function, an important change has taken place in the sourcing of IT activity. Most visibly, senior executives of other Fortune 500 companies have followed Kodak's example and signed long-term contracts worth hundreds of millions of dollars with IT outsourcing 'partners'. Examples include Continental Airlines, Continental Bank, Enron, First City, General Dynamics, McDonell Douglas, and Xerox (for details see Ambrosio 1991; Hamilton 1989; Hopper 1990; Huber 1993; Mehler 1992). In the UK, large organizations such as British Aerospace, BP Exploration, the Inland Revenue, and Philips Electronics have followed suit (see Willcocks and Fitzgerald 1994). CIOs and other prominent members of the IT community have responded with warnings of the dangers of surrendering management control of a 'strategic asset' (Bergstrom 1991; Buck-Lew 1992; Ganz 1990; Krass 1990). In many cases, these predictions have proved valid, with 'strategic partnerships' experiencing severe problems. Some companies have paid out huge sums to extricate themselves from contracts and rebuild their in-house capability (for a discussion see Lacity and Hirschheim 1993a and Willcocks 1995). On the other hand, CIOs who have adamantly refused to deal with outsourcing vendors have met personal misfortune when their own organizations have failed to demonstrate value for money. These high-profile events have tended to obscure the real phenomenon, a significant and irreversible move to what we call the selective sourcing of IT activity. Our findings suggest that the key question for executives is not 'should we outsource IT?', but rather: '*where* and *how* can we take advantage of the developing market for IT services?'

During two three-year research programmes in the USA and Europe, we have created and tracked in-depth case studies of IT sourcing in more than forty medium-sized and large companies and public-sector bodies. Full details of the case study findings can be found in Lacity and Hirschheim, (1993*a*) and Willcocks and Fitzgerald (1994).[1] We conducted nearly 150 interviews with business executives, chief information officers, outsourcing consultants, and vendor account managers. Our case study sample includes large and small organizations across many sectors—airlines, banking, chemicals, electronics, food manufacturing, government, petroleum, retail, and utilities. These organizations represent a spectrum of sourcing decisions. Some companies signed ten-year, multi-billion dollar contracts for the provision of all IT services. Others opted for short-term deals which cover only a subset of IT activities. Around a quarter rejected external bids in favour of in-house IT provision. Of these companies, several achieved substantial improvement in the internal service, while the remainder experienced little or no change for the better.

Looking across these case studies, two general findings stand out. First, unsuccessful outcomes were associated with an extreme choice of either total outsourcing or total in-house provision. Secondly, successful outcomes were based upon:

- careful selection of which IT activities to outsource;
- a rigorous process of evaluation and vendor selection;
- thoughtful tailoring of contract terms and duration;
- active and detailed management of the vendor relationship.

The present chapter addresses primarily the first issue. We have reported elsewhere on our findings in the other three areas (see Fitzgerald and Willcocks 1994; Lacity and Hirschheim 1993*b*; Willcocks *et al.* 1995). Here we reflect on and utilize the case study findings in order to develop a decision-making framework to guide the selective sourcing of IT activity.

Illustrative Outsourcing Experiences

Before developing the framework, it is useful to look in detail at some illustrative examples of ways in which organizations have been choosing to utilize the external market for IT products and services. This will provide a springboard for the ensuing discussion. We have been finding a large diversity both in types of sourcing arrangement and also in outcomes. Consider the following five case histories, drawn from our research base.

1. The CEO from a diversified services company decided to outsource

[1] The US research study was carried out by Mary Lacity together with Rudi Hirschheim, Professor at the University of Houston. The European study was carried out by Leslie Willcocks and Guy Fitzgerald, Cable and Wireless Professor of Business Information Systems at Birkbeck College, University of London. We acknowledge the significant contribution that our colleagues Rudi Hirschheim and Guy Fitzgerald have made to the research base and thinking on which this chapter is based.

his entire IT department after being approached by a vendor. The vendor presented itself as a 'partner' that would reduce the CEO's IT costs by 20 per cent during a ten-year period. After a few high-level meetings, the CEO declared 'let's make a marriage.' Contract negotiations were swift, as each side was anxious to commence the relationship. Internal lawyers quickly constructed a fixed-fee contract which stipulates that the vendor will provide the same service levels that the internal IT department provided in 1988. Even though the CEO and vendor agreed that the relationship would be managed as a 'partnership', the contract motivated the vendor to maximize their own profits, primarily by charging excess fees and reducing service levels. For example, the first month into the contract the vendor sent an enormous 'excess' bill for services the CEO assumed were covered in the contract. Service levels fell—for example, the vendor took seventeen working days to provide users with logon IDs or access to data sets. The vendor instituted a virtual monopoly—the company could allegedly buy software elsewhere, but the vendor would not allow anyone but vendor employees directly to access the data centre. Thus, when the company hired another software house to build an application, the vendor argued that the system could not be implemented without giving the maintenance contract to the outsourcing vendor. The business unit leaders became so frustrated they used their discretionary funds to procure alternative IT solutions in order to circumvent the outsourcing contract. This case provides an example of relative failure through what we would call 'total' outsourcing, with the company also experiencing major problems with the concept of 'partnership'.

2. Senior executives from an equipment manufacturer outsourced the conversion to a totally new operating environment. They reasoned that the vendor was in a better position to perform the conversion and to provide continued management after installation. In addition, senior management viewed IT as a commodity, further suggesting that outsourcing would enable them to focus on 'core' activities. They soon discovered that it was unwise to outsource what they did not understand because they could not evaluate vendor performance. For four years participants questioned the vendor about the escalating costs of IT. When the vendor provided justifications for the expense, participants lacked the technical knowledge to validate the response. When IT costs rose to 4 per cent of sales, participants terminated the contract early and brought the environment back in-house. IT costs subsequently dropped to $1\frac{1}{2}$ per cent of sales. This company also provides an example of a 'total' outsourcing failure, with the lack of success this time rooted in the company outsourcing what they did not understand.

3. Senior management in a major US bank placed every department under severe pressure to cut headcount and save cost. The European arm had already done much to rationalize and consolidate data-centres,

development, and maintenance. In five years IT costs dropped from $35 to $20 million. In 1992 senior managers decided to outsource data-centre operations, but not application development or networks. The objective was to save a further $5 million a year. At this stage management felt that applications development was too critical to outsource and networks too difficult to outsource. As of 1994 the contract was deemed successful, with anticipated cost savings being achieved. The vendor achieved such savings by cutting down on hardware, consolidating maintenance agreements, and reducing the headcount. The vendor provided a lower remuneration package to the seventy-one transferred staff. The client was responsible for generous redundancy terms. There were economies of scale in including the data-centre in the vendor's established management and support infrastructure. A large up-front payment to the vendor also made a lower price possible. The bank monitored performance tightly, though this was found to take up an inordinate amount of management time. A further downside was that vendor profit margins were so slim that it adhered to minimum performance requirements as far as possible. The case provides an example of relative success through what we would call 'selective' outsourcing. However, though the cost-savings targets were being achieved, it was clear that a lot of active management of the vendor needed to be carried out over the life of the contract.

4. Senior executives at a telecommunications company decided to outsource after reading about Kodak's success. They rightfully perceived that the internal IT department was not cost competitive due to a strong labour union which promoted inefficient work practices. In particular, the labour union specified narrow job descriptions which caused excessive manpower. For example, data-centre managers were forbidden to touch the hardware and software, a union manager was required on every shift, and both a manager and a worker were called in for emergencies. Although the IT manager had tried on numerous occasions to negotiate better terms, the strong labour union resisted. Only after the request for proposal attracted two external bids did the labour union agree to allow the internal IT department to include revised union rules in their internal bid—the labour union either had to succumb or risk losing the entire work-site. The internal IT subsequently reduced headcount by 46 per cent. The case provides an example of relative success through what we would call 'outsourcing challenge'. Here outsourcing provided a lever: the threat of outsourcing served to empower the internal IT department to reduce costs.

5. An IT manager from a chemicals company initiated an outsourcing evaluation when he realized users were buying PC-based solutions without consulting him. Although his superiors were not cognizant of the situation, he felt his contribution to the company would come into question. He delegated the evaluation process to his subordinates, who would potentially lose their jobs if IT was outsourced. They created a request for

proposal and invited external bids from several small outsourcing vendors. Of the three vendors that submitted bids, only one indicated a moderate savings of 7 per cent. The IT manager believed that the outsourcing evaluation confirmed that current IT costs were not unreasonable, so he continued to manage IT in the same manner. Senior executives, however, questioned the validity of the evaluation and remained unconvinced of the value they received from IT expenditures. Six months after the evaluation the IT manager was fired and replaced with a manager with an accounting background. The case provides an example of relative failure through 'outsourcing challenge'. The outsourcing evaluation turned out to be merely a political process, with dire consequences for the IT manager.

It is clear from these case studies that those charged with making IT sourcing decisions in organizations are faced with a range of factors and circumstances in an environment of increasingly uncertain and rapid technological and business change. None of this makes decision-making for effective outcomes easy. However, the major difficulties tended to be experienced in the organizations that outsourced most of their IT assets and services.

Of the fourteen organizations that chose what we call the 'total outsourcing' route (more than 80 per cent of the formal IT budget spent on contracting-out IT services), five admitted experiencing serious difficulty. Some obvious lessons emerged from the 'total outsourcing' experiences. We found that in practice structural features of the IT services market, of the vendor–client relationship, and of the client organization's position after outsourcing favoured vendor opportunism rather than customer purchasing power. While the most obvious protection against vendor opportunism is a comprehensive requirements statement enshrined in a contract, we found full contractual protection particularly difficult to achieve in 'total outsourcing' situations. We also found the alternative 'strategic partner' type of arrangements suggested by Henderson (1990) also difficult to achieve and sustain (Lacity and Hirschheim 1993*a*; Willcocks 1995). Furthermore, the motive for 'total outsourcing' was often to eliminate a burdensome in-house IT function or deal with serious financial problems. In such cases important aspects of the IT service were often defined as 'commodity' and outsourced in an unbundled package, and complex business, technical, and economic factors were treated in an undifferentiated manner.

Leaving IT entirely in-house could also be problematic, mainly due to failure to unbundle IT-based activities and effectively compare and contrast in-house service with what could be provided by the market. However, an interesting finding was that in our sample on seventeen occasions the bid of an internal IT department was formally evaluated as superior to the bids of external vendors that had access to the best resources and scale economies. The reasons for this will be considered later in the chapter. It did emerge, however, that vendor economies of scale have been oversold. It was also clear that internal IT departments start with a potentially significant price advantage because of external vendors' need to generate a profit. Our evidence suggests that 'in-house' should always be an option but never a policy. Our case study 'outsourcing challenge' successes achieved cost savings not because they remained 'in-house', but because an outsourcing challenge highlighted the further opportunities for savings. But both external and internal circumstances change, and so, therefore, can the case for outsourcing.

In comparison, of sixty-three 'selective outsourcing' decisions (in twenty different case study organizations), forty-three were characterized by interviewees as 'successful' and a further thirteen as 'relatively successful'. While selective outsourcing was hardly problem-free this represents a strikingly higher level of satisfaction than that encountered in the 'total outsourcing' organizations. Compared to those that totally outsourced IT, 'selective outsourcing' organizations seemed to have a better ability to absorb and overcome contract performance difficulties. They also demonstrated a greater retention of bargaining power, and also found greater opportunities for additional cost savings. They also showed more insight than their peers in both the other groups in identifying non-cost benefits from outsourcing. Rather than debate whether IT as a whole was a core or non-core activity for the host organization, they disaggregated IT activity and differentiated between areas in which in-house resources could distinctly add value, and areas of 'non-problematic' IT activity which could be outsourced to vendors. They also took opportunities to use the external market on a short-term basis, for example, to maintain systems based on old technologies so as to buy time to create a new technology platform.

How can we make sense of this rich set of findings? And what guidelines can be offered to those charged with making IT sourcing decisions? It became clear that selective outsourcing most often offers a middle way towards effective sourcing of IT. However, even those that had selectively outsourced IT sometimes found they had chosen the wrong activity to outsource, or the wrong contractual relationship for their needs, or that anticipated cost savings and benefits failed to materialize. We now develop in detail a decision-framework to assist in the development of a viable IT sourcing strategy. First, we outline the distinctive features of IT sourcing that need to be considered before a decision can be entered into. Then we provide a framework for analysing the significant business factors that affect IT sourcing decision.

The Distinctive Features of IT Sourcing

Business has long operated on the premiss that many necessary activities are properly and beneficially contracted to external and specialist suppliers.

In recent years this idea has been reinforced by exhortations to focus in-house resources on core activities, to construct the networked organization or the hollow corporation (Drucker 1991; Prahalad and Hamel 1991; Quinn 1992; Quinn *et al.* 1990). If activities as diverse in nature and impact as component manufacturing, distribution, and advertising are routinely con-tracted out, why does IT outsourcing require special attention and treat-ment? Our work identifies four respects in which the IT field is distinctive. An understanding of these is the basis for a selective and successful sourcing strategy.

First, most businesses have by now invested in a wide variety of IT applications. Some IT activities uniquely enable business operations and management processes, for example, on-line reservation systems. Other IT activities merely provide standard functions common in most organizations, such as electronic mail. Rather than treating IT as a single homogenous function, we urge senior executives to analyse the *Business Factors* which identify the role of each major strand of IT activity. They are then able to protect and nurture those activities on which the future of the business may depend.

Secondly, IT capability continues to develop at an often-bewildering rate. In emerging areas of IT use, the business cannot generally predict its future needs with the precision required by most forms of contract. We shall describe how *Technical Factors* guide the choice of supply source, and the form of supply arrangements.

Thirdly, no simple basis for judging the economics of IT activity exists (see Bergstrom 1991 and Willcocks *et al.* 1995 for a full discussion). Although large operations lead to economies of scale for some IT activities, such as mainframe operations, small-scale operations for other IT activities, such as the development of new systems, often leads to better price perform-ance. In some cases companies find that technically outdated—but oper-ationally robust—technology is cheaper still. And our evidence suggests that IT management processes may have a greater influence on costs than size of operation or any particular choice of technology. Hence man-agement cannot assume that external vendors will enjoy scale or scope advantages. Management, therefore, must assess a range of *Economic Fac-tors* to arrive at sourcing decisions.

Figure 20.1 draws together these first three factors, and represents the first level of our selective sourcing framework. But the fourth and most important distinctive feature of IT sourcing is the scale of switching costs. In most areas of business operation, management can protect itself against poor sourcing decisions in a number of straightforward ways—by dual sourcing of component supply, annual contract review of its advertis-ing agency, and so on. These techniques, however, are largely ineffective for IT. The costs of re-sourcing an IT activity from in-house to external, or from one vendor to another, are usually considerable and potentially

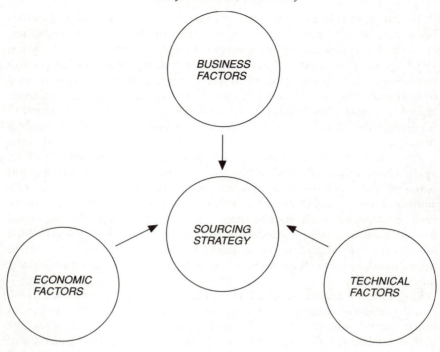

Fig. 20.1. *Selective sourcing factors*

massive. Vendors understand and may exploit this. Analysis of the Business, Technical, and Economic Factors protects the organization against the risk of enforced switching costs, by identifying the type of supplier and style of relationship appropriate to each major area of IT activity.

We now expand the basic framework of Figure 20.1 by proposing and explaining a decision matrix for each set of factors in turn. These matrices seek to capture the key learning from our research case studies. They aim to represent a structure for management discussion and decision, not a mechanistic methodology. If business and IT executives can agree how to map their IT activities onto these matrices, the framework provides a guide towards an effective sourcing strategy.

Making Sourcing Decisions: The Business Factors

Conventional wisdom suggests that IT activities which the business considers 'strategic' or 'core' should remain in-house, while 'non-strategic' or 'non-core' activities are outsourced (see, for example, McFarlan and Nolan 1993; Quinn and Hilmer 1994). Our research suggests that this delineation

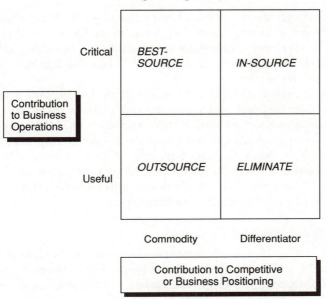

Fig. 20.2. *The business factors matrix*

is too simplistic. We recommend that IT activities are positioned against two separate dimensions of business contribution: competitive position and business operations.

Contribution to Competitive Position

IT activities can be divided between 'commodities' and 'differentiators', depending on their expected contribution to the business's positioning in the market-place.

An IT activity will be a commodity if it is not expected to help distinguish the business from its key competitors. In marketing language it is seen as a qualifier rather than an order winner. While the activity must meet certain performance criteria, there is no reward for over-performance—indeed, high performance will be a negative factor if it implies an increase in costs. The objective for any commodity activity should be to meet the required threshold level of performance at minimum cost. Examples of IT activities which are likely to be classified as commodities are development and operation of the firm's basic administrative systems, or provision of data-centre services.

Differentiators, on the other hand, equate to potential order winners, the IT activities that are expected to help the business achieve competitive advantage. High performance of correctly identified differentiators will be rewarded by increased revenue. Hence the objective for a differentiator activity should be to outperform key competitors. Examples of IT activities that may be classified as differentiators include systems which help reduce time-to-market or those which underpin the introduction of a new value-added customer service.

Over time, established differentiators will tend to become commodities as competitors respond and customer expectations grow. For example, the first banks to adopt automatic teller machines (ATM) enjoyed a short-term competitive advantage, but competitors quickly responded. As a result, ATMs have become a necessary cost of doing business. Meanwhile, firms will continue to search for the next set of differentiators. The task of classifying IT activities as commodities or differentiators requires insightful analysis of the competitive market-place.

Contribution to Business Operations

While the competitive-position dimension questions the *type* of contribution made by an IT activity, the business-operations dimension considers the *extent* of that contribution. The business-operations dimension therefore represents more of a continuum, with the labels 'critical' and 'useful' signalling extremes rather than two discrete categories. Hopefully, all IT activities will be considered at least 'useful' in the sense that the business operates better because they exist. But a number of IT activities will properly be classified as 'critical' because the basic operations of the business are now highly dependent upon them. For example, a petroleum refining business classifies its process control systems as critical because of the extent of their impact on quality, safety, and productivity. But the company views its employee scheduling system as merely useful, making an incremental contribution to productivity, but not central to their capital intensive business. The classification of IT activities along the business-operations dimension requires an understanding of where IT provides leverage in the business structure.

Mapping an IT activity's contribution to competitive position and business operations results in a preliminary diagnosis of which IT activities are candidates for outsourcing. But the first potential benefit of the mapping process is to surface different perspectives on the contribution being made. Corporate business executives quite commonly assess as merely 'useful' what their IT management are convinced is 'critical'. Business unit executives may take a territorial approach, classifying their own IT systems as 'differentiators' rather than 'commodities'. The matrix can be used to focus and refine the views of the various stakeholders by reaching a consensus on which IT activities fall into each of four categories:

'Critical-differentiators' *IT activities which are not only critical to business operations, but also help to distinguish the business from its competitors.* A European

ferry company considers its reservation and check-in systems to be 'critical-differentiators'. The company has similar ships to those of its main rival and operates from the same major ports across the English Channel between Britain and France. Its competitive strategy is to differentiate through service, including the speed and ease with which passengers and their cars complete the boarding process. Information systems are instrumental in constantly making innovations in this respect. While the company outsources a number of its IT activities, the reservation and check-in systems are retained in-house. This protects their ideas and expertise and enables rapid innovation.

In some parallel situations, we have seen organizations boosting their in-house IT capability by bringing in specialists from an external vendor. However, these 'outsiders' work alongside in-house people, under the company's own management—making this an 'in-sourced' solution.

'Critical-commodities' IT activities that are critical to business operations but fail to distinguish the business from competitors. A major airline views its IT systems which support aircraft maintenance as 'critical-commodities'. Like its rivals, the airline must maintain its fleet to specification or face very serious consequences. However, the maintenance activity and supporting systems respond to the mandated requirements of the manufacturers and regulatory authorities. The airline would receive no benefit from over-performance. Although the airline has not yet outsourced these systems, it is in principle prepared to do so. Because of the risks involved for the business, such a decision would be based on clear evidence that an external vendor could meet stringent requirements for quality and responsiveness, as well as offer a low price. The policy is 'best source', not cheapest source. A more standard 'critical-commodity', such as the provision of an emergency/standby computer centre, is commonly outsourced by businesses because a number of high-quality vendors are available.

'Useful-commodities' The myriad IT activities that provide incremental benefits to the business, but fail to distinguish it from competitors. In our experience, most businesses volunteer payroll and benefit systems as the first examples of 'useful-commodities'. We have met exceptions. A security guarding firm saw their payroll system as a differentiator because on-time payment attracted the better-quality staff in their industry, leading to superior customer service. Even 'useful-commodities' must be carefully identified as a function of business circumstances.

'Useful-commodities' are the prime candidates for outsourcing. External vendors are likely to have achieved low costs and prices through standardization. The business makes further gains if it can free up internal management time to focus on more critical activity. But the expectation of outsourcing must be validated through analysis of the technical and economic factors.

'Useful-differentiators' IT activities that differentiate the business from competitors, but in a way that is not critical to business success. 'Useful-differentiators' should not exist, but we have found that they frequently do. One reason is that the IT function is sometimes isolated from the business and subsequently pursues its own agenda. For example, the IT function of a paint manufacturer created a system that precisely matched a paint formulation to a customer's colour sample. IT managers envisioned that the system would create competitive advantage by meeting customers' wishes that paint should match their home furnishings. However, senior management had established the company's strategy as colour innovation. They failed to market the system because it ran counter to their strategy, and the system became an expensive and ineffective distraction. The system was eventually eliminated.

A more common reason for the creation of 'useful-differentiators' is that a potential commodity has been extensively reworked to reflect 'how we are different' or to incorporate the 'nice-to-haves'. This was an extensive phenomenon in one electronics company, resulting in very problematic and high-cost software maintenance. The CIO of the company has now implemented a policy requiring that all needs for 'useful' systems be met through standard software packages, with strict limits to customization. In effect, he has eliminated the 'useful-differentiators' by turning them into 'useful-commodities' based on outsourced software.

In summary, the Business Factors Matrix guides policy on the *source* of supply, based on an IT activity's role within the business. But it is important to be clear about exactly what the sourcing options are. We now proceed to detail the sourcing options for IT.

Clarifying Sourcing Options

Having considered the business factors that need to influence IT sourcing decisions, we need to clarify in more detail what sourcing options are available to organizations. As we outlined earlier, high switching costs are an important feature of the IT services industry. The existence of these switching costs puts vendors in a strong bargaining position whenever the business seeks to clarify or change its requirements. Many companies in our research sought to rise above these difficulties by selecting vendors as 'strategic partners'. All too often this approach to the IT sourcing relationship proved less than helpful. There is a considerable literature on such 'strategic partnerships' in the IT-outsourcing context, most of it positive, though some commentators—from experience or research—qualify this picture or attempt to develop a basis for more-effective partnering practice (see Henderson 1990; Hopper 1990; Huber 1993; Moad 1993; Willcocks 1995). One IT director in a major retail and distribution company provided a typical opinion amongst many of our case study organizations: 'There is a lot of rubbish talked about partnerships . . . I think it's nice to work together but its never a true partnership, unless you have a joint financial venture.'

In most of the cases we investigated, viewing vendors as 'partners' prompted companies to sign flimsy contracts, reasoning that the vendor would flexibly adapt to changes under the spirit and trust of 'partnership'. In actuality, vendors deferred to the original contract—which strongly favoured the vendor—to address changes. We only found two arrangements in which the language of 'strategic partnership' was justified. Even in these cases, detailed contracts specify the exact nature of the partnership by defining shared goals, such as profits generated from the sale of jointly developed software. Thus, the common experience was that vendors must be managed against contracts that enable the business to leverage its future bargaining position and to counterbalance the inherent disadvantage of switching costs. As one systems director put it: 'Basically we negotiated a tight contract and then put it to one side, which was the intention, so that we could run the thing as a partnership. But you've got to be protected.'

To help clarify the variety of contracting options, we offer a structure and language to help companies think through the contracting process. Our case study organizations expressed some frustration over the terms 'outsourcing' and 'insourcing'. In many ways, 'outsourcing' is not a new concept. External providers such as service bureaux, facilities management companies, contract programmers, and consulting firms have been used since the early days of data processing. Equally confusing was the term 'insourcing', which was used to describe a variety of sourcing options, such as managing and delivering IT services solely through the in-house function, bringing previously outsourced activities back in-house, or buying-in vendor resources but managing them internally. Figure 20.3 provides a consistent set of concepts for thinking through the IT sourcing options. It suggests that a wide variety of contracting strategies can be used to manage vendors, from buying in resources as part of an in-house team, to contracting out the entire delivery of an IT activity. In general, participants' contracts can be categorized based on two dimensions: purchasing style and purchasing focus.

We identify two purchasing styles: transaction or relationship. The transaction style involves one-off contracts with enough detail to serve as the original reference document. The relationship style involves less detailed, incentive-based contracts based on the expectation that customer and vendor will do business over many years.

We identify two purchasing focus options: resource or result. With a resource option, companies buy-in vendor resources, such as hardware, software, or expertise, but self-manage the delivery of the IT activity. With a result option, vendors manage the delivery of the IT activity to provide the company with the specified results.

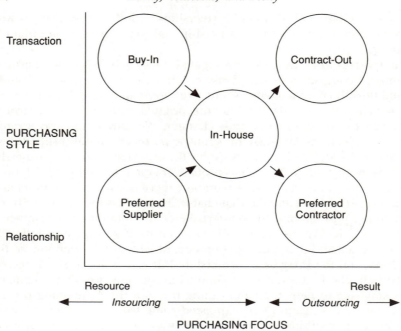

Fig. 20.3. *Information technology—the sourcing option*

Combining purchasing style and focus, four distinct ways of using the external IT market emerge, which we label 'buy-in', 'contract-out', 'preferred supplier', and 'preferred contractor'.

With a *buy-in* strategy, companies buy vendor resources to meet a temporary resource need, such as the need for programmers in the latter stages of a new development project. In these cases, companies are often unsure of the exact hours needed to complete the coding, so they sign contracts that specify the skills required and *per diem* cost per person.

With a *contract-out* strategy, the vendor becomes responsible for delivering the result of the IT activity. This strategy is most successful when the companies can clearly define their needs in an airtight contract. The contract must be complete because it will serve as original reference to manage the vendor (see Lacity and Hirschheim 1993*a*; Richmond *et al.* 1992). For example, companies often use a contract-out strategy to outsource data-centre operations. In these contracts, precise service levels, service level measures, escalation procedures for missed measures, cash penalties for non-performance, adjustments for volume increases or decreases, and termination clauses are clearly specified.

With a *preferred supplier* strategy, companies intend to develop a close relationship with a vendor in order to access their resources for ongoing IT activities. The relationship is managed with an incentive-based contract that defines *complementary* goals.

For example, one company engaged a preferred supplier to provide contract programmers whenever they were needed. The contract ensured complementary goals—the participant received a volume discount in exchange for not going out to tender when programmers were needed. The vendor was motivated to perform because they relied on a steady stream of revenue.

With a *preferred contractor* strategy, companies intend to engage in a relationship with the vendor to help mediate risk. The vendor is responsible for the management and delivery of an IT activity. To ensure vendor performance, the company tries to construct an incentive-based contract that ensures *shared* goals. For example, when one company decided to reduce costs by outsourcing data-centre operations and support of existing systems, they mediated risk by entering into a joint venture with a software house. By establishing a jointly owned company, they created shared goals which prevented vendor opportunism.

There remains, in Figure 20.3, the *in-house* arrangement. We found this option having a critical role to play even when organizations were spending over 80 per cent of the IT budget on contracting out or on preferred contractors. All forms of contract run larger risks if certain capabilities are not retained in-house:

- ability to track, assess, and interpret changing IT capability, and relate this to the needs of the organization;
- ability to work with business management to define the IT requirements successfully over time;
- ability to identify the appropriate ways to use the market, to help specify and manage IT sourcing, and to monitor and manage contractual relations.

We refer to the buy-in, preferred-supplier, and in-house options collectively as *insourcing* options, because in all of them in-house management retain full visibility and control of the IT activity. We refer to the contract-out and preferred-contractor options as *outsourcing* options, because in each of them in-house management pass control of the IT activity to the external vendor.

Having clarified the sourcing options we shall now describe the Technical Factors Matrix that helps to guide policy on the nature of the relationship between the organization and its internal or external IT source.

Making Sourcing Decisions—The Technical Factors

The different options detailed in the last section may present different switching costs. From our research we have identified that it is technical factors that tend to determine the importance of switching costs. In some cases technical factors enable fixed-priced contracts based on fully detailed service requirements. In these cases switching costs are low because many vendors can be substituted in the case of breach of contract. In other cases technical factors prevent companies from fully articulating their IT needs in detailed contracts. Instead, contracts serve as enabling agreements which specify the vendor's responsibilities and rewards as requirements change over time. By specifying complementary or shared goals in the contract, the company minimizes the risk of switching vendors midstream.

The critical task is to select a sourcing option which fits the IT activity in question, based on an analysis of technical factors. We have identified the dominant technical factors to be the technology maturity underlying the IT activity and the extent to which one IT activity is integrated with others within the organization. Together these form the dimensions of our Technology Factors Matrix.

Degree of Technology Maturity

We describe an IT activity as having low technology maturity when the technology itself is new and unstable, when the business has little experience of a technology which may be better established elsewhere, or when the business is embarked on a radically new use of a familiar technology (Feeny *et al.* 1989*a*, *b*). Examples include an organization's first venture into imaging or client-server technologies, or development of a major network to support a new business direction of globalization. In each of these instances, requirements will emerge over time as the organization accumulates experience with the technology. By contrast, we can describe an IT activity as having high technology maturity when it represents well-established use of familiar technology. Mainframe-based data-centre operations and accounting systems will be high-maturity IT activities for most organizations. In these cases the business has conquered the learning curve and reached a point where current requirements are well specified and reasonably stable.

Degree of Technology Integration

IT activities vary considerably in terms of interaction and interdependence. Some activities, such as a desk-top publishing application or a support service for PCs, can usually be managed on a self-contained basis. They have a low degree of technology integration. But a typical production scheduling system has multiple connections with, and dependencies on, other related systems, such as order entry, inventory control, and purchasing. Any changes to the production scheduling system produce potential changes to the related systems and vice versa. This IT activity—and there are many others—has a high degree of technology integration. Any sourcing arrangements for this activity must protect the company's future ability to keep the activity in step with other related activities.

Once again, the resulting matrix (Fig. 20.4) is a device to structure and stimulate discussion between senior business and IT executives. In this case, IT executives may be expected to take a leadership role. But business executives need to understand and agree the positioning of IT activity across the matrix. Otherwise they will be reluctant to accept the consequences for sourcing strategy which are based on the four resulting matrix categories:

Low integration—high maturity   IT activities which are well established in the business and have limited linkages with other activities.

In the simplest case, an IT activity exhibits high technology maturity and low technology integration. The activity is well understood and easily separated out. Switching costs are probably less high than usual for both these reasons. Unless Business and Economic Factors indicate otherwise, the activity can be 'contracted-out' using a detailed service specification and a fixed-price contract.

Among our case studies, a chemicals company successfully contracted out support for personal computers. The IT executive noted that adoption of PCs within the company had been growing rapidly for some time, forcing him into regular and poorly received requests for additional headcount. By outsourcing on a detailed two-year contract, he reduced costs and also avoided further requests for staffing.

Limiting the contract length is an important message in relation to this category. A typical view from our research was that three years was the maximum period for which one could assume requirements would be stable. In a counter-example, a petroleum company signed a ten-year deal to outsource its mainframe operations. Well within that time scale, 'client-server' technology appeared as a more attractive platform for many of their existing systems. The outsourcing contract represented financial barriers to migration. The company found it had three options: break the contract at great expense, pay the vendor high fees to amend the contract, or develop client-server systems outside (and in addition to) the contract.

Low integration—low maturity   IT activities which represent new ventures but have limited linkages with other activities.

Most organizations engage in a few IT activities which have low technology integration and low technology maturity. A pilot application of a new technology is the most common example. The important points here are first, that the company is not yet ready to write a detailed specification and invite vendor bids. The company does not yet understand how best to

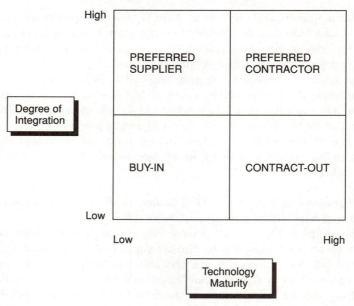

Fig. 20.4. *The technical factors matrix*

apply the new technology within its business context. On the other hand, the company may well benefit from an injection of external expertise to support its voyage of discovery. The recommendation is to 'buy-in' this expertise, but to integrate the external resources into its internal team. The business retains full management control and visibility of the project, capturing as much learning as possible about the technology and its application. The vendor is paid on the basis of resources actually used, and is perhaps offered an incentive bonus which becomes due if the project meets its business goals.

One of our case study companies used this pattern to develop its first 'expert system' application—a discrete system module designed to calculate sales tax for material transfers. A specialist expert systems vendor seconded resources to the in-house team under a 'buy-in' contract. The project was completed successfully, and the in-house IT staff now had the capability to take full charge of the ongoing support and development of the system.

High integration—low maturity   IT activities with strong linkages to other already established ones, but which themselves break new ground in the application of technology.

A more complex situation arises when an IT activity represents a combination of low technology maturity and high technology integration. Although the future shape of the activity is initially uncertain, it will undoubtedly impact upon and require changes to other existing organizational activities. If vendors are selected to play a role in the development of such activities, careful contracting with reliable vendors that understand the business interfaces is required.

A factory automation project at a fragrance and food manufacturer highlighted the difficulties of contracting 'high integration-low maturity' activities. During the course of the project management became aware that the new system had profound implications for the existing systems in almost every other department of the business. The project was contracted to two external vendors which had high levels of expertise in factory automation, but lacked any wider understanding of how the business operated. The project took four years instead of two, cost twice as much as anticipated, and still failed to meet many of its objectives. The company had outsourced the entire project, rather than engage a 'preferred supplier' who worked regularly with the business and who could have brought a holistic approach to the new development.

An alternative example (see Elam and Morrison 1988; Lasher *et al.* 1991) concerns the financial services organization USAA which invested in imaging technology to replace paper records such as customer letters with an electronic file. The company first explored the technology through a discrete R&D project in which they involved a vendor specializing in imaging. Senior executives reached a point at which they were convinced of the benefits of large-scale adoption, but they realized that many of their existing systems would now be affected. At this stage the company turned to its preferred IT supplier, a vendor with a very broad product line, with whom it had worked for many years. Resisting the vendor's instinct to develop a detailed fixed-price agreement, the company set up an enabling, resource-based contract. The project was completed successfully, providing competitive advantage for both the business and its supplier, which had established a reference site for its own imaging products.

High integration—high maturity   IT activities which are well established and understood, but have complex linkages with other activities.

In the final category of high technology integration and high technology maturity we generally find the existing information infrastructure of the business, the operational control systems and databases. Corporate-wide electronic mail services, integrated with other facilities at each work station, might form another example. Because such activities are well established and understood, it is possible to create a detailed specification with a view to outsourcing them. The problem is that changes in other, less mature, activities may drive changes to future specifications. Given inevitably high switching costs, an outsourcing vendor would have a strong bargaining position when negotiating the necessary amendments to the contract.

We therefore recommend a 'preferred contractor' approach for this category, outsourcing only if a vendor is persuaded of long-term benefits beyond the price paid for its services. Such benefits might take the form of an agreed preferred access for the vendor to other work, or the vendor's continuing relationship with a particularly prestigious client.

A large clothing and household goods retailer believes it has set up such an arrangement with one of the biggest outsourcing vendors. In a ten-year deal, the vendor will provide almost all the company's IT services. In addition, the retailer and the vendor will share profits from exploitation elsewhere of the retailers existing and future systems. For example, the vendor has already proposed to market the retailer's data models, which will generate profits for both parties. In the words of one of the directors of the retail business: 'We believe, as they do, that we are working together to make the profit pie bigger rather than just arguing over who gets the biggest piece.' The success of the deal depends on these attitudes being maintained, and on the expectations of a bigger profit pie being achieved.

From their different perspectives, business factor analysis and technical factor analysis identify whether and in what form the outsourcing of an IT activity makes strategic sense. To determine whether outsourcing makes commercial sense, we move to an analysis of economic factors.

Making Sourcing Decisions: The Economic Factors

One of the drivers of many large IT outsourcing deals has been the feeling of the business CEO that: 'This is a specialist area. The main vendors must by now be better at it than we can be, and they must have access to greater economies of scale.' While the assumptions of these CEOs are frequently mistaken, they have correctly identified the two dimensions that determine the economics of IT activity—economies of scale and managerial practices. These two parameters which underpin our framework of analysis in Figure 20.5 require further explanation.

Scale of In-House IT Activity

There are indeed economies of scale in some aspects of IT activity. For example, there is convincing evidence that data-centres begin to reach economies of scale at 150 'MIPS' (processing power equivalent to one large mainframe). However, constant changes in price/performance at every level of hardware—a unit of today's computing power will cost 30 per cent less next year—produces a sort of leap-frog effect in terms of optimal scale. With some IT activities, economies of scale are reached at a small size. For example, small development teams are markedly more productive and successful than larger ones. Thus, the assumption that vendors will always be more economically efficient due to larger size must be thoroughly questioned.

In-House IT Management Practices

A number of management practices can have a major impact on the level of IT costs. They include chargeout mechanisms which motivate business users to manage demand, consolidation of operating centres, standardization of software, automation of IT operations, archiving of inactive data, and employee empowerment to reduce supervision costs. Whether or not these practices are adopted is partly a function of the culture of the in-house IT department. One of those in our research has such a strongly cost-conscious culture that even the most senior IT executives were found working overnight to lay cable, saving the cost of a contractor. Other practice leaders have generated a marketing culture which also leads to cost efficiency. The CIO of a petroleum company sells 10 per cent of his capacity to external customers for this purpose. Through competition with external vendors, his staff has developed a focus on customer service and price which benefits in-house as well as external customers. On the other hand, we found many laggard IT departments which have not implemented management practices known to improve cost efficiency. As we shall describe, this was sometimes due to constraints imposed by the business.

Mapping IT activity onto the economic factors matrix requires an understanding of external standards and practice. Many of the companies in our research used the services of specialist IT benchmarking businesses, which have accumulated databases of performance and practice in hundreds of companies. Use of the matrix in Figure 20.5 leads to four possible conditions.

Practice laggard—subcritical scale   IT activities are poorly managed and are on a scale which is known to be inefficient.

When in-house scale is subcritical and management practices are lagging external comparators, a business can often achieve rapid improvements through *outsourcing*. For example, the incoming senior management of an electric supply company found they had inherited a fragmented IT operation whose staff had conspicuously weak technical skills. In the two years after they outsourced the bulk of IT activity costs fell by 30 per cent while service improved significantly.

But reference to business and technical factors may suggest the need to see outsourcing as a step within a longer-term strategy. Another of our case study companies set up a health-care insurance business in 1990. Lacking scale and experience in IT, they contracted for all their systems and operational support from an external vendor. Under the agreement,

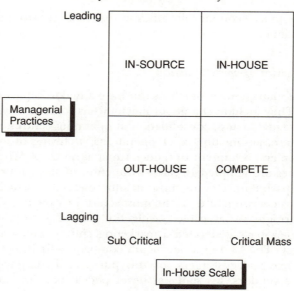

Fig. 20.5. *The economic factors matrix*

however, the vendor's role was steadily reduced. After three years the business had acquired critical mass and a good understanding of successful IT management practices. The company took back full control of the IT activities which it saw as critical to its future business operations.

Practice laggard—critical scale IT activities are on a scale which enables efficiency, but in place management practices lead to poor results.

When an in-house IT function with inherent scale advantages fails to exploit them through good management practices, senior executives often look to external vendors. If IT management plead for a change to improve, senior executives ask: 'If you could reduce costs, why haven't you done so already?' The frequent answer, according to our research companies, is that previous attempts to reduce costs have been thwarted by the IT function's lack of power, by inertia in the business organizations, or by outright user sabotage. Once senior executives threaten IT outsourcing, users realize that the practices they have been resisting will be implemented—either by an external vendor or the in-house staff. Because most users prefer the familiar in-house staff over unknown vendors, they generally allow IT management to submit an internal bid based on adoption of efficient practices.

The experiences of a large food manufacturer illustrate the point. Senior executives perceived that IT costs were too high and resolved to outsource the large corporate data-centre. The IT executive had previously tried but failed to reduce costs by persuading a large number of product-based business units to agree on a standard set of software. Despite his efforts, each business unit insisted on keeping their own operating systems, utilities, report generators, electronic mail, statistical packages, and spreadsheet packages. The chargeback system exacerbated the problem by putting software costs into overheads, so that if a business unit introduced a new software package the cost was spread across all business units. But when senior executives went out to tender, the in-house IT function beat off two external vendors. Their winning low-cost bid was based on elimination of the redundant software and of the consequent excess services and support staff. Within three years the in-house IT function reduced costs by 45 per cent.

The strong message from our research is that if IT activity falls in this category, senior management should look for the 'best source' based on competitive bids from external vendors and the in-house function. If executives compare vendor prices only against current IT costs, they are likely to invite vendors to benefit from 'picking the low lying fruit'. So the IT function should be asked to *compete*.

Practice leaders—critical scale IT activities are well managed and operating at above the minimum efficient scale.

When an in-house function achieves critical mass and a leadership position in management practices, outsourcing offers no long-term economic benefits. IT activities can remain 'in-house'. However, short-term incentives have prompted some companies with excellent IT functions to outsource. For example, the CFO at a transportation company signed a ten-year outsourcing contract after his company went bankrupt. The outsourcing arrangement brought in a multi-million dollar cash infusion, protected information systems assets from creditors, and transferred over 1,000 employees to a more stable company. In this extreme case of business distress, outsourcing provided a lifeboat to a sinking ship.

For most financially viable organizations, however, outsourcing from this category provides no economic advantage. Still, some companies choose to outsource for non-economic benefit, such as to focus in-house resources on more-critical activities. For example, a large retailer decided to develop a new generation of operational systems. As part of its plan, the company outsourced support and maintenance of the existing systems. Although the outsourcing contracted provided no direct economic or service benefit, it enabled the retailer to focus its management and technical resources on the new generation.

Practice leaders—subcritical scale IT activities are well managed, but do not have full access to economies of scale.

In-house IT functions which lack critical mass but adopt good management practices can deliver surprisingly good results. In our research, a number of small IT functions provided excellent service at low cost. Through practices such as software standards, automation of IT operations, purchase of used equipment, and self-managed work-groups they were able to match the prices of large-scale external vendors. For example, a telecommunications company runs a small data-centre at a cost comparable to larger vendors by adopting efficient practices.

Outsourcing IT activity from this category on the basis of lack of scale would be equivalent to divestiture of a high-quality business. The market value is much higher than the asset value. We suggest that senior executives consider whether *insourcing* is a superior way forward. IT management excellence can be exploited by building activity to critical mass through external revenue and resources. Both costs and contribution can potentially improve.

The economics factors matrix is the third element of our selective sourcing frameworks. It neither dominates nor defers to the other two. Business, technical, and economic factors represent three different and complementary perspectives. Sometimes their implications will represent consistent prescriptions, sometimes conflicting ones. If senior executives choose to give particular weight to one dimension, the other two dimensions can indicate the potential risks. We suggest that these three frameworks, based on the experiences of the many outsourcing cases we have examined, can help senior executives both avoid the pitfalls of 'quick-fix' thinking, and also explore the variety of options available in IT sourcing decisions.

The Outlook For IT Sourcing Strategy

After a lengthy and obscure infancy, the IT services industry burst into growth when Eastman Kodak and others decided to outsource their IT functions. Our work suggests that there are some clear lessons to be learned from the hectic activity of the past few years which can guide the development of an IT sourcing strategy. Specifically, we have argued for:

Selective Outsourcing

The central conclusion from our work is that successful outsourcing is selective outsourcing. The IT function cannot be outsourced as a single commodity, since activities within it differ widely in terms of their contribution to the business. On the other hand, outsourcing cannot be totally rejected on the grounds that the IT function is one large strategic asset, of which no part can be entrusted to the external market. A policy of selective sourcing creates the appropriate environment for efficient IT. Selective sourcing challenges complacency and any internal barriers to good management practice, and allows companies to exploit the external services market as it evolves.

Tailored Contracting

The stability of requirements varies widely from one IT activity to another. Contractual arrangements must be based on an understanding of the nature of each activity and tailored to encourage appropriate vendor behaviour. Writing a detailed contract for a new application is pointless because requirements cannot be adequately specified up front. Equally, vague talk of 'partnership' is no substitute for a set of fully defined service-level requirements when an established operational system is involved. Companies must select contractual arrangements just as carefully and thoughtfully as they select the activities to be outsourced.

Economic Analysis

Outsourcing vendors frequently quote prices which look to be very attractive compared with current IT costs. Business executives should not rush to embrace such bids without understanding the size and reasons for differences between vendor and internal costs as well as prices. In some cases the vendor may be trying to buy market share in a fiercely competitive sector. Once the contract is signed, the vendor may recoup losses by charging exorbitant excess fees for any change, realizing that customers are captive given the high switching costs. Unless the vendor is seen to possess a sustainable cost advantage, price advantage may be short-lived.

On balance, we have found that outsourcing vendors currently play a significant but a minority role in the sourcing of IT. In a 168-organization survey to support the European end of our case study research, we found that in the organizations which used IT outsourcing, the outsourcing contracts averaged 24 per cent of the total IT budget. When the very few organizations that totally outsourced IT were removed from the statistics, this figure averaged 13 per cent (Fitzgerald and Willcocks 1993, 1994). No doubt this proportion will grow over time as a higher percentage of IT activities falls into the 'mature' and 'commodity' categories. But as long as IT exhibits a high rate of innovation in technologies and products, many IT activities cannot be contracted out without high levels of risk.

Our case study research strongly suggests that the prospect for the in-house IT function is that its share of the total IT budget will gradually decline, but that high value-added 'demand side' activities will remain in-house. Such activities include:

- tracking new technology and interpreting its potential relevance to the business;

- working with business management to identify and define new applications;
- actively managing contractual relationships with vendors under a selective sourcing strategy.

These arguments are developed further in Chapter 13 by Willcocks and Fitzgerald in this volume.

As a final point, there is a danger that the publicity on IT outsourcing distracts too much senior executive attention towards IT sourcing and away from IT exploitation. For most organizations IT continues to represent a potential enabler of new ways of doing business, as well as underpinning today's operations. The constant innovation of the IT industry means that the IT function is not a peripheral support function that can safely be contracted out in its entirety. Effective sourcing policies enable the business to take advantage, where appropriate, of the market for IT services, while protecting its own vital future interests.

References

Ambrosio, J. (1991), 'Outsourcing at Southland: Best of Times, Worst of Times', *Computerworld*, 25/12 (25 Mar.).

Bergstrom, L. (1991), *The Ins and Outs of Outsourcing*, Darien: Real Decisions Corp.

Buck-Lew, M. (1992), 'To Outsource Or Not?', *International Journal of Information Management*, vol. 12, pp. 3–20.

Drucker, P. (1991), 'The Coming of the New Organization', in W. McGowan (ed.), *Revolution in Real Time*, Boston: Harvard Business School Press.

Elam, J., and Morrison, J. (1988), *United Services Automobile Association*, Harvard Business Case 9-188-102, Harvard Business School, Boston.

Feeny, D., Earl M., and Edwards, B. (1989*a*), *IS Arrangements to Suit Complex Organisations*, OXIIM Research and Discussion Paper 89/5, Templeton College, Oxford.

—— (1989*b*), *Integrating the Efforts of Users and Specialists*, OXIIM Research and Discussion Paper 89/5, Templeton College, Oxford.

Fitzgerald, G., and Willcocks, L. (1993), *Information Technology Outsourcing Practice: A UK Survey*, London: Business Intelligence.

—— (1994), 'Contracts and Partnerships in the Outsourcing of IT', in *Proceedings of the International Conference in Information Systems, Vancouver, Canada, December 13–15th*.

Ganz, J. (1990), 'Outsourcing: Threat Or Salvation?', *Network Management*, vol. 10, pp. 24–32.

Henderson, J. (1990), 'Plugging into Strategic Partnerships: The Critical IS Connection', *Sloan Management Review* (Spring), 7–18.

Hopper, M. (1990), 'Rattling SABRE—New Ways to Compete on Information', *Harvard Business Review*, 68/3 (May–June), 118–25.

Huber, R. (1993), 'How Continental Bank Outsourced Its "Crown Jewels"', *Harvard Business Review* (Jan.–Feb.), 121–9.

Krass, P. (1990), 'The Dollars and Sense of Outsourcing', *Information Week*, 259 (26 Feb.), 26–31.

Lacity, M., and Hirschheim, R. (1993*a*), *Information Systems Outsourcing: Myths, Metaphors, and Realities*, Chichester: Wiley.

—— (1993*b*), 'The Information Systems Bandwagon', *Sloan Management Review* (Fall), 73–86.

—— and Willcocks, L. (1995), *Are Information Systems Outsourcing Expectations Realistic? A Review of US and UK Evidence*, Oxford Institute of Information Management Working Paper 95/1, Templeton College, Oxford.

Lasher, D., Ives, B., and Jarvenpaa, S. (1991), 'USAA-IBM Partnerships in Information Technology: Managing the Image Project', *MIS Quarterly* (Dec.), 551–65.

McFarlan, W., and Nolan, R. (1993), *IT Make Or Buy—The Strategic Challenge*, Harvard Business Case N2-194-031, Harvard Business School, Boston.

Mehler, M. (1992), 'The Age of the Megacontract', *Information Week* (13 July), 42–5.

Moad, J. (1993), 'Inside an Outsourcing Deal', *Datamation* (15 Feb.), 20–7.

Prahalad, C., and Hamel, G. (1991), 'The Core Competence of the Corporation', *Harvard Business Review*, vol. 63, no. 3, pp. 79–91.

Quinn, J. (1992), 'The Intelligent Enterprise: A New Paradigm', *Academy of Management Executive*, vol. 6, no. 4, pp. 44–63.

—— and Hilmer, F. (1994), 'Strategic Outsourcing', *Sloan Management Review* (Summer), 43–55.

Quinn, J., Doorley, T., and Paquette, P. (1990), 'Technology in Services: Rethinking Strategic Focus', *Sloan Management Review*, vol. 31, no. 2, pp. 79–87.

Richmond, W., Seidman, A., and Whinston, A. (1992), 'Incomplete Contracting Issues in Information Systems Development Outsourcing', *Decision Support Systems*, vol. 8, pp. 459–77.

Willcocks, L. (1995), *Collaborating to Compete: Towards Strategic Partnerships in IT Outsourcing?*, Oxford Institute of Information Management Working Paper 94/11, Templeton College, Oxford.

—— and Fitzgerald, G. A. (1994), *A Business Guide To I.T. Outsourcing. A Study of European Best Practice in the Selection, Management and Use of External IT Services*, London: Business Intelligence.

Willcocks, L., Lacity, M., and Fitzgerald, G. A. (1995), *IT Outsourcing in Europe and the USA: Assessment Issues*, Oxford Institute of Information Management Working Paper 95/2, Templeton College, Oxford.

21

The Changing Environment for IS Professionals: Human Resource Implications

J. DANIEL COUGER

Introduction

One of the key challenges of the 1990s is involvement of IS organizations in more of the information processing activities of the firm. That statement may evoke surprise, until one considers that only 5 per cent of the information in the typical firm is contained in data-processing files and records. According to research by Sprague (1991), 95 per cent of the information required to conduct business is in document form. IS has just begun to include the valuable information contained in documents, particularly those from external sources. The dissatisfaction with the IS organization's ability to impact more of the information activities of firms is causing management in some firms to reassign responsibility for some IS activities to operating departments.

This chapter derives three scenarios for the near-term potential IS environment. It is anticipated that one of these scenarios will be representative of the IS environment for the large majority of organizations. The qualifications of IS personnel to operate successfully in each of these environments are then identified. These qualifications involve: skill set, experience, and interest. Next, an analysis is made concerning the degree to which these qualifications can be developed for existing IS personnel. IS personnel have some unique characteristics that affect their ability to make the transition to the changing IS environment.

The projections and recommendations of this chapter are appropriate for non-profit and governmental organizations as well as profit-making organizations. However, to simplify terminology, the term 'organization' will be used to delineate functional organizations, and the term 'corporation' will be used to represent the overall organization.

Scenario One—Natural Evolution of Present IS Environment

For many organizations, the IS environment has for many years been comprised primarily of maintenance and enhancement of a large set of applications, supporting the marketing, operation, distribution, and management control functions of the firm. The term 'operation' is used instead of 'production' to permit the scenario to apply to organizations in the service industries and government activities, as well as organizations that produce physical products.

Accordingly, a smaller percentage of the IS budget is spent in the following areas:

1. developing applications for *other* activities within each of the above-listed functional areas, which were previously not cost-effective for automation, such as expert system applications;
2. developing applications in other parts of the company, such as planning and human resource management;
3. linking of applications, through teleprocessing and database integration;
4. helping users utilize PC-based applications and access mainframe-based applications.

The bulk of the existing applications has been written in third-generation languages. The newer applications are being written primarily in higher-level languages. The corporation expenditures for IS are largely controlled by the central IS group. Exceptions are expenditures for personal computers and related software; however, the central IS group often has approval authority over these purchases in terms of standards or vendor policy.

Scenario Two—User Development of Their Own DSS and Tailored Applications

In many organizations users are developing some of their own applications. This result is due to the large application development backlog, the rapid improvement of user capability, and the availability of simplified application development tools. Already, in many firms the user-department expenditures for computing are more than 50 per cent of those spent by the central IS organization. The large integrated databases are also maintained by the IS organization, but many sub-databases are developed and maintained by the user organizations, for example, the customer database by the marketing organization, the cost database by the finance organization.

The IS organization has the prime responsibility for developing the technology architecture for the corporation, for protocols, standards, and guidelines, for supporting users in selection of off-the-shelf software, and for training and guidance of users in their development of applications with fourth-generation tools.

Scenario Three—Application Development/Processing is Transferred to the User Organizations

This scenario represents a revolutionary change, where the central IS organization is primarily a technology planning and support area, providing expertise in each of the technology areas needed by the firm. The user areas have complete control of their own application development, maintenance of applications, and processing most of those applications. The major databases reside in the organizations that logically support them, for example, the customer database in the marketing organization, the product database in the manufacturing organization, and the financial database in the financial organization.

This scenario has been adopted in several large corporations. As an indication of the trend, since 1991 more than half of the graduates of the IS programme in my college have been hired directly by users—for application development. In these companies users are no longer satisfied with using PC-oriented packages; they are hiring graduates of professional IS degree programmes to develop and process their own computer applications.

Most of the budget for IS resides in the user areas. They choose to develop their applications or even to outsource IS. There may be a mainframe processing facility shared by many organizations and administered by the central IS group, but many of the departments have their own mini- as well as microcomputers.

Figure 21.1 represents the three scenarios, on a continuum where central IS development/maintenance of applications is at the left and user development/maintenance is at the right.

Qualifications and Interests of IS Personnel

Scenario One

The *skills* required for personnel under the Scenario One environment represent natural evolution—acquisition of new skills to utilize the latest tools for application development, such as integrated CASE tools. Persons maintaining applications need to acquire new technology skills as well, such as re-engineering tools/techniques. *Experience* with, or knowledge of,

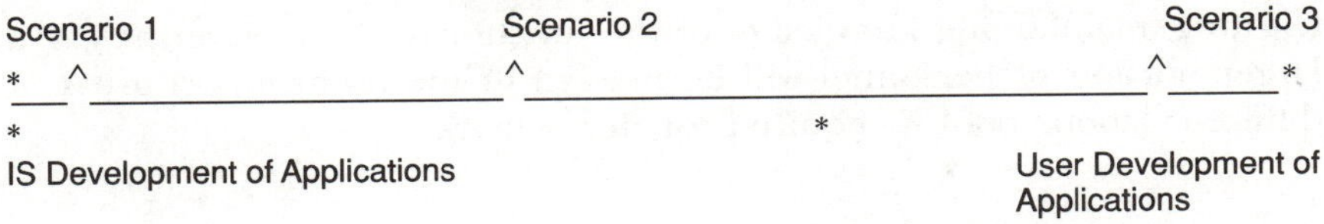

Scenario 1   Scenario 2   Scenario 3

*   ^   ^   ^   *

* _____|_____|_____*_____

IS Development of Applications   User Development of
                                                                     Applications

Fig. 21.1. *Continuum of IS involvement in application development*

existing applications will continue to be important because most of these applications were developed before structured technology became common, placing a great deal of emphasis on knowing the hard-to-decipher logic of the application.

Interests of personnel here will continue to be technically focused, for example, (1) third-generation type of programming practice, (2) database design, and (3) network design. A small number of persons whose interest is less technical and more consultation-oriented will continue to be involved in Information Centre type of work—training and helping users utilize PC-based systems and access mainframe-based systems. Some personnel are satisfactorily making the transition to the use of fourth-generation tools for new application development. Others are disenchanted with the lessening of technical skill requirement associated with many of the fourth-generation tools.

Scenario Two

In the Scenario Two environment a bi-modal distribution of *skills* is more evident:

Mode One—technically oriented personnel develop and maintain large transaction processing applications, design and maintain large databases, perform network design/support and system software support.

Mode Two—business-function oriented personnel help users develop decision support systems and tailored applications in each functional area of the corporation. These persons must also possess the technical skills associated with understanding and utilizing the software needed for these applications.

Experience requirements for the two modes of work differ significantly. For Mode One, the traditional IS experience is important. For Mode Two, the knowledge of the application area, that is, the business function, is paramount. Technical knowledge is also necessary, but not at the level of Mode One personnel.

The qualification area of *interest* is a major delineator. At present, a minority of IS professionals are interested in spending a lot of time acquiring expertise on business functions. The majority believe that the time required to maintain a proficiency in specialized technical areas precludes learning/maintaining knowledge of the functional areas. Nevertheless, a larger portion of personnel will be needed in the user-support areas. A different labour pool is required for this activity.

Scenario Three

The problems listed under Scenario Two are intensified in the Scenario Three environment. The proportion of personnel needed for the central IS organization is small compared with that working in the user areas. *Skills* needed for success in each area differ considerably. In-depth technical skills are needed for the central IS group while broad generalist skills are needed for most IS personnel working in the user areas. Only a small number of high-level technical personnel will be needed by each user group doing its own database development and processing. The central group continues to be the first to assimilate the latest technologies, for example, AI, neural networking.

Experience requirements will likewise be quite different. The user areas will hire people whose experience is primarily in the area of application and secondarily in IS. The central IS group will be looking for even greater technical expertise due to the need to provide technical support in each functional area.

Interest differences of the individuals working in these two areas is even more pronounced. The central IS group will appeal to persons with specialist interests, while the user IS groups will appeal to persons with generalist interests. However, the central IS group will be involved more in consulting than in performing the work themselves. Some IS personnel have little interest in consultation-oriented activity and have difficulty making the transition.

Changing Role of IS Organization

Roles

The changes from a Scenario One to Scenario Three environment represent a major paradigm shift. The IS organization is no longer the principal developer of computer applications; that role has shifted to the user organizations. As shown in Figure 21.2, IS takes on the roles of consultant, facilitator, adviser, and systems integrator. Instead of determining a system architecture with the task of persuading elements of the corporation to agree with the plan, it advocates compatibility of equipment and software across organizations. It still develops standards but now must convince the various user organizations of the value of adherence of standards. While it

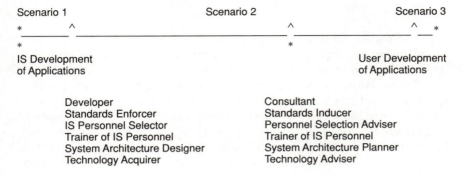

Fig. 21.2. *Alternative roles of the IS organization*

previously both selected and acquired the technology for the corporation, it now advises on those areas. If the corporation continues the policy of a central mainframe with satellite systems in various user organizations, the central IS group will have the principal say on the configuration of the mainframe. But if the corporation decides on a complete decentralization approach, the central IS group may be relegated to an advisory role on computer equipment. However, it may have the primary role in designing and operating the teleprocessing and telecommunications network to link the decentralized installations.

Its overall role is to scan the technology horizon and to advise how to keep the corporation current and competitive, both in hardware and software. While its role in applications development has changed, it still can have a major advisory impact. Although the user organizations are specialists in their functional areas and now are interacting with people in the same discipline in other companies to learn where computer technology is beneficial, the central IS organization is still the expert on potential uses of the technology. Therefore, a partnership arrangement between the two can ensure competitive advantage for the corporation in its use of technology.

Pipeline for Personnel

The personnel selection and training role for IS personnel, even those destined for the user organizations, should remain with the central IS group, regardless of scenario. This approach ensures consistency and quality of personnel. Central IS can serve as the pipeline for preparing personnel for all areas of the firm—both those who remain in the IS organization and those who will be working for the user organizations. This training not only includes technical training but training in system standards and methodology, to ensure quality and transferability of applications.

Approaches to Obtaining Qualified Personnel

The approaches for obtaining qualified personnel would *not* be the same for all three scenarios. The degree of specialization within the central IS organization increases along the continuum from Scenario One to Scenario Three. Hiring persons fresh out of a computer-science degree programme would not be as appropriate for the Scenario Three central IS organizations. More experience would be required. Also, these people will be performing consultative kinds of work, aiding the applications developers residing in the functional areas of the organization. There is a need for more training to help these personnel acquire better interpersonal skills.

For application development in the user organizations, a primary source of personnel is the user organizations themselves. Most user managers prefer to select people in their own organizations who have the domain knowledge and who have interest in technical matters, then provide the necessary technical training. Managers in these areas already know the qualifications concerning experience level and interest in terms of business knowledge. They believe it is easier to provide technical training than to locate persons who already have the technical skills but must be motivated to acquire the necessary business knowledge.

It is ironic that this approach was often used when organizations introduced computers thirty years ago. Because of the shortage of system analysts, personnel were transferred from user areas and trained in analysis techniques.

The Unique Characteristics of IS Personnel

The unique characteristics of IS personnel are a major factor in their ability to make a successful transition to organizations working in the new scenarios. Our research on behavioural characteristics of IS personnel over the past decade revealed that the majority of people attracted to the IS profession have some extreme differences from the general corporation population.

Using a survey instrument developed and validated by the field of psychology (Hackman and Lawler 1975), and job diagnostics survey, we were able to make direct comparisons with 500 other occupations in the USA. Our modifications preserved the original questions and added a section to get additional information. Our instrument was validated in 1978 (Couger and Zawacki 1980) and has been used to develop a database on seventeen job types within the IS field, from data entry personnel to CIO. The database on US personnel contains information on more than 15,000 persons. The instrument has also been used to gather information on IS personnel in ten other countries, (Couger *et al.* 1991*a*; Couger and Motiwalla 1985; Tompkins and Couger 1991); that database also exceeds 15,000 persons.

The interesting result of the surveys is that the unique characteristics of IS personnel are common to all the countries surveyed, despite highly different cultures. The diversity of culture is illustrated by the list of the countries where the surveys were conducted: Austria, Thailand, Republic of China, Taiwan, Hong Kong, Singapore, South Africa, Israel, Finland, Australia, and the USA.

One of the significant differences between IS personnel and other occupations concerns the behavioural characteristic of growth need. Of the 500 occupations surveyed in the USA, analysts and programmers exhibit the highest mean GNS (growth need strength). Personnel attracted to the analysts and programmer positions have an extraordinarily high need for challenge, for learning and developing beyond where they are now. IS managers must constantly evaluate tasks assigned to analysts and programmers to ensure that they continue to stretch these individuals.

A second characteristic in which analysts and programmers differ substantially from other occupations concerns the need for social interaction. SNS (social need strength) of analysts and programmers is the lowest of all 500 occupations. Persons with low SNS do not naturally seek out activities which involve a great deal of interaction.

A third characteristic is a high need for feedback. Analysts and programmers need to know how well they are progressing toward their individual goals and objectives.

The ability of personnel with these characteristics successfully to make the transition from a Scenario One environment to that of the other two scenarios is questionable. In a Scenario One environment analysts and programmers spend most of their time with IS people. While forays out to meet with users occur regularly, most of their time is spent in the IS area, working on the details of analysis, design, and programming with personnel possessing similar SNS/GNS.

In the Scenario Three environment analysts and programmers actually work for the users. They spend all their time in the user area, interacting continuously with persons with much higher SNS. There is also the question of whether they will consider the more generalist type of work as challenging as technical work.

Conclusions

Organizations have been trying to transfer large numbers of COBOL programmers to the fourth-generation languages/CASE technology environment. Some personnel are slow in making the transition because they believe they are giving up some of the technical skills required for 'professional' programming. They are micro-oriented and have difficulty changing to a macro-orientation. Yet such a transition appears much easier than the one where programmers are asked to become much more knowledgeable about business functions, in order to provide better support to user organizations. They do not possess experience in these areas and often lack an interest in spending their time acquiring business knowledge. These people become frustrated in a company that moves to the Scenario Three environment, where all application development personnel report directly to user organizations. Instead, many are relocating to companies that are in the Scenario One or Two environment.

Managers of analysts and programmers in a Scenario Three environment need to devise ways to show high GNS personnel that the work of designing and implementing the new wave of applications, those key to growth and survival of the corporation, is even more challenging than past assignments. Managers need to show that the work of automating the remaining 95 per cent of the corporation's information is both important and challenging.

Behavioural studies show that, although few people are able to change their basic needs, they can change their behaviour. If managers convince analysts and programmers that future advancement is based on an ability to communicate well, and to be successful at interpersonal activities, these personnel have the motivation to become proficient in these skill areas. They do not change their basic need for social interaction but they can change their behaviour to become more effective in interacting. If analysts and programmers can be convinced of the challenge of improving interactive skills, the impetus to change is supported by the individual's high need for growth.

Despite their inherent behavioural circumstances, most analysts and programmers can be motivated by the special challenges of those tasks associated with Scenario Two and Three environments. These personnel can successfully make the transition to the new environments if their managers understand their unique characteristics and plan transition activities to prepare IS professionals properly for the new environments.

The interesting question, of course, is whether a Scenario One or Two environment will even exist for the latter 1990s. Some IS executives have failed to recognize the need for their organization to be more business-knowledgeable and responsive to user needs, and have had a Scenario Three environment forced on them by upper management. Others have advocated such a change.

The IS organization has no less of a leadership role under the Scenario Three environment than under the other two. To enable the corporation to maintain its technical competency, the IS organization has the principal leadership role. Under a Scenario Three environment, IS must use a great deal more subtlety in its leadership—more persuasive and less prescriptive. Just as some COBOL programmers have difficulty in transition to the Scenario Three environment, some IS managers find difficulty in such a change. They, too, may need more training in the consultative, behavioural skills. As a consequence, the challenge is significant. The paradox is that companies need technical leadership even more in this era of rapid technology change. Since the trend to the Scenario Three type environment is evident, the IS managers who can make the transition have an excellent future ahead of them.

References

Couger, J. D., Burn, G., Dengate, G., Farn, C. K., Ma, L., Tompkins, H., and Weber, R. (1991*b*), 'Comparison of Motivational Norms for Pan-Pacific Computer Personnel vs the United States', *Proceedings, Pan-Pacific Conference V11* (June), 3 pages.

Couger, J. D., Burn, J. M., Ma, L., and Tompkins, H. (1991*a*), 'Motivating IT Professionals—The Hong Kong Challenge', *Proceedings, Hawaii International Conference on Systems Sciences* (Jan.), 524–9.

Couger, J. D., and Zawacki, R. A. (1980), *Motivating and Managing Computer Personnel*, New York: Wiley.

Couger, J. D., and Motiwalla, J. (1985), 'Occidental vs Oriental IS Professionals' Perceptions on Key Factors for Motivation', *Proceedings, International Conference on Information Systems*, Indianapolis (Dec.), 105–13.

Hackman, J. R., and Lawler, E. E. (1975), 'Employee Reactions to Job Characteristics', *Journal of Applied Psychology*, vol. 60, no. 2, pp. 159–70.

Sprague, R. H., Jr. (1991), quoted in 'Critical Issues in Information Systems Management, 1991–1995', *I/S Analyzer* (Jan.), 9.

Tompkins, H., and Couger, J. D. (1991), 'Cross Cultural Comparison of Information System Personnel in the Pacific Basin Versus the US', *Proceedings, Hawaii International Conference on Systems Sciences* (Jan.), 530–7.

22

The Hybrid Manager

DAVID J. SKYRME

Introduction

The challenges facing organizations in the 1990s require the skills of a special kind of manager—the hybrid manager. A hybrid manager is someone who blends the skills of information management and business management. Although the need for such people has been recognized for several years, the topic has only recently come into vogue. This is due to the growing evidence that hybrid managers can make a significant contribution to an organization's success.

This chapter starts with background on the concept of hybrid managers and why they are needed. Their contribution in different areas of information management activity is then described. This is followed by a discussion of the competences that they require and how they can be developed. Finally, a framework is offered which puts hybrids in their wider organizational context and helps identify factors for performance improvement.

The material for this chapter is drawn mainly from the results of a research project into hybrid managers carried out by the author. There were three main strands of research—a literature survey; in-depth interviews with directors, senior managers, and project team participants (in both the IS function and business units) in eight UK organizations; and a questionnaire survey.

Background

The term 'hybrid manager' was first coined by Keen in 1988 and more formally defined by Earl (1989) as: 'people with strong technical skills and adequate business knowledge, or vice versa . . . hybrids are people with technical skills able to work in user areas doing a line or functional job, but adept at developing and supplementing IT application ideas.'

Earl also defined two similar roles: leaders—'executives in user areas who can drive the exploitation of IT in their business'; and impresarios— 'the few executive managers in the IS function who can propel the organization into strategic consideration of IT'. The distinctions between these roles tend to be lost in conversation, the term 'hybrid manager' being used as a surrogate for all three. Note that a hybrid manager does not have to be a manager in the IT function, or come from an IT background. In fact, some of the more successful hybrid managers have moved into IT after following careers in business functions. Others believe that they can achieve more by directly managing business activities.

The clamour for hybrid managers has grown significantly during the last few years. An example is the British Computer Society's (BCS) appeal for the UK to develop 10,000 hybrid managers by 1995 if the country is to remain competitive in world markets. Their report (Palmer and Ottley 1990) makes a persuasive case for hybrid managers, including the following grand claims:

the payoff for organizations is significant. The presence of hybrid managers seems to enable organizations to see the opportunities for change, manage it better and control project delivery.

Who [else] can conceive and implement, in the line organization, systems that will win global customers and beat global competitors be it on time to market, cost, quality, service or any of the dimensions which are used to measure competitiveness[?]

The need for managers with both IT and business competence has become more marked as IT has become more pervasive and has evolved into a more pivotal role within business. Two complementary sets of data continue to reinforce this need. First, surveys of MIS issues consistently place 'alignment with business strategy' as the top issue (Niederman *et al.* 1991). Secondly, surveys of CEOs and senior business managers show concern about the return from their IT investment and even lack of confidence in their MIS departments (see, for example, Tomlin 1989). Hybrid managers seem one natural way of building bridges between the line and IS function to solve these issues.

Other evidence supports the case for hybrid managers. Many 'competitive edge' applications of IT emerge from 'champions' in the line who understand the implications of IT, rather than from IS or as a result of strategic IT planning (Earl and Runge 1988). Also, the senior IS management role is evolving to one that is more business oriented (Hartog and Rouse 1987). Finally, a conclusion from the cases researched in the five-year MIT 'Management in the 1990s' programme was that organizational success will increasingly depend on 'managers who understand the implications of IT for business strategy' (Scott-Morton 1990).

The questionnaire survey conducted by the author in early 1990 further supports the case. Senior IT and business managers were asked to rank MIS issues along with the contribution that they believed hybrid managers could make towards improving the situation. Ninety per cent of the eighty-eight respondents believed that hybrid managers would help with the top issues that they had ranked as follows:

1.   alignment of IS with business needs;
2.   coping with changing business needs;
3.   identification of strategic IT opportunities;
4.   improving IS–line relationships;
5.   convincing senior management of the strategic value of IT.

What special attributes do hybrid managers, therefore, bring to bear on these important issues? What is their unique contribution? How do they see their role? These were the questions explored in the interviews.

Roles

The hybrid manager's primary role is to enable the business to maximize the benefits of IT. It is fundamentally a bridge-building role between IT and the business with the following components:

- helping business managers understand and make better use of IT— how it contributes to winning business strategies and better perform- ance; how it impacts organizational change;
- making IT specialists more aware of the business and organizational context—the business strategy, information needs, organizational problems, issues, and opportunities;
- building successful partnerships between business units and the IS function—creating mutual benefits, pooling skills to solve complex business problems, developing a spirit of co-operation.

The role is also pro-active. Most hybrid managers see themselves as 'driving change'. On the one hand they urge business units to new levels of performance through the strategic application of IT. On the other hand they encourage the IS function to become more client-oriented and improve the level and quality of information services.

To understand more precisely what their role involves, it is convenient to consider the three major areas of information systems activity:

- *direction*—setting the vision and strategic direction for IT's contribu- tion to business needs; identifying and evaluating IT-enhanced busi- ness opportunities; determining the portfolio of applications;
- *development*—the process of systems development including the impact of new systems on organizational structures and processes; the man- agement of expectations and change;
- *delivery and support*—the provision of a full range of IS services, includ- ing user support, guidance, and trouble-shooting.

Continued successful outcomes in each of these areas require ever closer co- operation between the IS function and the business. Furthermore, today's dynamic business environment demands continual interaction between IS and their clients to adjust continually to these changes.

So far most of the publicity about hybrid managers has been focused on the glamour of senior-level managers and their contribution to business strategy. However, the research results confirm that hybrid managers bring positive benefits in all three areas, including development and delivery. Moreover, hybrid managers are needed at all organizational levels in all departments. The following sections elaborate these points.

Direction

Of all three areas, this is one where a senior hybrid manager can make the most impact. Those at board level can provide IT input on all important business decisions and make sure that strategic IT is put and kept on the top-management agenda. The interviews conducted as part of the research project identified the following as the particular contributions that hybrids make:

- making the business aware of the existing and potential capabilities of IT;
- envisioning new possibilities for the application of IT, but tempering it with an assessment of its practicalities;
- assessing the benefits and risks associated with new technological advances;
- reinforcing the business benefits of IT to line managers;
- ensuring IS managers are aware of business issues and opportunities;
- showing the IS function how it can respond to emerging and changing business needs.

These contributions show a combination of visionary thinking combined with a large dose of pragmatism. Many hybrid managers feel that they have helped their organizations develop 'better business visions'. These are visions of business activities and processes enabled and enhanced by IT. In addition, though, a good hybrid manager will give top management the confidence that this vision can and will be implemented. This will be done by building durable partnerships between the IS function and the business at senior management level. This takes time, but when it has been achieved the hybrid IT director holds the respect of the CEO and business peers. Unfortunately, this ideal state is reached in far too few organizations.

There are several well-publicized examples where hybrid managers have achieved this status and their organization has benefited. Colin Palmer, when a hybrid manager at Thomson Holidays, successfully introduced the TOPS reservation system for travel agents, and became deputy managing director of Thomson Tour Operations. John Watson, director of sales and regions at British Airways was one time information management director and his experience and success in overseeing the building of a competitive IT infrastructure no doubt helped him make this executive level transition. Unipart is a company in the competitive services sector which has several hybrid managers on its board of directors. Their backgrounds range from DP to retail marketing. Their hybrid skills have allowed them to develop a vision of the business as an integrated set of customer-facing 'systems'. In the space of a few years the company has been transformed into a leading performer in its sector. These, and many other, examples show the major business improvements that can be achieved through hybrid manager involvement in direction-setting activities.

Development

It is a stark reality confirmed from many surveys that most IT projects fail to be delivered on time and to budget, and fail to meet users' expectations. Many failures can be traced to inadequate understanding of the real business needs or to failure to address organizational and human factors.

Several approaches offer some help in addressing these issues. Structured methods (such as Yourdon and SSADM) have helped to improve the rigour of analysis and design. Hybrid development teams—a mix of users and IT specialists working side by side—bring together different perspectives and knowledge. The research interviews also identified another, but little-acknowledged, route for improvement—the hybrid pair. This consists of an IT specialist and a user representative working closely together over long periods of time.

While these approaches help, hybrid managers bring further improvements. A project manager with a hybrid's leadership qualities can enhance his or her team's general effectiveness. Hybrid managers, in the part-time role of business sponsor or steering-committee chairperson, can bring new insights or direction to the team. The research interviews identified the following as the additional contributions that hybrid managers bring to project development:

- providing insights at the scoping stage that direct effort to important aspects from the business perspective;
- assessing the programming effort needed to achieve certain desired functionality, thus making better trade-offs in function allocation between human and machine;
- continually monitoring the relevance of project activities against a backcloth of ever-changing business requirements and priorities;
- managing users' expectations;
- giving early anticipation of likely implementation issues;
- scoping the magnitude of the organizational changes needed and thus determining the nature of the implementation 'roll-out';

- creating a feeling of ownership by both parties: helping IS people see their responsibilities to the business; making line managers and users regard the new system as theirs.

The main skills used here are sensing, interpersonal, and negotiation skills. The hybrids' experience helps them anticipate the impact of new systems and the likely reactions of different groups of people who have an interest in the outcome. They see which decisions made during a project will be difficult to change, and bring appropriate people together in a timely fashion to help make them.

The interviews revealed several cases where the timely intervention of a hybrid manager had brought about significant changes in project direction, resulting in a better outcome. One case involved the development of a marketing system. The marketing manager, a hybrid, was able through his combined business and IT experience to determine that 90 per cent of the benefits could be gained in a much shorter time-scale than pursuing the 100 per cent perfect solution as recommended by the analysts. Since 'time to market' was a competitive advantage, this important trade-off, which might not otherwise have taken place, was made. In another case, a hybrid manager was able to suggest short-cuts in the normal analysis methods that lopped five months off the project time-scale.

Delivery and Support

The conventional wisdom is that hybrid managers have little to offer in this activity area as compared to direction and development. The research interviews suggest that this situation is changing. Organizations are scrutinizing more closely each of their operations, including information services, for their cost-effectiveness and customer service. For information services this is resulting in a shift of emphasis towards a more commercial and market-oriented operation, and an increase in consultancy-type services.

Service-level agreements are one vehicle through which user expectations are clarified and the IS function commits to a given level of service for a given price. Like development, this is very much a bridging activity between business needs and IT means. Therefore, who is better equipped to develop and manage such agreements than hybrid managers?

One organization studied during the research has recently reorganized their IS department into a separate business unit. This new unit has appointed 'account managers' to liaise with the other (non-IS) business units. These positions are normally filled by hybrid managers, who know about both IT and the business of the unit with which they liaise. One of their responsibilities is the development and management of service-level agreements between IS and the business. These agreements cover all the services that IS can provide—project management and development as well as delivery, support, and maintenance of hardware and software systems.

Characteristics

By definition a hybrid manager has competence in both business and IT. Also needed, though, are general management skills, particularly those of a 'soft' nature, for example, communications and interpersonal skills. Successful hybrid managers also seem to possess certain personality traits, such as the desire to drive change. The possible set of characteristics of a hybrid manager are shown in Table 22.1 (Earl and Skyrme 1992).

Business Knowledge

As well as a good grounding in general business principles hybrid managers must have a good understanding of the industry they work in. Kotter (1982) in his work on general managers has pointed out that business and organization knowledge is cumulative. Successful hybrid managers are, therefore, likely to have remained in the same or related industry for many years, and according to Keen (1988) to have spent some time (two to three years) in each job.

IT Knowledge and Experience

Although there are hybrid managers with in-depth programming experience, specific knowledge at a detailed level is less important than understanding the *capabilities* of IT. Successful hybrid managers put a focus on information. They explore ways on which technology can access, process, and distribute it. They know about price-performance trends. They have learnt how to trade-off functionality versus cost and time-to-market. They rely on tapping into specialist expertise as they need it. Hence, they must also be competent at selecting, managing, and communicating with IT specialists.

Organization Specific Knowledge

Knowing 'how to get things done around here' is an important, often overlooked, skill. Length of time with an organization helps the process of developing this capability. Good hybrids exploit their personal networks which they have developed over years. This can pose problems for newcomers to an organization, although in periods of change this is less of a handicap. One newcomer devoted significant time during his first

Table 22.1. *Characteristics of hybrid managers*

Aspect	Specific attributes	Critical skills
Business knowledge	Business fundamentals Functional knowledge Understanding firm's business	Business instinct to spot opportunities
IT knowledge and experience	IT fundamentals Project management Applications Methods Providers	Confidence to ask and challenge
Organization specific knowledge	Familiarity with culture, structure, and processes. Knowing key people and their motivations	Knowing how to get things done
Management skills	Cognitive Intuitive Information sensing Interpersonal Motivation Negotiation Listening and communication skills	Ability to get things done
Personal characteristics	People oriented Outgoing Energy and enthusiasm Commitment and integrity	Willingness to learn

few months getting to know many senior managers in the organization and how decision-making processes worked. A useful adage is: 'know-who is as important as know-how'; and it often turns out that the person to know is not the obvious one from formal role definitions.

General Management Skills

Time and time again the interviews highlighted effective communications and interpersonal skills as the most important competence. Since much of a hybrid manager's job is concerned with building organizational partnerships, he or she needs to be able to develop good working relationships with peers, subordinates, and superiors. Good judgement is also important: 'I know that I can trust John's ability to deliver on time.' They show many of the cognitive skills that Kotter identified in successful general managers—intuitive thinking, problem-solving, being able to see the 'big picture'. They can think 'outside the box' and to see things in unusual ways.

A noteworthy characteristic is their ability to move rapidly between levels, at one moment addressing the wider business context, at the next delving into the depth of detail needed to make decisions about the implementation of an IT system.

Personal Characteristics

When one meets successful hybrid managers, one is immediately struck by their energy, enthusiasm, and commitment. They actively want to drive change; they are dissatisfied with the *status quo*. They proliferate ideas, but they are also very interested in people. Work is currently in progress to assess the personality profiles of successful hybrid managers using standard personality tests. Such tests have been carried out on DP staff and managers in general (e.g. Couger and Zawacki 1980). They show that in aggregate the DP population is very introverted. It has the lowest social affiliation needs of all professional categories and is generally low on communication skills.

Although it is too early to make sweeping conclusions, it would appear that only a small proportion, say 10–25 per cent, of existing DP people would make suitable hybrid managers. The personality-profile average of the DP population also helps to explain why some of the more successful hybrid managers come from non-IT backgrounds. However, we would expect this pattern to change as the nature of the IS function changes and it attracts people with different personalities.

Taking all characteristics together, there is now sufficient knowledge to define, in some level of detail, the profile of a hybrid manager. The BCS did this in 1990 by introducing a new hybrid manager stream in their Professional Development Scheme. This scheme acts as a reference for careers in the information management profession in the UK. The new stream gives definitions of roles, skills, knowledge, and experience needed for hybrids at several organizational levels, up to IT director.

Developing Hybrids

Most organizations need to develop many more hybrid managers. Many of today's senior hybrid managers readily admit that their careers have been somewhat haphazard and largely unplanned. They seized opportunities as they arose, taking on jobs that broadened their experience beyond their specialism. Such opportunism must give way to a more sustained and systematic approach if hybrid managers are to be developed in the quantity needed. New partnerships are needed between education and industry. Changes are needed in organizations' career planning, training, and management-development programmes.

A notion that is useful for scoping this challenge is that of career trajectories (Keen 1988). This is a plot of an individual's career against two axes—business and IT experience (Fig. 22.1). Traditionally, professional careers, and particularly DP ones, have led to many people following a career path closely following one of the axes. Hybrid development requires more lateral career moves to gain the mix of experiences needed. Keen (1988) and Hartog and Rouse (1987) are among those experts that believe that IS professionals should move into other functions within their first four or five years of work.

Higher Education

The long-term solution to developing more hybrid managers probably rests largely with the higher education sector—at least in the UK. Until recently undergraduate education has been very specialized. Many IS departments have already turned away from recruiting predominantly computer scientists and are seeking entry-level graduates with a broader mix of knowledge and skill. Digital Equipment Corporation in the USA has done this.

In response to this need, higher education in many countries now offers more undergraduate courses where information technology can be studied in combination with business-related subjects. Thus, several 'business information management' courses have been specifically created to develop hybrid potential. These courses usually provide team-based project work, and often include periods of industrial placement.

Despite these moves, there remains much to be done. More institutions need to offer such courses. Many need to shift their emphasis from imparting knowledge to developing skills around its practical application. In particular, more attention needs to be given to helping students acquire the 'softer' communications and interpersonal skills required by hybrid managers. Project team-work helps, but the educational focus is usually on output (content) rather than the process to get there. Students usually receive little explicit instruction or help on team processes or feedback on their interpersonal skills.

Organizations can play an important part in helping the education sector develop the necessary skills. First, they can expose students (and staff) to some of their own management training. Thus, Digital through its DECollege programme in the UK works with higher education to help them develop change management skills. Students on placement with Digital have training periods specifically devoted to developing team skills, self-awareness, leadership, and communications. For most participants it is often their first exposure to such development.

Secondly, they can take an active role in teaming up with educational establishments. The co-operation between Unipart and the University of

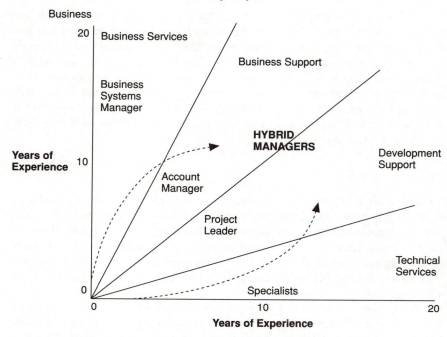

Fig. 22.1. *Career space and career trajectories*

Salford provides a good example of this. Unipart sponsors some of the students, advises on the curriculum, and provides some of their own staff to give seminars and lectures. They also provide business projects for student teams and have a senior director on the programme's management board.

MBA Programmes

MBA courses provide a good means of developing a wider business perspective after a period at work. Several organizations send their aspiring IT managers on such courses to broaden their skills. Some companies, such as Pfizer, recruit MBAs directly into their IT department. However, a survey undertaken in 1990 by the British Computer Society of the IT content of MBA courses in the UK shows them lacking good hybrid content. Information management is often a poor stepcousin to topics such as business strategy and finance. Where IT is addressed, it is too often treated as a totally separate discipline rather than being woven into the teaching of other topics. Again, organizations can help rectify this situation by working directly with educational institutions on tailor-made MBAs. Thus, General Electric in Fairfield, Connecticut, was an early starter in running a joint programme with Purdue Graduate School of Management to help their IS staff gain MBAs.

A fast-growing sector of MBA provision is that of distance learning. This gives practising managers, usually in their thirties, opportunities to broaden their skills with minimal disruption to their careers. Highly valued are those courses which provide opportunities for project work within the current job and organization context. Some MBA courses are now being specifically designed to help IT professionals make the transition to hybrids. Henley Management Centre in the UK, for instance, has launched such a course, which is sponsored by several large companies. Teams from these organizations work on relevant business problems during the course, so creating a bridge between theory and practice that many courses lack.

Other Training and Development Routes

Organizations have much to do to increase their pool of hybrid managers. One need is to help established specialists and senior functional managers get some hybrid competences. They also need to provide hybrid career paths and development opportunities for junior staff at the lower end of career ladder. Finally, they need to create a continuous learning environment that will help all employees to stay abreast of developments in the business and technological environment.

One response to the first need is the use of short courses and seminars. Business schools, as an example, run courses on strategic information management for senior business managers. Many companies organize one-to-three day 'Strategic IT' seminars run by for them by outside consultants. The IT specialist is catered for by industry 'trends and update' seminars delivered by industry experts. However, it appears that few companies use any of these methods on a wide enough scale. More needs to be done, in terms of offering a continuous programme of such events so that as many managers as possible receive ongoing education in regular bursts. Companies can increase access to such programmes through use of video-conferencing technology. Some multinational corporations run regular world-wide seminars with live video links that bring the world's leading experts in front of larger numbers of managers on a wide range of business topics.

More experiential methods are advocated for developing 'soft' management skills, such as communication and change management. In-house management development programmes feature widely here. Some specialist training organizations now run short courses especially for IT professionals to help them develop such skills. One such organization offers one-week courses on 'Hybrid Skills for Project Managers' and 'Communications Skills for IT Professionals'. A stumbling-block, though, is the attitude of some IT managers, who feel that the only training that their staff need is in technical specialities.

Perhaps the best recognized route for developing hybrid managers is through participation in IT projects. Many hybrids who started their careers as non-IT specialists got their first experience of IT in this way. They gain exposure to IT capabilities and techniques, but retain a focus on what it will do for their business.

If projects are to realize their full potential as a hybrid development route, though they must be viewed as such. This means making some changes to their conventional *modus operandi*. For a start, one or two people on each project team should be recruited purely for furthering their development needs, rather than necessarily being the best for the project. Also, OD (organization development) techniques and facilitated workshops should be used to guide individual and team learning, for example, through reflecting on their ongoing successes and failures. A growing practice is the collocation of members of a project team in a client business unit. All these methods, with a little planning and some attention to learning needs, offer a very natural way for IT specialists and business people to learn much more from each other.

Those organizations that have a track-record in developing hybrid managers put personal and management development high on all their management agendas. Human Resource (HR) managers and specialists will be very evident within the business and the IS function. Every individual will have a personal career and development plan that matches individual aspirations with organizational needs. They will have career paths that encourage cross-functional moves. Secondment and job rotation between IT and business will be a supported practice. They will move individuals temporarily onto three-to-six month assignments, perhaps with other managers as part of a company wide task-force. Mentoring is another approach being adopted by some of these companies. Individual development is supported by mentors or coaches, not in their direct reporting line. The questionnaire survey results shows that few of the practices are in widespread regular use.

Formal Hybrid Programmes

To date, only a small minority of organizations have put in place a formal programme for developing hybrids. Two companies, that have, Unipart and Esso UK, have gained significant benefits by doing so.

For Esso, developing hybrid managers is one aspect of a wider IS–business partnership programme that was started a few years ago. This programme also includes joint planning processes, physical location of IT specialists in business units, and service level agreements. Hybrids are developed by transferring a targeted number of people each year from the line to IS and vice versa. There is well-developed career planning and all staff have ample opportunity to receive appropriate education and training. A strong HR focus is very evident within the IS department. It must be said that Esso has a tradition of developing people with cross-functional experience. For them, developing IT hybrids seems a natural extension to developing other kinds of hybrid managers (e.g. marketing or purchasing hybrids). Esso claim impressive results from this programme. For example, over 90 per cent of IT projects now are completed on time and within budget.

A slightly different approach has been adopted by Unipart, a UK supplier and distributor of automotive replacement parts and spares. They have a hybrid programme in all but name. Hybrids are built into role and job descriptions. Thus, the characteristics required by an IS 'account manager' is that of a hybrid manager. It is a formal requirement that the job plans of most individuals will have a section devoted to developing hybrid skills. Individuals are encouraged to seek the education and development they need. However, they are not spoon-fed—the responsibility is placed firmly on the individual to pursue appropriate development opportunities. In pursuit of developing its competences for the future, the company runs various in-house training programmes with the help of external consultants—'managing for excellence' being one such module. It has also built strong links with education and training establishments, including local schools.

Companies like Esso and Unipart, though, are the exception rather than the norm. Although many IT managers say they support the development of hybrid managers, the evidence on the ground is that more needs to be done to address the fundamental career, education, training, and development shortfalls. For example, a PA Consultants' Report (Sparrow 1990) revealed that only 48 per cent of IS departments surveyed in the UK attempted any form of career planning, with only 7 per cent using systematic career development. Only with concerted attention in these areas will organizations develop the hybrid managers they need to make significant inroads into solving the issues highlighted at the beginning of this chapter.

Bridging Mechanisms

Hybrid managers are only one of several ways of building bridges between IS and business. One of the aims of the research was to investigate the relationships of hybrid managers to other mechanisms and to the wider organizational context. Different ways of bridging have been well reported in the literature (Drury 1985; Lodahl and Reditt 1989). In the first report on this research (Earl and Skyrme 1990), these bridging mechanisms were divided into three categories—organizational and structural, group, and individual. However, the research interviews quickly revealed the importance of *processes* as a means of bridging. A revised table therefore includes this new category as well as renaming and refinements in the other categories. (Table 22.2).

Position mechanisms give formal recognition and legitimacy to IS–line partnerships. They define roles and structures that should encourage closer integration of IT into the business. Composition concerns the knowledge and skills that come together in working teams and committees. Processes define the methods and procedures that are used to achieve common IS–line agenda outcomes. The people category focuses on the development of hybrid competences by individuals and has been discussed earlier in this chapter.

The eight research cases were analysed to see how their context affected use of mechanisms and what factors gave rise to success and failure. The reader is cautioned against drawing definite conclusions from a sample of only eight organizations, but some important patterns were noticeable.

First, hybrid managers were evident in all the successful cases. These organizations also tended to use more of the mechanisms listed in Table 22.2 and practice them more widely. Hybrid managers seemed to complement and enhance the other bridging mechanisms. Another noticeable characteristic of the successful organizations was the continuous flow of ideas emanating from interviewees and the probing questions they asked the interviewer! These are characteristics of high bandwidth communication and positive attitudes to learning, features one might expect as a prerequisite of effective bridging.

Further, although hybrid managers were always present in the more successful organizations, they were by no means absent in the least successful ones. One such organization had a career structure that encouraged the development of hybrid managers and used several other bridging mechanisms. Their poorer performance was obviously due to other factors.

What emerges from the analysis is that some factors exert more influence than others. Particularly useful insights into which these were came from analysis of which context variables had changed, and which had not, in three of the cases that had been in turn-around situations. The net result of a detailed analysis of the research data leads to a proposed framework of enablers (Table 22.3).

Hierarchy of Enablers

Operating at the highest level of the hierarchy is a set of organizational factors, any one of which can largely negate the positive influences of

Table 22.2. *Bridging mechanisms*

Type	Mechanisms
Position	Decentralized or federal structures
	IT Director on CEO team
	Liaison Roles
	Co-location
	Siamese structures*
Composition	IS strategy committee
	Cross-functional steering teams
	Multi-disciplined project teams
Processes	Joint business planning
	Top team gets regular exposure to IT
	Systems development methods
People	Hybrid managers
	Personal relations
	Secondment
	Job Rotation
	Cross functional job moves

Note: * Siamese structures are matrix structures where an IS manager will formally be part of a business management team and a corresponding business manager will also be part of the IS management team.

the factors at lower levels. Thus, poor intermeshing of responsibilities and processes were the obvious inhibitors in some of the least successful organizations, for example, project planning and manpower planning not synchronized with or closely connected to budgeting. Two of the turn-around organizations had senior management and CEO changes which generated a more positive view of IT. In one of these the culture had noticeably changed from one of departmental independence to one of interdepartmental co-operation (interdependence).

At the second level of the framework are several practices (the levers) that contribute to better IT–line relationships and IS performance. While each one by itself can result in improvements, there seems a synergistic effect between them. Hybrid managers and bridging mechanisms feature here. The implication is that the hybrid is more likely to be successful where more of these levers are being properly used. One lever that warrants specific mention is that of informal (but disciplined and purposeful) management styles. Openness, sharing, and trust between parties can be developed only by developing such a style. The business manager in one turn-around case had transformed the IS–line relationship he had inherited by adoption of this completely changed style.

At the bottom layer of the framework are the foundations, which give

Table 22.3. *Hierarchy of enablers*

Organizational context
- Supportive organizational culture—co-operative, trusting;
- CEO and board supportive of IT;
- Clear business vision;
- Aligned management process—planning; resource allocation;
- Synergistic structures—meshed responsibilities.

Levers
- Quality (joint) processes;
- Good use of systems methods;
- Multi-disciplinary, multifunction teams and team-work;
- IT Champions in Business;
- Partnerships—user involvement;
- Hybrid Managers;
- Good Project Managers;
- Positive attitudes to change and innovation;
- Informal working styles;
- Bridging mechanisms.

Foundations
- Widespread IT knowledge throughout organization;
- Current MIS skills set;
- Development of hybrid skills especially communication team building, interpersonal;
- Strong HR processes and commitment.

a measure of the competence in depth and breadth throughout the organization. Quite marked in one very successful organization was the widespread degree of computer literacy. They had been an early user of office automation, and everybody had had a terminal on their desk for several years. This made it easier to introduce new systems with little additional training.

The general effect of the hierarchy is that the impact of hybrid managers will be augmented when used along with other mechanisms. Also, it will be much harder for them to be successful without a supportive organizational culture. Finally, the organization's breadth and depth of skills will determine how far successes can be duplicated. Thus, the success of the Esso hybrid manager programme should not be viewed in isolation. It succeeds in part because it gets synergy by being part of a wider partnership programme and has strong business sponsorship. Esso also have strong foundations and a supportive culture. It is the combination of these enablers that explains their success.

A Management Agenda

Solving the problems of IT–business integration noted at the beginning of the chapter requires many changes. Educational institutions, trainers, and consultants all have a role to play. It is commercial organizations, though, who have the motivation to take a lead. IT managers, business managers, and HR managers must join forces on an agenda for change.

The table of bridging mechanisms (Table 22.2) and the framework of enablers (Table 22.3) can be used as a basis for assessing the effectiveness of IS–business partnerships. Thus, the intensity of use of different mechanisms and their outcomes are one set of indicators. Another is the measurement of factors in the hierarchy and their degree of alignment and synchronization. The following check-list, based on the capabilities, levers, and enablers listed in Table 22.3, is offered as a quick check for determining priority areas for improvement.

General

- Is the division of IT responsibilities between the IS function and the business commensurate with the organization structure and its external environment?
- To what extent do you regularly audit IT issues including quality of IS–business partnerships?
- How would you characterize your environment regarding stability, change, predictability, and so on? Do the processes and output of corporate strategic plans reflect this?
- How are your IT resources and investment divided between improving efficiencies in current business operations and general strategic advantage applications? Is the balance appropriate? If not how can it be shifted?
- To what extent would you describe (a) the organization, (b) the IS function as an innovative, changing, responsive, and learning organization? What programmes are in place to develop these attributes?

Organizational Enablers

- Have you recently audited your climate and culture, assessing such factors as attitudes to IT, change, mutual trust, and interdepartmental co-operation?
- How much does the language in everyday use, when referring to other departments, reflect a spirit of co-operation versus competition?
- How consistent are key management structures and processes? What are the blockages to improving alignment between them?
- Is your business and IT strategy clear, articulate, and well communicated throughout the organization?
- To what extent are the CEO and the board knowledgeable and avid believers in the strategic benefits of IT? What could you do to change these attitudes for the better?

Levers

- To what extent do you employ the different bridging mechanisms listed in Table 22.2. Have you developed ways of measuring their extent and their effectiveness?
- How many hybrid managers and team leaders do you have in your organization? Have you discovered your hidden hybrids?
- To what extent do you have in place active programmes and joint activities and processes that help develop the IT–line partnerships? Should you be doing more? Pick one key area for joint improvement.

Foundations

- To what extent do human resource and people considerations feature in management decisions about the business and IT?
- Does your organization have well-developed processes and measures to develop organizational capabilities and competences? To what extent would you regard all your employees as computer-literate?
- Do you have an effective programme of liaison with educational establishments? Do you sponsor hybrid courses and take students on industrial placement?
- Do you have an active programme of career development geared around competences rather than merely grades and structures?
- Do you carry out team development activities for project teams and senior management teams? Are your IT specialists encouraged to attend courses in self-awareness, personal development, and 'soft' skills?

Summary

This chapter has identified the special contributions of hybrid managers towards solving important information management challenges. These contributions apply to development of winning business strategies, systems development, and the provision of effective IS services. As well as business and IT competence, hybrid managers must have good general management skills, especially 'soft' interpersonal skills.

With a few notable exceptions, organizations are not doing enough to develop the hybrid managers they will need to solve these challenges. Education, career planning, management development, and training all need critical reappraisal in the light of the need to develop more hybrid managers. Attention must also be given to the wider organizational context and the range of bridging methods that can usefully be deployed to improve IT–business integration. A framework for considering these factors has been described.

References

Amoroso, D. L., Thompson, R. L., and Cheney, P. H. (1989), 'Examining the Duality Role of IS Executives: A Study of IS Issues', *Information Management*, 17/1 (Aug.), 1–12.

Couger, J. D., and Zawacki, R. A. (1980), *Motivating and Managing Computer Personnel*, New York: Wiley.

Drury, D. H. (1985), 'A Survey of DP Steering Committees', *Information and Management*, 9/1 (Aug.), 1–7.

Earl, M. J. (1989), *Management Strategies for Information Technology*, Hemel Hempstead: Prentice-Hall.

—— and Runge, D. A. (1988), 'Gaining Competitive Advantage from Telecommunications', in M. J. Earl (ed.), *Information Management: The Strategic Dimension*, Oxford: Oxford University Press.

Earl, M. J., and Skyrme, D. J. (1992), 'Hybrid Managers: What Do We Know About Them?', *Journal of Information Systems*, vol. 2, pp. 169–87.

—— (1990), *Hybrid Managers: What Do We Know About Them?*, Research and Discussion Paper, RDP 90/6, Oxford Institute of Information Management, Templeton College, Oxford.

Hartog, C., and Rouse, R. A. (1987), 'A Blue Print for the New IS Professional', *Datamation*, 33/20 (15 Oct.), 64–9.

Keen, P. G. W. (1988), 'Rebuilding the Human Resources of IS', in M. J. Earl (ed.), *Information Management: The Strategic Dimension*, Oxford: Oxford University Press.

Kotter, J. P. (1982), *The General Managers*, New York: Free Press.

Lodahl, T. M., and Redditt, K. L. (1989), *Datamation*, 35/4 (15 Feb.), 78–83.

Niederman, F., Brancheau, J. C., and Wetherbe, J. C. (1991), 'Information Systems Management Issues for the 1990's', *MIS Quarterly*, vol. 15, no. 4, pp. 475–500.

Palmer, C., and Ottley, S. (1990), *From Potential to Reality: Hybrids—A Critical Force in the Application of Information Technology in the 1990s*, London: British Computer Society.

Scott-Morton, M. S. (1990) (ed.), *The Corporation of the 1990s: Information Technology and Organizational Transformation*, Oxford: Oxford University Press.

Sparrow, P. (1990), *Human Resources in Information Systems*, London: PA Consultants.

Tomlin, R. (1989), *Business Success and IT—Strategies for the 1990s*, London: Amdahl Executive Institute.

23

The Chief Information Officer: Past, Present, and Future

MICHAEL J. EARL

Introduction

The post of IT director probably appeared on the organization chart of large corporations in the early 1980s (Diebold Research Group 1984), while the title 'Chief Information Officer'—or CIO—hit our consciousness a few years later. The CIO label was perhaps a recognition that the Information Systems function had become critical in many organizations and that therefore its most senior executive deserved parity with, say, the Chief Financial Officer. By the end of the decade, the post—if not the title—was common in large organizations. It could be a main board position reporting to the CEO, or located one or two levels below, reporting to a board member.

As Applegate and Elam (1992) imply, the rise of the CIO marked the transition from what might be called the DP era to the Information Era. Perhaps three forces were at work. First, as new information technologies arrived and began to converge with computing, somebody was required to oversee the formation and execution of technical policies and standards required in architecting and building the IT infrastructure (Rockart *et al.* 1982; Elam *et al.* 1988). Secondly, this explosion of information processing created an activity in need of leadership and a production function in need of management which required more than the skills of a technical specialist (Rockart 1982; Hurley and Ko 1991). Indeed, as the size of IT budgets increased, it became difficult to resist the notion that a corporate officer should be appointed to ensure that information resources were efficiently and effectively deployed. Then, as it became clear that IT could be a source of strategic advantage, or at least an essential strategic capability, it was argued that a senior general manager should be charged with integrating IT decisions with business development (Synott 1987; Cash *et al.* 1992).

By 1990, however, the turnover rate of CIOs was attracting attention so that one waggish article redefined CIO as 'Career Is Over' (Rothfeder 1990). Turnover rates of about 30 per cent have been reported (Hurley and Ko 1991), and indirectly confirmed by two recent studies of CIO roles (Applegate and Elam 1992; Grover *et al.* 1993). These trends raise at least two questions. First, for individual CIOs, it would seem important to understand what is required to ensure survival in the role. Secondly, we also might ask whether the role will survive in organizations or in what ways it might change.

This chapter seeks to address these questions, first by drawing on research done by the author in 1991 and 1992, and secondly by 'reasoned speculation' drawing on workshop discussions with the CIOs in 1994. The research took advantage of an opportunity suggested by the sudden demise of a number of well-known CIOs in the UK in 1990 and 1991. Ten 'famous name' IT directors who had suddenly lost their jobs to the surprise or anxiety of their industry peers were studied in comparison with ten 'survivors', matched by industrial sector. The aim was to explore the requirements, competencies, practices, contexts, and impacts of the CIO position using the lens of survival. The outcome was the identification of ten factors which could be critical to survival. In their own right, they may have the following practical implications:

1. as a basic toolkit for CIO survival—or perhaps CIO improvement;
2. as a guidance for those concerned with recruiting and developing IS executives;
3. in furthering our understanding of the role of the CIO;
4. in generating propositions about effective IS management.

On the other hand, these 'critical survival factors' could represent only an historical view. Three years later the context may have changed substantially. Certainly, the technological environment is somewhat turbulent and the economic assumptions of the 1980s do not translate too well into the 1990s. So the workshops in both the UK and USA have sought to update these views for the present and to derive a sense of the future challenges for the IS function and its leadership. This chapter will suggest that the challenges of the role of the CIO are not likely to get any easier. Indeed, the future looks even more demanding.

Analysing the Past

Two sources drove the framework for analysis in the survival study (Fig. 23.1). The claims of normative literature and results of prior research were combined with some 'conventional wisdoms' heard amongst IT practitioners. Unfortunately, findings from other recently published studies of CIOs were not available when this investigation began in 1991, and therefore they will be used here to support retrospectively the framework or to make sense of the results. The framework was operationalized through

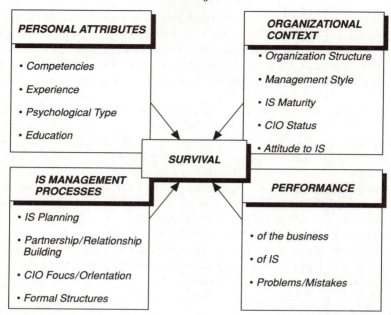

Fig. 23.1. *Framework for analysis in survival study*

an interview questionnaire which created fifty-one variables which might distinguish survivors from non-survivors.

Survival

Survival, the 'dependent variable', was not judged to be either good or bad or even a proxy measure of effectiveness. Indeed, there are several inferences that can be drawn from the turnover rates reported earlier. The job of CIO may be very difficult or unnecessary, the non-survivors be incompetent or no longer appropriate, or their host organizations either be weak in information management or a hostile environment in which to lead the IS function. Conversely, survivors may be lucky or adroit careerists rather than effective or valued—or they may work in organizations which cannot evaluate CIO performance. What we can assert with some confidence, however, is that ineffective CIOs are less likely to survive than effective ones, and most CIOs would prefer survival to non-survival. Furthermore, in looking for market tests of effectiveness, survival is one obvious candidate.

In terms of research methodology, the states of survival and non-survival provide the basis of a classical test of differentiation or discrimination. As, for example, in work done on corporate failure (Altman 1968), we can unambiguously delineate two populations (or samples) and search for discriminating independent variables—not necessarily to predict non-survival, but to suggest what contributes to survival.

IS Management Process

The assumption behind this set of independent variables is that if survival were in any way related to effectiveness, the emphasis and type of IS management processes could be influential. Because one of the rationales for creating the role of CIO has been the need to integrate IT investment decisions with business strategy development (Elam *et al.* 1988; Cash *et al.* 1992), we might assume that strategic IS planning is an important IS management process which CIOs should activate or encourage. Secondly, because several writers have stressed the need to be entrepreneurial in scanning both the business and technology environments (Synott and Gruber 1981; Rockart 1982; Synott 1987; Hurley and Ko 1991), we might expect that CIOs should adopt a proactive posture in IS planning. Indeed, Grover *et al.* (1993) reported that CIOs ranked entrepreneurship as their most important role. Three models were used to examine the degree of proactive IS planning: Parsons's (1985) linkage strategies, Hodgkinson's (1991) strategic management styles for corporate IS departments, and Earl's (1993*a*) strategic IS planning approaches.

Since information systems increasingly cross functional and other organizational boundaries, and since many strategic IT application ideas come from line managers, past writers have stressed the need for CIOs to be good at relationship-building (Rockart 1982; Brown *et al.* 1989; Hurley and Ko 1991; Cash *et al.* 1992). Grover *et al.* (1993) found that CIOs ranked the spokesman role (characterized as building relationships with others) as their second most important activity. Indeed, this would seem necessary in improving IS–user partnership as prescribed by Henderson (1990). Thus, emphasis on relationship-building is an obvious candidate survival factor. The CIO–CEO relationship is another. It was assumed to be important in the Feeny *et al.* (1992) study and if, as several writers have argued, the CIO is expected to be a member of (or contribute to) the general management team in order to integrate IS and business strategies, a good CEO relationship would seem to be necessary. Some have argued that CIOs could eventually become CEOs (Rockart 1982; Synott 1987).

Proactive planning and relationship-building both suggest that the CIO should spend significant amounts of time outside the boundaries of the IS function. Indeed, a study by Ives and Olson (1981) found that IS managers emphasized management of downward relationships, perhaps at the expense of working with peers and superiors. In an earlier study of IS leadership (Earl *et al.* 1986), recording whether CIOs were internally or externally focused, or sought a balance, was found to be a simple way of analysing their agendas. This test was used here.

Finally, 'folklore' and anecdotes from executive search consultants suggested that potential CIOs, when being interviewed, often were keen to
explore whether formal management processes were in place and encouraged. Were there steering committees, are there planning processes, was
there a clear mandate for the CIO, and so on? How much the CIOs stressed
such formal administrative infrastructure, therefore, was ascertained.

Personal Attributes

A job specification for the CIO could be expected to list requisite
competences and experience. A number seem to follow from the earlier
descriptions of the CIO role and several writers have speculated on them.
Given the operational nature of the IS function—running data-centres,
networks, and development shops—together with the need to work with
vendors, the requirement to manage specialists and the need to formulate technology policies and plan architecture, technological know-how
would seem essential (Rockart *et al.* 1982; Synott 1987; Earl 1989). This
was assessed. Also, years of IS experience were recorded on the assumption
that much technological knowledge and updating have to be gained 'on
the job'.

However, the arguments for relationship-building and teamwork imply
that communication, networking, and political skills are also important
(Rockart *et al.* 1982; Donovan 1988; Brumm 1989). These were assessed
under the collective label of social skills. On the basis that integrating with
others also requires an understanding of an organization's culture and
'how things get done around here', a similar assessment of organizational
know-how was made.

If CIOs are to help to discover opportunities for strategic IT applications, we can also assume the need for business knowledge (Synott 1987;
Earl 1989). This, plus industry knowledge, was assessed and years of general management experience recorded. Synott and Gruber (1981) suggested
that the CIO needs general management skills to balance the specialist
skills. Recently Applegate and Elam (1992) noted that newly appointed
CIOs tended to have considerable general management experience. Alter
(1990) reported that CEOs prefer a CIO with a business background as
well as technological experience.

It was felt that a complementary, and perhaps more objective, assessment of some of these aptitudes and competencies could be achieved by
use of a psychometric test. The Myers–Briggs test of psychological preference was chosen for two reasons. It is widely used in organizations and
thus is familiar to many CIOs. Secondly, the instrument has been used to
compare managers at large with IS professionals (Lyons 1985), with results
suggesting that IS professionals are a little different, for example, being

more introverted than the average manager. We might expect, given the apparent need for networking, communication, entrepreneurship, and leadership, that some degree of extroversion was helpful in the CIO role. Equally other preferences, such as perceiving rather than judging, could be influential. In other words, psychological preference could be a factor contributing to survival in its own right.

Education could be equally important in a role expected to combine technological and managerial competencies. Formal qualifications of CIOs were recorded in order to explore this dimension.

Organizational Context

CIO folklore often seems to relate to context. For example, as the IS function has become generally more decentralized or federal in nature (von Simpson 1990; Hodgkinson 1991), do the power, influence, and visibility of corporate CIOs diminish, especially as their command of the total IS budget reduces (Applegate and Elam 1992)? Or does the need for technology policy-making and functional leadership become more important for a centralized IS function within a decentralized host—as implied by some writers (Rockart *et al.* 1982; Cash *et al.* 1992; Grover *et al.* 1993)? The structure of the host organization and of the IS function could influence survival.

Management style, particularly the degree of formality or informality, could enhance or limit the extent to which CIOs can be entrepreneurial, build relationships, or formulate sustainable policies. Pyburn's (1983) classification of styles in his IS planning study was applied to explore this variable.

Appointment of a CIO could reflect an organization's maturity in IS management (Benbasat *et al.* 1980; Ein Dor and Segev 1982) and thus IS-mature organizations could be more conducive to survival, since the role is likely to be appreciated. Alternatively, IT could be more critical as the organization matures; certainly Grover *et al.* (1993) found that the managerial scope of the CIO's job increased with IS maturity. A stage model which emerged from a prior, broader IS leadership study was used to examine these conjectures (Earl *et al.* 1986).

Given the need espoused earlier for CIOs to operate at the top levels of the company (Synott 1987; Cash *et al.* 1992), we can expect a concern with reporting level and hierarchical status. Indeed, the proportion of CIOs reporting to board level or to the CEO is increasing (Raghunathan and Raghunathan 1989; Applegate and Elam 1992). Data on reporting level and involvement with top-level decision-making were therefore collected.

A final, potential contextual variable is the organization's attitude to IS. This could be either a given or something the CIO can influence, but it is not uncommon to hear CIOs complain of low interest in IS and low regard for the IS function. Whether there was an agreed view on the potential contribution of IT to the organization, and the ambitions held, were solicited using a nominal scale.

Performance

It would not be surprising if performance failures led to CIO dismissal. Indeed, Gibson and Nolan's (1974) 'stages theory' was partly founded on crises stimulating a change in management and the IS manager. Thus, personal assessments of the performance of IS were collected, as seen through the eyes of the CIO. Also CIO mistakes and problems were documented and analysed.

Equally, although there are many variables and time-lags mediating any relationship between business performance and the survival of the CIO, disappointing business results can lead to changes in top management. Business performance, therefore, was recorded using an ordinal scale.

Methodology

The sample size and construction were driven by availability of 'famous name' non-survivors. Ten were approached and readily agreed to participate. In order to take out any industry effect in the analysis, ten survivors were then chosen, matched by industry type. The survivor of each matched pair had to have been in the job longer than the non-survivor. At the time of study the mean tenure of non-survivors was 7.3 years and of survivors 8.8 years. It was felt that richer data could be collected if most individuals had been in post for several years rather than for a short tenure. All the subjects had occupied the highest level in the IS function in their organization and reported to the CEO or an executive one or two levels below. Not one interviewee had the formal title of CIO; IS director or IT director were the most frequent labels.

Clearly, there is a risk that a survivor could become a non-survivor the day after he or she had been studied. The data were collected in the first half of 1992. Three years later seven of the survivors were still in post. Another retired from his company. Two were promoted to more senior positions outside IS, but in the same organization. Of the ten non-survivors, only two took up another CIO position.

The data were collected by two means. First, semi-structured interviews were conducted with all the CIOs for between two and four hours. An interview questionnaire was used, designed around the framework for analysis in Figure 23.1. Subsequently, the respondents were asked to complete the Myers–Briggs questionnaire on psychological preferences; two survivors chose not to. Most of the interview questions were closed and the

respondents selected the questions themselves, that is, without any interpretation by the author. Three types of data were collected:

1. factual, descriptive data such as age, reporting level, and so on;
2. self-assessment scoring using four-point ordinal scales, for example,
   to measure technological know-how or social skills. Scale anchors
   were provided for the respondents;
3. positioning on classifications or taxonomies, for example, Earl's
   (1989) planning approaches or Pyburn's (1983) management styles.

Before most of these closed questions were asked, an open version also
was posed. This allowed collection of experiences, reflections, anecdotes
and 'raw' reactions before the respondent could be biased by the closed
question. This had two benefits. Where there was not an obvious way of
constructing a reliable measure of a candidate variable, it could be assessed
by simple content analysis of the interview notes of whether and to what
extent the variable was mentioned. Secondly, similar content analysis could
be done to search for any unanticipated but seemingly evident discriminating factors. Clearly this is more qualitative and subjective evidence and
an ordinal scale from 1 to 7 was constructed for these factors.

All the 'measures' were based on the CIOs' perceptions. It could have
been useful to capture the views of both user managers and general
managers on some of the variables, in the spirit of triangulation. However,
access to the organizations of several of the non-survivors proved difficult.
Most previous studies of CIOs have collected data only from CIOs.

Comparison of two data-sets allowed use of classical statistical analysis.
Although the sample sizes were small, tests of significance were used to
establish differences on a univariate basis, selecting a test according to the
variable type. If a measure was derived by content analysis of the responses
to open questions, the variable had to be significant at the 1 per cent level
to be judged a 'critical survival factor', because of its qualitative, interpretative nature. Others were classified as critical to survival if they were significant at the 10 per cent level or better. Since such tests of significance and
cut-off points could be inappropriate for small samples, percentage fre-
quencies for each variable were calculated and, where possible, are dis-
closed in discussing the results in the next section.[1]

Finally, since much of the data comprise *self-perceptions* of the CIOs, there
is a risk that non-survivors could be more self-critical than survivors.
Certainly, non-survivor interviews were deeply reflective and sometimes
quite graphic. However, as the next section demonstrates, contrasting

[1] Methodology employed in the survival study is discussed more fully elsewhere, including
disclosure of the questionnaire, statistical tests and results, and simple, descriptive data on
each CIO. See M. J. Earl, *The Chief Information Officer: An Analysis of Survival*, Centre for
Research in Information Management, London Business School, Sussex Place, Regents Park,
London NW1 4SA.

comments and incidents recorded from survivors and non-survivors did seem to substantiate the discriminating factors.

Critical Survival Factors

Five variables were significant at the 1 per cent level and five at the 10 per cent level. These are presented within the structure of the framework for analysis in Figure 23.1. This permits discussion of both significant variables and some of the more notable insignificant ones.

Personal Attributes

IT Know-How was significant at the 10 per cent level. One-hundred per cent of survivors felt confident or competent in understanding and discussing technical details of information systems and IT, whereas only 50 per cent of non-survivors did so. Survivors typically believed that they could have a good argument with specialists on technical matters, whereas non-survivors felt either 'naked' on technology or relied on being briefed by others on technical matters.

One non-survivor admitted that he 'realised the importance of architecture several years too late'. Another reflected that 'I was never able to break through the jargon and camouflage when discussing development problems'. One ex-CIO reflected: 'I overestimated the degree to which social skills could overcome technology know-how. You can't swan through IT issues—the techies will stand by and watch you fall off the cliff.' Another admitted: 'I don't understand the technology and after 5 years my peers thought I did. But my ignorance affected priority-setting, architecture decisions, dealing with suppliers and understanding operational crisis.' So poor technology know-how may not be a disadvantage in the short-term, but before long can be a severe handicap.

Survivors spoke of IT becoming ever more complex, of the industry moves towards 'openness' increasing options, of the rate of technological change and thus the need not only to be confident on technical matters but to be continuously updating oneself. One commented that: 'You can't communicate without a sound technology base.' Another opined that: 'A technical background helps; you feel at ease.'

We might expect the head of a specialist function to be a competent specialist, and thus this result may not seem surprising. It is perhaps relevant to note that of the non-survivors, 50 per cent were not career-IS professionals (see below), and thus it could be likely that they would feel 'technologically disadvantaged'—even though on average non-survivors had been in post for 7.3 years. Perhaps the more specialist a function is the more important functional expertise becomes. Feeny *et al.* (1992) found that CIOs with good CEO relationships were continuously informed on technological developments and were able to interpret their significance to the business in which they worked.

IS Experience may be the obvious means of developing IT know-how, especially for many who are too old to have received formal education in IT. On several measures of IS experience—number of years, percentage of career in IS, predominant experience in IS—survivors tended to have been career IS professionals. Indeed, having twenty-one years or more experience in IS was significant at the 5 per cent level. Only 10 per cent of non-survivors had this depth of experience compared with 90 per cent of survivors.

Experience may teach people the challenges of IS and prepare them for the leadership role. As one immigrant into IS put it: 'It took me 18 months to understand the function, whereas usually it had taken me six months to understand a new job. I couldn't get to the basics, fix the problems and make things happen.' In contrast, a survivor with a career in IS suggested that 'experience gives you instinctive technical knowledge. You nearly always know the right questions to ask.' Another observed not only that IT was complex, 'but there are always a hundred and one things to sort out'.

Experience in IS, therefore, seems likely to teach you judgement. Feeny *et al.* (1992) found that CIOs who had made their career in IS were more likely to have excellent CEO relationships. Applegate and Elam (1992) observed that in recruiting CIOs, CEOs preferred candidates with strong business backgrounds and strong IT backgrounds. Faced with a choice on these dimensions, however, they tended to opt for strong business and general management skills. This may not be sound practice if IS experience matters. Indeed, data collected in this study also indicates that the 'put in a business manager to sort it out' tactic may work for a time, but not in the longer run. Of the total sample, six had been given this mission; only one survived.

Social Skills also seemed significant at the 10 per cent level. Seventy per cent of survivors felt that they were perceived to be strong on matters of leadership, teamwork, communication, and motivation. Only 30 per cent of non-survivors were so confident. Several of the survivors had received company awards in recognition of these more managerial skills, for example, symbols such as diplomas, plaques, and commendations, or added roles such as task-force chairing, non-executive directorships of other lines of business, and role model work.

Non-survivors often confessed to weaknesses in social skills and sometimes to aversion to the more communicative, political, and expressive sides of the job. In other words, there is perhaps a need for both a social 'intent' as well as social skills. For example, a survivor talked of 'creating win-win situations and not win-lose tussles'. A non-survivor confessed to being 'comfortable on presentations and one to one meetings—but I do not like politics, I'm intolerant of slow people . . . if only things had been more rational'.

The Feeny *et al.* (1992) study also suggested the importance of these competences and of proactive team roles. The Myers–Briggs data collected here on psychological preferences, therefore, could be expected to be relevant. Indeed, one seemingly significant psychological categorization was discovered. Survivors (70 per cent) tended to be extroverts whilst non-survivors (60 per cent) were more introverted. This tendency perhaps could be isolated as an eleventh critical survival factor. However, two survivors declined to complete the Myers–Briggs questionnaire and so this result should be treated with care. Nevertheless, it could be an important factor. Other surveys (Lyons 1985) have found that DP professionals on average are more introverted than the managerial population at large. If social skills matter for survival, we could infer that the typically introvert, DP professional would be a risky appointment as a CIO.

Sensitivity was significant at the 1 per cent level. This is the capacity to sense what is important to the organization, not only business direction but management priorities and organizational values. 'Be dynamic, but only in what the company is ready for', said one survivor. Conversely, a non-survivor had continued to champion and develop an adventurous IT application which neither senior management nor the users believed offered any strategic advantage. In retrospect he believed that a new CEO finally despaired and that this was one reason why the CIO was dismissed. In other words, survivor CIOs seem to be good tacticians.

One element of sensitivity was often stressed: the ability to distinguish a significant sea-change in the organization which should be heeded from a passing squall which could soon be forgotten. Some survivors had been willing to retreat, retrench, and reorient for two years or more in order not to be a martyr to a short-term difficulty and miss a longer-term goal, for example, a one-time shared vision. 'It's important for us to save functional cost because revenues are flat', remarked one sensitive survivor. A non-survivor had done the opposite and resisted discussion of budget cuts because he believed IT investments should be protected.

A third aspect of sensitivity is appreciating when to conform and when to challenge. At least four non-survivors attributed their departure in large part to failing to conform or to hectoring executives to be different. One reflected: 'Being antagonistic once or twice works, but in the long run it is wearing on people.' Another concluded that 'you have to manage the world as it is and not as you would like it to be'. A third had doggedly resisted decentralization of IS to match the host organization structure because he felt that the breakup of a corporate architecture would be damaging to the business. However, top management saw few connections or synergies across the new divisions to consider this a risk.

'Sensitivity' may seem like a recipe for compliance and being reactive. However, as we shall see later, leadership and being proactive are not
prohibited. Sensitivity is probably more about avoiding misfit behaviour,
and understanding what is acceptable to the organization at different
points in time, and about sensing when the IS function itself is being
asked to change. It may have been displayed by the CIOs in the Stephens
et al. (1992) study who showed 'skill in reading situations and responding appropriately'. In the current study, 70 per cent of the survivors had
actively demonstrated these qualities. None of the non-survivors had, and
40 per cent had experienced substantial problems of this sort.

Non-significant personal attributes of note included industry know-how,
organizational know-how, and business know-how. Industry know-how was
assessed by recording years of experience in the respondent's current industry. The two CIO sets could not be distinguished on this basis, suggesting
that either industry knowledge does not matter or that it is necessary but
not sufficient for survival.

The same sort of conclusions can be made about organizational know-
how, which was assessed by the CIOs positioning themselves on a continuum
of acceptance by, and integration with, the top influencers and decision-
makers in their firm. However, as certain of the significant management processes below would seem to require knowledge of 'how to get things done
around here and how to influence those that count', we might guess that
organizational know-how also is necessary but not sufficient for survival.

Business know-how was assessed also on a self-reporting scale: 90 per
cent of survivors and 80 per cent of non-survivors felt that they were either
credible businessmen or were businessmen first and technologists second.
In other words, this competence also may be necessary but not sufficient
for CIO survival.

IS Management Processes

Building a *shared vision* for the contribution of IT to the business was
significant at the 1 per cent level. This variable emerged from content
analysis of the interview data and 60 per cent of non-survivors talked about
problems in this domain. Some were concerned about the lack of a sense
of direction in the business. 'There was not enough vision at the top', or
'I desperately asked about the vision for the business', or 'There was
no group strategy', were typical complaints. Others criticized the focus of
the business. 'It was a very short-term sort of business', or 'The CEO was
very vague when it came to vision', are indicative observations. Organizational changes were sometimes blamed for destroying visions and visioning.
'The movers and shakers left when *he* was appointed CEO', recalled one
CIO. Another believed that organizational decentralization had led to dilution of belief in, and commitment to, a corporate IS strategy. Finally, some

non-survivors had realized that they had been creating and promoting a vision of their own. Typical revelations included: 'The global IS strategy was my vision alone', or 'The Board was not a team and I felt personal ownership of IS', or 'I couldn't get people to understand what the business was really about rather than what they thought it was about'.

Ninety per cent of survivors made no such complaints and several emphasized the importance of both constructing a shared vision and constantly pursuing it. Four elements were emphasized. First, survivors tended to have secured such a vision and were clearly concentrating on achieving it. 'My job is to keep administrative costs down', was the focus of a CIO in an insurance company. Secondly, they had a good feel of what a sensible vision looked like. 'You have to understand the few areas where IT can add value', or 'agreeing what is important from the company's point of view', or 'setting a target to make a significant difference to the business', were emphasized. Next, they underlined the shared and collective nature of a vision. 'However it is discovered, you must share the vision', was one view. Another CIO had created a vision team of senior executives whilst another reflected: 'My role has been to facilitate visioning by senior management.' Finally, this factor seems to be constantly on survivors' minds. 'The day you think you have finished discovering and agreeing the direction to go, you're gone', or 'selling a business-oriented IS vision is crucial', were typical sentiments.

Pursuit of a shared vision as a survival factor is strongly hinted at in the Feeny *et al.* (1992) study of CIO–CEO relationships. An identity of vision—to transform the business—strongly believed in by both parties typified effective relationships. Furthermore, the CIOs were in part catalysts to business thinking. Of course, some contexts may be more propitious than others for developing and internalizing a shared vision (see below). However, survival seems in part to depend on it and survivors tended to work to facilitate vision-building whatever the constraints. Developing a shared vision for the contribution of IT can be seen as a combination of several of the required IS management process characteristics called for by past writers on CIOs noted earlier, for example, entrepreneurship, proactive IS strategic planning, and working with managers outside the IS function as well as within it.

Indeed *proactive IS planning* appeared to be a survival factor, in that three closely related variables in this domain were significant at the 10 per cent level. Using Earl's (1993a) taxonomy of strategic IS planning approaches, survivors tended to be involved in the business-led or organizational approaches and not the other three, more bureaucratic or technocratic, approaches. Approaches adopted by non-survivors were more varied, only 40 per cent following the two more proactive or interactive approaches.

Survivors did not wait for application requests but instead actively sought to understand the business direction and to discover user needs. They got involved with strategy-making processes, such as task-forces, management team meetings, executive retreats, and workshops. Non-survivors rarely had any mandate for such interaction with the business; survivors did, and were expected to contribute to business thinking as well as to IS strategy-making. Using Parsons's (1985) framework of linkage strategies, 80 per cent of survivors placed themselves in 'centrally planned' or 'leading edge', categories whilst non-survivors placed themselves across the full range of Parsons's categories, including those which gave IT a passive role in the business.

This combination of proactive IS mandate and strategic information systems planning approach was perhaps substantiated by the variable 'strategic management style' which used Hodgkinson's (1991)[2] categorization of corporate IS management behaviour. All survivors adopted a strategic leadership style, being expected to work with others to align IS with business strategies and to take initiatives on IT policies. In contrast, 60 per cent of non-survivors adopted a strategic guidance style, being cautious about too much interaction with the business on IS planning and settling for guidelines rather than policies on important technological matters.

Relationship-Building as predicted from analysis of past work, appeared critical at the 1 per cent level. Ninety per cent of survivors emphasized how important relationship-building was in their work. Non-survivors, in contrast, were generally either frustrated or inactive on this front.

Survivor CIOs actively built relationships with their peers and superiors, getting to know them and working with them. Building relationships over time with those in power, with other functional heads, with one's superior, and with those who are likely to sponsor strategic IT applications was stressed by most survivors. Many writers have emphasized the importance of senior management relationships, partnership, or networking (Rockart 1982; Donovan 1988; Cash *et al.* 1992). Stephens *et al.* (1992) found their CIOs devoted much time to working with senior executives and gaining peer acceptance and Feeny *et al.* (1992) suggested that relationship-building was necessary in building shared visions of how to transform business through IT.

Relationship-building may be a political imperative for any senior manager today (Kotter 1982), but in the CIO role it makes particular sense for several reasons:

- to help identify new applications for IT and 'market' new opportunities;
- to influence perceptions of the role of IT and to update peers on technological change;
- to build a shared vision of IT's contribution to the business;

---

[2] Also reported and updated in Chapter 12 of this volume.

- to build coalitions for the support of IT investments and the IS function;
- to help understand the business and the organization;
- to influence perceptions of your own actual and potential contribution to the business;
- to enable working across functional and other organizational boundaries.

How did survivors emphasize this survival factor? They talked of proactively getting to know peers and superiors, taking sometimes two years to 'interest and educate' a new senior executive, of 'reaching out' to discover colleagues' interests and problems and helping to resolve them, of 'serving but not being subservient', of 'lengthy and continuous regeneration of educating executives'. A long-time survivor recalled that he had suffered a bad relationship with one colleague after a good spell, but had now purposely rebuilt the relationship.

Non-survivors, on the other hand, often reflected that they should have spent more time building alliances even when it seemed time-consuming. 'I didn't spend enough time on winning users' minds, educating and helping them. It was a mistake', one commented. Some complained of little interaction with management peers and of 'not being seen as an equal'. One non-survivor observed 'there was a network mafia and as a recruit from the outside, I never was admitted'. Another admitted he concentrated on downward relationships and did not enjoy the 'diplomacy and politics' required in a corporate role.

One particular relationship, that with the CEO, also was significant at the 1 per cent level. Feeny *et al.* (1992) found that CIOs with good relationships worked at it and many writers have emphasized the importance of 'top management support' and 'CEO involvement' in IS management. It is thus perhaps not surprising that a good *CEO relationship* appears to be a critical survival factor, not least for the following reasons

- to secure ultimate support for IT investments and the IS function;
- because different CEOs bring different values and priorities for the organization and it is important to understand them ('sensitivity' perhaps);
- because many IT issues are cross-functional and CEO involvement in resolving and managing them is crucial;
- because a shared vision of the contribution of IT to the business is important and unlikely to be achieved unless the CEO is both shaping and backing it;
- to enable the CIO to be recognized as a potential member of policy groups, task-forces, operating committees, and the like;
- because ultimately the CEO can influence the 'hiring and firing' decisions at top level.

Several of the survivors revealed that the importance of IT's contribution to development of the business had been largely due to the CEO's early vision. Another claimed that he owed his position and survival to much earlier days when he had proved his credibility to the CEO by sorting out an IT crisis. A survivor of ten years standing observed that there had been a new CEO every two years; 'each one was very different with different values and I had to get to know each one and be flexible in my style and actions.' Another of similar tenure, stressed: 'I must be near the CEO and on the one hand have a clear view of his expectations of me and on the other hand educate him about IT.' Survivors would make sure that they discussed business-related issues with their CEO. Some encouraged their CEO to join them on very occasional visits to demonstrations, vendor events, or seminars. If away-days or retreats were used for strategic reviews of IS, they would engage the CEO in planning the event.

Non-survivors, in contrast, often recalled graphic experiences in the CEO relationship. Three attributed their dismissal to the arrival of a new CEO who had doubts about either the importance of IT or about the performance of the IS function or, indeed, was just applying a new management broom. Three others had difficult relationships, in each case the CIO despairing or fighting rearguard actions rather than adjusting or seeking to rebuild consensus. Another reflected that 'IT went off the Managing Director's agenda. With subsequent organizational changes, I became more remote from the MD and then when we had a bad patch, I had no support or sponsor.' One non-survivor, when appointed, found he had strong support from the CEO and built a good relationship. A successor CEO had many reservations about IT and the CIO had a natural reluctance to spend time working on the CEO's attitudes and harnessing his support. In retrospect, he concluded that 'the CIO must earn credibility with the CEO, by whatever route, including informal means'. Some non-survivors also—perhaps validly—opined that there was neither any progress likely with IT nor any future for a proactive CIO under a particular CEO. 'He was the wrong guy to take IT forward, he was obsessed with costs'; 'our visionaries have left since he was appointed'; 'he went around rubbishing IT', were some of the comments. A relationship, in other words, is two-way and both the CIO and CEO have to work at it, as Feeny *et al.* (1992) have shown.

Performance

Credibility of IS performance is significant at the 1 per cent level. Survivors strove for excellent functional performance. Indeed, 80 per cent of survivors described how important performance credibility was in their personal philosophy or described significant events which had accorded them credibility in the organization. Only 10 per cent of non-survivors did likewise; however, 50 per cent of them felt that they had experienced a credibility problem or suffered from a significant crisis which had destroyed their credibility.

Survivors emphasized three aspects of performance:

1.   a track record of delivering IT applications and operations reliably;
2.   meeting wider performance measurement criteria, especially financial or budgetary targets;
3.   being willing to respond to user IS needs.

Several survivors felt that the credibility of the IS function depended on establishing a good track record. 'If the organization is not satisfied with operations, the whole view of IS is affected', was a typical view. In particular, exhortations about how IT can transform the business sound hollow if users are experiencing organizational failures and development delays. 'You can't sell the sizzle if you don't deliver', quipped one survivor. Indeed, another CIO suggested 'that if you get operational performance right it leads to other opportunities'. A CIO from the insurance sector, recognizing that IT underpinned most business processes, commented: 'We are a factory and we must be first class.' He also reflected that 'IS has a good reputation for delivering which is why I am still here'.

These survivors were not hands-on operational executives, just as Feeny *et al.* (1992) and Stephens *et al.* (1992) found. However, the 'internal' side of the job was important to them. They appointed reliable managers below them and were often quick to step in if problems arose. More than this, however, they made credibility a visible issue inside and outside the IS function. Examples included receipt and analysis of performance bulletins at 07.30 hrs. each day, ensuring a significant application was delivered every nine months, constructing operational targets and cost measures, and setting department standards, for example, in quality, higher than elsewhere in the company.

Meeting financial control performance criteria was felt by some survivors to be necessary to show that IT is not treated differently from other areas. This may be especially true after an era of year-on-year expenditure growth. One non-survivor attributed the beginning of his exit to incurring a budget deficit for the first time and not reacting quickly enough to pressures to remedy it.

Being willing to respond to user needs and problems was widely seen by survivors as necessary in building relationships, in demonstrating that IT can deliver rather than promise, and sometimes in discovering significant application development opportunities.

Non-survivors had corresponding reflections and incidents to report. 'The function lost credibility and so did I'; 'Not dealing early enough with the credibility issue was a mistake'; 'The perception of the function's performance, as opposed to the reality, was a problem.' This last reflection relates to a variable which was significant at the 10 per cent level. Whereas there was no significant difference in how survivors and non-survivors viewed the performance of IS, there was in how they thought their business viewed it. Non-survivors generally downgraded the latter estimate more than did survivors. As this is a very fragile measure, it seems reasonable not to isolate it as a discriminating variable but to conflate it with credibility. It does reinforce how important the perceptions of users are in establishing credibility and it does suggest that perceptions should be managed. However, when one non-survivor commissioned a user-satisfaction survey, the results were disappointing and added impetus to the CIO's downfall. Perceptions can only be managed, perhaps, if the reality is satisfactory in the first place.

The emphasis on credibility is somewhat at variance from the indications of the Feeny *et al.* (1992) study. CIOs with good CEO relationships seemed to be valued more for their wider contribution to the business than for being excellent at managing IT resources. However, it seems reasonable that non-credible IS performance would lead to non-survival. Indeed, as executives tire of the hype of IT, perhaps CIOs have to make credibility a priority.

Business Performance was not found to be a discriminating variable. The measure used—an ordinal, descriptive scale to capture the business's own view and to provide a clean-cut independent variable—was somewhat fragile. However, it is well known that more quantitative and time-series figures are problematic, not least in terms of causality, lags, and definitions.

In short, if performance matters in CIO survival, it is the perceived performance of IS, perhaps more managerially termed credibility or track-record.

Organizational Context

The Organization's Attitude to IT appeared significant at the 10 per cent level. Interviewees were asked to summarize *their* perception of the organization's expectation of the contribution of IT—whether IT was seen as a support tool, a critical resource, a means of transformation, or whether expectations were unclear. Their view of the perception of their superior or boss also was sought. Ninety per cent of survivors opined that both their superior and their organization believed IT was critical or transformational as opposed to either a 'support tool' or 'unclear'. Furthermore, 80 per cent of survivors claimed that there was a complete alignment of expectations amongst the CIO, his or her superior, and the organization at large. Conversely, only one non-survivor claimed such alignment. Ninety per cent of the non-survivors inhabited organizations where expectations apparently varied across the range.

Survivors often worked on this factor by arranging IS education programmes for business executives, taking executive teams away on strategy
discussions, building IS–user partnership programmes, and encouraging
the formation of multi-disciplinary teams to study application opportunities. In addition they would work on their superiors through one-to-one
mechanisms. As one survivor put it: 'The CEO sees IT as an enabler of
transformation and a critical factor in business success. The Finance Director sees IT as a back office technology and cost-cutter. The Finance
Director is my boss—I haven't fixed him yet.' In contrast, a non-survivor
was more passive: 'my boss wanted to retrench and run the business among
the old more traditional lines, and we didn't agree.'

Non-survivors often thought their company's attitude was at variance with
their own (correct) one. 'There was a mismatch in perception between what
I thought I was doing, namely, developing IS's strategic role and what they
thought, which was essentially a support role.' A slightly different frustration was voiced thus: 'they aspired to transformation but did not understand what was required or face up to the changes required.'

The organization's attitude to IT can be thought of as a given or as a
controllable. It may be the product of a shared vision or a necessary condition for achieving one. Perhaps importantly, none of the remaining contextual variables proved significant. Survivors and non-survivors inhabited
a mix of host organizational structures and IS functional configurations.
Survivors apparently had no reporting advantages over non-survivors either
in terms of hierarchical level or to whom they reported. Respondents
found it difficult to position themselves on two-stage models of IS maturity, expressing the view that organizations tend to vary in evolution both
across units and technologies. Evidence about IS maturity, therefore, was
lacking. Finally, survivors seemingly had no advantages in either formality
or extent of administrative infrastructure.

Learning From the Past

Earlier, four potential benefits of this study were suggested. The ten discriminating variables (Fig. 23.2) do suggest a basic *tool-kit* for CIO survival.
There is evidence that a mix of technical and managerial skills is essential, similar to the model of the 'hybrid manager' proposed by Keen
(1986) and studied by Earl and Skyrme (1992).[3] In particular, the 'survival factors' of relationship-building, CEO relationship, sensitivity, social
skills, proactive IS planning, building a shared vision, and the organization's attitude to IT point to the CIO being a good politician. On the
other hand, credibility, IT know-how, and IS experience suggest that the
CIO also must be able to deliver. However, the importance of IS experience

---

[3] And further discussed by Skyrme in Chap. 20 of this volume.

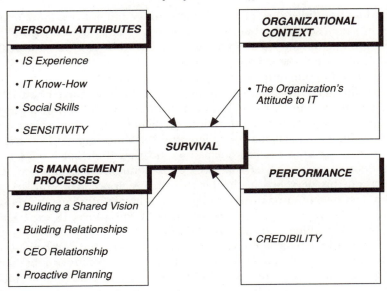

Fig. 23.2. *Critical survival factors*

suggests that 'hybrid' qualities can be acquired without any substantial link or business career development.

Some of the non-significant factors, however, add another dimension to the survival tool-kit. It was noted above that several conventional wisdoms relating to organizational context appear unhelpful. It seems that survival depends more on what you do than on the attributes of the environment in which you work.

Those responsible for *recruiting and developing* CIOs could draw at least three conclusions. First, despite a trend to the contrary in the UK in the 1980s, it seems unwise to appoint general managers with no IS experience to the position of CIO. Experience appears to matter, particularly per-haps in the matter of IT know-how and achieving credibility. The trend in the USA reported by Applegate and Elam (1992) of appointing CIOs who possess both strong business and strong IT backgrounds seems healthier. However, they did report a move away from promoting career IT pro-fessionals and opting for strong business and management skills where a choice had to be made. Our study of CIO survival cautions against such trade-offs.

Secondly, recruiters and HR managers can use the survival factors as an inventory of requisite competencies and develop profiles and assess-ment methods to match. How to develop CIOs is another matter. Should general managers have some IS experience as they advance their careers so that they have potential to be CIOs? Or should career IT managers who show wider aptitudes and interests be encouraged to acquire more experience 'in the business' so that they can return to be CIO with a good mix of skills? Since *considerable* IS experience seems to be associated with CIO survival, the latter strategy may be preferred.

In developing our understanding of the *role* of CIO, the results do suggest that the demands are wide-ranging. It could be the range of attributes required and the need to be both a functional specialist and a general manager at large in the organization, particularly working across other functions, that are particularly challenging. Yet Mintzberg (1971) observes that all managers are in fact specialists and that their roles tend to be dependent upon the functional area and hierarchical level where they work. From his perspective, the picture that is drawn from the 'critical survival factors' could be unsurprising. It is, however, perhaps the technological overlay represented by the variables IT know-how, IS experience, and credibility which add the 'risk premium'.

Two quotations from interviews provide some graphic confirmation of the demands of the role: 'I've done all the main executive jobs in the management team and the role of IS Director is the most difficult job by a street' (a non-survivor CIO). 'I want to take up the CEO job again—but I only get offered CIO jobs. I want four times the rate for being a CIO that I would accept for being CEO' (a non-survivor and former CEO).

To reinforce this picture, we can add a comment from a CEO interviewed in another study by the author: 'If you ask me how well my IS Director is doing, I cannot answer you simply. He has the most difficult job in the company' (a CEO).

Thirdly, do the 'Critical Survival Factors' in the IS management processes domain suggest any lessons for *managing IS* in general? All four indicate the importance of high integration and interaction between the IS function and the organization at large—in a processual sense. Practically, such a perspective perhaps is embodied in the partnership models of Henderson (1990) and the organizational approach to strategic IS planning of Earl (1993a).[4]

Analysis of the performance domain adds one other facet. 'Credibility' may be all-important, especially in an industry and function where hype can overtake reality. It is perhaps worth remembering that IS has a production function (even if outsourced) and this also may distinguish the CIO role from some other top-management positions.

Pulling the ten critical survival factors together in a more geographical way, we can perhaps historically see four imperative roles for the CIO as depicted in Figure 23.3. The significant variables of building a shared vision, proactive planning, and creating a positive attitude in the organization

---

[4] Further developed in Earl's 'An Organizational Approach to IS Strategy Making' (Chap. 7 of this volume).

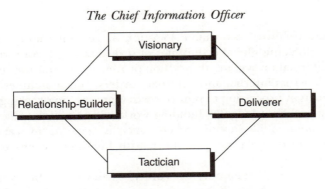

Fig. 23.3. *Four roles of the CIO*

towards IT suggest that the CIO needs to have some of the qualities of the *visionary*. The emphasis on credibility together with the attributes of IT know-how and IS experience may underline the qualities of a *deliverer*. The added and perhaps judgemental attribute of sensitivity indicates that the CIO also may have to be a *tactician*. This ability may be one that one is 'born with' as well as one learnt through the hard school of experience and possibly honed by strong social skills. These latter skills should help in building relationships with peers, superiors, and the CEO. In other words, the CIO also has to be a *relationship-builder*.

This picture is based on data collected in 1991 and 1992. It could reflect to some extent times past. The future may be different. More than likely, these roles are still required for some time to come. They represent, perhaps, what is required to integrate information technology with the organization and its management. Workshop discussions held in 1994 suggest that four further roles are required into the next decade.

From Past to Future

Four sets of challenges can be posited for the second half of the 1990s. They are summarized below. This perspective on the future demands on the CIO becomes somewhat polemical.

Business Challenges

Most large organizations in 1995 appear to have one or two major IT projects under way. For some, the need for global systems is apparent as enterprises firm up their understanding of global business strategies as described in the chapter by Earl and Feeny in this volume. We see increased internationalization of sources and markets and the need for systems which analyse performance, co-ordinate logistics, or cement trading alliances. Others are pursuing global economies of scale and need world-view management information systems, transaction processing systems with interfaces which work across internal and external borders, and sometimes rationalized information processing to reduce costs. Many are now seeking transfer of learning and knowledge by building world-wide networks, shared databases, and common 'life support' systems, such as electronic mail and groupware. The CIO is concerned, in short, with building systems that cross boundaries.

Business Process Reengineering (BPR), as described by Earl in this volume, is another thrust. This requires more systems which enable thinking and functioning across intra- and inter-organizational boundaries. It also, evidently, needs to embody the view that information systems alone achieve very little. A more socio-technical perspective on change is required. And we see CIOs being asked to lead BPR projects because they are perceived to understand and know their business's processes and maybe can bring a proactive but relatively neutral drive to business change.

A third thrust is the renewed search for, and investment in, systems which *inform*. The pursuit of an information edge (Earl *et al.*, forthcoming) can be seen in an ever-increasing purchase of external information, the development of enquiry and analysis systems (not to mention executive information systems), the emergence of new information roles in organizations, and the demands to 'put the "I" back into IT'. The complexity involved in building systems which inform and are easy to use should not be underestimated. And the need to invest in educating and reskilling both users and designers is becoming apparent.

The final thrust that we might observe is the demand in some divisional organizations to build shared service organizations (Short and Konsynksi 1992). Here administrative, information-intensive activities such as payroll processing, accounting, cash management, and the like are rationalized, consolidated, and centralized into one separate business unit. This unit becomes an information processing business.

One distinctive feature of all these business challenges is the systemic character of the responses. The resultant business changes are 'information systems plus', where the plus is organizational change, human resource development, and process thinking. They also tend to be cross-boundary investments, both inside and outside the organization. In these senses, the CIO is being asked to be a *systems thinker* as well as a visionary.

Technology Challenges

Several key trends are identifiable. For example, it is already clear that much information processing in organizations now takes place in a workstation environment. Specialist terminals as well as the pervasive personal computer dominate data processing in the 1990s. Companies are standardizing on desk-top architectures, often at the level of the operating system and associated application packages.

This distributed computing is evolving quickly into client-server configuratives. These are demanded, also, it seems, by more customer-facing systems and in-process information access. The technology platforms of the past are becoming outdated. In parallel, software and development methods are under change. Object-oriented programming techniques are being adopted both for conceptualizing system design and new IT architectures and for reusable and perhaps more rapid systems development. Enterprise-wide package-based applications are on the increase and it is not unusual for organizations to expect to buy as many IT applications as possible rather than 'make' them. Computer-aided software engineering (CASE) is still evolving and CASE-based application packages look promising (Hofman and Rockart 1994). Certainly, what are known as JAD (joint application development) and RAD (rapid application development) are the jargon of the mid-1990s. The CIO is having to encourage innovation in software development.

On top of these trends, business managers are demanding 'open systems' in at least two senses. First, they expect portability of applications across IT platforms and across boundaries. Secondly, they expect applications and technologies to be able to work together and share data. Some of the business challenges outlined earlier explain these demands.

At the same time, however, new information technologies continue to enter our organization. Multi-media computing is one example and the increasing interest in the 'Internet' and evolving 'information super-highways' is another. So the CIO is having continuously to forecast, track, evaluate, and introduce new technologies.

Meanwhile the IT industry itself is 'in churn'. The dominant manufacturers of the past do not look so omnipotent today. Software vendors are as important as hardware vendors. New suppliers rise up with each new technology and more and more service organizations offer consultancy, outsourcing, and systems integration. The CIO has had to become an industry-watcher too.

The consequence of this technological turbulence, combined in some ways with the new demands of business, is that large corporations are re-architecting their IT infrastructure. We hear anecdotal evidence of organizations taking on major re-architecting projects, with the observation that the cost will be 'somewhere between US$200m and 400m', often in one area of the business alone.

So the message from the past may have been that the CIO has to be a deliverer. He or she now has to be an *architect* too. We can guess, therefore, that IT know-how and IS experience continue to be essentials. We can also guess that quite often there will be a tension between acting as the deliverer, satisfying our needs relatively quickly, for example, or maintaining a reliable service, and introducing new technologies and rearchitecting.

Conceptual Challenges

By the end of the 1980s we were beginning to see significant changes in the context of business information processing. The obvious example in the western and developed economies was the impact of recession. As financial pressures increased, managements asked about the rising total cost of IT, the returns on their IT investments, and the affordability of what had become the costs of doing business in the IT-era. So it is not surprising that IS departments have been downsizing, aided by the relentless power-performance improvements of computing, and outsourcing data-centre operations, communications networks, PC maintenance, and systems development to third parties.

At the same time, questions of value for money became conflated with issues of user satisfaction and so practices of Total Quality Management, Customer Responsiveness, and Service Level Contracting have been imported into IS departments from the domain of operations management. By the mid-1990s these practices are becoming 'intensive and serious' as, for example, companies strive for six sigma levels of quality in their IS activities.

And a combination of rapid business change and environmental uncertainty have led managements to demand both flexibility and quick response in systems development. Rapid systems-building is becoming not only a matter of adopting new methods, but a question of redefining user–specialist relationships and re-examining make or buy policies. Indeed, a philosophy of rapid building is being applied through culture-change programmes in IS departments.

All these challenges, of course, raise questions of performance measurement in IS. We might expect some CIOs to institute new performance metrics in order to stimulate change. Certainly, we can suggest that to be a tactician is necessary in the sense of being sensitive to changes in the host organization's expectations of IS. But for the next few years CIOs may have to be more proactive in engineering change in their own function. They will have to be *reformers* too.

Organizational Challenges

Three important trends are apparent in organizing IT activities. First, as argued in Chapter 10 of this volume, by Earl *et al.*, large organizations continue to adopt federal IS structures, but often more various and complex than in the 1980s. The result is the location of IS groups and their managers at different levels of the organization. And some corporate CIOs who feel they have considerable responsibility but less authority may believe that it is more satisfying, or safer, to be a divisional IS executive rather than a corporate functional leader. Certainly, they are more likely to have many more distributed IS managers with whom they must work. They will have to build relationships at multiple levels.

A more recent and perhaps significant trend is the shift of information processing power to end-users. Not only are staff and managers at all levels of the organization likely to be competent work-station users, but some of them will have the capability to design, develop, and operate their own local applications. In some organizations the price of graduate or post-graduate recruitment is both a competitive remuneration package and a bundled configuration of a power PC, C++ programming, and high storage, multimedia accessories. These 'power-users' can then build their own analysis routines, financial instruments, software modules in products, or new information-based services. The IS function meanwhile may feel the need to preside over the architecture within which the power-users work, to ensure good practice and eventually to build industrial strength replacement applications. The CIO becomes as much concerned with user relationships as with business unit ones.

Finally, as the outsourcing movement gathers momentum and IS departments find they are dealing with ever more suppliers in a multi-vendor world, CIOs find themselves at the hub of many alliances. In other words, the CIO becomes an *alliance-manager* with third parties, business unit IS executives, and groups of power-users.

Four New Roles

The speculations above are suggestive of four further roles for the CIO of the future. These are combined with the four suggested by the past to produce Figure 23.4. They may be extensions of past role requirements, and to an extent each new role is related to one from the past. Thus they are depicted in pairs. Whether or not these pairings are valid, the picture suggests one message. The role of the CIO is not likely to get any easier. And the requirements suggested by the analysis of CIO survival in the past seem relevant for the future.

Conclusion

The study of CIO survival has highlighted ten critical survival factors, each of which would seem necessary for effective performance as well as holding on to the job. It also indicated several factors which do not influence

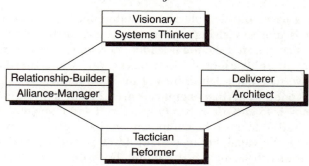

Fig. 23.4. *Eight roles of the CIO*

survival. Many of these related to organizational context, which suggests that CIOs should make the best of the conditions which they face. There is no evidence that generically the 'career is over' for CIOs. All non-survivors were replaced and the survivors remain in post—or have moved on to be replaced by others. Moreover, the ten critical survival factors in part suggest why the role is necessary—to facilitate a business vision for IT, to ensure good delivery, to help IS adapt as circumstances change, and to keep information management on executives' agendas.

The look into the future does not suggest that the IS function is likely to die or the role of CIO wither away. The responsibilities and emphases of the IS function look set to change, perhaps in the direction of the residual body presented by Willcocks and Fitzgerald in this volume, or perhaps evolving into something quite different as the next generation of technologies is assimilated.

Meanwhile, the demands on the CIO seemingly expand and a mix of technological and social skills remains essential to cope. So the epithet of the special, general manager still seems appropriate in describing the CIO role.

We have seen a few, insightful studies of CIOs in the early 1990s. They inform us as much about how to manage IS at large as about how to fulfil the job of functional leader in IS. It would seem that such studies should be continued, not only to understand the CIO role better but to document how it evolves and what is required for survival into the next millennium.

References

Alter, A. (1990), 'Good News, Bad News . . .', *CIO*, 3/4 (Jan.), 18–29.
Altman, E. I. (1968), 'Financial Ratios, Discriminant Analysis and the Prediction of Corporate Bankruptcy', *Journal of Finance*, 23/4 (Sept.).

Applegate, L. M., and Elam, J. J. (1992), 'New Information Systems Leaders: A Changing Role in a Changing World', *MIS Quarterly*, 16/4 (Dec.), 469–90.

Benbasat, I., Dexter, A. S., and Martha, R. W. (1980), 'Impact of Organisation Maturity on Information System Skill Needs', *MIS Quarterly*, 4/1 (Mar.), 421–34.

Brown, E. H., Karwan, K. R., and Weitzel, J. R. (1989), 'The Chief Information Officer in Smaller Organisations', *Information Management Review*, vol. 5, no. 3, pp. 31–45.

Brumm, E. (1989), 'Chief Information Officers in Service and Industrial Organisations', *Information Management Review*, vol. 5, no. 3, pp. 31–45.

Cash, J., McFarlan, F. W., McKenney, J., and Applegate, L. (1992), *Corporate Information Systems Management: Text and Cases*, Homewood, Ill.: Irwin.

Diebold Research Group (1984), *The Chief Information Officer Concept*, New York: Diebold Research Group.

Donovan, J. L. (1988), 'Beyond Chief Information Officer to Network Manager', *Harvard Business Review*, vol. 66, no. 3, pp. 134–40.

Earl, M. J. (1989), *Management Strategies for Information Technology*, Hemel Hempstead: Prentice-Hall.

—— (1993*a*), 'Experiences in Strategic Information Systems Planning', *MIS Quarterly*, 17/1 (Mar.), 1–24.

—— (1993*b*), *The Chief Information Officer: An Analysis of Survival*, Centre for Research in Information Management Working Paper 93/3, London Business School.

—— and Skyrme, D. (1992), 'Hybrid Managers: What Do We Know About Them?', *Journal of Information Systems*, 2/3 (July).

—— Bensaou, B., and Rockart, J. F. (forthcoming), *A Comparative Study of Information Systems in Four Countries*, Centre for Research in Information Management, London Business School.

—— Feeny, D. F., Hirscheim, R. A., and Lockett, M. (1986), *Information Technology. Executives' Key Education and Development Needs: A Field Study*. Oxford Institute of Information Management RDP 86/10, Templeton College, Oxford.

Ein-Dor, P., and Segev, E. (1982), 'Organisational Context and MIS Structure: Some Empirical Evidence', *MIS Quarterly*, 6/3 (Sept.), 55–68.

Elam, J., Ginzberg, M., Keen, P., and Zmud, R. (1988), *Transforming the IS Organization*, Washington, DC: ICIT Press.

Feeny, D. F., Edwards, B., and Simpson, K. (1992), 'Understanding The CEO/CIO Relationship', *MIS Quarterly*, 16/4 (Dec.), 435–48.

Gibson, C. F., and Nolan, R. L. (1974), 'Managing the Four Stages of EDP Growth', *Harvard Business Review*, 52/1 (Jan.–Feb.), 76–88.

Grover, V., Jeong, S. R., Kettinger, W. J., and Lee, C. C. (1993), 'The Chief Information Officer: A Study of Managerial Roles', *Journal of Management Information Systems*, 10/2 (Fall), 107–30.

Henderson, J. C. (1990), 'Plugging into Strategic Partnerships: The Critical IS Connection', *Sloan Management Review*, 31/3 (Spring), 7–18.

Hodgkinson, S. L. (1991), 'The Role of the Corporate IT Function in the Large Multi-Business Company', unpublished D.Phil. thesis, University of Oxford.

Hofman, J. D., and Rockart, J. F. (1994), *Application Templates: Faster, Better and Cheaper Systems*, Center for Information Systems Research Working Paper, no. 270, Sloan School of Management, MIT (July).

Hurley, M. A., and Ko, C. N. (1991), 'The IT Organisation and the Role of the

Information Technology Executive: A New Confidence', Nolan Norton & Co, Canada (Fall).

Ives, B., and Olson, M. H. (1981), 'Manager or Technician? The Nature of the Information Systems Manager's Job', *MIS Quarterly*, 5/4 (Dec.), 49–63.

Keen, P. G. W. (1986), *Competing in Time: Using Telecommunications for Competitive Advantage*, Cambridge Mass.: Ballinger.

Kotter, J. P. (1982), 'What Effective General Managers Really Do', *Harvard Business Review* (Nov.–Dec.), 156–67.

Lacity, M., and Hirschheim, R. (1993), *Information Systems Outsourcing: Myths, Metaphors and Realities*, New York: J. Wiley & Sons Inc.

Lyons, M. L. (1985), 'The DP Psyche', *Datamation*, 31/16 (15 Aug.), 103–10.

Mintzberg, H. (1971), 'Managerial Work: Analysis from Observation', *Management Science*, 18/2 (Oct.), 97–110.

Parsons, G. L. (1985), *Fitting Information Systems Technology to the Corporate Needs: The Linking Strategy*, Harvard Business School Teaching Note 9-183-176.

Pyburn, P. J. (1983), 'Linking the MIS Plan with Corporate Strategy: An Exploratory Study', *MIS Quarterly* (June).

Raghunathan, B., and Raghunathan, T. S. (1989), 'Relationship of the Rank of Information Systems Executive to the Organizational Role and Planning Dimensions of Information Systems', *Journal of Management Information Systems*, 6/1 (Summer), 111–26.

Rockart, J. F. (1982), 'The Changing Role of the Information Systems Executive: A Critical Success Factors Perspective', *Sloan Management Review*, 23/1 (Fall), 3–13.

——— Ball, L., and Bullen, C. V. (1982), 'Future Role of the Information Systems Executive', *MIS Quarterly*, 6 (special issue), 1–15.

Rothfeder, J. (1990), 'CIO is Starting to Stand for Career Is Over', *Business Week* (26 Feb.), 78–80.

Short, J. E., and Konsynski, B. (1992), *Baxter International: Shared Services in Alberquerque*, Harvard Business School Case no. 9-1-3-016.

Stephens, C. S., Ledbetter, W. N., Mitra, A., and Ford, F. N. (1992), 'Executive or Functional Manager? The Nature of the CIO's Job', *MIS Quarterly*, 16/4 (Dec.).

Synott, W. R. (1987), 'The Emerging Chief Information Officer', *Information Management Review*, 3/1 (Mar.), 21–35.

——— and Gruber, W. H. (1981), *Information Resources Management*, New York: Wiley.

von Simpson, E. (1990), 'The Centrally Decentralised IS Organisation', *Harvard Business Review*, 68/4 (July–Aug.), 158–62.

24

Integrating IS and the Organization: A Framework of Organizational Fit

MICHAEL J. EARL

Strategic Management of IT

Much of this volume has been concerned with the integration of IS activities with the organization. Underpinning these concerns, perhaps, is the notion that information resources should be efficiently and effectively managed. This is one available definition of information management. When surveys are done of the most important issues facing the managers of the IS function, we find they rarely change. Different language may be used, contemporary rhetoric introduced, and priorities alter, but they are usually concerned with how to get strategic advantage from IT and how to align IS strategy with business strategy, how to organize the IS function, and how to manage the ever-changing boundaries between users and specialists, and how to plan and build IT infrastructures and cope with the latest technologies (see, for example, Brancheau and Wetherbe 1987; Niedermann *et al.* 1991). These are as much general management issues as specialist, functional issues since they potentially affect organizational effectiveness. This issue-set therefore is described increasingly as the strategic management of IT.

In the early 1980s one indicator of the 'elevation' of such issues in organizations was the formulation of so-called IT-strategies. As a result of action research in a number of companies, I called for a distinction to be made between IT strategy and IS strategy (Earl 1987). This was, quite simply, because I found that most of the IT strategies of the time were strong on technology issues and technical terminology and weak on identifying application needs and business thinking. I suggested two levels or domains of information strategy: IS strategy, concerned with the firm's required information systems or applications set, or the 'what' question; and the IT strategy concerned with the technology and infrastructure-building set, or the 'how' question.

This distinction today may seem obvious and somewhat immature, but then it was found useful by many general managers and IS executives. A number of implications followed from the distinction. The IS strategy should be demand-led and business-driven, very much influenced and owned by general managers, and formulated wherever an identifiable business or competitive strategy was being pursued. We would expect there to be an IS strategy for every division or strategic business unit—and also corporately. These strategies would change as the business environment changed.

The IT strategy, conversely, was likely to be supply-oriented and functionally driven, very much the province of the IT professionals and often formulated primarily at corporate or group level where issues of efficiency, good practice, business-unit integration, economies of scale, and corporate control were emphasized. There may be areas of local discretion, but some architectural coherence was sought. Indeed, later (Earl 1989) I suggested that the terms 'IT strategy' and 'architecture' were largely synonymous. IT strategy, for reasons of integration and surety of supply, might have to be more stable than IS strategy, it was argued.

The observation that there were both—in the classical language of business strategy—strategic business unit (or local) and corporate (or global) questions in the strategic management of IT very soon led me to suggest graphically (and rather glibly) that IS strategy and IT strategy should be linked with corporate strategy and business (SBU) strategy (Earl 1988), and a diagram of these four domains was put on the dust-cover of this volume's predecessor. The message was not developed, however, other than to stress the need for linkage with the wider set of business strategies.

One year later strategy-making in IT was revisited (Earl 1989) and a third level or domain from the information resource perspective added. The notion of an Information Management (or IM) strategy was introduced, being concerned with putting the management into IT or with which way was IT to be managed. This was organization-based, relationships-oriented, and management-focused. It included questions such as the mission and organization of the IS function, control and accounting for IT, and design of the management processes required across all the IT activities of an organization. As opposed to 'the what' and 'the how' questions, IM strategy was seen to be concerned largely with the 'who', in that it spells out responsibilities, relationships, and roles and even in its more control-oriented components is concerned with guiding personal or functional actions and assessing subsequent performance.[1]

The three-domain (or box) diagram no longer included linkages to the wider business strategies, although these were written about in the 1989 book. Over the subsequent years the 'model' was developed through teaching and advisory work to become the 'information strategy triangle' in Figure 24.1. This was much more explicit about the responsibilities for each

---

[1] Originally (1989) I used the shorthand of wherefores, but this is not so appropriate and is used in another domain below. I am grateful to David Feeny for alerting me to 'the who'.

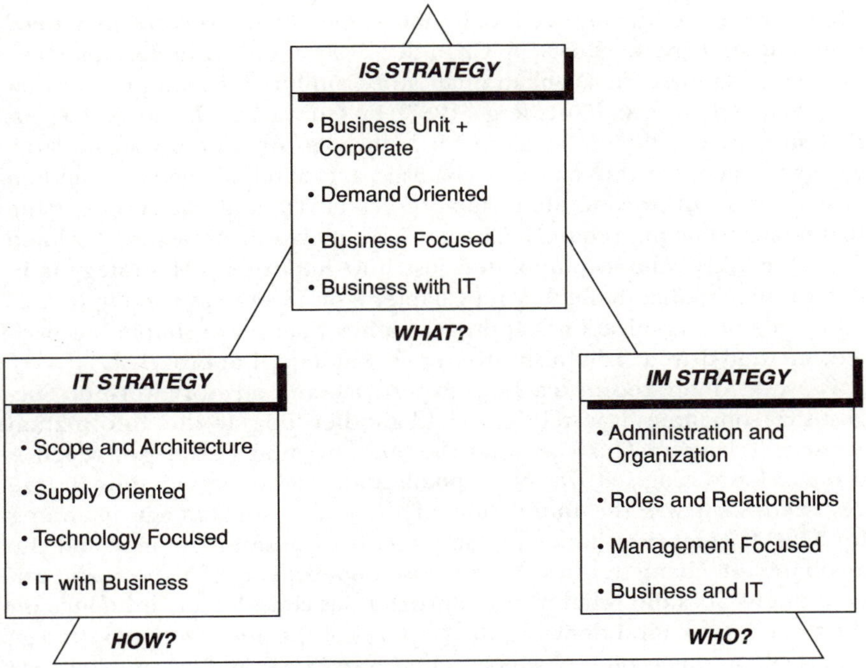

IS STRATEGY

• Business Unit + Corporate

• Demand Oriented

• Business Focused

• Business with IT

WHAT?

IT STRATEGY

• Scope and Architecture

• Supply Oriented

• Technology Focused

• IT with Business

HOW?

IM STRATEGY

• Administration and Organization

• Roles and Relationships

• Management Focused

• Business and IT

WHO?

Fig. 24.1. *The information strategy triangle*

domain, subtly, but importantly, suggesting a different balance between the IS function and general management in each.

IS strategy and Strategic Information Systems Planning remain a challenging issue for IS managers (Niederman *et al.* 1991) and a rich area of research for academics (Boynton and Zmud 1987; Lederer and Sethi 1988; Earl 1993). IT strategy and the associated architecture or infrastructure questions currently seem to be even more pressing for IS managers (Niederman *et al.* 1991), but under-researched (Boynton and Zmud 1987; Earl 1987). IM strategy questions never seem to die, partly perhaps because both technology and organization are constantly changing. Recent IM research would include studies of outsourcing (Lacity and Hirschheim 1993), the role of the CIO (Earl and Feeny 1994), and work reported in many of the chapters in this volume.

I would argue now, however, that IM strategy is the keystone of Information Strategy. Not only are IM issues recurring and frequently poorly addressed, but it is through the processes of Information Management (as delineated by IM strategy) that questions of both IS strategy and IT strategy are resolved. It is the organizational issues in the strategic management of IT that matter most. To use the parallel of strategic management at large, whilst we can see from a rational analytic view that structure may need to follow strategy, as shown by Chandler (1962) and as underpins many models of strategic fit (Venkatraman and Camillus 1984), a process view as developed by, say, Mintzberg (1987) or Quinn (1977) would suggest that strategy may follow structure. It is through organizations that strategies are made, and thus naïve, mechanistic, and simply aligned organization designs may not provide the adaptation, creativity, and entrepreneurship that strategy-making requires. Chapter 5 on global IS strategies (Earl and Feeny) in this volume pinpointed just how important IM strategy is in determining global IS needs. And Chapter 8 on IS strategy-making by Earl advocated an organizational approach rather than more simple business-led, method-driven, administrative, or technological approaches.

However, more-recent teaching experience and advisory work do suggest that sometimes it is helpful to add another 'box' to the 'Information Strategy Triangle'. This I will call the 'Organization's Strategy', which is very similar to King's (1978) conceptualization of the 'organizational strategy set' which was the foundation of his model for strategic planning for MIS. It comprises both the components of business strategy and the attributes or characteristics of the host organization. This domain can be thought of as the 'wherefores', in that it has considerable influence on the three information domains; the contents of the organizational strategy set are often 'on account of which'[2] choices in IS, IT, and IM strategies are made. Perhaps Gilbert's 'why and wherefore' substantiates the use of this shorthand.[3]

However, we also have to note that IT has the potential to offer new or alternative strategic choices in this domain, and so whilst the organization's strategy may influence strategic decision-making in the information domains in the long run, there is a possible feedback or iterative loop in the reverse direction. Finally, to defend the label of this 'box' when we talk and write of 'strategic choice', we apply the term to both business direction-setting and organizational design. The 'organization's strategy' comprises these two aspects because they are both critical factors in information strategy, as we shall see.

Bringing the four domains together, provides an 'organizational fit framework' (Fig. 24.2) which is explained and developed in the rest of this chapter. It provides, I hope, a practical and integrating denouement to this volume. Its purpose is to provide a guiding framework for the strategic management of IT or, more prosaically, for integrating information resources with the organization. Below is a set of typical questions that have to be addressed in information strategy. The 'organizational fit framework' does not answer them. However, it formalizes them into strategy

---

[2] An *Oxford English Dictionary* explanation of 'wherefore'.
[3] 'Never mind the why and wherefore', in Gilbert and Sullivan's *HMS Pinafore*.

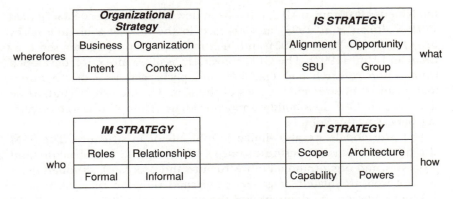

Organizational Strategy			IS STRATEGY	
Business	Organization		Alignment	Opportunity
Intent	Context		SBU	Group

IM STRATEGY			IT STRATEGY	
Roles	Relationships		Scope	Architecture
Formal	Informal		Capability	Powers

wherefores ... *what*

who ... *how*

Fig. 24.2. *The organizational fit framework*

sets and thereby indicates what management processes are required to ensure the questions are raised and answered:

- What IT applications should we develop to yield competitive advantage?
- What technological opportunities should we be considering?
- Which IT platforms should we be building and what IT policies do we need?
- Which IT capabilities should we be nurturing and which can we acquire from the market-place?
- How should IS activities be organized and what is the role of the IS function?
- What is management's role in IS/IT matters and what IT capabilities are required of today's managers?

The framework proposes not only that a complete information strategy has to address the four domains in Fig. 24.2, but also that they are inter-related. The notion of 'fit' proposes a consistent set of relationships, which are continually changing and thus should be mutually adapting.

Strategic Alignment

The notion of fit is just one of the similarities between this organizational fit framework (OFF) and the strategic alignment model (SAM) of Henderson and Venkatraman (1989, 1993). SAM is based on the need for strategic choices in the external domain (environment) and internal domain (organization) to be consistent and on the need for integration between the IS function and the organization. These two dimensions of strategic fit and functional integration give SAM a theory base and an elegance which is appealing. Indeed, from its origins in the Management in the Nineties Program at MIT, it has been developed by others (MacDonald 1991; Luffman *et al.* 1993) and assessed in the field at a broad level by Broadbent and Weill (1993) and in a much narrower, tighter sense by Chan and Huff (1993). The OFF, conversely, is more inductive, developed from action research and teaching, and perhaps is issue-driven rather than justified by strategic theories of the firm. On the other hand, as we shall see, the OFF does build on much evidence from IS research, including papers in this volume.

The two models are also similar graphically or in structure. The SAM also has four domains: business strategy, IT strategy, IS infrastructure and processes, and organizational infrastructure and processes, although these are not well articulated. It is also concerned with the relationships, or linkages, between the domains and the fit, or integration, between IS/IT and the business. Again, these linkages could be better developed. The purpose of the SAM, however, is also to guide the strategic management of IT and its spirit is that alignment is a dynamic matter.

Henderson and Venkatraman (1993) have articulated the strategic alignment model in terms of the requisite strategy perspectives of top management and IS management respectively and of the performance criteria that might be applied to IS. This helps us understand the management and organizational processes required of the SAM, but there is likely to be much more required in understanding the process of alignment. This is a tall order and involves research into processes and method. These may be developed in the future. Also required would be an examination of when and whether *misalignment* might be valid, not least to trigger the search for realignment in the dynamic worlds of organizations and IT. Even more controversially, if organizations are, in a sense, themselves information systems, and if information flows have to cross internal and external organizational boundaries and information resources be shared by all, should some elements of information strategy be above or somewhat removed from a current conceptualization of alignment between the business and its organization? After all, this line of argument is tentatively suggested by the evidence of global information management presented by Earl and Feeny in this volume.

These same critical questions can be posed of the organizational fit framework. The SAM and OFF models are compared again later.

Organizational Fit

The OFF (Fig. 24.2), then, comprises Earl's three domains or sets of Information Strategy, their interrelationships, and their integration with the organization's strategy. It provides a formal way of identifying and conceptualizing the questions of information strategy. It also helps general management see the need both for integrating information management with the organization's management processes at large and for participating in this integration. At its most basic, it provides a high-level check-list of factors to consider in integrating information strategy with the business.

Each domain, or box, comprises two 'components' and two 'imperatives'. These, it is claimed, are necessary to achieve organizational fit. They may not be sufficient; but they have been found to make a substantial contribution. 'Components' are subsets or different horizons of each domain or set. 'Imperatives' are factors or considerations which must be taken into account and not forgotten. The lines of connection between each domain in Figure 24.2 represent the interrelationships. They are two-way and will be described in terms of management processes that are likely to be required to ensure organizational fit. The detail of the domains has been refined as the OFF has evolved. The character of the processes required to bring about the interrelationships is more conjectural, but is derived from results of diverse research projects.

Organization's Strategy

The organization's strategy domain comprises the components of business strategy and organizational choices. These need to be clarified for all aspects of information strategy-making. It is not unusual for the business strategy especially to be vague, rather high-level, and not necessarily agreed (Bowman *et al.* 1983; Lederer and Mendelow 1986). This is why some organizations find that they have to revisit business strategy before embarking on information strategy. Clarification is required (Earl 1989).

Business Strategy, as becomes evident in IS strategy, is formulated at both the corporate and the SBU level. The former is concerned with mission, in the sense of what businesses we are in and not in, and thus with the shape of the business portfolio, with shareholder value (or not for profit analogues of added value), and desired or distinctive resources and capabilities. These are the essentials of corporate strategy, defined and described by Andrews (1980), Ansoff (1987), and others. SBU strategy is more concerned with competitive positioning, product-market choices, and managing the value chain as classically explained and analysed by Porter (1980).

Organizational choices comprise the chosen organizational structure or design, the management control system, and the formal policies and procedures by which the enterprise is supposed to be managed. Although these may be determined by the environment in which the enterprise is located (Lawrence and Lorsch 1967), there is a degree of strategic choice (Child 1973) often made by the CEO and mediated by top management.

One way of clarifying business strategies and organizational choices is by seeking the official, creative view of 'strategic intent' (Hamel and Prahalad 1989), a construct which captures both what strategic advantage is being sought and how. *Intent* forces a crystallization of purpose, an operational orientation, a focus or criterion in making choices, and a level of directional stability, since intent is somewhat timeless. In business strategy it is a statement of 'what we are about' and can exist at corporate and local levels. In organizational choice, it can be seen as the formal definitions, configurations, and instruments of structure and control. Intent, then, is one imperative.

The second, complementary, imperative is *context*. Formulation and implementation of business strategy take place in a context which can change. It can be important in making choices in both IS and IT strategy to be sensitive to current context. Earl's study of CIO survival reported in this volume highlights this point. There may be occasions when changes of emphasis in IS direction, IT infrastructure-building, or IM policies are required. Obvious examples are the need to economize when the firm's financial performance is under threat or the need for rapid systems delivery in periods of turbulent change.

Organizational context is just as important. It can be thought of as the ethos of the organization, the management style, or the culture. These are all 'soft' words and concepts, but can be thought of as 'how things are done round here', 'what values are sacrosanct', 'which flavours are changing', and the like. Context includes the informal side of organizational choice. It especially influences IM strategy in terms of how to put management into IT, for example, selecting an appropriate approach to strategic information systems planning. It may influence the tolerance to IT strategy and acceptance of its requisite policies and standards. It may condition the notion of what is a practical IS strategy, especially in terms of ambition and granularity. Important aspects of context include the informal networks and shared values formed by management development programmes, the preferences and habits in decision-making behaviour, the traditional attitudes to risk, and the emerging beliefs and rhetoric as times change.

These components and imperatives of the organizations' strategy, then, need to be articulated and heeded in information strategy-making. Because they may be unclear, disputed, or not formalized, they must first be clarified. Thus, the character of the process by which the organization's strategy influences the information strategy domains (Fig. 24.3) is *clarification*. There are several ways of achieving this and they may be organization-specific. But clarification is essential.

IS Strategy

The IS strategy domain comprises the components of alignment and opportunity. It is well established (Earl 1988; Henderson and Venkatraman 1989) that IS strategic planning is concerned with identifying the applications required to support business strategy (the alignment question), and

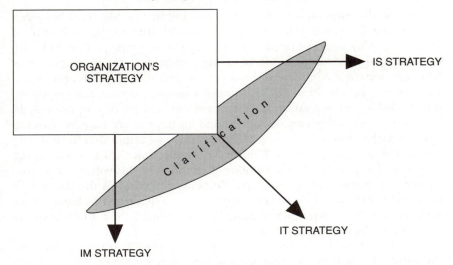

Fig. 24.3. *The clarification process*

with searching for more innovative uses of new technologies which can be exploited to enable business to be done differently or new businesses to be developed (the opportunity question). The alignment and opportunity questions form the agenda of IS strategy.

The *alignment* question is dependent upon the clarification process described above, and several methods and approaches are available and used for this in IS strategy planning (Earl 1993). They range from procedural forms of planning, to techniques such as critical success factors (Rockart 1979) or Business Systems Planning (IBM 1981), or more processual approaches such as Earl's Organizational Approach described in Section II of this volume. Earl's discovery that identifying and pursuing a few themes in IS strategy seems to lead to success argues for the process of clarification and the search for intent as inputs from the organizational strategy set. These may help also in finding IS opportunities.

The *opportunity* question, however, seems to be tackled as much through management processes which resemble those identified as necessary for product innovation (Earl 1988). In addition, the opportunity search may require a more aggressive consideration of new, emergent and future technologies. Henderson and Venkatraman (1989) in their strategic alignment model argue that firms should define their technological scope, or have a sense of which technologies in the market-place could become the enablers of new strategic thrusts. This issue of technology tracking and visioning needs further research.

These two questions or components of IS strategy have to be addressed on at least two levels of the organization: the SBU and the Group levels.

These are the imperatives. IS strategy-making at the *SBU level* has been emphasized for some years. This was probably due to the influence of Porter's (1980) conceptualization of competitive strategy. This SBU orientation had the beneficial effect of suggesting that, (a) product-market strategies were not complete without consideration of IS needs and opportunities (or threats), and (b) IS strategies should become the responsibility of SBUs and not an abstract and remote activity of corporate staff. However, it also may have backgrounded another need: namely, IS strategies at higher levels. In Figure 24.2, therefore, we argue that IS strategies are needed at *group* level too. This can be a collection of SBU's and/or the corporate level, implied in a number of chapters in this volume. It is concerned sometimes with global capabilities, as described in the chapter by Earl and Feeny, with new ways of organizing, as described by Sampler, or with the search for synergy and added group value. In the 1990s corporations are revisiting this level of IS Strategy.

Thus the character of the process by which the IS strategy influences the other domains is *innovation*. IS strategy can influence the organizational strategy, for example, by pursuing synergy more aggressively than before, because investment in information systems may be a more appealing route than structural pursuit of organizational integration. IS strategy may prompt questions of IM strategy, for example, configuration of some aspects of the IS function along process lines, as Business Process Redesign takes effect. The IT strategy may be impacted as IS opportunities enlarge the technological scope and as the need to experiment demands new technical abilities. Some guidance on these innovation processes is given in Section II of this book, especially in Lockett's chapter. This linkage process is depicted in Figure 24.4.

IT Strategy

The IT strategy domain comprises the components of scope and architecture. *Scope* is concerned with which technologies are to be formally included in the information strategy. There are at least two reasons for this. The first was discussed above; it can be important to agree which technologies in the market-place of the future are likely to offer business threats and opportunities. This set of technologies has been sometimes dubbed 'killer technologies'. These will be scanned, forecast, evaluated, and experimented with.

The second reason is to agree which current technologies are to be included in the IT strategy and architecture planning. These will be underpinning today's information processing. By implication, this usually means considering such technologies and their custodians in the IM strategy process. In the early 1980s debates were often engaged on whether telecommunications should be included in the IT domain, and sometimes whether

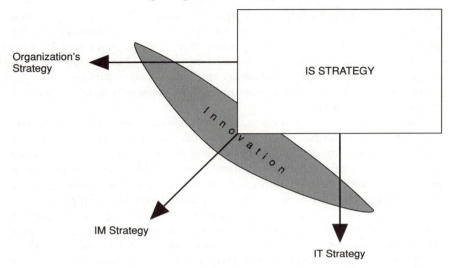

Fig. 24.4. *The innovation process*

manufacturing technologies were in the set. In financial services it was easy to see that where telecommunications underpinned distribution channels they should be included. In process industries the debate was often about process control computing. Today the issue could be about media technologies and information services. For instance, at the London Business School a decision was taken in 1990 to include both audio-visual services and library information processing in the scope and bring the departments into the IS division. They became 'core technologies' alongside computing and telecommunications.

The second component of IT strategy is *architecture*. This is the technology framework which drives, shapes, and controls the IT infrastructure. Architecture is a somewhat nebulous concept in both theory and practice and is variously defined and conceptualized. Periasami (1994) has derived some interesting perspectives from empirical work. Architecture can be seen to comprise at least the elements of computing, communications, data, and applications and can be conceived of in four levels of certainty, namely, parameters, schemas, policies, and plans (Earl 1989).

An architecture plan is required to ensure technological integration where it is needed, to guide technical choices as new technologies and methods became available, to ensure efficient (especially reliable) and effective delivery of the IS strategy, and to provide a technological model of the business when technology-dependent business decisions are being made.

The imperatives in IT strategy are capability and powers. *Capability* is the set of skills, knowledge-assets, and activities needed to be especially competent, if not 'leading-edge', in the core or killer technologies that make up scope. For example, one might be cautious of outsourcing the planning and experimentation around these technologies and be concerned to maintain both expertise and experience. Equally, as Couger's chapter demonstrates, it is important to decide what capabilities must be retained in the IS function as computing and other technologies become ever-more distributed.

Powers are required to implement and monitor the architecture. The policies (or standards) behind architecture will often be perceived by users and managers as camouflage in discussions about information strategy and constraints on free and dynamic use of technology. Because architecture does sometimes matter, reserved powers may be necessary in order to exercise technology stewardship and functional leadership. An analogy is limits on foreign exchange exposure set by corporate treasurers and controllers on commercial managers in divisions. However, because standards battles are divisive and stressful and because it makes sense to encourage experimentation, innovation, and learning, experience suggests that reserved powers should be few and thus architectures be of minimal design.

IT strategy requires as inputs clarification from the organization's strategy. For example, guidance on risks, time to market, and other parameters mentioned earlier are required. Increasingly, affordability is a common factor as the economics of information processing is examined by corporations and the viability of technology-based business processes and products reassessed. The innovation thrusts from IS strategy are another input, suggesting, for example, the boundaries between formal system-development methods and more experimental approaches or indicating where a new technological capability should be nurtured.

The output from IT strategy can be thought of as a process of *foundation*. This is concerned with the ways in which infrastructure is to be built and with the management of architecture. Questions of IM strategy will be influenced by the imperatives of scope and powers. For example, today not only does the centralization versus decentralization of IS resources have to take note of this issue, so does the ever-moving boundary between users and specialists. Questions of organizational strategy also may be influenced by IT strategy. Organizations now talk of 'business architecture'. For example, there are anecdotes of how strategic alliances and mergers have foundered on incompatible technology. Conversely, business strategy options may be increased by the properties of the IT infrastructure. For example, one retailer has been able to pursue aggressive product promotion campaigns because of the software and data capabilities built into its EPOS platform (Earl and Feeny 1994). Finally IS Strategy may be constrained by the architecture principles, for example, robustness and integration are properties often traded off against systems flexibility and rapid delivery. Conversely, the inherited foundation may contain latent IS opportunities, which is one reason why bottom-up evaluation of existing infrastructure is useful in IS strategy formulation (Earl 1989). These linkage processes are depicted in Figure 24.5.

IM Strategy

The components of the IM Strategy domain are the roles and relationships that need to be defined in managing IT activities, especially the IS function.[4]

Roles is concerned with who has what responsibility and authority for information resource policies and actions both inside and outside the IS function and at different levels of the organization. The chapters in Section III address these questions, particularly those dealing with the balance between centralization and decentralization and users and specialists. As the Earl *et al.* chapter argues, these questions never go away, for the determining factors of technology and organizational characteristics change so often.

Relationships are equally important. Central to the Feeny *et al.* chapter on users and specialists is the argument that these two groups need to work together in different areas in different ways at different stages of technology maturity. These ideas can be translated into policies for project management, service level agreements, outsourcing, and the like. In the chapter on CIOs by Earl, relationships with both the CEO and with peers and superiors turn out to be crucial. This need, and the competencies to make it happen, can be built into information management development programmes. Skyrme's chapter on hybrid managers is relevant here.

The imperatives in this domain are attention to both the formal organization (the intent) and the informal (the context). We have learnt that effectiveness in IS is unlikely if the functional organization is at odds with the structure and style of the host organization. This is the simple message of the chapters by Earl *et al.* and by Hodgkinson in Section III. Both are concerned more with the *formal* organizational arrangements. However, the *informal* nature of organizations can be just as influential. Too much attention paid to the structure of the IS function, the creation of IM committees, and the hierarchical states of the CIO can be counter-productive in organizations where initiatives and decisions are made by consensus, via networking and lobbying or in critical groups and teams. Some IS executives have a tendency to demand an organizational context of formal structures, bureaucratic procedures, and neat and tidy processes in their

---

[4] Functional strategies and their missions often adopt the language of 'roles and relationships' used here. I am conscious that in social psychology 'role' often refers to interactions and relationships. An alternative description of the components of IM strategy therefore might be responsibilities and relationships.

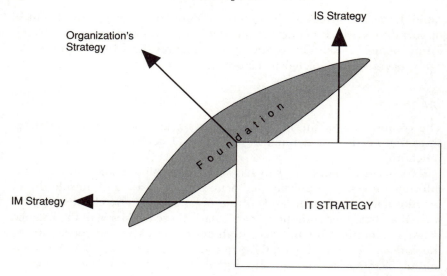

Fig. 24.5. *The foundation process*

belief in a rational world. The reality of much organizational behaviour is much more informal.

Indeed, some of the chapters in this volume have emphasized the informal side of IM. Earl observes that CIOs need to be good at politics and have strong social skills, especially to aid relationship-building. Beath finds that project champions are often unofficial and work informally with the CIO. Conversely, some roles and behaviours which may have existed only informally could be improved by some formalization. Edwards argues this for project sponsors and sponsorship. Mumford perhaps is calling for more explicit, official, and formal enactment of participative systems development.

The imperatives of IM strategy, namely, roles and relationships, need to fit both the formal and informal aspects of organizations. Furthermore, they will themselves have formal and informal management processes. The IS strategy may suggest new roles and relationships and the need for changes in nuance. The IT strategy will demand formal and official management adjustments from time to time.

The output linkages from the IM strategy domain can be described as processes of *constitution*. Instead of organizing and managing IS, people now talk of 'governance' of the IS function, perhaps in recognition of the many stakeholders, including external ones. Constitution is offered as a noun to describe this process. It can influence the setting of the organization's strategy, for example, when tensions or fault-lines in design of the host organization become manifest as IM issues. It can affect the capability and effectiveness of IS strategy-making, for example, in encouraging teamwork as advocated by Earl (1993) and partnership as advocated by Henderson (1990). It can influence the quality of IT strategic decisions, and the subsequent buy-in to them, by education, development, and propaganda programmes. The notion of constitution indeed reminds us that political initiatives should be on the IM agenda as much as structural and rational considerations. The process of constitution is depicted in Figure 24.6.

OFF in Perspective

The organization fit framework is offered as a model of information strategy, perhaps answering the questions 'how do I know an information strategy when I see one?' and 'what do we have to do to develop one?' More precisely the OFF:

- suggests three domains of information strategy as an output and prescribes the components and imperatives of each;
- adds a fourth domain, the organization's strategy, with which information strategy must connect;
- indicates how all the domains interrelate and outlines the nature of the linking processes;
- provides a check-list for developing an information strategy and a framework of analysis to ensure organizational fit.

The framework is not, however, either necessarily complete or fully validated. It leaves unanswered some important questions. The first is detail on the mechanics and dynamics of the linking processes. Researchers continue to work on this question. Secondly, it is not proven whether 'fit' is entirely about internal consistency or whether fit may sometimes be offset, because of the special characteristics of information flows and processes in organizations discussed earlier. And, of course, we have not proved that organizational effectiveness is dependent upon fit. However, the construct has been found useful in analysis of an organization's information strategy, particularly in determining matters of IM strategy—which are essentially organizational.

These critical questions can also be asked of the strategic alignment model, which is similar. The major differences are first that SAM is more deductive out of strategic management theory. OFF is more inductive out of information management issues. The driving assumptions of both frameworks are similar, namely the need for alignment or fit and the search for functional (or IT activity) integration with the organization. However, SAM leans mostly towards strategic positioning and alignment whereas OFF is founded on organizational capability and congruence. Finally, SAM may be more of a conceptual framework and OFF a managerial check-list.

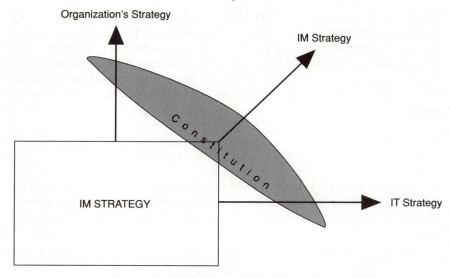

Fig. 24.6. *The constitution process*

These differences are nuances. The two frameworks are substantially similar. They are intended to help with the strategic management of IT. It is recognized that both alignment and fit are dynamic concepts. And the frameworks are predicated on strategic choices having to be made and on organizations differing in how they make them.

Finally, there may be two remaining differences. Because the OFF comprises three information domains, not two, IS managers may relate to it more easily; this is one possible benefit of its being issue-driven. Secondly, the OFF has been used to close and integrate, loosely, the chapters in this book. In other words, if it adds little incremental value over the SAM to practitioners and researchers, at least it brings an organizational dimension to information management!

References

Andrews, K. R. (1980), *The Concept of Corporate Strategy*, Homewood, Ill.: Irwin.

Ansoff, H. (1987), *Corporate Strategy*, Harmondsworth: Penguin.

Bowman, B., Davis, G., and Wetherbe, J. C. (1987), 'Three Stage Model of MIS Planning', *Information and Management*, 6/1 (Aug.), 11–25.

Boynton, A. C., and Zmud, R. W. (1987), 'Information Technology Planning in the 1990s: Directives for Planning and Research', *MIS Quarterly*, 11/1 (Mar.), 59–71.

Brancheau, J. C., and Wetherbe, J. C. (1987), 'Key Issues in Information Systems Management', *MIS Quarterly*, 11/1 (Mar.), 22–45.

Broadbent, M., and Weill, P. (1993), 'Improving Business and Information Strategy

Alignment: Learning from the Banking Industry', *IBM Systems Journal*, vol. 32, no. 1, pp. 162–79.

Chan, Y. E., and Huff, S. L. (1993), 'Investigating Information Systems Strategic Alignment', *Proceedings of the Fourteenth International Conference on Information Systems, Orlando*.

Chandler, A. D. (1962), *Strategy and Structure: Chapters in the History of American Enterprise*, Cambridge, Mass.: MIT Press.

Child, J. (1973), 'Strategies of Control and Organizational Behaviour', *Administrative Science Quarterly* (Mar.).

Earl, M. J. (1987), 'Information Systems Strategy Formulation', in R. J. Boland, Jnr., and R. A. Hirscheim (eds.), *Critical Issues in Information Systems Research*, Chichester: J. Wiley.

—— (1988), *Information Management: The Strategic Dimension*, Oxford: Oxford University Press.

—— (1989), *Management Strategies for Information Technology*, Hemel Hempstead: Prentice-Hall.

—— (1993), 'Experiences in Strategic Information Systems Planning', *MIS Quarterly*, 17/1 (Mar.), 1–24.

—— and Feeny, D. F. (1994), 'Is your CIO adding value?', *Sloan Management Review* (Spring).

Hamel, G., and Prahalad, C. K. (1989), 'Strategic Intent', *Harvard Business Review*, 66 (May–June).

Henderson, J. C. (1990), 'Plugging into Strategic Partnerships: The Critical IS Connection', *Sloan Management Review*, vol. 31, no. 3, pp. 7–18.

—— and Venkatraman, N. (1989), *Strategic Alignment: A Framework for Strategic Information Technology Management*, CISR Working Paper, no. 190, Centre for Information Systems Research, Massachusetts Institute of Technology, Cambridge MA (Aug.).

—— (1993), 'Strategic Alignment: Leveraging Information Technology for Transforming Organizations', *IBM Systems Journal*, vol. 32, no. 1, pp. 4–16.

IBM Corporation (1981), *Information Systems Planning Guide*, Business Systems Planning, GE20-0527-2, 3rd edn.

King, W. R. (1978), 'Strategic Planning for Management Information Systems', *MIS Quarterly*, 2/1 (Mar.), 22–37.

Lacity, M. C., and Hirschheim, R. A. (1993), 'The Information Systems Outsourcing Bandwagon', *Sloan Management Review* (Fall), 73–86.

Lawrence, P. R., and Lorsch, J. W. (1967), *Organization and Environment*, Division of Research, Boston: Harvard Business School Press.

Lederer, A. L., and Mendelow, A. L. (1986), 'Issues in Information Systems Planning', *Information and Management*, 10/5 (May), 245–54.

Lederer, A. L., and Sethi, V. (1988), 'The Implementation of Strategic Information Systems Planning Methodologies', *MIS Quarterly*, 12/3 (Sept.), 445–61.

Luftman, J. N., Lewis, P. R., and Oldach, S. H. (1993), 'Transforming the Enterprise: The Alignment of Business and Information Technology Strategies', *IBM Systems Journal*, vol. 32, no. 1, pp. 198–221.

Macdonald, K. H. (1991), 'Business Strategy Development: Alignment and Redesign', in M. S. Scott-Morton (ed.), *The Corporation of the 1990s: Information Technology and Organizational Transformation*, Oxford: Oxford University Press.

Mintzberg, H. (1987), 'Crafting Strategy', *Harvard Business Review*, 66/4 (July–Aug.), 66–75.

Niederman, F., Brancheau, J., and Wetherbe, J. C. (1991), 'Information Systems Management Issues for the 1990s', *MIS Quarterly*, 15/4 (Dec.), 475–500.

Quinn, J. B. (1977), 'Strategic Goals, Plans and Politics', *Sloan Management Review*, 19/1 (Fall), 21–37.

Periasami, K. P. (1994), 'Development and Usage of Information Architecture: A Management Perspective', unpublished D.Phil. Thesis, Wolfson College, Oxford.

Porter, M. E. (1980), *Competitive Strategy*, New York: Free Press.

Rockart, J. F. (1979), 'Chief Executives Define Their Own Data Needs', *Harvard Business Review*, vol. 57, no. 2, pp. 81–93.

Venkatraman, N., and Camillus, J. C. (1984), 'Exploring the Concept of "Fit" in Strategic Management', *Academy of Management Review*, vol. 9, pp. 513–25.

INDEX